A Catechetical
DICTIONARY
for the

CATECHISM
of the
CATHOLIC
CHURCH

by Joseph A. Fisher, Ph.D.

ACADEMY OF THE IMMACULATE
NEW BEDFORD, MA
2016

A Catechetical Dictionary for the Catechism of the Catholic Church is a book prepared for publication by the Academy of the Immaculate [academyoftheimmaculate.com], POB 3003, New Bedford, MA, 02741-3003.

Nihil Obstat

Peter Damian Fehlner, F.I.
Censor Librorum

Imprimatur

✠ Edgar Moreira da Cunha, S.D.V., D.D.
Bishop of Fall River, Massachusetts
December 16, 2014

The nihil obstat and imprimatur are official declarations that a book or pamphlet is free from doctrinal or moral error. No implication is contained therein that those who grant the nihil obstat or imprimatur agree with the contents or statements expressed.

ISBN: 978-1-60114-076-0

In Dedication to:

my beloved wife
in gratitude for sixty-one years of married grace,
whose constant example, edification, guidance, support,
collaboration, and editorial assistance
made this effort possible;

our seven beloved children and thirteen grandchildren
as a legacy of their parent's faith
to guide them in their life-long journey of Faith;

my Catechism students who shared their
journey of faith
in hours of edifying discourse and Christian friendship.

Ut in omnibus glorificetur Deus

Acknowledgments

I wish to thank the many persons, who played a role in the development of this *Catechetical Dictionary*, beginning with Fr. Chris Zugger and the students who studied *The Catechism of the Catholic Church* with me at Our Lady of Perpetual Help Byzantine Church in Albuquerque and my adult catechism students at the Shrine of St. Bernadette also in Albuquerque, New Mexico.

The privilege of conducting catechism seminars for the Carmelite Sisters of Santa Fe, New Mexico was particularly inspirational and resulted in a permanent spiritual bond with the community. Their prayers for the success of my catechetical efforts must be credited for the providential graces which guided the development of this *Catechetical Dictionary*.

The idea for this *Dictionary* began simply enough with students asking for definitions of words used in class. I soon learned that there were words which I could not define to my own satisfaction and that definitions were difficult or impossible to locate readily available in dictionaries. My wife suggested I collect these into a word list that could serve other catechism students.

For ten years I searched philosophy and theology texts, books on spirituality, catechetical materials and theological dictionaries gathering bits and pieces which were gradually compiled into what I called *A Catechetical Dictionary* intended as an instructional aid prepared specifically for persons studying *The Catechism of the Catholic Church*.

Interested in affiliating with other catechists for support and development, I attended a conference of the Marian Catechists in La Crosse, WI. I mentioned my *Dictionary* to His Eminence Raymond Leo Cardinal Burke (then Archbishop), who recommended that I speak with Theresa Knothe, National Coordinator of the Marian Catechist Apostolate. Luna Chou, a consecrated Marian Catechist, put me in contact with Fr. Peter Damian Fehlner, F.I., who, recognizing a potential value for catechesis, graciously reviewed the entire manuscript for accuracy and orthodoxy, and offered valuable suggestions to make it more effective and comprehensive. I am particularly grateful for his important role in making possible the publication of the manuscript.

I also wish to express my deep appreciation to the Academy of the Immaculate which thoroughly reviewed the manuscript for publication and prepared the layout.

I thank Theresa Knothe, National Coordinator of the Marian Catechist Apostolate and her staff for their formation program for Consecrated Marian Catechists. The spiritual development which it provided and the catechetical study courses by Fr. Hardon have enriched me both spiritually and academically.

I also wish to express special appreciation to my beloved wife for her encouragement, helpful suggestions, and editorial assistance in reviewing each entry. I thank my son, Andrew Fisher, for his editorial assistance. Vickie Hamilton and Teresa Gregory were kind enough to read the manuscript and shared their suggestions and impressions.

A bibliography of sources consulted in compiling the definitions is offered both to acknowledge them as sources and to recommend them for more comprehensive understanding of the definitions offered.

If this *Catechetical Dictionary* can facilitate the study of *The Catechism of the Catholic Church* and make the splendor of its Truth more accessible to others my efforts will be well rewarded.

Feast of Our Lady of Guadalupe, 2016.

JAF

About This Dictionary

This Dictionary is designed as an aid in the study of *The Catechism of the Catholic Church* (*CCC*) by offering definitions of important words used in the numbered paragraphs. It differs from other dictionaries because it identifies and italicizes important words within the definitions themselves. To ensure that the definition itself is understood, these italicized words are defined as separate entries in the dictionary.

An entry word followed by a number indicates that the word is used in that paragraph of the *CCC*. Italicized entry words without numbers refer to words defined in the dictionary which are not found in the *CCC* itself. As an example:

The entry 'Amen 1062' indicates that this word is used in paragraph 1062 of the *CCC*.

Within the definition of 'Amen' the word *assent* is italicized. The word *assent* is defined as an entry in the dictionary which, in turn, further refers the reader to Consent 1627.

Italicized words provide a network of references revealing the organic unity of the *CCC* because, as one defines words, one simultaneously learns how they are related to other concepts in the *CCC*.

When the dictionary is used with reading materials other than the *CCC*, these features make it a useful resource for relating the defined word with the doctrine of the *CCC*.

The use of italicized words within the definitions also helps adapt the definitions to the experiential level of the reader.

This *Catechetical Dictionary* is offered in the hope that it will foster wider interest in *The Catechism of the Catholic Church* by clergy, religious, laity, recent converts and others interested in Catholicism.

These features are intended to make the Dictionary a useful tool in catechetical programs, seminary education, deaconate preparation, adult faith formation classes, RCIA, and home schoolers.

A

A mensa et thoro

'A mensa et thoro' is a Latin phrase used in *Canon Law* dealing with marriage. Its literal meaning is 'from table and bed,' or more commonly 'from bed and board.' It refers to a limited kind of *separation* of *spouses* that does not dissolve the marriage bond or other *obligations*, but relieves the partners from the *duty* of *cohabiting* or living together. See Adultery 2380.

Abbey

In the Roman rite, an abbey is a monastery having at least twelve *monks* or *nuns* as members of the community. They are governed by an *abbot* or *abbess*. Some abbeys of monks are exempt from the jurisdiction of the local *Bishop*, but most are subject to a bishop. Though abbeys are independent of one another, they maintain an association with other abbeys of the same *order* in a federation called a *congregation*. Smaller houses, or offshoots of an abbey, are called *priories*. Priories remain either financially or jurisdictionally dependent on their founding abbey or *motherhouse*. See Particular church 833.

Abbey nullius

An abbey nullius is an *abbey* that belongs to no *diocese*. It is separated both territorially and jurisdictionally from the diocese in which it is located. The *abbot* of such an abbey may or may not be a *bishop*, but he always exercises ordinary *authority* and *jurisdiction* similar to that of a bishop within his territory. The abbot shares some of the prerogatives and privileges of a bishop, such as wearing a violet *skullcap* or *zucchetto* and having his name said during *Mass* in the prayers of petition. He may administer the *sacrament of Confirmation* and *consecrate churches*, functions ordinarily reserved to the Bishop.

Abbots of an abbey nullius are usually named by the *Supreme Pontiff* except when the *monks* of the abbey have been given the right to elect him. Since the changes in the *Code of Canon Law promulgated* in 1983, no more such abbeys are to be erected except for a special reason. An abbey nullius is now called a *territorial abbey*. See Particular church 833.

Abbot/Abbess

The head of a *monastery* of

monks is called Father Abbot. The *superior* of a monastery of *nuns* is called an Abbess. See Superior, religious.

Abnegation 37

Abnegation refers to acts of self-denial, renunciation of self, or self-sacrifice.

Abortion 2271

Abortion is the removal from or deliberate killing of an *embryo* or *fetus* in the womb. In former ages, abortion meant only the deliberate removal of a fetus from the womb before it was able to survive on its own outside the womb. Killing of the fetus within the womb was known as *feticide*. Embryo and fetus are different names for a baby or *human person* within the womb at various stages of development in preparation for birth or normal exiting of the womb. Whether it is called abortion or feticide, the malice of the act is the same: that of killing an innocent person.

Deliberate abortion constitutes an unspeakable, cowardly, and heinous crime against an innocent and defenseless *human being*. It is a *mortal sin* and incurs the penalty of *excommunication*, if this penalty is known at the time, for the mother who permits it and all who are associated with procuring the abortion. This penalty applies to anyone involved in seeking or implementing an abortion as well.

The penalty of excommunication is attached to this crime in order to emphasize the great *evil* and *injustice* it represents. *Catholics*, however, who have committed abortion should not despair of God's forgiveness but should seek *absolution* in the *sacrament of Reconciliation*.

Catholics who vote for candidates who openly support legalized abortions share in the crime committed by all who partake in or avail themselves of the abortions resulting from the legislation.

Abrogate/abrogates

Abrogate comes from the Latin word 'abrogare,' to repeal. It means to cancel, annul, or repeal. See Sunday 2175.

Absolute chastity

Chastity may be either *absolute* or *relative*. In the case of single *persons*, it is absolute, meaning that it requires total *abstinence* from all *sexual intercourse*. In marriage, the *virtue* of chastity is relative. It requires that the sexual *appetite* be under the control of right reason. See Chastity 915.

Absolution 1459

Absolution is the *forgiveness of sin*, which is conferred by the priest with the words, 'I *absolve* you from your sins in the name of the Father and of the Son and of the Holy Spirit.'

Christ granted the Church the power to forgive sin in Mt 16:19 when he said to Peter, 'I will give you the keys to the *kingdom of heaven.* Whatever you bind on earth will be bound in heaven and whatever you loose on earth shall be loosed in heaven.'

The words of absolution imply the physical presence of the *penitent.* Confession by telephone, internet, or mail is *invalid.* See Penance 1460.

Absolve

Absolve means to loose from or free. It is the judicial act by which a *priest* remits the *sins* of a *penitent* who has *contrition,* has confessed his sins, and has promised reformation of life.

The minister must have *faculties* to hear confessions. These are granted by the *Bishop* of the *diocese.* The words of *absolution* must be pronounced in the presence of the *person* to be absolved. Absolution by telephone cannot be given. See Secret of the Sacrament of Reconciliation 2490. Also see Absolution 1459.

Absorbed

Absorb comes from the Latin word 'absorbere,' meaning to suck up or drink into. The Church is careful to say that *human nature* was assumed rather than absorbed by God in the *Incarnation.* If it were absorbed, the human nature would have been changed into the preexisting *divine nature* and destroyed. To say that human nature was assumed means that it became *substantially* united to the *Second Person* without ceasing to be really distinct from the divine nature. See Human nature assumed not absorbed by Christ 470.

Abstain/Abstinence 2043

Abstinence comes from the Latin word 'abstinere,' meaning to refrain from or hold back. Abstinence is a *moral virtue* related to *temperance,* which controls or regulates the use of food in the interest of the *soul.*

When it is undertaken for the benefit of the soul, it is also referred to as *penitential abstinence,* such as the practice of refraining from the eating of meat on Fridays in honor of the *Passion* of Christ. The practice of abstinence is not intended to deny the goodness of *created* things or to punish the body. Its purpose is to unite the *person,* through the practice of *self-sacrifice,* to the sacrificial love of *Christ* and to free him from self-indulgence, which hinders devotion in prayer and ardent *charity.*

Abstinence differs from *fasting.* Abstinence refers to the regulation of the use of food or drink. Fasting refers to refraining entirely from food. Abstinence and fasting are often combined in practice.

Sexual abstinence refers to

refraining from *lawful sexual intercourse* at certain times for specific reasons. This abstinence is called *periodic continence* when it is practiced by married couples as a free and mutual decision for regulating *conception* according to natural methods approved by the Church. See Regulation of procreation 2368.

Abstract

The word abstract comes from the Latin word 'abstractus,' meaning to draw from. It is something thought about apart from any particular example or object. It refers to anything that is not *concrete* or specific. It may also describe something that is not easily understood because it is purely theoretical and not practical or applied. In this sense it is the opposite of concrete and specific. See Analogy. Also see Analogy of faith 114.

Accident/Accidental

In *Scholastic philosophy*, the word accident refers to a being whose *nature* it is to exist in another being as in a *subject*. Color is an accident because it does not exist alone but in something. Red exists as a color of something.

In philosophy, accident is distinguished from *substance*. Substance refers to a being whose nature it is to exist in and of itself and which does not require anything else in

which to inhere as in a subject. An apple is a substance because it can exist independently. Its red color is an accident because it does not exist alone but in something. Accident is a being because it exists or can exist. See Person 251. Also see Substance 251. Also see Hypostatic union.

Acclamation

Acclamation comes from the Latin word 'clamare' meaning to cry out. Acclamations are used in the *Mass* as the response of the congregation *assenting* to the words of *Christ* or to the actions of the *celebrant*. They emphasize significant parts of the *liturgy*. Five acclamations are sung during an *Ordinary Form* Mass. They are: the *Alleluia*; the *Sanctus*; the Memorial acclamation; the Great *Amen*; and the Doxology to the Lord's Prayer. See Eucharistic Prayer.

Accruing 2294

To accrue is to grow gradually or increase over a period of time.

Acedia 1866, 2094, 2733

Acedia, or accedie, is another name for *sloth*, and comes from the Greek for *negligence*, a lack of concern, or loss of interest. See Sloth.

Acolyte

An acolyte was the highest of the four *minor orders* in the Western Church. An acolyte's duties included lighting the candles, assisting in *processions* and during the reading of the *Gospel*, preparing the water and wine, and generally assisting as ministers in Church services. One who received the order of acolyte was given a candle and an empty *cruet*. The minor order of acolyte has been suppressed; however, the lay ministry of acolyte continues to exist in the Church, as redefined by Pope Paul VI in 1973. "The acolyte is appointed in order to aid the *deacon* and minister to the *priest*. It is his duty, therefore, to attend to the service of the altar and to assist the deacon and the priest in liturgical celebrations, especially in the celebration of *Mass*" (*Ministeria Quaedam*, 6). One is admitted to the ministry of acolyte by the prescribed liturgical rite. The acolyte may serve as *extraordinary minister of Holy Communion* and may publicly expose the *Blessed Sacrament* for *adoration* and afterward repose it, but he may not impart Eucharistic *Benediction*. "In accordance with the ancient *tradition* of the Church, institution to the ministries of reader and acolyte is reserved to men" (*Ministeria Quaedam*, 7). See Extraordinary minister of Holy Communion, Benediction, Minor orders.

Acquiescence/Acquiesce

Acquiescence means to give consent or agree to, quietly without protest but reluctantly. See Complete or full consent 1859.

Act

Act comes from the Latin word 'agere,' meaning to do, doing, or moving. It means a thing done or a deed. In *Scholastic philosophy*, act is not the same as action; rather it is the result of action or the perfection attained by action.

Because, philosophically, it is a first notion, act cannot be understood except in relation to its opposite, *potency*. Potency implies imperfection, and act implies *perfection*. Potency refers to what a thing may be; act refers to what it becomes or is.

Act may also refer to a court decision or legislation. See Judgment. Also see Act of the will; Act of man.

Act of contrition 1451

An act of contrition is a prayer of *repentance* expressing sorrow, regret, or affliction of *mind*, and detestation for *sins* committed accompanied by a *firm resolution* not to sin again. It is required for the reception of the *sacrament of Penance* or *Reconciliation*.

An act of contrition is called an act of *perfect contrition* when it expresses sorrow for sin out of pure love of God who is all goodness.

An act of contrition is called an act of *imperfect contrition* when the sorrow for sin is accompanied by fear of punishment. Imperfect contrition is also called *attrition*. Imperfect contrition is sufficient for forgiveness by *sacramental absolution*. See Perfect Contrition 1452. See Imperfect contrition 1453.

Act of man

Acts of man are *natural acts* performed by man as opposed to animals. They include bodily processes, instinctual behaviors, and behaviors that are *non-volitional*, that is, not intentional or the result of *judgment*. Only acts that are *intentional* or deliberate are correctly referred to as *human acts*.

Acts of man do not involve deliberate choices or a *judgment* of *conscience*. Because they do not involve a judgment about what is morally right or wrong, they are not *moral acts*. See Father of his acts 1749; Also see Human act 154; Moral act.

Act of the will

An act of the *will* is a deed that proceeds from the will's having *knowledge* of the *end* to which that deed is directed. Acts of the will are also called *human acts* and are distinguished from *acts of man* which do not involve the exercise of *free will*. See Intellectual agent. Also see Human act 154; Act of man.

Active life

Active life refers to human life insofar as it is occupied with *created* things as distinct from the *contemplative* life.

The active life is that portion of a *person's* life concerned with external activity in contrast with the internal concerns of *prayer* and *divine worship*. See Contemplative.

Actual/Actually

Actual refers to something that is not *potential*. It is something that really exists as opposed to merely being possible. Actually refers to the *act* of being real, not potential. See Real Presence.

Actual grace

Actual grace is that grace which moves or assists the *soul* with interior helps to acts of *supernatural virtue*, at certain times. Actual grace is subdivided into *grace of operation*, which excites the *mind* to action, and *grace of cooperation*, which assists in an operation already begun.

Actual graces are passing helps or movements of the soul by God in contrast to *habitual* or *sanctifying grace*, which is a permanent state. See Grace 2000.

Actual intention

An actual intention is a deliberate choice or determination of the *will*, which once made, exerts here and now a positive influence on a *person's* activity and is accompanied by attention of the *mind*. See Intentional homicide 2268. Also see Habitual intention; Virtual intention.

Actual sin

Actual sin refers to *sin* committed by an individual. It is distinguished from *original sin*, which is a condition into which every man is born as the *consequence* of the fall of Adam and Eve in the Garden of Eden. As a result of original sin, man is born with a darkened *intellect* and weakened *will*. See Original sin 389.

Actuality

Actuality is the state of being real as opposed to being potential or possible. See Beauty 341.

Addiction/Addictive

The word addiction comes from the Latin word addicere meaning to give consent. Addiction is a condition in which a *person* becomes physically dependent on something or controlled by a strong *habit* of irresistible craving for an object or experience. An addiction may center on narcotic drugs, sexual pleasure, food, or drink, among other things. Things that cause addiction are called addictive. See Gluttony 1866. Also see Enslavement 2414.

Adjuration

Adjuration is a command given in the name of God to do something. It takes the form of a *prayer*, called *exorcism*, in which the Church asks publicly and authoritatively, in the name of Jesus Christ, that a *person* or object be protected against the power of the evil one and withdrawn from his *dominion*. See Exorcism 550.

Adonai 209

Adonai is a *Hebrew* word meaning 'my lords,' the plural of majesty. The *mysterious* Hebrew name of God, which he revealed to Moses, means 'I am Who Am.' The *Jews* never spoke the name of God because it was considered too sacred to be uttered aloud. Instead, they used the term Adonai, literally 'my Lords,' as a substitute for *Yahweh*.

Thus, in Lk 1:43, Elizabeth says to *Mary*, 'What is this that the Mother of my Lord should come to me?' 'Mother of my Lord' here means Mother of Yahweh or of God.

God's name appears in the Old Testament as Yahweh (JHWH) or *Jahveh* (JHVH). In English versions of the *Bible*, the word Lord is used for the Hebrew JHVH. In their Scriptures, the Jews read the sacred name as Adonai.

Adopted sons/Adoption

In *Baptism* the *soul* receives *sanctifying grace*, which makes it a child of God, an *heir to heaven*, and a partaker in the *divine nature*. Because by grace, *Baptism* makes us partakers in the divine nature, it is called an adoption as sons. See Sacramental grace 1129. Also see Theosis; Child of God 526.

Adoration 2628

Adoration is the acknowledgment by man that he is "a creature before his *creator*. It exalts the greatness of the Lord who made us and the power of the Savior who sets us free from *evil*" (CCC 2628).

Adoration is the homage of supreme *worship* rendered to God alone as creator, the supreme good, and the thrice holy, *sovereign*, and transcendent being. Such worship is the first act of the *virtue of religion*. As distinct from all other acts of reverence, it is called *latria* and is reserved for the worship of God himself.

The reverence reserved to the *Blessed Virgin* is called *hyperdulia*, meaning extended praise in recognition of her unique place and role in the *mystery of salvation* as *Mother of God*. Though she is first among the *blessed*, the *veneration* accorded her is altogether different from the adoration accorded to God. However, because she is the *Mother of God*, it is also different from that accorded the blessed.

The praise and respect rendered to the *angels* and *saints* is called *dulia*.

Adore 2097

To adore means to praise and exalt God. In *adoration*, we humble ourselves before him acknowledging, with respect and absolute submission, our nothingness as creatures who would not exist but for him.

Adulation 2480

Adulation is servile flattery, homage, or the exaggerated and *hypocritical* praise of another, usually to gain favor with or control over them. It is a *grave* fault if it makes one an accomplice in another's *vices* or *grave sins*. It is a *venial sin* when it only seeks to be agreeable, to avoid *evil*, to meet a need, or to obtain *legitimate* advantages.

Adultery 2380

Adultery is marital *infidelity*. When two *persons* have *sexual intercourse* and at least one of them is married to another person, they commit adultery.

Christ condemns even the mere desire of adultery. The sixth commandment forbids it absolutely. The *prophets* see adultery as the sin of *idolatry*, because infidelity to one's *spouse* also involves infidelity to God, which is idolatry. Under the *Mosaic Law* this was punishable with death.

Adultery is an *injustice*, which injures the sign of the *covenant*, which the *marriage bond* really is, and it transgresses the rights of the other spouse. It undermines the institution of *marriage* by breaking the contract on which it is based. Adultery compromises the good of human generation and the welfare of children who need their parents' stable union. Adultery has become an increasing problem in modern society largely due to the accessibility of *artificial contraception*.

Adultery is always, in addition to an offense against the sixth commandment, a sin against the *virtues* of *chastity* and *justice*. If both parties are married, each one incurs a double sin of injustice. Even if married persons give consent to their partner's adultery, it does not alter the sin because marriage rights are *inalienable*.

Adultery of a spouse entitles the injured partner to claim a *juridical separation a mensa et thoro* (from bed and table) and even the right to refuse *marital intercourse*.

The granting of a separation does not mean the partners are free to remarry. In cases where one party commits adultery, the other has the right to separation for life, but the *marriage bond* remains for both parties.

If *civil divorce* is the only way to ensure legal rights, the care of children, or the protection of inheritance, it can be tolerated and does not constitute a *moral* offense, but it in no way allows the partners the right to remarry.

The practice of artificial contraception is an intrinsic evil whether practiced outside of marriage or within marriage. When married persons practice artificial contraception in any form, they weaken their moral sensitivity and fail to appreciate the gravely sinful character and injustice of artificial contraception. They fail to respect the dignity of their partner and the high calling to *holiness*, which is part of the sacramental *grace* of *Matrimony*. They turn *marital intercourse* into an act of mutual *masturbation*.

Advent 524

The first part of the liturgical life of the Church focuses on *Christ* as the light of the world. It begins with Advent, which celebrates the anticipation of the coming of Christ in the *Incarnation*. The word 'Advent' comes from the Latin word 'adventus,' meaning 'coming,' referring to the coming of Christ.

Advent is the *liturgical season* of *hope*, preparation, and *repentance*. It has a two-fold character. It is a preparation for the commemoration of *Christmas*, the humble coming of the Lord in Bethlehem, and it directs our *minds* and *prayers* to the *second coming* of the Lord at the end of time.

Evidence from as early as the mid-fourth century shows that the Church observed a period of preparation for Christmas.

At first, the period of Advent varied considerably. In some places, it began as early as mid-November on the feast of St. Martin. For St. Francis of Assisi and the Franciscans, the penitential part of Advent began and still begins the day after November 1, the *Solemnity* of All Saints. In other places, it was of shorter duration.

Today, the penitential season of Advent begins on the *Sunday* nearest the feast of St. Andrew (Nov. 30). It is the first day of the liturgical year and lasts from the first Sunday of Advent to *Christmas* (Dec. 25).

Formerly, the *penitential* character of the period of Advent varied. In Gaul, where the season was longer, Advent was observed with an emphasis on *penance* and looked more to the end time and the *parousia*. The *Ambrosian Rite*, still in use, observes a six-week period of Advent.

The *Roman* liturgical practice of Advent during the twelfth century was codified by the *Council of Trent* but given much of its present form by the liturgical reform following the *Second Vatican Council*.

The season begins with the preaching of John the Baptist calling for *repentance* and *reformation of life*. The season as a whole is divided into two parts. The first centers on the Lord's second coming and continues through December 16. During this period, the *Gloria* is not used so that the song of the *angels* might be repeated with greater freshness on Christmas. The *Alleluia* is recited before the *Gospel* as an indication of the expectant joy of the season. Readings from Isaiah dwell on God's visitation, consolation, and *redemption*. The *Gospels* portray Christ as the fulfillment of ancient *prophecies*.

On December 17, there is a shift in emphasis, and events associated with Christ's birth receive more prominence. The Gospels of Matthew and Luke, which proclaim important *Messianic* prophesies, are read.

The season is noted for the 'O *Antiphons*,' which have been set to especially beautiful melodies. Advent always begins with *Evening Prayer* I of the Sunday closest to November 30 but no later than December 3. The Fourth Sunday of Advent must be *celebrated* even if it falls on December 24. The Fourth Sunday of Advent is *Marian* in character, accenting the Marian character of the entire season. Advent ends with Evening Prayer I of Christmas. See Parousia 830; Liturgical seasons.

Advocate

Advocate comes from the Latin word 'advocatus,' meaning one called upon to plead. It is a title of *Christ* who is our advocate with the Father. The *Holy Spirit* is also called the Advocate or *Paraclete* by Christ himself (Jn 14:16) whom he promised to send to defend the *Christian* believers against their accuser, the *devil*.

In the great *Marian Antiphon, Salve Regina* (Hail, Holy Queen), *Our Lady* is invoked as 'our Advocate' with Christ. In this title, St. Francis of Assisi associates *Mary* with the Holy Spirit and addresses her as *'Spouse of the Holy Spirit,'* both of whom are made advocates, protectors and, guides of the *Franciscan Order*. Within the Franciscan *tradition*, the title *'Spouse of the Holy Spirit'* is understood to designate the *mystery* of the *Immaculate Conception*. See Counselor 692.

Advocate of God

The advocate of God is the *person* who serves as the promoter of the cause in the *canonization* process. He has full *authority* to examine the candidate's life, *virtues*, writings, reputation for holiness, and any *miracles attributed* to the person's intercession. See Canonization.

Advocatus Dei

Advocatus Dei is Latin for *Advocate of God*. See Advocate of God.

Aeiparthenos 499

Aeiparthenos is from the Greek word 'aion,' meaning ever, and 'parthenos,' meaning

virgin or maiden. Ever-virgin, Aeiparthenos, and the Latin 'Semper Virgo' are titles of the *Blessed Mother* professing her *virginity* before, during, and after giving birth to *Christ*.

Aesthetics

Aesthetics is the branch of *philosophy* that seeks to explain the *nature* of *beauty*, the modes of its *apprehension*, and the *psychological* responses to it. Many modern philosophers consider aesthetics to be a branch of psychology and deny its objective *reality* contending that it has no reality outside the comprehending *mind*. Since *divine* beauty is the cause of *being*, aesthetics is properly a branch of *ontology*. See Beauty.

Aeviternity/eviternity

Aeviternity or eviternity means never-ending time. It refers to that form of eternity possessed by *angels* and men. Angels were eternal only after they were *created*. Man's eternity begins with his death and *resurrection*. For angels and men, eternity has a beginning but no end.

The state called aeviternity is ascribed to *spiritual* creatures as part of their *essence* because their spiritual *nature* or *substance* cannot change once they are called into being by their *Creator*. They cannot change because spirits and human *souls* have no parts. Man's risen body will be transformed into a *glorified body* in order to enable it to share in the *immortality* of the *soul*.

The body of man in Eden was granted the *preternatural* gift of immortality: in this case, imperfect, or conditional immortality inferior to the perfect immortality of the glorified body. See Eternity; Preternatural gift.

Affective prayer

Affective prayer is a form of *prayer* in which there is less need for the assistance of mental reflection to move the *soul* to an awareness, desire and, love of God.

Meditative prayer, which begins with spiritual reading, reflection, and thinking, gradually grows into affective prayer, which requires little or no reflection to stir up awareness, desire, and love of God.

As one grows further in *perfection*, the obstacles to the working of the *Holy Spirit* are removed. The increased awareness, desire, and love of God become gifts of the Spirit in *contemplative prayer* and are not subject to the *will* of man. See Meditation 2705.

Affinity

The word affinity comes from the Latin term 'affinitas,' meaning nearness or relationship. In reference to *marriage*, affinity describes the relationships between *persons* that are established as a result of a validly contracted marriage.

The spouses acquire a blood relationship with blood relatives of their *spouse*. The blood relations of either spouse are related to the other spouse in the same *line* and *degree* as they are by *consanguinity*. This makes marriage between blood relatives in the *direct line* of a deceased husband or wife *invalid* unless a *dispensation* is granted. See Diriment impediment. Also see Nullity of marriage 1629.

Agape

Agape is that kind of *love* manifested toward another in need. It is marked by *generosity* without concern for reward. Closely related to *agape* is *philia*: that kind of love of friends based on common *values*. Contrasted with it is *eros*, a kind of love based on sexual attraction but which can also be of an *aesthetic* nature. *Storge* is the form of love found among family members.

The Church has used agape to refer to the meeting of the faithful for meals before the *liturgy*. See Love 218.

Age of consent

Canon Law sets the age at which a person can *consent* to *marriage* as sixteen for men and fourteen for women. See Age of discretion. 1457.

Age of discretion 1457

The Church fixes different ages at which *baptized per-*

sons incur certain *obligations*, enjoy certain privileges, or are allowed to enter special *states of life*. Each of these ages can be referred to *generically* as an age of discretion. The *age of reason* refers to the age at which a person is deemed capable of making *moral* decisions for himself and becomes morally responsible for his acts. The age of reason is commonly held to be about the age of seven years.

At this age, the *obligation* of *confession*, for those prepared for it, and *Mass* attendance are incurred. The obligation for confession refers to the duty to confess serious *sin* at least once a year. Those who have been initiated into the *Most Holy Eucharist* are bound to the obligation of receiving *Communion* at least once a year.

At this age, one may receive the *sacrament of the Sick* or *Extreme Unction*. In the *Latin Rite*, a person does not ordinarily receive *Confirmation* before this age.

The age of fourteen can also be referred to as the 'age of discretion.' It properly refers to that age at which a person becomes capable of making weighty decisions such as the choice of *vocation*. This roughly corresponds to the age of *puberty*, fourteen for boys and twelve for girls.

At the age of fourteen, one is bound by the laws of *abstinence* but not *fasting*.

Marriage contracted before the age of sixteen for boys and fourteen for girls is *invalid*.

At the age of eighteen, the obligation of fasting is binding. It ceases at the beginning of their sixtieth year for both men and women.

Candidates for the *permanent diaconate* can be admitted to the diaconate only when they have completed their twenty-fifth year if unmarried or their thirty-fifth year if married. "Those who are destined for the priesthood are to be admitted to the *order* of Diaconate only when they have completed their twenty-third year" (Canon 1031, § 1). Candidates must have completed their twenty-fifth year to be ordained a *priest*. They must be at least thirty-five years old to be consecrated a *bishop*. The *episcopal conference* may determine the norm by which a higher age is required for the *presbyterate* and permanent diaconate (Canon 1031, §3).

Religious cannot make *temporary profession* before eighteen years of age and before completing a year of *novitiate*. In order to be *valid*, the year of novitiate must be completed after the sixteenth year of age has begun. *Perpetual vows* may be made after the time for temporary profession has elapsed if the person is judged suitable. To be admitted to perpetual profession, the person must be at least twenty-one years of age and have completed at least three years of temporary profession.

Age of reason

The age of reason refers to the age at which a *person* becomes capable of making *moral* decisions, usually about seven years of age, but sometimes earlier and, in the case of mentally handicapped persons, sometimes considerably later. It is the age at which a person incurs the *obligation* to observe the *legal* and *moral* prescriptions of the Church, including the obligation to attend *Mass*. See Age of discretion 1457.

Agent

An agent is the *person* or means that performs or brings about an action or produces some result.

An agent may also be a person empowered to act for another as his representative. See Means.

Aggression

Aggression is an unprovoked attack on another accompanied by a self-assertive and hostile attitude. Aggression is opposed to *patience*. See Wrath 1866.

Agility

Agility is a quality *attributed* to the *resurrected body* by *Scholastic theologians*. Agility is the ability of the resurrected body to pass from place to place with great speed, which makes the body a perfect instrument of the *soul*. See Resurrection of the dead 992. Also see Glory 293.

Agnostic

An agnostic is a *person* who believes that it is impossible to know whether God exists or not since knowledge of God is beyond human *reason* and since reason is incapable of understanding anything besides physical laws. See Gnosticism 285. Also see Agnosticism 2127.

Agnosticism 2127, 2128

Agnosticism is a *philosophical theory* that holds that it is impossible to know whether God exists or not since he is beyond human *reason*. It holds that reason is incapable of understanding anything besides *physical laws*. For *agnostics*, man cannot grasp such *concepts* as *immortality* or the existence of God.

In some cases, agnostics do not deny God but allow for the existence of a *transcendental* being that is incapable of revealing itself. In other cases, the agnostic makes no *judgment* about God's existence, declaring that it is impossible to prove, or even to affirm or deny.

Agnosticism may represent a certain search for God, but it also expresses a certain *indifferentism* and a sluggish *moral conscience*. It is often equivalent to practical *atheism*.

Akathistos 2678

Akathistos is a *litany* to the *Blessed Virgin* prayed as a substitute for the *Divine Office* in the *Byzantine Church*. It is called the standing hymn because it is always sung standing.

Akolouthia

Akolouthia is a lengthy form of the *Divine Office* used in the *Byzantine Rite*. Originally the language used was old Greek, but now the Slavonic, Arabic, Rumanian, Georgian, Finnish, and Albanian languages are also in use. See Byzantine Rite.

Alexandrian Church /Liturgy/Rite

Alexandria, located in Egypt at the mouth of the Nile, played an important role in the life of the early Church. It was *evangelized* by St. Mark and produced great leaders like St. Clement (150–215 A.D.), St. Athanasius (296–373 A.D.), and St. Cyril (d. 444 A.D.). It was the home of a famous *catechetical* school under Clement (150–215 A.D.) and Origen (185–254 A.D.).

Alexandria was honored by the early Church as the second city of Christianity. The *Patriarchate* was considered second only to Rome and enjoyed *ecclesiastical* supremacy over the East.

The Church in Alexandria rejected the *Council of Chalcedon* as a capitulation to *Nesto-rianism* and fell into schism. Their Christology has been criticized as *monophysitism*, but they reject the term in favor of miaphysitism, which emphasizes the unity and divinity of Christ but without denying his humanity like monophysitism does. Recent *dialogue* has contributed to resolving this dispute. See Coptic Church/Rite. Also see Oriental Orthodox; Eastern Church.

All Saints

A *solemnity celebrated* on November 1 to honor all saints. In the USA and some other countries it is a *holy day of obligation*.

Allegorical sense 117

The allegorical sense of *Scripture* refers to a specific way of understanding Scripture. It is also called the *typical sense* or the *mystical sense*. It involves not only the meaning that a passage has in itself, the *literal meaning*, but also refers to some truth or event of which it is a type, symbol, or foreshadowing. It expresses meaning under the guise or appearance of something else to which it has an aptly suggestive resemblance, for example, 'Thou art Peter and upon this rock I will build my church' (Mt 16:18).

Allegorical sense, especially in the writings of the *Fathers of the Church* and of great *medieval theologians*, such as St. Bonaventure (1221–1274

A.D.), is often used to connote one of the three forms of the *spiritual or mystical sense* that a *biblical* text may possess. The allegorical sense deals with what we must believe, the *anagogical sense* with what we must hope, and the tropological with what we are obliged to do to please God.

Allegory/Allegorical

Allegory refers to a particular kind of literary device in which one thing is used to represent another for purposes of instruction. An allegory is a story in which *persons*, events, or things have a hidden or symbolic meaning. Allegory is used to teach ideas and principles by associating them with things already known in another context. A *parable* is a form of allegory. See Parables 546.

Alleluia

Alleluia means 'Glory to him who Is' and occurs in many *Psalms* as an expression of joy and praise. It is even sung in *heaven* (Rev 19:1). It is also used in almost every *liturgical prayer* of the Church. See Marana tha 671. Also see Aramaic terms used in the liturgy.

Alms

Alms refers to the food, clothes, or money given to the poor. The word comes from the Greek 'eleemosyne,' which is related to the word 'eleos,' meaning pity. It is the source of the English word eleemosynary, an adjective pertaining to alms or *charity*.

Giving *alms* to the poor is one of the chief witnesses to fraternal *charity* and is most pleasing to God. See Works of mercy 2447.

Altar 1182, 1383

The word *altar* comes from the Hebrew word 'mizbeah,' meaning 'place of sacrifice.' An altar is the table on which the *Sacrifice of the Mass* is offered. The Christian sacrifice of the Mass must always be offered on an altar, *altar stone*, or *antimension* when possible.

Out of reverence for the Mass, which is both a sacrifice and a meal, the altar must be covered with at least one cloth. A cross easily visible to the people should be on the altar or somewhere near to it. A *bishop* or *prelate* having the necessary *faculties* must *consecrate* the new altar on which sacrifice is to be offered.

The altar, altar stone, and antimension were required to contain relics of one or more martyrs in *memory* of the time when Mass was *celebrated* on the tombs of martyrs in the *catacombs*.

Although the General Instruction for the Missal issued by Pope Paul VI no longer requires that relics be part of the altar, it recommends the ancient practice of enclosing them in the altar *sepulcher* or under the altar itself.

There are different types of altars. A *permanent or fixed altar* consists of a single stone, which forms the table. A fixed altar has three parts: a top of stone, supports for the top, and a sepulcher or place in which bones of a saint or martyr have been sealed. If the altar stone is only a part of the table it is called a *movable altar*.

An altar or altar stone has five crosses cut into it to represent the five wounds of Christ. Many altars in the U.S. are not fixed and must have an altar stone set in them. This stone is in fact the *altar of sacrifice*.

A *church* may have more than one altar, in which case, the *main altar* or *high altar* is the one in the center of the *sanctuary*. Every altar should have a *title*. The title of the high altar or altar of sacrifice is the same as the name of the church.

In the *Byzantine Church*, there is only one altar in a church, and it is always clear of the east wall. In a large church where there are other altars in side *chapels*, those other altars are considered separate churches. Only one *liturgy* is celebrated at an altar in a given day.

An altar may be covered by a canopy called a *baldachino*. It may be either suspended from the ceiling or attached to a wall. It may be made of any material but should be ornamented with tapestry or other fabric. At times it is made of wood or stone supported by four pillars. Perhaps the most famous and beautiful baldachino is the one over the main altar in St. Peter's in Rome. A baldachino is also referred to as a *ciborium* or *baldachinum*. See Tabernacle 1379. Also see Altar stone; Fixed altar; High altar.

Altar of repose

The altar of repose is the *altar*, pedestal, or niche on which the *Blessed Sacrament* is reserved from the evening of *Holy Thursday* until *Good Friday*. After Mass on Thursday, the ciborium, covered with a white silk veil, is carried in procession to the altar of repose while singing the *Pange lingua*. The altar of repose is decorated with flowers and candles. To ensure that the Blessed Sacrament is not left unattended, at least until midnight, it is customary for the faithful to spend some time in prayer before the Blessed Sacrament during the time of repose. See Mass of the Presanctified.

Altar of the new covenant 1182

"The altar of the New Covenant is the Lord's Cross from which the *sacraments* of the *Paschal* mystery flow" (CCC 1182). It is on the *altar*, which is the focal point of the *covenant* of the new law, that the sacrifice of the Cross is made present under *sacramental signs*.

The altar of the New Covenant is also the table of the Lord to which the *faithful* are invited to share in the *mystery of salvation*. In *Eastern liturgies*, the altar is the symbol of the tomb, a sign that Christ truly died and is truly risen.

Altar stone

An altar stone is a smaller piece of stone set into the table on which the *sacrifice of the Mass* is *celebrated*. It is used when the altar itself is not a single piece of stone. This arrangement is called a *moveable altar* as opposed to a *fixed altar* in which the entire top of the altar is a single stone. See Altar 1383.

Ambiguities 28

Ambiguities are uncertainties that cause confusion or lack of clarity. When something is unclear, we say it is ambiguous.

Ambition

Ambition is an *inordinate* desire for honors and success. A desire is inordinate when it strives for that which is not deserved or is sought after by unlawful means or for unworthy motives. Modest ambition is not only blameless but praiseworthy. See Pride 1866.

Ambo 1184

Originally, an ambo was a small platform for the *proclamation of the Gospel* and *Epis-*

tle. It is also called the *pulpit* or *lectern*.

Ambrosian hymn

The Ambrosian hymn is a beautiful *hymn* of thanksgiving. Although known as the Ambrosian hymn and doubtless prayed by St. Ambrose, St. Ambrose himself probably did not write it. It is called the *Te Deum* because these are the first two words of the hymn. The well-known popular hymn: 'Holy God We Praise Thy Name,' is a paraphrased English translation. See Te Deum 168.

Ambrosian Rite

The Ambrosian Rite refers to the ancient *liturgy* of the Church and province of Milan, but how much of it is really attributable to St. Ambrose is questionable. Today it is generally regarded as a use of the *Latin Rite*, though there are considerable differences in usage and formulae used in the *Mass* and *Divine Office*. It is still in use in most *churches* of the Archdiocese of Milan. Pope Pius XI belonged to this *rite*. See Advent 524.

Amen 1062

Amen is a transliteration of the Hebrew word 'Aman,' meaning to show oneself dependable or to know that one is secure because of *faith*. Amen also means certain or true, indicating *assent* or affirmation. The root meaning of the word "expresses solidity, trustworthiness, faithfulness. And so we can understand why 'Amen' may express both God's faithfulness towards us and our trust in him" (CCC 1062). In Latin, 'fiat,' so be it or so be it done, often expresses the meaning of the Hebrew 'Aman.'

In the *New Testament* Amen is used by *Jesus* in the phrase, 'Amen, I say to you.' It is translated as 'truly' or 'in truth.' Jesus uses the word to emphasize that his words are certain and reliable and binding on himself and others. In Rev 3:14 Jesus calls himself 'the Amen' to affirm that he is a faithful and true witness.

The Creed's final Amen confirms and repeats its first words: 'I believe.' Christ is the definitive Amen of the Father's love, and he completes our Amen to the Father. See Marana tha 671. Also see Aramaic terms used in the liturgy.

Amend/Amendment

Amend comes from the Latin word 'emendare,' meaning to correct. To amend means to make better, improve, remove faults, or correct. It plays a necessary role in the improvement of one's conduct.

The amendment of life is part of true *contrition* and takes the form of a firm resolve to avoid the occasions of *sin*. See Penance.

Anagogical sense (of Scripture)
117

The anagogical sense of Scripture refers to the interpretation of scriptural realities and events "in terms of their eternal significance" (CCC 117) or what we are to hope for. It is a secondary *spiritual* or *mystical sense*, leading us to our true homeland, e.g., interpreting the Church as a sign of the *heavenly* Jerusalem.

Analogy

Analogy comes from the Latin word 'analogia,' meaning in due ratio, or in a fixed relationship or proportion. Analogy, according to the *Fourth Lateran Council* (1215), is an important tool in *theology* used to explain unknown or mysterious beings by means of partial similarities with things already known and that are otherwise unalike, such as God and creatures. This kind of analogy, to be distinguished from *metaphor* and *simile*, is also called the *'analogy of being.'* It is not to be confused with the *analogy of faith*.

Analogy is useful for explaining things because it compares point for point unrecognized similarities between things making it easier to understand them.

In using analogy, the features of something that is familiar and *concrete*, are used to explain something unfamiliar and *abstract*. It also points out similarities between things that are not usually associated with one another, creating a *harmony* between them. See Analogy of faith 114.

Analogy of Being

Analogy, according to the *Fourth Lateran Council* (1215), is an important tool in *theology*. When it is used to explain unknown or *mysterious beings* by means of partial similarities with things already known but that are otherwise unalike, such as God and creatures, it is called the analogy of being. This type of analogy is distinguished from *metaphor* and *simile*. See Analogy.

Analogy of faith 114

The analogy of faith refers to the *coherence* or consistency of the truths of the faith "among themselves and within the whole plan of *Revelation*" (CCC 114) so that one part of the whole does not destroy or contradict the rest.

It also refers to the consistency in reasoning or the *harmonious* connection of the various truths so that they join together to form a coherent whole.

Anamnesis 1103, 1354, 1362

In Greek, anamnesis means remembrance, commemoration, or memorial. In the *Latin Rite*, it refers to the *prayer* after the *Consecration*, which recalls the death, *Resurrection*, and glorious *Ascension* of *Christ*.

The purpose of the prayer is not simply to recall these events of the past but to make their presence in the *celebration* of the *Eucharist* felt by those participating in it.

Anaphora 1352, 2770

The anaphora is the *Eucharistic prayer* of thanksgiving and *consecration*, which is the heart and summit of the *celebration* of the *Mass*. It is the part of the *Eucharistic* celebration that includes the *consecration*, *oblation*, and *communion*.

In the Western Church, the anaphora is called the *Canon of the Mass* when referred to Eucharistic Prayer I of the *Roman Missal*. Because at times parts of the Canon were not spoken aloud, it was referred to as the *secret* of the Mass. The recitation of the final words spoken in a louder voice, as in the case of 'for ever and ever,' is called an *ekphonesis*.

Anathema

Anathema is the word used in *Canon Law* to refer to a form of *excommunication* imposed with the full ceremonial of the *Pontificale Romanum*. The term was used instead of *excommunication* in condemnatory *doctrinal decrees* of early Church *councils* to exclude one from the reception of the *sacraments*. Anathema signifies total separation from the *faith*. The pronouncement of anathema has not been used since the *Second Vatican Council*.

The Greek word 'anathema' originally referred to either objects of *consecration* or *execration*. It was in the latter sense that it came into use in both the *Old* and *New Testaments* as a *curse*, ban, or sentence of *reprobation*. See Marana tha 671.

Anathema sit

Anathema sit is a Latin phrase meaning 'Let it (him) be *anathema*.' Anathema is the formal pronouncement used by Church *councils* since early times to signify total separation from the *faith* for either *apostasy* or *heresy*. St. Paul used the term in referring to those separated from the *Christian* community for teaching false *doctrine*. In *post-apostolic times*, it was used frequently against *heretics* as a form of condemnation, ban, or *curse*. 'Anathema sit' is different from *excommunication* and may be directed to either *persons* or teachings.

Excommunication generally refers to an exclusion from participation in *ecclesial* functions. Anathema sit focuses on the *belief* that is not consistent with the *revealed truth* preached by the Church. See Marana tha 671.

Anchorite

The word anchorite comes from the Greek word 'anachoretes,' meaning to retire. It refers to a *person* who lives alone and away from society for purposes of religious meditation. It can mean recluse or hermit. See Monk.

Angel 328

Angels are *spiritual*, personal, and *immortal* creatures. Angels are *persons* because they have an *intellect* and *free will*. Because they are spirits, they are immortal. Angels *glorify* God without ceasing and serve as God's messengers to man.

Angel is also the name of one of the angelic *choirs* in *heaven* whose members exercise the ministry of heavenly messengers. Angel in Greek means messenger. In the Book of Revelation (ch. 2 and ff.), the term is also used to designate bishops as messengers of Christ to the *churches* or dioceses committed to their care. See Choirs of angels.

Angelical Salutation

The Angelical Salutation is a name for the prayer called the *Hail Mary* because these are the words used by the *Angel* Gabriel when announcing the *Incarnation*. See Hail Mary. Also see Appendix of commonly used prayers; Marian prayers.

Angelus

The Angelus is a devotion in honor of the Incarnation commemorating the *Annunciation* of the *angel* Gabriel to the *Blessed* Virgin. Traditionally, it is recited at six A.M., noon, and six P.M.

It is believed that the evening Angelus owes its origin to the curfew bell, a signal for evening prayer. The Angelus is replaced by the prayer *Regina coeli (Queen of heaven)* during the *Easter season*. See Appendix of prayers; Marian prayers; Angelus.

Anger 2302

Anger as a *vice* is an aggressive desire for *revenge* in the face of opposition. As one of the *irascible emotions*, it is a strong feeling of displeasure over opposition or *injustice* demanding removal of the opposition or correction of the injustice, and punishment of the offender. Anger as a vice is one of the *capital sins*. It is opposed to the *virtues* of peacefulness and meekness. Feelings of spontaneous anger are normal and not sinful simply as an emotion.

To become angry in moderation and for a just cause may be *licit* and even praiseworthy. Such anger is referred to as *righteous anger*, such as when the money changers in the *temple* roused *Jesus* to anger (Mt 21:12). It is not a *Christian virtue* to remain mild in the face of injustice when this attitude is the result of *apathy* or self-serving non-involvement.

When one gives way to feelings of anger out of proportion to the offense, anger becomes gravely sinful and may lead to other *sins* such as *blasphemy*, *scandal*, *battery*, or even *killing*. Such anger also blinds the *intellect*.

Anger as a vice is also called *rage*, *wrath*, or *ire*. Anger generates *indignation*, *rancor*, *blasphemy*, *violence*, *insult*, and *resentment*. It is opposed to the virtues of *patience*, *long suffering* and *equanimity*.

Animation

Animation simply means to enliven. The early *Church Fathers* taught that just as Eve was taken from Adam's side and enlivened by her *soul*, so also the Church, the *New Eve*, is taken from the side of the crucified *Christ*, the *New Adam*, and enlivened by the *Holy Spirit*. The flow of water and Blood from the side of Christ on the Cross is a *sacramental sign* of the animation of his Bride the Church through the *sacraments* of *Baptism* and the *Eucharist*. See Bride of Christ 796.

Animi Cruciatus 1431

Animi Cruciatus is a Latin phrase meaning torment or affliction of the *soul* or *spirit*. It is used to refer to the salutary pain and sadness that accompanies the true *conversion of heart* and *repentance*.

Annuario Pontificio

The Annuario Pontificio is the official annual directory of the Roman *Catholic Church.* It contains essential information about the *Pope, Roman congregations, dioceses, religious, and secular institutes, prelates,* and curial officials and a summary of the principal offices and activities of the Church's central administration. It is under the direction of the *papal* secretary of state. See Roman Congregations.

Annulled

An act is annulled when a competent *authority* has declared it to be *invalid* and *void.* Applied to *marriage,* a *decree* of *annulment* is a judgment by competent authority that a marriage *contract* never existed between two people. See Irrevocable 393.

Annunciation

The Annunciation is when the *Angel* Gabriel announced to the *Blessed Virgin Mary* that she had been chosen to be *Mother of God,* and when she pronounced her 'Fiat,' that is, consent, or agreement, to become the Mother of the *Second Person* of the *Trinity.*

This moment of the *Incarnation* is *celebrated* liturgically as a *Solemnity* on March 25, nine months before *Christmas,* the birth of *Jesus.* See Fullness of time 484.

Anointed with the Spirit 438

The name *Christ* (from the Greek for anointed, a translation of the Hebrew word Messiah) means he who was anointed. He was anointed by the *Holy Spirit* by being given his divine *mission* at the Incarnation. His *messianic consecration* was revealed in his earthly life, especially at the moment he was *baptized* by John when God anointed him with the Holy Spirit and with power that he might be revealed to Israel as the *Messiah.* See Messiah 437.

Anointing 1293

The use of oil as a refreshing unguent or salve was very common in ancient times, but its origin and precise symbolism as a sacred *rite* are hard to trace. What is clear is that the religious purpose of *anointing* was to make *persons* or things *sacred,* that is, set aside for *religious* purposes.

In the Church, anointing consists in tracing a cross on persons or things with *holy oil.* Anointing is a sign of joy and abundance. It also soothes, cleanses, and limbers, so it is a sign of healing.

"The pre-baptismal anointing with the *oil of catechumens* signifies cleansing and strengthening" (CCC 1294).

Anointing with the *oil of the sick* expresses healing and

comfort. Anointing with the *oil of chrism* in *Confirmation* and *Holy Orders* is a sign of *consecration* to the *mission* of Jesus Christ.

Anointing of the Sick 1513

Anointing of the Sick is the name now used for the *sacrament* also known as *Extreme Unction*. Because this *anointing* was administered to the dying, it was called extreme, i.e., 'last' anointing or unction. This sacrament, however, is intended not only for those in their last moments of life but also for the seriously sick and the aged or others who are in danger of death. It is administered so that they may receive their health if it be conducive to their *salvation* and to provide them with strength to bear their suffering. Only *baptized persons* who have attained the use of reason may receive this sacrament if they are seriously sick. A person condemned to death is not sick and should go to confession and receive *viaticum*, but he should not be administered the Anointing of the Sick.

The first *grace* of this sacrament is the gift of strength, peace, and the courage to overcome the difficulties that attend serious illness or the frailty of old age. It is given by the *Holy Spirit* to renew *faith* and trust in God, strengthen individuals against *temptations* of the *devil*, and help them overcome discourage-ment and anguish in the face of death. It is meant to lead the sick person to healing of the *soul* and also of the body if it is God's will. If the person to be anointed is unable to *confess* and repents of the sins he has committed, his sins are forgiven. *Deacons* may not administer this *sacrament*.

Anthropomorphic

Anthropomorphic comes from the Greek 'anthropos,' meaning man, and 'morphos,' meaning form. It refers to the *attribution* of human qualities to God. It is a common literary device used in the *Old Testament* in referring to God and his relations with men.

In general, it refers to the attribution of human properties to something that is not human, such as the deity, animals, or a natural phenomenon or force. See Neopaganism. Also see Cult of the body 2289.

Antichrist 675

Antichrist is the title of a great personal opponent who will arise against Christ and his *kingdom* and who is expected to appear on earth before the end of the world.

Antimension

An antimension is a square piece of silk or linen cloth decorated with symbols of *Christ's Passion* and into which is sewn a small bag containing relics of saints or martyrs. It is placed on an unconsecrated table when such is used by the Byzantines for offering the sacrifice of the *Mass*. It is equivalent to the *altar stone* used in the West for a portable altar. See Altar stone.

Antiphon

Antiphon comes from the word 'antiphona' in Latin meaning alternating. An antiphon is a short verse from a *psalm* or *scripture* recited before and after a psalm or between verses of a psalm. Antiphons are also recited before and after *canticles*, such as the *Benedictus, Magnificat,* or *Nunc Dimittis*. An antiphon is always recited before and after each psalm during the hours of the *Divine Office*.

When verses of psalms are recited alternately by two choirs or by a choir and the *congregation*, the recitation is referred to as *antiphonal*. See Psalter 2585.

Antiphonal

Antiphonal refers to the recitation of verses of psalms alternately by two *choirs* during the *Divine Office* or by a choir and the *congregation* on other occasions. See Psalter 2585.

Antitype

A type is anything that represents, *foreshadows*, or symbolizes something else. The fulfillment of the thing fore-shadowed is called an anti-type. See Type 117.

Apathy/Apathetic

Apathy comes from the Greek 'apatheia,' meaning incapable of suffering or insensitive and lacking *emotion* or interest, especially in circumstances that call for a show of emotion.

Apathy has generally come to mean lack of emotion, interest, or sensitivity in general. It is a listless condition marked by sluggishness or *sloth*.

In the Greek *theological* sense of the word, apathy does not exclude all this, but it is applied to a higher, *spiritual* form of sensitivity and charity. Thus when a *virgin* is said to be apathetic in Greek, this does not mean she is insensitive but merely that she does not yield in forms of sensuality associated with *sexual intercourse*. See Sloth 1866.

Apocrypha/Apocryphal

The word apocrypha comes from the Greek word 'apokryphos,' meaning hidden. The Latin form of this word is 'apocryphus,' meaning not *canonical*. Applied to *Scripture*, it refers to books whose origin is not certain and whose *inerrancy* is not guaranteed.

During the two centuries just before and after the birth of Christ, a number of books were in circulation, which though of purely human origin, claimed divine *inspiration*. These were called apocryphal because they lacked guarantee of *divine revelation* and were not allowed for use in liturgical *service*. Although on the whole they were *pious* legends and not particularly harmful, some contained *heretical* teachings.

Pope Gelasius in 494 used the term apocryphal to designate 1) heretical forgeries, 2) books revered by the ancients but not included in the *canon*, and 3) works of early Christian writers who erred in some points of *doctrine*. Today the term is used to refer to those books that were rejected by the Church for inclusion in the *canon*.

The apocryphal *Gospels* are *pious* literature containing many details of the infancy of Christ not mentioned in the *canonical Gospels*, such as the history of the *Blessed Mother* and Joseph the foster-father of *Jesus*.

Apocrypha may also refer to seven books, Sirach, Wisdom, Baruch, 1 & 2 Maccabees, Tobit, and Judith, included in the *canon* of the *Old Testament*, which were not counted in the *Hebrew Bible*. This situation gave rise to the term *deuterocanonical*, which means second canon, because *Protestants* believe the *Council of Jamnia*, a *Jewish* Council held c. 90 A.D., reputedly excluded these seven books from the list of inspired books, but not enough is really known about

the activities of this Council to be certain of this.

Origen, in the third century, defended the right of the Christians to use these books even if the *Jews* disapproved them. The Church could not be bound by the decisions of the Pharisees at *Jamnia* because the only source from which she could receive the Old Testament writings as inspired was the *Holy Spirit* himself through the *Apostles*. The Apostles in their teaching appealed to Old Testament scriptures as the *Word of God*. Guided by the *Holy Spirit*, they *consecrated* its *authority* and gave it abiding *value* as the guide to *faith* by the community. The *Council of Trent*, in 1546 A.D., formally declared that all the books of the Old Testament, including the deuterocanonical books, were to be accepted with equal devotion and reverence. *Protestants* call these books 'pseudepigrapha,' meaning false writings, that is, writings falsely claiming to be inspired. See Canon of Scripture 120.

Apollinarianism

Apollinarianism was a *heresy* that denied that *Christ* had a complete *human nature*, that is, that he did not have a real human *will* and *reason*. It teaches that the *divine Logos* substituted himself for the absent human spirit, thus making of Christ's incomplete human nature a single nature, a mixture partly human and partly divine. Apollinarianism anticipated the fifth century *monophysitism* (one *person* and one nature in Christ) condemned by the *Council of Chalcedon* in 451 A.D. The Church teaches that Christ has both a complete human nature and a complete *divine nature*: two really distinct natures united in one person. See Heresy 817, 2089.

Apologist

Apologist comes from the Greek 'apologia,' the prefix 'apo-,' meaning away from, and the word 'logos,' meaning speech or word. An apologist is one who writes or speaks in defense or justification of some *doctrine*, *belief*, or action. It was a title of honor in the early Church given to writers, especially those called *Fathers of the Church*, who defended the Church and her teachings. Today the term refers to *persons* versed in *theology* who teach, speak, or write in defense of the Church and her teachings.

Though the word apologetics is associated with the word apology, it is not an acknowledgement of some fault, injury, or insult or an expression of regret or a plea for pardon but a verbal defense. See Apostolic Fathers. Also see Fathers of the Church 11.

Apolyticon

An apolyticon is the short *hymn* that precedes dismissal in the *Byzantine* Liturgy. See Byzantine Rite. Also see Rite 1203; Troparia 1177.

Apophatic

Apophatic refers to knowledge based on negation. Man's rational understanding of God is largely apophatic, that is, based on negation or knowing what God is not. For example, knowledge of his infinity is based on an attempt to remove all known limitations. See Trinity, Holy 232, 234.

Apostasy 817, 2089

Apostasy, from the Greek word 'apostasia,' meaning 'standing apart from,' is an act by which a *baptized person*, after accepting the *Christian faith*, rejects it by its total repudiation. An *apostate* is automatically *excommunicated*.

The abandonment of Christianity by a person baptized in the Church but raised in a non-Catholic *sect* from infancy does not entail the guilt of apostasy.

The complete abandonment of the actual practice of the faith is not apostasy. A person, however, is an apostate who joins a non-Christian religion or who falls into a profession of unbelief, such as *atheism*, *materialism*, *agnosticism*, *rationalism, indifferentism, or* 'free-thought.'

Apostate

An apostate is one who is guilty of *apostasy*. See Apostasy 817.

Apostle

Apostle comes from the Greek word 'apostolos,' meaning one who is sent, or a *missionary* from the Latin for 'one who is sent,' often to deliver a message, hence a messenger.

Christ chose twelve Apostles to accompany him during his *public life* and called them to be particular witnesses whom he sent out to spread his *Gospel*.

The Apostles were Saints Peter, Andrew, James the Greater, his brother John, Thomas, James the Less the cousin of *Jesus*, Jude (Thaddeus) his brother, Philip, Bartholomew, Matthew, Simon Zealotes, and Matthias (chosen by lot after the *Ascension* to show that Christ rather than Peter determined the choice) who replaced Judas Iscariot.

Saints Paul (chosen directly by Christ on the road to Damascus), Barnabas, and Luke the Evangelist are also considered Apostles (although the latter two not in the strict sense because not chosen by Our Lord directly), although Luke is not mentioned in the *Canon of the Mass*. The Apostles were the first *Bishops*, and Peter was the first *Pope*.

The period of Church history during which the Apostles were still living is called the apostolic age or *apostolic times*. See Bishop 861. Also see Apostolic times.

Apostles' Creed 194

The Apostles' Creed is a form of the *Creed* that is so called because it is rightly considered a faithful summary of the *beliefs* of the *Apostles*, or *apostolic faith*. Its great *authority* arises from the fact that it is the Creed of the *Roman Church*, the *See of Peter*. It is *attributed* to the Apostles themselves. Tertullian (c. 200 A.D.) quotes the earliest form of this Creed. It has been known in its present form since about 525 A.D. The complete present version has been used since about 750 A.D. It is the form of the Creed used in the *rites* of *Baptism* and *Ordination* in the Roman Church. The *Eastern Churches* only use the *Nicene Creed*, authorized by the first *Council of Constantinople* in 381 A.D. See Creed 13.

Apostolate 863

Apostolate is derived from the word '*apostle*,' meaning emissary or *missionary*. It refers to work accomplished on behalf of the Lord, by the nonordained or *lay* members of the Church. This term is properly used in referring to *ecclesial* work done by *laypersons*.

Ministry is properly used in reference to *clerical* duties of the *ordained* ministry. The term '*extraordinary minister of Holy Communion*' can be justified in reference to *laity* only because they perform a *duty* ordinarily reserved to the *clergy*.

Protestants use the term *ministry* for nearly anything related to church activity. Since they lack a *sacramental* clergy, the term does not create for them any confusion of *doctrinal belief* or *hierarchical* rank.

Apostolic catechesis 1724

Apostolic catechesis is the *catechetical instruction* passed down from the *Apostles*. In its content, it is no different from that taught in the Church today.

Apostolic Constitution

An Apostolic Constitution is the highest form of *ecclesiastical* legislation and is issued by the *Pope* himself. The term *papal bull* was used to describe such documents in the past. In Roman congregations, it is abbreviated as 'ap. con.'

Apostolic constitutions deal with fundamental questions of Church life and practice. They are official texts *promulgated* or published in the 'Acta Apostolicae Sedis' (Acts of the *Apostolic See*). See Congregation.

Apostolic faith

Apostolic faith refers to the *faith* as it was preached by the *Apostles* themselves. See Articles of faith 191.

Apostolic Fathers

In general, 'Apostolic Fathers' refers to those Christian writers of the first two centuries considered the most *eminent* witnesses of the *orthodox* Christian *doctrine*. They may be younger contemporaries of the writers of the New Testament, who flourished during the first half of the second century and whose *sanctity* is generally recognized. Among those commonly classified in this grouping are: St. Clement of Rome (*Pope*), St. Ignatius of Antioch, St. Polycarp (*disciple* of St. John the Evangelist and teacher of St. Irenaeus), Quadratus, and Aristedes. All of these were acquainted with one or more of the *Apostles*, in particular Peter and John.

St. Justin and St. Irenaeus are sometimes listed with this group of earliest Christian writers, but they are more properly included with the *apologists* of the last half of the second century.

By *virtue* of their priority in time and closeness to the Apostles and their companions, the Apostolic Fathers constitute the most valuable witnesses to the early faith and sources of *theological tradition*. The *authority* of these Fathers may be great, but it is not unlimited. Only when they show a morally unanimous agreement on a *doctrinal* issue, is it considered decisive and *valid* evidence for doctrinal teaching.

The study of the writings of the Fathers is called *Patristics*. It is strongly encouraged by the Church. See Fathers of the Church 11.

Apostolic letter

An apostolic letter is a document issued by the *Holy See* or *Roman Curia*. It is a brief document used for lesser appointments, erecting or dividing territories, designating *basilicas*, and approving religious institutes. See Ecclesiastical decrees.

Apostolic preaching 76

Apostolic preaching refers to the message of Christ, which the *Apostles* handed on through their spoken words.

Apostolic See

The Apostolic See refers to the *diocese* of Rome. It is applied to the *Pope* as successor of Peter and the *persons* and offices directly under his *authority*. It is also referred to as the *Holy See* or *See of Peter*. See Holy See. Also see Pope 882; Ecumenical council 884.

Apostolic succession 77

Apostolic succession refers to the authoritative and uninterrupted transmission of the message, *mission*, and powers given by *Christ* to St. Peter and the *Apostles* by their *legitimate* successors. See Pope 882.

Apostolic times

The term Apostolic times refers to the period of Church history during which the first *Apostles* were alive. Apostolic times ended with the death of St. John, who died in 96 A.D. This period is also referred to as the apostolic age. See Apostle.

Apostolic Tradition

Apostolic Tradition is the living transmission of the preaching of the *Apostles* and the written message of *salvation* inspired by the *Holy Spirit*, which have been conserved in the *deposit of faith* through *apostolic succession*.

The development of Tradition follows two lines: 1) the better understanding of and penetration into *revealed truth* and 2) the constant application and adaptation of this *truth* to the historical, *cultural*, and religious situations facing man over time. In this process, the Church is *infallibly* guided by the *Holy Spirit*. See Trinity, Holy 232, 234, 237.

Apostolic work

Apostolic work is the work of an *apostle*. All the baptized are to share in the work of *evangelization* and to carry out the original *mission* entrusted by Christ to the Apostles.

Apostolate refers to any service to the Church that advances her and furthers her mission, such as pious works and participation of the *laity* in various ministerial, *social*, and educational programs in their *parish* or *diocese*.

At times, apostolic work refers to a ministry. Ministry, however, more properly refers to the work of *ordained* ministers and not to the work of laymen. See Dominicans.

Apparent good

An apparent good is something judged to be good for a being but that is not actually good for it. A true good is always consistent with the *ultimate end* of man. See Values. Also see Hierarchy of values 1886.

Apparition

An apparition is a *supernatural* vision in which a *person* or object not accessible to human powers is seen and often heard. Because illusions or hallucinations are common and might be the influence of an *evil spirit*, the Church requires proof that it is a true apparition before approving its *authenticity*. *Scripture* testifies that there have been many apparitions that are certainly of *divine* origin. See Shrine.

Appendage

An appendage is anything attached or affixed to something else or in some way dependent. See Particular church 833.

Appetite/Appetency

Appetite or appetency is the tendency or desire for one thing rather than another. See Soul 363.

Appetite, Irascible

An appetite is a spontaneous inclination toward something that is perceived as good and suitable or a withdrawal from something that is perceived as evil or not suitable. When the inclination is toward an object in the sensitive order, it corresponds to desire and is called a *sensitive appetite*. Because the *passions* reside in the sensitive appetite it is also called the *concupiscible appetite*. When the inclination toward an object is *knowledge* of an *intellectual* order, it is called intellectual appetite or *will*.

The word irascible comes from the Latin word 'irasci,' meaning angry. When the object of the appetite is difficult to attain because of obstacles and *anger* is aroused, the appetite is called irascible. See Irascible emotion/appetite. Also see Anger 2302.

Appetitive

The term appetitive refers to man's power of choice and ability to initiate actions ordered to attaining what he deems desirable. It is called his appetitive *power*.

Catholic *theology* distinguishes between two kinds of *appetite*: *intellectual*, and *instinctual*. The intellectual or spiritual appetite is known as the *will* because it is only activated by the exercise of *free choice*. The *instinctual appetite*, however, requires only sense stimulation to be activated.

Intellectual appetite involves two types of affection: the love of something for its own sake and the love of something because it is advantageous or useful. When a thing is loved for its own sake, it is loved for itself simply because it is good, *just*, or *holy*. The love of the *divine* goodness for its own sake differs from loving it because it is advantageous to us.

Contrition for *sin* is distinguished on this basis. Sorrow for offending the goodness of God is *perfect contrition*. Sorrow because of fear of punishment is *imperfect contrition* or *attrition*.

The love of something because it is useful or convenient may or may not be sinful depending on whether what is desired as useful is in conformity with the *divine law*. See Soul 363.

Apprehend/apprehension

The verb apprehend or the noun apprehension means to take hold of mentally or to perceive or understand something. See Omniscient. Also see Truly human knowledge of Christ 473.

Apprenticeship in self-mastery
2339

The apprenticeship in self-mastery refers to the continuing struggle to gain control of *concupiscence*. The practice of *chastity* can be considered a sort of apprenticeship.

Man's dignity requires that he be able to follow freely the dictates of his *conscience* and be moved from within, not by blind impulse or external constraint. He must rid himself of all slavery to passions. He does this by learning self-mastery, which enables him, with the *grace* of God, to choose freely to do what is good. Self-mastery grows through training by a *person's* striving to live a life of *virtue*.

The virtue of chastity by tempering, regulating, and moderating *sexual* desires, thoughts, and actions, fosters the development of true *freedom*. Through it, man maintains the *integrity* of the powers of life and *love* placed in him. This integrity ensures the unity of the person and opposes behavior that would impair it.

Self-mastery is a long and exacting work. It can never be considered totally acquired but must be pursued with renewed effort at all stages of life.

Aramaic terms in the liturgy

A number of Aramaic words are frequently used in the *liturgy*. The most common words are *'Alleluia,' 'Amen,' 'Hosanna,'* and *'Marana tha.'*

Alleluia means 'Glory to Him who Is' and occurs in many *Psalms* as an expression of joy and praise. It is even sung in *heaven* (Rev 19:1). It is also in use in almost every *liturgical prayer* of the Church.

'Amen' means 'So be it' or 'Certainly.' It was used in the *synagogue* and in private prayers of the *Jews*, frequently indicating the end of a prayer or *hymn*. The Church has adopted this usage as well.

'Hosanna' is a shout of triumph and rejoicing from Ps 118:25 and means 'Save us we pray.' It was shouted by the crowd at the Lord's entry into Jerusalem before his *Passion*. It has a prominent place during the *Sanctus* of the *Mass* and *Palm Sunday* liturgies.

'Marana tha' is an Aramaic term, meaning 'O Lord, come' or 'The Lord is near.' It is used dramatically at the end of the Book of *Revelation* where St. John writes, 'The one who gives this testimony says, "Yes, I am coming soon Amen!" Come Lord Jesus' (Rev 22:20). See Hosanna 559.

Archangel

See Choirs of angels.

Archbishop

An archbishop is a *bishop* who governs a diocese and presides over a grouping a dioceses which, taken together, form an ecclesiastical *province*. The bishops of the other dioceses are known as *suffragan bishops*. The archbishop can call the *suffragan bishops* to a *provincial council* and

acts as the first judge of appeal for these bishops, but he has immediate *jurisdiction* only in his own diocese. He is often called a *Metropolitan* because of the importance of his *see* city. Archbishops receive the *pallium* as a sign of this office. See Metropolitan; Suffragan bishop; Archbishop, titular.

Arianism

Arianism was a *heresy* that taught that Jesus was not truly *divine* but the greatest of God's creatures. It held that Jesus was God's Son but not a son in being and *substance* with the *Father*. Because Arianism teaches that Christ was *created*, it holds that there was a time when the *Son* did not exist.

This was perhaps the most important heresy with which the Church had to deal during its first *millennium* of history. It still remains a popular heresy for those whose faith in the *divinity* of *Jesus' Person* is weak or non-existent. The *Council of Nicaea* formally condemned it in 325 A.D. and defined that Christ was one in being, *consubstantial*, with the Father. Arians adopted the *Nicene Creed* but continued to believe that there was a time when Christ did not exist. See Heresy 817.

Aridity in prayer

See Dryness in prayer 2731.

Ark of the covenant 2578

The ark of the covenant is the structure that God ordered Moses to build of acacia wood. It was to be two and a half cubits long and one and a half cubits wide and plated inside and out with pure gold. Inside the ark were placed the *Tables of the Law*, a golden urn containing *manna* and the *Rod of Aaron* (Heb 9:4). The *Israelites* carried these with them in their wanderings in the desert. Because from the ark God communicated his *will* to Moses, it came to be regarded as the guarantee of God's presence among the Jews. It disappeared after the fall of Jerusalem in 587 B.C. The Ark of the Covenant is also a type of the *Virgin Mother*. See Mercy Seat 433.

Armed resistance 2243

Armed resistance refers to the use of force to overcome *aggression*. See Just war doctrine 2309.

Armenian Church/Rite

The *Catholic Church* was established in Armenia by St. Gregory the Illuminator (257–322 A.D.) where it flourished for several centuries. St. Gregory is called the Illuminator because he brought the light of *faith* to the Armenians. Although the *Apostles* Bartholomew and Jude (Thaddeus) preceded him, it was Gregory who persuaded king Tiridates III to accept the faith.

After the defeat of the Armenians by the Persians in the seventh century, the Armenian Church fell into *schism*. They reject the *sacrament of Anointing of the Sick*, permit *divorce* up to three times and are generally *Monophysites*. Today there are about 160,000 *Armenian Catholics* in union with Rome under the *spiritual* leadership of the Armenian Catholic Patriarchate of Celicia. An Armenian *exarchate* was established in New York in 1981 A.D.

When the Armenian Church was organized in the fourth century, the *liturgical* usage of Cappadocia, combined with some Syrian customs, was adopted. The *lectionary* resembles that of the fifth-century Jerusalem, and over time *Byzantine*, Antiochene-Syrian, and various Roman influences left by the *Crusaders* were incorporated. See Oriental Church. Also see Rite 1203; Eastern Church.

Aromatic

Aromatic refers to having an aroma or smelling sweet, spicy, fragrant, or pungent. See Balsam.

Articles of faith 191

Articles of faith are those specific truths that must be believed "particularly and distinctly" (CCC 191).

Articles of faith include whatever truths the Church has defined or *explicitly* laid down for *belief*. After being taught, a *person* who refuses to adhere to the *revealed* truth proposed by the *Magisterium*, even on a single article, loses *theological faith* by that refusal. All truths proposed must receive the same kind and *degree* of *assent* because they are all equally true. To reject one *truth* of faith, therefore, is to reject them all.

It is customary to reckon the number of articles of the *Creed* as twelve. The number twelve symbolizes the fullness of the *apostolic faith*.

Artificial birth control/artificial contraception

The use of devices that prevent *insemination*, or of drugs that render the womb sterile or prevent ovulation is referred to as artificial birth control or, more often, *artificial contraception*. Because such practices contradict the purpose of the *conjugal act*, they are in themselves *intrinsically* and gravely *evil*. Such practices do great harm to both the *integrity* of *marriage* and the love of family.

Sexual intercourse should be the physical expression and *consummation* of a permanent commitment of exclusive love. It should bond and increase affection by the mutual pleasure of complete self-giving of *spouses* to one another and their family. This is impossible when the ultimate purpose of the act is deliberately avoided.

Such intercourse is simply mutual *masturbation* and a shameful, degrading use of another for selfish pleasure.

When married *persons* practice artificial contraception in any form, they weaken their *moral* sensitivity and fail to appreciate the gravely sinful character and injustice of *adultery*. They fail to respect the *dignity* of their partner and the high calling to the *holiness* that is part of the *sacramental* grace of *Matrimony*. See Regulation of procreation 2368. Also see Artificial contraception; Contraception 2370.

Artificial insemination

Artificial *insemination* is a *fertilization* technique that entails the intrusion of a third party into the role of husband and wife in *conception*. It includes such procedures as the donation of sperm or ovum and use of a *surrogate womb*.

By this means, conception is achieved by doctors using a procedure that fertilizes an egg producing an *embryo*. It establishes the *dominion* of technology over the origin and destiny of *persons*. Such a *dominion* is in itself contrary to the dignity and equality that must be common to parents and children.

Such procedures are gravely *immoral*. When the techniques involve only the married couple to enable conception of their own child, it is perhaps less reprehensible but remains morally unacceptable. Just as it is wrong to prevent conception artificially, it is wrong to cause conception artificially outside of the *conjugal act* and so outside the womb because only God can decide when and where to create a child.

These procedures are immoral because they dissociate procreation from *conjugal love*. Such procedures bring a child into existence by a means other than by two persons freely giving themselves to one another in the state of marriage. See Heterologous artificial insemination and fertilization 2376.

Artophorion

The artophorion is the *tabernacle* in the *Byzantine Church*. See Tabernacle 1379.

Ascension

Ascension refers to the bodily departure of *Christ* into *heaven*, in the presence of his *Apostles*, on the fortieth day after his *Resurrection*. See Mysteries of the Incarnation 512.

Ascesis 1734, 2015, 2340

Ascesis comes from the Greek word 'askysis,' meaning bodily exercise or training. It refers to the practice of *self-discipline*, particularly that undertaken *voluntarily* for the love of God or for *spiritual* improvement.

Ascesis may refer to either internal or external disci-

pline. It is internal when it is applied to the control of the *mind* or *heart*. It is external in the renunciation implied in the *evangelical counsels* or in forms of bodily *mortification* directed at controlling the *appetites* to make them conform to right *reason* and *divine law*.

At least some self-discipline is required as a condition for *salvation* because Christ tells us, 'If thou wilt be perfect, go, sell what thou hast, and give to the poor' (Mt 19:21). And elsewhere, 'If any man will come after me, let him deny himself, and take up his cross, and follow me' (Mt 16:24).

Asceticism/Ascetical

Asceticism refers to the practice of *ascesis*, or *self-discipline* in all its forms, particularly when it is undertaken out of love of God and a desire for *spiritual* improvement. See Ascesis 1734.

Asexual reproduction

Asexual reproduction is *reproduction* without the union of male and female germ cells, in such a budding in which a new individual develops from a bud on the parent stalk. Another form is fission, where the parent organism simply divides into two or more parts, which develop into new individuals. See Reproduction.

Ash Wednesday

Ash Wednesday is the first

day of the season of *Lent*. It takes its name from the ceremony of placing ashes of *blessed* palms on the forehead with such words as, 'Remember man thou art dust and unto dust thou shalt return.' See Lent.

Aspersion

Aspersion is a *valid* but *illicit* manner of administering *Baptism*. In Baptism by aspersion, water is sprinkled on the head, not poured. See Baptizein 1214.

Assent

Assent is the act by which the *intellect* recognizes and accepts some *proposition* as true in the *theoretical* or *speculative order*, as distinct from the kind of *knowledge* based on *experience* alone. Although one accepts the *truths* proposed by *faith* solely on the *authority* of God's having revealed them by the *assent of faith*, this is not done without a prior *recognition* of the *credibility* of divine *revelation* derived from experience.

In *marriage*, assent refers to the internal acceptance of another as a permanent partner in marriage. See Consent 1627.

Assent of faith

Assent of faith means that a *person* gives assent to a *truth* that he does not understand but accepts as *revealed* on the *authority* of God and of the Church. See Assent.

Assisting grace

Assisting grace is another name for *grace of cooperation*. It is the form of *actual grace* that assists us in an operation already begun and accompanies every *supernatural* act. It may also be called *concomitant grace* or *cooperating grace* because it is associated with the use of *human freedom* in carrying out the *will of God*. See Grace 153.

Assumed a human nature 470

At the *Incarnation*, the *Second Person* of the *Holy Trinity* became *man*. In doing so, he neither divested himself of his *divinity* nor merely *absorbed* a *human nature* into his *divine nature*. The Church teaches that, while retaining his divine nature, the Second Person of the Trinity assumed a human nature and became man. He remained one Person possessing two real and distinct *natures*, one divine and one human.

Assumption of the Blessed Virgin 966

The Assumption is the taking of the body and the *soul* of the *Blessed Virgin Mary* into *heaven* on the completion of her earthly life before the general *resurrection* and *judgment*.

The *dogma* of the Assumption was defined in 1950 A.D.

This dogmatic definition does not mean that the Assumption became a new *revelation*. It is a declaration that this *mystery* was *implicit* in the *deposit of faith* from the beginning and is now expressly recognized as an *article of faith*.

Astrology

Astrology is a form of *divination* based on the *theory* that the stars and planets influence *human* affairs. Before 1543 A.D., astrology formed a partial basis for *astronomy*, but it has since been separated for scientific reasons. Astrology uses a map of the sky at the time of birth to determine one's tendency to disease, and liability to certain fortunes or calamities.

It is wrong to believe in astrology because it involves contradictions. It claims uniform influences on all *persons* born on the same day in the same place which prove later to be unmistakably different. It claims to predict accurately the future, which depends on the exercise of *free will*.

Such thinking contradicts the *doctrine* of free will and leads to a *fatalistic* view of *man's* destiny. It has been formally condemned by the Church. See Magi.

Astronomy

Astronomy is the science that treats of stars, planets, and other heavenly bodies and their composition, motion, and relative position and size. See Astrology.

Athanasian Creed 192

The Athanasian *Creed* is an official statement of *Catholic doctrine* principally regarding the *Holy Trinity* and the *Incarnation*. Many claim it was probably composed during the lifetime of St. Athanasius who died in 373 A.D., and was perhaps used by him. Others date it a little later, during the lifetime of St. Ambrose, and place its origin in the West rather than in the East.

Atheism / atheistic 2124

Atheism, sometimes called *infidelity*, is the rejection of *belief* in God or a denial of God's existence. There are different forms of atheism.

A common form is *practical materialism*, which restricts man's needs and aspirations only to space and time.

Another form is atheistic *humanism*, which falsely considers *man* to be an *end* in himself and the sole maker with supreme control of his own *destiny*.

A common characteristic of atheism is that it seeks the liberation of man through *social* and *economic* means alone. This poses a danger in efforts to remedy social ills if those efforts are concerned only with the *material* needs of man.

Because it denies or rejects the existence of God, atheism is a *sin* against the *vir-*

tue of religion. Believers can contribute to the rise of atheism by being careless about their instruction in the *faith*; by presenting its teachings falsely; by failing in their religious, *moral*, or social duties; and by concealing rather than revealing the true *nature* of God and of the faith.

Atone/Atonement

Atonement is the satisfaction of a *legitimate* demand or *reparation* for an offense. When the atonement is equal to the offense, it is adequate. Because *sin* is an offense against an *infinite good*, sinful *man* is unable to make proper atonement. Atonement for *sin* can only be made by a *Divine Person*.

The day of expiation is the day set apart by the *Jewish* people for observing the *Day of Atonement* for sin. Atonement could not obtain *forgiveness* under the *Old Law*. For this reason, the Old Law is called the *Law of Bondage*. Man was required to keep it but was not able to free himself from sin by his observance of it. See Day of Atonement 578.

Attribute/Attribution

As a noun, attribute is a characteristic or quality of a person or thing. The act of attributing is called attribution.

Attribute as a verb means to assign or ascribe something to someone as its source, such as authorship. See Preternatural attributes.

Attrition 1453

Attrition is another term for *imperfect contrition*. Attrition is sorrow for *sin* that is motivated by fear of punishment or revulsion for the sin itself rather than an act of perfect love for God. The motives for attrition are good, but since of themselves they do not flow from a pure love of God, attrition does not forgive *mortal sin* without *sacramental Confession*.

Like *contrition*, attrition requires *authentic* rejection of *sin* for religious motives. In *Confession*, attrition becomes contrition because the sacrament perfects attrition with the grace of God or *charity*.

Augur/Augury

In ancient Rome, an augur was one of a body of officials who interpreted *omens* as being favorable or unfavorable in connection to a public or private undertaking like war, *marriage*, etc.

Augury is the practice of *divination* from omens or the formal ceremony conducted by the augur in making his determination. Some examples of omens include the flight of birds, the study of bird entrails, the tossing of stones at random and studying the patterns of sprinkled grains, the study of the sky and planets, etc. The consultation of augurs was very popular among the aristocracy and rulers of Rome. See Omen.

Aumbry/Ambry

An aumbry is a cupboard or niche located on the *Gospel* side of the *altar* used to store the *holy oils*. See Holy oils.

Auricular confession

Auricular comes from the Latin word 'auricula,' meaning ear. Church law imposes the obligation of confessing grave sins committed after *Baptism* to a qualified priest. It is called auricular confession because confession is normally made by word of mouth and heard by the priest before he gives *absolution*. See Communal celebration of penance 1482. Also see Individual confession.

Auriga virtutum 1806

'Auriga virtutum' is a Latin phrase that means charioteer of *virtues*. It is used to describe *prudence* because it guides the other virtues by setting the rule and measure for them.

Prudence immediately guides the *judgment* of *conscience* by assisting in the application of *moral* principles to particular cases without error. It overcomes doubts about the good to be achieved and the evil to be avoided.

Authentic/Authenticity

Authenticity refers to the quality, reliability, or genuine-

ness of a *belief* or item. See Sphragis 698.

Authentic teachers 2034

Authentic teachers are those endowed with the *authority* of Christ to preach the *faith* to the faithful entrusted to them. *Bishops* in union with the *Supreme Pontiff* are authentic teachers of the faith in their *dioceses*.

Authenticate

To authenticate is to represent something as genuine and able to be accepted or believed as trustworthy or reliable. See Authenticity Also see Notaries.

Authority 1897, 875

Authority is the quality that *persons* or institutions possess that gives them the right to expect *obedience* from those under their authority. Authority makes observance of the laws or orders they give binding in *conscience*.

Every human community needs an authority to govern it. The proximate foundation of that authority lies in *human nature* itself as *created* by God, with the *natural law* of God inscribed in the heart of each *human being* (cf. Rom 2:14–15). The role of authority or *divine law* in *society* is to ensure, as far as possible, the *common good* of society.

Authority does not derive its moral *legitimacy* from itself but from God. Legitimate authority imposes a *duty* of obedience and respect toward those who exercise it.

Autonomous

Autonomous comes from the Greek 'autos,' meaning self, and 'nomos,' meaning law. Something that is autonomous can function independently of others or is a *law* unto itself. See Human person 2222. Also see Person 251.

Autopsy 2301

An autopsy is a detailed examination and dissection of a body that is made especially to determine the cause of death or damage done by disease. It is also called a *post mortem*.

Autopsies can be *morally* permitted for legal inquests or for scientific research.

Auxiliary Bishop

When the pastoral needs of a *diocese* warrant it, one, or several Auxiliary Bishops may be appointed at the request of the *diocesan Bishop*.

Auxiliary Bishops are bishops deputed by the Holy Father to assist the diocesan Bishop in the performance of his *episcopal* functions in very large dioceses. They share in the same fullness of *sacramental orders*, but they do not have *ordinary jurisdiction* in the diocese and do not have the *right of succession* in the diocese. See Bishop 861.

Avarice 1866, 2536

Avarice is the inordinate love of wealth, *material* goods, or worldly honors and their attendant power. St. Paul calls it the root of all evil in 1 Tim 6:10. It is opposed to the *virtues* of *justice* and *liberality*. Avarice is a *capital sin*. From avarice proceed hardness of *heart* toward the poor, *inquietude* of *soul*, faithlessness, treachery, and fraud.

Prayer, almsgiving, detachment, and simplicity of life help one to overcome avarice.

Avatar

In Hinduism an avatar is a god who comes to earth in bodily form, a sort of incarnation of the god. See Hindu. Also see Centering prayer; contemplation.

Ave

Ave is a name for the *Hail Mary* because the first word of the *prayer* in Latin is Ave. See Hail Mary. Also see Rosary.

Axiom

Axiom comes from the Greek word 'axioma,' meaning *authority* or an authoritative sentence. It is used today to refer to an established *principle* of *law* or *science* that is accepted as true. In *logic* and mathematics, it refers to a statement that needs no proof because its truth is self-evident. See Lex orandi, lex credendi 1124.

B

Babylonian exile

The Babylonian exile was the 70 year period of *Jewish* history during which the inhabitants of Judah and Jerusalem were forced to live in exile in Babylon from c. 606 B.C. to c. 537 B.C. Because of the relatively benign Babylonian treatment, many *Jews* preferred not to return to Israel after Cyrus' decree that they were free to return. See Exile.

Baldachino/Baldachinum

A baldachino or baldachinum is a canopy that covers the *altar*. It may be suspended from the ceiling or attached to a wall. It may be of any *material* but should be ornamented with tapestry or other fabric. At times, it is made of wood or stone supported by four pillars, as the famous baldachino over the main altar in St. Peter's. A baldachino is also referred to as a *ciborium*. See Altar 1182.

Balsam

Balsam is gummy *aromatic* oil obtained from certain types of a balsaminaceae tree. Balsam is mixed with olive oil in preparing *sacred chrism*. See Sacred chrism 1183. Also see Holy oils.

Banns

Banns of *marriage* refer to the public *ecclesiastical* announcement of the names of *persons* intending to marry. The purpose of the publication is to discover possible *impediments* and to prevent a secret marriage. The 1983 edition of the *Code of Canon Law*, Canon 1067, stipulates that the *episcopal conference* is to issue the norms concerning the examination of the parties and banns or other appropriate means for carrying out the necessary inquiries that are to precede marriage. See Mixed Marriage 1633.

Baptism 1213, 1214

Baptism is the *sacrament* instituted by *Christ* by which a *person* is incorporated into Christ and is cleansed of *original sin* and *actual sin*. It is administered by the pouring of water on the head while saying the words, 'I baptize you in the name of the Father, and of the Son, and of the Holy Spirit.'

Through Baptism, a person becomes a member of the Church and is infused with the *theological virtues* of *faith*, *hope*, and *charity*.

Baptism is the first sacrament and gives access to all the others by enabling the baptized to receive the other sacraments effectively. Without Baptism, no other sacrament can be received *validly* or *licitly*. Because Baptism confers an *indelible* or *permanent character* on the soul, this sacrament cannot be repeated.

By virtue of their Baptism, all Christians have a *sacerdotal* function and dignity called the *priesthood of the faithful* or *baptismal priesthood*. With Christ and the *ordained minister*, they offer *worship*, sacrifice, and glory to God. Their role in the *Eucharistic celebration* reflects this priestly function.

By Baptism, Christians are called to live the *Word of God* and to bear witness to all nations in his name. They are, therefore, a *prophetic* people.

Although the ministerial priesthood and priesthood of the baptized are grounded in the *priesthood of Christ*, they differ in *essence* and not merely in *degree*. *Ministerial priesthood* requires reception of the sacrament of *Holy Orders*, and exercise of the priesthood of the faithful depends on exercise of the *ministerial priesthood*.

Baptism of blood 1258

Unbaptized *persons* who suffer death for the sake of the *faith* or some Christian *virtue* are "baptized by their death for and with Christ" (CCC 1258). Because death precludes the possibility of receiving the *sacrament* of *Baptism*, the person's willingness to die under these conditions implies the desire for the sacrament, and, if they were to survive, they would still need to be baptized. Therefore, 'Baptism of blood' is not a sacrament, but is called 'baptism' since it "brings about the fruits of Baptism without being a sacrament" (CCC 1258).

Baptism of desire 1258

When sacramental *Baptism* is impossible, an act of *perfect contrition* with a desire for Baptism "brings about the fruits of Baptism without being a *sacrament*" (CCC 1258). Because it is not Baptism in the full, sacramental sense, even though the *person* receives sufficient grace for *salvation*, they not only can, but must, receive Baptism if it becomes possible.

'Baptism of desire' is most clear in the case of *catechumens*, who explicitly desire Baptism and are "already joined to the Church, they are already of the household of Christ" (CCC 1249). However, it is also possible for someone who is "*ignorant* of the *Gospel* of *Christ* and of his Church, but seeks the truth and does the *will of God* in accordance with his understanding of it" (CCC 1260) to be saved through an *implicit* desire of Baptism, that is, that had they known of Baptism, they would have *explicitly* desired it.

However, *Vatican II* teaches that "often men, deceived by the *evil one*, have become vain in their reasonings and have exchanged the truth of God for a lie, serving the creature rather than the Creator." Because of this, though it is possible for those who are ignorant of the Gospel to be saved by an implicit desire for Baptism, "the Church fosters the missions with care and attention" (Vatican II, *Lumen Gentium*, 16). See Missionary mandate 849.

Baptism of infants 1252

The practice of baptizing infants is an *immemorial tradition* in the Church. Infants are to be baptized soon after birth, but no definite time frame is set by *Canon Law*.

Non-Catholic infants may be baptized even against their parents' wishes when there is present danger of death. Otherwise they may be baptized only with the consent of at least one parent or guardian and when there is an assurance that the child will be raised *Catholic*.

Abandoned children whose parents are unknown are to be baptized conditionally when there is no evidence of previous *Baptism*.

Baptism of the Holy Spirit

Baptism of the Holy Spirit is an *experience* shared by members of the *Charismatic Renewal* or *Catholic Pentecostals* through which they are renewed and filled with *grace* and special gifts, such as healing or speaking in tongues. They meet weekly to pray, share the *Spirit*, and testify about personal *faith* moments. See Charismatic gifts 768.

Baptism of water 1238

'Baptism of water' refers to the *sacrament* of *Baptism*, in which the candidate either is immersed in water or has water poured on the head while the minister of the sacrament says the words, 'I baptize you in the name of the Father, and of the Son, and of the Holy Spirit.' See Baptism of blood.

Baptism, Sacrament of 977, 1213

Baptism is the first of the seven *sacraments* and the chief sacrament of forgiveness. It grants access to the other sacraments. Baptism forgives original and personal *sin*, bestows a new life in *Christ* and the *Holy Spirit*, and incorporates a *person* into the Church, the *Body of Christ*.

Baptismal creed 189

The baptismal creed is the first '*profession of faith*' made by the candidate during the *rite* of *Baptism*. In the case of *infant Baptism*, the *creed* is recited by all those attending, and the *sponsors* speak for the child. In the Western Church, this profession of faith is made using the *Apostles' Creed*.

Baptismal font

A baptismal font is the decorated stone, metal, or wooden receptacle that contains the *baptismal water* used for the solemn administration of *Baptism*. Every *church* must have a baptismal font. See Baptistry 1185.

Baptismal name 2156

The Baptismal name conferred at *Baptism* refers to the name of a *saint*, who, because he has lived a life of exemplary *fidelity* to the Lord, can serve as a model and personal *advocate* of the *person* baptized before God. A person may take the name of a Christian *mystery* or Christian *virtue* as a Baptismal name. Parents, *sponsors*, and the *pastor* must ensure that the name given is not foreign to *Christian* sentiment.

Baptismal priesthood 1268, 1669

By their *Baptism*, all Christians receive a *sacerdotal* function and *dignity* called the Baptismal priesthood or *priesthood of the faithful*. Together with Christ and the *ordained minister*, the baptized offer *worship*, *sacrifice*, and *glory* to God. Their role in the *Eucharistic celebration* reflects this priestly function.

Although the *ministerial priesthood* and priesthood of the baptized are grounded in the *priesthood of Christ*, they differ *essentially* and not only in degree.

Baptismal seal or mark

In the sacraments of *Baptism*, *Confirmation*, and *Holy Orders*, the *soul* is imprinted with the *indelible seal* of the *Holy Spirit* as a *sign* of ownership, of the *person's faith*, and of both the expectation of the *blessed* vision of God and the hope of the *resurrection*.

The sign is indelible because it remains even in one who loses the *state of grace*. It signifies that one who has received these *sacraments* has a special relation to Christ. It is called a *character* because it confers a permanent quality that distinctly identifies the individual with unique abilities that enable him to perform certain works in the Church.

This seal or permanent mark is Christ's pledge of eternal life. It is also called the seal of the Lord or *Dominicus character*. See Seal of the Lord 1274. Also see Dominicus character 1274.

Baptismal water 1238

Baptismal water is water especially *consecrated* by a prayer of *epiclesis* either at the time of *Baptism* or at the *Easter Vigil* (cf. CCC 1238). In the prayer of epiclesis, the Church asks God that, through his Son, the power of the *Holy Spirit* may be sent upon the water, so that those who will be baptized in it may be "born of water and the Spirit" (CCC 1238) and so be incorporated into Christ and share his life. The relation of water and the Spirit in Baptism suggests a parallelism between our rebirth to *eternal life* and the birth of *Jesus* to human life through the *Virgin Mary* and the power of the Holy Spirit. Therefore, it also suggests Mary's role as our spiritual Mother.

Baptistry 1185

Originally, the baptistry was a building separate from, but near the *church* where the *sacrament of Baptism* was administered. Only through Baptism could one outside the church enter it. Today, it signifies the part of the church that is set aside for Baptisms and contains the *baptismal font*. After the main *altar*, the baptistry is the most *sacred* part of the church. As part of the *liturgical* reform, it is encouraged in the *Roman Rite*.

Baptized

See Baptism.

Baptized in Christ

Baptized in Christ refers to a *person* who has received the *sacrament* instituted by *Christ* by which he is incorporated into Christ and cleansed of *original sin* and *actual sin*. See Baptism 1213. Also see Born of a virgin 502.

Baptizein 1214

Baptizein is a Greek word meaning 'plunge' or 'immerse.' The central *rite* of the *sacrament* of *Baptism* is the plunge into the water, which symbolizes the *catechumen's* burial with *Christ* from which he arises with Christ as a new creature. It is for this reason that the *sacrament of regeneration* is called Baptism.

Baptism may also be *validly* administered by pouring or sprinkling water on the head. Baptism by sprinkling is called *aspersion*. Baptism by aspersion is *valid* but *illicit*. Baptism by immersion was once universal in the Church and is still practiced in the *Oriental Church* as part of the liturgical reform. It is encouraged in the *Roman Rite*.

Barbarians

The term barbarian was first used to refer to non-Greeks or non-Romans. It originally meant alien or foreigner but gradually came to refer to any civilization regarded as primitive or savage. See Benedictines.

Basileia 2816

Basileia is a Greek word meaning kingdom. In the *New Testament*, it may be translated as an *abstract* noun meaning kingship, kingdom, or reign. The *Kingdom of God* prayed for in the *Lord's Prayer* lies ahead of us. It is brought near in the *Word Incarnate*, is proclaimed through the *Gospel*, and has already come in *Christ's* death and *Resurrection*. The Kingdom of God means Christ, whom we desire to come daily. He is the Kingdom of God, in whom we shall reign at our resurrection.

Basilica

'Basilica' originally meant a house or palace of a king (from the Greek word meaning king) and later used to designate the house or palace of *Christ* the King and Victor. It is a title of honor given to certain *churches* of religious or historical importance. There are two kinds of basilicas: *major basilicas*, which include four great churches in the city of Rome: St. John Lateran, St. Peter, St. Paul and St. Mary Major, and two in Assisi: St. Francis and St. Mary of the Angels; and *minor basilicas*, which include other important churches in Rome and other parts of the world. The major basilicas are also known as *patriarchal basilicas*. Celebration of *Mass* on the main *altar* of the Archbasilica of St. John Lateran is normally reserved to the *Pope* alone.

Basilicas enjoy special privileges, such as special *indulgences* and a distinctive emblem called an 'ombrellino,' a red and yellow striped umbrella. The colors represent the *papal* colors. Basilicas also have a bell on a staff, which was once used to announce the arrival of the Pope. The basilica also may display the papal coat of arms in or over the main entrance. See Cathedral.

Beatific vision 1028

The beatific vision is that immediate and absolutely clear vision of God which constitutes the primary *felicity* of *heaven* and the *ultimate end* of *man*. By the beatific vision, the *souls* of the *blessed* see the *divine essence* directly, clearly, and openly as he is in himself as one and triune. It is through this immediate vision of God that the blessed share in divine *happiness*.

The first object of the beatific vision is the vision of God as he is in himself, in the perfection of his *Trinitarian nature*. Such *supernatural knowledge* is not proper or even accessible to *human nature*. Hence, the *intellect* of the blessed is supernaturally enlightened for this purpose by a special grace called the *lumen gloriae*.

The secondary object of the beatific vision is the *revelation* of all the *mysteries* believed in, through *faith*, while on earth and confers a distinct knowledge of things exterior to God whether actual or possible.

Those who enjoy the beatific vision have the sight, *recognition*, and enjoyment of those whom they loved on earth. They have knowledge of the prayers and *veneration* addressed to them by those still on earth and can *intercede* for others before the throne of God.

Beatification

Beatification is the third stage in the process of *canonization*. The first stage, during which the *person* is referred to as *'Servant of God'*, begins when the local *Bishop* petitions the *Congregation for the Causes of Saints*. This starts a careful inquiry, so careful it may take many years, into the person's life, writings, *sanctity*, and alleged *miracles*. If the congregation agrees that the person lived a heroically holy life, the person is given the title *Venerable*. With the approval of a miracle worked through the Venerable's *intercession* and the *Pope's* approbation, solemn beatification takes place, and public *veneration* of the *Blessed* is permitted. An *Apostolic letter* is issued, and from this time the person is referred to as *Blessed* or *Beatus*. After beatification, another miracle must be proven to have taken place through the intercession of the Beatus before the person is formally canonized or declared a saint. See Canonizing 828. Also see Promoter of the Faith.

Beatitude, eternal

Properly speaking, beatitude refers to the state of the *blessed* in *heaven*. On earth, we move toward beatitude by acts prompted by the movement of *grace* toward *virtuous* behavior and as *gifts of the Holy Spirit*.

The beatitude to which God calls man is referred to as the *Kingdom of God*, the vision of God, the joy of the Lord, and entering into God's rest. With beatitude, we become partakers of the *divine nature* and of *eternal life* and share the joy of *Trinitarian* life. Beatitude surpasses all understanding and comes as a free gift of God in the form of a special *grace* called the *lumen gloriae*.

The call to beatitude confronts *man* with *moral* choices. To achieve beatitude, man must freely purify his heart of *evil instincts* and seek the *will of God* before all things. It is by morality that true happiness is found in God alone who is the source of everything *good* and of all *love*. The *Decalogue* describes the path that leads to beatitude.

Sustained by the grace of the *Holy Spirit* and the workings of the Word of *Christ*, man is able to bear the fruit of *holiness* in the Church to the glory of God and his own beatitude. See Hope 1817, 2090.

Beatitudes 1716

The Beatitudes are the words of *Jesus* found in Mt 5:3–12 and Lk 6:20–23 in which he pronounces *blessings* on the *poor in spirit*, those who mourn, the meek, those who hunger for *righteousness*, the merciful, the clean of heart, the peacemakers, and those persecuted for the sake of righteousness.

The acts referred to in the Beatitudes are acts of *virtue* arising from the influence of *actual grace* in the soul moving it to practice the *gifts of the Holy Spirit.*

As a literary form, the Beatitudes are found in the *Old Testament* and in the Greek literature of the time of *Christ* associated with the salvific deeds of God.

The rewards of the Beatitudes define suffering on earth within the context of God's saving plan and show how sharing Christ's Cross is the beginning of *eternal life.*

Beatus/Beati

Beatus, meaning *blessed*, is a title conferred in the third step in the process of *canonizing* a *saint*. The process of *canonization*, which requires an inquiry into the *person's* life, writings, *sanctity*, and alleged *miracles*, begins with the local *Bishop*. If his investigation reveals that there is merit to the person's reputation for *holiness*, the Bishop passes the investigation to Rome for further review. At this stage, the person is called '*Servant of God.*'

In Rome the investigation continues. It is exceedingly thorough and may continue many years. When the investigation is successfully completed and the *Pope* approves, solemn *beatification* takes place. At this time the person is referred to as Blessed (Beatus). See Beatification. Also see Canonizing 828.

Beauty 341

The formulation of a definition of beauty is a difficult one because it is manifested in such a variety of forms. The Catechism explains that beauty is the recognition by the *intellect* of the order and harmony of *creation* resulting from the diversity of beings and the relationships that exist between them.

This order and harmony is discovered by *man* progressively as he learns more about the laws of nature and the *interdependence of creatures.* Beauty is found not only in *material* things but especially in *spiritual* things because beauty is a reflection of the *infinite* beauty of the Creator and inspires respect and submission of man's *intellect* and *will* to him who creates and sustains all.

Philosophy considers beauty to be a function of the *cognitive faculty* of the *soul* and an *intuitive knowledge* and delight in what is known. There are three general *attributes* of being: unity, truth, and goodness. These are *transcendental* attributes of all being, but being and beauty are not convertible ideas.

The attribute of *unity* implies the idea of 'indivision' or 'undividedness' in a being's inner reality, which separates it from all other things. The attribute of *truth* consists of the conformity of a being with its *nature*. A thing is what it is by virtue of its nature and *essence*. The attribute of goodness means that every positive reality is *good* and in some way perfect because actuality itself is a kind of perfection. The notion of perfection of being gives rise to the attribute of beauty.

There are three particular elements or properties that must be present in a thing for it to be styled beautiful. They are 1) integrity or completeness, 2) proportion or balance, and 3) clarity or splendor. Integrity or completeness is the first recognizable property of beauty. The presence of any defect or mutilation makes an object unpleasant to behold. Because it causes disturbance, irritation, and unrest in the *mind* it hinders *aesthetic* enjoyment. When this disturbance is minimal, it may not entirely prevent enjoyment in the object as a whole because we can still recognize some degree of beauty, such as would occur from a false note in a pleasant melody.

Proportion or balance is a second requisite for beauty. The mind experiences aesthetic pleasure in perceiving orderly arrangement. The sound of instruments of an orchestra being tuned is not beautiful, but when the sounds of the same instruments are related into an intricate harmony, they become a beautiful symphony.

The third element of beauty is clarity or splendor. What is beautiful must attract and charm by its appearance. The beauty of an object emerges with a kind of compelling force that elicits an active and absorbing response on the one contemplating it. Beauty inspires a spontaneous joy and delight in the *heart* by its splendor, which floods the heart with emotion.

Beauty is always associated with the good. In finite things, beauty never appears in absolute form or purity because no finite thing is perfect. Beauty is always a foretaste of the perfect beauty and goodness of God. The order of excellence or goodness of *created* beings is proportionate to the degree to which they possess these three attributes of beauty.

St. Thomas simply defines beauty as that which pleases when seen.

Beget/Begetting

To beget means to *procreate*, to bring into being or to father. See Reproductive rights. Also see Procession of Divine Persons; Begotten.

Begotten

The manner in which the *Divine Persons* are related to one another is called *procession*. The Son is said to proceed from the Father by *gener-ation*. It is through procession by generation that the Son is the only begotten of the Father before all ages.

Because procession is an *eternal* aspect of the *Trinity*, it cannot be understood as meaning that the processions follow as cause and effect or in sequence as in creatures. See Procession of Divine Persons.

Being

Being is anything that is or can be. It includes whatever exists or can possibly exist. Possible things or beings can exist in the *mind*, as *imagination* or as a statement. They can also exist outside the mind. If a thing does not *actually* exist but could exist, it is a possible being.

In *philosophy*, being is what is real and corresponds to the *essence* of a particular thing. It is the opposite of unreal, that is, something that implies an inner *contradiction*, such as a square circle. See Accident.

Belief/Beliefs

Belief is the *assent* to something on the *authority* or trustworthiness of the words of another. All belief, therefore, includes an *act* of the *will*, which commands the intellect to accept something that is not evident or apparent based on the trustworthy words of another.

According to the motive for giving assent, belief may be human or divine. Human belief is based on the authority or trustworthiness of another *human being*. Such belief may prove wrong. Belief based on God's word in *revelation* is *divine faith*. It accepts something as true because it is revealed by God who is absolutely trustworthy because he is *Truth* itself.

Because the *assent of faith* is an assent to *supernatural* truth, it requires the gift of *grace* and is accepted as absolute truth. See Believed with divine and catholic faith. Also see Dogma 88; Faith 26, 146; Faith as a theological virtue 1814.

Believed with divine and Catholic faith

To believe with *divine faith* means to believe those truths of faith that are *explicit* and direct *revelations* of God and must be believed as true on the *authority* of God who reveals them. To believe with *Catholic* faith means to believe something is true on the *infallible* authority of the Church teaching that a *truth* is contained in *divine revelation* and is part of the *deposit of faith* preserved by the *Church* in *Sacred Tradition*. See Heresy 817.

Benedictines

Benedictines refers to a *monastic order* of *monks* established by St. Benedict c. 529 A.D., who is considered to be the father of western *monasti-*

cism. They live in *community* observing the *Rule* of St. Benedict and dedicating themselves to work and *prayer*. There are Benedictine *nuns* who observe the same rule.

The Benedictines are credited with saving the best in Greco-Roman *culture* from the onslaughts of the *barbarians* by incorporating that culture into a new Christian Civilization and embracing the converted barbarian peoples. See Order 1537.

Benediction

Benediction is a short name for *Benediction of the Blessed Sacrament*. See Benediction of the Blessed Sacrament. Also see Eucharistic species 1373.

Benediction of the Blessed Sacrament

Benediction of the Blessed Sacrament is a short service consisting of the singing of the hymn 'O Salutaris Hostia' with *incensing* of the *Blessed Sacrament*, prayers in honor of the Blessed Sacrament, a period of silent *adoration*, and the singing of the *hymn* 'Tantum Ergo' together with incensing. This is followed by a *blessing* with the *Sacred Host* and the recitation of the *Divine Praises*. It is often simply referred to as Benediction. See Eucharistic species 1373.

Benedictus

The Benedictus is the *canticle* of Zachary (Zechariah)

recorded in Lk 1:68–79 after his announcement that his son would be called John. It is a song of thanksgiving for the visit of the Lord (brought by *Mary* to the house of Zachary) and the proximate delivery or *redemption* of Israel (symbolized by the healing of Zachary), to be announced by his son who is to be given not his father's name, but John, meaning gift or *grace* of God.

Liturgically, it is used at *Lauds* in the *Divine Office*. See Antiphon. Also see Canticle.

Benefice

A benefice is a permanent *ecclesiastical foundation* or endowment consisting of a *sacred office* or *duty* and the right to annual revenue. Four things are necessary for a benefice: 1) that it be set up according to *Canon Law*, 2) that it have a right to revenue, 3) that it have an *ecclesiastical office*, and 4) that it be permanent. Beneficed *clergy* have free use of their income to the degree necessary to live in a manner befitting their state but must spend what is *superfluous* on the poor and good works. See Right to private property 2403.

Beneficence

Beneficence comes from the Latin word 'benefacere,' meaning to do good. Beneficence is the fact or quality of being kind, doing good, or being charitable. See Fruits of charity 1829.

Benevolence/benevolent

Benevolence is a *virtue* that disposes one to promote the welfare of others. It is a form of *charity*, which seeks what is good for another without self-interest. See Creation 279.

Benignity

Benignity is kindness or *mercy* toward others and a willingness to serve them with *love*. It prompts us to serve others by word and deed. See Fruits of the Holy Spirit 1832.

Bible/Biblical

'Bible' is the name given to the book of *Sacred Scripture*. The Bible is divided into two parts, the *Old Testament*, containing forty-five books (or forty-six, when Lamentations is counted as distinct from Jeremiah), and the *New Testament*, consisting of twenty-seven books. These books contain the words by which God reveals himself to man in human words. The human authors wrote in their own words but under the *inspiration* of the *Holy Spirit*, so these books have God as their author. The Church holds that what the *inspired* sacred writers affirm is to be regarded as affirmed by the *Holy Spirit*. They firmly, faithfully, and without error teach the *truth* which God wished to reveal for the sake of our *salvation*. See Sacred Scripture 102, 109.

Biblical Commission

The Pontifical Biblical Commission was established in 1902 A.D. by Pope Leo XIII to promote biblical studies and to guard against *doctrinal* errors. In 1971 A.D., Pope Paul VI completely reorganized the Commission and joined it to the *Congregation for the Doctrine of the Faith*. See Congregation for the Doctrine of the Faith.

Bind and loose 1445

Bind and loose refers to the power given by Christ to the *Apostles* to exercise supreme *authority* to rule the Church and to forgive *sins* (Mt 16:19). The words bind and loose mean that whomever the Church excludes from her *communion* will be excluded from communion with God and whomever she receives anew into her communion will be received anew into communion with God. Whoever is reconciled with the Church is reconciled with God.

Birth control

Birth control refers to the practice of engaging in *sexual intercourse* while simultaneously *deliberately* preventing *conception*, which is its natural purpose. The use of barriers or drugs for the purpose of preventing *fertilization* during *sexual intercourse* is always *gravely disordered* and sinful and does great harm to both *marriage* and family. See Regulation of procreation 2368.

Bishop 861

The word bishop comes from the Greek word 'episkopos,' meaning overseer or supervisor from 'epi,' over, and 'skopos,' one who watches. A bishop is the supreme overseer of a *diocese*. The Church defines bishop as one who has received the fullness of the *sacrament* of *Holy Orders*. His *consecration* makes him a successor to the *Apostles* and an *authentic teacher* of the *Gospel*.

Bishops are responsible directly to the *Pope* but do not act in the name of the Pope or as his delegate. Bishops have *authority* by reason of their office, but in the exercise of their authority, they are subject to the authority of the Pope as head of the Church and require from the Pope the power of *jurisdiction* to exercise their power of *orders legitimately*.

A *Coadjutor Bishop* is a bishop *deputed* by the Holy Father to assist a *diocesan* bishop in the performance of *episcopal* functions. He shares in the same fullness of *Sacramental Orders* and has the *right of succession*, but he does not have the same ordinary jurisdiction in the diocese. Upon vacancy of the *episcopal see*, he immediately becomes

the Bishop of the diocese after he has legitimately taken possession of it.

When the pastoral ends of a diocese warrant it, one or several *Auxiliary Bishops* may be appointed at the request of the diocesan Bishop.

They are deputed by the *Holy Father* to assist a diocesan bishop in the performance of *episcopal* functions in very large dioceses. They share in the same fullness of Sacramental Orders, but they do not have *ordinary jurisdiction* in the diocese and do not have the right of *succession* in jurisdiction.

Black Friars

See Dominicans.

Black magic

Black magic is the name given by modern writers to the kind of magic that involves the *invocation* of the power of *devils*. Black magic is gravely opposed to the *virtue of religion*. See Magic 2117.

Blasphemy 2148

Blasphemy is the uttering against God either inwardly or outwardly of words of hatred, reproach, or defiance. It also includes speaking ill of God or failing in respect toward him in one's speech by misusing God's name. The prohibition of blasphemy extends to language about Christ's Church, the *saints*, and *sacred* things. In itself, it is a *grave sin* because it is a direct offense against the *person* of God. The *second commandment* of the *Decalogue* expressly forbids blasphemy.

Blessed / Blessedness

Blessed is a title formally granted to a *person* who has been beatified (declared blessed) by an official declaration of the Church by the process of *beatification*.

In general, blessed refers to any person, place, or thing closely associated with God enjoying *divine* favor.

Blessed is used to describe anything that has been set aside for devotional purposes by a special *prayer* said over it, often accompanied by sprinkling with *holy water*. See Holy water. Also see Canonizing 828; Beatus.

Blessed Mother

Blessed Mother refers to the *Blessed Virgin Mary* as the *Mother of God*. See Aeiparthenos 499.

Blessed Sacrament

The *Eucharistic species* is also called the Blessed Sacrament. It is the Body, Blood, *soul*, and *divinity* of Christ under the appearance of bread and wine. See Eucharistic species 1373.

Blessed Trinity

Blessed Trinity is another term for *Holy Trinity*. See Trinity, Holy 232.

Blessed Virgin Mary

Blessed *Virgin Mary* is a title of the Mother of *Jesus Christ* and the greatest of *Christian* saints. See Immaculate Conception 491.

Blessing(s) 1078, 1669, 2626

A blessing is a prayer invoking God's power and care on some *person*, place, or thing. Some blessings confer a permanent status, such as the *consecration* of persons to God or setting something apart for *liturgical* use. A blessing *dedicates* persons, places, or things to a *sacred* purpose and attaches some *spiritual value* to them.

The Church imparts a blessing by using a prescribed formula invoking the name of *Jesus* while making the *sign of the Cross*. In a general sense, anyone may bless by invoking the *divine* favor, such as is done in the blessing before meals or in making the sign of the Cross on oneself.

"Blessing expresses the basic movement of *Christian prayer*: it is an encounter between God and *man*" (CCC 2626). One of the ways God communicates with man is through his blessings or gifts. Through blessing, God's gift and man's acceptance are united in *dialogue*. The prayer of blessing is man's response to God's gifts. Because God blesses, the *heart* can, in return, bless the source of every blessing.

The whole of God's works is a

blessing, but in the Church's *liturgy*, the divine blessing is fully revealed and communicated. When man blesses God, blessing means *adoration* and surrender to his creator in thanksgiving.

Blood relations/relationship

Blood relationship may be either direct or collateral. A *collateral line* or relationship exists between two *persons* who have a common ancestor. A *direct line* or relationship arises through the begetting of offspring.

The direct line has as many *degrees* as there are *generations*. The degree in the collateral line is the total number of persons in both generational lines traced to the common ancestor, excluding the ancestor.

In the direct line, *marriage* is *invalid* in any degree whether generation is illegitimate or natural. In the collateral line, it is invalid to the fourth degree inclusive. See Consanguinity.

Boasting 2481

Boasting is bragging or talking about one's deeds or abilities in a way that shows too much *pride* and satisfaction with one's self. It is distasteful and inclines one to exaggeration and pride. Boasting can cause resentment in others, thus, leading them into sin.

Boasting may take the form of *irony*, which *disparages* another by *maliciously cari-*caturing* some aspect of his behavior, possessions, or personal traits, thus, making the boaster look better by contrast.

The habit of boasting can be overcome by practicing the *virtue* of *humility* and by the prayerful awareness that any good one has he has received from God and should be used for the benefit of others. Trying to cultivate an appreciation of the talents and gifts of others also helps a boastful person to pay less attention to himself.

Body of Christ 787, 789, 790, 1381

Body of Christ is used to refer to a number of different realities. First it refers to the *human* body that *Christ* assumed at the *Incarnation* through *conception* in the womb of the *Virgin Mary* by reason of which he became truly man. The Body of Christ also refers to his *glorified Body* in *heaven* and his *Mystical Body*, the Church.

Body of Christ refers to the same *Incarnate* Body, Blood, soul, and *divinity* sacramentally present in the *sacrament of the Eucharist* under the appearances of bread and wine. In this *sacrament*, Christ is truly and substantially present and united to each *person* receiving him in *Holy Communion* as a *mystical* member of that very Body.

Body of Christ can also refer to the Mystical Body of Christ, the Church, the intimate communion that Jesus shares with all his *disciples* by their *Baptism*. Here the Church is viewed *metaphorically* as a body whose head is Christ and whose members are the *faithful*. This image keeps in focus both the unity of the Church with Christ and the diversity of her members.

The Church is not the same as a physical body whose members or parts do not enjoy personhood. On the other hand, the Church is not merely a moral body or corporation whose members are united merely by *legal* bonds. The communion of the baptized is in and through the real Body of Christ. Cf. the *encyclical* of Pius XII, *Mystici Corporis*.

Body of Christ also means the daily Bread of the *Our Father*, which, taken literally, refers directly to the *Bread of Life* as the Body of Christ. See Epiousios 2837. Also see Eucharistic species 1373; Substantially contained 1374; Transubstantiation 1376.

Body-soul

This hyphenated word is used to indicate that *man* is a composite of body and *soul* rather than a body inhabited by a soul. The body and soul in man are substantially united as body-soul. They are not two separate complete *natures* but a single complex nature. The *human* body cannot exist independently of the soul.

But the soul can continue to exist, even if in death the body is separated from it. With the separation of body and soul at death, a *human nature* ceases to exist until reconstituted in the *resurrection*. See Dualism 285. Also see Hylomorphism.

Bonds of Church unity 815

The multiplicity of peoples and *cultures* gathered together in the unity of the Church is always threatened by sin; therefore St. Paul (Eph 4:3) exhorts *Christians* to maintain the unity of the *Holy Spirit* in the bond of peace. This bond of unity rests above all in *charity*, which binds everything in perfect *harmony*. The *visible bonds of communion in the Church* are 1) The profession of one *apostolic faith*, 2) the celebration of *liturgy* and *sacraments*, and 3) *apostolic succession* by means of the sacrament of *Holy Orders*.

Born from above 526

Born from above refers to the new life of *grace* that God gives those who believe in his Son, whom he sent to bestow on men a share in his *divine nature* making them *adopted sons* of God and *heirs of heaven*.

Baptism effects an *ontological* change, that is, a change in the very *nature* of those who receive it. Through *Baptism*, a *person* is born again into the *supernatural* order and begins to live supernaturally, that is, in a way that is beyond his *created* nature as a man. This baptismal rebirth enables men to *share in the divine life* through grace so that their *natural acts* acquire a *supernatural* character through sharing in the life of *Christ* while they are still on the earth.

Born of a virgin 502

God, in his saving plan, willed that his Son be born of a virgin to manifest his absolute initiative in the *Incarnation. Jesus* has only God as Father. The *Son Incarnate* was never estranged from the Father when he *assumed a human nature*. This means he remained God. He is, in his *divine nature*, the Son of the Father by virtue of his *divinity* and naturally the son of *Mary* by virtue of his human nature. Therefore, as one *Person*, Christ is both *Son of God* and Son of Mary precisely because Christ is one Person with two *natures*.

By being conceived by the *Holy Spirit* in Mary's womb, Jesus became the *New Adam* who inaugurates a *new creation*. The first Adam was of the earth; the second is from heaven.

By his *virginal conception*, Jesus also ushers in through *Baptism* the new birth of children adopted in the *Holy Spirit* through *faith* in Jesus Christ. In his *Gospel*, St. John tells us that this participation

in Jesus' *divine life* is not of the blood nor of the flesh nor of the *will* of man but of God (Jn 1:12). This life of *adoption* is *virginal* because it is entirely the gift of the *Spirit*. This is what is meant by saying that the Church gives virginal birth to those who are *baptized in Christ*.

Mary's *virginity* is also a sign of her *unadulterated* and undivided gift of self to God's will. It is her *faith* that enables her to become Mother of the Savior. As virgin and Mother, Mary is the symbol and most perfect realization of the Church, which, by receiving the *Word of God* in faith, becomes herself a Mother bringing forth sons conceived by the Holy Spirit and *born of God* into a new and *immortal life* by the Holy Spirit.

The Church herself is a virgin who keeps the faith pledged to her *spouse* in its entirety and purity.

Born of God 526

Born of God refers to the new *supernatural* life of the *soul* that has been *imbued* with *sanctifying grace*. The soul is said to be *born from above* because of the new supernatural life bestowed on it by the Holy Spirit at *Baptism*.

Born under the law 422

Christ assumed the *human* condition by being born of a woman and born under the *Law* in order to achieve the two-fold object of the *divine plan*: to *redeem* those condemned under the Law and to confer divine *sonship* on all mankind. The Spirit of Christ, the *Holy Spirit*, gives the *Christian* his sonship and the inheritance of God's Kingdom (Cf. Gal 4:4 ff.).

By being born of woman, Christ became subject to the *Mosaic Law*. By submitting to the Law of *circumcision*, he becomes capable of falling under its curse. The curse of the law refers to the *consequences* that result from non-observance of the Law. Just as the promises of the *covenant* must be fulfilled, so the curse or punishment consequent on non-observance of the Law of the covenant must also be endured as the condition for fulfillment of the promises. *Redemption* includes both the fulfillment of the covenant and undergoing its curse.

Both the promise and the *curse* are *irrevocable*. In Gal 3:13, St. Paul says that Christ has removed the curse of sin from man by himself becoming a curse. That is, he bore our guilt to achieve our *redemption*.

The Law only served to reveal the deficiencies of *human* conduct, but it could neither cure nor *atone* for them. St. Augustine taught that God gave man the Law so that he would seek *grace* and that he gave grace so that man could observe the law. Christ cured and atoned

for human deficiencies by redeeming man through the *Sacrifice of the Cross*. The curse Christ took upon himself consisted of all the penalties due to the human race for its *transgression* of God's *Law*. By his death, Christ completely negated the curse of sin and merited for man the grace to keep the Law.

Bread of Life

Bread of Life refers to the *Blessed Sacrament* or *Eucharist*. In the *Lord's Prayer*, it is referred to as 'artos epiousios.' 'Artos' means bread, loaf, or food.

The use of the Greek word *epiousios*, meaning super-essential, is translated as 'daily bread' in the Lord's Prayer. This word occurs nowhere else in the *New Testament*. Here it signifies a repetition of 'this day' to confirm us in trust without reservation. It also signifies what is necessary for life, what is good and what is sufficient for subsistence.

Taken literally, it refers directly to the Bread of Life, the *Body of Christ*. Finally, in another sense, it refers to the *Day of the Lord*, the feast of the kingdom to come, which is anticipated in the *Eucharist*. See Epiousios 2837.

Breaking of bread 1329

Breaking of bread is the action by which Christ's *disciples* at Emmaus recognized him after the *Resurrection*.

Jesus used this *rite*, part of a *Jewish* meal, when at the *Last Supper* he took bread, blessed it, broke it, and gave it to his disciples saying, 'Take and eat: this is my body' (Mt 26:26).

For this reason, the *sacrifice of the Mass* is frequently referred to as the breaking of bread.

Bride of Christ 796

In 2 Cor 11:2, St. Paul refers to the Church as the Bride of *Christ* as does St. John in Rev 22:17. This *metaphor* occurs expressly nowhere else in the *New Testament*. The *nuptial* nature of the relationship between Christ and the Church, however, is often explained elsewhere in the *New Testament* (e.g. Eph 5:21–32) as well as in early Church writings. The theme of Christ as *Bridegroom of the Church* was anticipated by the *prophets* and announced by St. John the Baptist.

Bridegroom of the Church

Christ is seen as the *New Adam* of the *new creation* in 1 Cor 15:22 and again in Rom 5:12. The early *Church Fathers* taught that just as Eve was taken from Adam's rib so the flow of water and Blood from the side of Christ on the Cross is a *sacramental sign* of the *animation* of the *New Eve*, his Bride the Church, through the *sacraments* and the *Eucharist*. See Bride of Christ 796.

Bronze serpent 2130

In Num 21:4–9, Moses made a bronze serpent (also known as a *seraph* serpent) and mounted it on a pole so that anyone who had been bitten by the snakes God sent among them would recover.

Jesus, sometimes given the title of Seraph, mentioned this symbol in Jn 3:14 where he compared his own purpose to the bronze or seraph serpent. By being lifted up on the Cross, he gave *spiritual* healing to all who are afflicted by *sin*. As *faith* was necessary for those looking upon the bronze serpent to be healed, so faith is necessary to receive the healing of *salvation* from the Cross. See Graven image 2129.

Brute

Brute means lacking in the ability to think. It is also used to refer to the animal impulse in man or *sensuality*. See Reproductive rights. Also see Understanding 1095, 1101.

Buddha/Buddhist

Buddha, the founder of Buddhism, was called the Sage of India and the Enlightened or Awakened one. He was born in what is today Nepal about 563 B.C. and was named Siddhartha Guatemala. Early in life, he gave himself over to severe penance but finding such life without meaning became a holy beggar.

While meditating in 531 B.C.,

he *experienced* an enlightenment in which he saw the visible world as empty and changing. His insight became the primary spiritual influence of the Asian world for twenty-five hundred years.

Buddhism contains four basic teachings: 1) suffering is universal in a changing world; 2) suffering is the result of desire; 3) extinguishing desire will remove suffering; and 4) the way to do away with desire lies in the practice of eight things: right understanding, right purpose, right speech, right conduct, right work, right effort, right mindfulness, and right *contemplation*. Buddha died in 483 B.C. See Centering Prayer.

Byzantine Rite/Church

The Byzantine Rite refers to the system of forms, *ceremonies*, and *prayers* found in the *worship* and in the administration of the *sacraments* originally employed by the Church of Constantinople. This *rite* now is used by all the *Eastern Orthodox* Churches and those Byzantine Churches in union with Rome.

This rite employs the *Divine Liturgy* of St. John Chrysostom and a lengthy form of the *Divine Office* called *'Akolouthia.'* Originally, the language used was old Greek, but now the Slavonic, Arabic, Rumanian, Georgian, Finnish and Albanian languages are also used. Statues and musical instruments are forbidden in *church*.

Holy *Communion* is given under both *species* with a spoon. The *sanctuary* is separated from the *nave* by an *iconostasis* or partition covered with beautiful *icons*. It contains doors that are opened during specific parts of the *liturgy*. The chant is unusually beautiful and often sung in *harmony*. The abundant use of icons is intended to represent the *communion of saints* who share in the life of the Church even in heaven. See Oriental Church. Also see Rite 1203; Eastern Church.

C

Calced

See Discalced.

Calumny 2477

Calumny, also called *slander*, consists in making false remarks, which harm the reputation of another and gives occasion for false *judgments* concerning them. Calumny harms the *reputation* of another by spreading lies about him. It is an offense against *charity* and *justice*. *Gossip* is frequently calumny.

The *gravity* of the *sin* of calumny is proportionate to the degree of injury it causes to the reputation and good name of the *victim*. Because it injures another's reputation and good name, one guilty of calumny is bound in *justice* to retract his statements and restore the good name of the *person* offended, so far as possible. Because such injury is difficult to remedy, one should be especially careful to avoid the sin of calumny at all cost.

Calumny is an offense against the *virtues* of *charity*, truthfulness, and justice. Calumny is often caused by *envy*, *anger*, or *resentment*. It can be avoided by refusing to judge others and rejecting occasions of gossip. Prayer, *examination of conscience*, frequent *confession*, and reception of *Holy Communion* are strong helps to avoid such *sin*.

Calvary

Calvary is the hill outside of Jerusalem where Christ was *crucified*. See Sacrifice of the Cross.

Camaldolese

Camaldolese is the name of a religious order founded in 1012 by St. Romuald (950–1027 A.D.) at Camaldoli in Italy. It was a branch of the *Benedictines* whose ideal was a minimum of communal ties. Because St. Romuald left no written rule, the order's *traditions* varied over the centuries, but it always favored long fasts, *hermitages*, periods of silence, and manual labor. See Contemplative.

Canon(s)

The word canon comes from the Greek word 'kanon,' meaning rule. It represents a standard against which other things are measured.

The body of laws by which the Church is governed is called *Canon Law*.

Sacred writings admitted to *Scripture* as *authentic* according to the rules set by the Church are called *canonical.*

The fundamental unvarying part of the *Mass* is called the *Canon.*

The list of saints recognized formally by the Church is called the *canon of saints.* See Canon Law. Also see Apocrypha.

Canon Law

From the time of the early Church, the *decrees* governing conduct based on *faith* were called *canons.* These were collected and given names reflecting the source of their *promulgation,* such as the *Apostolic* Canons and the Canons of the *Council of Nicaea* or of the *Council of Chalcedon.* Gradually the term canon came to be restricted to matters of *discipline* only. Pronouncements regarding faith were called *Dogmas.*

The 1983 *Code of Canon Law* refers to the 1752 rules or canons related to faith, *morals,* and discipline prescribed for *Christians* by *ecclesiastical authority.* These canons provide the norms for good order in the Church by enunciating the *rights* and duties of individuals according to the status and rank given them by *Christ.*

The Latin name for the Code of Canon Law is *Codex Iuris Canonici.* The Latin word 'Ius' literally means authority as the basis of right. It focuses attention on rights and duties

both of *religious superiors* and subjects based on the authority of God. The Church's primary concern is with protection of the rights and duties of all parties. Another Latin word 'lex' more accurately corresponds to English usage of the word law.

The use of Ius (Right based on divine authority) instead of Lex (Law) suggests the spirit and perspective of the Codex, which is to specify and protect the rights of individuals rather than to control misbehavior.

All who are *validly baptized* are subject to the *prescriptions* of Canon Law regardless of whether they formally consider themselves members of the Church or accept her authority. This is because the character imprinted on the *soul* by *Baptism* makes it subject, authoritatively, or by right, to those whom Christ appointed to rule his flock. The Church, however, specifically exempts from some of the canons non-Catholics who have been baptized.

The most recent Code published for the Western Church was promulgated in 1983 A.D. The present Code is universal so far as the *Latin Church* is concerned and *abrogates* all previous laws contrary to it. A parallel code for the *Eastern Catholic Churches,* known as the Code of Canons of the Oriental Churches (in Latin, *Codex Canonum Ecclesiarum Orientalium*), was promulgated in 1990 A.D. See

Ecclesiastical penalty 1463; Ecclesiastical law 1952.

Canon of saints

Canonization is the public and official declaration of the heroic *virtue* of an individual. It is accompanied by the official enrolling of the *person's* name in the register or canon of saints. It bestows the title of *saint* on the individual, allows him to receive public *liturgical* honors, establishes a day for the celebration of his *feast*, permits the public *veneration* of his *relics*, and allows the *dedication* of *churches* in his honor. See Canonization.

Canon of Scripture 120

The Canon of Scripture refers to the list of inspired books that the Church acknowledges and accepts as part of the *Apostolic Tradition* revealed by God as *valid* components of *Sacred Scripture*, also called the *Bible*. *Inclusion* in this canon serves to distinguish sacred inspired writings from *profane* writings.

In 382 A.D., Pope Damasus I published a complete list of the *inspired* books of the Bible, which he declared were accepted by the universal *Catholic Church*. That list contains 46 (some count 45 by considering Jeremiah and Lamentations as one book) books for the *Old Testament* and 27 books for the *New Testament*. In the list he provided, he was careful to exclude from

the *biblical* canon all *apocryphal* writings that had *insinuated* themselves into various communities in the East.

The list of Pope Damasus includes the twenty-seven books of the *Old Testament* found in the *Septuagint* translation. It also includes seven books that were declared apocryphal by the *rabbis* attending the *Council of Jamnia* about 90 A.D.

The Church, however, is not bound by the decisions of the *Pharisees* at Jamnia because the only source from which she could receive the Old Testament writings as inspired was the *Holy Spirit* and the teaching of the *Apostles*. The Apostles in their teaching appealed to Old Testament Scripture as the *Word of God* thereby *consecrating* its *authority* and giving it abiding *value* through its being used by a community guided by the *Holy Spirit*.

The *Council of Florence* in 1439 A.D. repeated the canon of Pope Damasus I as the Roman Catholic canon of the Bible. In 1545, the *Council of Trent* solemnly restated the teaching of Pope Damasus and the Council of Florence.

Because the *inspiration* or *divine* authorship of particular books can only be made known by the Divine Author himself, any criterion by which to judge the inspired or *canonical* character of a book must include a divine witness. Such testimony or witness is only found in the *Tradition* coming from *Christ* and his Apostles, which is preserved in the Church and supported by her authoritative pronouncements.

Because inspiration is different from the power of inspiring, which depends on the dispositions of the reader at the time of the reading, the Church never held that the divine inspiration of a book could be judged by its effects on the *mind* or *heart* of the reader. To be inspired, the book must have God as its author.

Canon of the Mass

The Canon of the Mass is the part of the *Eucharistic liturgy* that begins after the *offertory* and ends before the *communion*. It refers to *Eucharistic Prayer* I in the 1970 *Roman Missal*. It is also called the *anaphora*. It begins with the prayer 'Te igitur' (to you therefore) after the '*Sanctus*' (holy) and ends with the 'Great Amen' before the *Pater Noster*. It is called the Canon because its form is fixed. The Canon forms a single Eucharistic *prayer*.

In the *Eastern Liturgy*, the Canon of the Mass is called an anaphora. See Anaphora 1352.

Canonical/Canonically 105

When something is officially approved, established, or sanctioned by the Church, it is said to be canonical.

Canonical Age

Canonical age refers to the age that the Church prescribes for the reception of the *sacraments* of *orders* and *matrimony*, for profession of the *vows of religion*, and for entering the *novitiate*.

The term may also be used to refer to the age at which a *person* incurs the *obligation* to observe certain *legal* and *moral* prescriptions of the Church, such as *fasting* and *abstinence*. See Age of discretion 1457.

Canonical form

Canonical form refers to the manner or way in which an *act* must be administered in order to conform to the requirement of *Canon Law*. See Convalidation of marriage.

Canonical Gospels

A canonical Gospel refers to one of the four *Gospels* by Matthew, Mark, Luke, and John approved as *authentic* and included in the *Canon of Scripture* in the *New Testament*. See Apocrypha. Also see Canon of Scripture.

Canonical penalty

A canonical penalty is a punishment imposed by *Church Law* on a *person* who has committed an offense identified in the 1983 *Code of Canon Law*. It consists in the deprivation of some *temporal* or *spiritual* benefit imposed for an *ecclesiastical* offense.

Canonical penalties may be either *expiatory penalties* or *censures*. Canonical penalties are incurred not because of the *intrinsic* wickedness of an act but because of the circumstances attending it and the serious *consequences* involved. They may be incurred in three ways: automatically, by an administrative act of a *superior*, or by an *ecclesiastical* judge in the course of a trial.

Censures are *medicinal* in nature, that is, they are intended for the correction of the offender. Expiatory penalties, on the other hand, aim to satisfy justice by the punishment of the offender.

Ecclesiastical penalties must not be confused with *penances* or other spiritual exercises imposed during the *sacrament of Reconciliation*, which are part of the *moral* order and issued for moral offenses. Canonical penalties belong to the *legal* order and are only imposed for legal offenses. See Ecclesiastical penalty 1463.

Canonical penance

Canonical penance refers to the prayers and good works, such as *fasting*, *almsgiving*, *pilgrimage*, and *retreat*, imposed by *ecclesiastical authority* on those guilty of offenses against *Canon Law* in order to obtain release from *canonical penalties*.

According to the 1983 *Code of Canon Law*, *public penance* may not be imposed for secret offenses. Canonical penance must not be confused with *sacramental penance*, which refers to the good works prescribed as a requirement for *absolution* in *Confession*, precisely in order to help one *reform* his life. See Penance 1459.

Canonization

Canonization refers to the public and official declaration of the heroic *virtue* of an individual. It is accompanied by the official enrolling of the *person's* name in the register or *canon of saints*. It bestows the title of *saint* on the individual, allows public *liturgical* honors, establishes a day for the celebration of his *feast*, permits the pubic *veneration* of his *relics*, and allows the *dedication* of *churches* in his honor. Of course, a person does not have to be canonized to become a saint because one can enjoy the *beatific vision* without having been canonized.

The process of canonization begins when a group of people approach their *Bishop* and propose an individual of outstanding virtue as worthy of canonization. The Bishop, working with the *advocates*, initiates an investigation into the *holiness* of the candidate. If the investigation seems promising, the Bishop submits his findings to the *Congregation for the Causes of Saints* for further study and examination. If the Congregation approves, the candidate is referred to as *"Servant of God."* Permission is given for *veneration* usually in a particular region or country, but it does not include permission to display this servant's image in church or to mention his name in the *Divine Office* or the *Mass*, which normally is reserved to public veneration in the proper sense.

The Congregation for the Causes of Saints examines the candidate's virtues to establish that the individual did indeed practice heroic virtue or died a martyr's death. If so, the Congregation prepares a report. When the *Pope* accepts this report, the person is called *"Venerable."*

At this time, a second more extensive scrutiny of the candidate's holiness is undertaken. This examination is undertaken under the supervision of a person called *"Advocatus Dei"* or *Advocate of God*. He serves as the *"promoter of the cause"* and has full *authority* to examine the candidate's life, virtues, writings, reputation for holiness, and any miracles *attributed* to the person's intercession. It is no longer the devil's advocate but the *Relator* who supervises this. A *Promotor of the Faith* called the "Advocatus Diaboli" or *Devil's Advocate*

may be appointed. His *duty* is to raise all possible *legitimate* objections to approval. This post may be held also by the Relator or by a person distinct from the Relator.

With the approval of the congregation, a decree of heroic virtue is issued by the *Holy See* and approved by the Pope. The process of inquiring into the person's life, writings, *sanctity*, and alleged *miracles* continues. This investigation is exceedingly thorough and may take many years. Customarily, one miracle attributed to the intercession of the candidate is required for *beatification*.

When the investigation is successfully completed and the *Pope* gives his approval, the solemn beatification ceremony takes place. At this time, the person is referred to as *Blessed*.

After beatification, another miracle must be proven to have taken place through the *intercession* of the Beatus before the person is formally canonized. His name is entered in the canon of the saints, and he is formally declared a saint.

In the case of a *martyr*, the requirement of two miracles is not necessary for Sainthood. See Canonizing 828.

Canonizing 828

Canonizing is the act of giving *solemn* official *sanction* or approval by the *authority* of the Church. The act or *rite* of canonizing a *person* is one by which the Church solemnly proclaims him to have practiced heroic *virtue*, to have lived in *fidelity* to God's *grace*, and to be in *heaven*. His name is entered on the roll of saints. Canonized saints are *venerated* by the universal Church as saints.

Canons

A canon is a *priest* whose *duty* it is to sing the *Divine Office* in a *cathedral*. Canons are appointed by their *Bishop* and have a right to a *choir stall* in the *cathedral choir*, a voice in the *chapter*, and a share in the revenues of the cathedral chapter. In Medieval times, they were required to live in the cathedral city and sing the Divine Office in the cathedral, but their rights and duties varied from country to country as did their dress.

The canons who formed the chapter determined the character of the cathedral. When the canons are drawn from the *secular clergy*, the cathedral is diocesan. When they are members of a *religious order*, the cathedral is *monastic*.

In *medieval* England, there were two kinds of cathedrals corresponding to the types of canons who administered them. There were nine *secular foundations* and eight *religious foundations*.

Secular canons did not take the *vows* of *poverty*, *chastity*, and *obedience*. They did not necessarily live in a *community* as the religious canons who took religious vows. See Sanctuary.

Canticle

A *canticle* is a song of praise. There are fourteen canticles in the *Old Testament* and three in the *New Testament*. These latter are as follows: the *Benedictus* sung by Zachary on regaining his power to speak (Lk 1:68–79); the *Nunc Dimittis* recited by Simeon at the presentation of Christ in the *Temple* (Lk 2:29–32); and the *Magnificat*, which Mary, in response to Elizabeth's greeting, sang in thanksgiving for the graciousness of God in fulfilling his promise to send a Savior to Israel (Lk 1:46–55). See Benedictus. Also see Magnificat 2619.

Canticle of Mary/Magnificat

Canticle of Mary is the English name for the Magnificat. It was spoken at the time that Mary visited her cousin Elizabeth.

The prayer is called the Magnificat because that is the first Latin word of the 'Canticle of Mary.'

In this canticle, Mary is responding to the greeting of Elizabeth and addresses God in praise and proclaims his graciousness in fulfilling his promise to send a Savior to Israel. It is recorded in Lk 1:46–55. See Appendix of prayers; Marian prayers; Magnificat.

Capital sins 1866

Capital sins are those sins that engender, are the source of, or give rise to other sins or *vices*. The capital sins are *pride, avarice, envy, wrath, lust, gluttony,* and *sloth* or *acedia*. Capital sins are also called the *deadly sins*.

Capitalism 2425

Capitalism refers to an economic system in which owners of capital resources or those in control of the means of exchange or money lend these to manufacturers or traders in exchange for a share in the profits of the enterprise. Manufacturers or traders need capital to develop their business, but the lenders' only interest in the business is the return on their investment. This gives rise to a tendency for manufacturing and trading to be carried out solely for the sake of money. The success of the business comes to be expressed in terms of profit or loss rather than the *common good*.

The profit motive can result in the destruction of small businesses and individual *responsibility* when it concentrates control of areas of business in the hands of a few large companies. This can expand into an international domination by a process called *globalization*.

Capitalism is not unlawful itself, but the profit motive may easily lead to abuses, which the Church *unequivocally* condemns.

Capsula

A capsula is a round, flat container consisting of two glass disks between which a *consecrated Host* is placed when it is set in a *monstrance* for exhibition during *adoration* or *Benediction of the Blessed Sacrament*. It is also called a *lunette* or *lunula*, little moon, from its shape. See Tabernacle 1183.

Cardinal virtues

The cardinal virtues are *prudence, justice, fortitude,* and *temperance*. They are called cardinal *virtues* because they play a pivotal role as the source and controlling influence over all other virtues. See Virtue 1803.

Caricaturing

Caricaturing is depicting or imitating a *person* by exaggerating certain features or manners to make him appear ridiculous. See Boasting 2481.

Carmelite Rite

The Carmelite *Rite* is a use of the *liturgy* proper to the *Carmelites*. It is based on the *Rite of the Holy Sepulcher* used by the *Latin Church* in Palestine during the twelfth and thirteenth centuries.

It differs from the *Roman Rite*

in that the bread and wine are prepared at the beginning of Mass and between the *Epistle* and *Gospel* at *High Mass*. The *Salve Regina* is recited before the Last Gospel. There are also differences in the administration of the *sacraments* and the burial service. The *chant* used is unique to the Carmelites.

St. Teresa of Avila and St. John of the Cross chose to use the Roman Rite for their reform (*Discalced* Carmelites), and so only the Carmelites of the Old Observance (Calced) used the Carmelite Rite. See Latin Rite.

Carmelites

The complete name for the male Carmelites is The Brothers of the Order of the Most Blessed Mother of God and Ever Virgin Mary of Mount Carmel. It claims descent from *hermits* living on Mount Carmel under the direction of Elias and Eliseus, but their documented history began in 1155 A.D. with a *hermitage* founded there by St. Berthold.

The reformation of the order began with the efforts of St. Teresa of Avila and St. John of the Cross in the sixteenth century and resulted in two independent branches of the *order*. The Calced or Shod Carmelites (who wear shoes) are referred to as the Old Observance and is the parent stem. The original rule regarding *fasting* and *Divine Office* has been modified, but their Medieval liturgy

has been retained. The second branch is called the *Discalced* (or barefoot or Teresian) Carmelites. They practice perpetual *abstinence* and observe special fasts. In addition to their *monastic* duties, they engage in ministerial work and preaching.

The *nuns* of the order were founded in 1452 A.D. and with *papal sanction* live a *mitigated* rule. The convents founded by St. Teresa in 1562 A.D. follow the primitive or non-mitigated rule. Both branches have very similar *constitutions*. Nuns live in *poverty*, have strict *enclosure*, observe perpetual abstinence and silence, recite Divine Office in choir, and are devoted to mental prayer and manual labor. See Latin Rite. Also see Order 1537.

Carnal covetousness 2517

Carnal covetousness is an inordinate and *culpable* desire of possessing that which belongs to another or to wish or love things that are fleshly or sensual. It is an inordinate desire for what is *material, temporal*, and *secular* rather than spiritual. It offends against *charity* and *temperance. Prayer*, frequent reception of the *sacraments*, and exercise of the *corporal* and *spiritual works of mercy* increase charity and temperance.

Carnal covetousness can be overcome with earnest prayer and *meditation* on spiritual goods. A spirit of *mortification* manifested by *fasting* and *almsgiving* helps one to overcome inordinate attachments and desires.

Carthusians

Carthusians is the name of an *order* of *monks* founded by St. Bruno in 1084 A.D. They lead the life of *hermits* and practice perpetual *abstinence*. Their sleep is interrupted every three hours for the recitation of the night office, and they always wear a *hair shirt* called the *cilicium*. They live in *cells* with provisions for prayer, eating, sleeping, and manual work in a small garden. They meet on *Sundays* and *feast days* for *communal prayer*. For recreation, they go for a long walk once a week.

Carthusian *nuns* are strictly *inclosed* and *contemplative*. They follow the same rule as the men except that they eat together daily, but they do not walk outside their grounds. Wearing the cilicium is optional, and they retain the privilege of the *consecration of virgins*. See Contemplatives. Also see Consecrated persons 1672.

Cassock

A cassock is a close fitted, ankle length black robe used by *clerics* as their distinctive garb. See Clerical orders. Also see Clerics 934.

Catacombs

Catacombs are underground tunnels that served as the burial places in which *Christians* of Rome buried the dead during the first three centuries.

Designed like the *Jewish* burial places, they began as family vaults, which by Roman law enjoyed a protected *immunity* from disturbance. Because they were safe places, early Christians *celebrated Mass* there during time of *persecution*. Over time, they grew to become long tunnels filled with hundreds of niches into which bodies were placed. Mass was celebrated over the tombs, which served as tables or *altars*.

The custom of burying *relics* of saints in the *altar stone* recalls these times. At least twenty-five catacombs have been discovered. St. Callistus and St. Sebastian, two of the most famous catacombs, lie close to the Appian Way, an ancient road leading out of Rome. See Altar 1182.

Catechesis 5, 426, 2688

Catechesis is a word from the Greek meaning instruction by word of mouth; hence, it refers to the oral instruction given to *catechumens*. The act of passing on the *faith* through such instruction is called *catechizing*. At the heart of catechesis we find a *Person, Jesus Christ* the only Son of the Father.

Catechetical instruction

Catechetical instruction refers to the *systematic and organic* teaching of the *faith*, especially by *oral instruction*. See Apostolic catechesis 1724.

Catechism 11

A catechism is a basic text used for instruction in the principles of the *Catholic faith*; it was often written in a question-answer format. It is the most *fundamental* and reliable source of knowledge regarding the teaching of the Church in *faith* and *morals*.

Catechism of the Catholic Church, The

The *Catechism of the Catholic Church*, promulgated by St. Pope John Paul II on August 15, 1997 A.D., presents an *organic synthesis* of the *essential* and fundamental content of *Catholic doctrine* regarding both *faith* and *morals* in light of the *Second Vatican Council* and the whole of the Church's *Tradition*.

Catechizing

The act of passing on the *faith* through *oral* instruction is called *catechizing*. The word comes from *catechesis*, a word from the Greek meaning instruction by word of mouth. It refers to the *oral* instruction given during the *catechumenate*. Those who receive the instruction are called *catechumens*. See Catechesis 5, 426, 2688.

Catechumenate 1230

The catechumenate is the process of spiritual formation required of one preparing to fully embrace the *Catholic faith*. During their catechumenate, *persons* are introduced into Catholic *parish* life and are called *catechumens*.

During this period, catechumens are considered candidates for reception into the Church. Candidate comes from the Latin 'candidus,' meaning white, in reference to the white robes worn at Baptism symbolizing purity of heart.

The period of the catechumenate includes a series of preparatory liturgical rites acting as liturgical landmarks that culminate with the reception of the Sacraments of Christian initiation. See RCIA 1232.

Catechumens

The word catechumen comes from the Greek word 'Katecheen,' meaning 'to put into the ear,' because the *Word of God* leading to *faith* begins with hearing the Word of God presented in the Gospels.

Catechumens are those who are receiving instruction in the faith in preparation for *Baptism*. See RCIA 1232. Also see Catechizing 1232.

Categories

In metaphysics, categories are the primary ways in which finite beings can exist. The two basic categories are *substance* and *accident*. When something exists independently and does not require something else in which to exist, such as a book or dog, it is called a substance. When a thing requires something else in which to exist, such as color or size, it is called an accident. There are nine types of accidents: quantity, quality, relation, action, passion, place, time, posture, and habit.

In logic, a category is one of the supreme *genera* to which all *predicates* can be referred or reduced. See Divine nature. Also see Substance 251; Accident.

Categorize/categorization

To categorize means to classify into groups. A category is a supreme *genera* under which *knowledge* of things is classified. Genera is the plural form of genus, which in *logic* refers to a class of things comprised of *subordinate* classes. There are two such genera: *substance* and *accident*. Under substances are classified all things that exist of themselves, that is that have no need of another subject or support to exist, such as a tree or animal. There are things that cannot exist except in something else, such as color or number. They need a *subject* in which to inhere in order to exist. These are called accidents. See Transcendent 285.

Cathedra 1184

Cathedra refers to the seat or throne of a *Bishop* set up in his *cathedral church*. The Bishop's church is called a cathedral because it contains the *chair of the Bishop*. The chair is a symbol of his *authority*. See Cathedral.

Cathedral

Cathedral, from the Latin 'cathedra,' meaning chair, is the title given to the *church* of a *Bishop*. The Cathedral is honored as the principal church in a *diocese* and contains the *chair of the Bishop*, the symbol of his *authority*.

Cathedral choir

See Canons.

Catholic 830

Catholic is a word derived from the Greek word 'katholicos,' meaning universal. The name *Catholic Church* is used to identify the Church established by *Christ* himself and which he entrusted to the *Apostles*. The Church is Catholic because she is universal and possesses the totality of Christ's teaching and *authority*. She faithfully transmits all the teachings of Christ.

A Catholic is a *baptized person* who does not adhere to a non-Catholic religion. A *good Catholic* is one who practices his religion to the best of his ability.

Catholic Church

Catholic is a word derived from the Greek meaning universal. Catholic Church identifies the Church established by *Christ* himself and which he entrusted to the *Apostles.* See Catholic 830.

Catholic Epistles

Catholic *Epistles* refers to those Epistles addressed to the Church in general. Individual Catholic Epistles are called by the names of their authors. See Epistle.

Catholic pentecostals

Members of the *Charismatic renewal* are also referred to as *Catholic pentecostals.* See Charismatic renewal. Also see Pentecostals.

Catholic worker movement

The Catholic worker movement was founded by Dorothy Day and Peter Maurin in New York in 1933 A.D. Its purpose was to motivate the interest of Catholics and others to address the plight of the poor in the United States and identify with those suffering from *poverty* and oppression. It began with the opening of the House of Hospitality, where the unemployed, hungry, or desperate could receive food and shelter.

The movement and its *philosophy* were promoted by the Catholic Worker. It *espoused* applying the *social* teaching of the *Catholic Church* to improve society by eliminating the impersonal dehumanizing practices of much of modern culture. It openly criticized *capitalism*, but was opposed to *communism.* Worker houses are still functioning today. The movement laid a foundation for efforts of *Vatican II* to involve lay Catholics in *social* action and reconstruction. See Distributism.

Cause/Causality

A cause is the principle in virtue of whose action something originates and on which that thing is dependent. It gives existence in some way to another or is the reason for the existence of another *being.* Whatever cannot be the *reason* for its own being must have a cause that is the reason it came to be.

Causality is the influence of a cause in the production of or in the changes that take place in a *material* being. See Divine plan.

Cause (beatification)

A cause is the preliminary inquiry and the subsequent processes involved in *beatification* and *canonization.* See Canonization.

Celebrant

A celebrant is the *priest* who actually says or sings the *Mass* as distinguished from the other *ministers* who assist him. See Solemn Mass.

Celebrate/Celebration

To celebrate means to perform a *ritual religious ceremony* publicly and formally. It also means to give public honor and praise or to observe an anniversary with festivities. See Liturgy of the Mass.

Celebret

In cases in which an unknown priest is to *celebrate* Mass, he must have a *celebret*, a document signed and sealed by his *Bishop* stating that the holder is a *priest* and is free to say Mass. See Celebrant.

Celibacy

In general, celibacy refers to the state of being unmarried. The Church uses the term in a similar manner but distinguishes between lay and *ecclesiastical* celibacy required of the *clergy*.

The Church has always fostered the celibate life in the lay state as a means of living a life more completely focused on the love of the kingdom by following *Christ's* teaching in Mt 19:10–12. One of the *charismata* of *religious life* is found in the self-imposed celibacy of men and women who desire to devote themselves completely to following Christ. See Celibate 1579.

Celibate 1579

Celibate refers to the state of a *person* who, for the sake of the *kingdom*, practices perfect *continence*, that is, *self-control* in the matter of *sexual appetite*. By observing perfect continence, the celibate completely renounces the possibility of matrimony and, therefore, any use of the procreative power or sexual appetite. Married persons must also practice self-control with regard to the sexual appetite in the married state but not perfect continence. See Celibacy.

Cell

A cell is the separate room of a *monk*, *friar*, or *nun* or the habitation of a *hermit*. See Carthusians.

Celtic Rite/Church

The Celtic Rite refers to the various rites in the British Isles that existed from the earliest presence of Christianity in Celtic lands until the Synod of Cashel in 1172. It was confined to the poorer elements of Celtic society rather then the colonial Roman communities. The barbarian invasions of the fifth century isolated the Celtic Church from the rest of Europe, but the arrival of St. Augustine at Canterbury in 603 started, albeit with much opposition, the renewal of ties with Rome. Particular controversies were the date of *Easter*, the way of baptizing, the tonsure, and the evangelization of the Saxons. The Synod of Whitby in 664 ended the independence of the Celtic Church and acknowledged the authority of Rome. However, the name continued to be used until the invasion of England in 1066 by the Normans under William the Conqueror. It endured in Ireland until the reorganization of the Irish Church by the *Council* of Cashel in 1171. See Gallican Rite.

Cenacle

The cenacle is the upper room in which Christ and his *Apostles celebrated* the *Last Supper*. This was also the room in which Christ appeared after the *Resurrection* and in which the *Holy Spirit* descended upon the Apostles on *Pentecost*. See Pentecost 696.

Cenobite

Cenobite is the name given to monks who live a common life in a monastery. The term originates from the Greek 'konoibion,' meaning common life. It is used to distinguish such monks from those known as hermits since they do not lead a life in common. See Monk.

Censure

A censure is an *ecclesiastical* or *canonical penalty* by which a *baptized person* who is guilty of an offense against *ecclesiastical law* and who stubbornly resists *authority* is deprived of certain *spiritual* benefits until he *repents* and is *absolved*. Censures are only imposed for *grave* external and *consummated* crimes and are intended for the cor-

rection of the offender rather than the satisfaction of *justice* and the punishment of the offender. There are three kinds of censure: *excommunication*, *suspension*, and *interdict*. See Ecclesiastical penalty 1463.

Centering prayer

Centering prayer is a method of attempting to acquire the gift of *contemplation* by removing obstacles to it. It seeks to achieve this by preparing human *faculties* to cooperate with the gift. It requires a form of *incantation* by the repeated *chanting* of a sacred word or *mantra* to empty the *mind* of all thought.

Centering prayer originated in the mid-seventies out of *dialogues* of a Trappist *monk* with *Buddhist*, *Hindu*, and *Zen* masters. The techniques it employs are neither *Christian* nor *prayer*. These techniques function at the level of human *faculties* and not as a gift of *grace* freely bestowed by God. The Church cautions *Catholics* against engaging in centering prayer. See Contemplative prayer 2709. Also see Contemplation.

Ceremony/Ceremonial/Ceremonies

Ceremony refers to any action, gesture, or movement used during *divine* worship or the administration of a *sacrament*. When the ceremonies that are part of *public worship* are viewed as part of a complete system of forms, actions, ceremonies, and *prayers*, they are referred to as a *rite*. See Rite 1203.

Certain conscience

Conscience is said to be certain when it adheres to one side of a *practical contradiction* without fear about the *truth* of the opposite. The certain conscience has no doubt about the goodness of a choice. One must always follow the dictates of a certain conscience. See Conscience 1706, 1776, 1778.

Certitude

Certitude is the firm *assent* of the *mind* to a *proposition* without fear of error. There are three kinds of certitude: 1) *metaphysical* certitude, when the opposite is inconceivable, such as two and two are four; 2) *physical* certitude when something cannot be otherwise according to the *laws of nature*, such as the earth rotates on its axis; and 3) *moral* certitude, when it should not be otherwise according to *moral law*, such as parents must care for their children. See Major logic.

Chair of the Bishop 1184

The chair of the Bishop is the chair or throne set up in a *Bishop*'s *cathedral* as a *symbol* of his *authority* over his *diocese*. The chair is called a *cathedra* in Latin, from which the name cathedral, refer-

ring to the Bishop's *church*, is derived.

Chaldean Church/Rite

Today's Chaldean Catholics are descendants of former *Nestorians* who returned to the Church in the sixteenth century. Today, they are found chiefly in Mesopotamia and Persia and number about 96,000. They are governed by the *Patriarch* of Babylon. They follow the *Gregorian calendar*, and, in their *liturgy*, they use the Syriac language.

Chaldeans receive Communion under both species separately. The *words of institution* are sung aloud. Their *churches* have a wall between the *nave* and *sanctuary* with an opening in the middle. The *altar* always faces the east wall, and the *baptistry* adjoins the sanctuary. Men and women are separated in church. In their churches they do not use *crucifixes* or pictures but they display plain crosses. The Chaldean *Rite* is also called the Assyrian or Persian *Rite*.

The Chaldeans preserve the custom of the *Holy Leaven* to emphasize the continuity of the *Eucharist* by a unity of the bread used. Each time the bread is baked, it is mixed with some dough from the previous baking and *leavened* with a bit of *Holy Leaven*, which has been handed on from age to age in each church.

The legend is that, at the baptism of the Lord, St. John the

Baptist caught the water that fell from the *Body of Christ* in a vessel. Before his death, he gave the vessel to John the son of Zebedee to keep till it would be required.

At the *Last Supper*, Christ gave a loaf to each *Apostle* but he gave two loaves to John, one to eat and the other to keep as the Holy Leaven. Later, when Christ was pierced on the Cross, John saw the water and Blood as signs of the *mystery* of regeneration. He collected it in the loaf of the Holy Leaven and mixed it with the water from the baptism of Christ, which the Baptist had given him and divided it among the Apostles.

The leaven is renewed on *Holy Thursday*. What remains in the vessel is mixed with dough, salt, and olive oil to leaven the whole. Nestorians hold this as one of the *sacraments*, and no liturgy may be *celebrated* without it. The reason the Western Church *anathematized* Nestorius, according to the legend, is that, when he fled Constantinople, he took all the Holy Leaven with him leaving the rest of the Church without it.

Although the legend is without basis in reality, it affords an interesting insight into the Eastern mind. See Oriental Church. Also see Rite 1203; Eastern Church.

Chalice

A chalice which should be made of some precious metal or plated with gold, is used to hold the wine that will become the Precious Blood of *Christ* during the *consecration* of the *Mass*. Any *priest* may bless a chalice.

Glass or pottery are not suitable *materials* for a *chalice*. They are easily broken, causing spillage of the Precious Blood, or they may be porous, and the chalice, consequently, may not be properly purified after use. See Offertory 1350.

Chamberlain

Chamberlain is the title given to different classes of officials serving the *papal* court and to those who serve in the apartments of the *Pope*.

The list of official chamberlains include; 1) The Chamberlain of the Holy Roman Church who is the *Cardinal* who administers and cares for the revenues of the *Holy See*, convenes the College of Cardinals and, at the death of the Pope, becomes head of the College of Cardinals. 2) The Chamberlain of the Sacred College is a Cardinal who records the business of the *Consistories*. 3) The Chamberlain of the Roman *clergy* is a Cardinal and president of the Roman *secular clergy*. See Prelature. Also see Papal household.

Chamberlain of the Holy Roman Church

See Chamberlain.

Chamberlain of the Roman Clergy
See Chamberlain.

Chamberlain of the Sacred College
See Chamberlain.

Chancellor
The Chancellor is the *diocesan* official responsible for the department of the diocesan *Curia*, which is entrusted with the care and custody of official *diocesan* documents. In the 1983 *Code of Canon Law*, the Chancellor may be a *cleric* or lay *person*. The Chancellor may be assisted by secretaries or *notaries*, who may be *laypersons*. See Diocese 833.

Chant/Chanting
See Gregorian chant.

Chaplains of His Holiness
The title Chaplain of His Holiness refers to a type of *domestic prelate*. He is addressed as *Monsignor* in Italian or My Lord in English. Such Monsignori are mostly *honorary prelates* without special *jurisdiction* or power. In Europe (including England) *bishops*, as well as prelates without *episcopal character* but with *jurisdiction* and power, are also addressed as My Lord or Monsignor. See Prelature.

Chaplet
A chaplet is a string of beads on which prayers are counted as they are recited. It is a gen-eral name for the *Rosary* or other devotions recited with the aid of beads. There are various kinds of chaplets. One popular chaplet is that of the Chaplet of Divine Mercy.

Literally, a chaplet is a wreath or crown. It comes from the French word 'chaplet,' meaning cap. See Rosary. Also see Divine Mercy Chaplet.

Character
Character comes from the Greek word 'charakter,' meaning an engraved or stamped mark. In English, the word character refers to the *moral* qualities of a *person* based on *temperament* and developed by *free choice*. Character is that which distinguishes a *person* as an individual. It includes both the habitual *virtues* and the failings that make a person a distinct moral individual.

Character represents the integration of one's *nature* and moral habits as they are expressed in daily living. See Substantial form.

Character, sacramental 1121
"The three *sacraments* of *Baptism*, *Confirmation*, and *Holy Orders* confer, in addition to *grace*, a *sacramental character* or '*seal*' by which the Christian shares in Christ's *priesthood* and is made a member of the Church according to different states and functions. This *configuration* to *Christ* and to the Church, brought about by the

Spirit, is *indelible*; it remains for ever in the Christian as a positive disposition for *grace*, a promise and guarantee of *divine* protection, and as a *vocation* to *divine worship* and to the service of the Church. Therefore these sacraments can never be repeated" (CCC 1121).

Charism(s) 798, 799, 800, 801, 1508, 2003

Charism is the Anglicized form of the Greek word *charismata* denoting a special gift or *grace* of the *Holy Spirit*, which directly or indirectly benefits the *common good* in building up the Church.

Charismatic gifts do not necessarily indicate *sanctity* or the reward of merit since they are given for the service of others. Charismata make the *Christian* fit and ready to undertake various tasks and *offices* for the renewal and building up of the Church.

Charisms are granted primarily for the good of others rather than the *person* receiving them. Charisms named in 1 Cor 12:8–11 include *wisdom*, *knowledge*, *faith*, healing, *mighty and wondrous deeds*, *prophecy*, *discernment*, varieties of *tongues*, and *interpretation of tongues*. Collectively, such charismatic gifts are referred to as charismata, graces given every Christian for the fulfillment of his role in the Church.

Charism of infallibility 890

The *Roman Pontiff* enjoys the gift of *infallibility* by *virtue* of his office as *supreme pastor*. This gift is called the *charism* of infallibility and extends to matters of *faith* and *morals*.

Infallibility is also present in the body of *bishops* when, gathered with Peter's successor, they exercise the supreme *Magisterium*, especially in an *ecumenical council*. This extraordinary manner of exercising the Magisterium is complemented in an ordinary manner exercised by the bishops when each, in union with the *Pope*, teaches in his *diocese* on matters of faith and morals.

Infallibility is the supreme participation in the *authority* of *Christ* by virtue of which the teaching of the Church cannot err. This infallibility is ensured by a charism or special *grace* of God and extends as far as does the deposit of *divine revelation* and those elements of *doctrine*, including morals without which the saving *truths* of the faith cannot be preserved, explained, or observed.

What the supreme Magisterium proposes as doctrine for *belief* as divinely revealed and as the teaching of Christ the *faithful* must adhere to with the *obedience of faith*.

Charismata

Charismata is the plural form of charisma, a Greek word

meaning favor or kindness, and refers to special gifts to individuals arising from the goodness and kindness of God. In a broader sense, it refers to those *graces* granted every Christian for the fulfillment of his work in the Church.

Charismata thus refers collectively to those special *spiritual gifts* freely given by the *Spirit* for the *common good* of believers. The English word *charism* comes from this Greek word and refers to a single gift. See Charism 798.

Charismatic Gifts 768

The word 'charisma' in Greek means favor or kindness. Charismatic gifts are also referred to as *charismata*. They are extraordinary *graces* granted to individuals primarily for the benefit of others rather than the one receiving them.

Charismatic Renewal

Associated with *charismatic gifts* is the Charismatic Renewal, a movement in certain Western Churches to restore the *charismata* or spiritual *gifts of the Holy Spirit* (especially speaking in tongues, healing, and prophecy) to a central place in the life and *worship* of the Church. It is promoted through the Charismatic Renewal of *Catholics*. Its members are called *charismatics*.

The *Charismatic Renewal* has received cautious support of the American *Bishops*, Popes Paul VI and John Paul II because of some historical problems with *Protestant* charismatics who denied the *authority* of bishops and the *value* of the *sacraments* as well as embracing *biblical fundamentalism*.

In recent years, the movement has been characterized by strong adherence to the Pope, and a biblically rooted devotion to the *Eucharist* and the *Blessed Virgin*. See Charismatics.

Charismatics

Charismatics are members of the *Charismatic Renewal* or *Catholic Pentecostals*.

Charity 1822

"Charity is the *theological virtue* by which we *love* God above all things for his own sake, and our neighbor as ourselves for the love of God" (CCC 1822). Charity is infused into the soul at *Baptism* and is necessary for *salvation*. Charity is the highest *virtue* and the source of all other virtues.

By charity, we love the *blessed* in *heaven*, the *souls* in *purgatory*, and all men on earth, even our enemies, as God loves them. The practice of the *moral* life animated by charity gives to the *Christian* the *spiritual* freedom of *children of God*.

Charm

A charm is a word, text, act, or

object supposed to have *occult* power to bring something to pass. The use of charms is *superstitious* and forbidden to *Catholics*. See Superstition 2111. Also see Virtue of religion 2096, 2125.

Chastity 915, 2337, 2339, 2346, 2365, 2368

Chastity is the *virtue* by which single *persons* exclude all indulgence in voluntary pleasure arising from the *sexual appetite* and that controls the use of sexual appetite according to the dictates of *reason* by those who are married.

The virtue of chastity enables us to love others with an upright and undivided heart because it tempers, regulates, and moderates sexual desires, thoughts, and actions, subjecting them to the control of reason instead of blind *passion*.

Chastity may be either *absolute* or *relative*. In the case of single persons, it is absolute and requires total *abstinence* from all *sexual intercourse*. In *marriage*, the virtue of chastity is relative. It requires that the sexual appetite be under the control of right reason.

Even in marriage, *lust* for a *spouse* is forbidden because lust renders the other person an object to be used for selfish purposes. Thus, St. Paphnutius before the *Council of Nicaea* taught that a man's intercourse with his wife is chastity. Married sex must

always be a giving of oneself to another and not the using of another. All persons, single, or married, must be chaste.

Chastity is one of the *fruits of the Holy Spirit*. It is a *moral virtue* and the fruit of *spiritual* effort by which the *grace* of the *Holy Spirit* enables one whom the water of *Baptism* has regenerated to imitate the *purity* of Christ.

Chastity is sometimes confused with purity, which more properly refers to refraining from unlawful *sexual intercourse* or moral *corruption*. See Purity.

Chastity as a cultural effort 2344

Though *chastity* is an *eminently* personal task, it also involves a *cultural* effort because of the interdependence between personal betterment and the improvement of society. Chastity requires respect for the *rights* of others, especially the right to information and education that respect the *moral* and *spiritual* dimensions of human life.

Advertising must not offend *modesty* much less arouse *lust* in the presentation of merchandise. Clothing styles must respect the demands of modesty and avoid arousing lust in others as a means of controlling them. Attempts to sell goods in terms of *sexual gratification* offend by making light of *sin* and rendering *immorality* appealing.

Cherubim

Cherubim is the plural of the *Hebrew* word cherub. Cherubim were *angels* armed with flaming swords who were stationed at the gates of *paradise* to prevent man from returning there.

Two cherubim were built on top of the *Ark of the Covenant* facing one another and covering the *mercy seat* with their wings symbolizing that God does not see *sin* when granting his *mercy*. See Mercy seat 433.

Children / Child of God 526, 2222

The *Catechism* teaches that, in his goodness, God freely *created* men and invites them to become his *adopted sons* and *heirs of heaven* through *adoption* in Christ by *Baptism*. God reveals himself to men and makes them capable of responding, knowing, and loving him far beyond their *natural* capacity by means of *sanctifying grace* bestowed at Baptism.

By becoming children of God, we are *born from above* and *born of God*. Born from above refers to the new life of *grace* that God gives to those who believe in his Son whom he sent to *redeem* them and to bestow a share in his *divine nature* through *adoption* in Baptism. Born of God refers to the state of the *soul* that has been *imbued* with *sanctifying grace* through *Baptism*.

Christ liberates man from *sin*

by his death. His *Resurrection* opens the way to a new life of *justification* in God's *grace*. Justification is the victory over death caused by sin through *filial adoption*.

Filial adoption transforms men through sanctifying grace and makes it possible to follow Christ, to act rightly, and to attain the perfection of *charity*.

Because of our adoption as sons in Christ, we pray to God as *Abba*, Father, confident of his loving and *benevolent* providence.

Children of God and parents

Parents must regard their children as children of God, who *created* them and entrusted them to their care. They must respect their children as *human persons* made in the *image of God*. Parents are *obedient* to the *will* of their Father in *heaven* when they educate their children to fulfill his *law*. See Children of God 2222.

Chiliasm

Chiliasm is a word derived from the Greek 'chilioi,' meaning one thousand. It is the *belief* that, during the thousand years when Satan is bound, the *martyrs* of *Christ* will come to life and reign with Christ for a thousand years (cf. Rev 20), which *sectarians* use as a *biblical* basis for their theories. Some consider chiliasm synonymous with *millenarianism*. See Millenarianism 676.

Choir

The choir is the part of a *church* in which a body of singers perform the musical portions of the *Liturgy*.

In *monasteries* where the *Divine Office* is chanted, choir refers to the *stalls* used by the *monks* or *nuns* for this purpose. It is separated from the sanctuary by a carved partition or arranged in raised tiers or levels.

Choir also refers to those who are trained to sing at liturgical services. See Choir stalls. Also see Church 752.

Choir stalls

Choir stalls are the seats with kneelers located on two sides of the *sanctuary* that are provided for the *monks* in their monastery *church* or *priests* of a *cathedral* to sing the *Divine Office*. See Presbytery 1536. Also see Church 752.

Choirs of angels

An *Angel* is a pure *spirit* with an *intellect* and *will*. The number of angels is vast, beyond *human* reckoning. Each Angel is an individual *person* and differs from others in perfection, *nature*, and *grace*. Each angel is an individual species.

According to Isaiah, Ezekiel, and St. Paul, there are three hierarchies of angels, each one made up of three choirs. Seraphim, Cherubim, and Thrones form the first hierarchy. Dominions, Principalities, and Powers form the second. Virtues, *Archangels*, and Angels make up the third. Each choir of angels is distinct and has a status, dignity, and power all its own.

Each choir has certain duties and is traditionally represented by a different symbol. The first choir consists of the following: 1) *Seraphim* are symbolized by fire with six wings and eyes representing their special *zeal* and love for the Trinity. 2) *Cherubim* are represented with four-eyes and wings holding a book symbolizing knowledge; and 3) *Thrones*, are represented as kneeling in *adoration*. The second choir consists of: 4) *Dominations* depicted in royal robes wearing crowns of *authority*. 5) *Principalities* depicted carrying *scepters* and serving as guardians of individual countries. 6) *Powers* shown holding swords because they are charged with the destruction of *evil spirits*. The third choir consists of: 7) Virtues are charged with dispensing miracles. 8) Archangels are special messengers sent from God on important missions. Three of them are given names in *Scripture*. Michael drove Satan into hell, Gabriel announced the Incarnation to Mary, Raphael healed the blind Tobias. 9) Angels are angelic spirits who act as *guardians* and minister to the needs of man. They are usually represented beside *altars worshiping* the *Blessed Sacrament*. In icons they hold the instruments of Christ's Passion.

The three choirs of angels, together with the *saints*, stand before the throne of God as his heavenly court, as his army against *evil*, to assist him in governing *creation*, and to be his messengers to *man*. See Hierarchical 771.

Choleric

Choleric refers to a type of *temperament*. Temperament identifies a *person's* customary frame of *mind* or natural disposition. Persons with a choleric temperament are quick tempered, *irascible*, and easily irritated. See Temperament.

Chosen People

The term chosen people refers to the *Israelites*. In *Scripture*, God calls Israel his first-born. 'Thus says the *Lord*: Israel is my son, my first-born' (Ex 4:22). Elsewhere, he refers to them as a chosen *people*: 'For you are a people sacred to the Lord, our God. He has chosen you from all the nations on the face of the earth to be a people peculiarly his own' (Deut 14:2). Finally, God calls Israel his son: 'When Israel was a child I loved him, out of Egypt I called my son' (Hos 11:1). See Israelitica dignitas 528.

Chrism 1241, 1289

Chrism, also called *sacred chrism*, is olive oil mixed with *balsam* and blessed by the *Bishop* at the Chrism *Mass* on *Holy Thursday*. Chrism is used in the blessing of the *person* during the administration of the *sacraments* of *Baptism* and *Confirmation*, in the *consecration* of a bishop, and in the consecration of *churches*, *altars*, and *sacred* vessels.

Chrismation 1113, 1289

Chrismation is the name for the *sacrament* of *Confirmation* in the *Eastern Churches*. The name is taken from the *anointing* with the *oil* of *chrism*, which takes place during the administration of the sacrament of Confirmation.

Christ 436

The word Christ comes from a Greek translation of the *Hebrew* word *Messiah*, which means anointed. It became the name proper to *Jesus*, the *Word made flesh*, because he accomplished perfectly the *divine mission* that the word 'Christ' signifies.

Christian

A Christian is anyone who has been *validly* baptized. A professed Christian believes in the essentials of the Christian *faith* expressed in the *Apostles' Creed*. A *Catholic* Christian accepts the teachings of the Roman *Catholic Church*, participates in her *liturgical* and *sacramental* life, and gives allegiance to the *Bishop* of Rome and to the hierarchy. See Son of God 441.

Christian death 1682

Christian death refers to the end of earthly life. For the Christian, it inaugurates the end of his *sacramental life* and the completion of *spiritual growth*, which began with his birth in Christ at *Baptism*. It is the final conformity to the image of the Son conferred by the *anointing* of the *Holy Spirit*. It marks the beginning of participation in the *feast* of the *heavenly kingdom* anticipated in the *Eucharist* even if *purification* may still be needed before receiving the *beatific vision*.

Christian humanism 1676

Humanism is a system of thought, which arose during the late fourteenth century, based on an understanding of the *nature*, interests, dignity, and ideals of *man*, and which was sometimes completely *rational* in *nature* denying any role for *revelation* and *religion*. Christian humanism, by affirming the *eschatological* transformation of humanity, radically affirms the *dignity* of every *person* as a child of God. It combines the *human* and the *Divine*, reason, and revelation, giving each its proper role in the life of man.

Humanism becomes inadequate only when it assumes that the pursuit of man's earthly welfare and develop-

ment are conducted without reference to his *supernatural* end. St. John Fisher and St. Thomas More were examples of Christian humanists. See Humanism.

Christian iconography 1160

Christian iconography is the expression, in images, of the same *Gospel* message that *Scripture* communicates by words. Image and word illuminate each other. The Divine injunction in Deut 4:15–16 included a prohibition of every representation of God made by the hand of man. Nonetheless, already in the *Old Testament*, God ordained or permitted the making of images that pointed *symbolically* toward *salvation* by the *Incarnate Word*, as occurred with the *bronze serpent* and the *cherubim* on the *Ark of the Covenant*.

Basing its arguments on the *mystery* of the Incarnate Word, the second *Council of Nicaea* (787 A.D.) justified the *veneration* of *icons* of Christ, the *Mother of God*, the *angels*, and *all saints* because, by becoming *Incarnate*, the *Son of God* made it possible to represent God *authentically* and introduced a new *economy* of images.

Veneration of such images is not contrary to the first *commandment*, which prohibits *idols*, because the honor rendered the image passes to the one it portrays. The honor paid *sacred* images is respectful veneration, not *worship*, which is given to God alone.

Christian initiation

Initiation comes from the Latin word 'initiatus,' meaning to enter upon or into. *Christian* initiation is the process by which a *person* is received into full communion with the *Catholic Church*. It takes place in four stages:

1) The *pre-catechumenate* or inquiry stage generally starts in September as a series of meetings in which the person asks questions, gathers information, or corrects misunderstandings about the Church.

2) The *catechumenate stage* is a process of spiritual formation and an introduction to Catholic parish life.

3) Stage three is the election, which prepares the candidate for the reception of the *sacraments of initiation* at *Easter*. It begins the First *Sunday* of *Lent* and includes three *scrutinies*, *presentations*, and *anointing*.

4) The fourth stage, called *final initiation*, takes place at the *Easter vigil* when the catechumens are baptized, are confirmed, and receive their first *Holy Communion*. See RCIA 1232.

Christmas

The *Christmas season* follows *Advent*. It includes the time "from First *Vespers* (*Evening Prayer* I) of the Nativity of the Lord" (the evening of December 24) "up to and including the Sunday after *Epiphany* or after January 6" (*Universal Norms on the Liturgical Year and the Calendar*, 33).

Several practices in the celebration of Christmas merit special mention. In early times, the greater *feasts* were preceded by a *vigil* or a preparation day. The *faithful* observed the vigil in the *church* spending the night in fasting and prayer. This practice was abolished among the faithful and was restricted to religious orders who recite the night office, whereas the faithful observed the vigil simply as a *fast day*.

Though the vigils of other feasts were abolished, the vigil of Christmas was preserved, and, to this day, following ancient *tradition*, people gather in the church to attend *Mass*, which is offered during the night. By an ancient custom, the Pope offered three Masses on Christmas: the first in the Liberian *Basilica* or St. Mary Major, the second at the church of St. Anastasia, and the third in the Vatican Church. These Masses were celebrated at night, dawn (cockcrow), and in the daytime. In a *mystical interpretation*, the three Masses represent the three births of our Lord: 1) *begotten* of his Father before all ages, 2) born of the Blessed Virgin in the *Incarnation*, and 3) born in the hearts of the faithful through conversion and *Baptism*.

Christmastide

Christmastide extends over the length of the *Christmas* season. During this time, three great solemnities are celebrated: Christmas, the *Solemnity* of the *Mother of God*, and *Epiphany*. See Liturgical seasons.

Chromosome / Chromosomic inheritance 2275

Chromosomes are the threadlike particles in the *nucleus* of every cell. Composed of protein and DNA, they contain the *genes*, which govern the inherited characteristics of an individual.

Normal humans have 46 chromosomes, which are divided into 23 pairs, in their cells. At conception, one chromosome of each pair from the mother combines with a matching chromosome from the father to create a new individual possessing a new set of genes whose sum is a combination of those inherited from each parent. This passing on of the chromosomes constitutes chromosomic inheritance.

Church 751, 752, 754, 755, 757, 761

The word Church designates a convocation or assembly of the *People of God*, especially the *liturgical* assembly of the people called to *celebrate* the *Eucharist*.

Church also refers to a house of *prayer*: the place where the *liturgy* is celebrated, where the Eucharist is celebrated and *reserved*, where the presence of the *Son of God* is worshiped, where the *Divine Office* is sung, and where the *sacraments* are administered.

In the West, there is no uniformity of building or interior arrangement for churches. The liturgical requirements are few, but there must be at least one *altar*. The church must be divided into a *nave* to accommodate the worshippers and a *sanctuary* for the altar and its ministers. In large *Cathedral* churches, there is a place for the *choir* called *the presbytery* in which the *clergy* sing the Divine Office. In *parish* churches, there must be a *baptismal font* and a *confessional*. Seats and kneelers for the worshippers are common in *Latin Rite* churches. In the house of God, the *truth* and *harmony* of the elements that make it up should be signs that show *Christ* is present and active. See Oratory/oratories.

Church council

A Church council is a meeting of church leaders legally *convoked* by proper *authority* to discuss matters and affairs of *ecclesiastical* concern. See Council 465.

Church Fathers

See Fathers of the Church. Also see Apostolic Fathers.

Church is Holy 823

"'The Church... is held, as a matter of *faith*, to be unfailingly holy. This is because *Christ*, the *Son of God*, who with the Father and the *Spirit* is hailed as "alone holy," loved the Church as his Bride, giving himself up for her so as to sanctify her; he joined her to himself as his body and endowed her with the gift of the Holy Spirit for the glory of God.' The Church, then, is 'the holy *People of God*,' and her members are called '*saints*'" (CCC 823). See Coheir/ Coheirs.

Church Law/Ecclesiastical law 1952

A *law* is a rule of conduct enacted by competent *authority* for the *common good*. Such rules enacted to protect the *rights* and good order of the Church are called Church Law. Church Law is found primarily in the 1983 *Code of Canon Law*.

Church Militant

The Church Militant refers to the *souls* on earth still on their journey to *heaven*. It enjoys the *intercession* of the *Church Triumphant* in *heaven* and the *Church Suffering* in *purgatory*. The Church Militant is also called the *Pilgrim Church*. See Three states of the Church 954.

Church Suffering

The Church Suffering refers to the souls being *purified* in *purgatory*. It enjoys the *intercession* of the *Church Militant* and the *Church Triumphant* for release into the joys of *heaven*. The Church Suffering intercedes for the Church Militant in the *communion of saints*. See Three states of the Church 954.

Church Triumphant

The Church Triumphant is the Church of *glory*. It refers to the *faithful* in *heaven* who have achieved *spiritual* perfection. There they *intercede* with the Father for the *Church Militant* and the *Church Suffering*. See Three states of the Church 954.

Church's treasury 1476

The Church's treasury refers to the *infinite* and inexhaustible *value* that the *merits* of *Christ* and the *saints* have before God. It does not refer to the totality of *material* goods that the Church has accumulated over the centuries.

This treasury of merit is *dispensed* to the *faithful* by means of *indulgences*, which the Church attaches to certain *prayers* and good works.

Ciborium

A ciborium is the vessel in which *consecrated Hosts* are

kept and from which they are distributed to *communicants*. It resembles a chalice with a lid. Today, shallow plates are used for distribution of the consecrated Hosts in order to facilitate carrying the number of vessels needed for multiple *Extraordinary Ministers of Holy Communion*. *Chalices* are still used for distribution of the Precious Blood.

Ciborium may also refer to a *canopy* of wood or stone, supported by four pillars, covering the *altar*. Such a ciborium is also referred to as a *baldachino*. See Tabernacle 1379. Also see Altar 1182.

Cilicium

Cilicium is the Latin word for haircloth. It is another name for *hair shirt*, a *penitential* undergarment made of goat's hair worn next to the skin as *mortification*. The size of the garment varies from a vest or girdle to a waistcoat. See Hair shirt. Also see Carthusians.

Circumcision, Feast of the

Circumcision is the *rite* prescribed in *Judaism* and other cultures that involves cutting off the foreskin of a male. It was a sign of the *covenant* between God and his people Israel and *prefigured* the *Rite of Christian Initiation* (RCIA, RCIC) in *Baptism*. *Christ* was circumcised eight days after his birth in accord with *Jewish law*. The Feast of the Circumcision was *celebrated* January 1. Today, the feast is called The *Solemnity of the Mother of God*. See Feast.

Circumincession/Circuminsession

The communion or fellowship of *Persons*, each equally God, really distinct yet fully within each other without ceasing to be distinct, is called their circumincession (literally tending to be in each other) or circuminsession (literally sitting in each other). There is in God only one *nature* but three Persons. This is known as the *Holy Trinity*. The Greek term for circumincession is *perichoresis*. See Trinity, Holy 232.

Cistercians

The Cistercians refer to a strict *monastic* order following the *Rule of St. Benedict*. It was founded at Citeaux in 1068 A.D. by St. Robert of Molesme (1024–1110 A.D.). Its purpose was to establish Benedictinism on the austere lines that he considered to be its primitive spirit. St. Bernard of Clairvaux (1090–1153 A.D.) was perhaps its most illustrious member and is often considered to be its second founder. By the end of the thirteenth century, there were 680 Cistercian *abbeys*.

Cistercians led a life of silence, lived in a community, and devoted themselves mainly to *liturgy* and *prayer*. Strict rules of diet were followed, as was the rule regarding manual labor. The order became a pioneer in agriculture and trained others in its method. The decline of the order after the thirteenth century was followed by a rise of new reformed groups. See Contemplative.

Civil

Civil refers to that which pertains to citizens, their private rights and the *legal* protection of those *rights*, or their interrelationships. See Civil law 1952.

Civil divorce

Civil divorce is a declaration of *civil law* that a marriage bond is dissolved. In reality, it is a purely civil *act* that in no way dissolves a *marriage*, because marriage is, of its *nature*, indissoluble. 'Whoever *divorces* his wife and marries another, commits *adultery* against her' (Mk 10:11–12). See Divorce 1650.

Civil law 1952

Civil law refers to the rules governing human behavior that are established by the *secular authority* of the state.

Civil liberty

Civil liberties are the *inalienable rights* guaranteed to all men which cannot be abridged by *law* or custom. It includes the rights to think, to speak, and to act as one wishes without restraint except with regard to the interest of the *common good*. See Libertarian.

Clarity

Clarity is a quality *attributed* to the *resurrected body*. Clarity is the attribute of brilliance, luster, splendor, light, and *glory*. See Resurrection of the dead 992. Also see Glory 293.

Clarity (property of beauty)

See Beauty 341.

Class war

Class war refers to the constant *economic* and *political* struggle between different *social classes*, which *communism* claims exploits workers. It is described simply as the struggle between the *capitalists* who possess wealth and power, called the bourgeoisie, and poor workers, called the proletariat, who possess no wealth and power and, therefore, are oppressed. See Communism 2425.

Classical learning

Classical learning is education in the arts, *law*, medicine, and *theology*. See Monastery.

Clergy

Clergy is the designation of those who are *ordained* with the *sacrament of Holy Orders* for service to the Church as *deacons*, *priests*, or *bishops*. Today, entry into the *clerical state* takes place when the man is ordained a deacon. In earlier times, entry into the *clerical state* took place with the reception of *tonsure*.

Clergy is referred to as *secular clergy* when its members are not bound by a *vow* of poverty but by the rule of *celibacy* and a promise of *obedience* to their *Bishop*.

Clergy who are members of a *religious* community are bound by religious *vows*, live a community life, and are called religious clergy. See Clerical orders. Also see Cleric 934.

Cleric 934

A cleric is one who is a member of the *clergy*. Formerly, a man became a cleric by receiving *tonsure* during a ceremony in which his head was shaved and he was vested with a *surplice*. Tonsure prepared him for the reception of *minor* and *major orders*, but it was not itself considered to be an order. A man now becomes a cleric upon the reception of the *diaconate*.

The *priesthood*, diaconate, and *episcopacy* are referred to collectively as *clerical orders* and are conferred by the *sacrament* of *Holy Orders* instituted by Christ. *Holy Orders*, like *Baptism* and *Confirmation*, confers a *permanent character* or *indelible mark* on the *soul* and cannot be repeated. See Clerics. Also see Clerical orders; Holy Orders 1536.

Clerical orders

Clerical orders refer to the separate steps conferred on men receiving the sacrament of *Holy Orders*.

Traditionally, there were seven separate steps in the reception of Holy Orders in the Western Church. They were divided into major and minor orders. The *minor orders* were *porter*, *lector*, *exorcist*, and *acolyte*. They are no longer in use except by communities permitted to use the Extraordinary Form of the Roman Rite. *Major orders* were *subdeacon*, *deacon*, and *priest*. But the order of subdeacon is no longer in use. The *sacrament* of Holy Orders, like *Baptism* and *Confirmation*, confers a *permanent character* or *indelible mark* on the *soul* and cannot be repeated.

Holy Orders themselves are organized into a *hierarchy*, which includes the *episcopacy* (*bishops*), *priesthood*, and *diaconate*. Bishops (the episcopacy) have the fullness of priestly power. Priests and deacons exercise their ministry under the *authority* of the Bishop.

Cardinals have a high office, but that office does not represent another *sacred order*. Today, it is ordinarily required that cardinals be consecrated bishops, or at least be priests, but, before the *Code of Canon Law* of 1917, it was sufficient to be a member of the clergy, even if only in minor orders. The *Eastern Catholic Churches* have a different way of organizing major and minor orders.

Those in clerical orders are referred to as the *clergy*, and their customary garb is called a *cassock*. See Cleric 934.

Clerical state

Clerical state refers to the members of the *clergy* as a body of *persons* in the Church performing specific duties. See Clergy.

Clerics/Clerical 934

Members of the Church are divided into *clergy* and *laity*. Members of the clergy are called clerics and constitute the *hierarchy*, which is divided into *clerical orders* in the ranks of *bishops*, *priests*, and *deacons*. Since the *suppression* after *Vatican II* of *minor orders* and the *subdiaconate*, the term clergy refers only to the *ordained* ministers whose office is distinguished from the laity by virtue of the sacrament of *Holy Orders*, which they have received.

Religious and other *consecrated persons* are also members of the laity because, as religious, they do not receive the *sacrament* of Holy Orders. Ordained religious priests, however, are part of the clergy.

Cloister

Some *religious* live apart from the world in *cloistered monasteries*. In such monasteries, a specific area is designated as the *canonically enclosed* residence of the religious called the cloister. *Persons* who are not *professed* members of the *monastic* family are forbidden entrance. See Cloistered.

Cloistered

Cloistered is the adjectival form of cloister. It comes from the Latin word 'claustrum,' meaning a closed place. The place in which *religious* are secluded is called a *monastery* or *convent*.

Some religious live apart from the world in *cloistered monasteries*. *Contemplative religious* are commonly cloistered, some more strictly than others. The strictest form of cloister is the *'papal enclosure.'* See Eremitic life 920. Also see Consecrated persons 1672.

Coadjutor Bishop

A Coadjutor Bishop is a *bishop deputed* by the Holy Father to assist a *diocesan* bishop in the performance of *Episcopal* functions.

He shares in the same fullness of *Sacramental Orders* and has the right of succession, but he does not have the same *ordinary jurisdiction* in the diocese. See Bishop 861.

Code of Canon Law

The 1983 *Code of Canon Law* refers to the book of official laws of the *Latin Church*. It contains 1752 canons organized into seven books: Book One - General Norms; Book Two - The *People of God*, divided into three parts: 1) Christ's *faithful*, 2) the *hierarchical* constitution of the Church, and 3) Institutes of *consecrated life* and societies of apostolic life; Book Three - The Teaching Office of the Church; Book Four - The Office of Sanctifying in the Church, divided into two parts: 1) the *sacraments* and 2) other acts of divine *worship*; Book Five - The *Temporal Goods* of the Church; Book Six - Sanctions in the Church, which contains *penalties* for offenses in general and penalties for specific offenses; Book Seven - Processes, divided into five parts: 1) trials in general, 2) contentious trials, 3) special processes, e.g., *marriage*, 4) penal processes, and 5) administrative recourse.

The Latin name for the 1983 *Code of Canon Law* is *Codex Iuris Canonici*. Because the word 'Iuris' focuses attention on *rights*, the literal translation could be Code of Canonical Rights. The term suggests that the Church's primary concern is with protection of the rights and duties of all parties, both *superiors* and subjects. The term 'lex' in Latin more accurately corresponds to the English usage of the word *law*. The word law is consistent with the Latin word 'Ius,' which can also mean law or the *authority* underlying law, which focuses primarily on the order of society. See Canon Law. Also Canonical penalty.

Code of Canon Law, New

The 1983 *Code of Canon Law* is the name of the revision of the Code of Canon Law *promulgated* by Pope St. John Paul II on January 25, 1983 A.D. See Religious congregation.

Code of Hammurabi

Hammurabi was the king of Babylon around 1700 B.C. He is famous for his code of *law*. His laws date from his first year as king around 1728 B.C. The two hundred eighty-two judgments or paragraphs, which still remain, consist primarily of the verdicts of the king.

The code is not concerned with *religious* or *cultic* matters. Penalties include drowning, 'Lex Talions' or a 'tooth for a tooth,' fines, different kinds of restitution, and death. It recognized three *social* classes: freedman, state dependent, and slaves.

The code resembles *Hebrew* law in form, style, and content and may have influenced early forms of Israelitic law, but it differed in significant ways. 1) The Hebrews did not have an aristocracy. 2) Among the Hebrews, the state was not custodian of the law. 3) Hebrew law was more humane. 4) Hebrew law placed great emphasis on *ethics*. 5) Hebrew law showed a strong religious tone. 6) The Hebrew law was *covenant* centered.

See Torah. Also see Genesis; Code of the Covenant.

Code of the Covenant

The *Code of the Covenant* is a collection of humanitarian, *religious* laws formulated apart from *civil* laws. They are believed to be a distinctly *Israelitic* adaptation of the *Code of Hammurabi.* See Genesis.

Codex Iuris Canonici

The Latin name for the *Code of Canon Law* is *Codex Iuris Canonici*. See Canon Law.

Cognition/Recognition

Cognition comes from the Latin word 'cognitio,' meaning knowledge. In English, it refers to the whole process of knowing, including *perception*, *memory*, and *judgment*.

Recognition is acknowledgement or approval. See Cognitive.

Cognitive

The word cognitive comes from the Latin verb 'cognoscere,' meaning to know. The *intellect* is man's cognitive or knowing faculty and is referred to as the *mind*. The act of *cognition* refers to the process of knowing, normally terminating in a simple act of *assent* to some *truth* or to *Truth* itself. It includes *perception*, *judgment*, and *memory*. The intellect is considered to be a *faculty of the soul*. See Soul 363.

Cognitive faculty

In describing the powers of the soul, *theologians* commonly speak of two distinct faculties: *intellect* (cognitive power) and *will* (affective power). Mention is often also made of *memory*, either as a distinct faculty (St. Augustine and St. Bonaventure) or as a key aspect of the intellect (St. Thomas and Bl. John Duns Scotus). See Soul 363.

Cohabitation/Cohabiting

Cohabitation refers to living together as husband and wife outside of *marriage*. See Concubinage.

Coheir/Coheirs

A coheir is one *person* among others entitled to a share in the distribution of property at the death of another. See Union with Christ.

Coherence / Coherent / Coherently 114

Coherence is a quality or state characterized by *logical* or orderly relationship of parts. It is present when thoughts are consistent, that is, not *contradictory*, fit together, and are *congruent* with one another forming a unified whole.

Coitus

Coitus is another word for *sexual intercourse*. See Sexual intercourse.

Collateral line

Collateral line refers to the

type of family relationship that exists between *persons* having a common ancestor. It refers to the *indirect line of relationship* that exists between brother and sister, aunt and uncle, niece and nephew, first cousins, second cousins, etc.

Relationship in the collateral line is a *diriment impediment* to the fourth *degree*, but dispensations are possible in the third and fourth degrees of *consanguinity*. See Consanguinity.

Collect

The collect is a short prayer recited before the readings of the day having a direct reference to the *feast* of the day. Practically all collects are addressed to God the Father. It is called a collect because it is intended to call together the prayers of all the people.

Collection or offertory collection 1351

From the earliest times, Christians attending the *Eucharist* brought the bread and wine for the Eucharist, together with gifts to share with those in need at the *offertory* of the *Mass*. This gave rise to the custom of the offertory collection.

The term collection refers to the universal custom of gathering contributions of money from the *faithful* after the *Creed* for the support of the Church and the poor. The *medieval mass-penny* formed the link between these two customs.

The personal *mass-stipend* today reflects these traditional offerings.

Collectivism 1885

Collectivism refers to a *socialistic theory* of ownership or control of all the means of production, especially the land, by the whole community or state collectively for the benefit of the people as a whole.

The principle of *subsidiarity*, which is supported by the Church, differs from collectivism in important ways. It is opposed to all forms of collectivism because they do not set limits to state intervention in private ownership. It aims at a *harmonious* relationship between individuals and society in which each *social* unit can function without undue interference by higher order communities.

Collegial nature / Collegiality 1559

Collegial nature or collegiality refers to a characteristic of the *episcopal* office. *Episcopal consecration* confers, along with the *office* of *sanctifying*, the offices of teaching and of ruling. This office or service of *bishops* is carried out in union with the College of Bishops. The body of bishops is called a college because it is a union of *persons* associated as colleagues in the performance of their office and function.

Columbarium 701

A columbarium is a receptacle for reserving the *Eucharist* in the *tabernacle*. It was formerly made in the form of a dove, which is 'columba' in Latin, hence, its name. Today it is called a *ciborium* and has changed its shape to that more closely resembling a *chalice* with a cover.

Commandments

See Ten Commandments.

Commandments of the Church

The term commandments of the Church is another name for *precepts of the Church*. See Precepts of the Church 2041.

Commandments of the New Testament

The commandments of the *New Testament* are the *Beatitudes*. See New law 1965. Also see Law of the Gospel 1965, 1968.

Commemorate/Commemoration

A commemoration is any act that recalls the memory of some *person* or event. It is through *liturgical* commemorations that the mystery of *Christ*, the lives of *saints*, and other *sacred* events are kept alive among the *faithful*. The *Christian* calendar is built around such commemorations. See Holy Week.

Commission

A commission is a group of *persons* officially appointed to perform specific duties. See Holy Office. Also see Curia.

Common good 1906

The common good refers to the sum total of *social* conditions that allow *persons* either as individuals or as groups to reach their fulfillment more fully and easily. The common good focuses on those things pertaining to the happiness and prosperity of all.

The idea of the common good first presupposes respect for the person and protection of his fundamental and *inalienable* rights as an individual. Secondly, the common good requires the well-being and development of the group itself. Finally, the common good requires *peace*, that is, the stability and security of a just order.

Common of the Mass

The common of the Mass is the general name for all the prayers and *ceremonies* that do not change with various feasts. It is also called the ordinary of the Mass. See Anaphora 1352. Also see Canon of the Mass.

Common priesthood 1141, 1268

The common priesthood refers to the participation of the whole community of the *baptized* in the *priesthood of Christ*. Those baptized by *regeneration* and *anointing* of the *Holy Spirit* are *consecrated* to be a *spiritual* house and holy priesthood that they may offer *spiritual sacrifices* through participation in the *liturgical* celebrations.

The common *priesthood* is distinguished from the *ministerial priesthood* received by men who have been ordained by the *sacrament* of *Holy Orders* to offer sacrifice in the *person* of Christ and whose *ministry* makes possible the exercise of the common priesthood.

Communal celebration of Penance 1482, 1483

The communal form of the celebration of the *sacrament* of *Penance* is one in which a group of the *faithful* prepare themselves for *Confession* and then give thanks for the forgiveness they have received after *individual confession*.

In this option, the individual confession of *sins* and *absolution* are inserted into a *liturgy* of the *Word of God*. This consists of a *homily* with readings followed by an *examination of conscience* conducted in common, a communal request for forgiveness, the recitation of the *Our Father*, and common *prayers* of thanksgiving. This form of celebration most clearly expresses the *ecclesial* character of Penance.

Communal prayer 2664

Communal prayer is *prayer* offered aloud in a group. It is commonly called *vocal prayer* and may be official, that is, *liturgical*, as in the case of the *Divine Office*, or non-official, as prayer before meals or other spontaneous prayers offered in a group setting. A number of more frequently used vocal or communal prayers can be found in the Appendix of Prayers.

Communion

Communion is the act of sharing thoughts, *emotions*, and common interests with another. It also refers to a common profession of *faith* and practice of the same *religious rites*, especially sharing in or celebrating the Eucharist called *Holy Communion*. See Holy Communion 1331.

Communion, Holy

See Holy Communion 1331.

Communion in charity 953

Communion in charity means that the *faithful* form the *Body of Christ* and are individually members of it. Being grounded in the *communion of saints* and in *solidarity* with all men living or dead, the least act done in *charity redounds* to the profit of all.

Communion in sacris 1399

Communion in sacris refers to joining with others in sacred actions. Those *Eastern Churches* not in communion with Rome have *apostolic succession* and possess *valid sacraments*.

For *Catholics*, however, to join actively and publicly in *divine* worship with *Non-Catholics* is forbidden. Canon 1258 does allow *passive* and merely *material presence* at non-Catholic services, such as funerals and weddings, because of civic *duty* or respect.

Acting as a groomsman or bridesmaid in non-Catholic weddings is active assistance and, thus, unlawful. To be a *godparent* at a non-Catholic *Baptism* is forbidden absolutely. It is also forbidden to receive *sacraments* from non-Catholic ministers, even if these are *objectively valid sacraments*, except in certain circumstances precisely indicated by the *Code of Canon Law*: Canon 844, § 1–4, and 861, § 2.

All this is forbidden because to participate actively in non-Catholic *worship* implies a denial of *belief* in the Church and her teaching and subscription to another *faith*.

Communion in the faith 949

Communion in the faith refers to the *faith* of the Church, which was received from the *Apostles* and which is shared by all the *faithful*.

Communion of charisms 951

Communion of *charisms* refers to the special graces that are distributed by the *Holy Spirit* among the *faithful* of every rank. Each receives the manifestation of the Spirit for service in the *common good* so

that all may share in the *fruits of the* Spirit through them.

Communion of saints 1475

The communion of saints is a *"perennial* link of *charity* in *Christ* [that] exists between the *faithful* who have already reached their heavenly home [*Church Triumphant*], those who are expiating their sins in *purgatory* [*Church Suffering*] and those who are still pilgrims on earth [*Church Militant*]" (CCC 1475). In the unity of faithful under Christ, there is a wonderful exchange in which this *holiness* of one benefits others and "lets the *contrite* sinner be more promptly and *efficaciously* purified of the punishments for sin" (CCC 1475). The communion of saints is the ninth article of the *Apostles' Creed*.

Communion of the sacraments 950

The Catechism of the Catholic Church teaches that the Communion of the sacraments refers to the *sacraments* as *"sacred* links uniting the *faithful* to one another and binding them to *Jesus Christ"* (CCC 950). This is especially true of *Baptism*, by which we become part of the Church and are united to Christ. The *communion of saints* implies the communion of sacraments, which unites all of us to God and to one another. It is primarily the *Holy Eucharist* that brings this communion about most *efficaciously*.

Communion service

The *Catholic Church* has nothing corresponding to the communion service of *Protestant* bodies. The Protestant communion service is simply a commemoration of the *Last Supper* without *consecration*. Such a communion service has no sacramental character or efficacy.

The 'communion service' in the Catholic Church is referred to as '*Holy Communion* outside of Mass.' It is an extra-liturgical *ceremony* accompanied by prayers during which hosts consecrated in a previous *Mass* are distributed outside of Mass. The communion service is allowed outside of Mass when Mass is not celebrated or when Holy Communion is not distributed at scheduled times.

The communion service is usually conducted by a deacon who distributes *consecrated Hosts* to those wishing to partake of the Holy *Eucharist*. It opens with the sign of the Cross and an opening prayer for the community followed by *Scripture* readings, according to the liturgical calendar for the day. It may include first and second readings as well as the Gospel. The reading from Scripture is followed with the recitation of the *Lord's Prayer* and the distribution of hosts consecrated in a previous Mass. The *laity* may conduct a communion service with proper authorization. Since the service is devotional, the opening prayer may vary according to the *person* conducting the service.

Communion with the dead 958

Conscious of the *communion* of the members of the *Mystical Body* of Christ, the *Church Militant* honors with great respect the *memory* of the dead called the *souls in purgatory*. Our *prayers* for the dead are capable not only of helping them but also of making their *intercession* for us effective.

Communion with the saints 957

Communion with the saints refers to the *communion* of *Christians* with fellow pilgrims on earth and those who have entered *eternity* before us, which brings us closer to *Christ* through example, support, and *intercession*. We are in *communion* with the saints in *heaven* by virtue of their *intercession* for us and the bonds of *charity*, which bind us together. By their prayers, the souls of those in heaven and *purgatory* join us to Christ from whom issues all *grace* and life for the *People of God*. Through this communion with the saints, they hear our prayers and we receive the fruits of their intercession.

Communism / communistic 2425

Communism is a political *theory* advocating the common sharing of goods and the abolishment of *private ownership*. Under communism, all property is *vested* in the state, which organizes labor for the common benefit of all members according to the professed principle that each should work according to his capacity and receive according to his needs.

Atheistic communism exalts *matter* over *spirit* and rejects any need for God since the state provides for all human needs. It holds that *economics* is the foundation of civilization and that all other ideas whether *religious*, *social*, or *political*, depend on economics.

The Church has always utterly rejected atheistic communism and urges Catholics not to collaborate with *communists* in political or social efforts because of atheistic communism's many errors; especially its atheistic *materialism*, its doctrine of *class war*, its denial of individual *liberty* and *human rights*, and its contempt for *morality*.

Communitarian 1429

Communitarian refers to a member of a *socialistic* or *communistic* community or an advocate of communistic or *socialistic ideology*.

Commutative justice 2411

The word commutative comes from the Latin word for mutual exchange. Justice has reference to the community. Commutative justice is that form of justice which obliges us to respect the *rights* of others as required by the seventh commandment. It regulates the exchanges between *persons* and between institutions with strict respect to their rights. It strictly obliges all. It safeguards property rights, the payment of debts, and the fulfillment of *obligations* freely contracted. Without commutative justice, no other form of justice is possible.

Commutative justice requires that all who partake in a *theft* or who knowingly benefit from it are obliged to make *restitution* or *reparation* for the *injustice* in proportion to their *responsibility* and share in what was stolen. *Reparation* of injustice committed against another requires the restitution of the stolen goods to the owner. This reparation extends to all who directly or indirectly have taken possession of the goods of another and *obliges* them to restore those goods or the equivalent in kind or money. Restitution extends as well to the profit or advantages their owner would have *legitimately* obtained from them.

All who partake in *theft* or who have knowingly benefited from it are also obliged to make restitution in proportion to their responsibility and share in what was stolen.

Compassion/Compassionate
Compassion is the feeling of pity at another's sorrow or misfortune with the desire to alleviate it or even to suffer in place of that *person*. See Mercy.

Compensation
Compensation is anything given in return as an equivalent, such as *amends* for loss or damage. It also refers to payment for services, especially wages. See Restitution 2412.

Complaisance 2480
Complaisance is the action or *habit* of making oneself agreeable. It is the desire and care to please others or to defer to their wishes. Complaisance becomes sinful when it encourages or confirms another in *malicious* acts or *perverse* conduct.

Complementarity
See Difference and Complementarity 2333.

Complete or full consent 1859
Complete or full consent refers to the total acceptance of, agreement to, *compliance* in, *concurrence* with, or *acquiescence* with the *gravely evil nature* of something proposed by the *intellect*. Such consent implies an agreement or *concurrence* sufficiently deliberate

to make it a *culpable* personal choice.

Compliance
Compliance means to agree with or to grant a wish, a demand, or a regulation. See Complete or full consent 1859.

Compline
Compline is the hour of the *Divine Office* said after *Vespers* and before retiring for the night. Its English name is *Night Prayer*. See Liturgy of the Hours 1174, 1178.

Composure of heart 2699
Composure of heart is an *interior* condition of *mind*, feeling, and *demeanor* marked by tranquility, calmness, and collectedness. Composure of heart is the *consequence* of the peace of mind that attends a pure heart resting completely in the Lord.

Compunctio cordis 1431
Compunctio cordis is a Latin expression meaning *compunction* of *heart*. It refers to the pricking or stinging of the *conscience* or heart that accompanies true *repentance*. The *Fathers of the Church* refer to this form of repentance as *animi cruciatus*, that is, affliction of spirit.

Compunction
Compunction is the deep feeling of interior *repentance* of *heart* and feelings of remorse, *contrition*, and sorrow for *sin*

that accompany true repentance. It is accompanied by a sense of regret, an uneasiness of *conscience*, and a *salutary* sadness due to wrongdoing together with a firm resolve to avoid sin in the future. Compunction is also called contrition. See Examination of conscience 1454.

Concelebrate/Concelebrant

At times, more than one priest *celebrates* at the same *Mass*; in that case, one priest is designated as the main or principal *celebrant*, and those who say Mass with him are called concelebrants because they concelebrate, that is, celebrate together with the main celebrant of the Mass. See Celebrant.

Concept

A Concept is the mental representation through which the *mind* knows an object or *external reality*. See Agnosticism 2127.

Conception

Philosophically, conception is the process of forming a concept. Concepts are the mental representations of extra mental realities through which knowledge is acquired. Conception also refers to the first instant of life of a *human being*. Because at this instant the *person* is *created*, it acquires all the *rights* of a human being. See Concept; Agnosticism 2127. Also see

Heterologous artificial insemination and fertilization 2376.

Conception of Christ

The *Solemnity* of the *Annunciation* is *celebrated* on March 25, nine months before Christmas, the birth of *Jesus*. It celebrates the moment of the *Incarnation*. See Annunciation.

Conclusion

A conclusion is the last step of the *reasoning* process, which takes the form of a *judgment*, *decision*, or opinion. See Human reason. Also see Reason; Deductive.

Concomitant grace

Concomitant grace is another name for *grace of cooperation*. It is the form of *actual grace* that assists in an *operation* already begun and accompanies every *supernatural* act. It may also be called assisting or *cooperating grace* because it is associated with the use of *human freedom* in carrying out the *will of God*. See Grace 153.

Concrete

Concrete refers to things or events that have a *material* existence that can be *perceived* by the senses. It is opposed to *abstract*. See Abstract.

Concrete actions

Concrete acts are real and specific or particular. They are actions that can be perceived by the *senses*. See Virtue 1768, 1803.

Concubinage

Concubinage refers to *cohabitation* without a legal marriage. In *polygamous* societies, a concubine is a secondary wife of inferior position and without legal status. See Free union 2390.

Concupiscence 405, 1264, 1426, 1869, 2515

The Latin word for concupiscence is *concupiscentia*. In Latin, it is also called *fomes peccati*, that is, the fuel of *sin*. In general, it refers to the *temporal consequences of sin*, such as suffering, illness, death, and the frailties inherent in life. It also refers to the weaknesses of *character* and the inclination or attraction to sin that remain after receiving *Baptism*. Concupiscence must not be confused with *original sin*. It is only the consequence of original sin.

Concupiscence may also refer to any intense form of human desire, especially desires and inclinations toward bodily and fleshly pleasures. St. Thomas defined concupiscence as the *appetite* that tends to the gratification of the *senses*.

Concupiscence may also be referred to as *passion*. Passion is defined as a movement of the sensitive appetite accompanied by some bodily alteration. Neither concupiscence nor passion is *evil* in itself.

However, the goal toward which they are directed may be *lawful* or unlawful. Passion becomes sinful when free consent is given to a sinful act performed under its influence.

Christian *theology* gives concupiscence a particular meaning as a movement of the sensitive appetite contrary to the operation of *human reason*. St. Paul identifies it with the rebellion of the *flesh* against the spirit. Arising from the disobedience of the first sin, it unsettles man's *moral faculties* and, without itself being an offense, inclines *man* toward sin.

In *Scripture*, concupiscence usually refers to the desire for worldly things, the insubordination of the sensual appetite to the dictates of *reason*, or the general tendency of *human nature* toward sin as a consequence of the *fall*. As a result of the fall, man's *intellect* was darkened and his *will* weakened. Though these impairments of the intellect and will incline man to sin, he can always overcome them by cooperation with the unfailing *grace* of God.

Concupiscentia 406

Concupiscentia is a general Latin name given to movements of the sensitive *appetite* toward whatever the *imagination* portrays as good or desirable. Desire, love, and hate are forms of concupiscentia, which is called *concupiscence* in English.

Concupiscentia is identified as an effect of *original sin* inherited from our first parents consisting in a tendency to *evil*, which is insurmountable without *grace*. It is a *consequence* of the darkening of the *intellect* and weakening of the *will* caused by original sin. According to the *Council of Trent*, original sin is truly a *sin*. Concupiscence, however, is not a sin but a tendency derived from original sin that leads to personal sin. See Concupiscence 405.

Concupiscible emotions/appetency

Appetency is the tendency of one thing toward another. Concupiscible appetency is the propensity to enjoy a *good*. *Emotions* are forms of appetency.

In *Scholastic philosophy*, emotions are classified as concupiscible and *irascible*. The concupiscible emotions, or *appetites*, strive for the good and flee from the *evil*. This appetency corresponds to two fundamental emotions: 1) love of the good and 2) hatred of evil. These two basic emotions take the form of the desire for an absent good or abhorrence of an absent evil or the joy in the possession of a present good and sadness in the possession of a present evil. See Irascible emotions/appetency.

Concurrence

Concurrence means happening together or to be in agreement with. See Complete or full consent 1859.

Condescension 101

Condescension means to act with courteous disregard of difference of rank or position.

Conditional Baptism

Because *Baptism* confers a *permanent character*, mark, or *seal* on the soul, it may not be received twice. The *sacrament* of *Baptism*, in certain circumstances, may be administered *contingent* on some condition, which is stated in the words of administration, such as 'If you are not already baptized, I baptize you, etc.' It does not confer a *permanent character* or mark on the soul unless the *person* who receives it was not already baptized. *Absolution*, in the *sacrament of Penance*, may also be given conditionally when it is uncertain whether a person is still alive by using such words as, 'If you are alive, I *absolve* you, etc.' See Baptismal water 1238.

Confection

Technically, confection means to make, and is used in reference to the completion of an action that consists of words and actions together with the intention of making or bringing about the *valid* administration of a *sacrament* by one properly *ordained* as a minister. See Consecrated Persons 1672.

Confess/Confession

Confession is another name for the *sacrament of Penance* also called the *sacrament of Reconciliation*. As a sacrament of the *new law*, Confession is the *rite* in which, by the *absolution* of the *priest*, *sins* committed after *Baptism* are forgiven when they are confessed with sorrow and *purpose of amendment*.

Because sins are confessed to the priest, the sacrament is called Confession. Because it reconciles men with God and the Church, it is called Reconciliation. Because it requires sorrow and *repentance* for absolution, it is called Penance.

The general confession of sin made by the *faithful* at the beginning of *Mass*, called the *Confiteor*, and the Lord have mercy or *Kyrie Eleison*, which follows, are not sacramental in *nature*. Their purpose is to dispose the *heart* to repentance for sin and to foster the proper disposition to receive the *graces* of the Mass.

The *sacrament of Reconciliation* is usually administered in a private space in the *church* set aside for this purpose called a *confessional*. See Penance 1459.

Confession of faith

A confession of faith refers to a *creed*: an *authoritative* concise statement of general *beliefs* that must be accepted in order to be a member of the *Catholic Church*.

The same *faith* one confesses by the creed is also to be professed in the life of the believer. See Creed. Also see Faith 26, 146.

Confessional

Confessional is the name for the private space set aside for administering the *sacrament of Reconciliation*. It provides a seat for the *priest*, who is called the *confessor*, and a kneeler for the *penitent*. Often there is a screen between the priest and penitent. Confessionals have been required since the *Council of Trent*. See Church 752.

Confessor

The term confessor refers to the *priest* who hears the *confession* of the *penitent* and administers *absolution*. See Confessional.

Configuration/Configured or conformed to Christ 1272

By *Baptism*, we are configured or conformed to *Christ*, that is, we are given shape, formed, or molded to resemble him. Configuration refers to being shaped through instruction, training, or *discipline* to resemble Christ in our behavior and *values*.

Philosophically, the word 'form' refers to the ideal *nature* or *essential* character of a thing as distinguished from its *matter*. Conformation to Christ, thus, has the additional meaning of making our essential nature *holy* like that of Christ through cooperation with *grace*.

We are conformed to Christ when we answer the call of grace to practice *virtue*, renounce our *will* in favor of the *divine will*, and fulfill the *divine plan* with *obedience* and disinterested *love*. See Character.

Confirmation 1289

In the Western Church, Confirmation is the *sacrament of initiation* in which a *baptized person* receives special *gifts of the Holy Spirit*, is strengthened in *grace*, and is signed or sealed as a *soldier of Christ*. It is administered by the imposing of hands and by the *anointing* with *chrism* by the minister as he says, 'Be sealed with the Gift of the Holy Spirit.'

Like *Baptism* and *Holy Orders*, Confirmation confers a *permanent character* on the *soul* and cannot be received again. It is usually administered by the *Bishop*, but it can be administered by a *priest* whom the Bishop delegates.

Confiteor

The Confiteor is the *general confession* of *sin* made by the *faithful* at the beginning of *Mass* during the *penitential act* to prepare them to assist at Mass more worthily.

This public confession of sinfulness and request for the *prayers* of all present begins with the words, 'I confess to Almighty God and to you my brothers and sisters.' See Penance 1459. Also see Appendix of prayers; Prayers recited at Mass; Confiteor.

Confraternity

A confraternity is an association of the *faithful* erected by *ecclesiastical authority* to promote and exercise some work of *piety* or *charity*. See Rosary.

Congregation

A congregation is a gathering or assemblage of *persons* for a particular purpose. It may also refer to persons gathered together to live a *religious life* according to a *rule* under a *superior*. See Roman Congregations.

Congregation for Bishops

The Roman Congregation for Bishops is a body of *cardinals* whose purpose is to oversee all issues related to *Bishops*. It supervises the *Commission for Latin America* and the *Commission for the Pastoral care of Migrants and of Tourism*. See Roman congregations.

Congregation for Catholic Education for Seminaries and Institutes of Study

The Roman Congregation for Catholic Education for *Seminaries* and Institutes of Study is a body of *cardinals* which has *authority* over all institutions of *Catholic* education. See Roman Congregations.

Congregation for Divine Worship and the Discipline of the Sacraments

The Roman Congregation for Divine Worship and the Discipline of the Sacraments is a body of *cardinals* which has *authority* over the regulation and promotion of the *sacraments* and the *Liturgy*. See Roman Congregations.

Congregation for Institutes of Consecrated Life and Societies of Apostolic Life

The Roman Congregation for Institutes of Consecrated Life and Societies of Apostolic Life is a body of *cardinals* which oversees all aspects of *institutes* of *religious*, *third orders*, *secular* institutes, and *societies of apostolic life*. See Roman Congregations.

Congregation for the Causes of Saints

The Roman Congregation for the Causes of Saints is a body of *cardinals* which oversees all matters related to *beatifications* and *canonizations*. See Roman Congregations.

Congregation for the Clergy

The Roman Congregation for the Clergy is a body of *cardinals* which has *authority* over the *clergy*, including *discipline*, preaching, and care for the Church's *temporal goods*. See Roman Congregations.

Congregation for the Doctrine of the Faith

The Roman Congregation for the Doctrine of the Faith is a body of *cardinals* whose purpose is to safeguard the teachings of the *faith*, to examine *doctrinal* questions and writings, to promote *theological* study and, to oversee matters related to the *Petrine Privilege* in *marriages*. See Roman Congregations.

Congregation for the Oriental Churches

The Roman congregation for the *Oriental Churches* is a body of *cardinals* whose purpose is to oversee all relevant matters pertaining to the *Eastern Catholic Churches*. See Roman Congregations.

Congregation of the Evangelization of Peoples

The Roman Congregation of the *Evangelization* of Peoples is a body of *cardinals* which supervises all *missionary* activity across the globe and has control over various *societies*, unions, and *councils* to assist in the missionary undertaking. See Roman Congregations.

Congruent

Congruent comes from the Latin word 'congruere,' meaning to come together, to agree, or to correspond. The English word means the same: to agree, to correspond with, to be in *harmony* with, and to fit together. See Coherence 114.

Conjugal act

Conjugal act refers to *sexual intercourse* that is the *lawful* expression of *conjugal love*. See Conjugal love 1643.

Conjugal community 2201

Conjugal community refers to the common life lived by those who are married to one another. This community is established with the consent of the *spouses* in the *marriage ceremony*. This common life of spouses and their *family* is ordered to the good of the spouses and to the *procreation* and education of children.

Conjugal fidelity 2364

Conjugal fidelity refers to the quality of enduring *faithfulness*, *love*, and sharing of life in the *marriage* partnership established by the *Creator*, governed by his *laws*, and rooted in the *marriage covenant*. In the marriage covenant, both parties give themselves definitely and totally to one another with a personal and irrevocable *consent* until death. The covenant they freely contract imposes on them the *obligation* to preserve it as unique to them and is *indissoluble*.

By *fidelity* to their marriage covenant, the *spouses* enter into the *mystery* of Christ's fidelity to his Church, and, through conjugal *chastity*, they bear witness to this mystery before the world.

Conjugal love 1643

Conjugal love is a fixation of the *will* on the good of a *spouse*, which manifests itself in concern for the other's welfare, delight in his or her presence, and desire for his or her approval.

It is a state in which correspondence of wills makes of two one *spirit* in a totality that includes all elements of the *person*, the appeal of the body and *instinct*, the powers of feeling, *affectivity*, and *aspiration* of the spirit and will.

It consists in a deeply personal and intimate unity, beyond union in one flesh, which leads to the formation of one heart and *soul*. It is formed, *purified*, and completed by *communion* in *Jesus Christ*.

Such love demands *indissolubility* and fruitfulness in a definitive mutual self-giving that is ever open to the possibility of new life. Such openness is, by its nature, incompatible with *artificial contraception*, which *essentially* precludes true conjugal self-giving love.

By *conjugal love*, spouses are raised and *sanctified* making them the expression of specifically Christian *values* and *virtue*. The communion of conjugal love is confirmed, purified, and completed by communion with Jesus Christ given through the *sacrament* of *Matrimony*.

Connatural

Connatural refers to something that belongs to a *person* or thing by its *nature*, birth, or origin. It is something inborn or innate. It may refer to things that have the same or similar nature. See Eternal.

Consanguinity

Consanguinity refers to a *blood relationship* based on common ancestry.

Canon Law recognizes two mutually exclusive types of consanguinity: (1) *direct line*, in which two people share the same direct generational line (parent, child, grandchild, etc.); and (2) *collateral line*, in which two people who do not share the same generational line nevertheless share a common ancestor (*siblings*, first cousins, second cousins, etc.).

Degree by consanguinity refers to the proximity of relationship between two *persons*. In the direct line, the degree is the total number of persons in the generational line. The degree in the collateral line is the total number of persons in both generational lines traced to the common ancestor, excluding the ancestor.

An attempted *marriage* between two persons related by consanguinity in the direct line in any degree or in the col-

lateral line up to and including the fourth degree (in case of relation by reason of adoption, the second degree) is *invalid*. A *dispensation* can be sought in the case of consanguinity in the collateral line in the third and fourth degrees.

Marriage is never permitted if there is any doubt about the parties being related by consanguinity, either in the direct line or in the second degree of the collateral line.

Consanguinity may be compared to *affinity*, which is the relationship established between two persons by reason of a validly contracted marriage. See Affinity.

Conscience 1706, 1776, 1777, 1778

Conscience is a *judgment* of practical *reason* whereby a *person* recognizes the *moral* quality of a *concrete act* that he is going to perform, is in the process of performing, or has already completed or omitted. When making such a judgment, the *intellect* is called *conscience*. By *reasoning*, it determines the *morality of an act* by judging its conformity to *natural* or *revealed law* and develops a *moral sense* in *man*.

Conscience is distinguished from *synderesis*, which is the instinctive, infallible, and habitual knowledge postulated as the *first principle* of moral action: do good and avoid evil. Because conscience is the *subjective* norm of individual morality, one is never allowed to act with an *uncertain conscience* or *doubtful conscience*. For an action to be *morally* right, a *prudentially certain conscience* is sufficient, that is, it has solid enough reason to justify action by an ordinarily *prudent* man.

Conscience is divided according to the relationship that exists between the *mind* and *truth*. Conscience is said to be a *certain conscience* when the mind adheres completely to one side of a *practical contradiction* without fear that the opposite might be true. When this adherence is both *objectively* and *subjectively certain*, it is called a *correct conscience*.

When conscience is certain and something it believes is true is, in fact, objectively true, then the conscience is called a *right conscience*. One must always follow a right conscience.

When conscience is subjectively certain but believes that something is true that is objectively false, then it is called an *erroneous conscience*. An erroneous conscience must be followed, but the person must also try to learn what the Church teaches on the issue and try to form a correct conscience.

Conscience may be an erroneous conscience because of either *vincible* or *invincible ignorance*. Vincible ignorance is ignorance in the absence

of *knowledge* that a person can attain with reasonable effort. Invincible ignorance is an absence of knowledge under circumstances in which knowledge cannot be obtained without extraordinary effort. Morally *unintentional ignorance* can diminish or remove culpability.

The clear *voice of conscience* must always be obeyed as an *infallible* guide to right action but the conscience must be properly formed by seeking to learn what is truly good to the best of one's ability. What is right is learned from the teaching of the Church, not from popular opinion or practice.

Conscious/Consciousness

Conscious comes from the Latin word 'conscius,' meaning aware or knowing. To be conscious means to be aware of one's physical *sensations* and feelings, to know what is happening, or to be aware of what one is thinking, feeling, doing, or intending. See Deliberate act. Also see Sensation.

Consecrate

To consecrate means to set apart as *holy* for *religious* purposes. It is also applied in a unique way to the act of *transubstantiation* effected by the words of *consecration* in the *Mass* through which bread and wine become in truth the Body, Blood, *soul*, and *divinity* of *Christ*. See Consecration

1376. Also see Consecrated persons 1672.

Consecrated Host

A consecrated Host is one that has been changed into the *Body of Christ* by the solemn act of *transubstantiation* in the *Mass* when a *priest* pronounces the words. 'This is my body, etc.' See Transubstantiation.

Consecrated life 916

A consecrated life is a life dedicated to following Christ by the *profession* of the *evangelical counsels* within a *permanent* state. *Persons* who live such a life follow a *common rule* and generally live in a *community*.

Consecrated persons 1672

To consecrate refers to an *ecclesial rite* by which a *person* or thing is set apart exclusively for some *religious* use in the service of God. It is considered *superior* to and more *solemn* than a *blessing*. The act by which something is consecrated is called *consecration*. See Religious life. Also see Consecrated Virgin.

Consecrated virgin 922

A consecrated virgin is a woman who, having decided to live in the state of *virginity* or *perpetual chastity* for the sake of the *kingdom of heaven*, requests *consecration* from the Church. Virgins committed to following Christ more closely and who are not members of a *religious community* are consecrated by the *diocesan Bishop* according to the approved *liturgical rite* called the Consecration of a Virgin Living in the world. This rite of consecration is found in the Leonine *sacramentary* dating to the late fourth century. The prayers of this rite were restored largely unchanged in the *Pontificale Romanum* of 1970.

This early *rite* of consecration was always used for women living in the world as there were no women's religious communities at that time. Many feminine saints mentioned in the *Canon* of the *Mass* were all consecrated virgins who lived in the world. By this rite, the *Bishop* constitutes a virgin as a *sacred person*.

Women who live in a community follow a *religious rule*, take the *vows of religion*, and are consecrated by their Bishop or his delegate according to an approved liturgical rite in the *Rituale Romanum* by which they are constituted *sacred persons*. Not all virgins wishing to follow Christ outside of a religious community become consecrated virgins. See Consecration of virgins and widows 922, 923.

Consecration/Consecratory 1376

Consecration takes place during the *Liturgy* of the Eucharist, which consists of the presentation of the bread and wine, the consecratory thanksgiving, and *Holy Communion*.

Consecration, in respect to the *Liturgy of the Eucharist* or *Mass*, refers to the *solemn* act of *transubstantiation*, which takes place when the *priest* pronounces the words, 'This is my body, etc,' during the Mass and changes the *substance* of bread and wine into the substance of the Body, Blood, *soul*, and *divinity* of Christ.

Extraordinary ministers of Holy Communion must be careful not to refer to their task as administering the bread or wine. Such usage takes away from the *reverence* due the *Sacrament* and fails to acknowledge the effects of consecration.

Consecration of Holy Chrism
1297

Consecration of the *sacred chrism* (or holy chrism) is the *rite* in which the *Bishop consecrates* the *oil of chrism* during the Chrism Mass celebrated on *Holy Thursday*. The oil of chrism is used in the blessing of the *baptismal font*, during the administration of *Baptism* and *Confirmation*, in the ordination or consecration of a bishop, and in the consecration of *churches*, *altars*, and *sacred vessels*.

Consecration of virgins and widows 922, 923

The consecration of vir-

gins and widows refers to an ancient *rite* contained in the *Pontificale Romanum* by which a *bishop* solemnly consecrates a *nun* to a more intimate life with Christ. The rite resembles the ordination of a *deacon*; the nun is invested with a plain wooden cross, crown, black veil, ring, *stole*, and *maniple*, which she assumes again only on her fiftieth anniversary of profession and for burial.

The ceremony is now unknown except among the *Carthusians* who receive it four years after *profession* of their *vows of religion*.

This rite is different from that by which a *person*, for the sake of the kingdom, decides, with the Church's approval, to live in the state of *virginity* or *perpetual chastity* without belonging to a *religious community*. Such persons are consecrated by the *diocesan* Bishop according to an approved liturgical rite. They are considered *sacred persons* and referred to as *consecrated virgins*. Also see Consecrated person 1672.

Consent 1627

Consent is an act by which the *will voluntarily* complies with something presented to it as good.

The consent required for the *validity* of a *contract* or agreement must be an *internal consent* that is made with the intention of fulfilling the *obligations* involved.

Consent may be *silent consent* in cases which admit of such consent as in accepting a gift. When one party has given consent, a contract is made as soon as the other party also gives consent. In *marriage*, this is known as *matrimonial consent*.

Consent is distinguished from *assent* by which the *intellect* recognizes that something is true in the *speculative order* or right in the *moral order*.

When consent is only pretended, that is, inconsistent with what is being willed interiorly, it is called *fictitious consent*.

Consequence/Consequent

Consequence comes from the Latin word 'consequens,' meaning to follow after. A consequence is the result, outcome, or effect of some action or process. See Sources of morality 1750.

Consequent or cooperating grace

Consequent or cooperating grace is *actual grace* which moves or assists the *soul* at certain times to acts of *supernatural virtue*.

Actual grace enlightens the *mind* and stirs up the *will* to the work of *salvation*. In this arousal of the will there are two stages, first, there is a grace, which moves the will spontaneously making it incline to God. This is called *prevenient grace*. The sec-

ond stage involves *cooperating grace*, which continues to arouse the will and supports it while it acts.

Thus, it comes about that God moves us to grace through prevenient grace and then gives us the grace to accept it with cooperating or consequent grace which assists in an operation already begun. See Grace 35, 54, 153 1996, 1997, 2000, 2008.

Conservation

Conservation refers to the act of preserving something in existence. It is applied to God's act of preserving creatures in their existence. This is essential for creatures which serve as *secondary causes* required for the world to endure in time by fulfilling God's plan. See Immanent.

Consistory

A consistory is an assembly called together by the *Pope*. A *private consistory* is confined to cardinals. A *semi-public consistory* is composed of cardinals and *bishops*. A *public consistory* consists of cardinals, *prelates*, and *laymen*. A consistory may be ordinary or extraordinary. In an ordinary consistory, "all Cardinals, or at least those who are in Rome, are summoned for consultation on certain grave matters of more frequent occurrence, or for the performance of especially solemn acts" (Canon 353, § 2). "All Cardinals are summoned" to an extraordinary consistory, "which takes place when the special needs of the Church and more serious matters suggest it" (Canon 353, § 3). Only an ordinary consistory can be public. See Curia.

Consoler 692

Consoler is a common translation of the word *Paraclete*. Jesus is the first Consoler, but he speaks of another Paraclete whom he will send, the *Holy Spirit*, the *Spirit of Truth*, who will remain with the *Apostles* and their successors forever and teach them all things after he returns to the *Father*. The Paraclete *sanctifies* by convincing *man* of his sin via an interior *judgment* by which he acknowledges his *sin* and is moved to *repentance* and reformation of life.

Constitution/Constitutions

Constitutions are the *legislation* that governs the life and purposes of a *religious institute*. For *canonical* approval by the Church, institutes must receive positive and formal approval from the *Holy See* or the *Bishop* and have a *rule* or constitutions which determine their mode of governance and the rights and duties of their members. Each member must take the *vows of religion* publicly.

Councils issue *ecclesiastical decrees* also called constitutions. These are generally

legislative enactments of the Pope or council. *Papal* decrees are also found in *apostolic letters* and *motu proprios*. See Institutes 925. Also see Second Vatican Council.

Consubstantial 242, 253

Consubstantial means of the same *substance* or *essence*. Something is consubstantial with something else when it has one and the same substance or essence. The term is applied to the three *Persons* of the *Trinity* who are of but one substance and, thus, are only one God.

Consummated 1640

Consummated means completed, finished, done, or achieved.

Consummation of the earth 1048

The consummation of the earth refers to its completion or perfection. It is the time of its full and perfect development or the crowning and fitting goal in which all its purposes and tendencies are entirely fulfilled.

Contemplation

Contemplation is a form of *prayer* in which there are no images, ideas, or words. It cannot be produced in any human manner. It is not available whenever man desires it, nor does it depend on any techniques or methods. It depends entirely on the initiative of the *Spirit*. To contemplate is to gaze on the *divine* beauty and to be filled with its peace and joy. Such prayer is the calling of all *Christians*.

Meditation develops slowly into contemplation, as it forms one from the inside by the living presence of the Spirit who 'transforms us from one glory to another' (2 Cor 3:18).

Contemplation is always a gift of God and beyond man's control. St. Teresa of Avila says that *contemplative prayer* is a close sharing between friends, taking time frequently to be alone with him whom we know loves us. It is a form of inner prayer in which we can still *meditate*, but our attention is fixed on the Lord himself.

This understanding of contemplation is difficult to reconcile with what is known as *centering prayer*. See Contemplative Prayer 2709.

Contemplative

Contemplative is a word used to identify members of a *religious order* who are committed to the *worship* of God in a life dedicated to prayer. They live a *cloistered* life dedicated to *prayer* by living apart from the *active life* in the world, which, by its distractions and worldly cares, could hinder divine *contemplation*.

What exactly constitutes a contemplative life is a matter of dispute. It depends on the degree and strictness of the separation of the *community* from the world. Generally the *Carthusians*, *Camaldolese*, *Cistercians*, *Carmelites*, some *Dominicans*, *Poor Clares*, and some *Benedictines* are considered contemplatives. See Consecrated persons 1672.

Contemplative prayer 2709

Contemplative prayer is a form of wordless prayer that focuses on God's great goodness and gazes on the *mysteries* of Christ's life with *faith* and *love*.

Contemplative prayer is also called *mystical prayer*. It develops from *meditative prayer*, which consists in reading, reflecting, thinking, imagining, drawing *conclusions*, and conversing inwardly with the indwelling *Trinity*. The goal of *meditation* is to stir the heart to desire and love God.

Meditative prayer gradually grows into *affective prayer* in which there is less need for the assistance of mental reflection to move the *soul* to greater awareness and love.

Meditative and affective prayer may be initiated by the action of man, but, as one grows in *perfection* and the obstacles to the working of the *Spirit* are removed, this awareness, desire, and love of God become gifts of the Spirit. When this intimate awareness and love become *habitual* for a *person*, he has achieved the *contemplative* state.

Contemplative prayer is the poor and humble surrender

to the loving *will* of the *Father* in ever-deeper union with his beloved Son. It is a gift and grace, a gaze of *faith* fixed on *Jesus,* one which can only be accepted in *humility* and *poverty.*

Continence 1650

Continence is self-restraint in the matter of *sexual appetite.* It may be expressed either by due moderation in *marriage* or by *total abstinence* in the case of the unmarried. As a *virtue,* it restrains the *will* from consenting to movements of sexual desire.

Continence may also refer to refraining *voluntarily* from *sexual intercourse* in marriage for sufficient reason, but both parties must agree to it. Continence is sometimes loosely identified with *chastity.*

Contingent/Contingently

Contingent comes from the Latin word 'contingere,' meaning to touch. Contingent means dependent upon something else. What is contingent may or may not happen depending on conditions. See Conditional Baptism. Also see Contingent cause; Primary cause; Free will 1704, 1731.

Contingent being

A contingent being is a *being* whose non-existence is possible. See Theologia 236.

Contingent cause/contingency

Every *cause* except the *first* *cause* is a *secondary cause.* God wills that secondary causes act according to their *natures* either by *necessity* or by *contingency.* Causes are said to be necessary when their effects come about simply because, once acting, their natures do not depend on factors outside themselves to produce their effects. The weathering of stones is a direct and unavoidable *consequence* of the action of the climate, or moving water as in a riverbed. Other causes are said to be contingent. A contingent cause is one that depends on certain conditions and circumstances outside of itself in order to produce an effect. The growth of seeds is a good example because growth is only possible when temperature, moisture, and light are present in certain measure; without these, the seed cannot produce a plant. The growth of a seed is said to be contingent because it depends on conditions outside its control to take place.

A contingent cause is distinguished from a *free agent* or *intellectual* agent. God wills things to act in accord with their individual natures and their interdependencies. God does not impose necessity on either the activity of a *free will* or contingent causes. *Moral acts* are always contingent upon *free choice.* See Primary cause. Also see Divine plan.

Contraception 2370

Contraception is another word for *birth control*. It refers to the practice of engaging in *sexual intercourse* while simultaneously and *deliberately* preventing *conception*, which is its natural purpose. The use of artificial barriers or drugs for the purpose of preventing *fertilization* during *sexual intercourse* is always gravely disordered and sinful and does great harm both to the *integrity* of *marriage* and to the love of *family*. See Artificial birth control / artificial contraception. Also see Regulation of procreation 2368.

Contract

A contract represents the *consent* of two parties to do or exchange something, as in a compact or *covenant*. It can refer to a formal agreement of *marriage* or *betrothal*. In all cases, it is a mutual agreement concerning the transfer of a *right* and requires that the two parties agree to the same object and bind themselves in *commutative justice* to observe the agreement. See Consent 1627.

Contradiction/contradictory

A contradiction is a form of opposition between two *propositions* that differ in such a way that it is impossible to affirm or accept one without denying or rejecting the other. Two contradictory statements can neither both be true, nor

both be false. For example: 'No man is good' and 'Some men are good' are contradictory propositions. See Contrary. Also see Freedom of Exercise; Practical Contradiction.

Contrary/contrariety

Contrariety is a form of opposition between statements or *propositions* that exclude one another because what one affirms the other denies, such as 'All men are good' and 'No man is good.' When one of two contrary statements is affirmed, the other must necessarily be denied. Two contrary statements cannot both be true, but both may be false, for example 'All men are good' and 'No man is good' are contraries, and both are false because some men are good, but some are not.

Contrary statements differ from contradictory statements because, if we accept one statement of a *contradiction*, the other cannot be accepted.

Contrariety may also refer to the *freedom of contrariety*, which is the ability of the *will* to choose between a moral *good* and a moral *evil*. See Contradiction. Also see Freedom of Contrariety.

Contrition 1451

The word contrition comes from the Latin word 'contero,' meaning to rub away or pulverize. The Church uses the word to refer to the condition of being bruised in heart or filled with sorrow or affliction of *mind* for some fault or injury done.

Contrition is the sorrow for and the detestation of *sin* together with the firm resolution not to sin again.

When contrition is heartfelt, it is called *true contrition* and refers to the sincerity of the sorrow and firmness of the resolution to reform one's life.

When contrition arises from the motive of pure love of God, it is called *perfect contrition* or *contrition of charity*. When it arises from fear of *hell* or from revulsion for sin, it is referred to as *imperfect contrition* or *attrition*. At least imperfect contrition is needed to receive *absolution* in the *sacrament of Reconciliation*.

Contrition of charity 1452

Contrition of charity is another name for *perfect contrition*, which arises from the motive of pure *love* of God. By an act of perfect contrition, *mortal sin* is forgiven even before it is revealed in *Confession*, but the *obligation* to confess remains under pain of committing another mortal sin. Perfect contrition is sufficient for forgiveness of *venial sin* even without Confession.

Convalidation of marriage

The *convalidation* or validation of a *marriage* is the transformation of an invalid marriage to a valid one. A marriage is rendered *invalid*

by the presence of a *diriment impediment*, by a deficiency in *consent* on the part of one or both *spouses*, or by the failure to celebrate the marriage according to the prescribed *canonical form*.

In the case of an *impediment*, the impediment must have ceased in order for a marriage to be convalidated (a simple convalidation), which consists in a renewal of the consent on the part of one or both spouses. But if the impediment is public, then a new celebration of marriage must take place in which the spouses exchange consent according to canonical form (Canon 1158).

If there is a deficiency in consent on the part of one or both spouses, an exchange of consent by the spouses according to canonical form is required if the deficiency can be proven; otherwise consent can be given privately (Canon 1159).

If a marriage is invalid because it was not celebrated according to the proper canonical form, then a new celebration in which the canonical form is observed must take place.

An impediment may be dispensed by an act of the proper *ecclesiastical authority*, in which case the marriage already celebrated is recognized as valid; this is known as a retroactive validation or *sanatio in radice*. Renewal of consent is not required in this case, because the canonical effects are attributed to the marriage from the moment of its celebration in the past. A *sanatio in radice* is granted by the *Apostolic See*. The diocesan *Bishop* may grant a *sanatio in radice* in certain cases, except when *dispensation* from a given impediment is reserved to the Apostolic See or in the case of impediments pertaining to *natural law* or positive *divine law* that have ceased (Canon 1165, § 2). See Nullity of marriage 1629.

Convent

A convent is sometimes called a *monastery* or a *nunnery*. Convent comes from the Latin word 'conventus,' which means assembly and refers to a group of *persons* devoted to *religious life* under a *religious superior*.

The difference between a convent, a monastery, and a nunnery is a matter of usage. In English usage, convents were traditionally residences for women *religious* and some men religious. The name monastery was generally used for men religious and sometimes *contemplative* women religious. Nunneries, however, referred to residences for *cloistered* women religious. See Monastery.

Conversion/Convert 1426, 1989

Conversion is a radical reorientation of the whole life away from *sin* and *evil* and toward God. This change of *heart* or conversion is a central element of *Christ's* preaching, of the Church's ministry of *evangelization*, and of the sacrament of *Penance* or *Reconciliation*.

Conversion of heart 1430, 1888, 2608

Conversion is a *person's* turning away from *sin* and toward God. The *heart* is the seat of *consciousness* and the innermost sanctuary of the person where the *conscience* dwells. The conversion required by *Christ* must arise from the depths of the heart.

Before one prays, he should first reconcile himself with his brother as an indication of the *purity of heart* required to approach God. *Prayer* consists not only in saying, 'Lord, Lord' (Mt 7:21), but also in disposing the heart to do the *will* of the Father, which is conversion of heart. This conversion is required for true *repentance* and *reformation of life* after sin. It is also called inner *conversion* or *metanoia*.

Conversion of tears/Conversion of water

St. Ambrose speaks of two conversions, the conversion of water in *Baptism* and the conversion of tears of *repentance*. The *second conversion* of tears has a *communitarian* dimension because the Lord continually calls the whole Church to *repentance.* See Second conversion 1428.

Convincing of sin 1848

'Convincing of sin' refers to the "interior *judgment* of con-science" acknowledging one's *sin* and moving one to *repentance* and *conversion.* Conviction of sin is "a proof of the action of the *Spirit of truth* in man's inmost being,... a new grant of *grace* and love ... [and] a double gift: the gift of the truth of conscience and the gift of the certainty of redemption. The Spirit of truth is the *Consoler*" (CCC 1848).

Conversion must begin with this conviction concerning personal sin. The Consoler, the *Holy Spirit*, comes to convince man of his sin as the way to *sanctification.*

Convoke/Convoked

To convoke means to call together for an assembly or meeting. See Church council.

Cooperating grace

Cooperating grace is another name for grace of cooperation. It is the form of *actual grace* that assists us in an action already begun and accompanies every *supernatural* act. It may also be called *assisting* or *concomitant grace* because it is associated with the use of *human freedom* in carrying out the *will of God.* See Grace 35, 54, 153, 1996, 2008.

Cooperation in sin 1868

Cooperation in *sin* refers to incurring responsibility for the sins of others. Ways this can happen are: "by participating directly and *voluntarily* in them [these sins]; by ordering, advising, praising, or approving them; by not disclosing or not hindering them when we have an *obligation* to do so; [and] by protecting evil-doers" (CCC 1868).

Catholics who vote for any candidate who openly supports laws opposed to Church teaching or to the *natural law* are guilty, to some degree, of cooperation in that sin.

Coptic Church/Rite

The Coptic members of the *Alexandrian Rite* were received into *communion* with the *Roman Church* by Pope Benedict XIV in 1741, although their own *patriarchate* was restored in 1895 by Pope Leo XIII. The *liturgy* is conducted in Coptic, an early form of Egyptian, and contains elements of Greek and Arabic. It incorporates elements of the *Byzantine liturgy* of St. Basil, the *Alexandrian liturgy* of St. Mark, the liturgy of St. Cyril, and St. Gregory of Nazian-zus. Certain *feasts* use Coptic translations of these liturgies: St. Basil's being used for *Sundays*, St. Gregory's on certain *feast days*, and St. Cyril's during *Lent* and on *Christmas* Eve.

In 1947, there were 63,000

Coptic Catholics served by the *Patriarch* of Alexandria, three *suffragan bishops*, and an Egyptian *clergy*. *Celibacy* was made *obligatory* in 1898, but it is *dispensed* for priests converted from *Monophysitism*. Patriarchs and bishops are appointed by the *Holy See*. See Eastern Church. Also see Eastern rite.

Copulation

Copulation is another term for *sexual intercourse*.

Copyist

A copyist is a *person* who makes written copies of documents. See Scribes.

Coredemptrix/Coredemptress

Coredemptrix or Coredemptress is a title of the *Blessed Virgin* honoring her as unique cooperator with *Christ* in the work of *redemption*.

The brief, mysterious message of victory of the seed of the Woman over the brood of the serpent found in Genesis 3:15 is referred to as the *protoevangelium*. It is considered the first announcement of God's plan for man's redemption. The *Fathers* and *Doctors of the Church* have seen the woman announced in the protoevangelium as *Mary*, who, as the Mother of Christ the Redeemer, would be the *New Eve*. For this reason she is sometimes called the *Mother of all prophecy*.

Mary has been referred to as Coredemptrix by *theologians* since the fourteenth century. The title was used in documents of the *Holy See* by Benedict XV in 1918 and Pius XI in 1933. Pope St. John Paul II used it at least seven times. *Vatican II*, although it did not use the title, made repeated references to Mary's cooperation in the redemption. In *Lumen Gentium*, Vatican II used the word 'unique' to set in relief the role of Mary in the redemptive *sacrifice* of *Christ*, under him, but transcending that of any other believer because she was the *Mother of God*.

Though all the *baptized* contribute to the work of redemption by 'filling up what is wanting in the sufferings of Christ' (Col 1:24), they contribute nothing to the *objective redemption* as Mary did.

Christ alone is the primary, universal, and *sufficient cause* of our redemption, but Mary had a secondary, finite share in the process. Her role drew its *efficacy* from the merits of her Son. God accepted her share together with, but *subordinate* to, Christ's *sacrificial* action for the *salvation* of mankind. When Mary consented to become the Mother of God, she freely consented to his work of redemption.

Our Lord accepted the *will* of the Father to become *incarnate* to offer himself as sacrifice for our redemption, precisely in reference to the *Fiat* of Mary to be his Mother and so prepared his Body to be sacrificed (cf. Heb 10:5–10).

This *insinuates* the joint offering on *Calvary* of the *New Adam*, Christ-Redeemer, and the New Eve, Mary-Core-demptix. The Redeemer and Coredemptrix reverse the *consequences* of the joint *infidelity* of the First Adam and First Eve in the *Garden of Eden*.

The *Marian* teaching of Vatican II is found in Chapter Eight of Lumen Gentium. It forms the basis for understanding Mary's *discipleship*. The *Council Fathers synthesize* the *doctrines* about Mary in the *mystery* of Christ and the Church using as a foundation the *Church Fathers*. They establish Mary as a central figure in *faith* and *theology* because of her role in the *Incarnation* and the way she mirrors the central *truths* of the faith.

Since the time of St. Francis of Assisi (in the *antiphon* of his Office of the Passion), Mary's relationship with the *Trinity* has been described as that of Daughter and handmaid of God the Father, Mother of the Incarnate Son, and *Spouse of the Holy Spirit*.

Because of her unique *mission*, she was preserved from *original sin*. The Father willed that the consent of the *predestined* Mother should precede the *Incarnation* and, ultimately, the foundation of the Church.

Mary was related to Christ in five ways: 1) she shared in the redemption in a most sublime manner as its first and most perfect fruit; 2) as the spouse of the Holy Spirit she truly became the Mother of God; 3) by being completely free of sin she was the perfect faithful servant of her Son; 4) Mary freely cooperated in the work of redemption with perfect faith and obedience; and 5) Mary was the model of the perfect disciple, the one who heard the *Word of God* and kept it in perfect obedience (Cf. Alfred McBride, *Images of Mary*, p. 146).

Her close and unique relationship to the *salvific* work of the Incarnation is the basis for referring to her as Coredemptrix. See Fiat 2617. Also see Mediatrix.

Corporal

A corporal is a linen cloth about twenty inches square that is placed on the *altar* and on which the sacred vessels holding the *Eucharist* are always placed.

Corporal also means of the body or bodily. Corporeal is an obsolete form of the same word. See Tabernacle 1183.

Corporal works of mercy

The corporal works of mercy are acts of *charity* directed to the relief of the physical needs of others. They are as follows: feed the hungry, clothe the naked, shelter the homeless, give drink to the thirsty, care for the sick, visit prisoners, and bury the dead. See Spiritual works of mercy.

Corpus Christi

Corpus Christi is a feast of the *Blessed Sacrament* established in 1246 in the diocese of Liege. Its observance was extended to the universal Church by Pope Urban IV in 1264. Today, it is celebrated as the *Solemnity* of the Body and Blood of Christ on the first Thursday or Sunday after *Trinity Sunday*. See Pange lingua.

Correct conscience

A correct conscience is one that, recognizing the *moral* quality of a *concrete act*, adheres to one side of a practical *contradiction* with both *objective* and *subjective* certitude, that is, that the choice made is actually true and correct in itself (objective), and the individual believes it to be *true* and correct (subjective). A correct conscience chooses something as *good* that is, in fact, good in itself and also believes it to be true. One must always follow the dictates of a correct conscience. See Conscience 1706, 1776, 1777, 1778.

Corruption

Corruption is the improper alteration of something or an influence on something that renders it defective, *evil*, depraved, *unclean*, or subject to decay. See Rational animal. Also see Soul 363.

Cosmology

Cosmology is the study of the *corporal* universe and its ultimate constitution. See Systematic philosophy.

Cosmos/cosmic 1046

The cosmos is the *material* world or universe viewed as an ordered and *harmonious* system. *Revelation* affirms the common destiny of the material world and *man*. The whole visible universe is destined to be transformed so that the world, restored to its original state, will be at the service of the *just* and share in their *glorification* in the risen *Christ*. Cosmic is the adjectival form of cosmos.

Council 465

A council is a meeting of Church leaders legally *convoked* by proper *authority* to discuss matters and affairs of *ecclesiastical* concern. The word is synonymous with 'concilium,' a Latin term first employed by Tertullian around 200 A.D. Acts, chapter 15, refers to such a convocation called in Jerusalem, probably in the year 51 A.D.

Councils may be classified in a variety of ways.

Ecumenical councils are convoked for the whole world by the Pope or his *legates*. After confirmation by the Pope, *decrees* of such councils are binding on all *Christians*.

Plenary councils pertain to and are convoked by an *episcopal conference*, with the approval of the *Apostolic See*.

Provincial councils are assemblies convoked under the authority of the *Metropolitan* of a *province* and presided over by him. Their decrees bind only the province.

Diocesan synods are convoked by the *Bishop* of a *diocese* and presided over by him. Their decrees bind only in the diocese.

Council of Chalcedon 468

The Council of Chalcedon was the Church's Fourth *ecumenical council*. It was held at Chalcedon in 451 A.D. Its greatest work was the definition of our Lord's *nature* and *Person*. It condemned *Monophysitism*, which held that there is only one nature in *Christ* and that his humanity was entirely *absorbed* by his *divinity*. It also reaffirmed the condemnation of *Nestorianism*, which had already been condemned at the *Council of Ephesus* in 431 A.D. Nestorianism held that in Christ there were two *persons* joined together, God the Word and *Jesus* the *man*.

The Council of Chalcedon was rejected by the Copts, *Armenians*, and *Syrian* Jacobites, most of whom have remained outside of communion with both the Western and *Eastern Churches* ever since.

On the second *Sunday* in July, the *Byzantine Rite* commemorates the fathers of the five first councils, Nicaea I in 325 A.D., Constantinople I in 381 A.D., Ephesus in 431 A.D., Chalcedon in 451 A.D., and Constantinople II in 553 A.D.

Council of Constantinople III 475

The Council of Constantinople III, held in 680–681 A.D., was the sixth *ecumenical council*. It condemned *Monothelitism* by defining that *Christ* had two physical *wills*: a *human* will and a *divine will*. The human will is without division, change, partition, or confusion. The two wills are not contrary to each other, but the human will is always subject to the divine will. Christ has two wills because he has two *natures* in one *Person*.

Council of Ephesus 466

The Council of Ephesus was the third *ecumenical council*. It was held at Ephesus in 431 A.D. It condemned the heresies advanced by the *Nestorians* and *Pelagians* and formally approved the title of '*Mother of God*' for the *Blessed Virgin Mary*. It defined the *hypostatic union* as the *substantial* union of the divine and human *natures* in One *Person, Jesus Christ*. By the *Incarnation*, the *Sec-*

ond Person of the *Holy Trinity assumed a human nature.* In Christ, there is one *Divine Person* with two natures, one human and one divine; this is called the hypostatic union.

Council of Jamnia

The Council of Jamnia or Jabneel was a *Jewish* council held in Jamnia some time between 90 and 100 A.D. The city of Jamnia was located on the border of Judah about twelve miles from Joppa, which is today called 'Yebna.'

After the fall of Jerusalem in 70 A.D., many *Jews* settled in Jamnia and it became a seat of Jewish learning. It was here that the *canon* of the Jewish *Scriptures* was settled.

At that time, seven books, Sirach, Wisdom, Baruch, 1 & 2 Maccabees, Tobit, and Judith, which are accepted as part of *Old Testament* by the Church from the teaching of the *Apostles*, were excluded from the *Hebrew Bible* giving rise to the term *deuterocanonical*, which means second *canon*, in reference to them. It is believed that they were deleted in order to counter their use by the Church to support the *Messianic* claims of *Christ*.

Protestants accepted the canon of the Council of Jamnia and excluded these seven books from the list of inspired books. This gave rise to the differences between the *Catholic* and Protestant Scriptures at the start of the *Reformation*.

The differences between them were increased after the Reformation when other books that failed to agree with Protestant *theology* were also dropped from the canon.

The Church, however, retained all of these books because she is not bound by the decisions of the Jews at the Council of Jamnia. The only source from which she could receive the Old Testament writings as inspired was the *Holy Spirit* through the Apostles. The Apostles in their teaching appealed to Old Testament Scripture as the *Word of God* thereby *consecrating* its *authority* and giving it abiding *value* because it was used by a community guided by the Holy Spirit. See Apocrypha.

Council of Nicaea 465

Emperor Constantine (d. 337 A.D.) convened the first *ecumenical council* in 325 A.D. at Nicaea with the sanction of Pope Sylvester I. The principal work of the Council was the condemnation of *Arianism*, which taught that the Word was not the equal of the Father or true God but merely a more perfect creature. Arianism was one of the most widespread and devastating heresies that ever afflicted the Church. In opposition to it, the Council affirmed that the Son of God was eternally *begotten* of the Father. He was begotten, not made, of the same *substance* as the Father.

The Council adopted the term *homoousios*, a Greek word that means of the same substance, to express this idea.

The *Nicene Creed* was composed in response to the Arian Heresy. The Nicene Creed was reaffirmed in the Creed of the *Council of Constantinople* 381 A.D., which defined the *Holy Spirit* to be of the same substance as Father and the Son, a truth denied by the Arian followers of Macedonius. Hence, the form of the completed Creed is referred to as the Nicene-Constantinopolitan Creed. This Creed is the text for the *Profession of Faith* used in the liturgy.

Council of Nicaea II 476

The seventh *ecumenical council*, held at Nicaea in 787 A.D., condemned *Iconoclasm* and ordered the restoration of holy images in *churches*. Iconoclasm means the breaking of images. Iconoclasts rejected the use of images in the Church as being against the second commandment. The *Byzantine Rite* keeps a feast in honor of the fathers of this *Council*, known as the feast of Orthodoxy.

Respect for the *icons*, above all of Jesus, meant acceptance of the *Incarnation* and appearance of God in the flesh, which is capable of being depicted. Rejection of the images implied, above all, rejection of the *Incarnation*. Those *Christians* who became iconoclasts were sympathetic to *Muslim* teaching concerning the impossibility of the Incarnation and the mystery of the *Trinity*, which it presupposes.

Council of Orange

There were two *councils* of importance convened in Orange, in southern France, one in 441 A.D. and another in 529 A.D. They dealt with general matters of *ecclesiastical* discipline and reform. See Grace 35.

Council of Trent 406

The Council of Trent was the nineteenth *ecumenical council*. It was summoned by Pope Paul III and met between 1545 and 1563 A.D. The Council met in twenty-five sessions, and its decrees were confirmed by Pope Pius IV in 1564 A.D. It focused attention on issues raised by the *Protestant Reformation* and some needed reforms in Church discipline.

The Council issued decrees dealing with *Tradition* and *Scripture* in the Church and the understanding of the nature of *grace, sin, merit,* and *justification*. It also dealt in detail with *sacramental theology*.

Its disciplinary decrees dealt with reformation of the *liturgy* and the improvement of *seminary* formation and education. The Council had an immense impact on *Catholic* life and thought and prepared the ground for the work of *Vatican II.*

Counsel 1831

Counsel is one of the seven *gifts of the Holy Spirit.* It completes the *virtue* of *prudence* by enabling us to discern, without hesitation, the right course of action and by urging us to pursue it.

The gift of counsel supports and confirms the *virtue* of *hope* by helping us to recognize the deceits of *Satan,* who makes *evil* appear to be *good.*

Counsel guides us in the way of perfection by urging us to seek *divine* guidance. In cases where we must decide between two things that are both right and good, counsel shows us which would be more pleasing to God.

Counselor

Counselor is an advisor or *advocate,* one who speaks on behalf of another. The Greek word 'paraklitos' means advocate. *Jesus* called the *Holy Spirit* the *Paraclete.* In his Gospel, St. John called the Holy Spirit the Advocate. Paraclete, Advocate, Comforter and Counselor are all terms used in reference to the Holy Spirit. See Holy Spirit 702.

Counsels

Counsels are rules of perfection *voluntarily* assumed by those who have a *vocation* to do so. They are not perfections in themselves but instruments for strengthening *love* of God and neighbor. See Evangelical counsels 915.

Covenant 56

A covenant is a type of solemn agreement between two *human beings,* or between God and *man,* involving mutual commitments or guarantees.

In early *Hebrew* society, written documents were not in common use. Instead, the spoken word was invested with a *ritual* solemnity, which made it a sort of *concrete* reality that could not be *annulled* or retracted. For the *Jews,* a covenant was a solemn ritual agreement in which the covenanting parties mutually bound themselves by calling down curses upon them should they violate it.

Covenantal

Covenantal means having the quality or property of a covenant. See Covenant 56.

Covenantal Relationship

A *covenant* establishes an artificial blood kinship between the parties, second only to the blood kinship of family, signifying affection and loyalty. This relationship is referred to as a covenantal relationship. See Covenant 56.

Covet 2534

To covet is to long for or *inordinately* to desire that which belongs to another. The *sensitive appetite* leads us to desire pleasant things we do not have. In themselves, such desires are good, but they can exceed the limits of *reason* and drive us to desire inordinately and unjustly what belongs to another and prompt us to appropriate it for ourselves by violating the rules of *justice*, if necessary.

Coveting leads to *injustice*, *envy*, *jealousy*, insincerity, lying, *greed*, and *theft*. It is overcome by *prayer*, the practice of *self-denial, detachment* from *material* things, cultivation of *spiritual values*, and the reception of the *sacraments*.

Create/Created 295

To create means to bring forth into being out of nothing by a simple *act of the will*, without instruments of any kind and without any preexisting subject matter out of which to make something new. Only God can create because, being *omnipotent*, only he can confer existence or being by producing without instruments and without acting on pre-existent *matter*. Nothing can exist until he wills it, matter included. Creative activity in *man*, such as art, literature, or music, consists in reorganizing ideas or things that already exist and is not creation in the strict sense of the term.

Creation 279

Creation is the *act* by which, with a simple act of his *omnip-*otent will, God made, formed, produced, or brought into existence everything out of nothing. God *created* the entire universe and everything that is not himself and sustains everything in existence by an act of his loving and *benevolent providence*. Creation even extends to the *good* and order of what he brought into *being*.

God created *man* in his image and likeness by giving him *intellect* and *free will*. This made man a *person* capable of knowing and freely responding to God's loving call to union with him.

Creator 279

Creator refers to God as the one who made everything out of nothing.

Creche

Creche is a French name for the representation of the manger scene where *Christ* was born. It traditionally contains figures of Joseph, *Mary*, the Christ child, animals, shepherds, and the *Magi*. The practice arose in 1223 A.D. as a devotion founded by St. Francis of Assisi. It is also known as a *Manger* or *Crib*. See Christmas.

Credence table

The credence table is a table located in the *sanctuary* and on which are placed items required for *liturgical* functions. See Sanctuary. Also see Church 752.

Credentity, Motives of

Closely related to, but not identical with, the *motives of credibility* are the motives of credentity.

The credentity of Christian *revelation* is the convincing evidence for its truth, which imposes an *obligation* for it to be believed with a *divine faith* because, having been assisted by God's enlightening *grace*, one recognizes it to be of *divine* origin. See Motives of Credibility 156.

Credible/Credibility

Credible or credibility refers to the reasonable grounds for believing that something is true. See Assent. Also see Motives of Credibility 156.

Credo

The Latin word Credo is the first word of the *Nicene Creed* and the *Apostles' Creed*. It means 'I believe' and is used to designate the *profession of faith*. This profession of faith is used as part of the *Mass*. See Creed. Also see Appendix of prayers: Prayers recited at Mass: Credo.

Creed 13

Creed is a term derived from the Latin word 'credo,' meaning 'I believe.' The Church uses the word creed to refer to an authoritative and concise statement of the general *beliefs* that must be accepted in order to be a member of the *Catholic Church*. It contains those articles of belief that are regarded as *essential*.

The word creed usually refers to one of the three major *confessions of belief*, which are the *Apostles' Creed*, the *Nicene Creed*, and the *Athanasian Creed*. None of the Creeds used at different stages of the Church's life can be considered as superseded or irrelevant. The different expressions only serve to deepen the understanding of the *faith* of the Church over time.

The Creed is referred to as the 'Credo' from the first word of the Creed in Latin.

Cremation 2301

Cremation is the reduction of a corpse to ashes by burning as a way of disposing of it instead of burial or interment. The Church permits cremation, provided it is not intended to demonstrate a denial of *faith* in the *resurrection* of the body and the ashes are not preserved in the home or scattered over land or water, but are properly buried in blessed ground. Because the body became the *temple of the Holy Spirit* at *Baptism* and will rise again on the last day to share *eternity* reunited with the *soul*, human remains should be shown respect even after death.

Crib

See Creche.

Criminal law

Criminal law is that area of law that deals in any way with crimes and their punishment. See Code of the covenant. Also see Holiness code; Genesis.

Criteria for singing and music in the liturgy 1157

The musical *tradition* of the universal Church is of greater *value* than that of any other art because "as a combination of sacred music and words, it forms a necessary and integral part of solemn *liturgy*" (CCC 1156).

There are "three principal criteria: *beauty* expressive of *prayer*, the unanimous participation of the assembly at designated moments, and the solemn character of the celebration" (CCC 1157). Also "the texts intended to be sung must always be in conformity with Catholic doctrine. Indeed they should be drawn chiefly from the *Sacred Scripture* and from *liturgical* sources" (CCC 1158). A great example is the Church's long musical history found in the magnificent and rich tradition of *Gregorian Chant*.

"The harmony of *signs* (song, music, words, and actions) is all the more expressive and fruitful when expressed in the cultural richness of the People of God who *celebrate*" (CCC 1158). The primary purpose of all liturgical words and actions is the glory of God and *sanctification* of the *faithful*.

Criteriology

Criteriology is the part of *logic* that treats of the *validity* of the means whereby the *mind* attains *truth*, such as *human authority* or the truths used as principles of reasoning. It studies the *first principles* of human thought and their value as knowledge. See Logic.

Critical question, the

The issue of the trustworthiness of *human knowledge* is referred to as the critical question. See Formal logic. Also see Logic.

Crosier

The crosier or pastoral staff is a symbol of office used by the *Bishop* of a *diocese*. It usually has a crook at one end as a symbol of the Bishop's role in tending his flock. The other end is pointed, suggesting a prod for the spiritually lax.

The crosier is carried by the Bishop with the crook pointed outward; others who handle it keep the crook pointed backwards. The *Pope* does not use a crosier but a ferula, which is a staff surmounted with a cross. See Miter.

Crucified/Crucifixion

Crucifixion is a method of execution in which the *victim* is nailed or bound to a cross. It was adopted by the Romans and was commonly inflicted on those condemned *persons* who could not prove Roman citizenship. It was normally preceded by *scourging*. See Calvary. Also see Mass.

Crucifix

A crucifix is a cross to which a figure of *Christ* is attached. When the word cross occurs in the *liturgy*, a crucifix is to be understood. A crucifix must be placed on or near an *altar* on which the *sacrifice* of the *Mass* is offered. Due reverence is always given the Cross as the symbol of our *salvation*.

The crucifix did not come into general use in the Church until after the *Reformation* (1517–1641 A.D.).

A *blessed* crucifix is a *sacramental* and is commonly displayed in hospitals and homes. See Crucified.

Cruet

A cruet is a small pitcher. Cruets containing water and wine together with bread for *consecration* are presented at the *offertory* of the *Mass*. See Acolyte.

Crusade/Crusader

The Crusades were a series of wars undertaken to free the Holy Places from the hands of the *infidels* who refused *Christians* access to sacred sites. When volunteers became crusaders, they took a *vow* and received a small cross.

The name for the wars comes from the cross that the crusaders wore on their clothing. There were eight principle cru-

sades; the first began in 1095 A.D. and the eighth in 1270 A.D.

From 1099 A.D. to 1187 A.D., there was a Christian king of Jerusalem, but Christendom lost the Holy Land as result of internal dissension, imperial jealousy, and barbarous outbreaks, first in Jerusalem in 1099 A.D. and then in Constantinople in 1204 A.D.

After this, the name Crusade was applied to any expedition against *heretics* and infidels that received the *blessing* of the Church. After 1291 A.D., with the loss of the castle of Acre, the crusades degenerated into a series of expeditions of aggrandizement and plundering. See Armenian Church. Also see Maronite Rite.

Culpable/Culpability

Culpable means responsible for or *guilty* and blameworthy. See Negligence 1736.

Cult

Cult is a form of religious *worship* or *ritual* in honor or in *veneration* of a *person* or thing. See Disparity of cult 1635.

Cult of the body 2289

The cult of the body is a *neopagan* notion that promotes an exaggerated concern and preoccupation with the body. It sacrifices everything for the sake of the body or idolizes physical perfection and success in sports. By its selective preference for the strong over the weak, such conceptions can lead to the perversion of *human* relationships.

Proper care of the body is a serious *obligation* because of its role in *man's spiritual* development. Man is a *body-soul* composite, and the body shares equally with the *soul* in the *dignity* of man. It will also share in the eternal punishment or reward with the soul. For this reason, the Church always shows respect for the body and insists that it be reverenced as the *temple of the Holy Spirit* even after death.

Culture/Cultural

Culture is the totality of a people's *traditions*, attitudes, customs, institutions, art, and language. A *person* both forms culture and is formed by it. See Benedictines.

Curia

The curia of a *diocese* is the *legal* court of a diocesan *bishop* which helps him administer the diocese. The curia generally consists of the *Vicar General*, *Chancellor, ecclesiastical judges*, and others who act with the Bishop's *authority*.

The *Roman Curia* consists of those bodies that assist the *Pope* in administering the Church. These include the *Congregations*, Pontifical Commissions, Pontifical Councils, *Tribunals*, and Curial *Offices*. The diocese of

Rome has a diocesan curia of its own; distinct from the Roman Curia.

When curial officials are called together for a special meeting, it is called a *consistory*. See Diocese 833.

Curse

A curse, like a *blessing* and a *covenant*, is a solemn utterance that cannot be retracted or *annulled*. The word, particularly for the ancients, was empowered with a certain reality that allowed it to pursue its objective unfailingly.

Every covenant was *validated* by a curse. The *ritual* for forming a covenant is described in Gen 15:10. A *sacrificial victim* was killed and divided into two parts, which were laid on the ground. Those making the covenant passed between these parts and called upon themselves the fate of the slaughtered animals if they should violate the covenant.

Sin breaks man's covenant with God and calls down upon him the curse symbolized by the sacrificial victim. *Christ* took the curse of sin upon himself to *redeem* man. See Born under the law 422.

Cycles A, B, C

The liturgical celebration of the *mysteries of redemption* takes place in a yearly cycle of readings that provides the basic rhythm of the *Christian's prayer* life. Over a period of three years, the *Mass* readings from the *Old* and *New Testaments* of the *Bible* are divided into annual cycles: Cycle A, Cycle B, and Cycle C. New Testament readings other than the Gospels are used as the second reading on *Sundays* and major *feasts* in a three year cycle and in weekday Masses in a two year *cycle*. The *sanctoral cycle* of feasts remains the same each year. See Liturgical year.

D

Damnation

Damnation comes from the Latin word 'damnum,' meaning loss. It refers to the state of *eternal punishment* and *reprobation* in *hell*. Reprobation literally means rejection by God. The Church, however, very clearly teaches that damned *souls* are not actively rejected by God, who loved them even before they were *redeemed*.

Men are damned as the result of the exercise of their *free choice* by which they reject God's merciful *redemption*. All men were *created* to glorify God in eternal union with him in the joys of *heaven*. God still loves the damned, which he continues to keep in existence. See Hell 633, 1033.

Dark ages

The term 'dark ages' has been applied to the general period of history from the fifth to the fifteenth centuries, usually called the *Middle Ages*. Scholarship has rejected the expression dark ages as totally unjustified because it ignores the fact that, despite the wars and conflicts that plagued the period, it was remarkable for its enlightenment and achievements.

It may more correctly be called the Age of Faith. It was actually a period of outstanding learning and was filled with great men like Pope St. Gregory the Great, St. Bernard, St. Thomas Aquinas, St. Francis of Assisi, and many others. This time period also saw the rise of *monasticism*, the universities, and the riches of Gothic architecture. See Monastery.

Daughter of Sion (Zion) 489

Mary is referred to as the Daughter of Zion because 'The deliverer will come from Zion' (Rom 11:26), and she is his Mother. It is most appropriate to use 'Daughter of Sion' to refer to Mary, who was *full of grace* and from whom *Christ* came to earth to dwell among us in the bodily *temple* he received from her.

Sion or Zion is the *Hebrew* word for the hill where Jerusalem was built and where, according to *tradition*, both the institution of the *Eucharist* and the descent of the *Holy Spirit* took place.

The word *temple* is identified with the presence of God. Since the Temple was located in Jerusalem, it was considered to be the place where God dwelled. *Jesus* identified himself with the Temple dramatically when he said, 'Destroy this temple and in three days, I will raise it up' (Jn 2:18–20).

Sion is also used figuratively for the household of God, referring to either the Hebrews as people of God or the Church established by Christ. Since Mary is the pre-eminent member of the household of God, she is also known as the Daughter of Sion. In her is already personally achieved all that is being realized in the Church between *Pentecost* and the coming of Jesus in glory. For this reason, Mary is often called the Mystical City of God, the Heavenly Jerusalem, etc.

This title is frequently found in religious and *theological* literature, sermons, and even in the daily speech of *Christians* referring to the *kingdom of heaven*.

Day of Atonement 578

The Day of *Atonement* is also called the *Day of Expiation* or Yom Kippur. The *Jews* observed it on the tenth day of *Tisri* with a ceremony during which the *High Priest* made expiation for his own *sins* and the sins of the people. See Day of Expiation.

Day of Expiation

Expiation means *atonement*, which is an attempt to undo the wrong one has done by suffering a penalty and making *reparation*. It is closely related to *propitiation*, which

means to make *restitution* or to atone for fully.

The day of expiation is the day set apart by the *Jewish* people for observing the *Day of Atonement* for sins. Atonement is not forgiveness in the *Old Law* because it is impossible to make complete atonement for an offense against *infinite* goodness. It is also called the Day of Expiation or Yom Kippur. See Day of Atonement 578.

Day of the Lord

The Day of the Lord is referred to in Acts 2:20 as the day when *judgment* will be rendered upon the *just* and unjust for their life choices.

It is referred to as the *'parousia,'* the day of the *second coming* of Christ in judgment, in 1 Cor 1:8.

The day of the Lord is also considered to be the *'eighth day'* of re-creation, never to be followed by a ninth day. See Epiousios 2837. Also see Eighth day 349.

Days of abstinence 2043

Days of *abstinence* are days on which the faithful refrain from eating flesh-meat or soup made from meat.

Abstinence is distinguished from *fasting*, which is refraining from food, but may be combined with it.

Days of abstinence for the universal Church are Fridays throughout the year (unless they are solemnities), *Ash*

Wednesday and *Good Friday* (Canon 1251).

"The *Episcopal Conference* can determine more particular ways in which fasting and abstinence are to be observed" (Canon 1253).

"The law of abstinence binds those who have completed their fourteenth year" (Canon 1252).

It is helpful to identify certain misconceptions regarding the basis for the rules of abstinence from meat. 1) The Church does not forbid eating certain foods on the grounds that they are impure in the sense of the *Jewish proscribed* foods. The Church has condemned the *Gnostics* and *Manicheans* who counted flesh and wine as *evil*. 2) The abstinence required by the Church is to be reasonable and is not exacted of anyone whose health might be injured or who would be incapacitated from performing normal duties. 3) Finally, abstinence is a means, not an end. Abstinence pertains to the *Kingdom of God* only to the extent that it is performed by a heart enlivened by *faith* and love of God. Abstinence strengthens the *will* and increases awareness of the need for *reformation of life*. It is evidence of true remorse, *compunction*, and *repentance* for sin.

Daytime prayer

In the *Liturgy of the Hours*, Daytime Prayer is the hour said between Lauds and Vespers, and, depending on the time of day, is said as *Terce* (*Midmorning Prayer*), *Sext* (*Midday Prayer*), or *None* (*Midafternoon Prayer*). While there is only one set of *psalms* provided for Daytime Prayer each day, the *hymn*, reading, and final *prayer* differ according to the time of day.

De Fide

De fide is a Latin phrase meaning 'of faith.' It is used to identify those *doctrines* of the *faith* that are *infallibly* true. Their certitude derives ultimately from *divine revelation* and from the fact that they have been either defined by the Church's *solemn Magisterium* or taught by her *ordinary Magisterium* or her universal teaching *authority* as binding on the *conscience* of the *faithful*. See Doctrine.

Deacon

Deacon comes from the Greek word 'diakonos,' meaning servant. In Latin the word is 'diaconus.' It is the first major order of *Holy Orders* and the lowest *hierarchical* order of the Church.

The duties of a deacon are assisting at the celebration of *Mass*, reading the *Gospel*, preaching in *church*, administering *Holy Communion*, solemnly administering *Baptism*, *blessing marriages* in the name of the Church, taking *viaticum* to the dying, and officiating at funerals and burials.

There are two types of deacons: *transitional deacons*, who also will receive the order of *priesthood*, and *permanent deacons*, who will not be ordained priests. Deacons receive a *permanent character* on their *souls* and may not marry unless they were married when ordained. See Clerical orders. Also see Permanent deacon 1571; Transitional deacon.

Deadly sins
"Deadly *sins*" is another name for the *capital sins*. Because these sins are the roots of many other sins, they are called capital or deadly. See Capital sins 1866.

Deanery
A deanery is a territorial division of a *diocese*. See Diocese 833.

Death with dignity
'Death with dignity' is simply a euphemism for *euthanasia* and a *grave* violation of true human *dignity*.

Decalogue 1724, 1962, 2056
The word Decalogue literally means *'ten words'* and refers to the *Ten Commandments* revealed by God to Moses on Mount Sinai. See Ten Commandments. Also see Moral law 1950.

Declaration
A declaration is a formal statement or announcement. See Magisterium 83, 889, 890.

Decree
A decree is an *ordinance*, *edict*, or decision set by an *ecclesiastical authority*. Decrees of the *Pope* or of an *ecumenical council* are universally binding. See Ecumenical council 884. Also see Ecclesiastical decree.

Dedication
Dedication is the ceremony by which a building is set apart for *Divine Worship*.

Deductive/Deduction
When a reasoning process moves from a universal *premise* to a particular *conclusion*, it is called deductive. In deduction, a general truth is applied to a particular thing. For example: *Angels* are spirits. Gabriel is an angel. Therefore, Gabriel is a spirit. See Inference.

Defamation
Defamation comes from the Latin word 'diffamare' made from 'dis,' meaning from, and 'fama,' meaning fame. To defame means to attack or injure the reputation or honor of another by false statements, slander, or libel. See Slander.

Defender of the Bond
The Defender of the Bond is an official of an *ecclesiastical*

court appointed to uphold the *marriage bond* by every *lawful* means in all cases in which the dissolution of a marriage bond is under consideration or the *validity* of a marriage is challenged. He must be present in all such cases, and, if the court declares the marriage *null*, he must appeal to a higher court.

Traditionally, only a *priest* filled this office, but the revised 1983 *Code of Canon Law* allows non-*clerical persons* to fill it if they have a *doctorate* or *licentiate* degree in *Canon Law* from a *Pontifical Institute*. See Diocese 833.

Definition/Definitions

A definition is a statement that declares the meaning of a term or explains its *essence*. It may identify the nature of what it defines, identify its characteristic properties, relate how it comes into being, or explain its roots or sources.

A doctrinal definition is a statement of a religious *doctrine* of *faith* or *morals* or the solemn condemnation of an error made by a supreme religious *authority*. Such definitions either are made by the *Pope* or are made by *ecumenical councils* and confirmed by the Pope. See Solemn Magisterium.

Definitive or definitive manner
892

Definitive is used to describe a teaching of the Church that

has been formally declared to be *divine truth*. Definitive manner is used to describe solemn definitions or *dogmas* in the strict sense where not only is the content of this teaching declared to be divine truth, but also the manner of formulation is definitively fixed or made unchangeable. The *faithful* must accept such declarations and adhere to them with the *obedience of faith*.

Apart from solemn definitions *ex cathedra* of a *Pope* and formal *Dogmatic* pronouncements and *decrees* of an *ecumenical council*, the most frequent expressions of the mind of the Church are presented in the form of *encyclicals*. Addressed to all the faithful or to the Church in specific regions, they express the mind of the *Holy See* on matters of greater importance. Though not the usual form for *infallible* pronouncements, they definitely reflect the *ordinary Magisterium* and merit respect from the faithful.

Degree(s)

A degree is a successive step or level. It may be a stage in a process of attaining a status as in degrees of *Holy Orders* or a step in the direct line of descent. See Minor orders. See Degrees of blood relationship.

Degrees of blood relationship

Blood relationship is also known as *consanguinity*. It refers to *persons* having the same blood or ancestor, e.g., father and son, brother and sister, etc.

The degree of blood relationship refers to the proximity of relationship based on successive *generations*.

In the case of *direct line* consanguinity, the degree is the number of persons in the generational line (for example a grandfather-grandson relationship is third degree).

In the case of *collateral line* consanguinity, the degree is the number of persons along both generational lines, excluding the common ancestor (for example, a relationship between first cousins is fourth degree). See Direct line or lineal relationship.

Deification

Deification means making a god of a *created* thing by divinizing it. See Theosis.

Deifying or Sanctifying grace
1999

Deifying or sanctifying grace is the *gratuitous* gift that God makes to us of his own life. It is *infused* by the *Holy Spirit* into one's *soul* to heal it of *sin* and to *sanctify* it. This grace is received at *Baptism* and is the source of the work of *sanctification*. It is also the origin of the *indelible mark* that *Baptism* gives the soul. Because it gives us a share in God's own life, it is called deifying grace. However, deifying grace leaves the creature still a creature

and does not make the creature God by *nature*. Because it sanctifies the soul, it is also called sanctifying grace.

Deipara

Deipara is a Latin title for *Mary Mother of God*, meaning birth-giver to God or God bearer. It has nearly the same meaning as the Greek title of Mary as *Theotokos*. See Theotokos 495.

Deism 285

Deism refers to the teaching that God exists, that he *created* the world, that he established the *laws* according to which it works, and that he then left it to run by itself without further intervention.

Deists admit that there is a God but reject his *revelation*. *Catholics* believe that God created the world and lovingly continues to conserve it in being through his *providence*. The Church teaches that the order of *creation* is not complete in itself but is the stage on which God continues to reveal himself and to offer *salvation* to man, who chooses his *eternal destiny* through the use of his gift of *free will*.

Deliberate act

A deliberate act is a *human act* that is freely chosen in *consequence* of a *judgment* and proceeds from a *conscious act of the will*. Human acts are *moral acts*, that is, they can be morally evaluated as being either good or *evil* and make the *person* accountable for them and their intended *consequences*. See Human act 154. Also see Moral act.

Demon/Demoniac

A demoniac is a *person* possessed by the *devil*. See Exorcism 550.

Demonic possession

Demonic possession is the domination of a *person's* body by one or more *evil spirits*. The Church recognizes that this can occur and uses the *rite of exorcism* to liberate possessed persons. See Exorcism 550.

Denomination/Denominational

Denomination refers to a legally distinct group of believers, especially among *Protestants*. Different denominations can exist within a single Protestant tradition, such as among the Lutherans. They need not be different in their *faith* and *worship* or form of church government, but they can be. See Religion.

Denzinger

The term Denzinger is used to refer to the *Enchiridion Symbolorum, Definitionum, Declarationum de Rebus Fidei et Morum*, in English, '*Enchiridion* of Symbols, Definitions, and Declarations Concerning *Faith* and *Morals*.' It is a handbook or reference manual of definitions and declarations first compiled by the German *theologian* Henricus Denzinger in the mid-1800's and, subsequently, re-edited to the present day.

This Enchiridion has always been printed in the original languages in which the declarations were first issued, namely Greek or Latin. Approved Latin translations are provided for documents printed in the Greek. This is done to ensure accuracy in translation of language for these important pronouncements and teachings. See Enchiridion.

Deposit of divine revelation

Deposit of *revelation* refers to the same thing as *deposit of faith*. What is to be believed has been revealed by *Scripture* and *Tradition*. See Deposit of faith 1202.

Deposit of faith 1202

The deposit of *faith*, in Latin '*depositum fidei*,' is the body of *revealed truths* to be believed and those *principles* of conduct to be followed, which were given to the *Apostles* by Christ for the guidance of the *faithful*. It includes the truth of both *Scripture* and *Tradition* entrusted to the Church and its *Magisterium*.

The deposit of faith is preserved by the Church with the guarantee of *infallibility*. The term was not in common use before the sixteenth century, but what it connotes has always been familiar to the Church.

Depositum fidei

Depositum fidei is a Latin phrase that means the *deposit of faith*. See Deposit of faith 1202.

Depravity

Depravity is a state of corruption, wickedness, or *perversion*; it means *morally* bad. See Vice 1768.

Deputed

To be deputed is to be given *authority* to act as another's substitute or *agent*. See Auxiliary Bishop.

Derivative

Derivative means something taken from, descending from, or originating in other sources. It means non-original. See Righteousness 1224, 1991.

Desires of the spirit 2541

Desires of the spirit refers to a gift of the desire to conform to the *law* of God and the *grace* that turns *man's heart* away from *sin* and inspires in him a yearning for the *Sovereign* Good. This gift instructs man in the ways of the *Holy Spirit*, who alone can satisfy the *human* heart.

Despair 2091

Despair is a willful rejection of trust or *hope* for personal *salvation* from God. It is a refusal to believe in the power and *mercy* of God's *love* and accept the help needed for attaining salvation and the *forgiveness of sin*.

Despair is contrary to both *faith* and *charity*. In despair, one decides that it is impossible to fulfill the duties required for *eternal* salvation. Despair is contrary to God's goodness and *mercy*. It refuses to believe that the Lord is *faithful* to his promises and that his mercy endures forever. It may be described as a complete lack of hope, which is why it makes faith in God and love of God impossible to practice.

Despair is a *mortal sin* when it arises from distrust of God's goodness and *fidelity* but is a *venial* sin when it is the result of *melancholy* or fear due to personal weaknesses.

Despair must not be confused with anxiety. Fear or doubt lack the deliberate consent needed for despair.

Detachment

Detachment refers to withholding undue affection from creatures or *created* things. These undue affections are obstacles to *holiness* or to complete service of God or neighbor. Detachment is necessary for growth in holiness. See Covet 2534.

Detraction 2477

Detraction consists in the disclosure, without an objectively *valid* reason, of another's faults and failings to *persons* who did not know them. It harms another's reputation by telling *truths* about them that need not be shared with others.

Detraction is a *sin* against *justice* and *charity*. It is gravely sinful if the damage done to another is serious. One is always obliged to try to repair the damage. Because *reparation* of this damage is difficult and often impossible, one must try very hard to avoid such sins. One should pray for the person offended and apologize to him.

Deuterocanonical

After the fall of Jerusalem in 70 A.D., *Jews* settled in Jamnia, and it became a seat of *Jewish* learning. It was here that, in the *Council of Jamnia*, the *canon* of the Jewish *Scriptures* was settled.

At that time, seven books in the Catholic *Old Testament* (Sirach, Wisdom, Baruch, 1 & 2 Maccabees, Tobit, and Judith) were excluded from the *Hebrew Bible* giving rise to the term deuterocanonical, which means second canon, in reference to them. See Council of Jamnia.

Deuteronomic Code

The Deuteronomic Code is found in the books of the *Pentateuch*. It deals with prohibition of the *worship* of other gods, *prophets*, funeral observances, clean, and *unclean* food, offerings of the first-born, worship at a single *sanctuary*, the *Sabbath*, regulations regarding animal *sacrifice*, judges, *marriage*, and a host of other cultic and humanitarian regulations. It is not simply the *Ten Commandments* given by God on Mt. Sinai. See Genesis.

Deuteronomic tradition 2697

The Deuteronomic *tradition* refers to the instruction and guidance offered in the fifth of the five books of Moses. It is dominated by certain *theological* concepts, such as the election of *Israel* by *Yahweh* to be his people, the importance of observing the law especially the *repudiation* of foreign gods, a broad humanitarian concern for fellow *Israelites* as well as foreigners, and confidence in the power of Yahweh. It is also referred to as the *prophetic tradition*.

Deuteronomy

Deuteronomy is the name of the fifth book of the *Old Testament* and the last book of the *Pentateuch*, which is the name given to the first five books of the Old Testament.

The book is called Deuteronomy, or second *law*, because it contains a summary history of Israel until the death of Moses as well as the laws of the *Covenant*. See Graven image 2129. Also see Law of Moses.

Devil

The word devil comes from the Greek word '*diabolos*,' meaning slander. In a generic sense, it refers to those *angels* who joined Lucifer, called *Satan*, after his rebellion against God. His followers are called devils or *evil spirits*.

Devils, in their *nature*, are like other *angels*, pure spirits, but they have lost their *supernatural grace* and friendship with God through their prideful rejection of his *will*. In their pride, they desired to be like God without his *grace*, choosing instead to seek it by the powers of their own *nature*, which was indeed the most exalted in all *creation*.

To explain the fall of the angels, some *theologians* suggest that God revealed the *Incarnation* of the *Second Person* to them, and they foresaw that they would have to *adore* God in the form of a creature below their own nature and *venerate* his *Blessed Mother*, a woman, as their Queen. This they refused to do.

All subsequent rebellion against God is attributable to the fallen angel Lucifer. He brought about the fall of our first parents and their rebellion, which made *human nature* vulnerable to the allurements of the world, the flesh, and the devil through *concupiscence*.

The Church finds reason to rejoice in this ruinous fall and describes it in her *liturgy* as the *'felix culpa'* (happy fault), which merited such a *Redeemer*. It turned the burden of *concupiscence* into the means of *salvation* and of the conquest of evil and death in *man*. See Anointing of the Sick 1513. Also see Diabolos 2851.

Devil's advocate

In the process of canonization, the Devil's advocate, in Latin 'Advocatus Diaboli,' is the name given the *Promoter of the Faith*. If he is appointed, it is his duty to raise objections regarding the alleged *sanctity* of the *person*, the *validity* of *miracles attributed* to his *intercession*, or other possible difficulties that might limit the approval of his cause.

It is no longer the Devil's Advocate but the *relator* who supervises this process. The post of Devil's advocate itself may be held by the relator or a person distinct from the relator. See Promotor of the Faith. See *Canonization*.

Devotion / Devotional 2102

St. Thomas teaches that devotion is a readiness or willingness to dedicate oneself to things that pertain to the service of God. In devotion, one abandons himself to God in *prayer* and opens his *heart* to God's call. The life of prayer aims at promoting devotion. Devotion is the chief act of the *virtue of religion* and is acquired by earnest *meditation* on the love of God and his goodness.

Devotion is also used to describe the sensible or spiritual consolation felt in the service of God. It is called sensible devotion when the senses themselves are directly moved, as in the gift of tears. Devotion is spiritual when its source is in the *will*, as occurs in the *prayer of quiet*, and takes the form of inner peace and joy.

Sensible devotion can present dangers if it engenders the notion that love of God is not real unless it is felt. It can also give rise to *vanity* and to spiritual *pride* as though one were already a *saint*.

It offers great advantages when it encourages the *soul* in the service of God and the will to do *good*. We foster devotion through prayer, spiritual reading, and the *pious* reception of the *sacraments*. The opposite of devotion is *aridity*.

Diabolic/Diabolical

Diabolic comes from the Latin word 'diabolus'; it means devil-like. Diabolical means of the devil, very wicked, cruel, or fiendish. See Spiritism 2117.

Diabolos 2851

The Greek term diabolos literally means *slanderer* or accuser. It also refers to the *devil, Satan, the evil one*, the *father of lies*, the *fallen angel*, who viciously opposes God and his children (Rev 12:17). He totally opposes God's plan and the work of *salvation*.

'The Devil' is the title for the diabolical creature whose personal name is 'Satan.' He longs to bring suffering to believers (Rev 2:10); he is a devious schemer (Acts 13:10); he sneaks enemies of the Gospel into the Church (Mt 13:39); he claims *authority* over the world and gives it to whomever he wishes (Lk 4:6); he can prompt *persons* to *sin* (Jn 13:2). *Jesus* came in order to destroy the devil's work (1 Jn 3:8).

Diaconate 1536

The diaconate is the lowest level in the *hierarchy* of *Holy Orders*. Deacons receive an *indelible character* on their *souls* by this *sacrament*, which *configures* them to Christ. Deacons assist the *Bishop* and *priests* in the celebration of the *Divine Mysteries*. They assist in the distribution of *communion* and at *blessings* and *marriages*. Deacons also proclaim the *Gospel* at *Mass* and preach. They preside over funerals and baptisms and dedicate themselves to the various *ministries* of *charity*. A deacon may remain married if he is married before ordination, but, if his wife dies, he may not remarry.

Dialectics

Dialectics is a branch of *logic* that examines opinions or ideas by using *logical* argumentation. See Horns of a dilemma 589. Also see Logic.

Dialogue

Dialogue means to talk together or a conversation. Usually, it refers to an interchange and discussion of ideas in an effort to seek mutual understanding and harmony, as in ecumenical dialogue. See Protestant Reformation.

Didache 2760

The Didache is a short *treatise* written before the end of the second century presenting the teachings of the twelve *Apostles*. It is written in two parts. The first part is *moral*, and the second is *disciplinary* and *liturgical*. It was esteemed by some of the early Fathers to be second only to the *Bible* as a witness to the teaching and *praxis* or practice of the early Church. It is also referred to as 'The Teaching of the twelve Apostles.'

Die with Christ 1005

Dying with Christ refers to doing the Father's *will* instead of our own during our earthly life. *Christ's* life was given to the Father by his perfect *obedience*, even to death on the Cross. We die with Christ when we conform our wills to his will through *obedience* in *discipleship*, love of God, and *love* of neighbor.

At death, the *soul* leaves the body to be at home with the Lord if it has conformed itself to the will of the Father. *Union with Christ* is achieved by love, and *love* is manifested by keeping the *commandments*.

Diet of Speyer

The Diet of Speyer was an assembly called by Emperor Charles V on February 21, 1529 A.D. It was a reaction against the rise of *Protestant* reformers. It issued legislation that ended toleration of Lutheranism in lands with a *Catholic* majority but insisted on toleration of Catholicism in lands with a Lutheran majority. On April 19, 1529 A.D., a number of prominent leaders signed the 'Protest of Speyer', which defended *religious* toleration and inaugurated the term 'Protestants.' See Protestant.

Difference and complementarity 2333

The Catechism of the Catholic Church teaches that the concept of difference and *complementarity* between man and woman refers to those physical, *moral*, and *spiritual* conditions and qualities that make *man* and woman different but mutually perfecting and complementary. This difference and complementarity is oriented toward the goods of *marriage* and the flourishing of *family* life. The *harmony* of both the couple and *society* depends on how the complementarity of needs and mutual support between the sexes is lived out.

Dignity

Dignity comes from the Latin word 'dignitas,' meaning worth or worthiness. Dignity is the inherent quality of excellence of a *person* or thing, which deserves *recognition* and praise. See Christian humanism 1676.

Dignity in dying

'Dignity in dying' is simply a euphemism for *euthanasia* and a *grave* violation of true human *dignity*.

Diocesan Bishop

A diocesan bishop is a *bishop* who has been duly consecrated with *jurisdiction* over a *diocese*. See Auxiliary Bishop.

Diocesan synod

A *diocesan synod* is an assembly of selected *priests* and other members of the *faithful* of a *diocese* with their *Bishop* to discuss the needs of the diocese. See Synod 887.

Diocese/diocesan 833

The word diocese comes from a Greek word meaning administration. It refers to the territory governed by a *bishop*. Only the *Pope* can erect, alter, or divide a diocese. He does this through the Consistorial Congregation now called the *Congregation of Bishops*.

The Bishop organizes his diocese into *parishes* and *deaneries*. A territorial *prelature* and *territorial abbacy* are considered by *Canon Law* to be the equivalent of a diocese.

The administration of a diocese is carried out through the *curia*, consisting of the *Vicar General, Chancellor, Pro-*moter of *Justice, Defender of the Bond, synodal judges* and *examiners,* and *secretaries.* The *chapter of canons* where present also helps the Bishop rule his diocese and run it when the *see* is vacant. Also see Particular church 833. Also see Coadjutor Bishop.

Direct and intentional killing 2268

Direct and intentional killing refers to an act that takes the life of another by *consciously* directing one's activities toward that specific end. It is intentional when the result is foreseen and freely chosen as the purpose of the action. See Intentional homicide.

Direct line or Lineal relationship

Direct line or lineal relationship is the relationship between a *person* and his ancestors or descendants. It may move either by ascent or descent in a straight line, e.g., grandfather, father, son. See Line and degree.

Directly voluntary act

A directly voluntary act is an *act of the will* that *terminates* in an objective that is willed as an end in itself or as a means to an end. Such an act is also called a *voluntary act*. See Human act 154. Also see Act of man.

Diriment impediment

A diriment impediment is an

obstacle arising from *natural* or *Church Law* that prohibits *marriage* between *persons* having them and renders any attempted marriage between them *null and void*. A diriment impediment is also called an *invalidating impediment.*

A diriment impediment may arise from a condition in the *person*, from something he has done, or from some circumstance that arises from the relationship itself. The *Code of Canon Law* lists these impediments in Canons 1083–1094.

Diriment impediments are different from *prohibiting* or *hindering* impediments, which only make a *marriage illicit* but not *invalid.*

"The *local ordinary* can dispense his own subjects wherever they are residing, and all who are actually present in his territory, from all impediments of *ecclesiastical law*, except for those reserved to the *Apostolic See*" (Canon 1078, § 1). The Apostolic See must dispense of the impediments arising from Holy Orders, a public perpetual vow of chastity in a *religious institute* of pontifical right, and the putting to death of another for the purposes of marriage.

Impediments arising from *natural law* can never be dispensed. *Hindering* or *prohibiting impediments* were dropped in the 1983 Code of Canon Law.

The consent required for a valid marriage can be impeded by lack of sufficient reason, *violence*, grave fear, abduction, and clandestine secrecy. Failure to observe the *canonically* prescribed form of celebration renders a marriage invalid.

Impediments exist because of the Church's concern for the welfare of the individuals, for the institution of marriage itself, or for the effect of the marriage on the community.

Persons have the *right* to marry, but this is not an absolute right because it depends for its exercise on the capacity to fulfill the marital *obligations* and responsibilities. See Nullity of marriage 1629. Also see Impediment.

Discalced

Discalced comes from the Latin word 'calceus,' meaning shoe. It is used as an adjective to distinguish members of a *religious order* who wear sandals or shoes, called calced, from those who go barefoot, called discalced. See Carmelites.

Discern/Discernment 1676

Discernment is derived from the Latin word 'discernere,' meaning to distinguish and differentiate between. It is used to refer to the process by which a *person* sees through to the causes or sources of a decision, movement, or behavior. It aims at making a decision with the light of the *Holy Spirit*, so it can become a *grace*-filled human *judgment*.

There are two ways to verify what is discerned. First, any movement of the *interior life* that claims to be of God must affirm the basic *Gospel* message, be verified by *Scripture*, be echoed in the *Sacred Liturgy*, and be consistent with the lives of the *saints*. Second, at the practical level, it is judged by the fruit it produces.

Disciple/Discipleship

Disciple comes from the Latin word 'discipulus,' meaning learner. It refers to a student or follower of a teacher. The twelve *Apostles* were disciples of Christ.

Discipleship is the state of being a disciple. See Human work 2427. Also see Die with Christ 1005.

Discipline/disciplinary

Discipline refers to the rules of conduct required of members of the Church. Rules and regulations are made by the Church and are designed to maintain order among the *faithful* in matters of *liturgical* and *ecclesiastical law.* Failure to comply with them incurs penalties intended to correct or punish violations. See Ecclesiastical law 1952. Also see Ecclesiastical penalty 1463.

Discipline of the secret

The discipline of the secret was the custom during the first five centuries of Christianity of concealing entirely the most sacred *rites* and *doctrines* of the Church from the unbaptized to avoid *blasphemy*, *profanation*, and *persecution*. Through a long period of instruction and preparation, *catechumens* were enlightened by *degrees* as a test of their sincerity and to avoid improper instruction.

This discipline did not imply an initiation into a body of *esoteric* knowledge because all catechumens were fully instructed before they were allowed to receive the *sacraments of Christian initiation.* See Liturgy 1069.

Discursive prayer 2705

Discursive prayer is another name for *meditative prayer* or *meditation*. It consists in reflecting on a subject with the aim of stirring the *will* to greater *faith, hope, love, humility*, etc., and of forming resolutions that will reform one's life and draw one closer to *Christ.* See Meditation 2705.

Disordered will

Disordered will refers to a will that because of unruly *habits* or rejection of instruction in what is right, is upset in its normal function to choose what is morally good. *Addiction* to sinful habits, neglect in seeking to form a *correct conscience*, rejection of the teachings of the Church, yielding to *concupiscence*, neglect of prayer, and *spiritual sloth* all contribute to the development of a disordered will. See Soul 363.

Disparage

To disparage means to discredit, show disrespect or to belittle another. See Boasting 2481.

Disparity of worship or cult 1633

Disparity of worship or cult refers to an *impediment* that occurs when *marriage* is attempted between a *Catholic* and an unbaptized *person*. This is often incorrectly referred to as a *mixed marriage*.

According to Canon 1086 a marriage between a Catholic and an unbaptized person is *invalid*, unless a *dispensation* from the impediment is granted by the competent *ecclesiatical authority*. Such a *dispensation* is not to be granted unless conditions in Canons 1125 an 1126 are fulfilled. Canon 1125 requires the following: 1) that the Catholic party declares himself prepared to remove dangers of falling away from the *faith* and promises to have the children brought up in the Catholic faith; 2) that the other party is to be informed of these promises and made aware of the *obligation* of the Catholic party; and 3) that both parties must be instructed on the *essential* ends and properties of marriage. Canon 1126 provides that the *episcopal confer-*

ence is to establish the way in which these declarations and promises, which are always required, are to be made.

Dispensation 1635

A dispensation is a relaxation of the *law* in special circumstances.

The special permission given by the *Holy See* for a *person* to deviate from *Church Law* is called an *indult*.

Dispense/Dispensed/Dispensing

To dispense means to relax a *law* in a particular instance to permit something to be done *lawfully* under certain conditions. To be *valid*, a dispensation must be granted by one having the proper *authority* to grant it. See Dispensation 1635.

Dissident

Dissident is a name that has been applied to those *Eastern Churches* not in union with Rome to distinguish them from others of the same *rite* that are in union with Rome.

The term is appropriately applied to distinguish between *theologians* who oppose the teaching of the Church and *orthodox* theologians. Those who publicly opposed the teaching of Humanae Vitae (Of Human Life) by Pope Paul VI (1968 A.D.) condemning *artificial birth control* are dissidents and 'mirabile dictu' (Latin for 'wonderful to say,' or 'shockingly'), they continue teaching in *Catholic* universities. Such teachers often offer support and justification to various activist groups who oppose Church teaching on *moral* and *disciplinary* issues. Also see Eastern Church.

Dissimilitude 43

Dissimilitude is the condition or quality of being unlike, different from, dissimilar to, or diverse from something else.

Dissimulation 2468

Dissimulation is a pretense or an attempt to hide one's true feelings, motives, or *intentions*.

Distraction 2729

Distraction refers to a wandering of the *mind* and a lack of attention while at *prayer*. An attempt to remove distractions directly would be to fall into their trap. Simply returning the mind and *heart* to prayer is simpler and more effective. Distraction reveals where our attachments lie, and the humble awareness of this should awaken our preferential *love* for God and lead us to offer our heart resolutely to him to be purified.

Distributism

Distributism is offered as an alternative to the excesses of *capitalism*. It does not stress state ownership of income-bearing wealth but a fair distribution of wealth so as to support the *dignity* of all *families*. This is a program closely associated with the English Catholic writer G. K. Chesterton. He claimed that the differences between modern capitalism and *socialism* were merely incidental, both concentrating control of the means of production in the hands of a few powerful *persons*: the first in the hands of a few private persons and the other in the hands of a few powerful politicians. The views of Chesterton greatly influenced Dorothy Day, foundress of the *Catholic Worker movement*, and seem to have had a certain influence on the thought of *Popes* John Paul II and Benedict XVI. See Socialism 2425. Also see Catholic Worker Movement.

Distributive justice

Distributive justice is that form of *justice* that regulates what the community owes its citizens in proportion to their contributions and needs. See Justice 2407.

Divination 2116

Divination is the practice or use of *material* things to learn the future or other things not obtainable by *human* means of knowing. It can also refer to the attempt to foretell the future or discover the unknown through the aid of *evil spirits*.

Examples of divination are *palmistry*, *tarot cards*, *ouija boards*, *séances*, and horoscopes. Divination is gravely opposed to the *virtue of religion*. It betrays a certain lack of confidence in *divine providence* and an unwholesome desire to know hidden things.

Many who get involved with such things may not be serious about engaging in the activity, but they could give *scandal* and mislead others. The gravity of the *sin* depends on how much *faith* the *person* puts in the information obtained by such means. It is always prudent to avoid such behavior. When it involves *conscious* recourse to the *devil*, divination is always a *grave* sin.

Divine

Of or like God, inspired by God, sacrosanct. See Divine missions 258.

Divine economy 258

Divine economy refers to the *revelation* of God seen in his activity of creating and governing the world and especially in his plan for *salvation* in the *Person* and work of *Jesus*. Also see Divine law.

Divine faith

Divine *faith* refers to the *assent* of the *mind* to what has been told to us by God in *revelation*. It is distinct from human faith, which is assent given to what *human beings* tell us. See Believed with divine and Catholic faith.

Divine law

Divine providence in its governance of all creation bears the character of *law*. A law is the *ordinance* of *reason* ordering the *common good* given by the one responsible for it. Because it was conceived in *eternity*, it is called the *eternal law*. When the eternal law is used to determine what is right or wrong, it is called the *moral law*.

Eternal law may be physical or moral or be the fulfillment of some norm common to both. In physical laws this norm is fulfilled necessarily. The fulfillment of *moral law* depends on the *free will* of *human beings*.

The moral law has been revealed in two ways, naturally, and supernaturally. By *nature*, *man* comes to know the moral law through the light of reason from contact with creation itself, which reflects God's goodness and providence. Man comes to know the moral law from *divine revelation*, to which he can respond with the help of grace. This revelation is found in the communication of God's *will* through the *prophets*. He revealed his will perfectly through his Divine Son. See Ascesis 1734. Also see Will of God; Divine plan.

Divine life

All men are called to the *vocation* of *holiness*. A *person* is said to be holy when he lives in union with God in the state of *sanctifying grace*, which unites him to God and allows him to share in the divine life. This is called *moral holiness*.

Sanctifying grace is required for union with God because it is through grace that man shares in the divine life. Through grace, the *virtues* and *gifts of the Holy Spirit* are *infused* in the *soul* to strengthen and increase holiness in the life of man.

Holiness denotes union with God. Growth in holiness refers to the development or increase of moral holiness or union with God, which results from performing *morally good acts*. See Share in the divine life. Also see Sanctifying grace 1999, 2000; Union with Christ; Moral holiness.

Divine Liturgy

'Divine Liturgy' is the *Eastern Rite* term for the *Eucharistic Sacrifice*, which is called the 'Mass' in the *Latin Church*.

Divine Mercy Chaplet

The Divine Mercy *Chaplet* is a *devotional* prayer recited on rosary beads. It was introduced by St. Faustina to foster devotion to the *Divine Mercy*. It uses the prayer 'For the sake of His sorrowful *Passion* have mercy on us and on the whole world,' which is said in place of the *Hail Mary*. See Rosary.

Divine missions 258

A *mission* is a sending or being sent to perform some function or service. The Divine missions refer to the sending of the *Second* or *Third Person* of the *Holy Trinity* by the First, or of the Third Person by the First and Second Persons, for the production of a *temporal* effect revealing the Person outside the Trinity. The mission of the Son is the *Incarnation* of the Savior and *salvation*. The mission of the *Holy Spirit* is our *sanctification* and incorporation into *Christ*.

The temporal missions of the Second and Third *Divine Persons* outside the Trinity presuppose their *eternal processions* within the Trinity. To reveal the distinction of Persons and to make their life of *eternal fellowship* accessible to us, the Persons sent must first proceed eternally from the Father. Otherwise, there would be no real distinction of Persons within the unity of the Godhead. The Father, being the origin without origin of the divine processions, does not proceed and is not sent. He is not considered to have a mission in this sense. Rather, he is revealed and made accessible to us through the missions of the Incarnate Son and of the Holy Spirit. Through Christ and in the Holy Spirit we can pray: 'Our Father who art in heaven...'

Divine Mysteries (celebration of)

The celebration of the Divine

Mysteries is the Holy Sacrifice of the *Mass*. See Mass.

Divine nature

The *nature* of a thing or *person* refers to its *essence* considered as the ultimate *principle* of its *operations*. By essence, we mean the *act* of *being* which perfects and determines a thing in its *species*, that is, makes it to be the kind of thing it is. A *species* is a class of persons or objects possessing common *attributes*. Since the divine essence or being is absolutely unique, it *transcends* all *categories* and species into which *created* beings naturally fall.

Essence can be considered either as physical or as *metaphysical*. Physical essence refers to the fundamental and indispensable parts of a being, that is, those things that make a thing the kind of thing it is. Metaphysical essence refers to those aspects of a thing that make it understandable, that is, those things by which one knows what that something is.

Regarding the physical essence of God, we have to keep in mind that God is not a body made up of parts. Neither is he a creature, that is, made by some other cause. His essence is unique, not limited or confined in any way. In his physical essence, God is an *infinite* and indivisible pure spirit. Since God is unique, the only one of his kind, he cannot belong to any species.

God's metaphysical essence is concerned with what makes it possible for the *mind* to grasp what makes God knowable or intelligible. Some think it is his radical *infinity*, still others his boundless knowledge, and others still his subsistent being, but, in each of these ways, he is thought of as existing in himself, or self-existing. *Philosophically*, this idea is expressed as *'subsistent* being itself.' As God said to Moses, 'I am Who Am.' See Partakers of the divine nature 460. Also Will of God.

Divine Office

The Divine Office is the official daily cycle of the Church's public prayer. *Office*, 'officium' in Latin, refers to any *ecclesiastical* function or *duty*. Because of this, the Divine Office is often referred to simply as the 'Office.'

The practice of reciting the Divine Office began as a response to the command in Exodus that *priests* offer a morning and evening *sacrifice* (Ex 29:38–42). *Monastic* and eremitical (*hermit*) practice, as it developed in the early Church, adopted the *psalms* as the perfect form of *prayer*.

St. Benedict (480–550 A.D.) organized these psalms into hours of prayers for each day consisting of groups of psalms, prayers, and *scriptural* readings to be recited at set times. He provided that the entire *psalter* would be recited in a week. This schedule of times for prayer St. Benedict called the *Opus Dei* or the Work of God in keeping with his monastic motto, "pray and work." Except for *Prime*, this organization of prayer can be found in the Institutes and Conferences of St. John Cassian (360–435 A.D.).

The Divine Office, recited at regular intervals, gradually developed into the official prayer of the Church. It was a natural complement to the fullness of divine *worship* encountered in the *Eucharistic Sacrifice* and overflowing into the hours of daily life. This routine of prayer became the *Roman Breviary* promulgated by Pius V in 1568 A.D.

After the *Second Vatican Council*, Pope Paul VI (1970 A.D.) *promulgated* a new version of the Divine Office titled 'The *Liturgy of the Hours*.'

The names of the hours in the *Extraordinary Form* are: *Matins*, recited during the night; *Lauds*, recited at sunrise; Prime, the preparation for the day's work; *Terce*, the third hour of the day (9am); *Sext*, the sixth hour of the day (noon); *None*, the ninth hour of the day (3pm); *Vespers*, recited in the evening; and *Compline*, recited before retiring for the night.

In the revised *Liturgy of the Hours*, Matins was changed into the *Office of Readings* and is suitable for any time of the day, the hour of Prime

was suppressed, and *Daytime Prayer* is usually only said once in a day as either Terce, Sext, or None depending on the time. Other than these, the general structure of the day's hours in the Ordinary Form are the same. However, they are often referred to by their English name instead of the Latin: Lauds is *Morning Prayer*, Terce is *Midmorning Prayer*, Sext is *Midday Prayer*, None is *Midafternoon Prayer*, Vespers is *Evening Prayer*, and Compline is *Night Prayer*. See Liturgy of the Hours 1174 1178.

Divine pedagogy 708

Divine pedagogy refers to the teaching of God leading man to *moral* behavior and *virtuous* living. God gave the *Law* as a *divine* pedagogue, or teacher, to lead his people to *Christ*.

Divine pedagogy is distinct from *divine grace*, which enables man to keep the Law taught by God in *Scripture* by the life of Christ and by the guidance of the Church.

Divine Persons

In her teaching of the *dogma* of the *Trinity*, the Church professes one God in a *consubstantial* Trinity of three *Persons*, not three gods. The Persons do not share the *divinity* between them, but each Person is God, whole and entire. Each is what the other two are. By *nature*, there is but one God. The *Fourth*

Lateran Council (1215 A.D.) teaches that each Person is that supreme reality, namely, the *divine substance, essence,* and *nature.*

The Divine Persons are really distinct but in no way divided/ separated or divisible/separable from one another. God is one but not solitary. Father, Son, and *Holy Spirit* are not names distinguishing *modalities* of the *divine being.* They are distinct from one another in their *relations* of origin. The Father *generates,* the Son is *begotten,* and the Holy Spirit *proceeds.* The divine unity is *triune.*

The procession of the Word (Son) from the Father is called *generation,* and the procession of the Holy Spirit from the Father and the Son is called *spiration.* These processions are *eternal* and *immanent.*

Because the real distinction of Persons from one another does not divide the divine unity, the real distinction between them resides solely in the relationships that relate them to one another.

They are called Persons in view of their relations, but they are one in nature and *substance.* Because of this *substantial* unity, each Person is wholly in the other two Persons. This in-existence of really distinct Persons is known as *circumincession* in Latin and *perichoresis* in Greek. See Trinity, Holy 232, 234.

Divine plan

A plan is a scheme by which things are arranged and ordered or put together to achieve a common end or purpose. The divine plan is the ordering of the universe toward its end as revealed through *man's understanding* of the workings of God's *providence* in *creation* either by the use of *reason* or from *revelation.*

All men are *created* in order to attain their last end or ultimate goal. God's plan for man to attain that goal is called *divine providence.* Through his providence, God acts to carry out his divine governance. All *created* things have a place in his providence and are intended to give *glory* to God by assisting man to achieve his *ultimate end* not in a merely general way but as a unique and particular individual. It includes every detail of man's *being* and activity.

The providence of God is revealed to man's reason by means of the principle of *causality,* or the *primary cause.* Providence itself is not a means or medium outside the *divine nature;* rather, it is one with God and his *essence.* It is by divine providence that *secondary causes* act according to the *natures* that God gives them.

Some secondary causes act out of necessity, such as flame consuming wood. These are called *necessary causes.* Others act *contingently* or dependent on the nature of other things, such as how man, in order to attain his *ultimate end*, must choose good or how the growth of seeds depends on proper soil, sunlight, and moisture. These are called *contingent* or *dependent causes*.

The cause of man's free *acts* rests solely in his *free choice*. Because *voluntary acts* are entirely self-initiated, they are only determined by the free *act of the will*. Free choice acts as a contingent cause and providence does not impose necessity on such causes. Free will may or may not consent to pressure from without. It is impervious to anything except the *divine will* and *judgments* to which it freely accedes. See Individualism 2425. Also see Divine providence 302; Divine will; Question or problem of evil 309.

Divine praises

The Divine praises are the series of fourteen *blessings* recited after *Benediction of the Blessed Sacrament* before the *Sacred Host* is replaced into the *tabernacle*. They originated in the eighteenth century as an act of *reparation* for *blasphemy* and *profanity*. See Eucharistic species 1373. Also see Benediction of the Blessed Sacrament.

Divine presence

Divine presence refers to the existence of God acting in favor of his creatures. He is present first as the *cause* and object of the things he *created*. He is especially present by his *grace* in the *soul* of the rational creature who knows and seeks him. Cultivating the awareness of God's presence in the soul and the events of divine providence is necessary for growth in the spiritual life. See Prayer of quiet.

Divine providence 302

St. Thomas defines divine providence as the ordering of all things to their *ultimate end* (*Summa Theologica*, Q. 22, 1). This ordering of all things is also called the *divine plan*. Each thing God *created* has a particular role in this plan. Providence is not a merely general plan, but is particular and individual, and applies to the individual details of each *being's* function and activity.

Through his providence, God is the *primary cause* of governance in creation, but he has willed to use his creatures as *secondary causes*. Some secondary causes act by necessity as when fire consumes wood. Some secondary causes act *contingently*, that is, dependent on something else, such as seeds which depend on conditions for growth. The *acts of man* are contingent because they depend on his *free choice*. God does not impose necessity on *causes* that act contingently.

By *divine providence, creation*

was made incomplete and the purpose of creatures, particularly man, was to share in the completion of *creation*. By the use of *reason*, man develops the potentials of *nature*. By *procreation*, man shares in the creation of children, builds up the *Body of Christ*, and raises up *heirs to heaven*. By uniting their sufferings to those of Christ, the *baptized* share in filling up what is lacking in the suffering of Christ in his *Mystical Body* (cf. Col 1:24).

Divine revelation

Divine revelation is the manifestation to man of *divine truths* or realities beyond the power of his reason. Divine revelation is made manifest in *Scripture* and in the *Tradition* of the Church. God revealed himself personally in the *Incarnation* and continues to reveal himself through the teaching of his Church which alone is authorized as its repository and exponent. See Dogma 88.

Divine Sonship

Divine Sonship refers to becoming an adopted son of God by *Baptism*. In Baptism the *soul* receives *sanctifying grace*, which makes it a child of God, an *heir to heaven*, and a partaker in the *divine nature*. Baptism, by making men partakers in the divine nature, confers an *adoption* as sons. See Sacramental grace 1129. Also see Theosis.

Divine will

See Will of God.

Divinity

Divinity is the quality or condition of being divine. See Arianism. Also see Born of a virgin 502.

Divinity of Christ

Divinity refers to the *attribute* of being divine. It is the affirmation of *Christ's* true Godhead and, by virtue of the *hypostatic union*, a *Divine Person*.

Christ was not merely a messenger from God, not just a man of outstanding *virtue* and *wisdom* with the *mission* of *redeeming* man. The hypostatic union means that he was the only *begotten Son of the Father* from all *eternity*, who *assumed a human nature* and remained both true God and true *man*. See Arianism.

Divinization/Divinizing

Divinization is making something *divine*. The words come from deification. See Idolatry 2113. Also see Deification.

Divorce 1650, 2384, 2385

Divorce is a declaration that the *indissoluble marriage bond validly* entered into between a *man* and a woman is broken. *Civil* divorce, as far as it implies the right to remarry, is contrary to the *divine law* of the *indissolubility* of marriage, which binds all mankind, both *baptized* and unbaptized.

Civil *divorce* is an attempt to legislate the *dissolution* of the marriage bond, but it is a purely civil act that in no way dissolves the marriage bond, which, by its nature, is indissoluble. Divorce is expressly forbidden by Christ himself, 'Whoever divorces his wife and marries another, commits *adultery* against her' (Mk 10:11–12).

"If the divorced are remarried civilly, they find themselves in a situation that objectively contravenes God's law. Consequently, they cannot receive Eucharistic *Communion* as long as this situation persists. For the same reason, they cannot exercise certain *ecclesial* responsibilities. *Reconciliation* through the sacrament of *Penance* can be granted only to those who have repented for having violated the sign of the *covenant* and of *fidelity* to Christ, and who are committed to living in complete *continence*" (CCC 1650).

When a marriage has been declared *null* in *Canon Law*, it does not mean that a marriage has ended but that a true marriage never existed in the first place.

Where it is necessary to *terminate* the civil effects of their *invalid* marriage, the parties involved may apply for a civil divorce with the permission of their *Bishop*. In such cases, they are still free to marry because the *decree* of nullity merely affirms that there was no marriage.

For a *grave* reason, such as the Catholic education of the children, the *Bishop* may permit validly married *Catholics* to apply for civil divorce, but, in that case, they are not free to remarry.

Because the Church does not recognize civil divorce as evidence that a marriage contract no longer exists, *persons* who have received a civil divorce and wish to enter a marriage that will be recognized by the Church must obtain an *ecclesiastical dissolution*, such as the *Pauline* or *the Petrine Privilege* or a declaration of *nullity*.

A *valid* and *consummated* Christian marriage can only be dissolved by death. A non-consummated marriage between two baptized persons or between a baptized and a non-baptized person can be dissolved by *papal dispensation* for a just cause at the request of either party (Canon 1142).

Finally, to avoid misunderstanding, it is important to note that, when the term divorce is used in Catholic *theology* and law, it does not have the same implications as it does in secular law.

In forbidding divorce absolutely (cf. Mt 5:32; 19:6), Christ deprives all merely human *authority* of the right and power to dissolve the marriage bond. This power is reserved exclusively to God himself and to those whom he may directly authorize to act in his name in certain specified cases. The normal way God dissolves the marriage bond is death, after which, in *heaven*, 'they are not given in marriage' (Mt 22:30).

For a sacramental, consummated marriage, there are no exceptions to the rule that only death ends the marriage bond. In his *mercy* and wisdom, the Lord has given his *vicar* on Earth, the *Pope*, the authority to dissolve the marriage bond in cases of non-sacramental (when at least one party is not baptized) or non-consummated marriages. This does not authorize the spouses or any other merely human authority—civil or ecclesiastical—to pretend they can dissolve a valid marriage bond, even if it falls under those cases where the Petrine Privilege applies (cases which fall under the sole authority of the Pope). The most human authority may do is grant a legal separation to the spouses without the right to remarry.

Divorce is a grave offense against the *natural law* because it does injury to the covenant of *salvation* of which sacramental marriage is a sign. It is also *immoral* because it introduces disorder into the *family* and *society* and brings grave harm to the deserted spouse and to the children who are traumatized by the separation of their parents and torn between them.

Divortium in plenum a vinculo

Divortium in plenum a vinculo is a Latin phrase implying dissolution from the marriage bond, which must be determined by the competent *ecclesiastical authority*. "A marriage which is ratified and consummated cannot be dissolved by any human power or by any cause other than death" (Canon 1141). See Divorce 1650, 2384, 2385.

Divortium semi-plenum

Divortium semi-plenum is a Latin phrase signifying a situation in which the *spouses* are separated, but their *marriage bond* remains in force.

Married *persons* have a *duty* to live together ordinarily, but in cases of abuse, for example, or when there is danger to one of the spouses, they may be allowed to live apart. Their marriage *vows*, however, remain, and they are not free to remarry. See Divorce 1650, 2384, 2385.

Docile/Docility

Docile comes from the Latin word 'docere,' meaning to teach. In English it means easy to teach, manage, or discipline and tractable or obedient. See Spiritual body.

Doctor of the Church

Doctor of the Church is a title used since the *Middle Ages* to refer to certain *saints* whose writing and teaching offers outstanding guidance to the Church in matters of *faith*. As of 2016, in the Western Church, there are thirty-six Doctors of the Church: four women and thirty-two men. See New Eve 411.

Doctorate

Doctorate refers to the highest academic degree conferred by a *Pontifical Institute*. The *Licentiate* and Doctorate are graduate level degrees. See Defender of the Bond.

Doctrine/doctrinal

A doctrine is an individual *truth* of *faith* or *morals* held by the Church as part of the *deposit of faith* entrusted to her by *Christ*.

More specifically, it refers to particular formulations in the *Creed*, the definitions of *councils* confirmed by *papal authority*, or other *magisterial* pronouncements. Teachings defined in this manner bind the *faithful* as *authentic apostolic* teachings of the Church.

Doctrinal teaching authority is exercised as '*extraordinary Magisterium*' when a doctrine is formally declared as an article of faith or '*de fide*' by *papal definition* or by an *ecumenical council*. Teaching that has not been the subject of an explicit *dogmatic* formulation is taught by the '*ordinary Magisterium*.' Such teaching shares in the *charism* of *infal-*

libility and requires the *assent of faith*. See Infallibility 891. Also see Magisterium 83; Ecumenical council.

Doctrine, Development of

Develop means to gradually grow, build, expand, or become complete. Doctrine refers to carefully worked out sets of tenets, *beliefs*, or a *creed*. Dogma is a *truth*, tenet, or *doctrine* directly and *authoritatively* proposed by the Church for belief as an article of *divine revelation*.

Development of doctrine refers to the process by which meaning continues to be drawn out of the *deposit of faith* under the guidance of the *Holy Spirit*. It is also called dogmatic development. Such development always presumes that the truth of a mystery revealed in *Scripture* always remains unchanged; only the personal understanding of the truth by the believer may change.

Such development becomes necessary when a truth is contained only implicitly in the deposit of faith. For example, the doctrine of the *Immaculate Conception*, which was always accepted as part of the deposit of faith, was not *explicitly* defined until 1854 by Pope Pius IX.

The improved understanding that brings about such clarification is the fruit of prayerful reflection, study, and research by scripture scholars and *theologians*, the collective wisdom of the hierarchy in union with the Holy Father, and the guidance of the Holy Spirit.

Giving the *assent of faith* to the dogma thus clarified fosters in the *faithful* an increase in love and understanding of the truth of the faith and nurtures religious piety and a more fervent spiritual life.

Here are the seven criteria commonly used to distinguish *authentic* development from corruptions of doctrine as they are found in the classic work of Bl. Cardinal John Newman, *An Essay on the Development of Christian Doctrine*: Preservation of its Type; Continuity of its Principles; Power of Assimilation; Logical Sequence; Anticipation of the Future; Conservative Action upon its Past; and its Chronic Vigor. The "hermeneutic of continuity" proposed by Pope Benedict XVI for the interpretation of the documents of *Vatican II* reflects these notes of authentic development.

See Doctrine/doctrinal. Also see Deposit of faith 1202; Dogma 88.

Dogma 88

A dogma is a *truth*, tenet, or *doctrine* directly and *authoritatively* proposed by the Church for *belief* as an article of *divine revelation*. In the strictest sense, it is a doctrine solemnly defined both as to its content (what it says) and its formulation (the way it is said).

The *systematic and organic* study of the doctrine of the Church considering each article of *faith* in itself and its relation to other doctrines is called *Dogmatic Theology*.

Dogmatic pronouncements/proclamations

Dogmatic pronouncements are truths directly proclaimed by the Church with *Apostolic authority* which must be believed as part of *revealed truth*. See Dogma 88.

Dogmatic Theology

Dogmatic *theology* is the study of *Catholic doctrine*. It treats the teachings of the Church systematically as a whole as well as examining the *articles of faith* in relation to each other and in their own right. It includes Church doctrine in *Scripture* and *Tradition* and demonstrates how they are compatible with reason. It responds to *philosophical* objections and explains *logical* consequences of the *truths* the Church teaches. It is also called *Systematic Theology*. See Dogma 88.

Domestic church 1655, 2204

The domestic church refers to the *Christian family* as a community of *faith*, *hope*, and *charity* as a specific *revelation* and realization of *ecclesial communion*. It may properly be called a domestic church because it is a communion of *persons* and a sign and image of the communion of the Father, Son, and Holy Spirit. It reflects the Father's work of creation in the *procreation* and education of children and is called to partake of the *prayer* and *sacrifice* of Christ. It strengthens itself and grows in charity through daily prayer and reading of the *Word of God*. The Christian family has an *evangelizing* and *missionary* task within itself and in the world. See Ecclesia domestica 1656.

Domestic prelate

Domestic *prelate* is an honorary distinction conferred by the *Pope* on priests in *recognition* of special merit. They are considered members of the *papal household*. Their dress is very similar to that of a *bishop*. They are addressed as Very Reverend Monsignor. See Prelature.

Dominican Friars

Dominican Friars are members of the Dominican order. See Dominicans.

Dominican Rite

The Dominican Rite is a use of the *Latin Rite* proper to the *Dominican Order* approved by Pope Clement IV and St. Pius V. There are many similarities between the Dominican Rite and the *Extraordinary Form* of the *Roman Rite*. Chief dif-

ferences that distinguish the Dominican Rite are as follows: in the *proper* of the liturgy, the *chalice* is prepared by the *celebrant* at the *altar* before *Mass* begins; the *Gloria* and *Credo* are started in the center of the *altar* and are continued on the side by the *Missal*; the *host* and chalice are offered together; and during, the *Canon*, the celebrant's arms are extended. At the end of Mass, the *Salve Regina* is sung. Differences in the *Divine Office* are very slight. Their calendar *celebrates* a number of *Beati* proper to the order. See Latin Rite.

Dominicans/Dominican order

Dominicans are a *religious institute* founded by St. Dominic in 1215 A.D. under the title of Order of Preachers. They are a *mendicant order*, that is, they depend for their subsistence on the *charity* of the *faithful*. Their active work of preaching is rooted in *monastic* observance. The order is guardian of *Scholastic philosophy* and *theology*.

There are two orders attached to the Order of Preachers: *cloistered nuns* who follow a rule similar to that of the friars; and a third order, consisting of those who live an *active life* in the world doing *apostolic work* outside of the community. The efforts of the order have spread the *faith* around the world. See Friars Preachers.

Dominicus character 1274

Dominicus character is a Latin phrase used by St. Augustine meaning *'seal of the Lord.'* It refers to how the *Holy Spirit* has marked the *baptized* with the seal of *eternal life* for the day of *redemption*.

Dominion

To exercise dominion means to have power, rule, or control over something. See Spiritual direction 2690.

Donatism

Donatism is a *heresy* that holds that the *validity* of a *sacrament* depends on the *holiness* of the one who administers it so that, for example, a sacrament administered by a *heretic* would not achieve its effective *grace*.

A *council* was convoked by the emperor Constantine in 314 A.D. in the town of Arles to address the Donatist *schism* in North Africa. Despite appeals to the *Pope* in 313 A.D., the Synod of Arles in 314 A.D., and the emperor in 316 A.D., the movement continued to spread. St. Augustine, after becoming *Bishop* of Hippo in 397 A.D., worked to refute Donatism for fifteen years. After a conference called by the emperor in 411 A.D. failed to resolve the *doctrinal* dispute, a *persecution* of Donatists began, but the *sect* persisted until the invasion of the Arabs in the seventh century.

One beneficial result of the struggle was that the Church was forced to better articulate her understanding of the *sacraments* and how their *efficacy* depended on the power of *Christ* rather than the worthiness of the minister. However, in spite the doctrinal clarifications and the many tragic *consequences* of the Donatist heresy, many non-*Catholic* sects still subscribe to this key principle of Donatism. See Ex Opere Operato 1128.

Douay-Rheims Bible

The Douay-Rheims Bible is a translation of the Latin *Vulgate Bible* published in two parts in two different cities at different times. The *New Testament* was published at Rheims in 1582 A.D. The *Old Testament* was published between 1609 A.D. and 1610 A.D. at Douay.

The translation was made in order to avoid *heretical* tendencies found in other *Protestant* English translations of the day. The translation was not based on original *Hebrew*, Aramaic, or Greek texts but on the Latin Vulgate. It achieves a high standard of consistency with the Latin, but it was so literal that it often resulted in obscurity. Largely because of its reliability, it influenced the Authorized Version (King James Version) made in 1611 A.D. Although its prose was inferior to that of the Authorized Version, it served as the standard English language Bible of the *Roman Church* for 350 years.

Bishop Challoner made revisions of the Douay-Rheims Bible between 1749 A.D. and 1752 A.D. It is not really a version of the Douay-Rheims because it was altered and modified until very few verses of the original remained. Effectively, it is a new translation. Yet, it is still referred to as the Douay-Rheims Bible. It is the English Bible most used by *Catholics* because it cleared up obscure words and passages in the original version. See Righteousness. Also see Vulgate Bible.

Double consequence of sin
1472

Double *consequence* of *sin* refers to the Church's teaching that there are two kinds of punishment for sin, *eternal* and *temporal*. *Mortal sin* deprives us of *communion* with God and makes us incapable of *eternal life*. This punishment is called *eternal punishment*. When mortal sin is forgiven in the *sacrament of Reconciliation*, the eternal punishment is removed, but *temporal punishment* remains to be *expiated* through *penitential* practices and sharing the Cross of *Christ*.

Punishment for sin, whether eternal or temporal, is not a kind of *vengeance* inflicted by God from without but a natu-ral consequence arising from the very nature of sin.

Perfect contrition, which proceeds from an act of perfect *charity*, can attain complete *purification* in such a way that no temporal or *eternal* punishment would remain. For *Catholics*, the *sacrament of Reconciliation* is normally required for the remission of *mortal sin*. For the full remission of the eternal punishment due to mortal sin, acceptance of a penance is normally required to receive *absolution*.

Double effect, Principle of 2263

The principle of double effect operates when there is question of *abstaining* from an action because, in addition to a good effect, it will also produce a bad effect. It is *lawful* to perform the action that has a double effect provided:

1) the act itself is not wrong;
2) the doer intends and desires only the good effect and not the bad one;
3) the good effect is produced independently of and not by means of the bad effect; and
4) there is a sufficient reason for allowing the bad effect, for example, amputating a finger to prevent a life-threatening infection.

Double genuflection
See Genuflect 1378.

Doubtful or uncertain conscience

A doubtful or uncertain *con-*

science is one that is unable to decide whether an *act* conforms to the *moral law* or not. Morally, one is never allowed to act with a doubtful or uncertain conscience.

For an action to be morally right, a *prudentially certain* conscience is sufficient, that is, there is solid enough *reason* to justify an action by an ordinarily prudent *man*. See Conscience 1706.

Dour 409

Dour means hard, harsh, severe, bold, stern, or fierce.

Doxology 2641

A doxology is a formula of *praise*. The term comes from the Greek 'doxologia,' which is composed of the two words 'doxa,' meaning *glory*, and 'logos,' meaning word. There are two types of doxology: the *greater doxology*, which is the 'Gloria in excelsis' of the *Mass*, and the *lesser doxology*, which is the 'Glory be to the Father.'

The *Eastern rites* have traditionally added a doxology to the *Our Father*. In the *Byzantine Church*, the words are, 'For thine is the kingdom, the power, and the glory, Father, Son, and Holy Ghost, now, and forever, and world without end.' A similar doxology is found in the *Didache*, written in the second century.

A variation of this Eastern doxology, which omits the reference to the *Persons* of the *Trinity*, is added to the *Our*

Father among *Protestants*. This latter form was adopted in the *Latin Church* after *Vatican II*.

Dry Mass (missa sicca)

A dry Mass, or '*missa sicca*' in Latin, was the celebration of the *sacred liturgy* in which there was neither *offering* nor *consecration*. See Mass 1332. Also see Mass of the Presanctified.

Dryness in prayer 2731

Dryness in prayer, or *aridity*, refers to the absence of consolation or devotion during *prayer*. It may range from a lack of sensible *devotion* to complete desolation. It can lead to weariness of *soul* in doing *good* and the abandonment of the *spiritual life*. It can, when patiently endured, foster true *devotion* and fervor by making *piety* an affair of the *will* rather than the *emotions*.

Aridity is sent by God to those he is leading to himself in order to make them seek him alone and not his consolations. Aridity, however, is not always from God. It may be due to a careless spiritual life. In this case, one has to stir himself up by turning again to God and seeking his will more *consciously* through prayer.

Dualism 285

Dualism refers to the *philosophical theory* that man is composed of two *principles*, one *material* or bad and the other *spiritual* or *good*. In man, the good, spiritual principle is entrapped in the bad, material principle. This explanation of the *nature* of man and of the *problem of evil* is contrary to *Catholic* teaching.

Dualism can also refer to the *doctrine* that there are two ultimate and independent *first principles*, one good and the other evil, which are in eternal conflict. *Man*, caught in this *cosmic* struggle, is unable to affect its outcome.

Theologically, dualism refers to the doctrine, *attributed* to Nestorius, that *Christ* had one nature and two personalities, one *human* and one *divine*, instead of being one *person* with two natures, one human and one divine as the Church teaches.

Dulia

Dulia is the *praise* and respect rendered to the *angels* and the *saints*. See Adoration 2628.

Duplicity 2468

Duplicity is the act of being openly or secretly deceitful or double-dealing.

Duty

A duty is a *moral* obligation to do or to refrain from doing something. *Rights* and duties are complementary. Every right imposes a duty to respect that right. However, when one has a right he does not necessarily have the duty to exer-

cise it. The one who has the duty always has the right to fulfill it.

God is the only exception to the mutual dependence of rights and duties. He has all rights but no strict duties. See Grave obligation 2072.

Duty of citizens 2239

It is the *obligation* of citizens to contribute, along with *civil authority*, to the good of society in a *spirit of truth, justice, solidarity*, and freedom. The love and service of one's country follows from the *duty* of *gratitude* and belongs to the order of *charity*. Submission to *legitimate* authority and service to the *common good* require citizens to fulfill their roles in the life of the political community. These include observance of its laws, payment of its taxes, exercise of one's right to vote, and defense of the country.

Duty of reparation 2487

Every offense committed against justice entails the *obligation* of *restitution* or *reparation* even if the offense has been forgiven. If public reparation is impossible, it must be made secretly. The *duty* of reparation also concerns offenses against another's reputation and obliges in *conscience*.

Dynamic entity

Dynamic comes from the Greek word 'dynamis,' meaning power or strength. *Entity* comes from the Latin word 'ens,' meaning *being*. A dynamic entity is a force pro- ducing change or motion. See Prophetic formula.

E

Easter 1169

Easter is the *liturgical solemnity* commemorating the *Resurrection* of *Christ* from the dead. Easter is "celebrated on the first *Sunday* after the first *full moon* after the *vernal equinox*" (CCC 1170) because it is related to the *Jewish Pasch*. It is the Sunday of the Resurrection, the *feast* of feasts, and the most solemn of all *solemnities* because the Resurrection is the basis of the *Christian faith*. "If Christ has not been raised, your faith is futile and you are still in your *sins*" (1 Cor 15:17). Also see Easter mystery; Paschal mystery 571.

Easter candle

Easter candle is another name for *Paschal candle*. See New fire. Also see Easter vigil.

Easter duty

The Easter duty is the *obligation* imposed by the third precept of the Church to receive *Holy Communion* during *Easter* Time, that is, between the First *Sunday* of *Lent* and *Trinity Sunday* in the United States. See Precepts of the Church 2041.

Easter mystery

The Easter mystery is also called the *Paschal mystery*. It refers to the *Passion*, death, *Resurrection*, and *ascension* of *Christ*. See Paschal mystery 571, 1085.

Easter season 2042

Easter season refers to the *liturgical* period covering fifty days, extending from *Easter Sunday* through the *Solemnity* of *Pentecost*. It is also known as *Paschal Time* (or Easter Time). The first eight days of Easter Time constitute the *Octave* of Easter and are celebrated as solemnities.

Easter Triduum

The Easter Triduum begins with the Mass of the Lord's supper on *Holy Thursday* and concludes with *Vespers* on *Easter Sunday*. See Paschal mystery 571, 1085.

Easter Vigil 1217, 1254

The word vigil comes from the Latin word 'vigila,' which means a night watch or night hour. By *immemorial tradition*, the Church has kept the day preceding a *feast* as a day of preparation. The night services are held as spiritual preparation for the feast that gives the day its name.

The day before Easter is kept as a day of mourning for *Christ* in the tomb. That night, the Easter Vigil, which is especially solemn, includes the *blessing* of the *new fire*, the procession of the *Paschal* candle, the *Baptism* of *catechumens*, and the renewal of baptismal promises. Everything leads up to the joy of the *Resurrection* with the ringing of bells, the singing of the *Regina coeli*, and the new greeting of '*Christ* is Risen' and the response, 'Truly, he is Risen.'

Easter water

Easter water is the water blessed during the *ceremonies* of the *Easter Vigil* and used in administering *Baptism* to the *Catechumens*. During the ceremony, the *Easter candle*, representing *Christ*, is lowered into the water and raised up three times, symbolizing the death and *Resurrection* of Christ. See Holy water.

Eastern Church

'Eastern Church' is a term that, in a broad sense, describes those Churches that originated in Asia Minor, the Middle East, and parts of Eastern Europe, Africa and Southern Asia. They have customs and liturgical *traditions* distinct from that of the *Latin Church*, namely, those Churches whose liturgical

traditions and customs are derived principally from Rome.

The Eastern Churches can be broadly divided into three distinct communions: *Eastern Catholics, Eastern Orthodox*, and *Oriental Orthodox*. Eastern Catholics are those Churches which are in union with Rome. The Eastern Orthodox Church is a communion of independent national Churches who accept the first seven *ecumenical councils* and who separated from the *Catholic Church* during the eleventh century. The Oriental Orthodox is a communion of independent Churches who accept the first three *ecumenical councils*, but refused to accept the *Council of Chalcedon* and went into schism in the fifth century. All of these have valid sacraments and *apostolic succession*, and are thus Churches in the true sense of the term. The Eastern Orthodox and Oriental Orthodox were all, at first, in union with the *Pope* and the Catholic Church, but they currently deny the *authority* of the *Holy See*. See Nicaea II 476. Also see Rite 1203.

Eastern Catholic Churches

The Eastern Churches who are in union with Rome are called the Eastern Catholic Churches or *Oriental Churches*. They are fully Catholic and keep their own *liturgies, Canon Law* and customs by right just as the *Latin*

Church does. In *faith, morals*, and *obedience* to the Holy See there is no difference. See Eastern Church.

Eastern Orthodox Church

Eastern Orthodox Church refers to those *Eastern Churches* that have *valid orders* and share the same *faith* as the Latin or Western Church but do not accept the *authority* of the *Holy See*. The Eastern Orthodox accept the first seven *ecumenical councils*, and are not in communion with the *Oriental Orthodox*, who only accept the first three ecumenical councils. See Eastern Church.

Eastern Rite

The term Eastern *Rite* refers to *liturgical* practices of *Eastern Churches* that are distinct from the Western Churches in general and from the *Latin Rite* in particular. See Eastern Church.

Ecclesia domestica 1656

Ecclesia domestica is Latin for *'domestic church.'* The *Christian family* as a community of *faith, hope,* and *charity* is a specific *revelation* and realization of *ecclesial* communion. See Domestic Church 1655.

Ecclesial

Ecclesial means pertaining to the Church. See Presbyterate 1536.

Ecclesial communion

Ecclesial communion refers to the sharing of the *liturgical* life of the Church between its members.

The family participates in the Father's work of *creation* by the *procreation* and education of its children. Through mutual edification and support, it fosters growth in *Christian virtue* and shares in the *prayer* and *sacrifice* of *Christ* in the Christian community. See Domestic church.

Ecclesial communities

Ecclesial communities are assemblies of *baptized* believers united by a common *faith* and *Christian love*. They are not Churches in the proper sense because they lack a *valid* priesthood and do not *celebrate* the *Eucharist* as this is understood in the *Catholic Church*.

Those *Eastern Churches* not in communion with Rome are, nevertheless, Churches in the proper sense, because they enjoy a valid priesthood and *sacraments*. See Ecumenism.

Ecclesial tradition 83

Ecclesial tradition refers to the "various *theological, disciplinary, liturgical,* or *devotional traditions,* born in the local *churches* over time" (CCC 83) and through which the great *Tradition* is expressed. Ecclesial traditions may be modified or abandoned under the guidance of the *Magisterium*. See Tradition.

Ecclesiastical

Ecclesiastical means pertaining to the Church. It comes from the Greek word 'ekklesia,' meaning to call out. In *New Testament* usage, the word became 'ecclesia' in Latin and referred to the Church as the 'ones called out' or gathered in the work of the Lord.

St. Paul never thinks of the Church as a physical structure but as an assembly of dedicated *disciples* purchased by the Blood of *Christ* and a new race equipped with the leadership and *spiritual gifts* needed to build the *Kingdom of God* on earth. See Church 752.

Ecclesiastical decrees

Ecclesiastical decrees are official pronouncements called *constitutions* issued by *councils*. In a general sense, they include decrees of the Roman Congregations. More often, they are legislative enactments of the *Pope* or council. *Papal* decrees are also found in *apostolic letters*, and *motu proprios*. See Constitution. Also see Decree.

Ecclesiastical dissolution (of marriage)

Because the Church does not recognize *civil divorce* as evidence that a *marriage* contract no longer exists, *persons* who have received a civil divorce and wish to enter a marriage that will be recognized by the Church must obtain an *ecclesiastical* dissolution of the prior marriage or a declaration of *nullity*. See Divorce 1650.

Ecclesiastical foundation

An *ecclesiastical* foundation is an *endowment* consisting of a sacred office or *duty* and the right to annual revenue. Such a foundation is called a *benefice*. See Right to private property 2403. Also see Benefice.

Ecclesiastical law 1952

Ecclesiastical *law* refers to the rules governing human behavior established by the Church. It is not a repetition by the Church of the *divine* or *natural law*; rather, it is concerned with *liturgy*, *legal* procedures, and *penalties* associated with infractions of those laws. Most ecclesiastical laws can be found in the 1983 *Code of Canon Law*. Because ecclesiastical laws are *disciplinary* in nature and are made by the Church, they can be *dispensed* by *ecclesiastical authorities*. They may change over time to meet the needs of changing circumstances.

Ecclesiastical office

An ecclesiastical office is the *duty* of service associated with one's station or position in the Church or a task to be performed as an *obligation*. The three offices of the Church are to teach, to *sanctify*, and to govern. See Officium 1255. Also see Benefice.

Ecclesiastical penalty 1463

An *ecclesiastical* penalty is a *disciplinary* form of punishment imposed by the Church on a *person* who has committed an offense against *Canon Law*. It consists in the deprivation of a *temporal* or *spiritual* benefit as a punishment imposed by *legitimate* ecclesiastical *authority* for an ecclesiastical offense.

In general, a penalty intended for the betterment of the person is called corrective or *medicinal*. When a penalty is intended as punishment for an offense, it is called a *punitive* or *vindictive penalty*.

Because ecclesiastical penalties are specified in Canon Law they are also called *canonical penalties*. They are classified either as *expiatory penalties* or as censures. Expiatory penalties are punitive in nature and aim to satisfy *justice* by the punishment of the offender. *Censures* are medicinal in nature, that is, they are intended for the correction of the offender.

There are three kinds of censures: *excommunication*, *suspension*, and *interdict*. Such penalties are incurred not because of the intrinsic wickedness of an act but because of the circumstances attending it and the serious consequences involved.

Excommunication impedes a person's right to receive the *sacraments* or Christian burial until the person repents and is reconciled with the Church.

Suspension excludes a person either from *office* or *benefice* or both.

Interdict is an ecclesiastical censure by which members of the Church remain in communion with the *faithful* but are excluded from participation in certain *sacred offices* and reception or administration of certain sacraments.

An interdict on a state or *diocese* can only be imposed by the *Holy See*, but an interdict on a *parish* or a particular person can be imposed by the *Bishop*.

Ecclesiastical penalties may be incurred in three ways: automatically; by an administrative act of a *superior*, such as a bishop or *abbot*; or by an ecclesiastical judge in the course of a trial.

Ecclesiastical penalties must not be confused with *penances* or other spiritual exercises imposed during the *sacrament of Reconciliation*. These deal with the *moral* order in the *internal forum* of *conscience* rather than in the *external*, *public*, or *legal forum* and are issued for moral offenses rather than for crimes disturbing the *social* order. Penalties belong to the legal order and are imposed for legal offenses. See Excommunication.

Ecclesiastical tribunal

An ecclesiastical tribunal is a Church court. The Church court has *jurisdiction* over issues involving *Canon Law*. See Nullity of marriage 1629.

Economic/Economics

Economics is a science that investigates the laws that govern the production of goods and services, their distribution, ways in which they are consumed, and problems related to labor, finance, and taxation. See Communism.

Economy 1066

The term economy comes from the Greek word 'oikonomia,' meaning management of household or public resources. The term is used in the Church to refer to the management of *spiritual* goods, particularly the way they are produced and distributed. It may sometimes mean work, as in the *economy of salvation*. See Oikonomia 236.

Economy of salvation 705, 1066

The *Patristic* fathers referred to the *mystery* of *Christ*, which is fulfilled in history according to the ordered plan of God, as the economy of salvation or the *economy of the Word Incarnate*.

Economy of the Word Incarnate 1066

Patristic tradition calls the plan of God for all *creation* as confessed in the *Symbol* of *Faith* the *plan of the mystery* or the economy of the Word Incarnate. It is through the *mystery* of the *Incarnation* that the Father's plan for creation is accomplished. It is also called the *economy of salvation*.

Ecstasy/Ecstatic

Ecstasy comes from the Greek word 'ekstasis,' from 'ex,' meaning out, and 'histanai,' meaning to cause to stand. In English, it means to be beside oneself. It is an enraptured condition of body and *soul* in which there is a suspension of the senses. It begins with the fading of normal *sense perception* followed by an intense state. The body is not injured but is, rather, strengthened by the *experience*. Ecstasy does not usually last long.

The suspension of the senses is a *consequence* of the soul's being riveted on and totally absorbed in God. The results of ecstasy are positive. They include *holiness* of life, increased *love* and joy, patience, sorrow for *sin*, and the pursuit of *spiritual* insight.

Rapture is a sudden and violent form of ecstasy that cannot be resisted. It is possible to resist simple ecstasy at the outset only.

Many *saints* have received ecstasies from God as a *supernatural* gift, but, in itself, ecstasy is not required for *holiness*. See Prophet. Also see

Mystical union 2014; Ecstatic union.

Ecstatic union

Ecstatic union is a state of union with God marked by a vivid act of *contemplation* accompanied by the loss of sense life in which the *soul* is rapt in God and receives *spiritual* illumination. It can be so intense that the *soul* goes out of the body, as it were, and the senses are inhibited. In ecstatic union, the body is not injured but is, rather, strengthened. See Mystical union 2014.

Ecumenical council 884

An ecumenical council is a council that is convened by the *Holy See*, consisting of all the *bishops* of the world and others entitled to vote. The *decrees* of ecumenical councils have no binding *authority* until confirmed by the Holy See. Decrees issued at sessions over which the *Pope* presides in *person* require no further confirmation. If the Pope dies during the council, it is suspended until his successor reopens it because it must be confirmed by the new Pope.

The first seven ecumenical councils were convoked by emperors, but the Pope shared in the convocation. Subsequent councils were *convoked* by the Pope. In the Fifth Lateran Council, Pope Leo X stressed the principle that the right to convoke, approve, or dissolve general councils belongs to the Pope.

Ecumenism

Ecumenism refers to a modern movement toward *Christian* unity having *Protestant* origins in the Edinburgh World Missionary Conference in 1910 A.D. The *Second Vatican Council* issued a decree called *Unitatis Redintegratio* (The Restitution of Unity), which discusses the status of *ecclesial communities* separated from Rome. It formulated three basic *Catholic principles* for the practice of ecumenism based on the *premise* that overcoming the scandalous divisions among Christians requires *recognition* that Christ founded only one Church. The three principles are as follows: 1) *Christ* established his Church on the *Apostles* and their successors whose visible head and principle of unity was Peter and his successors as *Bishop of Rome*; 2) since the second century there have been divisions in Christianity but many now separated from visible unity with the successors of Peter are Christians and have a share, to a greater or lesser degree, in the life of grace whose fullness resides in the *Roman Church*; and 3) Catholics must do everything possible to foster the ecumenical movement.

The decree admits that responsibility for the *schisms*

of the sixteenth century lies with both Catholics and Protestants and that those born into separated communities and raised in them cannot be charged with *sin*. The *Catholic Church* accepts them with respect and affection as brothers.

The significance of the *decree* rests in the teaching that the life of *grace, theological virtues*, and *gifts of the Holy Spirit* are available to Christians outside the visible body of the Catholic Church. It continues with the statement that it is through the Catholic Church alone that the fullness of the means of *salvation* can be obtained.

The decree recognizes that *reconciliation* is beyond *human* power and that true hope for unity lies in the prayer of Christ for his Church. See Reformation. Also see Protestant.

Edict

An edict is a *decree, ordinance*, or decision set by an *ecclesiastical authority*. Edicts of the *Pope* or of an *ecumenical council* are universally binding. See Ecumenical council 884.

Efficacious / Efficaciously 1127

Efficacious means capable of producing an effect. *Sacraments* are efficacious because with certainty they produce in the *soul* their intended or appropriate effect.

Efficacy

Efficacy means effectiveness. See Donatism.

Eighth day 349

The eighth day is the day of Christ's *Resurrection*. The seventh day completed the first *creation*, and the eighth day begins the new creation. Never to end after it's dawning, it is the day in which God rests after the work of creation is completed with the Resurrection of Christ. The seventh day completed the first creation; the eighth day begins the new creation culminating in the greater work of *redemption*. It is the day of the Church.

Eisegesis

Eisegesis refers to inserting meaning into *scriptural* writings as opposed to exegesis, the determination of the meaning of a scriptural text. See Exposition. Also see Exegesis 116.

Ekphonesis

Ekphonesis is a Greek word meaning heightening of the voice. It refers to the final words of a prayer, which are spoken or sung aloud when the previous words are recited silently. An example of this is found in the *Extraordinary Form* of the *Mass* in the *Roman Rite*. At the end of the *Canon* of the Mass, the first part of the *doxology* is said silently, but the final words, "per omnia saecula saeculorum," are said aloud. See Anaphora 1352.

Elect

Elect is a term used by St. Paul in his letter to the Romans to refer to those who are chosen to merit *heaven* by the grace of the *redemption*. In general, it refers to the *faithful* as members of the Church. See Final purification 1031. Also see Purgatory 1031, 1472.

Elements of catechesis 6

Certain elements of the Church's *pastoral mission* are catechetical because they either prepare the way for *catechesis* or arise from the catechesis given. These elements of catechesis may be divided into the following: 1) the initial *proclamation* of the *Gospel* or *missionary* preaching to arouse *faith*; 2) an examination of the reasons for *belief*; 3) *experience* in *Christian* living in the community; 4) celebration of the *sacraments*; 5) full integration into the Christian community; and 6) *apostolic* and missionary witness to the *faith* (cf. CCC 6).

Elicit/Elicitation

Elicit comes from the Latin word 'elicere,' meaning to draw out. To elicit means to entice or cause to be revealed or to extract. See Human act 154. Also see Moral act.

Elohist

Scholarly criticism during the seventeenth and eighteenth centuries noted differences in the text of the *Pentateuch* that suggested multiple styles of writing. The first always used the divine name '*Jahweh*' for the divine name of God, and the second used 'Eloi,' or Lord God, for the *divine* name. The first usage was very formal and transcendent, the second made God more human-like.

The first source was called the *Jahwist* (J) source, written in Judah under King Solomon around the tenth century B.C., and has a strong Davidic emphasis.

After the fall of Solomon's kingdom and the separation of the north, an account was needed that would reflect the Northern Kingdom's anti-Jerusalem sentiments. This account is known as the Elohist (E) source, probably written after 900 B.C., and has a strong emphasis on Jacob. See Genesis. Also see Jahwist; Pentateuch.

Emanation/Emanationism 285

Emanation comes from the Latin word 'emanatio,' which means to flow out from or discharge. It refers to a process by which one thing comes from another.

In *philosophy*, emanation is a feature of a false theory called emanationism and refers to the out flowing of all things from the divine substance.

Emanationism is a *theory* that all *created* things are emanations of God and are particles of his *substance*. What emanates from God loses the perfection of the divine *substance* as it flows out. Emanation, according to this theory, is considered a necessary *attribute* of the divine substance.

Emanation gives rise to *pantheism* in which creation is considered to be part of God. This notion called emanationism was condemned by the First Vatican Council, which affirmed that God is absolutely simple and immutable, or unchangeable, and cannot pour out or share anything of his being. Emanationism denies that God created the earth out of nothing.

Ember Days

The Ember Days were the Wednesday, Friday, and Saturday between the Third and Fourth *Sundays* of Advent, between the First and Second Sundays of *Lent*, between *Pentecost* and *Trinity Sunday*, and in the third week of September. The name ember days comes from the Latin word 'emeto,' meaning to reap. Ember Days were intended to *sanctify* the four seasons and obtain God's *blessing* on the *clergy*. Ember Wednesday, Friday, and Saturday were especially set apart to pray for those who would receive *ordination* that ember Saturday. This very ancient usage is of uncertain origin. See Fast Days 2043.

Embryo 2271

Embryo is a name for a child in its earliest stages of development in the uterus, usually until the third month after *conception*. Thereafter, it is referred to as a *fetus*.

Eminent/Eminently

Eminent means to be higher than others in rank.

Emissary 858

Emissaries, from the Latin word 'missionarius,' are *persons* sent on a *mission* to gain information, to gain adherents, or to promote the interests of a cause. The Greek word for emissaries is 'apostoloi,' from which we get the word *apostle*.

Emotion

Emotion is a state that is characterized by strong feeling caused by the awareness of an object or situation. It is associated with an impulse to action and physiological changes in bodily function. See Aridity in prayer.

Empirically

Empirically is the adverbial form of 'empirical,' which comes from a Greek word meaning that which pertains to *experience*. It refers to something that can be demonstrated or proven by using methods of *science* based on the results of observation and experiment, rather than by *theory* or pure *reason*. See Proof for the existence of God 31.

Emulation

To emulate means to imitate or to try to equal or surpass. See New law 1965.

Enchiridion

Enchiridion means 'close at hand' in Greek and is used to refer to a handbook or reference manual. The best known enchiridion is the 'Enchiridion Indulgentiarum' or Enchiridion of *Indulgences*, which lists all the *prayers*, *devotions*, *pious* practices, or charitable works through which indulgences can be granted together with the conditions that must be met for receiving those indulgences.

Another important enchiridion is the 'Enchiridion of Symbols (Creeds), Definitions, and Declarations Concerning *Faith* and Morals,' usually referred to as *Denzinger* after the German *theologian* Henricus Denzinger who first compiled the Enchiridion in the mid-1800's. See Denzinger. Also see Indulgence 1471.

Encyclical

An encyclical is a letter from the *Pope* addressed to *patriarchs*, *primates*, *archbishops*, *bishops*, and the whole Church. Encyclicals are not necessarily *infallible* since the Pope could choose to speak formally *Ex Cathedra*, but, when they contain *doctrinal* teaching of the Church, *Catholics* are bound to give them interior and exterior *assent* and *obedience*. See Magisterium 83, 889, 890.

End

In *philosophy* and *theology*, the word end refers to that which is desired as the result of some *act* or process. It refers to the reason for which something exists or for which it is made, or its reason for *being*. See Sources of morality 1750.

End of man

The end of man refers to the purpose for which he was made, union with God in *heaven* where he will enjoy the *beatific vision*. See Beatitude 1719. Also see Beatific vision 1028.

End of marriage 2366

Fecundity is a gift. It is also the end or purpose of marriage, because conjugal love naturally tends to be fruitful. A child springs from the very heart of the *spouses*' mutual self-giving as its fruit and fulfillment. The Church teaches, therefore, that "each and every marital act must of necessity retain its intrinsic relationship to the *procreation* of human life" (*Humanae Vitae*, HV 11).

End time / End times 686, 715

The phrase 'end times' refers

to the age ushered in by the *redemption* and *Incarnation* in which the *Spirit* is revealed, given, recognized, and welcomed as a *person*. It may also indicate an indefinite period preceding the end of the world.

Energumen

Energumen is from the Greek word 'energoumenos,' meaning energetic or worked up. It was used to designate *persons* who were *possessed*, or *demoniacs*. The energumen, *catechumens*, and those doing *public penance*, were required to leave the assembly at the end of the *Mass of the Catechumens*. See Exorcism 550. Also see Public penitents.

Enlightenment, Age of

The Age of Enlightenment refers to an intellectual movement during the eighteenth century that had its origins in the scientific revolution. The central tenet of the movement was that the only reliable guide to *knowledge* was to be found in *reason* alone and not *faith*. The Church and the age of faith were seen as outmoded and as constraints on the power of human reason. Knowledge, prior to the Enlightenment, was seen as based on faith, the Church's *Tradition*, and *authority*. Many advocates of the Enlightenment became completely hostile to the Church.

This exclusive dependence on reason of the Enlightenment led to *secularism* because it rejected faith, Tradition, and *revelation* as sources of knowledge. Any source of knowledge was rejected if it was not based directly on observable and verifiable data. See Dark ages.

Enrollment of names

The third stage of the Christian initiation of adults prepares the candidate for the reception of the *sacrament of initiation* at *Easter*. It is called the Election or enrollment of names. The Rite of Election begins on the First *Sunday* of *Lent*. During the rite of election, the candidates' names are enrolled, and they are called to receive the sacrament of initiation. See RCIA 1232.

Enslavement 2414

Enslavement means, in the literal sense, being totally subjected to another *created person*, whether by capture, purchase, or birth, and completely divesting the person enslaved of freedom and personal rights, as in modern totalitarian political regimes.

Enslavement also refers to the impairment of freedom of one who is controlled by *habits* or *addictions*, which gravely reduce *freedom* of choice due to an obsessive and overpowering need for certain drugs or activities.

Any form of enslavement is *sinful* because it offends *human dignity*, which requires that *man* must always be free to choose the *good*, to determine his own behavior, and to conform himself to the *will of God* through the exercise of *virtue*.

Enslavement also has a metaphorical sense in *theology* when '*divine* slavery' or 'Marian slavery' (for example, St. Louis Grignion de Montfort) are discussed. Here the term is used to stress the perfect union of two persons in love without any suppression of that personal *dignity* and freedom characteristic of the *supernatural* order, but with reference to the willingness of such persons, in *union with Christ* crucified, to *sacrifice*, after his example, for the good of others, particularly for their *salvation*.

Entity/Entities

Entity comes from the Latin word 'ens,' meaning *being*. Entity refers to a thing that has definite individual existence or reality, whether in the *mind* or outside of it.

Envy 1866, 2538

Envy refers to feelings of sadness, resentment, or ill will occasioned by the goodness, excellence, achievements, or advantages of another that are perceived as a threat to one's own excellence or glory. Envy is a *capital sin*.

Envy may also be a sadness at the sight of another's goods and the immoderate desire to acquire them for oneself, even

unjustly. It can develop into hatred of another.

When envy results in *grave* harm to a neighbor, it is a *mortal sin*. Envy is a sin against *charity*, which moves us to be pleased at the good of others.

From envy flow *detraction*, *calumny*, murmuring, insolence, reproach, insulting or offensively contemptuous language or treatment, spite, and scornful rudeness.

Helps to overcome envy include the practice of *humility*, deference toward others, seeking to find *good* in others, and praying for others rather than judging them.

Eparchy 833

Eparchy is the name for a *diocese* in the *Eastern Church*. It refers to a community of the Christian *faithful* living in the *communion* of *faith* and *sacraments* together with their *Bishop*, who has been ordained in *apostolic succession*.

Epiclesis 1105, 1238, 1353, 1519, 2583, 2770

Epiclesis is a Greek word meaning '*invocation*.' It is an *intercessory prayer* in which the *priest* begs the Father to send the *Holy Spirit*, the *Sanctifier*, so that the offerings at the *Eucharist* may become the Body and Blood of *Christ* and so that the *faithful*, by receiving them, may themselves become a living offering to God. In the administration of every *sacrament*, there is a *prayer* of *epiclesis* calling down the *Holy Spirit*.

Epiousios 2837

Epiousios means 'daily.' This word occurs nowhere else in the *New Testament* except in the *Lord's Prayer*. In the Lord's Prayer, it is referred to as 'arton epiousios,' translated as our daily bread.

Here it signifies a repetition of 'this day' in order to confirm us in trust without reservation. It also signifies what is necessary for life as well as every good thing sufficient for *subsistence*.

Taken literally, it means 'super-*essential*,' referring directly to the *Bread of Life*, the *Body of Christ*. Finally, it means the *Day of the Lord*, the *feast* of the kingdom to come, which is anticipated in the *Eucharist*.

Epiphany 528

The *Solemnity* of the Epiphany *celebrates* the *manifestation* of *Jesus* as *Messiah* of Israel, *Son of God*, and Savior of the world. The Solemnity of the Epiphany *commemorates* the *adoration* of the wise men from the East (*magi*). Other epiphanies include the *baptism* of Christ in the Jordan and the wedding feast at Cana.

Episcopal/episcopacy

Episcopal and episcopacy mean pertaining to *bishops*. See Bishop 861.

Episcopal character

Episcopal character is a *charism* received by episcopal *ordination* through the imposition of hands and the words of *consecration*. By it, the *grace* of the *Holy Spirit* is given, and a *sacramental character* is impressed in such a way that the *Bishop*, in an *eminent* and visible manner, takes the place of *Christ* himself as teacher. By it, bishops are constituted as true and *authentic teachers* of the *faith* and become *pontiffs* and *pastors*. See Episcopate 1536. Also see Prelature; Roman Pontiff.

Episcopal conference

An episcopal conference is a gathering of *bishops* from a specific region jointly exercising their *pastoral* office. Each episcopal conference drafts its own statutes, which are reviewed by the *Holy See*. In the United States, the episcopal conference is called the United States Conference of Catholic Bishops (*USCCB*). See Synod 887.

Episcopal consecration

Episcopal *consecration* is the *rite* of conferring the fullness of the *sacrament* of *Holy Orders*. Episcopal consecration confers, together with the *office* of *sanctifying*, the offices of teaching and of ruling. By the imposition of hands and through the words of consecration, the *grace* of the *Holy Spirit* is given, and a *sacred character* is impressed in such a way that a *bishop*, in an *eminent* and visible manner, takes the place of *Christ* himself as teacher, shepherd, and *priest* and acts as his representative. See Episcopate 1536.

Episcopal jurisdiction

Episcopal jurisdiction refers to the *authority* given to the Church, and to *bishops* by virtue of their *consecration*, to rule the *faithful* for *spiritual* purposes.

Church jurisdiction can only be exercised by *clerics* and is attached to their *office*. It can only be exercised over their own subjects and in their own territories. In his *diocese*, the Bishop exercises the highest authority. The *Pope* has jurisdiction over the entire Church. See Power of the keys 553. Also see Vicar General.

Episcopal ring/Pontifical ring

Bishops, *abbots*, and Protonotaries wear a ring as a symbol of their rank and as a sign of commitment and *fidelity* to the *faith*. As the successor of St. Peter, the *Pope* has a ring, called the Fisherman's ring, with his *papal* seal signifying his supreme *authority*. It is broken at the time of his death. See Miter.

Episcopal vicar

A vicar is one who acts in the place of another. He performs acts of *authority* in an *ecclesiastical* office in the name of another *person*.

When a diocesan *bishop* has an *auxiliary bishop*, according to Canon 406, he should appoint him as his *Vicar General* or Episcopal Vicar. Vicars General and Episcopal Vicars act in the name of their residential Bishop. Both are called *ordinaries* because they possess the power attached to their *office*. Their power, however, is not personal but is exercised in the name of the Bishop. See Diocese. See Vicar General.

Episcopate 1536

Episcopate refers to the office of *Bishop*. From earliest times, the chief place among the offices of the Church has been exercised by bishops who, through their appointment to that *dignity* and responsibility and in virtue of an unbroken *apostolic succession*, are regarded as true transmitters of the apostolic line in both teaching and *authority*.

The fullness of the sacrament of *Holy Orders* is conferred by *episcopal consecration*. Episcopal consecration confers, together with the *office* of *sanctifying*, both the offices of teaching and of ruling.

Epistemology

Epistemology is the study of the *validity* or truth-*value* of human knowledge, based on *experience* and the use of the *intellect*. It deals with the *theory* of the origin, *nature*, grounds, method, and limits of *knowledge*. See Systematic philosophy.

Epistle

An epistle is a book of the *New Testament* written in the form of a letter to individuals or *churches*. There are twenty-one epistles. The fourteen epistles of St. Paul are named for the *persons* to whom they were written. They are referred to as the *Pauline epistles*.

Other epistles are called by the name of their author. Those epistles addressed to the Church in general are called the *Catholic epistles*.

The epistles to Titus and Timothy are called *Pastoral epistles*. They treat of the duties of the *episcopal office*. See Ambo 1184.

Equanimity

Equanimity refers to an evenness of *temperament* that is not easily disturbed or annoyed. See Wrath 1866.

Equivocation 2471

Equivocation is the use of words or expressions that have a double meaning with the intention to mislead. It is often the expression of a falsehood in the form of a *proposition* that is verbally true. Advertising provides many examples of equivocation.

Eremitic life 920

An eremitic life is one lived in a stricter separation from the world for the praise of God and *salvation* of the world but without necessarily professing the *evangelical counsels*. Those who live such a life are called *hermits*. Their life is a silent preaching of the Lord to whom they surrender their life because he is everything to them.

Eros

Eros is love viewed as a passion of either a *sexual*, an artistic, or a *spiritual* nature. It is an attachment to that which is beautiful and desirable. See Love 218.

Erotic

A thing is called erotic that arouses *sexual* feelings, sexual desires, or sexual love. It is the same as saying that a thing is *lascivious*. See Pornography 2354.

Erroneous conscience

An erroneous conscience is a conscience that is *subjectively* certain of the goodness of one side of a practical *contradiction* but which is *objectively* false in itself. The erroneous conscience thinks something is good that in fact is not good. One must follow an erroneous conscience until he learns that he is in error. However, an erroneous conscience does not exonerate one from the duty to always seek the *truth* and properly form one's conscience. See Conscience 1706.

Eschatological 326, 673, 2771
Eschatological is the adjective of *eschatology*. See Eschatology 673.

Eschatological icon 972
Mary is referred to as the eschatological icon of the Church because, in her, we contemplate what the Church already is in the *mystery* of her own *pilgrimage* of *faith* and what the Church will be at the *end of time*. The *Mother of God*, in the glory she possesses in body and *soul* in *heaven*, is both the image and the beginning of the Church as it is to be perfected in the world to come.

Eschatological joy
Eschatological joy is the state of the *blessed* in *heaven* consisting in the complete pleasure, satisfaction, delight, and *exultation* of both body and *spirit*, which consists in the *beatific vision*, that is, seeing God face to face. See Heaven 1023.

Eschatological significance 1186
Eschatological significance of the Church refers to the interpretation of the Church in the present time as the initial realization of the last things in the *Christian* life.

Eschatology 673
Eschatology is the area of *theology* dealing with last things, such as the *second coming* of *Christ* on the last day, human destiny, death, *judgment*, *resurrection of the body*, *heaven*, *purgatory*, and *hell*.

Esoteric
Esoteric refers to something intended for only a chosen few as a group of initiates. It also refers to knowledge that is beyond the understanding or knowledge of most people. See Discipline of the secret. Also see Liturgy 1069.

Essence
Essence is the *act* of *being* that perfects and determines a thing in its *species*. More simply, essence is that which makes a thing to be what it is. See Consubstantial 242.

Essential/Essentially
Essential refers to something necessary to the fundamental *nature* of a thing or something without which a thing cannot be. See Configuration.

Essential rite 1239, 1300, 1573
Essential *rite* refers to the formal words, procedures, and actions that constitute the *essence* of a *sacrament* and are necessarily, or indispensably, required for it to be that particular *sacrament*.
The essential rite is that formula and material belonging to the essence of a sacrament in such a way that, if absent, the intended outcome or effect does not take place; for example, the exact words of *conse-*

cration of the bread and wine are necessary for the *confection* of the *Eucharist*.

Eternal 290

Eternal is the adjectival form of eternity. See Eternity.

Eternal law 1952

Eternal law is used at times to refer to the *moral law*. It stresses the source of all law, which is God. It is revealed in the plan of God for creation as expressed in *revelation*.

Eternal life

Eternal life is the term used by *Christ* to describe the state of endless happiness of *heaven* to be enjoyed by the *just* (Mt 25:42). See Christian humanism 1676.

Eternal plan

The eternal plan refers to divine *wisdom* ordering and directing the actions and events of all *creation*. It is the expression of the unchangeable *decree* of the Creator binding on all creation directing it to the purpose for which it was *created*. In *man*, it provides the *grace* to use the *faculties* of *understanding* and *free will* to attain *holiness*. See Damnation.

Eternal punishment 1472

Eternal punishment refers to the lot of those who die without *repentance* for *mortal sin*, which renders them incapable of *eternal life*. Such *souls* are eternally lost because they choose to reject the *infinite love* and *mercy* of God and condemn themselves to *hell* forever.

Eternity

Eternal, in the strict sense of the term, is an *attribute* proper to the one and *triune* God alone. It describes the mode of duration in being found only in God. The divine *mode* of being is that of existence without beginning or end, never changing from moment to moment, but, as an ancient definition states, 'a totally simultaneous and perfect possession of life.' It is the exact contrary of a *temporal* life, or a life in time, which is not entirely simultaneous in an unchanging 'now' but one whose present moment is continuously becoming and continuously ceasing to be, viz., passing from the 'now' to the 'future'. Future, in Latin, means 'coming to be' as present and ceasing to exist as past. When this continuous succession ceases, temporal duration ceases. This is true both for individual beings and for the world as a whole. In a word, time is successive duration rather than simultaneous duration. What might come after the cessation of time is another question. It is commonly discussed under the heading of last things, or *eschatology*.

Because God is *eternal* being,

he is immutable, and, because God is eternal, he is infinitely perfect *being*, 'an ocean of being' according to the *Fathers of the Church*. God revealed his name to Moses as 'I am who am,' that is, he is being itself. God is pure *act*. Therefore, he exists as perfect and total act. His existence is not stagnant and immobile, like that of a stone. *Angels* who ended their trial period of existence in the *state of grace* and men who die in the state of grace can share eternal life endlessly, although not with the perfect *immutability* and fullness proper to God alone.

The form of duration that angels and men have who have entered into a state of everlasting bliss is known as *eternal life* or *immortality*. This state is called *eviternity* because it has a beginning but will have no end. This eternal life of bliss presupposes immortality in its subjects. Immortality is *connatural* to angels and to the human *soul*. In the case of risen man, it is also connatural to his *glorified body*. Those angels and men who have failed their trials also become immortal but not to a life of eternal bliss.

Strictly speaking, men, both *just* and unjust, do not enter eternal life until their resurrection, when body and soul are reunited: the just, to an eviternity of bliss, the unjust to an eviternity of unending torment in body as well as *soul*. The human soul, naturally immortal, enters a state of eviternal duration on death. The spiritual human soul, while united to the body before death, though immortal, is not yet in eternal life but is in time as long as it remains united to the body. Angels, not being united to a body, never existed in time in the proper sense of the term. Angels were *created* in eviternity. They cannot die because they have no body.

God's *preternatural* gift to man of immortality—or of not dying so long as he remained faithful to God's commands—did not make Adam and Eve eviternal before the *fall*. This is because this preternatural gift did not change the temporal character of duration proper to the human *person* composed of body and soul. With his fall from grace, man lost his *preternatural* immortality and became subject to death. After completion of his mortal pilgrimage, in preparation for heaven, man's soul is separated from his body in death. The body returns to the dust from which it came, and the soul permanently enters eternal life for better or worse. At this moment, the human person, in the *metaphysical* sense, ceases to exist until the *resurrection*. This is because, when the human soul no longer informs the body, man is no longer a complete *nature*, unlike the angels who are created as pure spirits without bodies. After death and before the *resurrection of the body*, the soul of man remains only a reflection of the person subsisting as a *body-soul* composite in time before death. See Eternal 290; Also see Eviternity.

Ethical/ethics

Ethics is the study of the *laws* determining right or wrong conduct on the basis of *natural reason* alone as opposed to *revealed truth*. Ethics rests on three principles of natural *philosophy*: 1) the existence of a personal God; 2) the *freedom* of *human will*; and 3) the *immortality* of the *soul*. Behavior that corresponds to *right reason* is called ethical.

Ethics differs from *morality*. The norm for determining right and wrong in morality is based on the relationship between a *human act* and the *person's ultimate end*. Human acts are good or bad according to whether they lead a person to or detract him from his ultimate end according to revealed truth. See Moral sense of Scripture.

Etymological sense of Scripture

See Primary sense of Scripture.

Etymology/etymological

Etymology is the study of the origin and development of words and phrases. It traces the history of words to their sources as a means of identifying the core concepts they represent. See Mass groat.

Eucharist/Holy Eucharist 1328

The word Eucharist comes from the Greek word 'eucharistia,' meaning thanksgiving. The Church uses this term to refer to the *sacrament* in which the Body and Blood of *Christ* are made really, truly, and substantially present under the form of bread and wine. In the Eucharist, Christ offers himself in sacrifice as the grace-producing spiritual food for the *faithful*. The Holy Eucharist is the real living Christ. Because a living body is not without its blood nor is living blood without the body, Christ is fully present under either form, bread or wine.

The Eucharist is a sacrament instituted by Christ who gave thanks at the *Last Supper*. He commanded his *Apostles* to do the same in order to perpetuate the Sacrifice of the Cross in *memory* of him.

The *matter of the sacrament* of the *Eucharist* is bread and wine; the *form* is the words of *consecration*. See Eucharistic species 1373. Also see Eucharistic Presence.

Eucharisted 1355

Eucharisted refers to the bread and wine that has been consecrated and become the *Eucharistic species*.

Eucharistein 1328

Eucharistein is the Greek word for the prayer of *blessing* and thanks offered especially during a meal proclaiming God's works of *creation*, *redemption*, and *sanctification*.

Eucharistic assembly 1329

The Eucharistic assembly refers to the members of the Church gathered for the *celebration* of the *Mass*. See Lord's supper.

Eucharistic celebration

The *Eucharistic* celebration is another name for the *Mass*. It is also called the *Eucharistic Sacrifice* and the *Eucharistic liturgy*.

Eucharistic liturgy

Eucharistic liturgy is another way of referring to the *Mass*.

Eucharistic prayer

The Eucharistic prayer is the central part of the *Mass*. It contains eight parts: the *preface*, *acclamation*, *epiclesis*, *consecration, anamnesis, oblation, intercessions*, and *doxology*. See Secret of the Mass.

Eucharistic presence

The word Eucharist comes from the Greek word 'eucharistia,' meaning thanksgiving. The Church uses this term to refer to the *sacrament* in which the Body, Blood, *soul*, and *divinity* of *Christ* are made really, truly, and substan-

tially present under the form of bread and wine. Eucharistic presence refers to Christ really present as the *Eucharistic species*. Also see Eucharistic species 1373.

Eucharistic Sacrifice

Eucharistic Sacrifice is another name for the *Mass*.

Eucharistic species 1373

The Eucharistic species is another name for the *Eucharist* insofar as retaining the *accidents* of bread and wine (appearance, color, taste, smell, quantity, etc.) after the conversion of the *substance* of the bread and wine into the Body and Blood of *Christ* (*transubstantiation*).

Eugenics 2268

Eugenics refers to the efforts to improve the human race through control of *hereditary factors* that affect mental and bodily health. It argues that the *marriage* of the unfit leads to an increase of hereditable defects in the population. This is cited as a justification for *birth control*, compulsory *sterilization*, and the prohibition of marriage for the unfit.

Eugenics is contrary to Church teaching and Christian practice. The Church does not interfere with a *person's* right to marry, provided that a person can give consent, understands the permanence of marriage, and be physically able to perform the *conjugal act*.

Eulogein 1328

Eulogein is a Greek word meaning *blessing*. The term 'eulogia' is applied to anything that has been blessed but especially bread. Blessed bread was given in early times to those, such as public *penitents*, who were unable to receive *communion*. The word is also used to refer to the *Blessed Sacrament* itself.

Euthanasia 2277

Euthanasia refers to any action or omission of action that, either of itself or by *intention*, causes the death of a handicapped, sick, or dying *person* as a means to escape suffering. Terms such as "mercy killing," "death with dignity", and "dignity in dying" are often used to signify and promote the practice of euthanasia. Because euthanasia is a murderous act, it is always forbidden and must never be practiced or promoted.

Evangelical counsels 915, 925, 1973, 2103

Besides *precepts*, the *New Law* also includes the evangelical counsels of *poverty*, *chastity*, and *obedience*. The good life of the *Gospel* always calls for a *generosity* that goes beyond exact observance of precepts. This ideal of wholehearted and free service takes the form of *counsels*.

"The traditional distinction between God's commandments and the evangelical counsels is drawn in relation to *charity*, the perfection of *Christian* life. The precepts are intended to remove what is incompatible with charity. The aim of the counsels is to remove whatever might hinder the development of charity, even if it is not contrary to it" (CCC 1973).

The evangelical counsels are gifts given to the Church by God. Certain individuals dedicate themselves in a special way to observe poverty, chastity, and obedience. The evangelical counsels are also called the *vows of religion*. They are rules of *perfection voluntarily* assumed by those who have a *vocation* to do so. They are not perfection but instruments for strengthening love of God and neighbor.

The observance of the evangelical counsels according to one's state in life is necessary for *salvation*. In the Constitution on the Church of *Vatican II*, all Christians are invited to observe the evangelical counsels according to their state of life by virtue of the universal call to *holiness*, but *religious* commit themselves to observe them by public vows or promises and in a more radical manner.

The counsel of poverty means the renunciation of the use or direct ownership of *material* goods in the case of religious and moderation and self-denial for others.

Chastity means perfect continence for single *persons*, *celibate priests*, and religious and absolute *fidelity* to one's *spouse* for those in the married state.

Obedience, for religious, means obedience to *superiors* in matters pertaining to their personal life. For priests who are not religious and for *laypersons*, it means accepting and following the will of the Church as closely as possible and faithfully serving those under whose direction they work. For superiors, it means commanding only what accords with God's *will* and never using one's *authority* for personal advantage or gain.

Evangelical instinct 1676

The Catechism of the Catholic Church teaches that the evangelical instinct is a principle of *discernment* through which the *faithful* "spontaneously sense when the *Gospel* is being served in the Church and when it is emptied of its content and stifled by other interests" (CCC 1676). It makes discernment possible.

Evangelical Poverty

Evangelical poverty refers to the renunciation of the use or direct ownership of material goods in the case of those who take the *vows of religion*. It refers to moderation in the use of material goods and pos-

sessing them in the spirit of *stewardship* and *charity* for those who do not take vows. See Evangelical counsels 915. Also see Poverty of heart 2544.

Evangelization/evangelize

Evangelization is the *proclamation* of the good news of the *Gospel*. It refers to the *religious* activity involved in preaching the message of the Gospel through the *ministry* of the Church and building it up for the glory of God.

By virtue of *Baptism*, every *Christian* is to make God known to the world and has the *obligation* of spreading the *faith*, especially through the *charismatic* gifts given him. The most important means of evangelization is leading a truly Christian life. The evangelized are those to whom the Gospel has been preached. See Conversion 1426.

Evening Prayer

The hour of the *Divine Office* said in the evening is called 'Evening Prayer,' or '*Vespers*' in Latin. It is one of the *major hours*, and the *Magnificat* (Lk 1:46–55) is sung during it. The liturgical observance of *Sundays* and *solemnities* begins the previous evening with Evening Prayer I, also called First Vespers. See Liturgy of the Hours 1174, 1178.

Ever Virgin

Ever Virgin refers to the *Blessed Virgin Mary* who was

a *virgin* before giving birth to *Christ*, while giving him birth, and for the rest her life. See Born of a virgin 502.

Evil 309

Evil is the absence of some quality or property that is an essential part of a complete *nature*. It is the absence of some *good* that should be present in a being in order for it to fulfill completely its natural potential. It is a privation of a good that should be present in a being.

Evil one

See Devil.

Evil spirit

The evil spirit refers to the *devil*. See Devil.

Ex cathedra

'Ex cathedra,' in Latin, means from the chair. It refers to an *infallible* pronouncement in which the *Pope*, exercising his *office* as shepherd and teacher of all Christians and in virtue of his supreme *apostolic authority*, defines a *doctrine* of *faith* or *morals* to be held by the universal Church.

The word *'cathedra,'* itself, refers to the *episcopal* throne and is used figuratively to indicate an official utterance of the most *solemn* kind. The throne symbolizes the *authority* supporting the *truth* of the utterance. See Magisterium 83, 889.

Ex opere operantis

'Ex opere operantis' is a Latin expression meaning 'by virtue of the work of the doer.' In reference to the *sacraments*, it refers to the fruitfulness of the conferral of sacramental *grace* as affected by the disposition or moral condition of the minister or recipient of a sacrament.

The Church teaches that the sacraments act *ex opere operato*, meaning that grace is conferred in virtue of the sacramental *rite* performed. "Nevertheless, the fruits of the sacraments also depend on the disposition of the one who receives them" (CCC 1128).

Because *sacramentals* impart grace depending on the disposition of the recipient and the *intercession* of the Church, they are unlike sacraments. Their efficacy depends on the disposition of the *person* using them. See Ex opere operato 1128.

Ex opere operato 1128

'Ex opere operato' is a Latin expression meaning 'by virtue of the work itself being done.' In reference to the *sacraments*, it means that they are *efficacious* because of the sacramental *rite* itself, regardless of the worthiness of the *minister* or recipient. The disposition of the recipient, however, does make the *sacramental grace* more or less efficacious.

The *belief* of the Church concerning the efficacy of sacraments rejects an explanation of that efficacy in terms of '*ex opere operantis*,' Latin for 'by virtue of the work of the doer,' which makes the effectiveness of the sacrament dependent on the personal *virtue* of the minister or recipient. This is not the teaching of the Church. This heresy in the ancient Church is known as *Donatism* and was condemned at the Council of Arles in 314 A.D.

Exact conscience

An exact conscience is a tender conscience, one sensitive to the *moral* dimensions of its decisions. See Fear of the Lord 1831.

Examination of conscience 1454

The examination of conscience refers to a careful review and evaluation of one's personal behavior, actions, and attitudes in order to discern one's *spiritual* condition. This implies that it must be done with sound *judgment*, honesty, and *integrity*. It should result in a spirit of *compunction* and a resolve to *amend* one's life in the future.

An examination of conscience may be made at any time, but it is usually a review of the day made before retiring. It is necessary especially before the reception of the *sacrament of Reconciliation* in order to be able to recount one's *sins*. In this case, it is a review of failings during the period since the last *Confession*.

The examination of conscience is a way of growing in *holiness* because it keeps one's sins and *human* failings before his *mind* and fosters the amendment of his life. There are two kinds of examination of conscience, general, and particular.

The *general examination of conscience* reviews one's relation to God and neighbor as contained in the *Ten Commandments* and the practice of various *virtues* associated with growth in holiness as expressed in the *Beatitudes* and *precepts of the Church*.

The *particular examination of conscience* focuses on a particular fault, virtue, or *duty*.

The examination of conscience is an important part of every Catholic's *spiritual life* as a way of making progress in the *Christian* life.

Examiners (Synodal)

A synodal examiner is an officer of the *diocesan curia*. This office was dropped in the revised 1983 *Code of Canon Law*, but the *Bishop* remains free to appoint *persons* to fulfill the duties of examiners. Their task is to conduct examinations of candidates for *pastor* and *Holy Orders* and of applicants for *faculties* to hear *Confessions* or to preach. They also advise the Bishop in the removal or transfer of pastors. See Diocese 833.

Exarchate

Exarch is the title of an *archbishop* or *bishop* of the Russian and Greek Catholics in the *Byzantine Church*. An exarchate is the area of an exarch's *jurisdiction*. It is like a *diocese* in the Western Church. See Armenian Church.

Excommunication 1463, 2272

Excommunication is the most severe *ecclesiastical penalty* imposed by *Canon Law*. It is a type of ecclesiastical *censure* that excludes an individual from the right to attend divine services, receive the *sacraments*, and exercise certain ecclesiastical acts. The excommunicated have no share in *indulgences* or in the public prayers and *Masses* of the Church, but the *faithful* should pray for them privately.

Excommunication is incurred automatically, or '*ipso facto*,' by the crimes of *apostasy*, *heresy*, *schism*, and *abortion* successfully procured. Absolution is reserved to the *local ordinary* or to a priest authorized by him.

Automatic excommunication is also incurred by the crimes of throwing away the *Eucharistic species* or retaining them for *sacrilegious* purposes, use of physical force against the *Roman Pontiff*, absolution of an accomplice in a sin against the sixth commandment, consecration of a *bishop* without pontifical mandate (including the one who is thus consecrated a bishop), direct violation of the *sacramental seal of confession*, the attempt to confer the sacrament of *Holy Orders* on a woman, and the attempt of a woman to receive such a sacrament. *Absolution* in these cases is reserved to the *Apostolic See*.

Absolution in cases of excommunication cannot be granted, according to *Canon Law*, except by the *Pope*, the *Bishop*, or a *priest authorized* by him. In danger of death, any priest, even if he is deprived of *faculties* for hearing Confession, can *absolve* a *person* from every sin and from excommunication.

Execration

Execration is an expression of utter detestation, abhorrence, and abomination of some object, *doctrine*, or *person*. It can constitute a *curse* that imprecates, damns, or utterly denounces as an abomination the object at which it is directed. The term is used in association with formal pronouncements by early Church *councils* to signify total separation from the *faith* for either *apostasy* or *heresy* or to refer to those it separates from the *Christian* community for teaching false doctrine.

Execration is called *desecration* when it refers to a separation of the sacred character inhering in a place or thing that has been *consecrated* or *solemnly blessed*. In the case of a *fixed altar*, it is desecrated if the *mensa* is separated from its support, if an anointed part is broken off, if the *relics* are removed, or if the *sepulcher* is opened or removed except by proper authorities.

Chalices or *patens* are desecrated by profane usage but not by regilding (restoring their gold plating). *Churches* are desecrated if the greater part of the outer walls is destroyed at one time.

Objects that have been blessed are not liable to desecration but may lose their *blessing* and any *indulgences attached* to them. See Anathema.

Exegesis 116

Exegesis is a word from the Greek meaning 'to bring out.' The term is used to refer to a process of determining the meaning of the text of *Scripture*. *Valid* exegesis must follow certain rules of interpretation, which are called *hermeneutics*.

Exegesis is different from *exposition*. Exegesis more properly refers to the processes used to determine the original meaning of a text. Exposition refers to the determination of a text's meaning for today. Because of the importance of the text of Scripture as well as difficulties in determining the correct translation of texts, exegesis has been practiced from earliest times.

This term is the opposite of *eisegesis*, which means reading meaning into a text. See Eisegesis.

Exegetes 119

Exegetes are *persons* who investigate and explain the truth actually conveyed by *Sacred Scripture*. They are also called Scripture scholars.

Exhortation

Exhortation means to urge earnestly by advice or warning. See Governing office 894.

Exigencies/exigent

Exigencies are conditions of pressing, urgent, or critical need or an absolute requirement. See Preternatural.

Exile

Exile refers to a period of *Jewish* history from the destruction of Jerusalem by the *Babylonians* around 587 B.C. to the rebuilding of Jerusalem by the Persians beginning around 537 B.C.

This period was particularly significant because, during the *Babylonian exile*, the Jewish national and *religious* consciousness moved to Babylon. During this time, the exiles came to think of themselves as *Israel* and did not include in their number the peasants who remained behind in Judea as captives. The exiles built houses, planted vineyards, married, and settled in Babylon. They accepted exile as a punishment from God, and Jeremiah urged them to await the good pleasure of *Yahweh*.

The exiles prospered in their captivity, and it was during this period that a great deal of work was done to systematize the *traditions* of Israel and the *sacred* books of the *Old Testament* already written. It was also during this period that the *Synagogue* made its appearance as a substitute for the *worship* of the *Temple*. See Genesis.

Exilic

Exilic is the adjectival form of exile. See Exile.

Exodus

Exodus comes from the Greek word 'exodos,' meaning departure. Exodus refers to the departure of the *Israelites* from Egypt described in the second book of the *Pentateuch*. See Genesis.

Exoneration

Exonerate comes from the Latin words 'ex,' meaning out, and 'onus,' meaning load. To exonerate means to free one of a burden or *obligation*. It is like a pardon. See Perjury 2152, 2476.

Exorcism 550, 1237, 1673

Exorcism refers to the driving out or expulsion of *evil spirits* from *persons* or things.

Properly speaking, exorcism is the public and *authoritative* act of the Church to protect or liberate a person or object from the power of the *devil*. It is the act of expelling an evil spirit by adjuration or the performance of certain *rites*. The *Rite of Exorcism* is the *liturgical* rite and *ceremony* used to expel evil spirits from persons in cases of *demonic* possession.

There are two types of exorcism, major and lesser. A *major exorcism* takes place in a case of demonic possession by means of adjuration, or a command in the name of God, and requires a formal *ritual*. *Lesser exorcisms*, which do not imply a state of possession, are used in *Baptism* and the *blessing* of water and salt.

In *Scripture*, exorcism is a manifestation of God's *sovereign* reign and power to conquer all evil. We witness to this in the *Lord's Prayer* when we say, 'Deliver us from evil,' meaning the evil one or the devil.

A simple exorcism prayer in preparation for Baptism invokes God's help in overcoming the power of *Satan*, the spirit of evil. When a person in danger of death is baptized without all of the formal ceremonies and later recovers, these exorcisms are supplied later because exorcism is treated as one thing with actual Baptism, which is a complete exorcism through death in *Christ*.

Although there is a distinction between things that are

exorcisable and things that are not, it is difficult to offer a precise rule. Generally, matter requiring *purification* before being fitted for human use, such as salt, water, and oil are subject to exorcism, but bread, wine, or candles are not.

Exorcist

The Fourth Council of Carthage in 396 A.D. prescribed a form for the *ordination* of exorcists, who are given the power to drive out devils by laying hands on the possessed. This prescription is still in use today. In the early Church, *exorcists* had general superintendence over *catechumens* as well as those possessed, who were called *energumens*. Catechumens, though not necessarily possessed, still belonged to the kingdom of darkness, and exorcisms were employed to snap the bond between the *soul* of the candidate and the *devil*.

Before *Vatican II*, 'exorcist' was the third *minor order*. One of the duties of those with the order of exorcist was to prepare the water for the *Holy Sacrifice*. This exorcism is now represented in the *Extraordinary Form of the Roman Rite* by the sign of the Cross the *priest* makes over only the *cruet* of water at the *Offertory* and not over that containing the wine. *Pope* Innocent I prohibited exorcists from exercising their *ministry* except with express permission of their

Bishop. The minor order of exorcist has been suppressed, but a priest appointed by his *local ordinary* may exercise the functions pertaining to an exorcist.

In the *Eastern Church* exorcists are not ordained, and anyone, *lay* or *cleric*, who has the gift may perform exorcisms, as was the case in the early Church. See Minor orders. Also see Exorcism 550.

Experience

Experience is the act of living through an event or the personal involvement in or observation of events as they occur. It may refer to everything that has happened to a *person* during his life. See Assent.

Experiential knowledge

Experiential knowledge is the accumulated *knowledge* a *person* gains through *sense experience*. See True human knowledge of Christ 473.

Expiate 1459

To expiate is to make satisfaction or *amends* for *sin*, that is, to do away with or extinguish the guilt of sin or to offer satisfaction for it by doing *penance*. See Day of Expiation.

Expiation 457, 604

Expiation is the action of making *atonement* or satisfaction for *sin*. See Expiate 1459.

Expiatory penalty

An expiatory penalty is a type

of *canonical penalty* that aims at the satisfaction of *justice* and the punishment of the offender.

Ecclesiastical or *canonical* penalties may be either expiatory penalties or *censures* and may be incurred not because of the *intrinsic* wickedness of an act but because of circumstances attending it and the serious *consequences* involved.

They may be incurred automatically, by an administrative act of a *superior*, or by an *ecclesiastical* judge in the course of a trial.

In contrast to expiatory penalties, censures are *medicinal* in nature and are intended for the correction of the offender. See Ecclesiastical penalty. Also see Canonical penalty 1463.

Explicit/Explicitly

Explicit means clearly stated or saying exactly what is meant. See Truth 215.

Exposition

Exposition, as used in *hermeneutics*, refers to the determination of a *scriptural* text's meaning for today. It gives rise to the dangers of *eisegesis*, which means reading into *Scripture* ideas and meaning originating from without the text.

Exposition is different from *exegesis*, which more properly refers to the process of determining the original meaning of a text. See Exegesis.

Expounding 26

Expounding comes from the Latin word 'exponere,' meaning to put out, to set forth, or to explain.

External

External means on or having to do with the outside of something. It is the opposite of interior and inner. See Concept.

External forum

Forum refers to the sphere within which the Church exercises her *judicial authority*. The forum may be *external* or internal. The external forum deals with matters concerning the public welfare of the Church. The internal forum deals with matters of *conscience* in the *sacrament of Penance*, or *Confession*, where sins are forgiven and matters of *morality*, such as guilt, *restitution*, and *responsibility*, are decided. See Ecclesiastical penalty 1463.

Extraordinary Form of the Roman Rite

The Extraordinary Form of the Roman Rite is the name given by Pope Benedict XVI in his *motu proprio Summorum Pontificum* (2007 A.D.) for the celebration of *Mass* and administration of the sacraments according to the liturgical books promulgated by Pope St. John XXIII in 1962. This was the final revision of the Mass liturgy first promulgated after the *Council of Trent* by Pope St. Pius V and, hence, is often called the *Tridentine Mass*. It was never suppressed with the promulgation of the reformed texts of the liturgy by Pope Paul VI in 1969. This latter manner of celebrating the *liturgy* was given the name *Ordinary Form of the Roman Rite* by Pope Benedict XVI in his motu proprio just cited. See Ordinary Form; Roman Rite.

Extraordinary Magisterium

Doctrinal teaching is exercised as 'extraordinary Magisterium' when it is formally declared as an *article of faith* or *'de fide'* by *papal definition* or an *ecumenical council*. See Magisterium 83, 889, 890. Also see Solemn Magisterium.

Extraordinary minister of Holy Communion

Extraordinary minister of Holy Communion is the title of lay *persons* commissioned by their *pastor* to assist in the distribution of the *Eucharist* at *Mass* or to carry the *Blessed Sacrament* to the sick. See Apostolate 863.

Extreme Unction 1512

Extreme Unction is one of the seven *sacraments*. It is also called the *Anointing of the Sick*. The application of the name 'Extreme Unction' to this sacrament appears to have derived from the fact that the sacrament was tradition-

ally administered to those in danger of death.

Today the sacrament is administered to the seriously ill as well as to the dying. It is administered for the recovery of their health, if conducive to their *salvation*, and for the strength to bear their sufferings.

"The first *grace* of this sacrament is one of strengthening, peace, and courage to overcome the difficulties that go with the condition of serious illness or the frailty of old age... [It] is a gift of the *Holy Spirit* who renews *faith* and trust in God and strengthens against the *temptations* of the *evil one*, the temptation to discouragement and anguish in the face of death" (CCC 1520). This assistance "is meant to lead the sick *person* to healing of the *soul*, but also of the body if such is *God's will*" (CCC 1520). If a person repents of the sins he has committed, these sins are forgiven in this sacrament.

Origen (185–254 A.D.) considers this last sacrament as a complement to that of *penance*. If the person in the state of *mortal sin* has *attrition* for his sins but is unable to receive priestly *absolution*, he is justified by the grace of Extreme Unction according to St. Thomas' argument that 'By extreme unction a man is prepared worthily to receive *Christ's* Body' (Summa Theologica, 3a, q. 65, a. 3). The minister of Extreme Unction must be a *priest*.

Extrinsic

Extrinsic refers to something that does not really belong to a thing with which it is associated or that acts upon a thing from without. See Grave matter 1858.

Extrinsically indissoluble

All *marriages* are intrinsically indissoluble, that is, they cannot be dissolved by the spouses themselves. A ratified and *consummated* marriage is both extrinsically and intrinsically indissoluble and can only be dissolved by the death of one of the spouses. Marriages lacking the fullness of a ratified and consummated marriage (either non-consummated or not between baptized *persons*) may, in certain cases, be dissolved by the *authority* of the Church. However, the state does not have the authority to extrinsically dissolve marriages through *decrees* of *divorce*, even though many governments have arrogated this authority to themselves. See Indissolubility 1644. Also see Pauline Privilege; Petrine Privilege.

Exult/exultation

Exult comes from the Latin 'exsultare,' meaning to leap for joy. In English, it means to rejoice greatly, to be jubilant, or to feel triumphant. Exultation is the act of exulting. See Eschatalogical joy.

F

Faculties of the soul

The *soul* has two faculties, or inherent powers: the *intellect* and the *will*. The intellect is man's *cognitive* or knowing faculty and is referred to as the *mind*. The will is his power to initiate of itself, to choose and tend toward attaining what is deemed desirable. See Soul 363.

Faculty/Faculties

In the realm of ecclesiastical law, a faculty is an *authorization* to act in a certain capacity. It is in this sense that *Canon Law* provides for granting a *priest faculties* to hear *Confession*.

It is the *Bishop* who grants *faculties* to *priests* to hear Confessions, serve as *pastors* and hold *diocesan* offices. It is the *Pope* who gives faculties to bishops to govern dioceses. See Diocese 833. Also see Particular church 833.

Faintheartedness

Faintheartedness or *pusillanimity* is the fear of doing great or difficult things, or of being easily discouraged. It is a lack of courage, or cowardliness. See Fortitude 1808.

Faith 26, 146

Humanly speaking, faith is trusting or accepting as true whatever a *person* tells us. Supernatural faith, a gift of God, makes possible *man's* response to God who reveals himself to man by bringing him light as he searches for the ultimate meaning of his life. More specifically, faith means accepting something as true relying solely on the testimony or *authority* of God. In *Scripture* faith is called "the assurance of things hoped for, the conviction of things not seen" (Heb 11:1). It can also refer to the object of *belief* and the sum of *truths* taught by the Church.

Faith is a conviction affecting the character, *will*, and behavior, as opposed to the merely *intellectual assent* to *religious* truth, which is more properly, called *speculative faith*. When faith affects behavior, it is called *practical faith*. Faith is also a *theological virtue*. See Theological virtues. Also see Faith as a theological virtue 1814.

Faith as a theological virtue 1814

"*Faith* is the *theological virtue* by which we believe in God and believe all that he has said and revealed to us, and that Holy Church proposes for our *belief*, because he is truth itself. By faith, 'man freely commits himself to God.'" (CCC 1814)

Those who accept the gift of faith must not only keep it but also profess it, confidently bear witness to it, and spread it. Service of and witness to the faith are necessary for *salvation*.

Faith can be considered from an *objective* or *subjective* point of view. In the objective sense, it refers to all the saving truths contained in the *Scriptures*, the *Creeds*, *council* definitions, teachings of the *Magisterium*, and writings of the *doctors* and *saints* of the Church.

In the subjective sense, it refers to the acts and dispositions by which these *doctrines* are believed and practiced. It is in this sense that faith is considered one of the three infused *theological virtues*.

Though subjective faith is primarily a disposition of the *intellect*, it also involves an *act of the will*. It is more than the *adoption* of a *conclusion* based on sufficient evidence or argument, it is the *grace* of God moving the will to believe. Faith is required for *salvation* and is infused into the *soul* at *Baptism*.

Faithful

Faithful is the name used to identify those who accept and follow the teaching of the Church or are members of the Church community. They are also called the *People of God*. See Evangelical instinct 1676.

Fall, The

The fall refers to the *original sin* committed by Adam and Eve in *Paradise*. As a *consequence* of this sin they lost the friendship of God, and the *preternatural gifts* of *immortality*, *integrity*, *impassibility*, and *infused knowledge*. Their *intellect* was darkened and their *will* weakened making it impossible for them to do good without the help of God's *grace*. See Concupiscence 405. Also see Preternatural gift. Also see Original justice 376.

Fall of the angels 392

The fall of the angels refers to the freely chosen and *irrevocable* rejection of God by the *angelic* spirits, which resulted in their being cast out of *heaven* into *hell* for all *eternity*. The *angels* were not forgiven because they absolutely rejected God's *mercy* even though they knew him far better than any other creatures. By their *free will* they chose not to obey God's plan for them but to reject it. The fallen angels are called devils. Lucifer, their leader, is called *Satan* or the *devil*.

After death *man*, like the fallen angels, will no longer be able to *repent* of his sin and turn to God by accepting his call to union with him and *eternal* happiness. During life, man always has the opportunity to repent and accept union with God by living in *sanctifying grace.*

We must pray daily for the grace of *final perseverance* because the devil always prowls about the world like a roaring lion seeking whom he may devour. The devil will try harder to deceive us at the hour of our death, but with God's ever-present *grace*, we can overcome all *temptation.* God will not allow us to be *tempted* beyond our strength.

Fallacious

Fallacious comes from the Latin word 'fallere,' to deceive. Something which is misleading, deceptive, erroneous, or defective in *logic* is said to be fallacious. See Free union 2390.

Fallen angel

The fallen angels are called *devils.* Lucifer, their leader, is called *Satan*, the father of lies or the evil one. See Diabolos 2851. Also see Fall of the angels 392.

Fallen nature

See Fallen state 404.

Fallen state

See Fall, The.

Fallible 1739

Fallible means being capable of error or failure.

False witness 2476

False witness is the *intentional* making of a statement or giving testimony, which is contrary to the *truth.* It takes on special gravity when it is made publicly and officially. Such a statement made in court is called false witness unless it is given under *oath.* Then it is called *perjury.*

False worship

False worship is offering *worship* to *created* things that is properly due to God alone. See Virtue of religion 2096.

Family 2202

A family consists of man and woman united in *marriage,* together with their children forming the primary *communal* institution. This institution exists prior to any recognition by public *authority*, which has an *obligation* to recognize and support it.

Fast/fasting

To fast means to refrain from eating food. See Precepts of the Church. Also see Fast days 2043.

Fast days 2043

Fast days are days on which the *faithful* are allowed to eat only one full meal. It is to be taken after noon. Drink is not limited, but liquids containing solids, such as soup, count as food. The *obligation* to fast binds those over eighteen "until the beginning of their sixtieth year" (Canon 1252); however, severe work, illness, or debility excuse a *person* from the obligation.

Fasting is imposed as an act of *penance* and physical *mortification* for exercise in *temperance* and for the health of *souls*. Traditionally, before *Vatican II*, fast days in the United States were all the weekdays of *Lent, ember days*, and the *vigils* of certain major *solemnities*—Pentecost, the Assumption, and Christmas—unless the solemnity fell on a Monday, the vigil being suppressed by the *Sunday*.

According to the present (1983) *Code of Canon Law*, only *Ash Wednesday* and *Good Friday* are fast days for the universal Church. The *episcopal conference* can determine more particular ways in which fasting is to be observed.

Fat Tuesday

The Tuesday before *Ash Wednesday* was the occasion for enjoying a festive meal during which the foods on hand, which would be forbidden during the Lenten fast, could be consumed. See Lacticinia. Also see Mardi Gras.

Fatal/Fatalistic

Fatalistic means characterized by the *belief* in the inevitability of all events and the belief that nothing can be done to change them. See Astrology.

Father, God the 232

The Father refers to God the Father, the First *Person* of the *Trinity*. *Jesus* revealed the Father not only as Creator of all things but also as Father in relation to his only, eternally *begotten*, and *consubstantial* Son.

When *Christians* refer to God as Father, it is because we are united to Christ at *Baptism* and *adopted* into *divine sonship*. Therefore, we become *children of God* not merely because we were *created* by God, but by participation in the eternal sonship of God the Son.

In liturgical prayer, "God" refers to the Father. See Trinity. Also see Son, God the; Holy Spirit.

Father of his acts 1749

Man is considered to be the father of his *moral acts* because they originate with him in both *intention* and action by virtue of his *free will*. Because man is the sole cause or origin of a moral act, it is *imputable* to him alone.

Acts can be classified either as *acts of man* or as *human acts*. Acts of man are simply acts performed by man as opposed to animals. They include bodily processes, *instinctual* behaviors, and behaviors that are not intentional or the result of *judgment*. Acts of man are not associated with *morality* because they are not deliberate choices.

Human acts are moral acts. They are freely and *deliberately* chosen in *consequence* of a moral *judgment* of conscience. They are deliberate and free acts of the *will* and are always judged as *good* or *evil*, that is, to be in accord with the *divine law* or contrary to it. A *person* is fully responsible and accountable for his moral acts and their intended consequences. See Moral act.

Father superior/Mother superior

Father or Mother Superior is the title of the *superior* of a *religious community*. See Superior, religious.

Fathers of the Church 11

The term 'Fathers of the Church,' or simply *Fathers*, refers to *Christian* writers of the first twelve centuries. Special importance is given to those of the first six centuries because they offer evidence of Church teaching and practice from the earliest times of the Church. The earliest of these writers from the last quarter of the first century and the first half of the second century are also known as *Apostolic Fathers*. They formed the basis for *theological tradition*.

Fathers of the Desert

The Fathers of the Desert were the *monks* and *hermits* of the early Church who developed the *religious* life and laid the foundations for all future *institutes* of perfection or *religious orders*. They lived in the deserts of Egypt during the third and fourth centuries after *Christ*. See Rule of St. Benedict.

Fear of the Lord 1831

The gift of fear of the Lord forms the foundation of all the other *gifts of the Holy Spirit* because it drives *sin* from the heart and fills it with *reverence* for the *justice* and majesty of God.

The gift of fear of the Lord does not arise from a *servile fear* and dread of the *wrath* or punishment of God. It inspires a *filial fear*, or holy awe, arising from the *experience* and *knowledge* of the utter *holiness* of God. It inspires a detestation of sin because it offends God's perfect love, *providence*, *justice*, and care for us. It is a fear of offending a loving Father.

Fear of the Lord is a *habitual* disposition of the *soul* by which it maintains a state of *reverence* before God with a child-like, filial dread of displeasing him or of being separated from him whom we love. It renders the soul submissive to *God's will* and causes it to avoid all sin. The best evidence of this gift is the possession of a tender and *exact conscience*. See Gifts of the Holy Spirit.

Feast

A feast is a special day set apart by the Church to give

special honor to God, the Savior, *angels*, *saints*, or *sacred mysteries of faith*. Some feasts are fixed, such as *Christmas* or the *Immaculate Conception*; others are moveable and occur on different days in different years because of the date of *Easter*.

Since *Vatican II*, feasts are divided into *solemnities*, feasts, and *memorials*.

Solemnities are days of greatest importance; they have a *vigil* Mass and are celebrated for a period of eight days, called an *octave*. In the *Ordinary Form* of the *liturgy*, only Easter and Christmas have octaves. No *octaves* are associated with the other solemnities. Other octaves are retained only in the *Extraordinary Form of the Roman Rite*.

Feasts are celebrated on one day only. Memorials may be obligatory or optional.

Sundays are in a class by themselves, as are the various *liturgical* seasons such as *Advent*, *Lent*, or Easter, which are called Sacred Times. The religious purpose of all feasts and seasons is to remind the *faithful* throughout the year of the great mysteries, *persons*, and events in the life and *tradition* of the Church. See Liturgical year 1168, 1171.

Feast of the Holy Redeemer

The feast of the Holy Redeemer is also known as the feast of *Saint Savior*. Saint Savior is a title given to some *churches*

dedicated to God the Son as Redeemer. The *titular feast* is *celebrated* on August 6. This feast, when referred to as the feast of the Holy Redeemer, is found only in the special calendar of some *dioceses* and *religious orders*. It is celebrated with proper *Mass* and *Divine Office* either on the third *Sunday* of July or on October 23. See Transfiguration 554. Also see Saint Savior.

Fecundity

Fecundity means fruitfulness. The gift of fecundity fulfills the purpose of *marriage* because *conjugal* love naturally tends to be fruitful. See End of marriage 2366.

Felicity

Felicity comes from the Latin word 'felix,' meaning happy or lucky. In English it means happiness or bliss. See Beatific vision 1028.

Felix Culpa

The Church finds reason to rejoice in the ruin of man through *sin* in the Garden of Eden by describing it in the *Easter Vigil liturgy* as "O happy fault [felix culpa] that earned for us so great, so glorious a Redeemer!" (Exultet, Third Edition of the *Roman Missal*). *Jesus*, as the *Redeemer*, turned the burden of *concupiscence* into the means of *salvation* by conquering sin and death. See

Diabolos 2851. Also see Devil; Original sin 389.

Fellowship 425

Fellowship refers to sharing things in common. The first *disciples* shared a common *faith* in *Christ*, which filled them with a common conviction and common *zeal* for proclaiming Christ. Their common work was to spread the *Gospel* and to lead others to faith in him by inviting them to enter into the joyful fellowship of their communion with Christ. This was their *missionary* mandate.

The fellowship of the early disciples also extended to sharing their *material* things. They shared all things in common, even their suffering at the hands of those who ridiculed their faith, hated them, and sought to put them to death.

Fellowship also extends to the missionary mandate of *Christians*. It is founded on the *eternal* love of the *Divine Persons* of the Most *Holy Trinity* (cf. 1 Jn 1:3). The Church's *nature* is missionary because she has her origin in the *mission* of the Son and the *Holy Spirit*. The purpose of that mission is to enable men to share in the fellowship of *communion* between the Father and the Son in their Spirit of *love*.

Fertility

Fertility refers to the quality of or the capacity for fruitfulness. It is a condition of *fecundity*, by which one is capable of achieving impregnation or fertilization. See Conjugal love 1643; Also see Fertilization.

Fertilization

To fertilize is to make fruitful or productive. See Artificial insemination.

Fetus

The term fetus refers to a child in the uterus after the third month of its *conception*, as it is being prepared for birth. Before that time, it is referred to as an *embryo*. See Embryo 2271.

Fiat 2617

Fiat, the Latin word for 'let it be done,' was the response of acceptance by the *Virgin Mary* to the announcement of the *angel* that she was to be the *Mother of God* (Lk 1:38). All *prayer* should reflect an acceptance of *God's will* according to this model.

Jesus employs this same word during his prayer in the Garden of Gethsemani, in accepting the Father's will concerning his *imminent* condemnation and death by *crucifixion* (cf. Mt 26:42). The same phrase is placed on the lips of Our Lord accepting the will of the Father to become *incarnate* and to offer himself as *sacrifice* for our *redemption*, "Sacrifice and offering you did not desire, but a body you prepared for me... Behold, I come to do your will, O God" (Heb 10:5, 7).

This is an allusion to the *fiat* or acceptance of Mary to become the Lord's Mother and so prepare a body to be sacrificed (Heb 10:5–10). With this is *insinuated* the joint offering on *Calvary* of the *New Adam* and *New Eve*, *Redeemer* and *Coredemptrix*, reversing the consequences of the joint *infidelity* of the First Adam and First Eve in the *Garden of Paradise*.

Coredemptrix is distinguished from *Mediatrix*. Coredemptrix refers to Mary's role in Christ's act of redemption; Mediatrix refers to her role in the mediation of the grace of redemption to mankind. See Mediatrix.

Fictitious consent

Fictitious consent is false or pretended consent or consent inconsistent with the thing being willed *interiorly*. It is, of course, not true consent. See Consent 1627.

Fidelity

Fidelity refers to faithfulness or devotion to *duty*, *obligations*, or *vows*. See Baptismal name. Also see Conjugal fidelity 2364.

Figure

A figure is something used to represent something else. It is a common literary device used in *Scripture*. Thus, for example, the Good Shepherd

is used as a figure of *Christ*. See Sacramental sign 1152.

Filial adoption

Filial adoption refers to becoming *adopted sons* of God through the *grace* of *Baptism*. See Adopted sons.

Filial boldness 2610

Filial boldness refers to the lack of fear that should characterize the *prayer* of one who accepts God as a loving Father. See Parrhesia 2778.

Filial fear

Filial fear is the kind of fear inspired by the gift of *fear of the Lord*. It arises from the *experience* and knowledge of the utter *holiness* of God and inspires a detestation of *sin* because of an awareness of how it offends God's perfect love, *providence*, *justice*, and care for us. It is a fear of sin because of how it displeases God. See Fear of the Lord 1831.

Filial piety 2215

Filial piety is the respect for parents derived "from gratitude toward those who, by the gift of life, their *love* and their work, have brought their children into the world and enabled them to grow in stature, *wisdom*, and *grace*" (CCC 2215).

Filial prayer 2599

Filial prayer is the *prayer* of children to their Father. In

God's *indefectible covenant* with every creature, God has always called people to prayer. It is with Abraham that prayer is first revealed in the *Old Testament*. The notion of prayer developed over time.

Moses became the most striking example of *intercessory prayer*, which was to be fulfilled in "the one *mediator* between God and men, the man *Christ Jesus*" (1 Tim 2:5). In the *Psalms*, David, inspired by the *Holy Spirit*, became the first *prophet* of *Jewish* and Christian prayer.

Christ, the true *Messiah* and Son of David, finally revealed and fulfilled the meaning of prayer. In the fullness of time, Christ, in his *human nature*, learned to pray from his Mother using the words and rhythms of the prayer of his people in the *Synagogue* and the *Temple*.

A newness of prayer was revealed in Christ. He prayed to God as a loving Father and taught his *disciples* to do the same, praying in Jesus' name. He also taught them the prayer of the *Our Father*. See Prayer.

Filial Respect
See Filial piety 2215.

Filial spirit toward the Church
2040
Filial spirit toward the Church refers to an attitude that resembles one of a child toward its mother. It should be one of love, reverence, and *obedience*.

Filioque 246
Filioque is a Latin word meaning 'and from the son.' It is used in the *Nicene Creed* to affirm that the *Holy Spirit* proceeds from the Father and the Son.

The term was first used in the sixth century in Spain. It also came to be used in the West but not immediately at Rome. The usage came under attack and was even forbidden by Pope Leo III (795–816 A.D.) in deference to the practice of the Greeks, but it was allowed again by Pope Benedict VIII (1012–1024 A.D.).

This dispute, which involved no change in *doctrine*, was a *disciplinary* matter occasioned by the need to defend an attacked *dogma*, as well as the desire to conciliate the Greeks and to reaffirm the pronouncement of the *Council of Ephesus* (431 A.D.), which made the Nicene Creed the definitive expression of *faith*. There was never a dispute over the doctrine itself but only over the need to add the expression to the *liturgical* Creed.

Final Anointing
Final *Anointing* is another name for the *sacrament of the Sick*, or *Extreme Unction*. It is also called the *Anointing of the Sick*. Because this sacramental anointing is administered to the dying, it is called

Extreme Unction, or Final Anointing. It may be administered only by an ordained *priest*. See Extreme unction 1512.

Final end

The final end is also called the *ultimate end*. See Ultimate end.

Final initiation

The fourth stage of Christian initiation is called Final initiation. It takes place at the *Easter Vigil*. At this time, the *catechumens* are baptized, are confirmed, and receive their *First Holy Communion*. With the reception of these *sacraments*, the catechumens become *neophytes*. See RCIA 1232.

Final perseverance 2016

Final perseverance refers to the continuance in a *state of grace* leading finally to a state of *glory*.

Final purification 1031

Those who die in God's *grace* and friendship but who are still imperfectly purified are assured of their eternal *salvation*. After death, however, they must undergo a final *purification* in order to achieve the *holiness* necessary to enter the joy of *heaven*.

"The Church gives the name *Purgatory* to this final purification of the *elect*, which is entirely different from the punishment of the damned" (CCC 1031). See Purgatory.

Finality 1740

Finality refers to an ultimate purpose or end.

Fire of hell

In the *New Testament*, it refers to the place and state of *eternal punishment*, which consists, primarily, in the deprivation of the enjoyment of the sight of God and, secondarily, in the infliction of positive physical punishment, often called the fire of hell.

Theologians agree that this fire is real and external to the *victim*. Although real, it is called fire by *analogy* to earthly fire because it is reserved for *resurrected* bodies of the damned. Because it is eternal, it must burn without consuming. See Hell 633.

Firm resolution

A firm resolution is one that will not yield easily under pressure and cannot be moved or shaken. It is a resolution that is unchanging and constant. See Act of contrition 1451.

First cause 308

A first cause is a *cause* that is absolutely independent of any other cause or *being* and on which all other *causality* depends. The first cause is God because only he has no cause and is the ultimate cause of all that is. The first cause is also called the *primary cause*.

First class relic

There are three classes of relics. First class relics are parts of a saint's body. *Second class relics* are things a saint used during his life. *Third class relics* are objects, such as cloth, that have been touched to a first class relic. Relics may not be sold or bought. See Altar 1383. Also see Popular devotion 1674.

First Holy Communion 1244

First Holy Communion refers to one's first reception of the *Eucharist*. In the *Latin Church*, this often takes place some years after *Baptism* and is preceded by a period of *catechesis*.

In the *Eastern Churches*, First Holy Communion is given at Baptism together with *Chrismation* or Confirmation. The three *sacraments of initiation* are *celebrated* and commemorated together with friends and *godparents*.

First principle

A first principle is a self-evident truth from which *conclusions* are drawn. These three self-evident truths are called primary *truths*: the first truth is one's own existence; the second truth is that it is impossible for a thing both to be and not to be at the same time in the same respect; and the third truth is that man's reason is capable of knowing truth. These three truths are spontaneous convictions of the *mind*, are accepted without question, and are never doubted by ordinary men.

These truths are contained implicitly in all man's statements and actions. *Man* is aware that he can make mistakes, but errors do not *invalidate* the *essential* capacity of reason to know truth from error. Man's life is regulated by his spontaneous conviction of the *validity* of these three primary principles, or truths. See Dualism 285.

First Solemn Communion

First Holy Communion is also referred to as First Solemn Communion when the occasion is accompanied by a special recognition of the first communicants during the liturgy to commemorate the event formally. See First Holy Communion 1244.

Fixed altar

A fixed altar is a type of *altar* in which a single stone forms the table. A fixed altar has three parts: a top made of stone, supports for the top, and a *sepulcher* (a place in which *first class relics* of a *saint* or *martyr* have been sealed). See Altar 1383.

Flesh 990

The term flesh is used to refer to the body of *man* in his present state of weakness and *mortality*.

Follow Jesus 2233

To follow *Jesus* means to accept his invitation to become his *disciple* and to "live in conformity with His way of life" (CCC 2233) by keeping his commandments. To follow Jesus is the first *vocation* of the *Christian*.

Fomes peccati 1264

'Fomes peccati' is a Latin phrase meaning 'the tinder for sin.' It is used metaphorically to refer to *concupiscence*. See Concupiscence.

Foreknowledge

Foreknowledge is *knowledge* of something before it happens or exists. Because God knows all things, he is called *omniscient*, which means 'all-knowing.' In his eternal 'present,' everything in time takes place because God's vision embraces the whole of our time in his *eternal*, unchanging 'now.'

God knows how *man* will use his *free will*, but this knowledge in no way determines what man will choose. God's knowledge does not predetermine who will go to *hell* by knowing how a *person* will use his free will.

Sin does not frustrate God's *will* because he wills man to be free. No matter how man uses his freedom, God is *glorified* because man uses his gift to make his choice, whether that is to accept God's gift of *love* or to come under his just

judgment by rejecting his love and violating the right order of *nature*. See Predestined. Also see Contingent cause; Mary's predestination 488.

Foreshadow/foreshadowing

Foreshadow means to indicate, to *prefigure*, or to suggest beforehand. See Typological 1094.

Forgiveness of sin

Forgiveness of sin refers to the pardon or remission of guilt for a *moral* offense. The Church teaches that *sins* are actually removed, not merely covered up, by the *merits* of Christ. Only God can forgive sin. God forgives the sins of those who are truly repentant either through an act of *perfect contrition* or through the sacraments of *Baptism*, *Confession*, and, under certain conditions, the *Anointing of the Sick*. See Despair 2091.

Form (Substantial) 365

Form is defined as that which makes a thing to be what it is. In terms of *Scholastic philosophy*, a physical body is composed of prime *matter* and *substantial form*. These are *part-principles*, which must both be present before a thing can exist.

Prime matter is what makes a thing to be bodily, but it must be infused with a substantial form, which gives it a specific character in order to exist as a particular thing. Prime matter cannot simply exist; it must exist as something.

Substantial form refers to that incomplete, physically simple part-principle that makes a thing to be what it is. See Substantial form.

Formal Logic

See Logic/logical. Also see Reason; Systematic philosophy; Material logic.

Forms of prayer 2625

Prayer is the lifting of the *heart* and *mind* to God. It may take various forms. *Mental prayer* is a purely internal mental act; *vocal prayer* is an external act expressed through oral language. According to its content, prayer may be classed as *adoration, petition, intercession, or thanksgiving.*

Prayer of adoration, or *blessing*, is man's response to God's gifts, returning blessing to God who is the source of every blessing. In it, man blesses God who has blessed him.

In prayer of adoration, man recognizes that he is a creature before his creator and exalts the greatness of the Lord who made him.

The *prayer of petition* expresses our awareness of our relationship with God and our complete dependence on him. In prayer of petition, we ask God for his blessings.

Prayer of intercession is a prayer of petition for others, leading us to pray as Jesus did.

He is the one intercessor with the Father on behalf of sinful men. To ask intercession on behalf of others is characteristic of a heart attuned to God's *mercy. Christian* intercession is an expression of the *communion of saints.*

Prayer of thanksgiving expresses *gratitude* to God for his many blessings. It characterizes the prayer of the Church in the celebration of the *Eucharist*, which gives thanks for the work of *salvation.*

The *prayer of praise* recognizes most immediately that God is God and gives him glory not for what he does but for who he is. Praise embraces the other forms of prayer and carries them toward him who is its source and goal.

The *Eucharist* contains and expresses all forms of prayer. It is a pure offering of the whole *Body of Christ* to the *glory* of God's name and is the *sacrifice* of *praise*. See Meditation 2705.

Fornication 2353

Fornication is *sexual intercourse*, or carnal union, between two unmarried *persons*. It is gravely contrary to the *dignity* of persons and *human* sexuality, which is naturally ordered to the *good* of *spouses* and the *generation* and education of children.

Fortitude 1808, 1831

"Fortitude is the *moral vir-*

tue that ensures firmness in difficulties and constancy in the pursuit of the *good*. It strengthens the resolve to resist *temptations* and to overcome obstacles in the *moral* life. The virtue of fortitude enables one to conquer fear, even fear of death, and to face trials and *persecutions*. It disposes one even to renounce and *sacrifice* his life in defense of a just *cause*" (CCC 1808).

Virtues related to fortitude are *munificence*, *magnanimity*, *patience*, and *perseverance*. *Faintheartedness* and *pusillanimity* are contrary to fortitude.

Fortitude is also a *cardinal virtue* and a *gift of the Holy Spirit*. As a *virtue*, it is the *habit* of facing difficulties and evils resolutely and resisting mere recklessness motivated by uncontrolled fear. Impatience reflects a lack of fortitude.

As a gift of the Holy Spirit, fortitude completes the *cardinal virtue* of fortitude. It enables the body and soul to bear trials otherwise unbearable without this special support of the Holy Spirit. It moves the soul to undertake wearisome labors and to suffer grievous pain with courage and perseverance. It is concerned with the control of rather than the absence of fear. It enables us to avoid being bowed beneath adversity or lifted up by success by instilling *humility*, which avoids both *pride* in success and *despair* in failure. See Moral virtues 1804.

Forum

Forum refers to the sphere within which the Church exercises her *judicial authority*. The forum may be external and internal. The *external forum* deals with matters concerning the public welfare. The *internal forum* deals with matters of conscience in the *sacrament of Penance* or *Confession*, where sins are forgiven and matters of *morality*, such as guilt, *restitution*, and *responsibility*, are decided. See Ecclesiastical penalties 1463.

Fourth Lateran Council

Five Church *councils* were convened in the Lateran Palace in Rome between the twelfth and sixteenth centuries. The Fourth Lateran Council, held in 1215 A.D., was the twelfth *ecumenical council* of the Church. Convened by Pope Innocent III, it is considered to be one of the most important Church assemblies held before the *Council of Trent*. Among its declarations were annual *Confession*, definition of the *doctrine* of *transubstantiation*, *communion* during *Easter Time*, and the condemnation of the Cathars and Waldenses. See Analogy of being.

Franciscan friars/Franciscans

Franciscan friars are members of the Franciscan Order, founded in 1209 A.D. by St.

Francis of Assisi (1181–1226 A.D.). The distinctive feature of the order is the obligation of poverty not only for individual members but also for each community. The friars earn their livelihood by manual work or by begging.

The name Friar (brother) is used to identify members of *mendicant orders*, such as the *Dominicans* and Franciscans. The Franciscan friars are also known as Friars Minor or Minorites, Cordeliers (cord bearers), Grey Friars (from the original color of their habit), or the Barefoot Brothers. See Mendicant order. Also see Friar.

Frankincense

Frankincense is a gum resin obtained from various Arabian and African trees. It is burned as *incense* and favored because of its fragrant aroma.

The Church uses it in *liturgical rites* as a symbol of the *prayers* of the *faithful* rising sweetly to the Lord. It is usually referred to simply as incense. There are various types of incense, each with its distinctive aroma.

Pagans used incense as an offering to the gods and, during the *persecution* of the Church, demanded that Christians offer incense to the emperor as a god or face a cruel death.

The *Jews* offered incense to God in the *Temple* in recognition of his *divinity* and as a symbol of their prayers rising to him.

Tradition holds that the *Magi* brought gold, frankincense, and *myrrh* to the Christ child at the *Epiphany* as symbols of his kingship, divinity, and humanity. See Shewbread 2581.

Fraternal

Fraternal comes from the Latin word 'frater,' which means brother. Fraternal correction refers to the loving concern that prompts one to help another to avoid making a mistake or to correct his behavior. See Intercession of the saints 956.

Fratricide 2268

Fratricide is the act of killing one's *sibling*.

Free agent or free cause

By *agent* we mean the *person* who causes or performs an *act*. When a person acts with *knowledge* and *deliberate* purpose by an *act of the will*, he is a free agent. See Contingent cause.

Free choice

See Free will 1704, 1731. Also see Free agent; Contingent cause.

Free thought

Free thought refers to the refusal to accept any *authority* outside oneself in matters of religious *belief*. It relies on the use of unaided *human reason* alone and excludes *revelation* entirely in forming religious belief. See Individualism 2425.

Free union 2390

In a so-called free union, a man and a woman refuse to give *juridical* and public form to a *liaison* involving sexual intimacy. The expression itself is fallacious since union can have no meaning when partners make no commitment to one another, each exhibiting a lack of trust in the other, in himself, or in the future.

The expression includes various situations, such as *concubinage*, rejection of *marriage* as such, or the inability to make long-term commitments. These all offend against the *dignity* of marriage, destroy the very idea of family, and weaken the sense of *fidelity*. All are contrary to the *moral law*, constitute *grave* sin, and exclude one from *sacramental communion*.

Free will 1704, 1731

Free will in man refers to the capacity of the *will*, when all conditions for action are present, to decide whether to act or not to act in one way or another. Freedom means that the will is not necessitated by its *nature* to act in any determined manner but is capable of determining its own action rather than being determined by some action distinct from its own.

Two conditions are required for the exercise of free will in regard to objects where one or the other may be chosen:

1) a normal state of attention, because the will can desire only what the *intellect* proposes to it as *good* and

2) an objectively indifferent *judgment*, leaving the will to choose as it prefers in accord with the *moral law*.

The will exercises freedom of choice in three ways:

1) *freedom of exercise or contradiction*, which means it can choose freely between acting or not acting;

2) *freedom of specification*, which means that the will can choose freely between acts of the will with specifically different objects; and

3) *freedom of contrariety*, which means that the will can choose freely between *acts* with contrary objects, one morally good and the other morally *evil*. In the religious sense, free will is the capacity to respond either positively or negatively to *divine grace* without hindrance.

Free will is also called *intellectual* or *spiritual appetency*. It is also referred to as freedom of choice. See Intellectual appetency. Also see Freedom 1731.

Freedom 1731

Freedom in creatures is the power, rooted in right *reason* and *will*, to act or not to act, do one thing or to do its *contrary*, to do this or something different, in a word, to perform *deliberate acts* on one's own responsibility. *Human* freedom is a force for growth and maturity in *truth* and goodness, which attains its perfection when directed toward God.

Freedom in creatures, however, is a participation in the perfect freedom of God's will. *Divine* freedom is that property of the *divine will* whereby God necessarily loves his own goodness and all creatures he freely chooses to create. That freedom is *infinitely* perfect and so differs from the freedom of the *created* will in the two ways that reveal the limitations of the created will.

First, unlike the created will, the divine will does not multiply acts of willing, even when willing specifically different things, for the divine act of willing is identical with the divine being. When God wills creatures, his willing is one, *eternal* action, whereby each of these creatures begins to exist outside of God in time.

Second, since God wills all other things only in willing his perfect goodness first, he cannot *sin*. Only by *grace* can the created will attain to such perfection as to will without multiplying acts of willing and will to *love* God, not as a possible option among many, but as the first direct, immediate, all absorbing object of his love. The *saints* in *heaven* are, by grace and *glory*, *impeccable*

and, therefore, perfectly free and happy like God.

Freedom of contrariety

Freedom of contrariety means that the free *will* can choose between *moral good* and moral *evil*, which are contraries. In the religious sense, free will is the capacity to respond either positively or negatively to *divine grace* without hindrance. The reason that the *created* will can choose to reject rather than to love God is that, during a time of *pilgrimage*, the divine goodness is not immediately made present to the will as all-lovable but only indirectly through creatures as one of many lovable objects. The so-called power to *sin* is not a positive power but a limitation on freedom and so is not found in God, whose *knowledge* and love of himself are really identical and cannot be separated. See Free will 1704.

Freedom of exercise or contradiction

Freedom of exercise or contradiction means that the created *will* can choose freely between acting or not acting. Perfect freedom, by definition, is *infinite* and so without need to multiply *acts* in order to specify its various preferences among *contingent* goods. God, being perfect, is not subject to this limitation on the power to will freely. See Free will 1704.

Freedom of specification

Freedom of specification means that the *will* can choose freely between one object of the will or another and determine which object shall be the goal of its choice. This specification of objects outside the *created* will requires a previous multiplication of *acts of the will* for as many objects as are willed. For the *divine will*, no such multiplication is a prerequisite for the multiplication of objects outside of God. See Free will 1704.

Friar

Friar comes from the Latin word 'frater,' meaning brother. Since the thirteenth century, it has been used to refer to members of *mendicant* orders, such as *Franciscans* and *Dominicans*.

A friar differs from a monk because a friar works outside the monastery. Monks work on the grounds of the monastery. See Dominicans; Franciscans.

Friars Preachers

Friars Preachers are members of the Dominican order founded by St. Dominic (1170–1221 A.D.). The Dominicans are known as the Order of Preachers and in England as the *Black Friars*. See Dominicans.

Fruits of charity 1829

The Catechism teaches that the fruits of *charity* are joy, peace, and *mercy*. Charity demands *beneficence*, or kindness, as well as *fraternal* correction. Charity is *benevolent*, fosters *reciprocity*, and remains disinterested and generous. It is friendship and *communion*.

Fruits of Holy Communion
1391–1398

Fruits of Holy Communion refer to the benefits received by those who communicate worthily. There are seven fruits of Holy Communion:

1) to increase one's *union with Christ*,

2) to preserve, renew, and increase the life of *grace* received at *Baptism*,

3) to wipe way *venial sin*,

4) to preserve one from *mortal sin*,

5) to unite one more closely to Christ and, through him, to all the Church,

6) to commit one to the poor by enabling him to see Christ in the poor, and

7) to form a sign of unity and a bond of *charity* in the Church.

Fruits of the Holy Spirit 1832

"The fruits of the Spirit are perfections that the *Holy Spirit* forms in us as the first fruits of *eternal* glory" (CCC 1832). The older versions of the *Vulgate* listed twelve fruits of the Spirit:

1) *Charity* (*love*) is a constant burning love of God and neighbor.

2) *Joy* is a *spiritual* gladness, happiness, pleasure, or delight that no trials or reverses are able to destroy.

3) *Peace* is a calmness, equanimity, or stability of *soul* despite adverse circumstances or events.

4) *Patience* enables the soul to bear trials with resignation to God's *will*. It manifests itself as meekness when it concerns dealing with others.

5) Kindness, also called *benignity*, is *mercy* toward others and a willingness to serve them with love. It prompts us to serve others by word and deed.

6) Goodness, so *essential* to *Christian holiness*, is more than avoiding *moral evil*. It implies a growth in love of God and neighbor born of participation in the life of *Christ*, his *sacraments*, and prayer.

7) *Generosity* is the *magnanimous* nobility of *mind* that makes one willing to give and share unselfishly with others.

8) Gentleness is kindness or courtesy toward others. It is that quality of patience and serenity that is opposed to harshness or *violence*.

9) Faithfulness is the ability to maintain allegiance, constancy, or loyalty to another and to adhere unwaveringly to God and to the *faith*.

10) *Modesty* enables man to observe moderation in all things. In reference to deportment and dress, it is relative and dependent on situations, such as *person* or place. What is immodest for a single person may not be for a married person. Modesty is allied with *temperance* and is found in moderation according to circumstance as recognized by a thoughtful mind and pure heart.

11) *Self-control* refers to control of *emotions*, desires, or actions. Because of *original sin*, man has lost the gift of easy self-control and must struggle against *concupiscence* but is still free to resist *temptations* to sin arising from his lower *nature*.

12) *Chastity* is a gift distinct from continence or self-control relating to the *virtue* of purity. Because the majority of Greek manuscripts list only nine fruits of the Spirit, newer translations of Gal 5:22–23 list only nine fruits, omitting generosity, modesty, and chastity.

The fruits of the Holy Spirit are acts produced by *virtue*; they are not virtues or *habits* themselves. One finds the fruits of the Spirit manifested when the infused *theological virtues* transform the *heart*, mind, soul, and will. They represent the harvest of the Spirit, brought forth by *grace*. They result from the need for *man's* fallen *nature* to undergo death of the flesh together with Christ until it ceases to have power over the mind and will. With the death of the flesh, God fashions a new creation in the initial stage of a *resurrected* life. The fruits of the Spirit are the effects of living one's life in the Spirit and man's resurrected relation to God.

Full communion with the Church

To be in full communion with the Church means to be united to and associated with her in all matters of religion, *creed*, *worship*, and *spiritual life*. This implies being fully compliant with her prescriptions and regulations, adhering to her *doctrines*, and uniting with the *faithful* and *hierarchy* in service and *obedience*. See Public penitents.

Full consent and complete consent 1859

Full and complete consent refers to the total acceptance of, agreement to, compliance or *concurrence* with, or *acquiescence* in the gravely *evil* nature of something proposed by the *intellect*. It implies agreement or concurrence sufficiently deliberate to make the choice a *culpable* personal act.

Full knowledge 1859

Full knowledge means complete awareness, *understanding*, and recognition of the sinful character of a proposed thought, word, action, or omission.

Full moon

Full moon is that phase of the moon when its disk is fully illuminated, which is the case when the moon is opposite the sun as seen from the earth. See New moon. Also see Lunar calendar; Synodic month.

Full of Grace 722

The *Angel* Gabriel addressed *Mary* as 'full of grace' at the *Annunciation* because she was entirely free from *original sin*. This does not mean that she was endowed with *grace* to the fullest extent possible or that she had all possible effects of grace. It means that she had all the grace needed for her to become the *Mother of God*. This itself was enough to exalt her above all men and *angels*.

Mary is a creature of God. All that she is and has is from him, but she is God's most perfect creature. For this reason, the homage paid to her is paid to God himself who *created* her in the highest state of perfection.

The *reverence* we show her because of her exalted role in the divine plan is called *hyperdulia*. We honor her not for what she is herself but because she is wholly God's. We *love* her because we love God.

From Mary, God receives the highest *glory* a creature can possibly give him. She is so perfect and she is bound so closely to the *Holy Spirit* that she is called his *Spouse*. As *Spouse of the Holy Spirit*, she is raised above all created perfection and accomplishes in all things the *will* of the Spirit who dwells in her from the instant of her *conception*.

In responding to the Angel, Mary calls herself the *handmaid* of the Lord. A handmaid is one who abandons her right to decide for herself and willingly allows herself to be commanded by the Spirit.

Her *humility* is of *obedience* and is the *human* basis of her complete openness to the will and grace of God.

Fullness of time 484, 702

The fullness of time refers to that point in the *chronology* of *temporal* events when a *salvific* act preordained by God takes place, for example, the *Annunciation*, the Nativity of *Christ*, the Last Day, etc.

Examples in *Scripture* include, 'But when the fullness of time was come, God sent forth his Son, made of a woman, under the *law*' (Gal 4:4), and elsewhere, 'That in the dispensation of the fullness of times, he might gather in one all things in Christ, both which are in *heaven*, and which are on earth; even in him' (Eph 1:10).

Fundamental

Fundamental means forming a foundation or the basic ground or root upon which a thing depends. See Refusing obedience to civil authority 2242.

Fundamentalism

Fundamentalism is the name given to the form of *Protestantism* that regards Holy *Scripture* as the complete, sufficient, and final *authority* on *faith*. It holds that *Scripture* is to be interpreted literally and that any *doctrine* not explicitly contained in it is to be excluded from belief. See Charismatic gifts 768.

G

Gallican Rite

Gallican Rite refers to the liturgy of ancient Gaul in particular, and to the family of non-Roman *rites* of the Western Church in general, used during the first millennium of Church history. Toward the end of the first millennium, the Gallican Rite was supplanted by the *Roman Rite*, while at the same time exerting an influence on the latter. The surviving *Mozarabic Rite* bears a strong resemblance to the ancient Gallican Rite. See Latin Rite.

Games of chance 2413

A game of chance is any game in which a wager (bet) is placed on the unpredictable outcome of some act or series of acts in which one takes some risk in hope of gaining some advantage.

When one participates without placing a wager and where simply winning is the reward, it is not gambling because it is done for entertainment alone and no risk of loss is really taken.

Typical games of chance include card games, dice, roulette, lotteries, racing, bookmaking, slot machines, etc.

The general term for such activity is gambling.

Games of chance are not in themselves contrary to *justice* but can become *morally* objectionable when they deprive someone of what is necessary to provide for his needs or the needs of others.

Unfair wagers and cheating at games constitute *grave* matter unless the damage inflicted is so slight that the one who suffers cannot reasonably consider it significant.

Garden of Eden

In Gen 2:15–16, we learn that God put the man whom he *created* in a *Garden of Paradise*. The garden is a symbol of *divine blessings*, called 'Eden,' the *Hebrew* word for pleasure or delight.

The *Septuagint* uses the Greek 'paradeisos,' to translate the Hebrew word 'pardes' the classical word for garden, or 'eden,' meaning pleasure. It became understood as a paradise or pleasure park, or more simply, the Garden of Eden. It is depicted as a place of delight, happiness, *blessedness*, and close intimacy with God.

The teaching of the Church regarding details of the state

of man in Paradise before the *fall*, focuses on his *original justice*, or *holiness*, and the *preternatural gifts* of *infused knowledge, integrity, immortality*, and *impassibility*. These preternatural gifts were above and in addition to the powers he enjoyed as part of *human nature* but not beyond those of his *created* nature, so they were not *supernatural* in character.

Attempts to locate Eden geographically have focused on the mention of four rivers: Phison, Gehon, Tigris, and Euphrates (Gen 2:10–14). Two of these rivers may refer to the Euphrates and the Tigris which still exist. The other two, Phison and Gehon, are more difficult to locate with certainty. It is possible that these rivers were named as *metaphors*, suggesting the great size of Eden by the territory between them. The general consensus is that the Garden of Eden was located east of Palestine, perhaps in northern Mesopotamia, but its precise location remains uncertain.

This garden of pleasure into which God placed man was dominated by two trees, the *tree of life* and the *tree of knowledge of good and evil*. The expression 'tree of life' was a common ancient symbol for immortality, according to the Jerome Commentary (JC. 2:8–9). In the *Douay-Rheims Bible*, the footnotes in reference to Gen 2:9 explain that the tree of life was so called because, by eating of its fruit, man would be preserved in a constant state of health, vigor, and strength and would not have died at all. The tree of life is said to typify the Cross, whose fruit is the *Eucharist*, the Bread of Life, or the *Body of Christ* given for us and the Blood he shed for us.

Regarding the tree of knowledge, the same commentary adds that the *devil* falsely *attributed* to it the power of imparting a superior kind of *knowledge* beyond that which God was pleased to give. Another interpretation holds that the tree of knowledge refers to the substitution of personal desire for the *law* of God as the criterion for discerning the difference between *moral* good and evil. Adam and Eve both chose to *sin* most grievously because they preferred their own *judgment* to God's and so pretended to be equal to God. When the serpent told Eve that she would not die because of disobedience, he was lying because, in fact, they would and did die as God had told them.

The *Semites* understood the word 'know' means to *experience*. By encompassing a polarity, to know good and evil signifies total knowledge and the totality of experience. The word evil need not necessarily be used in a *moral* sense because deprivation of a required *good*, such as sight, is *evil* but is not necessarily *immoral*. In the context, however, of the positive commandment given to our first parents, it would seem more probable that the totality here is that of moral experience. See Impassibility. Also see Original sin 389. Also see Preternatural gift.

Garden of Paradise

Garden of Paradise is another name for the *Garden of Eden*. See Garden of Eden.

Gehenna 1034

Gehenna is the name of a place near Jerusalem where, according to Jer 19:5, etc., children were burnt in sacrifice to Baal or Molech. It is used, figuratively, to denote *hell*, the place of future torment.

General absolution 1483

General absolution refers to the practice of giving *sacramental absolution* to a number of *persons* simultaneously without their having made previous individual *confessions*. It is used in cases of extreme need, such as immediate danger of death without sufficient time for a *priest* or priests to hear each *penitent's* confession.

Grave necessity can also exist when, given the number of penitents, there are not enough confessors to hear individual confessions

in a reasonable time so that penitents, through no fault of their own, would be deprived of *sacramental grace* or *Holy Communion* for a long time (cf. Canon 961, § 1, n. 2). It is up to the diocesan *Bishop* to determine whether such a condition actually constitutes grave necessity (Canon 961, § 2).

In the case of *general confession*, for the absolution to be *valid*, the penitent must have the intention of individually confessing each and all of his unconfessed grave sins when it becomes possible.

General confession

Neither the general confession of *sin* made by the *faithful* at the beginning of Mass, I confess (*Confiteor*), nor the Lord Have Mercy (*Kyrie Eleison*) is sacramental in nature. Their purpose is to dispose the heart to *repentance* for sin and to foster the proper disposition to receive the *graces* of the *Mass*.

General confession may refer to a *private confession* in which the penitent confesses so far as can be remembered all past sins. This is often made before entering a new *state of life*, such as *marriage* or *religious life*.

General examination of conscience

A general examination of conscience is a review of one's relation to God and neighbor as contained in the *Ten Commandments* and the *precepts of the Church* and the practice of various *virtues* associated with growth in *holiness* expressed in the *Beatitudes*. See Examination of conscience 1454.

General judgment

The general judgment refers to the *soul*'s final encounter with *Christ* at his *second coming*. At this time, the *resurrected* body and the *soul* will share in the reward or punishment of the whole *person*, and the *righteousness* of God's way will be made manifest and *vindicated* before all *creation*. It is also called the *last judgment*. See Particular judgment 1022.

Generalate

A generalate is the administrative headquarters of a *religious institute*. See Motherhouse. Priory.

Generation (blood line)

Generation refers to a stage or *degree* in the succession of natural descent. Father, son, and grandson represent three generations.

The number assigned to the generation of an individual who descends from a common ancestor is referred to as a *degree of blood relationship*. See Consanguinity. Also see Diriment impediment; Nullity of marriage 1629.

Generation (trinitarian procession)

In the *theology* of the Holy *Trinity*, the three *Persons* are distinct from one another by relations based on their procession. The *procession* of the Son from the Father is called generation. The procession of the *Holy Spirit* from the Father and the Son is called *spiration*. The Father does not proceed because he is the non-originated origin of the processions, that is, he is the First Person since 'first' has nothing prior to it.

The relation by which the Father is distinguished from the Son and then from the Holy Spirit is established by the procession of the Son, who is *begotten* by him, and by the procession of the Holy Spirit from him and the Son, who is 'spirated' by both. See Trinity, Holy 232.

Generic/Generically

Generic means inclusive or general, in reference to a whole class or group. See Troparia 1177.

Generosity

Generosity is the *magnanimous* nobility of *mind* that makes one willing to give and share unselfishly with others. See Fruits of the Spirit 1832.

Genes

Genes are the part of the *nucleus* of each living cell that governs *reproduction*. Genes determine body build, eye color, and many other characteristics including health. The nucleus is a central mass of *protoplasm* present in most animal and plant cells, which contains most of the *hereditary factors* necessary for such functions as growth and reproduction. See Chromosomic inheritance. Also see Genetic inheritance 2275.

Genesis

Genesis is the first book of the *Old Testament*. The word genesis comes from the Greek word 'genesis,' meaning beginning.

Genesis is also the first book of the *Pentateuch*, a name taken from the Greek 'penta-teuchos,' meaning book of five volumes. The *Jews* refer to these books as the *Torah*, the *Law of Moses*, or *Mosaic Law*.

Genetic inheritance 2275

Genetics is the part of biology that deals with the *heredity* and variation of the characteristics in plants and animals transmitted to offspring by genes in generation.

Genes are the units of heredity recognized as controlling *agents* in the expression of single characteristics of a *species*. These are passed down to offspring by the process of *fertilization*.

Genes occur at specific points on chromosomes, which are microscopic rod-shaped bodies into which the chromatin of a cell nucleus separates during the process of mitosis, or cell division. They carry the hereditary characteristics of the species. The totality of such transmitted characteristics is referred to as chromosomic or genetic inheritance. See Chromosome 2275.

Genocide 2313

Genocide is the deliberate and systematic extermination of an ethnic or national group to achieve a political end. The *Second Vatican Council* condemned genocide when it declared that 'offenses against life itself, such as murder, genocide, *abortion*, *euthanasia*, and willful *suicide*' (*Gaudium et Spes*, n. 27), are offenses against *human dignity* and are criminal *acts*.

Gentile/Gentiles

Gentile is the term that the *Israelites* use to refer to anyone who is not a *Jew*. The word comes from 'goyim' in *Hebrew*, which was used to designate one who is not of the chosen people, either out of contempt and dislike or as a warning. Since the time of St. Paul, it has been used by *Christians* to designate those who are neither Jew nor Christian. The *Bible* uses the word gentile for any *person* who is not *Jewish*. See Israelitica dignitas 528.

Genuflect 1378

The word genuflect is composed of the two Latin words

'genu,' meaning knee, and 'flectere,' meaning to bend, and it means to bend the knee.

In making a genuflection, one bends the right knee to touch the ground while the body remains erect. The *Sign of the Cross* is not made when genuflecting since the gesture is already one of profound *reverence*. Genuflection and the profound bow are considered as the two normal *ceremonial* reverences.

After *Vatican II*, in the Western Church, the profound bow may now replace genuflection.

It is customary to genuflect before the *Blessed Sacrament* before entering a pew in *church* if the *tabernacle* is visible. The bow is preferred in the *Eastern Churches*.

All genuflect when passing an *altar* at which the *Blessed Sacrament* is reserved, when a *relic* of the True Cross is exposed, and to the unveiled Cross on *Good Friday*. A genuflection was formerly made at the words 'and was made flesh' in the *Creed*. A bow has become the practice since *Vatican II* except on *Christmas* and on the *Solemnity* of the *Annunciation* (March 25), when a genuflection is still required. When Mass is *celebrated* according to the *Extraordinary Form*, a genuflection is still required.

A *double genuflection* consists of kneeling on both knees, bowing the head, and rising. It is made only before the Blessed Sacrament when it is exposed.

Gift of tongues

See Tongues, gift of. Also see Glossolalia.

Gifts of the Holy Spirit or Holy Ghost 1831

The gifts of the Holy Spirit are permanent dispositions that make *man docile* in following the promptings of the *Holy Spirit*. The gifts are further perfections of the *infused theological* and *moral virtues,* which instill in the *soul* a readiness to respond to *divine* guidance.

"The seven gifts of the Holy Spirit are *wisdom, understanding, counsel, knowledge, fortitude, piety,* and *fear of the Lord*" (CCC 1831).

Wisdom, understanding, counsel, and knowledge are *habits of the intellect.* Fortitude, piety, and fear of the Lord are *habits of the will.*

The gifts of the Holy Spirit complete and perfect the *virtues* of those who receive them and render them docile in readily following divine *inspirations*. By these seven gifts, the *intellect* and *will* are disposed to receive and act with the light and assistance of the Holy Spirit.

The gifts of the Holy Spirit are distinguished from *actual grace* and the *theological* and *moral* virtues that dispose the intellect and will to acts recommended by reason. The virtues complete and perfect the gifts, which reside in the soul together with habitual grace as long as the soul is in the state of *sanctifying grace*.

Globalization

Globalization refers to a concentration of production or distribution of goods in a few companies, enabling them to dominate particular commercial sectors. The problem with such a process is that it eliminates smaller production units or businesses and, thus, eliminates competition and destroys opportunities for individual economic initiative. See Capitalism 2425.

Gloria

Gloria is used in reference to the *major doxology* recited in the *Mass*. It begins with the words 'Glory to God in the highest,' hence it is called the Gloria. See Gloria in Excelsis Deo. Also see Appendix of Prayers - Prayers recited at Mass, Gloria.

Gloria in excelsis Deo

'Gloria in excelsis Deo' were the words the *herald angels* used to announce the birth of *Christ*. They are used to open what is called the *major doxology*, a *hymn* of praise to the *Persons* of the *Trinity*. Originally, the hymn was used only at the *Midnight Mass* on *Christmas*, but today it is used at all *Sunday* Masses outside of *Advent* and *Lent*

and *Masses for the Dead*, and at daily Masses only as prescribed for *solemnities* and *feasts* of the *saints* or special occasions.

This *doxology* is not used in *Eastern liturgies*, but, on Sundays and major feasts, the *Byzantine Church* includes an expanded form of it in the *Divine Office* for Orthros, which corresponds to *Matins* and *Lauds* in the *Latin Church*. See Te Deum 168. Also see Doxology 2641.

Glorification

Glorification refers to the state of the *resurrected body* at the *last judgment*. The Church teaches that the resurrected body is identified with the body man possessed while on earth, though it is not necessary to believe that the same particles of matter possessed at the moment of death will be reassembled for the purpose. The *soul* is not resurrected because it never dies and has no parts to reassemble; nevertheless the soul of man needs the body in order to be a *person*, or *rational animal*. See Resurrection from the dead 992.

Glorified body

Glorified body refers to the *resurrection* and *reanimation* of the bodies of the dead who are saved but not to those of the lost after the last *judgment*. The resurrected body, which will be rejoined to the *soul*, will be a true body having the same identity as the earthly body but only for the just in a glorified state, *immortal* and *incorruptible*.

St. Thomas *attributes* to the glorified body the attributes or qualities of *impassibility*, *clarity*, *agility*, and *subtlety*. Impassibility is freedom from suffering, defect, and *corruption*. Clarity is brilliance, luster, splendor, light, and glory. Agility is the ability of the body to pass from place to place with great speed and to be a perfect instrument of the soul. Subtlety is the complete *subjugation* of the body to the soul by its assuming a *spiritual character* without ceasing to be a body. This is sometimes referred to as a *spiritual body*. The risen body will remain in a state of youth.

The lost will also rise not to be glorified but to suffer eternally in incorruptible bodies. See Resurrection from the dead 992. Also see Resurrected body; Glory 293; Fire of hell.

Glorious mysteries of the Rosary

Meditation on a *mystery* of the *faith* drawn from the *Gospels* accompanies the recitation of each decade of the *Rosary*. These meditations are known as the mysteries of the Rosary.

The mysteries of the Rosary are collected into groups of related scriptural events referred to as the Joyful, Sorrowful, Glorious, and Luminous mysteries. The recitation of five decades and meditation on a set of mysteries ends with the prayer Hail Holy Queen.

The Glorious mysteries, used on *Sundays* and Wednesdays, are the Resurrection (Mt 28:1–10; Lk 24:1–12), The Ascension (Mt 28:16–20; Lk 24:44–53), The descent of the Holy Spirit (Jn 14:15–21; Acts 2:1–11), The Assumption (Jn 11:17–27; Rev 21:1–6), and The Coronation of Mary (Mt 5:1–12; Pet 3:10). See Rosary 971, 2678, 2708.

Glory 293

Glory is the English translation of the *Jewish* word 'kabod.' 'Kabod' means highly significant or impressive. It was used to express the ineffable awesomeness of God in the *Old Testament*. 'Kabod' was translated as 'doxa' in Greek.

St. Augustine defines glory as the outstanding *knowledge* of a *person's* goodness, which elicits praise and admiration for that person. St. Thomas, using this definition, distinguishes between formal glory and objective glory. Objective glory refers to the fundamental goodness of the person, which gives rise to a need to *praise* his excellence. The knowledge of goodness itself, which is the basis of glory, is called formal glory.

Formal glory can only be rendered by *intelligent* creatures. Because the remainder of creation cannot know God's goodness, which is required for formal glory, it can only contribute to God's objective glory by manifesting God's goodness.

God has perfect *knowledge* of his goodness and has, therefore, perfect glory. What is referred to as the 'glory of the blessed' is their participation in the divine glory. For this reason, the intellect of the blessed must be perfected by a *supernatural habit* or *grace*, which enables them to see and know God *intuitively*. This grace is called the 'Light of Glory' or *'lumen gloriae.'* To look upon God face to face requires a supernatural participation in the knowledge of *divine good* or objective glory.

The objective glory that man renders to God in *heaven* is perfect because it arises from the *supernatural* knowledge granted him by the grace of the *lumen gloriae.*

In the Book of *Exodus*, the glory of God went before the *Israelites* in the desert as a light and appeared to them on the mountaintop as a burning fire. It was thought of as God's abiding presence in the *Ark of the Covenant* and as a fiery presence in the vision that is recorded in chapter six of Isaiah.

In the New Testament, God's glory centers on Christ by revealing his *divinity. Jesus'* glory is explicitly declared at his birth, at the *Transfigura-*

tion, and in the predictions of his *second coming* in glory.

All humanity is called to share in the glory of the *Resurrection* by being physically transformed with *glorified bodies*. We do not know how the physical body will be glorified, how perishable *nature* will put on the imperishable, or how mortal nature puts on *immortality*.

The bodies of the *reprobate* will also rise immortal and incorruptible. Just as the body partakes in the *nature* of the *human person*, so it shall share in its eternal reward or punishment. It is the whole person who is punished or rewarded at the time of *judgment*.

Glory be to the Father

Glory be to the Father is the name for the *prayer*, 'Glory be to the Father, and to the Son, and to the *Holy Spirit*. As it was in the beginning, is now, and ever shall be, world without end. *Amen.'* It is referred to as the *minor doxology*. It is one of the most used prayers and is frequently added at the end of other prayers. See Rosary. See Appendix of prayers, Glory be to the Father; Minor doxology.

Glossolalia

Glossolalia is another name for the *gift of tongues*. See Tongues, Gift of. Also see Charisms.

Gluttony 1866

Gluttony, sometimes called *intemperance*, is the inordinate *appetite* for food, drink, rest, and recreation. From gluttony proceed drunkenness, loquacity, and other excesses. The *evil* of gluttony rests in the offense it causes against a *person's* own *dignity*. When it takes the form of an *addiction* it not only degrades a person but also leads to greater evils.

Gluttony is a *capital sin*. It is opposed to the *virtues* of *abstinence, temperance, prudence,* and *self-respect*. Gluttony can be overcome by *prayer, fasting,* the exercise of temperance in all things, and frequent reception of the *sacraments*.

Gnosticism 285

Gnosticism is the name given to a group of *heretical* teachings that flourished in the first three centuries. The common element of their teaching was that *salvation* is special knowledge and is possessed by only a few initiated *persons*. Gnosticism was of pre-*Christian* origin and included a corrupted mixture of Egyptian, Indian, and Judaic religions. *Gnostics* indulged in *magic* and even adopted some elements of Christianity. They taught that matter is a *corruption* of the *divine*, that *Christ* is only an *intermediary* between God and matter, and that existence is *evil* and must

be escaped through *knowledge*.

Marcion (d.c. 160 A.D.) and Valentinius (d. 160 A.D.) were famous *gnostics*, and St. Irenaeus was their greatest opponent. Gnosticism left an enduring mark on Church history. In his defense against this *heresy*, St. Irenaeus (c. 130–200 A.D.) wrote the earliest known treatise on Catholic *dogma*. In it, he formulated with greater precision and stated in greater fullness the Church's *doctrine* on the *Incarnation*, the *sacraments*, and the *authority* of the teaching of the Church.

Gnostics

Gnostics refers to those who adhere to some form of *gnosticism*. See Gnosticism 285.

Godchild

A godchild is a *person* who, when he receives the *sacrament* of *Baptism*, enters into a spiritual relationship with another person who is known as his *sponsor*. The latter assists at the administration of Baptism of the former and helps him to fulfill his duties as a member of the baptized *faithful*. See Godfather/Godmother/Godparents 1255.

Godfather/godmother/godparents 1255

A godfather or godmother (or godparent) is one who fulfills the role of *sponsor* of one who receives the *sacrament* of

Baptism. At least one *person* must be assigned as *sponsor*; *Canon Law* allows for the possibility of two sponsors, one male and one female.

In the case of infant Baptism, the sponsor(s) make the *profession* of the *Christian faith* on behalf of the person baptized. They guarantee his or her *religious* education and help the one baptized to lead a *Christian* life and to fulfill the obligations connected with it. See Sponsor 1311. Also see Spiritual relationship.

God's pedagogy 1950

God's pedagogy refers to the fatherly instruction and guidance of God. God instructs and guides man by prescribing the rules of conduct that lead him to his promised beatitude and proscribing (forbidding) the ways of *evil*, which turn him away from God and his *love.*

Golden rule 1970

The golden rule refers to the requirement of the *Law of the Gospel* that disciples make a decisive choice between two ways, the way to *heaven* or the way to *perdition*, by putting into practice the words of the Lord, 'Whatever you wish that men would do to you, do so to them: this is the Law and the *prophets*' (Mt 7:12). This is frequently expressed as, 'Do unto others as you would have them do unto you.'

Good

In general, a good is anything that is suitable of fitting for someone or something. Philosophically, it is that which all things tend toward or desire. The good is whatever is desirable and the object of *natural* or *supernatural* tendencies or *appetencies.* See Intellectual appetite.

Good Catholic

A good Catholic is one who adheres to and practices the *Catholic faith* to the best of his ability. See Catholic 830.

Good Friday

Good Friday is the Friday of *Holy Week*, which *commemorates* the death of *Christ* on the Cross. It is the only day of the year on which no *Mass* is said. The day is marked by special services: the reading of the *Passion*, the *Veneration* of the Cross, and a communion service using hosts *consecrated* the day before. See Dry Mass. Also see Mass 1332.

Goodness of being

Goodness is an *attribute* of *being.* Every positive *reality* is suitable or fitting for someone or something and is, in some way, perfect because *actuality* or existence itself is a kind of *perfection.* The presence of perfection in being gives rise to the attribute of *beauty.* See Transcendental attributes of being.

Gospel

Gospel refers to the four books of the *New Testament* written by Matthew, Mark, Luke, and John, which narrate the life and teachings of *Jesus Christ*. These are the only books about the life of Christ included in the *Canon of Scripture* but the term also applies to other records of the acts and words of Jesus contained in the New Testament. The entire Canon of Scripture is included in the command to the *Apostles* to preach the Gospel.

The Gospels of Matthew, Mark, and Luke are called the *synoptic Gospels* because they follow the same general plan and offer the same comprehensive view of the life and teachings of Jesus.

The Gospel of St. John is not classed as a synoptic Gospel because it was written to record special proofs of the *divinity* of Christ. See Ambo 1184.

Gossip

Gossip refers to idle chatter about others. The *morality* of gossip is related to the amount of a *person's* time it consumes and the nature of the content. It can reflect a failure in *justice* if it is done on an employer's time or a failure in *charity* when it causes damage to another's reputation. See Calumny 2477.

Governing office 894

An *office* is a service or *duty* that is a responsibility or function in the Church. The *hierarchy* of the Church consists of three offices, called the *teaching office*, the sanctifying office, and the governing office.

The primary governing office is exercised by *bishops*, who are *vicars* and *legates* of *Christ* and who govern their Churches by their *counsels*, by their *exhortations*, by their example, and by the *authority* and *sacred* power conferred on them by the Church. They exercise their power to govern personally in the name of Christ under the control of the supreme *authority* of the Church.

Bishops govern in their own right by virtue of their *episcopal consecration*. They are not vicars of the *Pope*, but his authority serves to confirm and defend their power. For this reason, the authority of the Bishop must be exercised in communion with and under the guidance of the Pope, who is responsible for the entire Church as *Vicar of Christ*. See Magisterium.

Grace 35, 54, 153, 1996, 2008

Grace is the favor (the free and undeserved help) that God gives to each *person* to freely respond to his call to become his child, his adopted son, and a partaker of the *divine nature* and *eternal* life.

Grace is a *supernatural* gift of God that enlightens the *mind* and assists the *will*. In a broader sense not restricted to gifts given as a means of *salvation*, grace is everything *man* receives from God: his existence, his talents, and all the goods of life that he enjoys.

Man has been *created* to see God face to face and is called to eternal life, but this is entirely beyond *human* power; therefore, God, in his *infinite* love, freely gives man the necessary means by which he can secure his end.

This necessary means is a supernatural grace and is beyond the power of *natural* man. The gift of supernatural grace elevates man to the supernatural order and is distinguished from gifts of the purely *natural order*.

Some graces are internal, affecting the *understanding* and the will. When they inhere in the *soul* as a permanent quality, they are called *habitual grace*, or *sanctifying grace*.

Habitual or sanctifying grace which inheres permanently in the *substance* of the soul, renews it by the fact of its presence. By it, men become *partakers of the divine nature*, are made objects of God's special *love*, and become heirs of *heaven*, coheirs with Christ, and sons of God.

Sanctifying grace in the soul can only be lost by the commission of *mortal sin*. Only *repentance* at the *instigation* of God by *actual grace* can restore it. For *Catholics*, this restoration implies reception of the *sacrament of Reconciliation*.

There are other graces that move or assist the *soul* at certain times to acts of *supernatural virtue*. These are called *actual graces*. Actual grace is subdivided into grace of operation, or *concomitant grace*, which excites the mind to action, and *grace of cooperation*, which assists in an operation already begun. Actual graces are passing movements of the soul by God.

Graces that are given to promote the *spiritual* good of others are called *charisms* or, in Latin, 'gratiae gratis datae,' meaning grace given *gratuitously*. These are named in 1 Cor 12:8–11 as *wisdom, knowledge, faith, healing, mighty deeds, prophecy, discernment, varieties of tongues*, and *interpretation of tongues*.

Other graces that are given for the recipient himself with the direct object of bringing him nearer to God by establishing and strengthening divine friendship, such as actual, habitual, or sanctifying grace, are called 'gratiae gratum facientes,' meaning graces that make man pleasing to God.

The Church teaches that grace is absolutely necessary for salvation and that, without the intermediary assistance and *inspiration* of the *Holy*

Spirit, man cannot believe, *hope,* love, or repent in order to receive the grace of *justification*. In no case can man *merit* the first grace by natural good works because it is always a free gift of God.

According to the *Council of Orange,* the very wish to rise from *sin* comes as a grace from God. So great is the weakness left by *original sin* that, before he is healed by Christ, man is necessarily turned away from his last end. Even a person in the *state of grace* needs the impulse of actual grace in order to think a *good* thought or perform a good deed.

Prevenient grace is grace that comes before, from the Latin 'pre' and 'venire,' meaning to come before. It refers to the actual grace that must precede sanctifying grace at the beginning of *justification*. It is the grace that first moves the soul to recognize God as its true good and *ultimate end* and that moves it to those acts of natural *virtue* that prepare it for the gift of sanctifying grace. Prevenient grace can be accepted or rejected. If it is rejected, that rejection is a human failure, but, if it is accepted, the grace accepted is still a divine and gratuitous gift. *Scripture* teaches that even the beginning of salvation is an entirely free gift of God and is in no way a human attainment. St. Augustine (354–430 A.D.) formulated this doctrine in opposition to *Pelagianism* (255–425 A.D.).

The world of grace, like the world of *nature,* must be sustained at each instant by the hand of God.

Grace before meals

Grace before meals refers to *prayers* recited before eating as a means of expressing thanks for God's gifts. See Appendix of prayers - Grace before meals.

Grace of cooperation/cooperating grace

Grace of cooperation is the form of *actual grace* that assists one in an operation that is already begun and accompanies every *supernatural* act. It may also be called *subsequent, assisting,* or *concomitant grace* because it is associated with the use of human *free will* in carrying out the *will of God.* See Grace 153.

Grace of original holiness 399

The grace of original holiness is the gift of God by which man was originally *created* in a state of being filled with *spiritual perfection, purity, sanctity,* and friendship with God. This state is also referred to as the state of *original justice.*

Graces of state 2004

Graces of state are special graces that accompany the exercise of the responsibilities of individuals living the *Chris-*

tian life, such as in *marriage*, or in serving a ministerial role in the Church in the *priesthood*.

Gratitude 2215

Gratitude is a *moral virtue* related to *justice* that disposes one to an awareness of kindness received together with a warm sense of appreciation and goodwill toward the benefactor and a desire to do something in return.

Gratuitous

Gratuitous means given without charge, freely, without *obligation*, without *cause*, or without justification. See Deifying or sanctifying grace 1999.

Gratum facientes

'Gratum facientes' is a Latin phrase that means to make pleasing or acceptable. It refers to *graces*, which are given by God with the direct object of bringing the receiver nearer to God and making him pleasing to God. See Grace 153.

Grave/Gravely disordered

Grave comes from the Latin word 'gravis,' meaning heavy. When something is gravely serious, it requires serious thought because it has important *consequences*. Things that are gravely disordered represent an important threat or danger to *morality*. Gravely disordered *acts* are *mortal sins* and destroy *sanctifying grace*

in the *soul*. See Birth control. Also see Grave sin.

Grave matter 1858

Grave matter refers to something that is serious and important in its nature. Gravity can be viewed either *extrinsically* or *intrinsically*.

Matter is judged extrinsically as serious when it is declared to be seriously contrary to *natural law* or *divine law* by *Scripture, Tradition*, or even human law.

It is judged intrinsically as serious when the object in itself is seriously contrary to God and his perfections or to the order that God intended to flourish among men, the *common good*, which we must preserve between our neighbors and ourselves.

Grave obligation 2072

A grave *obligation* is a *duty* that is weighty, or serious and important, and requires careful attention. The *Ten Commandments*, in their basic content, are binding under *grave* obligation.

A grave obligation is fundamentally *immutable*, that is, unchangeable. A negative obligation obliges always and everywhere. It is expressed as a prohibition, such as, 'Thou shalt not kill.' Positive obligations bind everywhere but not always, for example, the positive commands 'Keep holy the Sabbath day' or 'Honor thy father and thy mother.'

Grave sin

Grave sin refers to *mortal* sin, which destroys *sanctifying grace* in the heart of man and turns him away from God and his ultimate *beatitude*. For *Catholics*, sanctifying grace can only be restored by the *sacrament of Confession* or an act of *perfect contrition* accompanied by a resolve to receive the sacrament of Confession as soon as possible. See Sin 386. Also see Mortal sin 1855.

Graven image 2129

A graven image is a sculptured or hewn figure or any representation made by *man* for purposes of *worship* as a god. Because such images of animals or *human* likenesses were used in *pagan religions* as objects of worship, fashioning them was forbidden by God in *Deuteronomy*. Nevertheless, God permitted the making of images that pointed symbolically toward *salvation* by the *Incarnate Word*, as was the case with the *bronze serpent* and the *cherubim* on the *Ark of the Covenant*.

Great Lent

In the *Eastern Rites*, the *Lenten Season* is called the Great Lent to contrast it with the lesser rigor of *penitential* practice observed during *Advent*. In the *Byzantine Rite*, during *Lent*, a severe fast is observed. Meat, *lacticinia*, eggs, fish, oil, and wine are forbidden for forty-eight

days. On week days, the *Liturgy of the Presanctified Gifts* may be celebrated, but not the full *Divine Liturgy* (the *Mass*) itself. See Liturgical seasons.

Greed

Greed is the *inordinate* desire to amass limitless earthly goods. Greed is an offense against the *virtues* of *temperance* and moderation and one of the *capital sins*. See Capital sins 1866.

Greek Septuagint 213

The Greek Septuagint is a translation of the *Hebrew Scriptures*, or *Old Testament*, into Greek. It is also referred to as *LXX*, the Roman number 70, because seventy scholars in Alexandria translated it in the third century B.C. It was later adopted by Greek speaking Christians.

The quotations from the Old Testament used in the *New Testament* are taken from the Septuagint translation rather than from the Hebrew.

Gregorian calendar

In the sixteenth century, the Julian calendar *promulgated* by Julius Caesar in 46 B.C. was ten days out of line with the seasons and was causing agricultural and navigational problems. To resolve the problem, Pope Gregory XIII (1572–1585 A.D.) gathered a group of scholars supervised by Aloisius Lilius, who died before completing the project. The

Jesuit mathematician Clavius completed the task and, in 1582 A.D., the *Pope* issued a *papal brief* correcting the system for reckoning or calculating the calendar and removed ten days to correct the error, making the day after October 4, 1582 A.D., to be October 15. The Gregorian calendar is considered to be correct to within one day in 20,000 years.

It was quickly adopted by most of Europe. The Orthodox Churches have not adopted the new calendar and have retained the Julian calendar, which is now thirteen days behind. See Chaldean Church/Rite.

Gregorian chants or melodies

Gregorian chants or melodies refer to the music and words that are the official musical setting of the sung *liturgy* of the *Roman Rite*. Gregorian chant is referred to as Gregorian because it achieved its final stage of development under St. Gregory the Great (590–604 A.D.). It is official because it is the chant provided by *ecclesiastical authority* for all those parts of the liturgy appointed to be sung. See Criteria for singing and music in liturgy 1157. Also see O Antiphons; Advent 524.

Growth in holiness 2227

Holiness denotes union with God. Growth in holiness refers to the development or increase

of *moral holiness* or union with God, which results from performing morally *good acts*.

Sanctifying grace is required for union with God because it is through grace that *man* shares in the *divine life*. Through *grace*, the *virtues* and *gifts of the Holy Spirit* are infused in the *soul* to strengthen and increase holiness in the life of man.

Progress or growth in holiness is made by keeping the Commandments, accepting the *will of God* in all things, doing good works, and practicing virtue in cooperation with God's *grace*.

Guardian

Guardian is a title of certain *religious superiors*. See Superior, religious.

Guardian angel

Guardian angels are *heavenly* spirits (mentioned in Ps 91:11–12, Mt 18:10, and Acts 12:15) assigned to watch over each individual during life. *Belief* in guardian angels has been part of the constant *Tradition* of the Church based on *Scripture* and teachings of the *Fathers of the Church*. It has not been defined as an *article of faith*, but belief in guardian angels is binding as part of the teaching *Magisterium*. The universal Church *celebrates* the *Feast* of the Guardian Angels on October 2. See Prayer 2098, 2559.

H

Habit

A habit is a modification of behavior that is rendered fixed and constant through use. Once acquired, it can become a principle of activity making *acts* easier, more accurate, and more pleasant to produce. Once acquired, habits are difficult to lose. Habits, whether good or bad, are acquired through repetition. They can only be replaced by developing a contrary habit. See Enslavement 2414.

Habit, Religious

The habit of *religious* refers to their distinctive garb. Such garb is prescribed for religious as an outward sign of their religious *consecration* by the *Second Vatican Council*. See Novice.

Habits of the intellect

Wisdom, understanding, counsel, and *knowledge* are considered to be habits of the *intellect.* They complete and perfect the *virtues* of those who receive them and render the intellect docile and ready to obey *divine inspirations.*

By them, the intellect, which is a *faculty* of the *soul*, is disposed to receive and act with the light and assistance of the *Holy Spirit.* See Gifts of the Holy Spirit 1831.

Habits of the will

Fortitude, piety, and *fear of the Lord* are considered to be *habits* of the *will.* They complete and *perfect* the *virtues* of those who receive them and render the will docile and ready to obey *divine inspirations.* By them, the will is disposed to receive and act with the light and assistance of the *Holy Spirit.* See Gifts of the Holy Spirit 1831.

Habitual

Habitual describes behavior that has been acquired by continual repetition. Such behavior becomes fixed and customary and is repeated with ease and performed without need for direct attention.

Natural virtues are virtues that can be acquired through practice and become habits of doing good. See Natural virtues. Also see Habits of the will.

Habitual grace 2000

See Sanctifying Grace 1999, 2000.

Habitual intention

A habitual intention is an

intention that a *person* has made that no longer exerts a positive influence on his acts but has never been *rescinded.* It remains, as it were, dormant in the *soul* and, in the proper circumstances, can easily be reactivated. See Intentional Homicide 2268; Also see Actual intention; Virtual intention.

Hades 633

Hades is the Greek name for the god of the underworld. In later times, it came to refer to his kingdom, abode, or house. This name for the *nether world* is used in the *Septuagint* and *New Testament* Greek *Bibles*, where it is used to translate the *Hebrew* word *scheol*, the abode of the dead or departed spirits. Today, it is sometimes used in reference to *hell*, but Hades does not really refer to the permanent place of damnation, or hell, as we understand it.

Hagiographical 21

Hagiographical is the adjectival form of hagiography. It comes from the Greek 'hagiographia,' meaning holy writing. In a general way, it refers to anything pertaining to writings about holy topics or biographies of *saints*, such as *martyrologies*, and legends of holy people.

The third and final part of the *Hebrew Scriptures* is called the *Hagiographic Books of the Hebrew Scriptures*. They are holy writings that were not included in the *law* or *prophets*.

Hail Holy Queen

The Hail Holy Queen is the English translation of the *Salve Regina*. It is one of the oldest *Marian antiphons* in Western Christianity and has been used from early time in the *Divine Office*. The author is probably Hermannus Contractus (d. 1054 A.D.) After *Compline*, in Dominican usage, it is accompanied by a procession. In the *Carmelite Rite*, it is recited at the *altar* steps before the last *Gospel*, and it is recited before the *blessing* in the *Mozarabic Rite*. See Dominican Rite; Appendix of prayers.

Hail Mary

The Hail Mary is a familiar prayer addressed to the *Blessed Virgin*. It is called the 'Angelical Salutation' because it contains the words of the *Angel* Gabriel at the *Annunciation*. It is called the 'Hail Mary' because of the first words, and it is called the 'Ave' because of the first word in Latin.

It consists of three parts: a) Hail *Mary*, full of *grace*, the *Lord* is with thee (Lk 1:28); b) Blessed art thou amongst women, and blessed is the fruit of thy womb, *Jesus* (Lk 1:42); c) Holy Mary, *Mother of God*, pray for us sinners now and at the hour of our death. The first two parts are *scriptural*, and the third is added by the Church. The first two parts were in use during the twelfth century. The present form was fixed in 1568 A.D.

The Hail Mary is used in many *devotions* and is a major part of the *Rosary*. See Rosary. Also see Appendix of prayers.

Hair shirt

A hair shirt is a garment woven of goat's hair or other hair that is worn next to the skin as *mortification*. It may take the form of a girdle, vest, or waistcoat. Another name for hair shirt is *cilicium*.

It is in common use by *religious* men and women but is not restricted to them. For the *Carthusians* and the *Discalced Carmelites*, its use is prescribed by their *rule*. See Carthusians; Cilicium.

Hallowed 2807

Hallowed means made *holy*. Only God can make things *holy*, but, with the first petition of the *Our Father*, we enter into the innermost mystery of his Godhead and the drama of *salvation*. We ask the Father that his name be made holy by drawing us into his plan of loving kindness and making us holy and blameless before him. See Appendix of prayers - Our Father.

Handmaid of theology/faith

Philosophy is referred to as the handmaid of *theology* or *faith* because it is in the ser-

vice of theology and faith in three ways.

First, it prepares the groundwork for understanding theology and the concepts of faith by explaining such things as the *spiritual* nature of the *soul*, the existence of God, and other *truths* taught by the Church.

Secondly, though it cannot prove *revealed truths*, it can show that they are not contrary to *reason*.

Thirdly, whenever the provinces of philosophy and theology conflict with one another, philosophy must correct its conclusions according to the higher and more certain revealed truth of faith according to the maxim, 'Nothing can be true in philosophy which is false in theology.' This means that, when philosophy rejects the primary truth of *morals* or *religion*, it must be rejected as false. See Scholastic philosophy.

Happiness 1718

Happiness refers to the wellbeing or *blessedness* of a *person*. It *essentially* consists of that state of the *soul* in which man acts in accordance with perfect *virtue*. Perfect happiness is unattainable in this life but can be approximated to the extent that one lives a virtuous life.

Man desires happiness above all things because it is natural to his *intellect*. It leads him to knowledge of the *good* and guides his *will* to *act* in accord with God's plan.

Because happiness consists in possession of the *truth*, which is the good known by *reason*, the ultimate happiness is to *love* God by knowing and seeing him as the supreme *truth* and ultimate good. Perfect happiness consists in the *beatific vision*, the end to which God's love calls every man.

In this life, happiness consists in ordering one's life so as to acquire the habit of lifting up his *mind* and *heart* in *prayer* to God in whom alone he finds perfect happiness.

Harmony/Harmonious

Harmony refers to the combination of parts into an orderly whole. It may refer to the agreement in feelings, actions, ideas, or interests among *persons* in peaceable and friendly relations. It can refer to the *coherence* or consistency between *truths* or within parts of a plan so that one part of the whole does not destroy or contradict the rest.

Harmony also refers to consistency in *reasoning* or the orderly connection of various truths so that they join together to form a coherent whole. See Analogy of faith. Also see Visible bonds of communion 815; Congruent; Collectivism 1885.

Hatred 2303

Hatred refers to a strong dis-like or ill will toward another. Hatred may be directed toward a *person* himself or toward his behavior, attitude, or *evil* qualities.

Hatred directed toward another's wickedness or evil qualities is not necessarily sinful. Incompatibility with another's *character* and dispositions is not hatred because it does not arise from a spirit of ill will. It is not wrong to avoid such a person's company in order to avoid friction, but it becomes sinful if ill will is involved.

Hatred of God 2094

Hatred of God is a sin against *charity* and flows from *pride*. It is *gravely* contrary to *love* of God, whose goodness it denies and whom it presumes to curse as the one who forbids *sin* and inflicts punishment. See Hatred 2303.

Heart 368, 2517, 2563

In *theology*, heart refers to the innermost depths of one's being where one decides for or against God. The heart is the seat of *moral* personality, man's hidden center, which only God can know and fathom fully. The heart is the place of *truth* where one chooses *eternal life* or death, the seat of *conscience*, and a place of decision deeper than one's psychic drives. It is the place of encounter with God and the place of *covenant* with him.

In *Scripture*, the heart is the

source of thoughts, desires, and deeds. Out of the heart come such things as *evil* thoughts, murder, *adultery*, and *fornication*. Change of heart is a transformation of character. The *law* is found written in the heart of man.

Forgiveness of *sin* creates a clean heart. In the *New Testament*, the heart is the seat of divine operations of *grace*, which transform the Christian.

Heaven/Heavenly 1023

Heaven is the *ultimate end* and fulfillment of the deepest human longings, the state of supreme and definitive happiness, and the *eschatalogical joy* that consists in the *beatific vision*.

"Those who die in God's grace and friendship and are perfectly purified live for ever with *Christ*. They are like God, for they 'see him as he is,' face to face" (CCC 1023).

Heaven and earth 326

This phrase refers to everything that exists or to *creation* in its entirety. Earth is the world of men, and *heaven* is both the firmament and, by *analogy*, the world of the *angels* and *saints* and God's own place.

Heavenly kingdom

Heavenly kingdom is another way of saying *Kingdom of God*, or *kingdom of heaven*. See Kingdom of God.

Hebrew

The designation of Hebrew seems to have originated with Abraham and indicated that he belonged to an ethnic group distinct from the Amorites. His land was called the land of the Hebrews, and his God became the God of the Hebrews. The name Hebrew appears to have been applied to the *Israelites* by foreigners (Gen 39:14,17 and 41:12; Ex 1:6–19) or by Israelites when speaking with foreigners. After David founded the monarchy, the term Hebrew disappeared, probably because the monarchy afforded the Hebrews a place among foreigners.

The *canonical* books of the *Old Testament* were written in the Hebrew language for the most part but contain some portions written in Aramaic. The language is not called Hebrew in the Old Testament itself. It was known simply as the language of Canaan or as Judean, the language of Judah. Linguistically, *Biblical* Hebrew is considered as part of the northwest Semitic language group called Canaanite.

The written Hebrew language has twenty-two consonants written right to left using the Phoenician script, which did not make it possible to represent or distinguish all the consonantal sounds of classical Hebrew.

Hebrew is synonymous with *Jew*. See Jews.

Hebrew Bible

The *Jewish* or Hebrew Bible refers to the *Old Testament*. It is included in the *Canon of Scripture* as revealed by God through *revelation*. See Canon of Scripture 120.

Heirs of/to heaven

Through *Baptism*, one is *born from above* and receives the new life of *grace*, which God gives to those who believe in his Son, whom he sent to bestow on men a share in his *divine nature*, making them *adopted sons* of God and heirs of *heaven*.

As adopted sons with *Christ*, the natural Son of the Father, men become objects of God's special *love* and *partakers in the divine nature*, which is the reward or inheritance of heaven. See Children of God 526, 2222.

Hell 633, 1033

Hell is the state of definitive self-exclusion from communion with God and the *blessed*. It is the state or condition prepared for *Satan*, his subjects, and unrepentant sinners.

The punishment of hell consists in the pain of loss of the vision of God as well as sensible pain. It cannot be conceived of as a purely *psychological pain* because it has an *objective* content. Suffering is possible because both the body and *soul* of a *person* share in *damnation* or *glorification*. The bodies of the rep-

robate will rise immortal and incorruptible but not impassible and glorious.

While there is no systematic doctrine of hell in the words of *Christ*, he does refer to it as, 'the furnace of fire where there will be weeping and gnashing of teeth' (Mt 13:50), 'the hell of fire' (Mt 18:9), 'eternal punishment' (Mt 25:46), and 'exterior darkness' (Mt 25:30). The pains of hell can also be inferred from Mt 13:41–42; and Mk 9:43. The Church has defined the *eternity* of hell in its condemnation of Origen (185–254 A.D.), who held that all consigned to hell would ultimately be reconciled to God.

In the *Old Testament*, hell, or *Hades*, refers to the abode of the dead or departed spirits. In the *New Testament*, it refers to the place and state of *eternal punishment*, which consists, primarily, in the deprivation of the enjoyment of the sight of God and, secondarily, in the infliction of positive punishment, often called the *fire of hell*. See Resurrected body.

Henotheism

Henotheism is the *belief* in one god who is chief among several gods. See Theism.

Herald

Historically, a herald was an official who made *proclamations* or carried state messages. Today, it refers to a *person* who comes to announce something that is about to happen. See Major doxology.

Hereditary factors

Hereditary factors refer to those traits that one receives from the *genes* of his parents. Genes are the units of heredity recognized as controlling *agents* in the expression of single characteristics of a *species*. These are passed down to offspring by the process of *fertilization*. See Genetic inheritance 2275. Also see Chromosomic inheritance.

Heredity

See Genetic inheritance.

Heresy 817, 2089

Heresy is the obstinate post-*baptismal* denial or doubt of some *truth* that must be *believed with divine and Catholic faith* (cf. Canon 751).

As a *sin*, heresy is the formal denial or doubt by a baptized *person* of any *revealed truth* of the Catholic faith. As a crime, it consists in the outwardly persistent, stubborn, resolute, and obstinate holding to an opinion opposed to the teaching of the Church.

One guilty of the crime of heresy incurs *excommunication ipso facto*, a *censure* whose remission is reserved to the *local ordinary* or to any *confessor* approved by him.

Over the centuries, certain heresies have been widespread. The earliest heresies centered on the *Trinity*. Major

among these were *Gnosticism, Subordinationism, Montanism,* and *Manicheism.* Heresies dealing with Christ as the *Son of God* included *Arianism, Apollinarianism, Donatism, Pelagianism, Nestorianism, Monophysitism,* and *Iconoclasm.*

Heretic

A heretic is defined as one who, after being baptized, obstinately denies or doubts a *truth* which must be *believed with divine and Catholic faith* (cf. Canon 751).

An unbaptized *person* or one who ceases to practice his *faith* is not a heretic in the strict sense, nor are non-Catholic *Christians* or *Protestants* or persons baptized *Catholic* but raised in another faith. See Anathema sit.

Heretical

Heretical refers to opinions contrary to the teaching of the Church. See Heresy 817.

Hermit 920

A hermit is a *person* who lives the *eremitic life* in separation from the world for the praise of God and the *salvation* of the world.

Hermitage

A hermitage is the residence of a *hermit*, where he has privacy for *prayer*, or a place for *priests* to celebrate *Mass*. In some cases, hermitages are clustered around a *monastery*, where the *hermits* gather for *liturgical* services and community exercises. See Carmelites.

Heterodox

The word heterodox comes from the two Greek words 'hetero,' meaning other or different, and 'doxa,' meaning *belief* or opinion. In English, heterodox means opposed to or departing from correct belief established by *doctrine*. Heterodoxy inclines one to *heresy* and to be unorthodox. See Iconoclastic controversy.

Heterologous artificial insemination and fertilization 2376

Heterologous artificial insemination and fertilization is a *fertilization* technique that entails the dissociation of the roles of husband and wife in *conception* by the intrusion of a *person* other than the couple. It includes such procedures as the donation of sperm or ovum and the use of a *surrogate womb*.

In these cases, conception is performed by doctors by a procedure that fertilizes an egg and produces an *embryo*. It establishes the *dominion* of technology over the origin and destiny of persons. Such a dominion is in itself contrary to the *dignity* and equality that must be common to parents and children.

Such procedures are *gravely immoral*. When the techniques involve only the married couple, such as *artificial insemination*, it is, perhaps, less reprehensible but remains morally unacceptable. Just as it is wrong to prevent conception artificially, it is wrong to cause conception outside of and separate from the *conjugal act*. Only God can decide when and how to create a child.

These procedures are immoral because they dissociate the sexual act from the *procreative* act and bring a child into existence by an act other than that by which two persons freely give themselves to one another in the state of *marriage*.

Hidden life/years of Christ 533

The hidden life of *Christ* refers to the years that he spent at Nazareth subject to Joseph and *Mary*. After the birth narrative, the only events known of his infancy and childhood are his *presentation in the temple*, his flight into Egypt, and the finding in the temple.

The hidden life is contrasted with the *public life of Christ*. Of his thirty-three years on earth, only three, his public life, are revealed in detail in *Scripture*.

Hierarchical 771

Hierarchical means belonging to and grouped according to a regular gradation of orders, classes, or ranks. In *ecclesiastical* usage, hierarchy refers to a body of *persons* or things ranked in grades, orders, or classes, one above another.

Hierarchical in Greek is composed of 'hier,' meaning *sacred*, and 'arche,' meaning order. The Church considers the ranking of those in *Sacred Orders* as sacred because their office constitutes them as sacred persons.

The *Fathers of the Church* and the great *theologians* of the *Middle Ages* also used the term hierarchical in reference to the order of *Persons* in the Blessed *Trinity*, the *choirs of angels*, and the *faithful* as *lay* and *clerical*.

Hierarchical communion 1206

Hierarchical communion refers to the way in which the *faithful* share and participate in the governance of the Church under the *Pope* and *bishops* by their *fidelity* to the common *faith*, which the Church receives from *Christ*.

Hierarchical order

A hierarchy is a body of *persons* ranked in grades, orders, or classes, one above the other. In the Church, hierarchy refers to the *Pope*, *bishops*, *priests*, and *deacons*, who have different degrees of *authority* and function by virtue of the *sacrament* of *Holy Orders*. See Order 1537. Also see Hierarchy 873.

Hierarchy 873

The term hierarchy refers to the organization of the ranks and orders of the *ordained ministers* of the Church into successive grades. See Order 1537.

Hierarchy of creatures 342

Hierarchy of creatures refers to the arrangement of creatures ranked in grades, orders, or classes, one above another because of increased complexity or superior abilities.

Hierarchy of values 1886

The hierarchy of values is the organization or ranking of *values* from the most universal to the most particular and the subordinating of physical and instinctual dimensions to *spiritual* ones.

Because life is absolutely necessary for any other value to have meaning, it must rank highest among *human* values.

Human *social* values must always be concerned with the spiritual and *moral* aspects of life.

High altar

When a *church* has more than one *altar*, the high altar is the one in the center of the *sanctuary*. It is considered to be the *altar of sacrifice*.

Every altar should have a title. The title of the high altar, or altar of sacrifice, is the same as the name of the church.

In the *Byzantine Church*, there is only one altar in a church and it is always on the eastern side of the church, but separate from the wall. In a large church, if there are other altars in side chapels, they are considered to be separate churches. Only one *liturgy* is *celebrated* at an altar in a given day. See Altar 1182.

High Mass

'High Mass' may refer either to a *Solemn Mass* or to a *Sung Mass* in the *Extraordinary Form*, or a *Mass* in the *Ordinary Form* with more than usual *solemnity*, such as the use of *incense* and *sacred* music.

High Priest

Among the *Israelites*, the head of the *Temple* officials was given the title of High Priest. As the most important *person* in the *Jewish* community, he served as the head of their religious *cult*, as president of the *Sanhedrin*, and as chief representative of the people to the ruling officers of foreign powers. He had the sole right to officiate at the *liturgy* of the *Day of Atonement*. On that day, only he could set foot in the *Holy of Holies*. He lived in the *Temple* itself in order to be available for the *liturgical* functions. He was held to greater *ritual purity* or observance of the *law* because of his responsibilities as leader of the *Jews*. See Day of Atonement 578.

Hindering impediment

In the 1917 *Code of Canon Law* those *impediments* that rendered a *marriage* illicit but not *invalid* were called hindering or prohibiting impediments. Hindering impediments were dropped in the 1983 Code of Canon Law.

The impediment prohibiting a *mixed marriage*, however, still requires dispensation by the *local ordinary*. See Impediment.

Hindu/Hinduism

Hinduism is the religion practiced by the largest number of people in India. In one form or another, it has been the dominant factor in the cultic life of India for 2500 years. The meshing of Vedic with native religious *traditions* over time has resulted in Brahmanism, which, in turn, developed into Hinduism in about the fifth century before Christ.

Hinduism is founded on belief in a supreme personal *deity* who demands intense personal devotion. There are, however, a great variety of *beliefs* included in Hinduism. The most *worshiped* god is Vishnu, a sky god who provides providential care for people.

The worship of Vishnu is found in the scriptures of the Bhagavad-Gita, composed about the third century before Christ. In it, the highest form of religious life is affirmed in union with Vishnu through *love* and *devotion*.

The best expression of this teaching was found in records

of the appearances of Vishnu in bodily forms, called *avatars*. This developed into two distinct incarnations, one called Rama and the other called Krishna. There are a wide variety of lesser gods with a wide variety of temples containing images of gods suited to the likes and devotion of a broad range of devotees. A 'Hindu' is a believer in Hinduism. See Centering prayer.

Hoarfrost

Hoarfrost is the deposit of water vapor in solid form on a solid surface. See Manna.

Hodigitria 2674

Hodigitria (Hodegetria) is a title for *Mary* the *Mother of God* as 'she who shows the way' and is the 'sign of the way.' This term is also used for an image or statue of Mary pointing to *Jesus* as the way or 'the One that is the promised Savior.'

Holiness 2013

In general, holiness is used to describe the dedication or *consecration* whereby a *person* or thing is pledged to God's service or is made the object of his special protection or pleasure.

All men are called to the *vocation* of holiness. A person is said to be holy when he lives in union with God in the state of *sanctifying grace*, which unites him to God and allows him to share in the *divine life*. This is called *moral holiness*.

Holiness Code

The Holiness Code is a collection of *religious* and *cultic* regulations contained in the *Pentateuch*. It contains no *civil* or criminal law. The nature of its contents suggests that it was closely related to the priests in its origins. Found in different chapters of Leviticus from 17 to 26, it contains a remarkable series of moral *precepts* dealing with such things as *incest*, superstitious *worship*, filial responsibilities, qualities of sacrificial animals, *blasphemy*, slavery, *blessings*, and *curses*. See Genesis.

Holy Communion 1331

Holy Communion refers to the reception and consumption of the *Holy Eucharist* as the *spiritual* food of the *soul*, which, by being intimately united to the Body, Blood, soul, and *divinity* of *Christ*, shares in his *divine life*. In Holy Communion, Christ is received whole and entire under either species of bread or wine. In Holy Communion, Christ nourishes the soul with his own self, the *Bread of Life*, and makes it more acceptable to God.

The Holy Eucharist is also called the *Blessed Sacrament*. It was instituted at the *Last Supper* when Christ broke bread and gave it to his disciples saying, 'take and eat, this is my body,' and taking the cup of wine said, 'this is my blood which shall be given for you,' commanding them to do this in his *memory* (cf. Lk 22:19–20).

When Holy Communion is received with the sacrament of the dying, or *Extreme Unction*, it is called *Viaticum*. See Eucharist 1328. Also see Eucharistic species 1373.

Holy day/Holy day of obligation

A holy day refers to a *feast* day other than *Sunday* on which Catholics are bound by serious *obligation* to attend *Mass* and to *abstain* from "those works and affairs which hinder the worship to be rendered to God, the joy proper to the Lord's day, or the suitable relaxation of *mind* and body" (Canon 1247). The number of holy days varies among countries. In the United States, there are six: The *Solemnity of the Mother of God*, January 1; The *Ascension* of the Lord, forty days after *Easter*; The *Assumption of the Blessed Virgin*, August 15; *All Saints* Day, November 1; Mary's *Immaculate Conception*, December 8; and *Christmas*, December 25. In many areas of the United States, the Solemnity of the Ascension is transferred to the following Sunday. According to a decree promulgated by the *USCCB* in 1993, whenever January 1, August 15, or November 1 falls on a Saturday or Monday, one

is *dispensed* from the precept to attend Mass for dioceses in the USA. See Sunday Obligation 2180.

Holy Eucharist
See Eucharist 1328.

Holy Ghost
Holy Ghost is another name for *Holy Spirit*. See State of grace 1861. Also see Holy Spirit 702.

Holy gifts
See Sancta sanctis 948.

Holy hour
Holy hour is a pious devotional exercise consisting of mental prayer and *vocal prayer* in the presence of the *Blessed Sacrament* exposed in memory of the words of Christ to the *Apostles* with him in the Garden of Gethsemane, 'Could you not watch one hour with me?' (Mt 26:40). See Monstrance.

Holy Leaven
Holy Leaven is a custom of the *Chaldean Church* used to emphasize the continuity of the *Eucharist* by the unity of the bread used. Each time the bread is baked, it is mixed with some dough from the previous baking and leavened with a bit of Holy Leaven, which has been handed on from age to age in each Church. See Chaldean Church/Rite.

Holy Mass

See Mass.

Holy mysteries 774

In the *Eastern Church*, 'holy mysteries' refers to the saving work of Christ's *sanctifying* humanity, which is revealed and active in the Church's *sacraments*.

Holy of Holies

Holy of Holies in *Hebrew* means most holy. It is the name given to the innermost room of the *Temple*. The Holy of Holies contained the *Ark of the Covenant* on which rested two carved *cherubim* with wings, which covered the *kapporet* or *mercy seat*. The *High Priest* was the only *person* who was allowed to enter this room, and he could only enter it on the *Day of Atonement*. See High Priest.

Holy Office

The complete name of the Holy Office is The Sacred Congregation of the Holy Office, and it is now known as the *Congregation for the Doctrine of the Faith*. Its purpose is to safeguard the teachings of the *faith*, to examine *doctrinal* questions and writings, to promote *theological* study, and to oversee matters related to the *Petrine Privilege* in *marriages*. The *Theological Commission* and *Biblical Commission* are attached to it.

It is part of the *Roman Curia*. It was erected in 1542 A.D.

to supersede the Universal Roman Inquisition. See Roman Congregations.

Holy oils

The *Bishop* blesses three holy oils during the Chrism Mass celebrated on *Holy Thursday*: the *oil of catechumens*, the *oil of the sick*, and the *sacred chrism (oil of chrism)*. They are distributed to all the *churches* of the *diocese* and are presented to each church in a procession and ceremony. Each of the holy oils is kept in its own vessel and stored in an *aumbry* or niche set in the wall of the *sanctuary* on the Gospel side of the altar. The vessels are marked OI, Latin initials for 'oleum infirmorum,' or oil of the sick; OC, Latin initials for 'oleum catechumenorum,' or oil of catechumens; and OS, Latin initials for 'oleum sanctorum,' or sacred chrism (oil of chrism).

During the Chrism Mass, just before the *Lord's Prayer*, the Bishop blesses the oil of the sick with a *prayer* that it may bring health both to *soul* and body for those for whom it is used. After *communion*, the Bishop blesses the oil of catechumens. He then blesses the oil of chrism, which is olive oil mixed with *balsam*, reciting a prayer of consecration over the oil.

Holy Oil is used in the sacraments of *Baptism, Confirmation, Holy Orders*, and *Extreme Unction*. In Baptism, two oils are used, the oil of catechumens and the oil of chrism. The person baptized is anointed with the oil of catechumens, and, later, that person is anointed with the oil of chrism. The oil of chrism is used in the sacrament of Confirmation and in the consecration of a bishop, a *church*, or an *altar*. The oil of catechumens is used in *ordinations*, in Baptism, in the *blessing* of a *baptismal font*, and in the consecration of an altar. The oil of the sick is used in Extreme Unction and in the blessing of bells. See Sacred chrism 1183.

Holy Orders 1536

Holy Orders is the *sacrament* through which the *mission* entrusted by Christ to the *Apostles* continues to be exercised in the *Church* until the end of time. It is the sacrament of *apostolic* ministry. It includes three *degrees*: the *episcopate* or *bishops*, the *presbyterate*, or priests, and *diaconate* or deacons. Holy Orders is also called *Sacred Orders*.

The sacraments of *Baptism*, Holy Orders, and *Confirmation* confer an *indelible spiritual character* on the *soul* and cannot be received again. It is because these sacraments confer an indelible or *permanent character* on the soul that they cannot be repeated. See Baptism 1213.

Holy Saturday

Holy Saturday is the Saturday of *Holy Week*. It is part of the *Easter Triduum*. Holy Saturday evening, the *vigil* of *Easter*, is the traditional time to confer the *sacrament* of *Baptism*. In former ages, it was also an occasion to confer the sacrament of *Holy Orders*. See Paschal mystery 571.

Holy See

The term 'see' comes from the Latin word 'sedes,' meaning 'seat.' The *authority* of the *Bishop* over his *diocese* is symbolized by a chair located in the sanctuary of his *cathedral church*. *Cathedral*, from the Latin 'cathedra,' is another word for chair, and the church where the Bishop's chair is located is known as the cathedral church.

The Holy See is the Diocese of the *Bishop of Rome*. It is also referred to as the *See of Peter* or the *Apostolic See*. Apostolic See could refer to any see founded by one of the *Apostles*, but, when it is used with the definite article, it refers specifically to the see of the Bishop of Rome.

The Bishop of Rome is called the *Pope*. Because he is the direct successor of Saint Peter, he exercises supreme authority over the entire Church. Out of respect for his holy office, he is referred to as His Holiness, and his see is called the Holy See.

Apostolic See is also used to

designate the Pope as *Supreme Pontiff* and those closely associated with him in governing the Church. See Apostolic See. Also see Pope 882.

Holy Souls

The name Holy Souls refers to the souls in *purgatory*. The Holy Souls are the souls of the just suffering in purgatory in order to be purged of the *temporal punishment* due to their *sin*.

It is an *article of faith* that the souls in purgatory can be helped by the *prayers* and *sacrifices* of the *faithful* on earth. It is also an immemorial custom in the Church to pray to these souls, asking them to intercede for us with God. This practice is a beautiful expression of the *communion of saints*. See Communion of saints 1475. Also see Communion with the dead 958.

Holy Spirit/Ghost 702

The Church teaches that the Holy Spirit is the *Third Person* of the *Blessed Trinity, consubstantial,* coequal, and coeternal with the Father and the Son. The Holy Spirit is God. He is not *generated* but *proceeds* from the Father and the Son by a single *spiration*.

The presence of the Holy Spirit is revealed gradually in *Scripture* through divine action in *creation*. The Spirit of God moved over the waters in *Genesis* (Gen 1:2).

Joshua, upon whom Moses laid his hands, was filled with the Spirit, so the *Israelites* gave him their *obedience* (Deut 34:9). He came upon Isaiah and anointed him to bring glad tidings (Is 61:1). The Holy Spirit overshadowed *Mary* at the *Annunciation* (Lk 1:35). He descended visibly upon *Christ* at his *Baptism* (Mk 1:12).

St. John describes the Spirit as the *Counselor*, or *Paraclete* (Jn 14:26; 15:26), and the *Spirit of Truth* (Jn 14:16; 16:13). At *Pentecost*, the Holy Spirit descended visibly upon the *Apostles* and directed their activity (Acts 11:12).

Power over life pertains to the Holy Spirit, for, being God, he preserves *creation* in the Father through the Son. The *mission* of the Holy Spirit is *sanctification*, which he accomplishes by endowing the soul with *sanctifying grace* and strengthening it with the *gifts of the Holy Spirit: wisdom, understanding, counsel, fortitude, knowledge, piety,* and *fear of the Lord*. Thus, he makes Christ live in the *minds* and the *hearts* of the members of his *Mystical Body*. See Divine missions.

Holy Thursday

Holy Thursday, also called *Maundy Thursday*, is the Thursday of *Holy Week*. It *commemorates* the *Last Supper* of the Lord at which he instituted the *Holy Eucharist* and the *priesthood*. *Holy oils* are blessed on this day during the

Chrism *Mass* celebrated in the *Cathedral* church and then distributed to all the *churches* in the *diocese*. See Holy Week.

Holy Trinity

Holy Trinity is another term for *Blessed Trinity*. See Trinity, Holy 232, 233, 234, 237, 253.

Holy water

Holy water is a *sacramental* consisting of water that has been blessed by a *priest*. By its use, the *blessing* of God is called down on all who use it. It is a symbol of *spiritual* cleansing and is used during times of danger, such as storms and *temptation*, by sprinkling a few drops in the area.

It is most commonly used by dipping a finger into a font upon entering a *church* and reverently making the *sign of the Cross*. It is a *pious* custom to keep some holy water in the home in a small font near the door to be used in making the sign of the Cross.

There are two special types of holy water: *baptismal water*, which is blessed for use in conferring *Baptism*, and *Easter water*, which is specially blessed on *Holy Saturday* to be used during *Paschal Time*. See Sacramentals 1667.

Holy Week

Holy Week is the week preceding the feast of *Easter*. It begins on *Passion Sunday (Palm Sunday)* and ends on

Holy Saturday. The *liturgies* of the week *commemorate* the approaching suffering and death of *Christ*.

The *Gospel* narrative commemorating the Lord's entry into Jerusalem is proclaimed at the beginning of the *liturgy* of Palm Sunday.

On *Holy Thursday* in the morning, the Church *celebrates* the Chrism *Mass* with the *blessing* of oils used in administering certain sacraments. The *Easter Triduum* begins with the celebration of the *Lord's Supper* on Holy Thursday evening. *Good Friday* commemorates the death of Christ with the Liturgy of the Lord's *Passion*. On Saturday evening, the *Easter Vigil* celebrates the *Resurrection* of Christ and is the traditional time to confer the *sacrament of Baptism*. See Paschal mystery 571.

Home Shrine

A home shrine is a space in the home set aside for private *prayer* to foster family *prayer*. It may contain a copy of *Scripture*, *icons*, and even candles. At times, it is called a *prayer corner*. See Prayer corner 2691.

Homily

A homily is a short sermon that uncovers a *spiritual* message or explains some *Scriptural* passage by means of an instructional commentary and a practical application to *moral* or spiritual life. Since the *Second Vatican Council* the homily has become an integral part of *Mass*. See Communal celebration of penance 1482, 1483. Also see Liturgy of the Word 1154, 1349.

Homoousios 465

'Homoousios' is a Greek word meaning 'of the same substance.' The *Council of Nicaea* adopted the term in 325 A.D. in opposition to Arius (260–336 A.D.) who affirmed that the Son of God 'came to be from things that were not' and that he was 'from another *substance*' than that of the Father. See Council of Nicaea. Also see Arianism.

Homosexuality 2357

Homosexuality refers to the relations between men or between women who *experience* an exclusive or predominant sexual attraction toward *persons* of the same sex. *Scripture* presents homosexual acts as acts of grave depravity. *Tradition* has always declared that homosexual acts are *intrinsically* disordered.

Homosexuality is contrary to the *natural law* because it closes the sexual act to the gift of life. Such acts do not proceed from a genuine affective and sexual *complementarity* and cannot be approved under any circumstance (cf. CCC 2357).

Homosexuality, which is objectively disordered, constitutes a trial for those in whom it is found. They must be accepted with respect, *compassion*, and sensitivity, avoiding unjust discrimination (cf. CCC 2358).

"Homosexual persons are called to *chastity*. By the *virtues* of self-mastery that teach them inner freedom, at times, by the support of disinterested friendship, by prayer and *sacramental grace*, they can and should gradually and resolutely approach *Christian perfection*" (CCC 2359).

Honorary prelate

A prelate is an *ecclesiastical* dignitary of exalted rank or *authority* having *jurisdiction* by right of his office. The principal *prelates* are *bishops*, but there is a large class of prelates who receive the name and rank without any *office* or duties as a mark of *papal* recognition of service to the Church. They are called honorary prelates.

All prelates have the title *Monsignor* and may wear special dress according to their rank. See Monsignor.

Hope 1817, 2090

Hope is the *theological virtue* by which one desires the *kingdom of heaven* and *eternal life* as his happiness, placing his trust in *Christ's* promises and relying not on his own strength but on the help and *grace* of the *Holy Spirit*.

Hope is the disposition of

the soul by which it aspires toward God as its last end and the *spiritual* and *temporal* means necessary for its attainment, knowing that it cannot be attained by personal efforts unaided by grace, but only in cooperation with grace.

Hope keeps *man* from becoming discouraged, sustains him in times of abandonment, and opens his *heart* in expectation of *eternal beatitude*. It is directed primarily to God and indirectly to the *beatific vision*. Secondarily, hope looks to the *resurrection* of all and to the temporal and the spiritual good, happiness, and *blessings* of others.

Hope is necessary for *salvation* and is infused into the *soul* at *Baptism*. Sins against hope are *despair* and *presumption*.

Hope of the Beatitudes 1820

The eight *Beatitudes* express the *hope* of all mankind: the *poor in spirit*, those who mourn, the patient and long-suffering, those who zealously hunger and thirst for *justice*, the merciful, the *pure in heart*, the peacemakers, and those who suffer persecution.

The rewards promised constitute the hopes of mankind. They inspire commitment in the struggle against *sin* and courage in times of failure. They give fallen *man* cause for joy in the sure *knowledge* that his Lord will not forget him.

Horns of a dilemma 589

The horns of a dilemma is a phrase used in *dialectics* or argumentation to refer to a situation in which a *person's* response to a *proposition* will always condemn him by forcing a choice between two self-condemning positions.

The *Pharisees* tried to force *Christ* into a dilemma when they asked him to decide whether it was *lawful* to pay tribute to Caesar. Whatever his response might be, it would offend either the Romans or the *Jews*. He offended neither of them by responding 'render to Caesar what is Caesar's and render to God what is God's' (Mt 22:21).

Horoscope

The word horoscope comes from the Greek word 'horoskopos,' meaning observer of the hour. A horoscope is a chart of the positions of the stars and planets at the time of a *person's* birth prepared in an effort to tell his future. It also refers to the forecast made on the basis of such a chart. See Divination 2116.

Hosanna 559

'Hosanna' is an exclamation, meaning 'Save now' or 'Save, pray,' occurring in Psalm 118:25. It was in frequent *liturgical* use among the *Jews* as an appeal for deliverance and *praise* to God.

At the entry of *Jesus* into Jerusalem, it was shouted by

the Galilean pilgrims in recognition of his *Messiahship* (Mt 21:9, 15; Mk 11:9, 10; Jn 12:13). It has been used from early times in the *Christian* Church as a cry or shout of *praise* or *adoration*. See Marana tha 671. Also see Aramaic terms in the Liturgy.

Host

The word host comes from the Latin word 'hostia,' meaning sacrificial *victim*. It is the name given to the round wafer made of *unleavened* bread used for the *consecration* of the *Eucharist* consumed by the celebrant and distributed to the *faithful* at *Communion*. Host may also refer to a multitude of people, such as the heavenly host or an army. See Chalice.

Human

Human refers to something that belongs to or is typical of mankind. It may also refer to something produced by people showing qualities possessed by *man*, such as *rationality* or creativity. See Human faculties.

Human act 154

A human act is an *act* that is freely chosen in *consequence* of a *judgment* and that proceeds from a *deliberate act of the will*. Human acts are *moral acts*, that is, they can be morally evaluated as being either *good* or *evil*. Because they are freely chosen they make the

person accountable for them and their intended *consequences*. See Act of man.

Human being

See Human person 2222.

Human faculties

Human faculties refer to those things that *man* can do because of his *nature* as a *rational animal* in a union of body and *soul*. Viewed as animal, man has the powers of *sensation*, locomotion, growth, and *reproduction*. Viewed as *rational*, man has the powers of *intellect* and *will*. These are considered as the powers of his soul.

A faculty is the power by which something is done. The power to act may reside in the nature of a *person* or thing, or it may consist in an authorization to act in a certain capacity. In this sense, *Canon Law* provides for granting a *priest* the faculties to hear *confessions*. See Quietism.

Human freedom

Human freedom refers to the use of *free will* in determining *human acts*. See Assisting grace.

Human nature 404

Human nature refers to the *essential*, inseparable qualities or properties that give *man* his fundamental *character* as a *human being* and enable him to act in a way and for the *end* proper to his being.

Nature in this sense refers to the elements of a thing that constitute its being and that have existence only in so far as they flow from its *essence*. The nature of a being is identical with its essence, but considered as its ultimate *principle* of *operation*.

A human being is a *rational animal* that grows, acts, senses, has the power of locomotion, thinks, and wills. All these operations flow from his nature as a *rational animal*, which is his ultimate principle of operation. Human nature, thus, refers to the essential, inseparable qualities or properties that give man his fundamental character.

Human nature assumed not absorbed by Christ 470

The Church teaches that *Christ* did not absorb *human nature* but, rather, he assumed it. If Christ had *absorbed* human nature, it would have changed human nature into his preexisting *divine nature*, destroying the human nature. In Christ, however, human nature was assumed, that is, it became *substantially* united to the *Second Person* of the Trinity without ceasing to be really distinct from his divine nature.

The human nature of Christ is not something added to the *Divine Person* but is personified, or *subsists*, in the Divine Person of the Word. Thus, there is but one Person with two natures, one human and one divine. 'Neither was God the Word changed into the nature of flesh, nor his flesh changed into the nature of the Word' (*Denzinger* 219, 428). See Incarnation 461.

Human person/being 251, 252, 2222

A *person* is an individual, complete, *subsistent*, and *rational being. God, angels*, and men are persons, because, in all *creation*, they alone possess *intellect* and *will*.

God and the *angels* are persons without bodies. They are pure *spirit. Man*, as a human person, is a *body-soul* composite; his soul does not merely inhabit his body.

Personhood is the source of human *dignity* because it is the basis for the *image of God* in man. Being the image of God, man reflects the eternal Word who, in being the eternal Son of the Father, is the perfect image of God and who, in becoming man, makes man the most perfect *created* image of the Father. The term person is relational and connotes at once both a real distinction from other persons and a real *communion* with them.

Human reason

The word *reason* comes from the Latin 'ratio,' meaning to reckon, plan, or think. *Human* reason is the capacity of man to attain *truth* and to recognize the *validity* of derived ideas, *judgments*, and *principles* based on indirect evidence. It is his capacity to think and form *judgments*, to draw *inferences*, and to reach *conclusions*. See Reason.

Human rights

A *right* is a subjective *moral* power residing in the *person* possessing it by which he can claim something as due him. It is a moral power because it does not depend on might or physical force, and deprivation of it is an offense against *justice*.

There is a difference between acquired rights and human rights. Acquired rights have their immediate source in the state. Human rights, also called rights of *man*, however, are acquired at the moment of *conception*. They inhere in the human person and are, by their nature, inalienable. Their source is the *Eternal Law*.

They arise because the *duties* imposed on man by his *creator* require that he have the right to fulfill them. Every right implies a corresponding *duty* of others.

There are three categories of human rights, that is, rights of the human person as such. They all depend, first of all, on the basic right to life, from conception to natural death, that belongs to every *human person*.

They include *freedom* under God and *just law* to seek perfection following his *con-*

science, the right to engage in *religious* activity, the right to marry and raise a *family*, the right to reasonable possession of private property, and the right to be treated as a person, not a thing.

Civic rights include the right to equal suffrage and participation in politics, to political self-determination, to political affiliation, to freedom to investigate and discuss, to equal rights before the law and to equal opportunity to develop personal abilities.

Social rights include the right to choose one's work, to organize into unions, to receive just wages, to share when possible in management and ownership, and to have the social security of sharing equitably in the *material* and *spiritual* goods of society. See Communism 2425.

Human tradition

Human tradition is the *oral* transmission of the stories, *beliefs*, and customs of a people from one generation to another. It is distinguished from *Sacred Tradition* because human tradition has its origin in *natural* human *experience* while Sacred Tradition has its origin in the *revelation* of *divine truth*, which is preserved and handed down through time by the Church under the guidance of the *Holy Spirit*. See Oral Tradition.

Human virtues 1804, 1810

"Human *virtues* are firm attitudes, stable dispositions, habitual perfections of *intellect* and *will* that govern our actions, order our *passions*, and guide our conduct according to *reason* and *faith*. They make possible ease, *self-mastery*, and joy in leading a *morally good* life" (CCC 1804).

The virtuous man is one who freely practices the good. Human virtues can be perfected by the performance of *human acts* in conformity with them. Human virtue is acquired by education or training. The frequent repetition of any *act* develops natural *habit* patterns, which make the behavior easier and more skillful.

Natural virtue opens man to cooperation with *actual grace*. God gives man grace to perform good deeds and by performing them, man opens himself to further growth in *supernatural virtue* as well as in natural virtue.

Grace builds on *nature*. God gives man the grace to perform good deeds, and, by performing them, man opens himself to growth in *supernatural virtue* as well as natural virtue.

Vice is the result of frequent failure to choose morally good actions and makes sinning easier. Failure to repent for *venial sin* increases the likelihood of committing *mortal sin*. Man must repent of venial sin and struggle against it in order to avoid sliding unconsciously into sinful habits and eventually into mortal sin.

Human work 2427

Human work is the physical or mental exertion required to produce something or to achieve a goal. *Man* was *created* in the *image of God*, and it is his *duty* to share with God in the completion of *creation* by his work.

Work honors the *Creator's* gifts and talents, which man receives from God. Work can be *redemptive*. By enduring the hardship of work in union with *Jesus* who died on *Calvary*, man collaborates in a certain fashion with the *Son of God* in his redemptive work and shows himself a *disciple* of *Christ* by carrying his cross daily in the work he is called to accomplish.

In work, the *person* exercises and fulfills, in part, the potential inherent in his *nature*. The *value* of work stems from man himself, who is both its author and its beneficiary. Work is for man, not man for work. From work, each should be able to draw the means for providing for his life and that of his *family* and be able to serve the human community at large.

Humanism

Humanism is the name of the *intellectual*, literary, and scientific movement of the fourteenth through sixteenth centuries. It focused on an effort to base all art, learning, and culture on that of the classical Greek and Latin civilizations. It extolled pagan non-*Christian* writers who stressed the development of natural *human nature*.

Humanism was opposed to Scholasticism and excluded divine *revelation* from the Gospel as relevant to understanding man, devoting itself, instead, to human interests without reference to God or divine things.

As a modern non-*theistic*, *rationalistic* movement, humanism asserts that man has no need of *supernatural revelation* and assistance to achieve personal fulfillment, happiness, and *ethical* conduct because these can be achieved by the power of reason alone. Kant and Lessing during the eighteenth century brought humanism into conflict with *religion* by attempting to rationalize *theology* against religion. They discounted revelation entirely and considered independent self-learning via *reason* as the sole basis for understanding human nature and achieving man's *end*. See Christian Humanism 1676. Also see Protestant reformation.

Humility 2546, 2559

The term humility comes from the Latin 'humilis,' meaning lowly, which, in turn, is derived from 'humus,' meaning earth. Humility is the *moral*

virtue by which *man* understands his proper relationship to God and neighbor and recognizes that everything he is and has derives from God's loving goodness. It forms the basis for *authentic* love of others because it brings man into greater conformity to *Christ* who was 'meek and humble of heart' (Mt 11:29).

The Latin equivalent for Adam, formed from the slime of the earth, is 'homo,' from 'humus.' The virgin earth, from which Adam was formed, in *Scripture* and in the writings of the *Fathers of the Church*, is a type of the *Virgin* Mother, from whom and by whom the *New Adam*, or Christ, was formed.

Pride, the opposite of humility, degrades man. God, in becoming man, commends humility as worthy of God and, therefore, as the basis for becoming like the God who became man.

Humility is opposed to pride, *arrogance*, *vanity*, and immoderate *self-abnegation*. It enables a *person* to recognize and appreciate his own good qualities as gifts to be used to serve others.

St. Augustine says that humility is to know oneself. St. Thomas defines humility in terms not of lowliness but of selflessness.

It was through his humility that Christ brought humanity the gift of *salvation* by entering into man's *mortal* and sinful state. Humility, thus, comes from above and forms the basis for all other virtues because it makes true obedience possible.

Hylomorphic theory/hylomorphism

The hylomorphic *theory* was formulated by Aristotle (384–322 B.C.) and developed in *Scholastic philosophy* to provide a philosophical explanation of the *nature* of *material beings*. It holds that all physical beings are composed of *prime matter* and *substantial form*. These are two *part-principles*, neither of which can exist without the other.

Prime matter is undefined and primitive. It makes a thing to be bodily. It must be fused with substantial form in order to exist. Substantial form is the definite mode of existence, which gives prime matter a specific character and makes it a particular kind of bodily thing. In order for something to be a dog or a tree, for example, the form of 'dogness' or 'treeness' must be fused with prime matter. The form of the dog makes this material being a dog and not a cat; the matter makes such a being *corporal* rather than *spiritual*. Prime matter remains constant in any change and gives individuality to every corporal being. Substantial form accounts for the *actual* existence of different things with their distinctive properties and the changes that take place when one substance changes into another.

The use of the hylomorphic theory as an explanation is called hylomorphism. See Form 365.

Hymn

Hymn comes from the Latin word 'hymnus,' meaning song of *praise*. A hymn is a religious song of honor and praise. It may also be a song of petition addressed to God or to the *saints*. The hymns for *liturgical* use are taken from *Scripture* for the most part and may be based on some *mystery* of *faith*. Many countries have official books of *vernacular* hymns, which are sung at appointed places in the *liturgy*. See Ambrosian hymn.

Hyperdulia

As the new Eve, *Mary* is the spiritual Mother of all the living on earth in the time of *grace* and *redemption*. She is *venerated* with an honor above that given to any other saint, called 'hyperdulia.' It differs from divine *worship* 'latria,' which is given to God alone. When someone prays to Mary, she intercedes for him with her Son. She is the link binding men to God based on the fact that she is the *Mother of God*. See Adoration 2628.

Hypocrisy/Hypocrite 2468

Hypocrisy is a pretense of *virtue*. It is the attempt to appear better than one is or to be something one is not.

Hypocrite comes from the Greek 'hypocrites,' meaning an actor or a pretender. In English, hypocrite refers to a *person* who pretends to be what he is not or to be better than he really is, such as acting pious or virtuous without really being so.

Hypostasis 251, 468

Hypostasis is a Greek term meaning 'standing under.' It refers to the *subsistence* that underlies every *being* and makes it a really distinct *being* existing in its own right rather than belonging to another. A hypostasis is a complete *substance* existing entirely in itself as an incommunicable *entity*.

In Christian *theology*, it connotes the same idea that personal existence, or *person*, does in Latin. In reference to the unique *essence* or *nature* of the Godhead, it has the same meaning as *person*. A person is a hypostasis endowed with *reason*.

Hypostasis is distinguished from *nature*. Hypostasis is the bearer of the nature and the subject of a being. Nature is that through which the hypostasis *acts* and exists.

In *Incarnational* theology, '*prosopon*' often refers to the appearance of the *human* and *divine natures* of the *Incarnate Word* as a single person and hypostasis. This can also mean 'mere' appearance but not really one person. *Christ* has two natures, one *human* and one *divine*, but he is only one person, or hypostasis. Likewise, the *Trinity* is one nature and three Persons, or hypostases. The interpretation of prosopon as merely an appearance instead of as a hypostasis formed the basis for the *Nestorian heresy*.

Hypostasis is also distinguished from *substance*. There are three hypostases, or persons, in the Godhead, but there is only one substance.

The Church uses the term hypostasis to designate persons in the *Holy Trinity*.

Hypostatic union

The hypostatic union refers to the union of the *human* and *divine natures* in the one *Divine Person* of *Christ*. The *Council of Chalcedon* in 451 A.D. declared that the two natures of Christ are joined in the unity of one person, or *hypostasis*. The 'unity of one hypostasis' indicates a *substantial union* rather than an *accidental* union of two natures in Christ. The union of the two natures in Christ is real (against *Arianism*); there is no mere indwelling of God in man (against *Nestorianism*). Christ has a rational soul (against *Apollinarianism*) and his *divine nature* remains unchanged (against *Monophysitism*).

The divine Person of the Son, which *substantially* unites in itself two natures, according to St. Thomas, is a *subsistent substance* of a *rational* nature or, according to the definition of Richard of St. Victor, an incommunicable existence of an *intellectual* (rational) nature. See Hypostasis 251. Also see Substantial Union; Council of Ephesus 466; Incarnation 461; Person.

I

Icon

Icon comes from the Greek word 'ikon,' meaning image. Though the word may refer to any image, it has special reference to a type of image used in *Eastern Churches* instead of statues. A prominent characteristic of true icons is the technique of lighting the image from within instead of from the outside. Icons employ this unique lighting technique to suggest that they are really windows into *eternity*.

Icons are written, not painted, and a single icon may contain images of events separated in time and place but which constitute the *doctrinal* content of what the image represents. Writing an icon is a form of *meditation*, and the writer fasts and prays for *inspiration* and assistance during its production.

The name of the *person* who wrote the icon is never indicated on the icon. Instead, a request for *prayer* for the writer is often placed on the reverse side. These prayers contain sentiments such as: 'Written for the glory of God and in honor of (*saint*). Remember me when you are moved to prayer by this image.' See Iconoclasm.

Iconoclasm

Iconoclasm was a movement during the eighth and ninth centuries to eliminate the use of images or pictures called *icons* in religious *worship* in the Christian *Eastern Churches*. It was the *primary* issue in the *Iconoclastic Controversy*.

Iconoclasm was inspired by imperial enactments that opposed the use of images on the grounds that they fostered *idolatry* and prevented the conversion of Muslims and *Jews*. St. John Damascene composed a famous defense of the *veneration* of icons. Pope Gregory III condemned iconoclasm in 731 A.D. In 787 A.D., the *Council of Nicaea II* articulated the principle that the veneration accorded to images passes to that which they represent. In 814 A.D., iconoclasm enjoyed a resurgence in the East when the Byzantine Emperor Leo V ordered the destruction of icons and the persecution of those who opposed him. Many *monks* suffered *martyrdom* as a result.

The Byzantine Empress Theodora restored the veneration of images in 842 A.D. with a great feast in their honor, which is still kept in the Eastern Church as the feast of *Orthodoxy*.

In general, iconoclasm refers to the breaking or destroying of images, especially images and pictures set up as objects of veneration, which are regarded as fallacious or superstitious. See Nicaea II 476. Also see Iconoclastic controversy.

Iconoclastic controversy

The iconoclastic controversy involved the clash between positive and negative views, especially in the *Eastern Churches*, regarding the propriety of using images of *saints* called *icons* in *religious worship*. At the heart of the controversy was the acceptance or rejection of the *Incarnation*. Highly placed political figures in the *Byzantine* Empire favored the *heterodox* negative view. This called into question the *legitimacy* of depicting God in *human* form and *venerating* such 'icons' or images. Promotion of the *heresy* in the Eastern Roman Empire was much related to the influence and power of Islam as well as the heresy of *Monophysitism*. See Iconoclasts 2131. Also see Nicaea II 476; Iconoclasm.

Iconoclasts 2131

Iconoclasts were *persons* who subscribed to a *heresy* prominent around 726 A.D., which held that the *veneration* of holy images called *icons* was unlawful.

In 787 A.D., the *Council of Nicaea II* defined that both the figure of the *sacred* and life-giving Cross and holy images may be placed in *churches*, but the honor paid to them is only relative for the sake of their *prototypes*, and they are to receive veneration rather than *adoration*.

Ideology

Ideology refers to the body of ideas on which a particular political, economic, *social*, or religious system is based. It represents the *doctrines*, opinions, or way of thinking of a class or group. See Communitarian 1429.

Idol

Idol comes from the Greek word 'eidolon,' referring to an image to which *divine worship* is paid. This practice of worshiping graven images as gods is expressly forbidden by the second commandment of the *Decalogue*.

Images in *Catholic churches* are not idols because divine worship is not paid to them. They serve only as reminders of *Christ* and the *saints* and foster an atmosphere of *prayer*, much as a picture of a family member recalls the role of that person in one's life and makes him present through the memories the picture provokes. See Christian iconography.

Idolatry 2113

Idolatry is the *divinization*, by *worship*, of a creature in place of God and the giving of divine honor to a thing. Worshiping things like money, pleasure, power, race, or the state instead of the *Creator* is idolatry just as much as worshiping *pagan* gods or *demons*. Idolatry is a violation of the first commandment to have no gods except *Yahweh*. Idolatry is a *perversion* of man's innate *religious* sense.

Ignorance

Ignorance is the absence of *knowledge* in one who has the capacity of knowing. Ignorance may be classified either as *invincible* or *vincible*.

Invincible ignorance is the absence of knowledge under circumstances in which knowledge cannot be obtained without extraordinary effort.

Vincible ignorance is the absence of knowledge under circumstances in which knowledge can be obtained with ordinary effort.

When knowledge becomes necessary, for example, to form one's *conscience* properly, vincible ignorance becomes *culpable* at the point when a *person* neglects to become properly informed. See Unintentional ignorance 1860.

Ignorance of fact

Ignorance of fact is the absence of *knowledge* of either the *substance* of a thing desired or done or of some circumstance affecting it: for example, using salt in cake batter instead of sugar. See Unintentional ignorance 1860.

Ignorance of the law

Ignorance of the law is the absence of *knowledge* of the existence of a *law* or, when known, the absence of knowledge that a law includes a particular case. Ignorance of the law is called *invincible* when knowledge is absent under circumstances in which it could not be obtained except with extraordinary effort. It is called *vincible ignorance* when knowledge of the law could be obtained with ordinary effort.

Ignorance of a law may *invalidate* an act, but it does not prevent the effect of the law. Ignorance of the law or a penalty is never presumed unless the law makes specific provision regarding it, as in Canon 1096 of the 1983 *Code of Canon Law*, which provides that a *marriage* contracted in ignorance of the fact that marriage is ordered to the *procreation* of children through *sexual* cooperation renders the marriage invalid. See Unintentional ignorance 1860.

Illicit

Illicit means unlawful or forbidden. A *sacrament*, such as *marriage*, can be illicit and still be *valid*. When a marriage is *invalid*, there is no marriage; when it is simply illicit, the marriage is valid but unlawful. An illicit marriage may be made *licit* by securing the proper *dispensation*. See Validity 1635.

Image of God 705

St. Thomas teaches that *man* was made in the image of God, not according to his body, but by reason of his *intellect* and *will*.

By creating man in his image, God made man a *person*. By creating man in his likeness, God made man *holy*. Man was *created* with a *body* and a *soul*. His intellect and will are *faculties* of the soul but are exercised through the mediation of bodily *senses*. Man's will enables him to choose freely to conform or not to conform to the *divine plan* known by the intellect.

The divine image remained in man even after *original sin* because he did not lose his *nature* as person, but his likeness to God, or *holiness*, was lost.

While retaining his *divine nature*, the *Second Person* of the Blessed *Trinity assumed a human nature* and became man. By dying for our *salvation*, he restored the likeness of God by enabling sinful man to become holy through *grace* and *obedience*. God destined man for union with him, but man must choose that union freely. By the proper use of his will, in cooperation with *grace*, man is *justified* and conformed

to the image of *Christ*, who did his Father's will in perfect obedience.

The likeness of God in man, lost through original sin, is restored through *Baptism*, but the likeness to God is not perfectly restored in this world. Because of his *fallen state*, or *concupiscence*, man must continue to work out his salvation in pain and groaning. The grace of *redemption* and the presence of the *Holy Spirit* provide consolation and strength to man in his journey to *eternal* union with God.

Imagination

Imagination is an internal sense by which man is aware of or knows absent sensible things. The imagination is the faculty that retains and reproduces representations of absent *material* objects. The representation is called a phantasm, and it differs from *sensation* in being faint in intensity and transitory. There are four internal senses: imagination, sentient *memory*, sentient *consciousness*, and *instinct*. See Jansenism.

Imbue/imbued

Imbue comes from the Latin 'imbuere,' meaning to wet or saturate. When the *soul* is imbued with *sanctifying grace*, it is completely filled with the *theological virtues* of *faith*, *hope*, and *charity*, which inspire it with ideals and *emotions* drawing it to goodness, *truth*, and *holiness*. See Born of God 526.

Immaculate Conception 491

The Immaculate Conception is the *doctrine* that the *Blessed Virgin Mary* was, in the first instant of her *conception*, by a singular *grace* and privilege of God in virtue of the foreseen merits of *Christ*, preserved from all stain of *original sin*. This is called the Immaculate Conception and must not be confused with the birth of Christ or the *Incarnation*. The *Solemnity* of the Immaculate Conception is *celebrated* on December 8.

Immanent/immanence

Immanent comes from the two Latin words, 'in' and 'manere,' meaning to dwell or remain in or near. God is said to be immanent because he is present throughout his creation by his act of *creation*, *conservation*, and *providence*. Because he exists independently apart from his creation, God is also *transcendent*. See Transcendent 285. Also see Perichoresis.

Immemorial

Immemorial means extending back in time beyond any living *memory* or written records. See Infant Baptism 1252.

Imminent

Imminent comes from the Latin 'imminere,' meaning likely to happen soon or without delay or impending. It is often associated with danger, *evil*, or misfortune. See Montanism.

Immodesty

Immodesty refers to a lack of modesty. See Impurity. Also see Modesty 2521.

Immolation

Immolation is the act of offering a *victim* as *sacrifice*. The act of sacrifice requires the destruction of that which is sacrificed. This destruction radically changes the object sacrificed; the animal is killed or the wine is poured out.

When the destruction of the sacrificial victim or object is not actual but equivalent, the sacrifice can be *symbolic* or *mystical*. The sacrifice of the *Mass* is mystical but real. The separate consecrations of the bread and wine symbolize the separation of *Christ's* Body and Blood on the Cross. The Mass is referred to as the unbloody Sacrifice of the Cross made present on the *altar*. It is not a repetition of the Sacrifice of the Cross. Christ does not physically and in bloody fashion die again in the Mass but, transcending the limits of space and time, undergoes his real death on the Cross mystically and in an unbloody manner in virtue of the double *consecration*.

Immoral

Immoral describes any *act*

that is contrary to the *moral law* or to established norms of behavior. See Divorce 1650, 2384, 2385.

Immortal

Immortal means living forever, undying, or deathless. See Angels 328.

Immortality

Immortality is the *preternatural attribute* by which *man* in the state of *original justice* was, conditionally, free from dying. See Original sin 389. Also see Preternatural gift; Original justice 376.

Immune/Immunity

Immune refers to protection against something harmful or disagreeable. See Catacombs.

Immutable/ Immutability 1958

Immutable means permanent and unchangeable. In reference to *natural law*, it means that it is fixed throughout all of history and continues under the flux of ideas and customs and supports their progress. Even when it is rejected or denied, natural law is never destroyed or removed from the *heart* of *man*; it always resides in his *conscience*, calling him to his true purpose.

Immutable part 1205

Immutable, as applied to the *liturgy*, refers to the part of the liturgy that is *divinely* instituted and cannot be changed as opposed to those parts that may be changed to adapt to the *cultures* of recently *evangelized* peoples. For example, the words of *consecration* are immutable and cannot be changed.

Impassibility

Impassibility refers to freedom from *suffering*. It was a *preternatural gift*, which Adam and Eve enjoyed in the *Garden of Eden*. This does not mean that they were unable to feel pain but that they were free of the pain that resulted in *consequence* of their fallen state, such as the discord and heartbreak resulting from *infidelity* or from the excessive use of any of God's gifts.

Complete impassibility, or complete freedom from pain, suffering, subjection to decay, and *corruption*, is a quality of the *resurrected* body of the *just*. The condemned, however, will still suffer because they remain under the *dominion* of *sin*. See Original sin 389. Also see Preternatural gift; Glory 293.

Impeccable

Impeccable comes from the Latin word 'impeccabilis,' meaning without *sin*. Someone is impeccable when he is not able to commit *sin* or to do wrong. He is without *moral* defect, error, faultless, and flawless. God is, by *nature*, impeccable; men and *angels* become impeccable in the light of glory. See Freedom 1731.

Impediment

An impediment is an obstacle that prevents the *valid* reception of a *sacrament*. It can arise from some condition in the individual, from something the *person* has done, or from some relationship between parties.

There are different kinds of impediments: *Diriment impediments*, *prohibiting* or *hindering impediments*, and *impediments of natural* or *ecclesiastical law*. Hindering impediments were dropped from the 1983 *Code of Canon Law*. The impediment prohibiting a *mixed marriage*, however, still requires dispensation by the *local ordinary*. Impediments of *natural law*, for example, attempted *marriage* when one of the parties is already married, never change and can never be *dispensed*. Impediments of ecclesiastical law resulting from the *discipline* of the Church are subject to change.

The reception of valid *Holy Orders* confers a permanent mark, which cannot be removed by dispensation. Laicization only removes the right to exercise the office. However, because the impediment to marriage associated with Holy Orders is an ecclesiastical law, it may be dispensed when a *cleric* is laicized. See Affinity.

Impediments of ecclesiastical law

Impediments of ecclesiastical law result from the discipline of the Church. These are subject to change and may apply only in the Western Church. Such impediments are dispensable, but some may never actually be granted because of their gravity, such as dispensing the *impediment* to *marriage* associated with the *valid* reception of Holy Orders, except in cases of laicization. See Impediment.

Impediments of natural law

Impediments arising from *natural law* are obstacles that nullify and void the reception of a *sacrament* because they violate the natural law, for example, an attempted marriage by a *person* already in a *valid* marriage. Such impediments can never be dispensed because the natural law is *immutable*. See Impediment.

Imperfect contrition 1453

Imperfect *contrition* is sorrow for sin inspired by motives other than the pure love of God, such as fear of *hell*, loss of *heaven*, the foulness of *sin*, etc.

Imperfect contrition is sufficient for the *valid* reception of the *sacrament* of *Penance* but it must be genuine, include all *mortal sins*, include a resolve to avoid sin in the future, and detest sin as the greatest *evil*.

Imperfect contrition cannot

forgive *grave* sins without the sacrament of Penance. Imperfect contrition is also called *attrition*. Also see Perfect contrition 1452.

Implicit

Implicit comes from the Latin word 'implicare,' meaning to enfold, entwine, or entangle. Implicit means something suggested or understood although not clearly expressed. See Assumption of the Blessed Virgin 966.

Imprimatur

The imprimatur is a formal statement of a *bishop* granting permission to publish *ecclesiastical* material. It appears at the beginning of the publication together with a *Nihil Obstat*, a statement that the material contained is not contrary to Church teaching. See Nihil Obstat.

Impurity

Impurity refers to sins of *lust*, that is, *sins* against *purity*. Lust may be internal or external. Internal lust takes the form of thoughts or desires that are not carried out, such as taking pleasure in sexual thoughts and desires for unlawful sexual pleasure. External lust is the performance of impure *acts*, such as viewing *pornography*, undue *sexual* excitation, *immodesty*, *masturbation*, *fornication*, *adultery*, *incest*, *homosexuality*, association with *evil* companions, and certain types of entertainment and reading materials.

Aids to *purity* begin with guarding the eyes by becoming sensitive to the first suggestions of lust, which often begin with looking at things capable of becoming an occasion of *sin*, and avoiding the occasions where such sights or suggestions are most likely to occur. Frequent *prayer*, *Confession*, and reception of the *Eucharist* are sources of *grace* in the struggle against sin. Cultivating a *spiritual* life and regular spiritual reading will fill the *mind* with holy thoughts and inspire the desire for *holiness*. See Pornography 2354. Also see Lust 1866, 2351; Chastity 915.

Imputability 1735, 1860

Imputability refers to the assignment of responsibility or accountability for something in such a way as to make one guilty or worthy of *merit*.

Imputable /Imputation 2269

Imputable refers to the *attribution* of *moral* responsibility or accountability resulting from a *volitional act*, that is, an *act of the will*.

Imputability can be diminished or even removed because of *ignorance*, inadvertence, duress, fear, *habit*, or other *psychological* or *social* factors, which affect the degree of freedom of the will at the time of the act.

In persona Christi Capitis 1548

'In persona Christi Capitis' is a Latin expression meaning 'in the person of *Christ* the Head.' The phrase refers to the service of the *ordained minister*, who acts in the *person* of Christ himself who is present in his Church as Head of the *Mystical Body*, Shepherd of his flock, *High Priest* of the *redemptive sacrifice*, and Teacher of *Truth*.

In the hands of his own counsel 1730

In the hands of his own counsel means that *man* is left to decide for or against submission to God according to the dictates of *conscience* by the use of *free will*.

Inalienable right 1738, 2273

An inalienable right is one that cannot be removed or separated from a *person* because it pertains to his *nature* and, as such, is a natural *right*.

Incantation

Incantation is the *chanting* of sacred or magical words or formulas that are supposed to cast a spell, perform some *magic*, or produce a particular effect. See Mantra.

Incarnate

Incarnate means made flesh. The *Second Person* of the Blessed *Trinity* was made flesh in the womb of the *Blessed Virgin Mary* by the *Holy Spirit*. This event is cel-

ebrated as the *Incarnation*. See Incarnate word. Also see Incarnation 461.

Incarnate Son

The *Second Person* of the Blessed Trinity is the only *begotten Son of God*. When he *assumed human nature*, he became the Incarnate Son. See Incarnation 461.

Incarnate Word

Incarnate Word refers to *Jesus Christ*, who, while remaining the *Second Person* of the *Holy Trinity*, was born of the *Virgin Mary*, became flesh of our flesh, and dwelled among us for our *salvation*. See Incarnation 461.

Incarnation 461

The Incarnation refers to the act by which the *Second Person* of the *Holy Trinity*, the *Son, assumed a human nature* while retaining his *divine nature*. Through the Incarnation, the human and divine natures of the Second Person of the Holy Trinity are united in a single person. Because of his Incarnation, Christ is called the *Incarnate Word*. See Assumed a human nature 470. Also see Kenosis; Mother of God 971.

Incense/Incensing

Incense is a resin, or gum, that gives off a pleasant odor when burned. It is used in *religious ceremonies* because the smoke rising from it is a symbol of the prayer of the *faithful* rising like a sweet odor to God. See Solemn blessing 1245. Also see Solemn.

Incest 2388

Incest designates *sexual intercourse* between relatives or in-laws within any *degree*.

Incest is a *grave* sin against both *chastity* and *piety*. Incest between a parent and child is distinct in malice from that of other incestual relationships. Incest corrupts *family* relationships and marks a regression toward animality.

Inclosed/enclosed

Inclosed or enclosed (or cloistered) is a term applied to a member of a *religious institute* devoted to the *contemplative* life, whose legislation enjoins its members to observe a strict discipline of living within the bounds of a *canonically* enclosed residence known as a *cloister*. See Consecration of a virgin and widows 922, 923. Also see Consecrated persons 1672.

Inclosure/enclosure

An inclosure or enclosure (or *cloister*) is a specific part of a *monastery* that has been set aside as the residence of a *religious community*.

The legislation of a *religious institute* regulates the discipline of enclosure according to the nature of the institute. A *papal enclosure* is one reg-

ulated by norms originating from the *Apostolic See*.

"The diocesan *Bishop* has the faculty of entering, for a just reason, the enclosure of cloistered *nuns* whose monasteries are situated in his *diocese*. For a grave reason and with the assent of the *Abbess*, he can permit others to be admitted to the enclosure, and permit the nuns to leave the enclosure for whatever time is truly necessary" (Canon 667, § 4).

Inclosed religious may receive visitors in a parlor, where conversation takes place through a large screen or grill, which may be covered with a cloth. See Eremitic life 920. Also see Monastery.

Inclusus

The term inclusus referred to a *nun*, *monk*, or other *person* who, with permission of *ecclesiastical authority*, was voluntarily walled up in a cell with an opening through which food could be introduced and communication could take place. This custom is now obsolete, and the term inclusus is no longer recognized in the common language of the *faith*. See Consecration of a virgin 1672. Also see Inclosed.

Inconstancy/Inconstant

Inconstant means changeable, not remaining firm in *mind* or purpose, being unsteady or unreliable in affection or loyalty, or fickle.

See Right to trial marriage 2391.

Incorrupt/incorruptibility

Incorruptible means that a thing is incapable of decay or dissolution into its components. Since the *soul* is *spiritual*, it is a simple indivisible substance. It has no parts, so it cannot disintegrate or decay into any parts that make it up. After the *resurrection*, the body will become incorruptible. The body reunited to the soul is described as a *spiritual body*. See Glorified body. Also see Resurrection from the dead 992; Resurrected body; Glory 293.

Incredulity 2089

Incredulity refers to the neglect of revealed *truth* or the willful refusal to *assent* to it. It is the outright refusal to assent to some teaching or to follow it, that is, it is willful disbelief.

Indefectible/Indefectibility

Indefectibility refers to a quality of imperishable duration and *immutability*. It is applied to the Church, which will endure until the end of time. This unfailing quality in her constitution and ministration was promised by *Christ* himself, 'Behold I am with you always' (Mt 28:20).

Her indefectibility is seen externally in her triumph over obstacles and trials and internally by her faithful preserva-

tion of the teaching of the *Gospel*. See Filial prayer 2599.

Indelible spiritual character

1272, 1582

Indelible *spiritual character* refers to an irremovable *spiritual* mark or seal on the *soul* produced by the *sacraments* of *Baptism*, *Confirmation*, and *Holy Orders*. These sacraments effect an irrevocable, *supernatural* power in the soul to receive or to produce something *sacred*. Because of the permanent *nature* of this character, these sacraments cannot be repeated.

Indifference 2094

Indifference can refer either to the refusal to give *worship* to God because of *sloth* and the refusal to accept one's *obligation* to worship him or to the *belief* that one need not practice the one true *religion* because all religions are of equal *value*.

This neglect, or lack of *zeal*, in religious practice does not necessarily arise from contempt of religion. It can arise from the absence of care about it, the absence of zeal for it, or even doubt or uncertainty concerning it.

Though some *truth* may be found in all religions, the fullness of truth is found only in the *faith* expressed by the *Catholic Church* of Rome. Because one has the *duty* to seek truth, one has a general *obligation* to move toward that Church.

Indifferentism 2128

Indifferentism refers to the denial that the *worship* of God and practice of true religion is the *duty* of *man* or to a claim that one has the right to choose whatever form of worship one prefers.

Indignation

Indignation refers to *just anger* resulting from *injustice* or *ingratitude*. See Wrath 1866, 2302. Also see Anger 2302.

Indirect line of relationship

The indirect or *collateral line* of relationship is that which arises between *persons* having a common ancestor, such as brother and sister, aunt and uncle, nephew and niece, and first and second cousins. Such a relationship renders *marriage invalid* to the fourth *degree* in the collateral line. See Collateral line.

Indirectly voluntary act 1736

An indirectly voluntary act is an act that *terminates* in an object that is not itself willed as an *end* or means to an end but that is, in some way, foreseen as a possible outcome of an *act* that is directly willed, such as amputating someone's arm to save their life.

Indissolubility 1644

Indissolubility is that charac-teristic of the *valid marriage bond* that makes it impossible to invalidate, break, or dissolve while both *spouses* are living.

In some cultures, *marriages* are said to be *intrinsically indissoluble* but *extrinsically soluble*. When it is considered intrinsically indissoluble, neither the spouses themselves nor anyone else can dissolve the marriage. When marriage is held to be soluble by the external *authority* of the state, it is said to be extrinsically soluble.

The Church denies that the state possesses such power since power to dissolve, or end, a marriage by extrinsic authority is reserved exclusively to *Christ* or to someone directly and personally delegated by him. The *Pope* is the only delegate who has such power in certain, very restricted cases.

In the Church, all sacramental marriages are considered to be intrinsically indissoluble. Non-sacramental or *non-consummated marriages* can be extrinsically soluble in certain circumstances.

Individual confession

Individual confession refers to the act of confessing *sins* to a *priest* in private. It is also called *auricular confession* because sins are ordinarily confessed by word of mouth to be heard by the priest before granting *absolution*. See Communal celebration of penance 1482.

Individual liberty

Liberty is *freedom* as it relates to the individual who exercises it. Individual liberty is the *subjective* power of self-determination. Freedom is the absence of *objective* constraint or coercion by *civil* society in certain matters, such as *religion*, assembly, education, etc., in the exercise of individual liberty. See Individualism 2425.

Individualism 2425

Individualism is a doctrine that emphasizes the *rights* and *liberty* of a particular *person* over the rights of the family and society at large.

Individualism is offered as justification for actions contrary to God's *law*, such as the insistence by homosexuals on teaching children about their lifestyle, the insistence by adults on practicing *artificial birth control*, or the insistence by pro-abortionists that the rights of a mother are more important than the rights of her unborn child. Some call this attitude *free thought*.

The Church teaches that the rights of the individual must always be understood in the context of the *divine plan* and man's *obligation* to follow the *will of God* even when this requires the *sacrifice* of one's personal plans or desires.

Inductive

Logical reasoning from particular facts to a general *conclusion* is called inductive. For example, the conclusion that water boils at a certain temperature is reached from observing that water is repeatedly found to boil at a certain temperature. See Inference.

Indulgence 1471

An indulgence is the remission before God of the *temporal punishment* due to *sin* that has already been *absolved* of guilt by *Confession*.

Indulgences are derived through the action of the Church as minister of *redemption* from the *merits of Christ*, his Mother, and the *saints*. The *faithful Christian* who is duly disposed gains an indulgence under certain conditions, either from the *sacrament of Confession*, by *perfect contrition*, by the recitation of certain *prayers*, or by the performance of certain *acts*. An up-to-date list of indulgences can be found in the *Enchiridion* of Indulgences.

Indulgences may be partial or plenary. A *plenary indulgence* remits all temporal punishment due to *sin*. A *partial indulgence* remits part of the temporal punishment due to sin.

To gain a plenary indulgence, one must be free from the attachment to all sin, but this is not required for a partial indulgence.

Indulgences may be gained for oneself or for the souls in *purgatory*, but not for another living *person*. By attaching indulgences to special prayers and acts, the Church spurs the faithful to works of devotion, *penance*, and *charity*.

Indult

An indult is a license or special permission granted by the *Pope* for good reason authorizing something to be done that the *law* of the Church does not generally allow. See Dispensation 1635.

Indwelling of the Holy Spirit

Indwelling of the Holy Spirit refers to the presence of the *Holy Spirit* in a *person* in the *state of grace*. He is present both by means of the *grace* he imparts and by his *divine nature*.

The nature of this indwelling produces an *accidental* union, not a *substantial* union, with the *soul* and is an operation outside of God himself. All the activity of God outside of the *Holy Trinity* is common to all three persons, so the indwelling of the Holy Spirit implies the indwelling of all three Persons and is a manifestation of the *love* of the Father and the Son as well. It is through this indwelling that one becomes a *temple of the Holy Spirit*.

The immediate effect of this indwelling is *sanctifying grace*, by which the *mind* is able to understand something of the

mystery of God and the *will* is enamored of his goodness beyond the power of *reason* or the *natural affective* power of the *soul*. See Share in the divine Life. Also see Temple of the Holy Spirit 1695.

Inerrant/Inerrancy

Inerrancy means free from error or mistakes. Inerrancy is applied to God's *omniscience*, to the *knowledge* of Adam in the state of *original justice*, to the knowledge of *Christ*, to *Sacred Scripture*, and to the Church's infallibility. See Apocrypha.

Infallibility 891, 2035

Infallibility is that supreme participation in the *authority* of *Christ* by virtue of which the teaching of the Church in matters of *faith* and *morals* cannot err.

Infallibility is ensured by a *charism*, or special *grace* of God, and extends as far as does the *deposit of divine revelation* and those elements of *doctrine*, including *morals*, without which the saving *truths* of the faith cannot be preserved, explained, or observed.

Infallible

Infallible means unable to err. In the Church, it means the incapability of error in setting forth *doctrine* on *faith* and *morals*, especially when the *Pope* speaks 'ex cathedra' in official capacity as successor of Peter. See Infallibility 891.

Infant Baptism 1252

Infant Baptism refers to the practice of baptizing infants. It is an *immemorial tradition* in the Church that teaches that infants are to be baptized soon after birth; however, no definite rule is set by the 1983 *Code of Canon Law* regarding the child's age.

Non-*Catholic* infants may be baptized even against their parent's wishes when there is present danger of death. Otherwise, they may be baptized only if at least one parent or guardian gives consent and if there is an assurance that the child will be raised as a Catholic.

Abandoned children whose parents are unknown are to be baptized conditionally when there is no evidence of previous *Baptism*.

Infanticide 2268

Infanticide is the killing of an infant. The term infant refers to a child during the earliest period of life, even if it is yet unborn. When the child killed is still in the womb, infanticide is called *abortion*. Though the term infant is generally applied to toddlers, it may refer to any child, especially those less than seven years of age.

Inference

Inference comes from the Latin 'inferre,' meaning to bring in. It is a process of reason by which, from truths already known, one concludes to a *truth* previously unknown. Inference may be either *inductive*, meaning starting from particular truths and going to the general, or *deductive*, meaning starting from the general truth and going to the particular. See Human Reason. Also see Reason.

Infidel

The word infidel comes from the Latin 'infidelis' from 'in,' meaning not, and 'fidelis,' meaning faithful. Originally, the term referred to all non-*Christians*, but now it refers simply to unbelievers, such as *atheists* or *agnostics*. See Crusades.

Infidelity

Infidelity is a lack of *faith*. The lack of faith itself can come about in three ways. 1) Positive infidelity occurs when a *baptized person* sufficiently instructed rejects the faith. Positive infidelity is a *grave sin*. 2) Privative infidelity occurs when a person neglects to examine the grounds for *divine revelation* and does not admit his *obligation* to embrace the faith even when the grounds seem *credible*. Privative infidelity is sinful in proportion to the degree of *culpable negligence*. 3) Negative infidelity refers to the simple lack of faith in one who, through no fault of his own, has had no opportunity to learn it because it has not been adequately presented and because he is unaware of his *duty* to inquire about the faith. Negative infidelity is not sinful.

Because positive and privative infidelity always, in some way, involve a turning away from God, they may lead by degrees to *atheism*. Positive infidelity may occur in association with marriages of *mixed religion*. See Atheism 2124.

Infinite/Infinitely 202

Infinite means lacking any limits or bounds, extending beyond measure, lacking a beginning or end, possessing *perfection* without limit, or possessing the fullness of perfection. See Omnipotence 270.

Informed conscience 1783

An informed *conscience* is one, that has been developed in accord with the dictates of right *reason* and, therefore, is upright and truthful and conforms to the true *good* willed by the *wisdom* of the *Creator*. See Conscience.

Infuse/infused

Infused comes from the Latin word 'infundere,' meaning to pour into. It refers to qualities, ideas, or *graces* imparted or instilled without personal effort. See Prudence. Also see Sanctifying grace 1999, 2000.

Infused grace

Infused grace is another name for *sanctifying grace*. See Sanctifying grace 1999, 2000.

Infused knowledge

Infused *knowledge* refers to the *preternatural* gift of the *natural* and *supernatural knowledge* conferred by God on Adam and Eve. They were *created* as adults and were to be the first teachers of their children. Infused knowledge is not gained by *experience* but is given directly by God as a special *grace*. See Garden of Eden.

Infused virtue

Natural virtues are *good habits* that must be acquired through practice or repetition. The *supernatural virtues* of *faith*, *hope*, and *charity*, however, cannot be acquired through practice because, being *supernatural gifts*, they are simply beyond the capacity of *human nature*.

Infused virtues are imparted to the soul with *sanctifying grace* by *Baptism*. Sanctifying grace is a habitual gift, a stable *supernatural* disposition. It perfects the *soul* and enables it to live with God, to act by his *love* and to respond to his call to union.

Infused virtues surpass natural virtues because they directly and immediately relate *man* to God and lay the foundation for the life of the Spirit in the soul. Through them, man participates in the *divine life* and is prepared for a fuller union with God. Infused virtue ennobles *human nature*, making its actions *holy* and the pursuit of natural virtues easier.

By the supernatural virtue of faith, *reason* is given spiritual *understanding* and *wisdom*. By *hope*, man is strengthened in his aspiration for perfection. By *charity*, he is able to surrender to God in loving union.

Though man can do nothing by his natural power to increase the supernatural virtues, by responding to the movements of grace, he opens or disposes himself to receiving them more fully. Growth in the *theological virtues* is the ultimate aim of *Christian* life. See Theological virtues 1812.

Ingratitude 2094

Ingratitude is a *sin* against God's love. It is the failure or refusal to acknowledge *divine love* and to respond to it with love. It is being unthankful or ungrateful for God's manifold gifts. It may also refer to the same attitude toward a gift or favor from another *person*.

Inhere/Inherent

Inherent refers to that which exists in someone or something as a natural inseparable quality. See Right 1930.

Injustice

Injustice is any treatment of another in a way that violates his *rights*. See Commutative justice 2411.

Innate

Innate comes from the Latin 'innatus,' meaning born in. It refers to anything that exists *naturally* in something rather than being acquired by it. See Moral Law 1950, 1952.

Inner conversion 1888

Inner *conversion* refers to the change of *heart* by which the inner *man* is conformed more closely to the *will of God*. This conversion is required for true *repentance* and *reformation* of life after *sin*. It is also called *conversion of heart*.

Inordinate

Inordinate comes from the Latin word 'inordinatus,' meaning without order. It means disordered, lacking restraint, immoderate, or excessive. What is inordinate is opposed to the *virtue* of *temperance*. See Temperance 2341. Also see Wrath 1866, 2302; Anger 2302.

Inquietude

Inquietude means restlessness, uneasiness, or being internally disturbed. See Avarice 1866, 2536.

Insemination

Insemination refers to the *fertilization* of an ovum or impregnation that brings an *embryonic person* into being.

See Artificial insemination. Also see Heterologous artificial insemination and fertilization 2376.

Insinuate

Insinuate means to introduce an idea by windings and turnings. It refers to the developing of the *understanding* gradually and indirectly. See Coredemptrix.

Inspiration 105

Inspiration is the special influence of the *Holy Spirit* on the *minds* of the writers of *Sacred Scripture* by which God himself becomes the principal author of what is written. The human writer is the instrument used by the Holy Spirit in harmony with the *person's temperament* without *violence* to the free and *natural* use of his *faculties*. Inspiration is a special immediate action or *supernatural* impulse of the *Holy Spirit* in the *human mind* or *soul*. It also refers to the *divine* influence under which the books of Scripture were written. The *supernatural* impulse of the Holy Spirit and the divine influence under which Scripture was written are different from one another.

The *canonical* books of Scripture are not works that were written naturally and then 'approved' by the Church. Rather, they truly have as their author God, who willed to commit them to the Church as inerrant. It is in this way that the Church recognizes their inspired character.

Inspired

Inspire comes from the Latin word 'inspirare,' meaning to breathe into. In English, it means to breathe on or into. In respect to *Scripture*, it means to cause, guide, communicate, or motivate by *divine* and *supernatural* influence. See Sacred Scripture 102. See Inspiration 105.

Instigation

Instigation is the act of inciting, urging, or spurring to action. See Grace 35.

Instinct/Instinctual

The word instinct comes from the Latin word 'instigare,' meaning to goad or stimulate. An instinct is an inborn tendency to behave in a certain way. It is a *natural* nonacquired way of responding to certain stimuli. See Appetitive.

Instinctual appetite

An *appetite* is a tendency or desire for one thing rather than another. An instinctual appetite is one that requires only sense stimulation to be activated. It is distinguished from the *intellectual* or *spiritual* appetite, also called the *will*, which is only activated by the exercise of *free choice*. See Soul 363. Also see Free will.

Institutes/Institutes of Christian Perfection 925

The term institutes refers to *societies* of men or women, approved by *ecclesiastical authority*, whose members, in keeping with the *laws* of their association, take *temporary* and *perpetual vows* of *poverty*, *chastity*, and *obedience*.

Institutes are either *clerical* or *lay*. *Clerical* institutes are those in which a notable proportion of the members receive *Holy Orders*. Lay institutes are those in which only a few receive Holy Orders.

For *canonical* approval by the Church, institutes must receive positive and formal approval from the *Holy See* or the *Bishop* and have a *rule* or *constitutions* which determine their mode of governance and the *rights* and *duties* of their members. Each member must take the *vows of religion* publicly.

Institution narrative 1353

The institution narrative refers to the *scriptural* accounts of the institution of the *Holy Eucharist* (cf. Mt 26:26–30; Mk 14:22–25; Lk 22:14–20; 1 Cor 11:23–27).

Insurmountable

Insurmountable means impossible to overcome. See Tree of knowledge of good and evil 396.

Integrity

Integrity is the total absence of *concupiscence* in *prelapsarian man* by a *preternatural gift* of God. By virtue of this gift, man's whole sensitive and imaginative life was completely under the control of and ruled by *reason*. See Original sin 389. Also see Preternatural gift; Original justice 376.

Integrity (property of beauty)

See Beauty 341.

Integrity of creation 2415

Integrity of creation requires that all creation, plants, animals, and inanimate *beings*, be destined by their *nature* for the *common good* of past, present, and future humanity. Their use cannot be divorced from respect for *moral imperatives*.

Man's dominion over the earth is not absolute but is limited by concern for the quality of life of his neighbors, including the generations to come, and demands a *religious* respect for all *creation*, which was *created* for the common good of all men.

Intellect/Intellectual

The intellect is a *faculty* of the *soul*. It refers to *man's cognitive* or knowing faculty and is commonly referred to as the *mind*. The ability of the intellect to recognize truths that are self-evident is called *intelligence*. When, by thinking, the intellect determines by *logical* steps truths that are not self-evident, it is called *reason*.

When the intellect is aware of itself and the world, it is called *intellectual consciousness.* When the intellect, by reasoning, determines the *morality of an act* and judges its morality, it is called *conscience.* When the intellect retains its *knowledge*, it is called *intellectual memory.* See Soul 363.

Intellectual agent

When the cause of an action is a *person* acting with *knowledge* and a deliberate choice because of an *act of the will*, it called an intellectual agent. See Contingent cause.

Intellectual appetite/appetency

Catholic *theology* distinguishes between two kinds of *appetite, intellectual,* and instinctual. The intellectual, or *spiritual*, appetite is known as the *will* because it is only activated by the exercise of *free choice.* The instinctual appetite, however, requires only sense stimulation to be activated.

Intellectual appetite involves two types of affection, the *love* of something for its own sake and the love of something because it is advantageous or useful. When a thing is loved for its own sake, it is loved for itself simply because it is *good, just,* or *holy.* The love of the *divine* goodness for its own sake differs from loving it because it is advantageous to

man. See Soul 363. Also see Appetite/appetency.

Intellectual consciousness

Intellectual *consciousness* is the awareness by the *intellect* of itself and of the world outside it. See Soul 363.

Intellectual discernment

Intellectual discernment is the power or act of the *intellect* by which it discriminates among the different ways that *moral principles* apply to individual cases or situations. See Prudence 1806.

Intellectual memory

The act by which the *intellect* retains *knowledge* is called intellectual memory. See Soul 363. Also see Intellect/Intellectual.

Intellectual virtue

An intellectual *virtue* is a *habit* and disposition for *good*, primarily concerned with the development of the power to know *truth. Knowledge* of the truth is necessary for man to live a virtuous life. See Virtue 1768, 1803.

Intelligence/Intelligent

As a faculty of the *soul*, intelligence refers to the ability of the *intellect* to recognize *truths* that are self-evident. Generally, intelligence refers to the ability to learn and understand from *experience*, to retain *knowledge*, and to use it to solve problems. See Soul 363.

Intemperance

Intemperance is another name for *gluttony*. See Capital Sins 1866.

Intention/Intentional 1752

Intention refers to the aim, goal, or plan that inspires a mental or physical *act*. Intention resides in the acting subject and constitutes the *voluntary* source of action determined by it.

Intention, together with object and circumstance, is an *essential* element in the *moral* evaluation of an act because the intention is a movement of the *will* toward an *end*, or goal. One intention can direct several actions when they are directed to the same purpose. A given act may be inspired by several intentions acting simultaneously.

Intentional act

An act is intentional when the *will* directs one's activities toward a definite *end*. See Intentional homicide 2268.

Intentional homicide 2268

Intentional homicide is the taking of human life in an act in which death is sought as a definite *end* by the *will*.

Intercede

Intercede comes from the Latin word 'intercedere' from 'inter,' meaning between,

and 'cedere,' meaning to go. To intercede means to plead or make a request on behalf of another. See Intercession 1354.

Intercession 1354

Intercession refers to the prayers of one *person* or of the Church for others. A great intercession forms part of every *Mass*. It is a prayer for all ranks and *orders* in the Church. In the intercession, the *celebrant* names those for whom he wishes to *pray* in particular and makes a *commemoration* of the *saints*.

The Catechism of the Catholic Church teaches that the *Eucharist* is "*celebrated* in communion with the whole Church in *heaven* and on earth, the living and the dead, and in communion with the pastors of the Church, the *Pope*, the *diocesan bishop*, his *presbyterium* and his *deacons*, and all the bishops of the whole world together with their Churches" (CCC 1354).

In the Eucharist, the Church offers up her Head and herself entirely to the Father. "The *sacrifice* of *Christ* becomes also the sacrifice of the members of his Body" (CCC 1368). The Eucharistic presence on the altar makes it possible for all generations to be united with his offering. It is in this sense that 'Eucharistic intercesssion' refers to Christ as the one mediator or intercessor before the Father. The

Church "unites herself to his intercession with the Father for all men" (CCC 1368).

Intercession of the saints 956
Intercession of the *saints* refers to the practice of praying to them to intercede with God on one's behalf in virtue of the bonds of *fraternal charity* they have with him in *Christ*.
Because they are more closely united to Christ, the saints in *heaven* fix the whole Church in *holiness* by unceasingly interceding for us. By the concern of the Church in heaven, the members of the Church on earth are greatly helped in their weakness.

Intercessory prayer 2634
Intercessory prayer, also called *prayer of intercession*, is a prayer of *petition* on behalf of another. In intercessory prayer, one prays as *Jesus* did. "He is the one intercessor with the Father on behalf of all men, especially sinners" (CCC 2634). Asking on behalf of others is characteristic of a heart attuned to God's *mercy*. *Christian* intercession participates in *Christ's* prayer as an expression of the *communion of saints*.

Intercourse, marital
Intercourse refers to communication or dealings among people or to an exchange of products, services, ideas, or feelings.
Marital means pertaining to

marriage. Among the most intimate exchanges between *spouses* is *sexual intercourse*, referred to as marital intercourse. See Sexual intercourse.

Interdependence of creatures 340
Dependence comes from the Latin word 'dependere,' meaning to hang down. In English, it means to be influenced or determined by something else or to rely on something for support. The *Catechism* teaches that "God wills the interdependence of creatures" (CCC 340). The sheer diversity and inequalities of *creation* reveal that no creature is self-sufficient. "Creatures exist only in dependence on each other, to complete each other, in the service of each other" (CCC 340). Only by service to others is man able to practice *charity*. The basis for *solidarity* among all creatures arises from the fact that "all have the same *Creator* and are all ordered to his *glory*" (CCC 344).

Interdict
See Ecclesiastical penalty

Interior conversion 1430
Interior conversion is also called *conversion of heart*. It refers to the turning away from *sin* and toward the ways of *holiness* and conformity to the *will of God*. Conversion is

at the heart of the preaching of John the Baptist and *Christ*.

It comes about through hearing the *Word of God* and accepting it as the guiding principle of one's life. In the Church, it refers to the interior turning to God through *repentance*, the acceptance of Christ as presented by the Church's teachings, and living a *just* life with the help of *grace* from the *sacraments*.

Interior life

Interior life refers to the inner life and activity of a *person* taking place in privacy and not available to others. The interior life is called the *spiritual* life because its animating principle is the *Holy Spirit* by means of *sanctifying grace*.

The interior life is lived out in the spiritual *faculties* of *intellect* and *will*, although it affects the whole *person*, body and *soul*. See Discernment 1676.

Interior prayer 2664

Interior prayer is also called *prayer of the heart*. It consists in prayer that takes place in the *mind* and *heart* of an individual. See Prayer.

Interior repentance 1431

Interior *repentance* is the "radical reorientation of our whole life, a return, a *conversion* to God with all our *heart*, an end of *sin*, a turning away from *evil*, with repugnance toward the evil actions we

have committed. At the same time it entails the "desire and *resolution* to change one's life, with hope in God's *mercy* and trust in the help of his *grace*" (CCC 1431). True repentance and conversion is manifested by *fasting, prayer, almsgiving*, and the practice of *virtue*.

Interiority 1779

Interiority is the state of introspection or being turned inward and made aware of the self and its operations and state, in a word, to be present to oneself. It is important for each *person* to be sufficiently present to himself in order for him to hear and follow the dictates of *conscience*.

Intermediary

An intermediary is a *person* who *acts* between persons as an *agent* or medium for communication. See Gnosticism 285.

Internal consent

Consent is the act by which the *will voluntarily* complies with something presented to it as good. The consent required for the *validity* of a *contract* or agreement must be internal, that is, made with the intention of fulfilling the *obligations* involved. See Consent 1627.

Internal forum

The internal forum is that forum or sphere within which the Church exercises her *judicial authority* in matters of *conscience* in the *sacrament* of *Penance*, or *Confession*, where *sins* are forgiven and matters of *morality*, such as *guilt*, *restitution*, and *responsibility*, are decided. See Ecclesiastical penalty 1463.

Interpretation of tongues, Gift of

The gift of interpretation of tongues accompanies the gift of speaking in tongues.

The gift of *tongues* is one of the gifts given to the *Apostles* on Pentecost. It is also called *glossolalia*. The ability of hearers to understand someone speaking in a foreign language is the gift of interpretation of tongues. See Charism. Also see Glossolalia.

Interpretative intention

An interpretative intention is one that was never actually made but which would have been made if the *person* had thought about it. See Intentional homicide 2268.

Intrinsic/Intrinsically

Intrinsic refers to anything that belongs to the *nature* or *essence* of a thing and is not dependent on circumstances. See Soul 363. Also see Grave matter 1858.

Intrinsically evil act

An intrinsically evil act is an act that is *evil* in its very *nature* independent of external circumstances. It can never be justified on *moral* grounds. See Rape 2356.

Intrinsically indissoluble

A marriage is said to be intrinsically indissoluble because of its *nature*. Neither the *spouses* themselves nor any *human* institution can dissolve the *marriage bond*. See Indissolubility 1644.

Introit

The word introit comes from the Latin word 'introitus,' meaning 'to go in.' It is an introductory *rite* of *Mass* consisting of an *antiphon* or *hymn*, which may be either sung or recited, as the *priest* approaches the *altar*, kisses it, and proceeds to the place where he will greet the *faithful* and begin the *penitential act*. See Confiteor.

Intuition/Intuitive/Intuitively

Intuition comes from the Latin word 'intuere,' meaning to look upon or regard. In English, it is applied to direct *knowledge* acquired without the conscious use of *reason*. In intuition, the *mind* perceives something, without conscious attention or reasoning, as immediately evident, such as the insight into the meaning of *first principles* or primary *truths*.

Intuitive knowledge

Intuitive comes from the Latin word 'intuitus,' meaning 'to look at or regard'. Intuitive knowledge is direct knowing or learning without the conscious use of *reason*. It is an immediate *understanding*. See First principle.

Invalid/invalidate

Invalid means not binding under *law*, and invalidate means to *render null* and *void*. See Indissolubility 1644. Also see Ignorance of the law.

Invalid marriage

The word *invalid* comes from the Latin word 'invalidus' meaning weak, feeble, chronically ill, and disabled. An invalid *marriage* is one having no legal force and is considered void, empty, null, or not binding. Marriage may be declared null or lacking in legal force when it conflicts with a *natural*, *divine*, or *ecclesiastical* law that makes it impossible.

Such an obstacle is called a *diriment impediment*. It may arise from a condition in the *person*, from something he has done, or from some circumstance arising from the relationship between the persons attempting marriage. This would be the case in the absence of *matrimonial consent* or the omission of the proper *canonical form* of celebration required for *validity*.

When a diriment impediment is discovered, such a union must either be declared null by *judicial* process or *regularized* by *convalidation*.

In such a case, the union entered into, even in good faith, is in fact not a true marriage. The Church, after examination by an *ecclesiastical tribunal*, can declare a nullity of the marriage, that is, that the marriage never existed. In this case, the persons are still free to marry if natural *obligations* of their attempted union are discharged. See Convalidation of a marriage.

Invalidating impediment

Impediment is called 'impedimentum' in Latin. It comes from 'impedire,' meaning a hindrance. It is an obstacle that hinders the *validity* or legality of an *act* or prevents its effects. An impediment that specifically renders an act *invalid* and lacking legality is called an invalidating impediment. See Diriment impediment.

Inversion of means and ends
1887

An end is the *objective* or purpose for which a thing exists or for which an action takes place. A *means* is something that is necessary to achieve an end. The inversion of means and ends occurs when a means, which is intended to be used only to attain an end, is made an end in itself.

Eating and drinking are means of sustaining the *person* so that he can work out his *ultimate end, salvation*. When eating and drinking result in drunkenness and *gluttony*, they have become ends in themselves rather than a means to an end.

For example, means, and ends are inverted when persons are used merely as means to *sexual* pleasure, as occurs in the use of *artificial birth control*. It changes love into lust and destroys the personal *dignity* of another by using him or her only for selfish pleasure. Such *lust* makes the *Christian* commitment to serve others in *charity* difficult or impossible. Charity requires one to serve others rather than to use them.

Invincible ignorance

Invincible ignorance is absence of *knowledge* under circumstances in which knowledge cannot be obtained without extraordinary effort.

It is said to be *physically invincible ignorance* if the knowledge cannot be obtained by any amount of care and diligence.

It is called *morally invincible ignorance* if the knowledge cannot be obtained by the amount of care and diligence an ordinarily prudent *man* would exercise under similar circumstances. See Conscience 1706.

Inviolable fidelity 1646

Inviolable fidelity refers to the loyalty and commitment to a union, which cannot be violated. By its *nature, conjugal* love requires the inviolable

fidelity of the *spouses*. "This is the *consequence* of the gift of themselves which they make to each other... The 'intimate union of *marriage*, as a mutual giving of two *persons*, and the good of the children, demand total *fidelity* from the *spouses* and require an unbreakable union between them'" (CCC 1646).

Through the *sacrament* of *matrimony*, the spouses represent the fidelity of *Christ* to his Church as well as their fidelity and witness to their union.

Invocation

Invocation comes from the Latin 'in,' meaning in or down on, and 'vocare,' meaning to call. Invocation is the calling on God or a *saint* for *blessing*, help, *inspiration*, or support.

There is a special form of invocation referred to as *epiclesis*, derived from the Greek word 'epiklesis,' meaning invocation. It is an *intercessory prayer* in which the *priest* begs the Father to send the *Holy Spirit*, the *Sanctifier*, so that the offerings at the *Eucharist* may become the Body and Blood of *Christ* and that the *faithful*, by receiving them, may themselves become a living offering to God.

In the administration of every *sacrament*, there is a prayer of epiclesis calling down the Holy Spirit. See Epiclesis 1105, 1238, 1353, 1519, 2583, 2770.

Involuntary

Involuntary means not under the control of *free will* or contrary to one's intention or will. *Involuntary acts* are not *morally imputable*. See Negligence 1736.

Involuntary doubt 2088

"Involuntary doubt refers to hesitation in believing, difficulty in overcoming objections connected with the *faith*, or also anxiety aroused by its obscurity" (CCC 2088). It refers to a concern over what some Church teaching really means without actually refusing it. Such doubt is not sinful, but the *person* must seek the understanding that will remove it.

Ipso facto

'Ipso facto' is a Latin expression meaning 'by the fact, or act, itself.' It is used to indicate that a certain *consequence* follows a certain action or set of circumstances automatically. See Mixed marriage 1633.

Irrational

Irrational is derived from the Latin word 'rationales.' Irrational refers to a lack of power to *reason*, or senseless, absurd, or contrary to reason. It implies mental unsoundness. Animals are irrational because they lack the capacity to reason. Because of this, they are referred to as brute creatures. See Spiritual.

Irascible emotions/appetency

Appetency is the tendency of one thing toward another. Irascible appetency is the propensity to fight an *evil*.

Emotions are forms of appetency. In *Scholastic philosophy* emotions are classified as *concupiscible* or irascible.

When the *good* is difficult to attain or evil is difficult to avoid, the irascible emotions are aroused. These are classed as follows: 1) hope, which considers an absent good to be possible to attain; 2) despair, which considers a good to be impossible to attain; 3) courage, which views a threatened evil as conquerable; 4) fear, which considers an evil to be unavoidable; 5) *anger*, which is aroused by an evil that has already overcome the *person*. Though this classification does not include every possible emotion, such as surprise, pity, anxiety, etc., it adequately covers the primary and fundamental emotions, which are combinations of the others. See Anger 2302.

Ire

Ire is a strong feeling of resentment against another or an inflammation of the *mind* to an inordinate *aggression* against someone or something with a desire for *vengeance*.

Ire is also called *rage, wrath,* or *anger*. Ire generates *indignation, rancor, blasphemy, violence,* insults, and resentments. It is opposed to *patience, long suffering, equanimity*, and *charity*. See Anger 2302.

Irenics

Irenic means pacifying, peacemaking, or non-*polemic*. Irenics is the *doctrine* or practice of promoting peace among *Christian* churches having *theological* differences.

Irenical *theology*, or irenics, presents the points of agreement among Christians with a view to the ultimate unity of Christendom. See Polemical 575.

Irony 2481

Irony is speech that belittles or makes fun of others by mimicking some aspect of their behavior. Irony is an expression in which the intended meaning is the opposite of what is expressed.

Irrevocable 393

An act is irrevocable when it cannot be changed, repealed, *annulled*, or undone. It is absolutely unalterable and irreversible.

Because it was irrevocable, the *sin* of the *fallen angels* is unforgivable. Their choice to reject God is irrevocable. It is the irrevocable character of their choice, not a defect in divine *mercy*, that prevents their *repenting* and asking for God's mercy. Because after death *man*'s choice becomes irrevocable, there can be no repentance for men after death.

Israel/Israelites

Israel is the name given to Jacob by an *angel* after wrestling with him all night. He became the personification of the nation of Israel, and his descendants were called Israelites. See Deuteronomical tradition 2697.

Israelitic

Israelitic refers to that which pertains to the *Israelites*. See Code of the Covenant.

Israelitica dignitas 528

Israelitica dignitas is a Latin phrase meaning Israelitic *dignity*. The *Epiphany* showed that all nations now can take their place in the family of the *patriarchs* and are made worthy of the heritage of Israel. By this, the *gentiles* share the *dignity* of *Israelites* as *chosen people*.

J

Jahwist

Jahwist is a variant form of *Yahwist*. It refers to the author of one source of the *Pentateuch* called the J-source. The author regularly uses the word *Yahweh* for God, such as in Gen 2:4. It is generally considered to be the oldest account.

The name of the author for another source for the documents of the Pentateuch is referred to as *Elohist*, or E-source, because this author uses the word 'elohim' for God. See Genesis. Also see Elohist; Pentateuch.

Jansenism

Jansenism is a *heresy* that deals with the problem of *grace* and *free will*. This heresy taught that, as a result of *original sin, man* was no longer capable of acting freely and, therefore, acted under the compulsion either of *fallen nature* or of grace. This opinion makes *salvation* dependent solely on God and his grace.

There are two problems involved. First, God's grace is unquestionably effective, but, with free will, man can choose to reject it. If grace *nullifies* free will, man is no longer respon-sible for his acts because they are beyond his control.

Secondly, if only grace is necessary for salvation, *redemption* would require God to give it to all by virtue of universal redemption. In that case, it would cease to be a free, gratuitous *gift* and would become something owed to redeemed man. If man could make good *moral* choices without grace, he could achieve salvation without grace, and salvation would not be a free gift of God.

Jansenism is an effort to solve the problem between *freedom* and grace, but solves it by requiring either the elimination of freedom of the will in man or by compelling God to save him.

Salvation does depend on the gratuitous grace of God, but man is always free to respond or not to respond to it, as he chooses. Salvation then is chosen by man cooperating with the grace of God. See Heresy 817.

Jehovah

God's name appears in the Old Testament as *Yahweh* (JHWH) or Jahveh (*JHVH*). The word Jehovah grew from a false reading of the name of God as found in the current

Hebrew text. Yahweh is probably the correct pronunciation of the *sacred* name. See YHWH 206.

Jesus 430

The name of Jesus comes from the Aramaic word 'Yeshu,' meaning 'Jahweh is *salvation.*' This was the name given to *Christ* by God himself at the *Annunciation.* It signifies that the very name of God is present in the *Person* of his Son. It is the divine name, which alone brings salvation.

Jesus' hidden life 512, 513

Jesus' hidden life refers to the years in *Christ's* life that are not discussed in *canonical Scripture.* Nothing is known of the details of Christ's life in the years between when he was lost in the *Temple* at twelve years old and his baptism in the Jordan. These are called the hidden years.

Jesus' public life 512, 513

Jesus' public life refers to the three years preceding his death, during which time he preached *salvation* and worked wonders. Records of Jesus' public life are found in the *Gospels* of Saints Matthew, Mark, Luke, and John.

Jews/Jewish

Jew is derived from the *Hebrew* word Judah. The term 'Jew' may refer either to those who adhere to *Judaism* as a *religion* or to the members of any of the twelve Hebrew tribes.

After the death of Solomon (c. 932 B.C.), the twelve tribes divided into two kingdoms, Judah in the south and Israel in the north. The name Jew came to refer to the inhabitants of the kingdom of Judah, and the inhabitants of Israel were called *Israelites.* See High Priest.

Joyful mysteries of the Rosary

Meditation on a *mystery* of the *faith* drawn from the *Gospels* accompanies the recitation of each decade of *Hail Mary's* of the *Rosary.* These meditations are known as the mysteries of the Rosary.

The mysteries of the Rosary are collected into groups of related scriptural events referred to as the Joyful, Sorrowful, Glorious, and Luminous mysteries. The recitation of five decades and meditation on a set of mysteries ends with the prayer Hail Holy Queen.

The Joyful mysteries, used on Saturdays and Mondays, are The Annunciation (Lk 1:26–38), The Visitation (Lk 1:39–56; Jn 1:19–23), The Nativity (Mt 2:1–12; Lk 2:1–20), The Presentation (Lk 1:22–35), and the Finding of Jesus in the temple (Lk 21:44–50). See Rosary 971, 2678, 2708.

Judaism

Judaism refers to the religion revealed by God to the *Jews* through Moses and the *proph-*

ets. It is preserved in the Old Testament. See Circumcision 527.

Judgment

A judgment is an act of the *mind* pronouncing agreement or disagreement between two ideas. A judgment can also be an *act of the will* in favor of or against some *person*, thing, or idea. See Conscience 1706, 1776. Also see Human reason.

Juridical

Juridical refers to court proceedings or to matters related to the *legal* system. See Free union 2390.

Jurisdiction

Jurisdiction refers to the *authority* given by *Christ* to his Church to rule her members for *spiritual* purposes. Church jurisdiction can only be exercised by *clerics* and is attached to their *office*. It can only be exercised over their own subjects and in their own territories. The *Pope* has jurisdiction over the entire Church. See Power of the keys 553.

Just

A just *man* is one who is of good *moral* character, who is faithful to God's *law*, who has been delivered from *sin*, and who is innocent of blame. See Righteousness 1224, 1991.

Just wage 2434

The *legitimate* fruit of work is referred to as a just wage.

The refusal or withholding of wages can be a *grave injustice*. It is one of the *sins* that cry to God for *vengeance*.

In determining a fair wage, both the needs and contributions of each worker must be taken into account. Wages "should guarantee man the opportunity to provide a dignified livelihood for himself and his family on the *material*, *social*, cultural, and *spiritual* level" (CCC 2434).

Mere agreement to work for a given wage alone is not sufficient to *morally* justify the amount of wages to be received.

Just war doctrine 2309

The just war doctrine refers to the conditions required for *legitimate defense by military force.*

There are four conditions required for legitimate defense by military force. These conditions must be considered and all be present at one and the same time:

"– the damage inflicted by the aggressor... must be lasting, *grave*, and certain;

– all other means of putting an end to it must have been shown to be impractical or ineffective;

– there must be serious prospects of success;

– the use of arms must not produce evils and disorders graver than the *evil* to be eliminated" (CCC 2309).

Justice 2407

Justice, as a *cardinal moral virtue*, consists in the constant and firm will to give to God and neighbor what is due to them. Justice toward God is called the *virtue of religion*. It differs from *charity* because justice involves what is due to others by right. Justice rests in the distinction between a *person* and his neighbor. Charity focuses on the union that exists between the person and those he *loves*, which enables him to love his neighbor as himself.

Justice may also designate that state of holiness or general *moral* state of perfect harmony with the *will of God*, when, for instance, one is in the *state of grace* and in possession of all the *virtues* and not merely of the moral virtue known as justice.

Justice, as a *moral virtue*, disposes one to respect the *rights* of each individual and to establish in *human* relations the harmony that promotes both equity regarding others and the *common good*.

There are different kinds of justice. *Original justice* refers to the state of *holiness* in which God *created* man's first parents. *Commutative justice* is the *obligation* to respect the rights of others. It is required by the seventh commandment. It is distinguished from *legal justice*, which concerns what the citizen owes to the community, and *distributive jus-tice*, which regulates what the community owes its citizens in proportion to their contributions and needs. *Social justice* is the respect for the *human person* and the rights that both flow from human *dignity* and guarantee it. *Society* must provide the conditions that allow people to obtain what is their due according to their *nature* and *vocation*.

Because of its extent and implications, justice is one of the most important and far-reaching of the *virtues*. Together with *charity*, it governs man's relations with others.

Justice includes many virtues, notably, *religion, obedience, truthfulness, gratitude, liberality*, and *piety*. *Sins* against justice include any act that infringes on another's rights by damage to his property, such as *theft, calumny, detraction*, and *adultery*.

Offenses against justice always require *reparation* in so far as it is possible. See Virtue 1768, 1803.

Justification 1266, 1987

Justification is the gracious action of God that frees man from sin and communicates 'the *righteousness* of God through *faith* in *Jesus Christ*' (Rom 3:22). It is not only the *remission* of sins but also the *sanctification* and renewal of the *interior life* of *man* merited for him by the *Passion* of Christ.

Justification detaches man from *sin* and *purifies* his heart. It follows upon God's merciful initiative of offering man *forgiveness* which reconciles him with God. One accepts God's righteousness through *faith* in Jesus Christ, which establishes cooperation between God's *grace* and man's freedom.

Justification also refers to the change that takes place in a *soul* when it passes from a state of *sin* to one of *sanctifying grace*. It is the action whereby man is justified, or freed from the penalty of sin, and accounted as or made righteous by God.

By justification, man's being is made truly *righteous*, or just, by the infusion of sanctifying grace. Because man can lose sanctifying grace through sin, justification is continuous and progressive from the time it is received and is not a single enduring act of God.

K

Kapporet

On top of the *Ark of the Covenant*, there was a golden plate called 'kapporet' in *Hebrew* and translated as *mercy seat* or *propitiatory* in English. It was known as the place where *Yahweh* receives *atonement*. Above it were two *cherubim* facing one another with their wings overshadowing the kapporet signifying that God would not see the *sin* of the *Jews*. See Mercy seat 433.

Kenosis

'Kenosis' is a Greek word meaning emptying out. As understood by the Church, kenosis refers to the act by which the *Second Person* of the *Trinity*, Jesus, assumed a *human nature* while retaining his *divine nature*. Through the *Incarnation*, the human and divine *natures* of the Second Person of the Holy Trinity are united in a single person.

Christ emptied himself not by laying down his divinity but by concealing it. He, as God, assumed a human form and became like *man* in everything except *sin*.

Kenosis may also refer to a *heretical theory* of the Incarnation found in *Protestant* theology that holds that, when *God the Son* became *man*, he discarded his *divinity* and certain *divine attributes*. In their stead, he assumed purely human gifts and *attributes* and was unaware of his *divinity* until after the *resurrection*. This implies that he could not exercise *omnipotence* and *omniscience*, and was, therefore, no longer really divine. This opinion is irreconcilable with the Church's *doctrine* concerning the *hypostatic union*. See Incarnation 461.

Kingdom of God

The Kingdom of God originally referred to the *Jews*. They were the *people of God*, and he was their king. Later, the *Old Testament prophets* taught the Jews to expect a *Messiah* who was to come. This expectancy was heightened by the political condition of the Jews at the time of *Christ*. John the Baptist preached that the Kingdom of God was at hand in reference to Christ.

Jesus frequently referred to the Kingdom of God and the *kingdom of heaven*. In the *New Testament*, this referred to the *spiritual* rule of God by *grace*. The kingdom of heaven is not a purely future *heavenly* kingdom. It begins in this world with the *Incarnation*. As a spiritual power, God rules the earth through the Church. His rule will become perfect and will come to its fullness at the *end time*. See New earth 1043.

Kingdom of heaven

The kingdom of heaven is the same as the *Kingdom of God*. *Heaven*, as it is used in this context, is simply another way of saying God without mentioning the *sacred* name by substituting the designation of his abode for the name. See Kingdom of God.

Kingly office 908

The kingly office refers to the *duty* of *ordained ministers* to govern the Church and to provide for the *spiritual* needs of the *faithful*.

Kingly office of the laity

By virtue of their *Baptism*, the *laity* share, in their own way, in the kingly office and *mission* of the Church, especially by their *dominion* of self through the use of their *wills* with the support of the *grace* of God. See Kingly office 908.

Kiss of peace

The kiss of peace is a greeting exchanged among members of the community after the Angus Dei (Latin), or Lamb of God in the Mass. See Lamb of God.

Knowledge 1831

Natural knowledge is the clear *perception* of or grasp of *truth*. Knowledge as a *gift of the Holy Spirit*, is a *supernatural* clarity and grasp of the truths of *faith*, creation, and one's *duty* to God. This gift helps one to know these truths, to appraise their *spiritual value*, and to see the connections between them. The gift of knowledge enables one to see the utility of *created* things and to appreciate the magnificent *harmony* and order of all that God has done and revealed.

Knowledge is related to *prudence*. Prudence is a *habit* that enables *man* to view situations from different perspectives so as to decide what is the correct thing to do under given circumstances. The gift of knowledge aids the *virtue* of *prudence* by pointing out things that lead to God or that turn one away from him.

Knowledge can be considered as either practical or speculative. *Practical knowledge* is knowledge put to specific practical use to solve problems or to produce results. *Speculative knowledge*, or knowledge in the *speculative order*, simply enriches the *mind* with *truth*, without application to specific purposes. See Gifts of the Holy Spirit 1831.

Kontakion

A kontakion is a short *hymn* used in the *Byzantine Church* to *commemorate* the *feast* being *celebrated*. See Troparia 1177.

Kyrie eleison/Christe eleison

2613

'Kyrie eleision' is a Greek phrase meaning '*Lord* have mercy.' The Greek phrase 'Christe eleison' means '*Christ* have mercy.' These words are an acknowledgment of one's sin and a request for God's forgiveness.

In *Mass*, after the priest exhorts the people to prepare to *worship* God by repenting for their sins and asking for God's mercy, the people repeat after him the words, 'Lord, have mercy; Christ, have mercy; Lord, have mercy; (Kyrie eleison; Christe eleison; Kyrie eleison).' The words may be recited or sung in Greek or English.

In the early Church, before the Latin language became common, Greek was the language most used for celebrating Mass. The modern use of the Greek 'Kyrie eleison' recalls this ancient usage.

After the penitential act, the 'Kyrie eleison' is said unless it has already been said within the *penitential act*. The 'Kyrie eleison' is an important feature in the *liturgy* of the *Eastern Church*. See Confess/Confession; Penance 1459, 1460.

Kyrios 209, 446

Kyrios is a Greek word meaning *Lord*. It is the more usual name employed in place of the *sacred* same, *Yahweh*, to indicate the God of Israel.

L

Lacticinia

Lacticinia comes from the Latin word 'lac,' meaning milk. It refers to milk and foods made from milk as distinguished from eggs and meat. Lacticinia were formerly forbidden in the Roman Rite on fast days of *Lent*, but this is no longer the case. Their consumption is still forbidden or restricted on various fast days for all *Eastern Rites*. See Great Lent.

Laetare Sunday

The Fourth *Sunday* of *Lent* is called Laetare Sunday. The name is taken from 'Laetare,' the first word of the *Introit* of the *Mass* on that day. In Latin, 'laetare' means rejoice. On this day, the organ may be used, flowers may be placed on the *altar*, and rose-colored *vestments* are worn. The day is joyful because, on this day, the handing over of the *Apostles' Creed* takes place, which is the decisive moment in the preparation of *catechumens* for *Baptism*. It is indeed a time to rejoice. See Liturgical seasons.

Laity 897

All the *baptized faithful* who are not in *Holy Orders* or in some *religious* state approved by the Church are called the *laity*. Those in Holy Orders are called the *clergy*, those in the religious state are called the *religious*, and all others are called the laity or, simply, *laymen*. All the faithful incorporated into *Christ* through *Baptism* are the *people of God* and of the Church.

The laity participate, in their own way, in the *priestly, prophetic*, and *kingly* functions of Christ. Their role is priestly through their offering of themselves and their lives in *union with Christ* and his *sacrifice*. It is prophetic through their acceptance of the *Gospel* and their *proclamation* of it to the world. It is kingly because they belong to Christ the King and are called to rule themselves by living *virtuous* lives on earth in cooperation with the *grace* of God.

Lamb of God

Lamb of God, also called 'Angus Dei' in Latin, is the triple invocation, or *prayer*, that accompanies the fraction of the host by the priest in preparation for communion. It is recited or sung by the *faithful* in the *Mass* immediately following the *kiss of peace*. See

Appendix of prayers; Prayers recited at Mass - Lamb of God.

Lascivious

Something is called lascivious when it excites *lustful* desires. See Pornography 2354.

Last days 678, 732

The phrase 'last days' refers to the final time or age of the earth. The coming of the *Holy Spirit* caused the world to enter the 'last days,' which is the time of the Church. The *Kingdom of God* is already inherited, though not yet *consummated*, during these last days.

Last hour, the 670

The last or final hour refers to the final age of the world after which it will be renewed in *eternity*. It is also used to designate the last moments of life of an individual just prior to death.

Last judgment 1038

The last judgment is the final encounter with *Christ* at his *second coming* after the *resurrection* of the body. At the last judgment, the body will share in the reward or punishment of the soul, and the *righteousness* of God's way will be made manifest and *vindicated* before all creation. For this reason, it is also called the *general judgment*.

Last Supper

The Last Supper refers to the *Paschal* meal *celebrated* by *Christ* with his *disciples* the night before he suffered. It was at this celebration that he instituted the *Holy Eucharist* and commanded his *Apostles* to do the same in *memory* of him. See Eucharist 1328.

Latae sententiae 2272

'Latae sententiae' is the term used in the 1983 *Code of Canon Law* to refer to the automatic imposition of a *canonical penalty* as soon as the *ecclesiastical* crime has been committed. See Ecclesiastical penalty.

Latin Church

Latin Church refers to the Church of Rome, or the Western Church. Though the reference 'Latin Church' is useful, it actually embraces several *rites*: 1) the *Roman Rite* and its derivatives, such as the *Ambrosian* and *Mozarabic liturgies*, and 2) the rites of some *religious orders*, including the *Carmelite Rite*, the *Dominican Rite*, and the *Carthusian Rite*. See Rituale Romanum 168. Also see Latin Rite; Roman Rite.

Latin Mass

Latin Mass refers to the liturgy of the Mass in the *Roman Rite* that uses the Latin language.

There are two forms of the *liturgy* in the Roman Rite. The *Ordinary Form* uses the *vernacular*, that is, the language of the people as well as Latin, and the *Extraordinary Form* uses the traditional Latin. This difference gave rise to the term 'Latin Mass' in reference to liturgies that use the Latin language.

The Extraordinary Form is the Mass celebrated according to the *Roman Missal* published by Pope John XXIII in 1962, and the Ordinary Form is celebrated according to the Roman Missal promulgated by Pope Paul VI, which can be celebrated in Latin or in the *vernacular*. See Rituale Romanum 168. Also see Latin Church; Rite 1203.

Latin Rite or Roman Rite

Latin *Rite*, or Roman Rite, refers to the *ceremonies*, forms of *liturgical* worship, and administration of *sacraments* using the Latin language in the Western Church. The Western Church can also be referred to as the *Roman Church*, or *Patriarchate* of the West. See Rituale Romanum 168. Also see Latin Church.

Latria

Latria is the type of *worship* or *reverence* reserved to God alone as distinct from all other acts of reverence given to *created persons.*

Adoration is the acknowledgment by *man* that he is a creature before his *Creator*. "It exalts the greatness of the Lord who made us and the almighty power of the Savior who sets us free from *evil*" (CCC 2628).

Adoration is the homage of supreme worship rendered to God as the Creator, the supreme *good*, and the thrice *holy, sovereign, transcendent,* and *omnipotent being*. Such worship is the first act of the *virtue of religion*. See Adoration 2628.

Lauds

Lauds is the hour of the *Divine Office* said in the morning. It is also called *Morning Prayer*. It is one of the *major hours*, and the *Benedictus* (Lk 1:68–79) is recited or sung during it. See Liturgy of the Hours 1174, 1178.

Law 1951

A law is a rule of conduct enacted by competent *authority* for the *common good*.

Law of bondage

The law of bondage refers to the law of the *Old Testament*, which could not forgive *sin* but which required strict adherence. It is in contrast to the *law of freedom* in the *New Testament*, which sets *man* free from the *ritual* and *juridical* observances of the *Old Law*.

The day of *expiation* is the day set apart by the *Jewish* people for observing the *Day of Atonement* for sin. Atonement, however, is not forgiveness in the *Old Law* because it is impossible to make complete *atonement* for an offense against *infinite* goodness. See Day of Atonement 578. Also see Atonement; Law of freedom 1972; Old law 1952.

Law of freedom 1972

The law of freedom is the *New Law*. It is called the law of freedom not because it abolishes *law* as such, but "because it sets us free from the *ritual* and *juridical* observances of the *Old Law*, inclines us to act spontaneously by the prompting of *charity* and, finally, lets us pass from the condition of a servant... to that of a friend of *Christ*... or even to the status of son and heir" (CCC 1972)

Law of grace 1972

The *New Law* is called the law of *grace* because it confers the strength of grace to act *morally* by means of *faith* and the *sacraments*.

Law of love 1972

The law of love is another name for the *New Law* because the *love* that motivates it is service to God and neighbor. It moves one to *act* out of love *infused* by the *Holy Spirit* rather than out of fear.

Law of Moses

The Law of Moses refers to the legislation found in the books of *Genesis*, *Exodus*, *Leviticus*, *Numbers*, and *Deuteronomy*, which make up the *Pentateuch*. It is also called the *Mosaic Law*.

The content of the Law of Moses is divided into six parts: 1) the *Decalogue*, 2) the *Code of the Covenant*, 3) the 'Jahwist' *ritual* Decalogue, 4) the *Deuteronomic Code*, 5) the *Holiness Code*, and 6) the *Priestly Code*.

The Decalogue is also called the *Ten Commandments*.

The Code of the Covenant is a collection of humanitarian, *religious laws* formulated differently from *civil* and criminal laws.

The 'Jahwist' ritual Decalogue is a series of laws pertaining entirely to religious practices, prohibitions, festivals, and offerings.

The Deuteronomic Code contains various *cultic* and humanitarian regulations.

The Holiness Code is a collection of religious and cultic regulations which includes a series of moral *precepts* and an extended treatment of *marriage*.

The Priestly Code is directed toward those responsible for public worship. See Genesis.

Law of Sinai 577

The Law of Sinai is the *Decalogue* or *Ten Commandments*. It is also called the *Ten Words*. It was given to Moses by God on Mt. Sinai.

Law of the covenant

A *covenant* is a solemn agreement between two *human persons*, or between God and *man*, involving mutual commitments or guarantees. The binding power of the covenant gives it the character of *law*.

In the *Old Testament*, God entered into a covenant with Israel in which he promised his protection in return for exclusive loyalty. After Moses presented God's offer to the people, they replied as one, and the compact was sealed (Ex 19:5–8).

Years later, Jeremiah revealed that a *new covenant* would be offered, which would make an *eternal* covenant of peace with them (Ez 37:26). The new and *eternal* covenant was made at the *Last Supper* when *Christ* repeated the words 'This cup is the new covenant in my blood' (1 Cor 11:25). This is called the *New Covenant*.

In early *Hebrew* society, written documents were not in common use. Instead, the spoken word was invested with a *ritual* solemnity, which made it a sort of *concrete* reality incapable of being *annulled* or retracted. For the *Jews*, a covenant was a solemn ritual agreement in which the covenanting parties mutually bound themselves by calling down *curses* upon them should they violate it. In the New Covenant, man promises *fidelity* to the *commandments* of the Lord and curses himself with eternal damnation if he should not fulfill it. God promises man protection against the forces of *evil*, that is, the *graces* necessary for *salvation*. A covenant established an artificial blood kinship between the parties, second only to the blood bond of families, which signified affection and loyalty to kinsmen. Hence, in the New Covenant men become children of God through *Baptism*. See Born under the Law 422.

Law of the Gospel 1952

Law of the Gospel is another name for the *revealed law*, the guide to *human* behavior contained in the *Old* and *New Testaments*.

Lawful

Lawful means something permitted by law or legitimate. See Validity 1635.

Laws of growth (Chastity) 2343

Chastity and, indeed, all *virtues* have *laws* of growth that progress through stages marked by imperfection and, too often, by *sin*. Day by day, *man* builds the *virtue* of chastity through many free decisions with the help of *divine grace* and so gradually accomplishes *moral* good by developing virtue in stages.

Lay

Lay comes from the Greek word 'laicus,' meaning not *priestly*. In the Church, lay refers to the *faithful* who have not received the *sacrament* of *Holy Orders*. See Laity 897. Also see Institutes 925.

Lay Apostolate

Apostolate is derived from the word *'apostle,'* meaning emissary or *missionary*. It refers to work accomplished on behalf of the Lord, by the non-ordained, or *lay*, members of the Church. This term is properly used in referring to *ecclesial* work done by *laypersons*. See Apostolate 863.

Layman/layperson

A layman is any member of the Church who is not a *cleric* or *religious*. As a group, laymen are called the laity. Also see Laity 897.

Leaven

Leaven is any substance that causes fermentation. This causes dough to rise. When introduced into dough, it modifies the whole mass. It is a symbol of *moral* influence upon others.

The *Jews* ate unleavened bread, by command of God, in commemoration of the original *Exodus* in haste from Egypt. The unleavened bread was also a sign of sinlessness or of holiness. Thus, in the *New Testament*, the "old leaven... of malice and evil" is contrasted with the "unleavened bread of sincerity and truth" (1 Cor 5:8). But also, in the Gospels, *Christ* compares the *kingdom of heaven* to yeast, which leavens all who come under its influence. See Chaldean Church.

Lectern 1184

A lectern is a high moveable reading stand used to support the books containing the

readings used during *liturgical* services. It is also called an *ambo*. See Ambo 1184.

Lectio divina or spiritual reading 1177, 2708

Lectio divina is the reading of and *meditating* on the *Word of God* or writings of *spiritual* masters and making them a form of *prayer*. It also refers to any serious reading intended to bring the soul nearer to God by *exhortation*, *exposition*, *meditation*, or example in order to extend one's *knowledge* of the *faith* and *holy* things.

It may consist in reading material drawn from *Scripture*, the *Fathers of the Church*, or other spiritual masters, which more deeply reveals the meaning of a *mystery* of the faith or Church teaching. It is especially useful as preparation for *silent prayer* and *contemplation*.

Lectionary

A lectionary is the liturgical book containing passages of *Scripture* proclaimed during the Liturgy of the Word of the *Mass*. See Lector. Also see Cycles.

Lector

Formerly, lector was the second *minor order* in the Western Church. His duties were to intone the *lessons* and to bless the bread. At his *ordination*, he was handed a *lectionary*. The minor order of lector has been suppressed; however, the lay ministry of lector (also known as reader) continues to exist in the Church, as redefined by Pope Paul VI in 1973. "The reader is appointed for a function proper to him, that of reading the word of God in the *liturgical* assembly. Accordingly, he is to proclaim the readings from *Sacred Scripture*, except for the *Gospel* in the *Mass* and other *sacred celebrations*" (*Ministeria Quaedam*, 5). One is admitted to the ministry of reader by the prescribed liturgical *rite*. "In accordance with the ancient *tradition* of the Church, institution to the ministries of reader and *acolyte* is reserved to men" (*Ministeria Quaedam*, 7). However, "in the absence of an instituted lector, other lay people may be deputed to proclaim the readings from Sacred Scripture, people who are truly suited to carrying out this function and carefully prepared" (*General Instruction of the Roman Missal*, 101). See Extraordinary minister of Holy Communion. Also see Benediction; Minor orders.

Legal/Legally/Legalizes/Legalization

Legal means that something is in conformity with the *law* pertaining to certain *acts*. Legally means that something is done in conformity with the law. Legalize means to make something into conformity with the law. Legalization is the process of making some-

thing conform to the law. See Overzealous treatment 2278.

Legal age

See Canonical age.

Legal fiction

A legal fiction is something accepted as fact for the sake of convenience though not necessarily true. See Reproductive rights. Also see Pro-choice.

Legal justice 2411

Legal justice is concerned with what the citizen owes to the community and with whatever bears on the *common good* of the community. It is chiefly expressed by *civil law*. Civil law binds the *conscience* to the degree that it conforms to *moral law*.

Legate

Legate comes from the Latin word 'legare,' meaning to bind. A legate is a *person* sent to make the sender present to another.

A legate may also be an *ecclesiastical* representative of the *Holy See* with varying *degrees* of *authority* to act in its name. When a legate is the personal representative of the *Pope*, he is referred to as a legate 'a latere,' meaning 'from the side' of the Pope. See Ecumenical council 884. Also see Council 465.

Legend

Legend comes from the Latin

word 'legere,' meaning to read. A legend is a popular tale, which may or may not be true and which is often a mixture of both fact and fiction. In the plural, 'legends' refers to a collection of such stories about *saints* or religious subjects that are generally accepted as true. The Church never proposes legends as objects of *belief*, and *persons* remain free to accept or to reject them on the basis of scientific study, an examination of sources, and the reputation of those who accept and promote them. See Magi 525, 528.

Legitimate/legitimacy

A thing is said to be legitimate when it is *lawful* and permissible. See Legitimate defense 2263.

Legitimate defense 2263, 2309

Legitimate defense is the *lawful* and permissible right to protect one's self, other *persons*, *society*, and even property from attack or to ward off injury. See Legitimate defense by military force.

Legitimate defense by military force 2309

Legitimate defense by military force refers to the right to self-defense by military means. This right may extend to military engagement under certain conditions.

The *gravity* of such a decision makes it subject to *rigorous* conditions of *moral*

legitimacy. The following must exist at one and the same time before a nation can employ legitimate defense by use of military force:

"– the damage inflicted by the aggressor... must be lasting, *grave*, and certain;

– all other means of putting an end to it must have been shown to be impractical or ineffective;

– there must be serious prospects of success;

– the use of arms must not produce evils and disorders graver than the evil to be eliminated" (CCC 2309).

Legitimate seed

'Legitimate seed' refers to the descendants of David whom God will raise up *righteous* and *faithful* to the *Covenant* and innocent of any charge or accusation. *'Righteous seed'* also refers to the descendants of David who would remain faithful to the *Covenant* and walk in the ways of the Lord. See Righteousness 1224, 1991.

Leitourgos 1144, 1070

'Leitourgos' comes from a Greek word meaning 'liturgist,' that is, one who conducts the *liturgy*. It is taken from the Greek 'leitourgia,' meaning work or public work done on behalf or in the name of the people.

In a *Catholic* context, it refers to the *person* or persons who, in the name of *Christ*, carry out the work of public service on behalf of the *people of God* in the *celebration* of the *sacraments*, each according to his particular function in the unity of the one who acts in all, viz., Christ.

It may be compared to the use of the English word republic, which comes from the Latin word 'respublica,' from 'res,' meaning things and 'publica,' meaning of the people or public. It refers to persons contributing to the *common good* through common work.

Lent

Lent is a season of *penance*, lasting from *Ash Wednesday* up to but excluding the *Mass* of the *Lord's Supper* on *Holy Thursday*. Traditionally, it was, and still is, a time for the preparation of *catechumens* for the reception of *Baptism*. See Paschal mystery 571.

Lenten season

The second half of the *liturgical* life of the Church focuses on *Christ* as the life of the *Christian*. It opens with the great Season of *Lent* in preparation for *Easter*. The word Lent comes from the Old English, 'lencten,' meaning 'spring.'

The Lenten Season lasts from *Ash Wednesday* up to but excluding the Mass of the *Lord's Supper* on *Holy Thursday*. This period is observed as a preparation for the com-

memoration of the *Passion* and death of Christ.

Lent was also the traditional time for the preparation of *catechumens* for *Baptism* and the *reconciliation* of *penitents*. This is the reason for the laws regarding fasting and *abstinence*, the use of purple *vestments*, the silence of the organ, the absence of flowers on the *altar*, and the omission of the *Gloria* and *Alleluia* in the *liturgy*.

The Fourth *Sunday* of Lent is called *Laetare Sunday*. On this day the organ may be used, flowers may be placed on the altar, and rose-colored vestments are permitted.

The time from the Fifth Sunday of Lent to *Good Friday* is called *Passiontide*.

In the *Eastern Rites*, the *Lenten Season* is called the *Great Lent* to contrast it with the lesser rigor of *penitential* practice observed during *Advent*. In the *Byzantine Rite*, during *Lent*, a severe fast is observed. Meat, *lacticinia*, eggs, fish, oil, and wine are forbidden for forty-eight days. On week days, the *Liturgy of the Presanctified Gifts* can be celebrated, but the *Divine Liturgy* cannot. See Liturgical seasons.

Leo I, Pope

Pope St. Leo I, who reigned from 440–461 A.D., is one of two *Popes* given the title 'the Great'; the other was Pope St. Gregory I, who reigned from

590–604 A.D. Pope St. Leo I did much to strengthen the *papacy* and the position of the *Holy See* in the Church and the world. Emperor Valentinian III, who ruled from 425–455 A.D., granted the Pope full *jurisdiction* over the West, but the East did not recognize his *authority*. When, in 452 A.D., Attila the Hun was prepared to attack all of Italy, the Pope bravely met him at Mantua and persuaded him to withdraw.

Leonine sacramentary

The Leonine sacramentary is the oldest Latin sacramentary or *liturgical* book. It is erroneously *attributed* to *Pope* St. *Leo I*, who reigned from 440–461 A.D. It was in use from the fourth century to the seventh century and many of the *prayers* it contained are still in use. See Consecration of virgins and widows 922, 923.

Lesser exorcism

A Lesser *exorcism* is one that does not imply a state of *demonic possession* but invokes God's protection from the *evil one*. This type of exorcism is used in *Baptism* and the *blessing* of water and salt. See Exorcism 1673.

Lessons

Lessons are passages of *Scripture* read at *Mass*. They are now called the Readings, which refer to passages of Scripture, the writings of the *Fathers of the Church*, documents of the *Magisterium*, and lives of *saints* read during the *Office of Readings* of the *Liturgy of the Hours*. See Lector. Also see Divine Office; Liturgy of the Hours

Leviticus

The third book of the *Old Testament* is called Leviticus because it contains the *rituals* and *laws* pertaining to *Jewish priests* and their assistants, who were taken from the tribe of Levi and were set apart by God for service in the *sanctuary*. The book records the *consecration* of Aaron and his sons as the first *priests* and prescribes the *religious ceremonies* to be performed by the tribe of Levi. These can be divided into the following: the *rites* of sacrifice (Lev 1–7), the *consecration* and installation of priests (Lev 8–10), laws of *purity* (Lev 11–15), rituals for the Day of Atonement (Lev 16), and laws of *holiness* (Lev 17–27). See Law of Moses. Also see Genesis.

Lex orandi, lex credendi 1124

'Lex orandi, lex credendi' is a Latin phrase meaning the *law* of *prayer* is the law of *faith*. This is a form of the *axiom* of Pope St. Celestine I, 'The rule of prayer determines the rule of faith,' which means that the *liturgy* of *worship* is the chief instrument in the *tradition* or passing on of true *doctrine*. Because of this, observance of *liturgical* law is *essential* to true *orthodoxy*.

Liaison

Liaison comes from the Latin word 'ligare,' meaning to bind. Most frequently it refers to an *illicit* love affair. It also refers to a *person* who acts as a mediator between persons or organizations. See Free union 2390.

Liberality

Liberality is the *virtue* of being willing to share, to give freely, or to act with *generosity*. It is opposed to the *capital sin* of *avarice*. See Capital sins 1866.

Libertarian

Libertarian can refer to a *person* who believes in the *doctrine* of *free will*. It also may refer to a person who *advocates* full *civil liberty* regardless of *moral* implications. See Reproductive rights. Also see Pro-choice.

Liberty

Liberty is *freedom* with respect to the *person* who exercises or enjoys it. It implies more than a *subjective* power of self-determination and the absence of constraint or coercion.

For *Christians*, it includes liberation from *sin* and the freedom to exercise *free will* in *obedience* to the *moral law*. It can be viewed internally as the absence of necessity or determination, which enables *man* to choose freely between alternatives. Viewed externally, liberty is freedom from external necessity or force.

Different forms of freedom include *freedom of exercise or contradiction, freedom of specification*, and *freedom of contrariety*. See Individualism. Also see Free will, human 1704; Freedom 1731.

Liceity 1635

Liceity refers to the quality of an act by which it is made allowable, permissible, and *lawful* and is carried out in full accord with the *laws* governing such acts.

Licentiate

Licentiate is the second highest graduate level academic degree conferred by a *Pontifical Institute*. The highest level degree is the *doctorate*.

Licit/licitly

Licit means allowed or legal. See Baptism 1213.

Lie 2482

A lie consists in acting or speaking a falsehood with the intent to deceive. The Lord denounces lying as the work of the *devil*, the father of lies. "Lying is the most direct offense against the *truth*. To lie is to speak or act against the truth in order to lead someone into error" (CCC 2483). Because it injures *man's right* to know the truth, which is a necessary condition for every *judgment* and decision, a lie offends against the *fundamental* relationship with God and one's neighbor.

"The *gravity* of a lie is measured against the nature of the truth it deforms, the circumstances, the *intentions* of the one who lies, and the harm suffered by its *victims*" (CCC 2484).

"Lying is destructive of *society*; it undermines trust among men and tears apart the fabric of *social* relationships" (CCC 2486). As an offense against truth, lying also offends the ultimate truth, which is God himself.

Line and degree

Line and degree are ways of understanding *family* relationships.

The relationship between a *person* and his immediate ancestor or descendent is said to be a *direct or lineal relationship* because the line of descent is direct. It may be either ascent or descent in a straight line, for example, grandfather, father, son.

A *collateral* relationship exists between two *persons* who have a common ancestor, for example, siblings and cousins.

Blood relationship, also known as *consanguinity,* is either direct or collateral. Relationship incurred by a valid *marriage* (relationship with in-laws) is known as *affinity*.

Degree by consanguinity refers to the proximity of relationship between two persons. In the direct line the degree is the total number of persons in the *generational* line. Thus, grandfather and grandson are related in the third degree. The degree in the collateral line is the total number of persons in both generational lines traced to the common ancestor, excluding the ancestor. Thus, for example, cousins are related in the fourth degree. Degree by affinity is reckoned similarly. Thus, father-in-law and son-in-law are related by affinity in the second degree. Also see Consanguinity.

Line of blood relationship

Lines of blood relationship may be either direct or collateral. A *direct line* refers to direct relationships: parent, child, grandchild. A *collateral line* refers to relationships in which two *persons* share a common ancestor, for example, two *siblings*.

Direct lines have as many *degrees* as there are *generations*. Collateral lines have "as many degrees as there are persons in both lines together, not counting the common ancestor" (Canon 108, § 3). For example, siblings are related to the second degree in the collateral line, cousins to the fourth degree.

In the direct line of consanguinity and affinity, marriage is *invalid* in any degree, whether generation is legitimate or illegitimate. In the collateral line of consanguinity, it is *invalid* to the fourth degree inclusive. See Consanguinity.

Litany

A Litany is a form of *prayer* consisting of an *invocation* followed by a response.

There are numerous litanies in popular *devotional* practice, and they have very early origins. The only litany currently used *liturgically* is the Litany of the *Saints*.

The *'Kyrie eleison,'* or 'Lord have mercy,' is a *relic* of litanies formerly used in the *Mass*. They are still used as important features of the *Eastern Rite liturgy*. See Akathistos 2678.

Literary genres 110

Literary genre refers to the modes and the ways of thinking, feeling, speaking, and narrating. It comes from the Latin *'litterarius,'* meaning letter, or dealing with literature or books. Genre comes from *'genus'* in Latin meaning kind, race, stock, or family.

In regard to *Sacred Scripture,* "in order to discover the sacred authors' intention, the reader must take into account the conditions of their time, the literary genres in use at that time, and the modes of feeling, speaking, and narrating then current" (CCC 110).

Vatican II "indicates three criteria for interpreting Scrip-

ture in accordance with the Spirit who inspired it" (CCC 111).

1) One must pay close attention to the "content and the unity of the whole Scripture" (CCC 112). The books of Scripture may be of different genres, but they are all united by reason of the unity of God's plan "of which *Christ Jesus* is the center and heart" (CCC 112).

2) We must read Sacred Scripture "within the living *Tradition* of the whole Church... it is the *Holy Spirit* who gives her the spiritual interpretation of the Scripture" (CCC 113).

3) We must "be attentive to the *analogy of faith...* the coherence of the *truths* of faith among themselves and within the whole plan of *Revelation*" (CCC 114).

Literal

Literal comes from the Latin word *'littera,'* meaning letter. Literal means to use words exactly as written as opposed to imaginatively, figuratively, or freely. See Literal sense of Scripture 115, 116.

Literal sense of Scripture 115, 116

The literal sense of *Scripture* refers to the meaning conveyed by the actual wording of a passage as it was written. It is the etymological or *primary sense* of the words as distinguished from any *spiritual* or merely secondary meaning.

The literal sense is essential

for the proper interpretation of Scripture in order to know the *mind* and *intention* of the *inspired* author.

Liturgia horarum

'Liturgia horarum' is the Latin name for the *Liturgy of the Hours*. See Liturgy of the Hours 1174, 1178.

Liturgical catechesis 1075

Liturgical *catechesis* is the means by which people are initiated into the *mystery* of *Christ* by proceeding from the visible to the invisible or from the sign to the thing signified.
Catechesis refers to the instruction itself. It is called *liturgical* because the instruction concerns itself with the work of the *People of God* in the mystery of the Church and her *mission*. It is presented by means of local and regional *catechisms*.

Liturgical colors

The *vestments* worn in the liturgy of different seasons and feasts are symbolically associated with them.
Black is a symbol of death and mourning. It is suitable for *Masses* for the dead. At funerals, white may be worn in order to suggest the *Resurrection*.
Green is associated with *hope*, growth, life, and *fidelity*. It is worn on *Sundays* and ferial days of *Ordinary Time*.
Red is the color of blood and suggests *sacrifice* and *mar*-

tyrdom, *charity*, or the *Holy Spirit*. It is used on feasts of the *Apostles* (except St. John the Evangelist) and of *martyrs*, as well as on *Pentecost*.
Rose signifies subdued joy. It is only used on Gaudete Sunday (Third *Sunday* of *Advent*) and *Laetare Sunday* (fourth Sunday of *Lent*).
Violet signifies *penitence*. It is used during Advent and Lent.
White signifies innocence, *purity*, *virginity*, and joy. It is used on joyful feasts like *Christmas* and *Easter*, and on feasts of the *Blessed Virgin Mary*, *angels*, and *saints* other than martyrs. See Liturgical seasons.

Liturgical mysteries

Liturgical mysteries are the celebrations of *transcendent* events in the life of *Christ* from before his birth to his *Passion*, death, *Resurrection*, and glorious *Ascension* into *heaven*. It includes events that manifest the work of the Holy Spirit in the life of the early Church. See Liturgical seasons.

Liturgical seasons

In her loving solicitude for the eternal welfare of her children, Holy Mother Church, under the guidance of the *Holy Spirit*, earnestly strives to foster and enrich the *spiritual life* of her children. The spiritual life of the Church revolves around a *liturgical year*, which is divided into four *sacred seasons*, *Ordinary*

Time, and a *sanctoral cycle* of feasts.

The liturgical seasons are periods of time in the year during which all the different *mysteries* of *faith* are commemorated. The four sacred liturgical seasons, also called the *Proper of Seasons*, celebrate the life of *Christ* from before his birth, to his *Passion*, death, *Resurrection*, and glorious *Ascension* into *heaven* as well as an account of the life of the early Church. These sacred seasons are: *Advent, Christmas, Lent*, and *Easter*. The time between these sacred seasons is called *Ordinary Time*.

The sanctoral cycle is also called the *Proper of Saints*. It parallels the four *liturgical seasons* and commemorates the lives of the *saints* and *martyrs* who have suffered and have been glorified with Christ and who, by their lives, proclaim the *Paschal mystery* commemorated in the liturgical seasons.

Advent season

The first part of the liturgical life of the Church focuses on Christ as the light of the world. It begins with Advent, which celebrates the anticipation of the coming of Christ at Christmas. The word Advent comes from the Latin word 'adventus,' meaning coming, referring to the coming of Christ. Advent is a penitential season that begins on the *Sunday* nearest the feast of St. Andrew (Nov. 30). It is celebrated from the first Sunday of Advent until Christmas (Dec. 25). See Advent 524.

Christmas season

The Christmas season follows Advent. It lasts from First Vespers (Evening Prayer I) of the Nativity of the Lord (the evening of December 24) up to and including the Sunday after *Epiphany* or after January 6. The Christmas season is also known as *Christmastide*. During this time three great feasts are celebrated, Christmas, the *Solemnity of the Mother of God* (formerly the *feast* of the *Circumcision*), and the Epiphany.

Several practices in the celebration of Christmas merit special mention. In early times, the greater feasts were preceded by a *vigil* or a preparation day. The night before the feast was spent in prayer. This practice was abolished among the *faithful* and was restricted to *religious orders* who recited the night *office*; the faithful then observed the vigil simply as a *fast day*.

Though the *vigils* of other feasts were abolished, the vigil of Christmas was preserved, and, to this day, following ancient *tradition*, people gather in *church* to attend *Mass*, which is offered after midnight. By an ancient custom, the *Pope* offered three Masses on Christmas: the first in the Liberian *Basilica*, the second at the Church of St. Anastasia, and the third in the Vatican Church. These Masses were celebrated at night, at dawn (cockcrow), and in the daytime. In a *mystical interpretation*, the three masses represent the three births of our Lord: 1) *begotten* of his Father before all ages, 2) born of the Blessed Virgin in the *Incarnation*, and 3) born in the hearts of the faithful through conversion and *Baptism*. See Christmas.

Lenten season

The Lenten season marks the beginning of the second part of the Church's liturgical year that focuses on Christ as the life of the Church. The season of Lent is a preparation for the great feast of Easter. The word Lent comes from the Old English 'lencten,' meaning 'spring.'

The Lenten Season lasts "from Ash Wednesday up to but excluding the Mass of the Lord's Supper" on Holy Thursday (*Universal Norms on the Liturgical Year and the Calendar*, 28). This period is observed as a preparation for the commemoration of the *Passion* and death of Christ.

Lent was also the traditional time for the preparation of *catechumens* for *Baptism* and the *reconciliation* of *penitents*. This is the reason for the laws regarding fast and *abstinence*, the use of purple *vestments*, the silence of the organ, the absence of flowers on the

altar, and the omission of the *Gloria* and *Alleluia* in the *liturgy*, all of which symbolize repentance.

The fourth Sunday of Lent is called *Laetare Sunday*. On this day, the organ may be used, flowers may be placed on the altar, and rose-colored vestments are permitted. The day is joyful because, on the following Wednesday, Catechumens receive the 'aperitio aurium,' or opening of the ears, and the 'traditio symbolorum,' or the handing over of the *Apostles' Creed*, the *Our Father*, and the *Gospels*. These are decisive moments in the preparation of catechumens for the solemnities of *Holy Saturday*. In the Liturgical reforms of Pope Paul VI, these traditions take place on Laetare Sunday itself. Ever conscious of the joyful hope of the *Resurrection*, these liturgical events are ideally timed to anticipate the joys of Easter in the midst of the somberness of the great season of penance.

The period of time from the Fifth Sunday of Lent to Good Friday is called *Passiontide*.

In the *Eastern Rites*, the Lenten Season is called the *Great Lent* to contrast it with the lesser rigor of *penitential* practice observed during *Advent*. In the *Byzantine Rite*, during *Lent*, a severe fast is observed. Meat, *lacticinia*, eggs, fish, oil, and wine are forbidden for forty-eight days. On week days, Mass may not be celebrated, only the *Liturgy of the Presanctified* is allowed.

Easter season

Easter is celebrated on the first Sunday after the first *full moon* after the *vernal equinox* because it is related to the *Jewish Pasch*. It is the Sunday of the Resurrection, the feast of feasts, and the most solemn of all solemnities because the Resurrection is the basis of the Christian faith: 'If Christ has not been raised, your faith is futile and you are still in your sins' (1 Cor 15:17). The Easter season extends from Easter Sunday to the Solemnity of *Pentecost*.

Ordinary Time

In Latin, 'Ordinary Time' is called 'Tempus Per Annum,' literally meaning 'Time throughout the year.' In English, it is translated as 'Ordinary Time' because the Sundays of Ordinary Time are identified in numerical order. Ordinary Time may last thirty-three or thirty-four weeks, depending on the date of Easter.

The designation Ordinary Time is part of the post-*Vatican II* revision of the liturgical calendar. Before 1970 A.D., the Sundays of Ordinary Time were referred to as *Sundays after Epiphany* and *Sundays after Pentecost*, respectively.

Ordinary Time is divided into two parts that occur outside of the liturgical seasons that celebrate specific aspects of the mystery of Christ (Advent, Christmas, Lent, and Easter). According to *The Universal Norms on the Liturgical Year and the Calendar*, the days of Ordinary Time, particularly the Sundays, "are devoted to the mystery of Christ in all its aspects."

The first period of Ordinary Time is shorter. It begins on the Monday after the first Sunday after January 6, and lasts until *Ash Wednesday*.

The second division of Ordinary Time is much longer and begins on the Monday after Pentecost Sunday. It ends before First Vespers (Evening Prayer I) of the First Sunday of Advent, which marks the beginning of a new Liturgical year.

When Ordinary Time resumes after Pentecost Sunday, the selection of readings depends on the length of the season for the year. If it has thirty-four weeks, the number of the week to be used is that following the last week used before Lent. When there are thirty-three weeks, the week that would follow consecutively after Pentecost is omitted to ensure that the last two weeks of Ordinary Time proclaim the coming of the *Kingdom of God*.

The Liturgical readings chosen for thirty-four Sundays of Ordinary Time and their week days are ordered to instruction on how to live the Christian faith in daily life. It celebrates the complete mystery of Christ rather than a specific aspect of the mystery of Christ, as do the other seasons.

The celebration of Sunday in Ordinary Time gives way to feasts of the Lord and to solemnities. See Liturgical colors; Liturgical Year 1168, 1171.

Liturgical year 1168, 1171

The liturgical year refers to the sequence followed in the celebration of the *mysteries* of the Lord's birth, life, death, and *Resurrection* throughout the year, making it a year of *grace*. It begins on the First *Sunday* of *Advent*. It closes with the thirty-fourth week of *Ordinary Time*.

The *spiritual life* of the Church year revolves around the two great Solemnities of *Christmas* and *Easter*, which commemorate the birth and Resurrection of *Christ*, respectively. The Christmas season focuses on Christ as the light of the world. It includes Advent, Christmas, *Epiphany*, and the Baptism of the Lord. It falls in the winter when daylight is short in the northern hemisphere, reminding the *faithful* that Christ is the light of the world. The *Easter season* focuses on Christ as the life of the *Christian*. It includes *Lent*, Easter, the *Ascension*, and *Pentecost*. It falls in the spring when new life arises from the death of winter, reminding the faithful of the gift of eternal life in the Resurrection. This celebration

of the *mysteries of redemption* provides the basic rhythm of the Christian's *prayer* life. The readings from the *Old* and *New Testaments* of the *Bible* are divided into three cycles called *Cycle A*, *Cycle B*, and *Cycle C*.

The liturgical year also contains the *sanctoral cycle*, which celebrates each *canonized saint* with an appointed feast day to honor and commemorate his life.

Before *Vatican II*, the same readings were used each year for the *Masses* in the *Roman Missal*. The first reading was generally taken from a *Pauline letter* or a *Catholic Epistle*. The *Gospel* readings were generally taken from Matthew (34.8%) or John (30.0%), less often from Luke (16.3%), and rarely from Mark (3.4%).

Since the liturgical reform following Vatican II, much more material from the New Testament is included in the *lectionary* for Mass. The *Acts of the Apostles* is used on Sundays and weekdays during *Easter*. *The Gospels of Matthew* (85.5%), *Mark* (96.3%), and *Luke* (87.8%) are used semi-continuously on Sundays of *Ordinary Time* on a three year cycle. The Gospel of John (92.5%) is used generally during *Lent*, *Easter*, and some major *feasts*. Selections from all other New Testament books are used as the second reading on Sundays and *solemnities* in a three year cycle, and in weekday Masses in a two year *cycle*. See Liturgical seasons.

Liturgy/liturgical 1069

Liturgy comes from the Greek word *'leitourgia,'* which originally meant a public work or service in the name of or in behalf of the people. Now, liturgy refers to the participation of the *People of God* in the *work of God* through the *ministry* of someone *ordained* for this by *Christ* and approved by the Church. Liturgy refers not only to the celebration of *divine worship* but also to the *proclamation* of the *Gospel*.

Through the liturgy, Christ continues the work of *redemption* in, with, and through his Church.

Liturgy of the Eucharist 1346

The *Liturgy of the Word* and Liturgy of the Eucharist together form a single act of *worship* and a fundamental unity as the *Mass*. The Liturgy of the Eucharist consists of the presentation of the bread and wine, the *consecration*, and communion.

Liturgy of the Hours 1174, 1178

Liturgy comes from the Greek word *'leitourgia'* meaning a public work done in the name of the people or on their behalf. Hours refers to divisions of daily *prayers*. The Liturgy of the Hours is a means of sanctifying the day by continual prayer. The Liturgy of

the Hours is also known as the *Work of God* (*Opus Dei*) or *Divine Office*. Its official Latin name is "Liturgia Horarium."

Most English speaking countries use the translation entitled 'The Liturgy of the Hours.' However, some English speaking countries use a different translation entitled the 'Divine Office.'

Lauds (*Morning Prayer*) and *Vespers* (*Evening Prayer*), called *major hours*, are the hinges of the entire office and have the most important roles. *Daytime Prayer* is either said as *Terce* (*Midmorning Prayer*), *Sext* (*Midday Prayer*), or *None* (*Midafternoon Prayer*) depending on the time of the day; these are the *minor hours*. They are arranged so that those who recite only one of them do not miss any part of the four week *psalter*. The *Office of Readings* may be recited as a night office but is suitable for any time of the day. The prayer day ends with *Compline*.

The cycle of psalms is completed in a period of four weeks, and cycle of readings from *Sacred Scripture* offers a wide selection designed to harmonize with the readings of the *Mass*.

The daily readings in the Office of Readings offer a broad selection of spiritual riches. Readings in honor of the *saints* are arranged in a way that the foremost spiritual qualities of the saints and their significance for the life of the Church clearly emerge.

The *laity* are encouraged to pray the Liturgy of the Hours, and, to make it more accessible, the Church has approved several abridged versions. In the USA, the most common are entitled *Christian Prayer* and *Shorter Christian Prayer*.

Liturgy of the Mass

The Liturgy of the Mass is the same as the *Liturgy of the Eucharist*. It refers to the words, actions, and *ceremonies* prescribed for the proper *celebration* of the Church's supreme act of *worship* in making present on the *altar* the *Sacrifice of Calvary*. See Liturgy of the Eucharist 1346.

Liturgy of the Presanctified Gifts

During Lent in the *Eastern Rite*, the *Divine Liturgy* may be celebrated only on Saturdays and *Sundays* during *Lent*. On any other day, if a Eucharistic liturgy is celebrated, it is the Liturgy of the Presanctified Gifts. It is an evening service structured like a Eastern Rite *Vespers* but with a communion service at the end. The *consecrated Host* (called a 'lamb' in the Eastern Rites) is immersed in unconsecrated wine before the communion of the *laity* and *clergy*. See *Great Lent*. Also see Mass of the Presanctified.

Liturgy of the Word 1154, 1349

The Liturgy of the Word and *Liturgy of the Eucharist* together form a single act of *worship* in unity in the *Mass*. The Mass begins with the Liturgy of the Word, which consists of the gathering, readings from the *Old Testament* and memoirs of the *Apostles*, the *homily*, and the general *intercessions*.

The Liturgy of the Word is so called because it is through all the words of *Sacred Scripture* that God speaks the one single Word, who is his one Utterance and in whom he expresses himself completely. The Liturgy of the Word is an integral part of all *sacramental celebrations*.

The *lectionary*, its *veneration*, the place of *proclamation*, its audible and intelligible reading, the homily (which extends its proclamation), and the response of the assembly are all to be emphasized because they signify and nourish the *faith* of the assembly of believers. Liturgical words and actions are inseparable insofar as they accomplish what they signify.

Living transmission 78

Living transmission refers to the action of conveying or handing on from one *person* to another the teaching of *Christ* under the guidance of the *Holy Spirit* through *Tradition*. See Tradition.

Living water 2652

The *Didache* instructs that Baptism should be administered in the name of the *Father* and of the *Son* and of the *Holy Spirit* using living water. Living water refers to water drawn from a well, spring, or stream and is preferred to that drawn from pools or cisterns. Living water signifies divine vitality, *revelation*, and *wisdom* in the *Old Testament*. It was even applied to the *Torah*.

In *biblical* imagery, water is life and *salvation*. Jesus applies this figure to himself, promising to give living water, which is *eternal life*.

The *eschatological* Jerusalem cannot be conceived without its stream of living water, which issues from the temple flowing from East to West as a mighty river. All these images apply to *Christ*, the Church, and the *Kingdom of God* he came to establish among men. The Holy Spirit is the living water welling up to eternal life in the *heart* that *prays*.

Living Will

A living will is a *legal* document intended to ensure that a *person's* personal preferences are taken into account should they become unable to express them at the time they are needed. In the living will, persons indicate whom they want to make decisions for them and what types of treatment they wish to have or to refuse. Such documents should be prepared with great caution because it is difficult to know the future conditions under which they might be applied. Living wills are also called *loving wills*. See Euthanasia 2277.

Local ordinary

An *ordinary* in *ecclesiastical law* is a *cleric* with ordinary *jurisdiction* in the *external forum* in a specified territory. It generally refers to the *Bishop* of a *diocese* but may include other specific individuals having jurisdiction over certain *persons*. See Ordinary.

Logic/Logical

Logic is the *science* concerned with the correctness of the thinking process. It is the method of acquiring *knowledge* through the study and application of *reason* as the means of discovering *truth*. Only correct thinking leads to knowledge that is true and certain.

There are two aspects of logic. The science of correct thinking deals with the *legitimate* process of reasoning. It is called *formal logic*, *dialectics*, or *minor logic*. The other aspect of logic is called *material logic*, *criteriology*, or *major logic*. It deals with the truth and certitude achieved by reasoning, that is, its content rather than its formal structure. The study of logic is considered to be part of *metaphysics*. See Reason/

Reasoning; Systematic philosophy.

Logos

Logos means 'word' in Greek. It is used in reference to the *Second Person* of the *Blessed Trinity*. See Apollinarianism.

Long suffering

Long suffering means enduring injuries, *injustices*, offenses, troubles, and insults patiently. See Patience.

Lord 446

The name *YHWH*, by which God revealed himself to Moses, is rendered *'Kyrios,'* meaning Lord, in Greek. It became the more usual name to indicate the *divinity* of *Israel's* God. The *New Testament* uses this word in its full sense to refer both to the Father and to *Jesus*, the Son.

Lord's Day, The 1166

By *tradition*, the Church *celebrates* the *Paschal mystery* every seventh day. This day is called the Lord's Day or *Sunday*.

The Church celebrates Sunday, rather than Saturday (the *Sabbath*), as the Lord's Day because on it the Lord rose victorious to the Father.

"[It] is both the first day of the week, the memorial of the first day of creation, and the 'eighth day,' on which *Christ*... inaugurates the 'day that the Lord has made,' the 'day that knows no evening.'" (CCC 1166).

Lord's Prayer

In Lk 11:1, when one of his *disciples* asked, 'Lord teach us to pray,' *Jesus* himself taught his disciples to pray and entrusted to them and to his Church the *fundamental Christian prayer*, which is called the Lord's Prayer. It is found in the *Gospel* of St. Luke with five petitions and in a more developed form in St. Matthew's Gospel (Mt 6:9–13) with seven petitions.

The Lord's Prayer is treated comprehensively in Part Four: Section Two on *Christian Prayer* of *The Catechism of the Catholic Church*, beginning with number 2759.

The Lord's Prayer begins with the words, *Our Father*, from which it takes its name. The Lord's Prayer is also called The Our Father and the *Pater Noster*. See Prayer 2098.

Lord's Supper, The 1329

The Lord's Supper refers to the Eucharistic meal that *Jesus* took with his disciples on the night before he suffered and during which he instituted the *Eucharist*. Those who gather to *celebrate* the Eucharistic meal are called the *Eucharistic assembly*.

Love 218

Love refers to a union of the *will* with an object presented to the *intellect* as *good*. It is recognized by a strong affection, desire for closeness, and devotion to a *person* or thing.

It consists in solicitude for another's welfare, pleasure in their company, and a desire for their approval.

Love is the *essential act of the will*, but it has a strong effect on the sensory *faculties*. In mutual love, there occurs a correspondence of wills that makes the two one in spirit.

The Greeks distinguished between four kinds of love. 1) *Storge* is family love. It refers to the bond formed between an individual and persons, between animals and persons, and between persons and things around them. 2) *Philia* refers to the love of friends chosen because of mutual compatibility and similar *values*. 3) *Eros* is love viewed as passion of a sexual, artistic, or spiritual *nature*. It is attachment to the beautiful and desirable. 4) *Agape* is the kind of love that is manifested toward another in need. It is marked by *generosity* without concern for reward.

The Church has used agape to refer to the meeting of the *faithful* for meals before the *liturgy*. These love *feasts*, as they came to be known, grew into disorderly parties quite separated from the *liturgy* and became sources of *scandal*. In his day, St. Augustine complained about them. Eventually, the *Council of Laodicea*, in 363 A.D., forbade such feasting in Church.

The term *sacrificial love* is used *metaphorically* to apply to internal acts by which man, in the spirit of *self-sacrifice*, devotes himself to the service of God, the *reformation* of life, and the service of others in *obedience* to the command to love others as one loves himself for the love of *Christ*.

The distinctions among the various forms of love play a significant role in the process of *discernment* about *marriage*. Especially in contemporary culture, the influence of eros love can blind one to the absence of other forms of love required for the formation of a true Christian *marriage bond*. Those other types of love, together with God's grace, form the foundation for the *indissolubility* of the marriage bond.

In Christian writing love is distinguished as one of four types. 1) Marital or *sexual love* refers to feelings centered on the natural *appetite* to seek the good in *procreation*. It includes an *intellectual* element as well as a sensitive attraction toward another. Married love must be governed by *right reason*, that is, it must always seek the *spiritual* good and welfare of the beloved. *Spouses* become, by virtue of the *sacrament* of *Matrimony*, special channels of *grace* and expressions of God's will guiding the spouses to mutual *sanctification*. 2) Love of *benevolence* is love of another irrespective of his being a source of good to the lover. 3) Love of *complai-*

sance is love shown because of another's *inherent* lovableness with no thought of personal benefit on the part of the lover. 4) Love of *concupiscence* is love shown to another as a source of good to oneself.

As a *theological virtue*, love of God is called *charity*. *Habitual* charity is a *virtue* infused by God with *sanctifying grace*. It inclines the will to love God above all things with a love of benevolence and to love one's neighbor as oneself. By it, the intellect appreciates God as worthy of the highest love, and the will prefers him above all else. *Charity* makes possible on *man's* part the highest and most perfect realization of the essential act of his will: love. Charity is the love of God as he loves himself. Man, in loving God as God loves himself, loves all whom God loves and in the way God loves them. It is in this way that the *communion of saints* is essentially constituted as a communion and, hence, charity is the essence of the fellowship at the heart of the Church.

Habitual charity is the indispensable means of *salvation* and is inseparable from sanctifying grace. It can be destroyed only by *mortal sin*. Man's capacity to love God is derived from God's love for him. God's unreserved love is the motive for his creating man. Because of the nature of his love, he can demand such love in return. He makes such

love in man possible by the power of the *Holy Spirit* and by the *adoption* as sons he bestows on man in *Baptism*.

Loving Will

A 'loving will' is a form of *living will* by which an individual expresses his preferences regarding the types of care to be given should he become unable to express them himself. See Euthanasia. Also see Living will.

Low Mass

A 'Low Mass' is *Mass* celebrated in its simplest way. The *celebrant* is assisted by a server or two, everything is done at the *altar*, there is no liturgical singing, and *incense* is not used. This term is proper to the *Extraordinary Form*, but can also be used to describe a simply celebrated Mass in the *Ordinary Form*.

Lukewarmness 2094

Lukewarmness refers to a state in which a *person experiences* little warmth or depth of feeling, is indifferent and lacks *zeal*, enthusiasm, or ardor for *spiritual* things.

Lukewarmness is a sin against *charity* in which a person hesitates or is negligent in responding to *divine love*. It can imply a refusal to give oneself over to the promptings of charity.

It can arise from a lack of attention to spiritual things or from a neglect of *religious* practices and inclinations. It may be improved and overcome through *spiritual reading, prayer, meditation,* and the reception of the *sacraments.*

Lumen Gentium

'Lumen Gentium,' translated as "Light to the Nations," is a Dogmatic *Constitution* on the Church issued by the *Second Vatican Council.* It explains the *nature* of the Church as a natural sign and instrument of communion with God for unity among all men and characterizes the *mission* of the Church as a *sacrament* of human *salvation.*

It also clarifies the meaning of *episcopal collegiality,* holding that the community of *bishops* has no *authority* without dependence on and communion with the *Bishop of Rome.* See Coredemptrix.

Lumen gloriae

'Lumen gloriae' is the special *grace* given to the *blessed* that makes it possible for the *human intellect* to *experience* the *beatific vision* and to see God as he is in himself in all his *glory, perfection,* and *Trinitarian nature.* The beatific vision is impossible to *human nature* without this special *grace.* It is a *preternatural gift,* that is, beyond human nature but not contrary to it.

The *Trinitarian* nature is the first object of the beatific vision. The beatific vision also includes the *revelation* and understanding of the *mysteries* of everything that was known only through *faith* while on earth. The blessed also have the sight, *recognition,* and enjoyment of those whom they loved on earth. They also have *knowledge* of the *prayers* and *veneration* addressed to them by those still on earth. See Beatific vision 1028.

Luminous mysteries of the Rosary

Meditation on a *mystery* of the *faith* drawn from the *Gospels* accompanies the recitation of each decade of the *Rosary.* These meditations are known as the mysteries of the Rosary.

The mysteries of the Rosary are collected into groups of related *scriptural* events referred to as the *Joyful, Sorrowful, Glorious,* and *Luminous* mysteries. The recitation of five decades and meditation on a set of mysteries ends with the prayer *Hail Holy Queen.*

The Luminous mysteries, used on Thursdays, are The Baptism of Jesus in the Jordan (Mt 3:13–17; Mk 1:1–9; Lk 3:21–22; Jn 1:29–31), The Wedding at Cana (Jn 2:3–5, 7–10; Lk 6:27–28, 37), The Proclamation of the Kingdom (Mk 1:14–15; Lk 4:18–19), The Transfiguration (Mt 5:14, 16; Lk 9:30–33), and The Institution of the Eucharist (Jn 13:1; Mt 26:18; Lk 22:15–16). See

Mysteries of the Rosary 2678, 2708.

Lunar calendar

A lunar calendar is a calendar based on cycles of phases of the moon. The length of a month in the lunar calendar is the period of a *synodic month*, that is, the period of time between successive *new moons*. The lunar calendar is contrasted to the *solar calendar*, which is based on the period of time it takes for the earth to complete one full revolution around the sun in its orbit.

Lunette or lunula

A lunette or lunula is a circular receptacle consisting of two plates of glass encircled with gold that is used to hold the *Blessed Sacrament* upright when it is placed in a *monstrance* for *Benediction of the Blessed Sacrament*. It is also called a *capsula*. See Tabernacle 1183, 1379.

Lust/lustful 1866, 2351

Lust is "disordered desire for or inordinate enjoyment of sexual pleasure. Sexual pleasure is morally disordered when sought for itself, isolated from its *procreative* and *unitive* purposes" (CCC 2351). Lust is one of the *capital sins*, or *deadly sins*.

According to St. Augustine, lust quickly clouds better *judgment* and makes one vulnerable to different forms

of lust-*violence*. It can lead a *person* to *moral* blindness, to becoming inconsiderate, and to being inconstant. It can even lead to a hatred of God, *spiritual lukewarmness*, or even the total loss of *faith*.

Lust warps one's *perception* of others, compromises one's *intimacy* with others, and deepens one's isolation. One common *consequence* of lust is the *abortion* of an unborn child who was conceived out of lust instead of true *love*.

All forms of lust offend against *chastity* because they *pervert* the *conjugal act*, which is essentially the intimate self-donation of *spouses* to one another completely in *sacrificial* love.

Lust is opposed to justice as well as *charity* because it demeans the person who is the object of lust by using them rather than serving them. It is love of self as opposed to love of another.

The remedy for lust is *prayer*, *penance*, the reception of the *Eucharist*, and works of charity that help one to view others as something other than instruments for self-gratification.

The practice of instantly averting the eyes from tempting objects or persons and praying at the first awareness of a lustful desire or thought is a critical first step in overcoming lust. Frequent *confession* and the reception of *Holy Communion* together with *fasting* and *spiritual reading* are also important aids against lust.

Pornography is a particularly *addictive* form of lust. Pornography refers to any form of communication, whether written, graphic, or electronic, that is intended to excite *lascivious* or *erotic* feelings. The *evil* of pornography consists in removing sexual acts from the intimacy of the partners in order to display them to third parties.

Viewing pornography leads to *impure* thoughts and lustful behavior. Pornography is deeply addictive and destroys one's capacity for true intimacy.

The chief means of overcoming *addiction* to pornography are prayer, fasting, reception of the *sacraments*, and the guidance of a good *spiritual advisor*.

The sexual attraction and the affection that bind man and woman in *marriage* are very different from lust because they unite them in a holy *communion* of service to one another and their children in a sacrificial love. The goal of sexual attraction in marriage is to motivate the spouses to give themselves to each other, not to use each other to serve personal selfish needs.

LXX

LXX is the Roman number 70. It refers to the Greek Septuagint, which is a translation of the *Hebrew Scriptures* or *Old Testament*. The Septuagint translation of the Hebrew Scriptures was made by seventy scholars in Alexandria in the third century B.C. It was adopted by Greek speaking *Christians*. See Septuagint.

M

Macedonianism/Macedonians

Macedonianism is a *heresy* named after Macedonius, the *Arian Bishop* of Constantinople (d. 362 A.D.). He taught that there was a hierarchy instead of an equality between the *Persons* of the *Trinity*. His followers, called the Macedonians, denied the *divinity* of the *Holy Spirit*. Sts. Basil the Great (329–379 A.D.), Gregory of Nyssa (335–395 A.D.), and Athanasius (296–373 A.D.) fought against this heresy. It was formally condemned by the First Council of Constantinople in 381 A.D. See Heresy 817, 2089.

Magi 525, 528

'Magi' is the plural form of the word 'Magus,' meaning one skilled in magic or *sorcery*. A Magus was a member of the ancient Persian priestly caste, said by ancient historians to have been originally a *Median* tribe. In a wider sense, Magus refers to one skilled in Oriental magic and *astrology*, or an ancient magician or sorcerer. Others maintain, however, that Magus might also have simply indicated someone learned in *astronomy* and other *sciences* related to the study of the *heavens*.

The Magi are also called 'the wise men' because they saw a star, which they interpreted as a sign of the birth of a new king, and set out to find him and to pay him homage. They were wise because they were seeking God, who is true *Wisdom*.

Their visit is *commemorated* as the *Solemnity* of the *Epiphany*, the manifestation of *Christ* to the world beyond the *Jews*.

The number of Magi who saw the star in the East and visited the infant Christ is not known from any written records, but *tradition* holds that there were three. *Medieval tradition* gives their names as Gaspar, Melchior and Balthasar.

Magic 2117

Magic refers to the production of marvelous physical effects through the *invocation* of *evil spirits*. Such magic is also called *black magic* or *witchcraft*. Magic is gravely opposed to the *virtue of religion*. In this sense, magic is *gravely* sinful.

What is often called magic in the area of entertainment is really illusion and does not pretend to be achieved by the invocation of *evil* spirits. Such magic is not sinful.

Magisterium 83, 889, 890

Magisterium refers to the *divine authority* by which the Church infallibly teaches the *truths* revealed by *Christ*.

There are two forms of Magisterium: solemn and ordinary. The *solemn Magisterium* is exercised only rarely in formal and *authentic declarations* of *councils* or of the *Pope* teaching *ex cathedra*. This is at times referred to as *extraordinary Magisterium*.

The *ordinary Magisterium* is exercised continually in the universal practices associated with *faith* and *morals* and is referred to as the *universal Magisterium*. *Encyclicals* are part of the ordinary Magisterium and, as such, require the *religious assent* of the *faithful*.

Both forms are *infallible* as a whole. Generally, Magisterium simply refers to the teaching authority of the Church. See Teaching office.

Magisterium of the pastors of the faith 2033

The *magisterium* of the pastors of the *faith* refers to the *teaching office* of the Church in matters of faith and *morals* ordinarily exercised in *catechesis* and preaching with the help of *theologians* and *spiritual* authors. This would apply to *papal* instructions and *encyclicals*.

Magnanimity

Magnanimity comes from the Latin meaning large or great soul. It is a disposition to perform *morally good acts* of exceptional *generosity*, kindness, or *charity*. Because it is restrained by *prudence*, magnanimity differs from *impetuosity*, or brashness. It is the opposite of *pusillanimity*, which is the fear of doing great and difficult deeds out of cowardliness. Pusillanimity is also called *faintheartedness*. See Fortitude 1808, 1831.

Magnanimous

Magnanimous means large-hearted generosity, especially in overlooking injury or insult arising from *pettiness*. See Fruits of the Spirit 1832.

Magnificat / Canticle of Mary 2619

Magnificat is the name of the *canticle* of the *Blessed Virgin* spoken at the time she visited her cousin Elizabeth. The prayer is called the Magnificat because that is the first Latin word of the 'Canticle of Mary.' A canticle is a song of *praise*.

In this canticle, *Mary* responds to the greeting of Elizabeth by addressing God in praise and proclaiming his graciousness in fulfilling his promise to send a Savior to Israel. It is recorded in Lk 1:46–55. See Appendix of Prayers; Marian Prayers; Magnificat.

Major Basilica

See Basilica.

Major doxology

See Gloria in excelsis Deo.

Major exorcism

A major exorcism is the formal *rite* of *exorcism*, which is used by the Church in a case of *demonic* possession. It consists of an *adjuration* or a command in the name of God that the *demon* depart from the *person*. See Exorcism 1673.

Major hours

The major hours of the *Divine Office* are the *Office of Readings, Lauds (Morning Prayer)* and *Vespers (Evening Prayer)*. The last two are particularly important, being the "two hinges on which the daily office turns; hence they are to be considered as the chief hours and are to be *celebrated* as such" (*Vatican II, Sacrosanctum Concilium*). See Liturgy of the Hours 1174, 1178.

Major logic

The issue of the trustworthiness of *human knowledge* is referred to as the *critical question*. Since this question is concerned with the *mind* and knowing, it is the proper subject matter of *logic*. The department that answers the critical question is sometimes called major logic. It deals with the matter rather than the form of thought. It is also called *criteriology* or *epistemology*. In any case, its purpose is to test the *truth* and *certitude* of knowledge. See Logic.

Major orders

There were traditionally seven separate *degrees* of *Holy Orders* in the Western Church. They were divided into major and minor orders. The major orders were *subdeacon, deacon,* and *priest. Minor orders* were *porter, lector, exorcist,* and *acolyte.* After *Vatican II*, the minor orders and the major order of subdeacon were abolished in the Ordinary Form of the Roman Rite. *Priest* in major orders is taken in the sense of 'sacerdos' in Latin, one who is commissioned to offer the *sacrifice* of the *Mass.* A *bishop* is also a priest, and, for this reason, he cannot be *consecrated* unless he is already a priest. A bishop is consecrated by a separate *ordination* because he is given powers a simple priest does not possess, in particular that of ordaining other priests. To differentiate the two ranks of *priesthood*, bishops are known as *priests of the first order,* and simple priests are known as *priests of the second order.* See Clerics 934. Also see Clerical orders.

Malicious/maliciously

Malicious means being intentionally spiteful or doing something with *evil* and harmful intentions. See Boasting 2481. Also see Complaisance 2480.

Man

Man is defined as a living substance composed of a *material* body, which dies and is subject to corruption, and a *spiritual*, immortal *soul*. He is *created* to know, *love*, and serve God in this life and to be happy with him in *eternity*.

Man was created by God in his own image and likeness as male and female. In Latin the word 'homo' refers to *human being*. The Latin word 'vir' refers to a male *person*. Homo has no perfect English equivalent, but it is part of the Church's official vocabulary and can be found in every major document of the Church.

The Anglo-Saxon word man means rational animal. Philosophically, man is defined as a *rational animal*. See Image of God 705.

Man as a moral subject 1749

The phrase '*man* as a moral subject' means that he has *free will* and can make choices that can be evaluated *morally* and for which he is responsible.

Mandatum

Mandatum is a Latin word meaning *commandment*. It is used in reference to the occasion at the *Last Supper* in Jn 13:14 when *Christ* gave his *disciples* a *new commandment*. He told them to do to each other as he had done to them, referring to the washing of their feet as a symbol of service to others.

The Thursday of Holy Week is called *Maundy Thursday* because of the *mandatum* of Christ given at the *Last Supper*.

The term mandatum is also used to refer to the *episcopal recognition* of the *orthodoxy* of those who teach in Catholic colleges and universities. See Maundy Thursday.

Manger

See Creche.

Manichaeism 285

Manichaeism refers to the *heretical* teaching of Manes (d. 277 A.D.), who, in third century Persia, taught that there are two *eternal* first principles: God, the cause of all *good*, and *matter*, the cause of all *evil*. According to Manes, matter is the *spirit* of evil and is equal to God in power.

The followers of Manes were called the Manicheans. They rejected the *Old Testament* and were selective about what they accepted in the *New Testament*. They believed that the body is the work of the supreme bad principle, that *marriage* is wrong, and that *begetting* children is sinful.

Manifestation

Manifestation is the act of making something clear, evident, or obvious. See Theophany 204. Also see Epiphany 528.

Maniple

A maniple is a band worn on the left forearm by those in *major orders* during a *Mass* celebrated according to the *Extraordinary Form*. It is the distinctive badge of the *subdeacon*, who is invested with it during *ordination*. *Bishops* put it on after the *Confiteor* during *Mass*.

Historically, *Carthusian nuns* receive it during the *rite* of *consecration of virgins*. Today, the maniple is no longer in common use except in the *celebration* of the *Extraordinary Form* of the *Roman Rite*. See Consecration of virgins. Also see Consecrated persons 1672.

Manna

Manna was the *miraculous* bread, whose appearance was similar to that of *hoarfrost*, that God rained down onto the ground from *heaven* every morning for the *Israelites* in the desert. Each morning the people were to gather only the amount they needed for the day. Before the *Sabbath*, they were allowed to gather enough for two days. See Mercy seat 433.

Mantra

A mantra is a repeated *hymn* or word *chanted* or intoned as an *incantation* or prayer in Hinduism. See Centering Prayer.

Marana tha 671, 1130, 1403, 2817

'Marana tha' is an Aramaic term meaning 'O *Lord*, come' or 'The Lord is near.' It may appear either as 'maran atha,' meaning 'Our Lord has come,' or as 'Marana tha,' meaning 'Come, our Lord.' It is used dramatically at the end of the Book of *Revelation*, where St. John writes, 'The one who gives this testimony says, "Yes, I am coming soon. *Amen!*" Come Lord *Jesus*' (Rev 22:20).

The fact that St. Paul used the expression in his letter to the Church at Corinth suggests that this Aramaic expression was already known to them and was even used as a *liturgical invocation*. The expression seems to have arisen among the Palestinian communities and was passed to the Hellenistic Church at a very early time. It is probable that it was used in the *celebration* of the *Eucharist* where the 'coming' referred to both the *eschatological* coming, called the *parousia*, and the coming of the Lord in the Eucharistic banquet.

In discussing the institution of the Eucharist. St. Paul writes, 'For as often as you eat this bread and drink the cup, you proclaim the death of the Lord until he comes' (1 Cor 11:26). The Eucharist, thus, was considered an everlasting symbol and assurance of the parousia, the second coming of the Lord.

The *Catechism of the Catholic Church* teaches that, though it is already present in the Church, *Christ's* reign is yet to be fulfilled, so she prays above all in the Eucharist to hasten his return by saying 'Marana tha,' 'Our Lord come.'

Marcionism 123

Marcionism refers to a series of *heretical* teachings named for *Bishop* Marcion, who *seceded* from the Church in 144 A.D. He taught that *Christ* was only a manifestation of God opposed to the God of the *Old Testament*. He rejected the Old Testament and all but selected parts of the *New Testament* as revelations of an inferior and *evil* principle. He also held that *matter* was worthless, that there would be no *resurrection* of the body, and that married *persons* should not be *baptized*.

Marcionism, one of many manifestations of *gnosticism*, was eventually absorbed by *Manichaeism*.

Mardi Gras

Mardi Gras is French for *Fat Tuesday*. See Fat Tuesday.

Marian

Marian is an adjectival form of *Mary*. It refers to anything relating to or specifically about the *Blessed Virgin*, such as her *virtues*, *cult*, *devotional* practices, scriptural references, art, literature, or *theology*. See New Eve 411.

Marital intercourse

Intercourse refers to communication or dealings among people or an exchange of products, services, ideas, or feelings.

Marital means pertaining to *marriage*. Among the most intimate exchanges between *spouses* is *sexual intercourse*, referred to as marital intercourse. See Sexual intercourse.

Maronite Church, Rite

The Maronite Church is an *Eastern Catholic Church* in communion with Rome. It is the Church of most Arabic speaking Syrians living in Lebanon. The name comes from St. Maron (d. 410 A.D.), a Syrian *hermit*. Three hundred and fifty *monks* in the *monastery* of St. Maron were later killed for their loyalty to the *Council of Chalcedon*, which had condemned *Monophysitism*. During the Arab conflict of the seventh century, the *patriarchs* of Antioch moved to Constantinople, leaving the Chalcedonians in Syria without a patriarch. The monks of St. Maron and local *bishops* then elected the first Maronite patriarch in 685 A.D.

The *Crusaders* brought the Maronites into contact with the *West*, and the Maronite patriarch attended the *Fourth Lateran Council* in 1215 A.D. Strong ties to Rome over time have resulted in a certain Latinization of the *liturgy*, but the use of Syriac in the liturgy has been retained. The *Divine Liturgy* is the Syrian liturgy of St. James. Married men may receive *Holy Orders*. Maronites are now under the Patriarch of Antioch and have some 350,000 members in Syria, Palestine, Egypt, and Cyprus. See Oriental Church. Also see Rite; Eastern Church.

Marriage 1603

Marriage is the intimate union of a man and woman in a community of life established by the *Creator* and endowed with its own proper powers.

Since God directly formed man and woman, their mutual *love* becomes an image of the absolute and unfailing *perpetual* love with which God loves *man*.

Scripture affirms that man and woman were *created* for one another: 'It is not good that man should be alone' (Gen 2:18). In Genesis, Adam says that woman is the 'flesh of his flesh' (Gen 2:18–25). As man's helpmate, woman represents the dearest of all things given by God who faithfully comes to man's help. Therefore, a man leaves his father and mother and cleaves to his wife, and they become one flesh' (Gen 2:24).

The *Lord* himself teaches (Mt 19:3–9) that becoming one flesh signifies an unbreakable union of two lives by recalling what the plan of the Creator had been in the beginning.

Marriage is one of God's most beautiful gifts to man. Marriage is the basis for *family*, its purpose, and its guardian. It is an image of the Church.

Marriage bond 1640

The marriage bond is the bond that comes into existence only by a *valid* marriage and continues to exist even if the *spouses* are physically separated.

The bond of marriage between two *baptized persons*, *Catholic* or not, is a *sacramental* bond. The *consummated* sacramental bond cannot be dissolved by any power on earth.

The unique *covenantal* relationship between a man and a woman, which is ordered to the well-being of the spouses and the *procreation* and upbringing of children, comes into existence when marital *consent* is exchanged.

Marriage consent

See Matrimonial consent 1625.

Marriage covenant

See Matrimonial covenant 1601.

Marriage or matrimonial consent 1625

See Matrimonial consent 1601.

Martyr

A martyr is a *person* who chooses to die rather than renounce the *faith* or *Chris-*

tian principles. See Martyr-dom 2473.

Martyrdom 2473

"Martyrdom is the supreme witness given to the *truth* of the *faith*: it means bearing witness even unto death" (CCC 2473). Martyrdom is the most perfect imitation of *Christ*. Those who suffered martyrdom in the early Church were the first to be regarded as saints.

Technically, martyrdom refers to the established fact that a *person* has died as a martyr and is eligible to have his cause introduced for *can-onization*.

Marvelous exchange 526

The marvelous exchange refers to the *Christmas mys-tery* in which God became *man*, was born of the *Virgin* and made men sharers in the *divinity* of *Christ*, who hum-bled himself to share in their humanity.

Mary

Mary is the name of the *Blessed Virgin*, the spotless *Spouse of the Holy Spirit* and Mother of the *Incarnate Word*, the Savior of the world (cf. Eph 1:4). She is the woman announced in the *protoevange-lium*, the *New Eve*, conceived without sin, the *Coredemptrix* and *Mother of the living*. See Immaculate Conception 491.

Mary's predestination 488

Predestination is the *fore-knowledge* by which, from *eternity*, God decrees what he will do in time.

From all eternity, the *Incar-nation* of the Son was part of the *divine plan*. God also willed that the Incarnation be preceded by the free *assent* of his predestined Mother so that just as woman, in Eve, shared in the coming of death into the world through *sin* so also a woman, his Son's Mother, should share in the coming of life.

Knowing this from eter-nity, God willed to prepare a body for his Incarnate Son by choosing *Mary*, a virgin betrothed to Joseph, to be his Mother. Because she was to become his Mother, God enriched Mary with appropri-ate gifts and *graces*.

Mary had freely to choose to cooperate with the divine plan. God's foreknowledge did not remove her *free will*. Because, as a creature, she needed divine grace to cooper-ate with his plan, God made her *full of grace*. Only by being totally free from sin could she give absolutely free assent, through *faith*, to her *vocation*. Therefore, by a singular grace and privilege of God and in virtue of the merits of *Christ*, Mary was *redeemed* in a more exalted fashion by reason of the *merits* of her Son and preserved *immune* from all stain of *original sin* from the moment of her *conception*.

The splendor of her unique

predestined *holiness* comes entirely from Christ. She was blessed more than any other *created person* with every *spiritual blessing* to be blameless before him in love before the foundation of the world. By the grace of God, she remained free of every *personal sin* her whole life long.

Mary's virginity 496

"From the first formulations of her *faith*, the Church has confessed that Jesus was conceived solely by the power of the *Holy Spirit* in the womb of the *Virgin Mary*, affirming also the *corporeal* aspect of this event: Jesus was conceived 'by the Holy Spirit without human seed" CCC 496).

Her son, in his *human nature*, was truly the *Son of God* in being born of her flesh and remained the Son of God in his *divine nature* while truly being *born of a virgin* by the *will* and power of the Holy Spirit.

The Church confesses Mary's real and *perpetual virginity* even in the act of giving birth to the Son of God made man and she *celebrates* Mary as 'Aeiparthenos,' the 'Ever Virgin.'

Mass 1332

The Mass is the sacrifice of the *New Law* in which *Christ*, through the ministry of the *priest*, offers himself to the Father in an unbloody manner under the appearances of bread and wine. It is also referred to as the *Sacred Liturgy*, Liturgy of the Mass, or *Divine Mysteries*.

The Mass is the same *sacrifice* as the sacrifice of the Cross, but the manner in which the sacrifice is *immolated* is different. On the Cross, Christ physically shed his Blood and was physically slain. In the Mass, there is no physical shedding of blood or physical death. On the Cross, Christ gained *merit* and made *atonement* for our sins; in the Mass, he applies this to us.

The Mass consists of the *Liturgy of the Word* (*Mass of the Catechumens*) and the *Liturgy of the Eucharist* (*Mass of the Eucharist*. Together they form a single act of worship in the unity of the Mass.

The Liturgy of the Word is so called because it is through all the words of *Sacred Scripture* that God speaks the *Incarnate Word*, who is his one utterance and in whom the Father expresses himself completely. In the Liturgy of the Eucharist, the *faithful* unite themselves to the sacrifice of the Son to the Father made present in the liturgy.

It is customary for priests to celebrate Mass daily, but it is not obligatory. In order to celebrate a second Mass in a day, priests only need a sufficient pastoral motive. However, on Christmas and *All Soul's Day* all priests may celebrate three Masses.

Some days in the liturgical year are known by the name of a saint, feast-day, or festival, to which the suffix '–mass' or '–mas' is applied, such as in Candlemas, Christmas, Martinmas, All Hallowsmass, Ladymass, and Marymass. Another Mass with a special name is *'Midnight Mass,'* which is celebrated in the middle of the night on *Christmas*.

The *Mass of the Dead* is also called a *Requiem Mass*, and is the Mass celebrated on All Soul's Day. It is also celebrated on the day a *person* dies; on the day of his burial; on the third, seventh, and thirtieth days after his death; and on the anniversary of his death.

Mass *obligation* refers to the duty for Catholics to attend Mass on all *Sundays* and *holy days of obligation.*

Before the sixth century, the Mass was called the offering, sacrifice, or mystery, depending on the aspect being given prominence. For example, 'yr offeren' (Welsh), 'an offeren' (Cornish), 't-aifrenan' (Irish), and 'an aifrionn' (Scottish) all mean 'the offering,' and refer to the Mass.

It is generally agreed that the word Mass comes from the Latin word 'missa,' which is an abbreviated verbal form of the Latin verb 'dimittere,' meaning to send away or dismiss. This could refer to either the dismissal of the catechumens, public penitents, and energumens at the end of the Liturgy of the Word, or it could refer to the final words of the Mass: 'Ite missa est,' translated as 'Go, the Mass is ended.' 'Missa' was shortened to Mass and came to be used to identify the service. The earliest known use of the word was in the last quarter of the fourth century.

In the *Extraordinary Form*, there are four specific ways of celebrating the Mass. While essentially the same Mass, they each have their own proper ceremonials. They are the *Pontifical Mass*, Mass celebrated by a bishop; the *Solemn Mass*, where a *deacon* and *subdeacon* join the celebrant; the *Sung Mass*, an intermediate style in which the priest is not assisted by a deacon or subdeacon and sings the parts of the Mass as in a Solemn Mass, its ceremonies are usually a mixture of the Solemn Mass and *Low Mass*; and the Low Mass. In the *Ordinary Form*, there are not several distinct ways of celebrating Mass; rather, there are many options which may be observed or left aside according to circumstances. See Mass of the Presanctified. Also see Private Mass.

Mass-groat

Mass-groat refers to the *offertory collection* of money made at Mass for the support of the Church and the poor. It was first called the *Mass-penny*. It came to be called a Mass-groat after the *denomination* of a coin called a 'grossus,' or thick coin in Latin, became the customary offering.

Etymologically the word 'grossus' means thick, in reference to the 'pfenninge,' which was a thick penny. It was worth about one-eighth of an ounce of silver in the fourteenth century, but its *value* varied considerably.

The Mass itself was called *The Offering* before the sixth century. See Mass penny. Also see Offering, The.

Mass of Obligation

The Mass of *Obligation* refers to the requirement that all Catholics attend Mass once on every *Sunday* and *holy day of obligation* unless prevented by illness, distance, or *grave* duties.

To be considered as fulfilling this obligation the *person* must be present at least from the *offertory* until after *Holy Communion*. If one involuntarily misses a considerable part, he must hear the corresponding part of another Mass if possible. See Mass.

Mass of the Catechumens

Since the time of St. Ambrose (340–397 A.D.) the *Mass* has been divided into two great parts referred to as the 'Missa catechumenorum,' or Mass of the Catechumens, and the 'Missa fidelium,' or *Mass of the Faithful*.

The Mass of the Catechumens is the part of the Mass from the beginning up to the offertory, exclusively. At this point the *catechumens, public penitents*, and *energumens*, who were excluded from the Mass of the Faithful, would be dismissed.

The Mass of the Catechumens consists of instruction of *Scripture*, the homily, a *profession of faith*, and the prayers of the faithful. Today it is generally referred to as the *Liturgy of the Word*. See Discipline of the Secret.

Mass of the Dead

The Mass of the Dead is the *Mass* appointed for *All Souls Day*; the day a *person* dies; the day of his burial; the third, seventh, and thirtieth days after his death; and the annual anniversary of his death. All the *proper* parts of the Mass refer to death, *judgment, resurrection*, and life.

The Mass of the Dead is also called a *Requiem Mass*.

Mass of the Faithful

The Mass of the Faithful is that part of the *Mass* containing the *offertory, consecration*, and *communion*, which, in earlier times, only the *baptized faithful* could attend.

Mass of the Presanctified

The 'Mass of the Presanctified' was the Eucharistic part of the *Good Friday* liturgy before 1955. While there was no *consecration*, many of the prayers and gestures of the normal *Mass* were used (but with important changes). The *celebrant* alone communicated, consuming the extra host that was consecrated the previous night at the Mass of the *Lord's Supper*. It was one of the last examples of a *missa sicca* in the *Roman Rite*.

This practice has been superseded by a brief *communion service* on *Good Friday*. Following the Adoration of the Holy Cross, the *Blessed Sacrament* is brought from the *altar of repose* and placed on the *altar*. After the priest and the people recite the *Lord's Prayer*, *Holy Communion* is distributed using hosts consecrated at the Mass of the Lord's Supper. See Mass 1332. Also see Liturgy of the Presanctified Gifts.

Mass-penny

The Mass-penny refers to the *offerings* of money made at *Mass*. It was also once called the *Mass-groat* after a denomination of coin called a 'grossus' in Latin, meaning thick. It was recognized from the thirteenth century in various countries of Europe. Its standard seems to have been one eighth of an ounce of silver in the fourteenth century, but its actual intrinsic *value* varied greatly. *Etymologically*, the word means thick, in reference to 'pfenninge,' which was a thick penny.

The offering of money at Mass is symbolic of the self-offering each individual should make in union with the offering of the *Eucharistic Christ*. The funds collected are used to maintain the Church and to support the *clergy*. See Collection 1351.

Mass stipend

It is *lawful* for a *priest celebrating* a *Mass* for the special intention of another to receive an offering, or stipend, to be used for his personal needs or at his discretion. Not more than one stipend may be received for the same Mass. The local *Bishop* or *legitimate* custom determine the amount of the stipend. It must not be considered as the purchase of a Mass or the sale of *spiritual* goods. See Collection 1351.

Masturbation 2352

Masturbation is the deliberate stimulation of the genital organs in order to derive *sexual* pleasure.

The *Magisterium* of the Church and the constant *Tradition* and *moral* sense of the *faithful* leave no doubt that masturbation is an *intrinsically* and *gravely* disordered act because any sexual pleasure sought outside of marriage is *essentially* contrary to its purpose.

The use of any artificial means of birth prevention is essentially a form of mutual masturbation involving two *persons*.

Material

Material is anything formed out of *matter*, perceivable by the *senses*, or measurable in some way. Material things are also called *corporal* because they are bodily and can be touched (tangible) and are known through the *senses* rather than through *reason*. See Dualism 285.

Material logic

Material logic is the division of *logic* that addresses the truth value of the reasoning process. It investigates the content of *reasoning*, not merely the process like *formal logic* does. It is also called *Major Logic*, *Criteriology*, or, in modern terms, *Epistemology*. See Logic/Logical.

Materialism 285

Materialism is the erroneous teaching that nothing can be known to exist except *matter*, its movements, and its modifications. It totally denies the existence of immaterial *substances* and holds that the *mind* is the function of purely *material* processes. It denies the existence of God and the immaterial *soul* in man.

Materialism results in the exclusive concern for material development and comfort and makes these the first consideration and purpose of life. This *belief* is incompatible with Christianity, which gives meaning to earthly existence as the means of attaining *eternal life* through *grace*.

Matins

In the *Extraordinary Form*, Matins is the first office of the day. It would be recited either in the evening of the previous day, during the night, or in the early morning. Depending on the day, it is composed of either one *nocturn* of nine *psalms* and three readings, or of three nocturns with three psalms and three reading each. See Divine Office. Also see Liturgy of the Hours 1174, 1178.

Matrimonial consent 1625

Matrimonial *consent* is the *essence* of *marriage* viewed as a *covenant* between a man and a woman. Matrimonial consent is the *act of the will* by which each party gives and accepts exclusive and *perpetual right* to those acts ordained for the *procreation* of children.

Internal consent of the *mind* is presumed in *law* to conform to the words and signs that constitute the marriage ceremony, but if either party, by an act of the will, excludes either the marriage itself or all right to the *conjugal act* or to any *essential* property of marriage, the marriage is *invalid*.

Consent given under the compulsion of fear is not *valid* consent. Matrimonial consent is also called *marriage consent*.

Matrimonial consent given

in a *sacramental* marriage is referred to as a *matrimonial covenant*. See Matrimonial covenant 1601.

Matrimonial covenant 1601

The matrimonial *covenant* is the mutual *solemn* agreement, fortified by an *oath*, through which a man and a woman establish between themselves a partnership for the whole of their lives and agree to do and refrain from doing certain acts.

The *spouses* enter into a solemn agreement to mutually *inviolable fidelity*, support, and loyalty by which each one's *faith* is pledged or plighted to the other.

This solemn promise constitutes the matrimonial covenant. This covenant, once *validly* established, is indissoluble, that is, it binds until death and cannot be broken by any *authority* other than the divine.

The term covenant is used instead of contract in *recognition* of the spiritual equality of the spouses and their capacity to make an agreement requiring the total gift of their whole *person* without reservation.

Matrimony

Matrimony is a *sacrament* in which a man and a woman, who are both *baptized* and free to marry, bind themselves for life in a *lawful* marriage and receive the *grace* to discharge the duties of their state.

Though the man and woman administer the sacrament to one another, the *ceremony* must be conducted according to the form approved by the Church. See Matrimonial covenant 1601. Also see Matrimonial consent 1625.

Matter

Matter is that which constitutes a body having characteristics that can be measured, such as size, weight, parts, mass, and volume. It is that which is not *spirit* or immaterial. See Prime matter; Hylomorphic theory.

Matter of a sacrament

The matter of a *sacrament* refers to sensible things or outward signs, *substances*, or acts, such as water for *Baptism*, *chrism* for *Confirmation*, and bread and wine in the *Eucharist*. Such matter receives *sacramental* significance from the accompanying form that consists of the words and actions necessarily used to perform the sacramental *rite* in order to confer grace. See Eucharist, Holy 1328.

Maundy Thursday

Maundy Thursday is the name given to the Thursday of *Holy Week*. The word is a *corruption* of the Latin word '*mandatum*,' meaning commandment, used when *Christ* gave his *disciples* a new *commandment* to wash one another's feet as he had washed theirs (Jn 13:4–17). See Holy Thursday.

Maxim

A maxim is a short principle or rule of conduct. See Rule of law 1904.

Means

A means is something that is not sought for its own sake but for the sake of something else, called an *end* or purpose. A means lies between an *agent* and an end and is used to help the agent reach that end.

Some means serve as intermediate ends and there may be a series of intermediate ends that each serve to bring the agent closer to an *ultimate end*. Such goods are sought as means of acquiring something else. Money may be sought as an intermediate end in order to pay for medical expenses. See Inversion of means and ends 1887.

Media/Median/Medes

Media was an ancient kingdom in the part of South West Asia now called Iran. Median is an adjective describing something pertaining to the country of Media, its language, or its culture. The inhabitants of Media are called Medes.

Media can also be the plural form of the word medium, which is a means or instrument, especially of communication, used to reach the general public, such as television, radio, newspapers, etc. See Social sin 1869.

Mediation

Mediation refers to the actions that are undertaken by a *mediator*. It is the process of effecting or bringing about *reconciliation* between disputing parties. See Mediator 65.

Mediator 65, 618

A mediator is one who intervenes between two parties, for the purpose of effecting reconciliation between them. For example, a mediator brings about a peace treaty or settles a dispute through *diplomatic* intervention, usually with the *consent* or invitation of the disputing parties. The process itself is referred to as *mediation*.

St. Paul writes, 'There is one God, and there is one mediator between God and *man*, the man *Jesus Christ*, who gave himself as a ransom for all, the testimony to which was given at the proper time' (1 Tim 2:5). Through his sacrificial offering of himself on the cross, Christ became both *victim* and *High Priest*, the unique mediator between God and man, gaining for man access to God's saving *mercy* and *grace*. The role of mediator is applied pre-eminently to Christ who, as the *Incarnate Word*, died to reconcile all mankind to the Father. He founded his Church to guide them in their journey to eternal life with the Father in heaven.

Christ is the only mediator in the sense that he personally brought about the reconciliation of man to God. He effected *salvation* through perfect *reparation* for sin. He made it possible for man, through him, to share *supernaturally* in the *divine life* and, through cooperation with *grace*, to *merit* salvation.

Mary, his Mother, is called *Mediatrix* by virtue of her cooperation in the *mission* of the Incarnate Word and the *salvific* mission of Christ. She is the dispenser of the graces bestowed on men by the *Holy Spirit* through the merits of the *Crucifixion*. By cooperating in the *Incarnation* and *redemption* by her motherhood she became a channel for the graces flowing from the death of her Son.

Christ is mediator because, though sent by God, he is our representative before the Father. In Lumen Gentium 8, *Vatican II* teaches that "Christ, the one mediator, established and ceaselessly sustains here on earth his Holy Church, the community of *faith*, *hope*, and *charity*, as a physical structure. Through her he communicates *truth* and grace to all."

By sharing in the *Mystical Body* of Christ, members of the *Church Triumphant*, the *Church Suffering*, and the *Church Militant* also share in the *salvific* mission of the Church through *efficacious intercessory prayers* for one another.

Mediatrix 969

The word mediatrix is a Latin word meaning *mediator*, or intermediary. Mediatrix is used as a title of the *Blessed Virgin* because 1) as *Mother of God* and *full of grace*, she occupies a middle position between God and his creatures; 2) because with *Christ* and under him, she cooperated in the *reconciliation* between God and *man*; and 3) because she distributes God's *grace* to man.

The title Mediatrix applies to the Blessed Virgin under two aspects. First of all, she gave her consent to the birth of Christ, the only source of all grace to mankind. Though Christ alone made full *atonement* for *sin* on the Cross, *Mary*, because of her unique relation to Christ as his Mother, shared in the work of his redeeming *Passion* and death as no other believer could or did. With Christ and under him, she cooperated in the reconciliation between God and man on *Calvary* through her direct consent to become the Mother of God and her intermediating *compassion*.

Several Church documents warn about the dangers of ascribing the title of *priest* to Mary or of depicting Mary in *sacerdotal vestments* so as not to confuse her with *min-*

isterial priests, namely, those who are priests by virtue of the sacrament of *Holy Orders*, or to imply that she, as a woman, could be and was ordained a ministerial priest.

Nonetheless, the Church does not deny that Mary, in some true sense, shares in Christ's priesthood. Since the earliest days of the Church, Mary has been called, in some sense, the Virgin Priest (Virgo Sacerdos). This is because Mary's share in the priesthood and victimhood of her Son is not merely by virtue of the *common priesthood*, as is the case for all other believers by reason of their *Baptism*.

Though Christ alone made full atonement for sin, this does not exclude, as *Vatican II* notes, the participation of others with him in various ways in the work of *redemption* and in the redemptive *sacrifice*.

Because Mary is associated with Christ in this work as his Mother and so participates in his Passion and death as no other, she alone is held to participate actively by her compassion in what is called the *objective redemption*, or the *sacrifice* of Christ on Calvary.

By her unique participation there, she makes possible the participation both of ministerial priests and of the common priesthood of the *faithful* in the *subjective redemption*, whose summit is the *celebration* of the *Eucharist*. This is why, on the point of death,

Christ entrusted or consecrated, in the *person* of St. John, *bishops*, and priests to his Mother in a special way. Mary's singular role (in the phrase of Vatican II) in the objective redemption, though *subordinate* to that of Christ, is direct and proximate and is the basis for her universal mediation of *grace* in the subjective order of redemption.

The second aspect of Mary as Mediatrix is derived from her maternity in the order of grace, whereby she is involved in applying Christ's redemptive grace to individual Christians. This is called subjective redemption, as distinguished from objective redemption, the latter of which refers to Christ's act of redemption on the Cross.

Mary's maternal *intercession* is not in itself necessary for the bestowal of divine blessings. In God's special ordinance, however, graces merited by Christ are conferred through the maternal mediation of his Mother. This interpretation of Marian mediation in the order of the subjective redemption is consistent with the teaching of Vatican II and of recent *Popes*, especially Pope St. John Paul II, who understands Jn 19:25–27 as affirming the maternal and not merely intercessory character of the Virgin Mother's universal distribution of all graces merited by Christ. See Fiat 2617.

Medicinal censure/penalty

Medicinal means having the properties of medicine, such as curing, healing, soothing, or relieving pain. See Canonical penalty 1463. Also see Ecclesiastical penalty 1463.

Medieval

Medieval means like or pertaining to the period of European history between ancient and modern times covering the years from 476 A.D. to 1450 A.D. This period is also referred to as the *Middle Ages*. See Canons secular/ regular.

Meditation 2705

Meditation is also called *discursive prayer*. It is a form of prayer that consists in reflecting on a subject with the aim of stirring the *will* to greater *faith, hope, love, humility,* etc., and of forming *resolutions* that will reform one's life and draw one closer to *Christ*.

Meditation engages thought, *imagination, emotion,* and a desire to mobilize the *faculties* necessary to deepen one's convictions of faith, to prompt a *conversion of heart,* and to strengthen one's resolve to follow Christ.

Meditation gradually grows into *affective prayer,* in which there is less need for the assistance of mental reflection to move the *soul* to such awareness and love.

Meditative and affective prayer may be initiated by the action of man, but, as he grows in perfection and as the obstacles to the working of the *Holy Spirit* are removed, this awareness, desire, and love of God become gifts of the Spirit in *contemplative prayer*.

Meditative prayer

Meditative prayer is the prayer from which *contemplative prayer* develops. It consists in reading, reflecting, thinking, imagining, drawing *conclusions,* and conversing inwardly with the indwelling *Trinity*.

It is distinguished from *lectio divina,* or *spiritual reading,* in that the emphasis is not so much on the reading as on the *pious* and *devotional* reflection resulting from it. See Contemplative prayer 2709.

Medium

In *spiritualism,* a medium is a *person* who claims to act as an *agent* between the dead and the living in order to communicate ideas and *experiences* from beyond the grave. Mediums are not recognized by the Church because spiritism is opposed to the first commandment. See Spiritism 2117.

Melancholy

Melancholy refers to a type of *temperament.* Temperament identifies a *person's* customary frame of *mind* or *natural* disposition. Persons with a melancholic temperament tend to be sad, depressed, gloomy,

and pensive. See Tempera-
ment. Also see Astrology.

Melchior
 See Magi.

Memorare
 The Memorare is a prayer to
the Blessed Virgin asking for
her intercession. See Appendix of prayers/Marian prayers.

Memorial 1363
 As part of the Mass, the
memorial is also called the
anamnesis. 'Anamnesis' is
a Greek word meaning calling to *mind.* In the *liturgy,*
the memorial is "not merely
the *recollection* of past events
but the *proclamation* of the
mighty works wrought by God
for *man.* In the *liturgical celebration* of these events, they
become in a certain way present and real" (CCC 1363). In
celebrating the *Eucharist,*
the Church *commemorates
Christ's Passover,* which is
made present because the *sacrifice* of Christ remains ever-
present. As often as the sacrifice is *celebrated* on the *altar,*
the work of *redemption* is carried out. It is made present,
not repeated.

Memory
 Memory is the power, process, or act of recalling to
one's *mind* previous *experiences* or facts and the ability
to perceive their implications
for the future. See Cognition.

Mendaciously 2855
 Mendaciously means in a
lying manner. It comes from
the Latin word "mendax,"
which means liar.

Mendicant order
 Mendicant orders are societies of *religious* who divest
themselves of all worldly goods
and support themselves by
the *alms* of others. St. Francis of Assisi and St. Dominic
were founders of the two major
mendicant orders, known as
the *Franciscan Friars* and
the *Preaching Friars,* respectively. See Dominicans. Also
see Franciscans; Order 1537;
Religious life 925.

Mental prayer
 Prayer may take various
forms. Mental prayer is a
purely internal mental act in
which one privately turns his
mind and *heart* to God in *adoration, praise,* thanksgiving,
petition, or *intercession.* It is
contrasted with *oral prayer,*
which is expressed audibly
and is the form of prayer used
in *communal prayer* or in the
liturgy. See Forms of Prayer
2625.

Mercy
 Mercy refers to refraining
from harming or punishing
an offender or to being kind
in excess of what might be
expected or demanded by *justice.* Mercy is also a forbear-
ance and *compassion* shown
to another.

The *infinite* mercy of God is most notably manifested in the *forgiveness* of *sin*. God is also infinitely *just* and *holy*. This can create a *dilemma*. To *reconcile* the contradiction presented by equally infinite *attributes*, it is customary to appeal to God's equally infinite *love*. However, this only complicates the problem further because it seems to make love more infinite than justice or mercy.

Sin is really an act by which *man* rejects God's love. Man's love is always a response to the *divine* call to union. God's call itself is never in question; only the response is at issue. Without *grace*, man can do nothing to answer the call and restore friendship with God. Forgiveness of sin ultimately depends on accepting the grace of *conversion*. God's mercy *essentially* consists in giving man the grace of conversion.

This gift of the grace of conversion, which is prompted by God's love, allows man to respond freely to God's call to union. Man's *justification* through conversion depends on his response to the call to union as a *contingent cause*. Mercy in no way represents granting man a reprieve from the *evil* of his sin. It must be seen as a new beginning rather than a *dispensation*. See Despair 2091.

Mercy killing

Mercy killing is another way of saying *euthanasia*. Euthanasia comes from the Greek 'eu,' meaning good or well, and 'thanatos,' meaning death. These terms both refer to any action or omission of any action that, of itself or by intention, causes the death of a handicapped, sick, or dying *person* as a means to escape suffering. Mercy killing, or euthanasia, differs from murder only in motive. See Euthanasia 2277.

Mercy seat 433

The mercy seat refers to a part of the *Ark of the Covenant*.

On top of the Ark of the Covenant, there was a gold plate called the 'kapporet' in *Hebrew*. It is translated as 'mercy seat,' or *'propitiatory,'* in English, the place where *Yahweh* receives *atonement*. Two *cherubim* facing each other were atop the Ark, so constructed that their wings overshadowed the 'kapporet,' where Yahweh meets Israel and reveals his commandments as from his throne. The overshadowing of the wings symbolized covering the eyes of God, who, in his *mercy*, would not see the *sins* of the *Israelites*.

Merit/Merited 2006

Merit is the reward that God promises and gives to those who love him and, by his *grace*, perform *good* works. One does not merit *justification* or *eternal* life, which are always given as free gifts of

God. The source of any merit one has before God is due to his acceptance of the *grace* of *Christ* working in him to do good.

Meritorious

Meritorious means deserving of reward or praise. See Spirit of detachment.

Messiah / Messianic 437

Messiah comes from the *Hebrew* word meaning *'anointed.'* It was commonly applied to kings who were anointed leaders. The Greeks translated Messiah as 'Christos' from which is derived the title *Christ*.

Metanoia

Metanoia comes from the Greek word 'metanoein,' to change one's *mind*, to *repent*, or to experience a *conversion*. The term is used in the Greek *New Testament* in reference to the *repentance, faith, Baptism*, and *confession* of *sins* necessary for conversion to new life in the *Spirit*. It is characterized by the change of *heart* from sin to the practice of *virtue*. Metanoia is essential to the pursuit of *Christian* perfection and fundamental to the teaching of *Christ*. It was the essential message of St. Peter in the very first sermon on *Pentecost*. See Conversion of heart 1430, 1888, 2608.

Meta-ousiosis

Meta-ousiosis is the expres-

sion used by the *Fathers of the Church* to express what takes place at the *Eucharistic consecration*. It comes from the Greek words 'meta,' meaning change, and 'ousia,' meaning being. Thus, it refers to the change of the total, not the partial, substance of the bread and the wine into *Christ's* Body and Blood.

The *Fourth Lateran Council* in 1215 A.D. first used the word *transubstantiation* in referring to this change of the total substance of bread and wine into the Body and Blood of Christ.

The *Council of Trent* formally called this *conversion* of the whole substance of the bread and wine into the *Eucharistic species* (the Body and Blood of Christ) transubstantiation. See Transubstantiation 1376.

Metaphor

A metaphor is a figure of speech containing an implied comparison in which words or phrases primarily used for one thing are applied to another, for example 'a curtain of light.' See Metaphorical sense. Also see Analogy.

Metaphorical sense

In *Sacred Scripture*, the metaphorical sense refers to the use of *metaphor* or *analogy* as a way of conveying the *spiritual* meaning of an inspired text. It is distinguished from the *literal sense*, or the etymological or *primary sense*, of the words. See Allegorical sense 117.

Metaphysical

The word metaphysical comes from the Greek 'meta,' meaning after, and 'physika,' meaning physics. It referred originally to the material in Aristotle's philosophy that followed upon his treatment of physics in the early collection of his works.

Metaphysical has come to mean that which is beyond the physical or *material*. As a field of study metaphysics deals with the *nature* of *being* or *essential reality*. See Divine nature.

Metempsychosis

See Reincarnation 1013.

Metropolitan

Metropolitan comes from the Greek, 'metro,' meaning great, and 'politan,' meaning ruler of a city, namely, ruler of a city greater than other cities near it. In the Western Church, the title Metropolitan is given to an *archbishop* who presides over a *province* containing other *bishops*, known as *suffragan bishops* because they depend on the suffrage (from the Latin: 'suffragium,' meaning 'support') of the Metropolitan or come under his influence and *authority*. Not all archbishops are metropolitans. See Council 465. Also see Suffragan Bishops; Archbishop.

Midafternoon Prayer

Midafternoon Prayer is the name of *Daytime Prayer* as recited after 3pm in the afternoon. In Latin, it is called *None*. See Divine Office. Also see Liturgy of the Hours 1174, 1178.

Midday prayer

Midday Prayer is the name of *Daytime Prayer* as recited between noon and 3pm. In Latin, it is called *Sext*. See Divine Office. Also see Liturgy of the Hours 1174, 1178.

Middle ages

Middle Ages refers to the period of history between 476 A.D. and the end of the fifteenth century. Some believe that during the middle ages, after 1100 A.D. to the end of this period, the highest realization of Christendom as a *cultural* unity built on a common *faith* was reached. See Doctor of the Church.

Midmorning Prayer

Midmorning Prayer is the name of *Daytime Prayer* as recited before noon. In Latin, it is called *Terce*. See Divine Office. Also see Liturgy of the Hours 1174, 1178.

Midnight Mass

Midnight Mass is the *Mass* of *Christmas* Day which is *celebrated* during the night in order to express the joy that burst upon the world with the host of herald *angels* singing,

'Glory to God in the highest,' to the shepherds. See Major doxology. Also see Mass 1332.

Mighty/Wondrous deeds

Mighty deeds are acts that can only be done with the help of *supernatural* power. They are usually referred to as *miracles*.

Miracles performed by *angels*, *prophets*, and *saints* are wondrous deeds done in the name of God and by his power to manifest the goodness of God. The miracles of *Christ* were performed by his own *divine* power and were performed so that people would know that he was truly God. See Miracle 548. Also see Charism.

Millenarianism 676

The term millenarianism is derived from the Latin root for 'one thousand' and refers to a *belief* that *Christ* will return to govern a *temporal* kingdom on earth for a thousand years before the end of the world. It is based on an excessively *literal* reading of the Book of *Revelation*. It is much like *chiliasm*. See Chiliasm.

Mind

The *intellect* is man's *cognitive*, or knowing, *faculty*, and it is referred to as the mind. See Soul 363.

Minister general

Minister general is the title of the *superior* of certain *religious* communities, especially *Franciscans*. See Superior, religious.

Ministerial priesthood 1120

Ministerial priesthood refers to those of the *faithful* who have received the *sacrament* of *Holy Orders* and are appointed to nourish the Church with the word and *grace* of God in the name of *Christ*.

This "ministerial priesthood is at the service of the *baptismal priesthood*. The ministerial priesthood guarantees that it really is Christ who acts in the sacraments through the *Holy Spirit* for the Church" (CCC 1120).

Ministry

Ministry is the work of *ordained clerics* who have the *duty* to govern, teach, and *sanctify* the people of God. The work of the *laity* in the Church is properly referred to as an *apostolate*.

The service of *extraordinary ministers of Holy Communion*, though done by *laymen*, is properly referred to as a ministry because the administration of the *Eucharist* is properly reserved to the ordained ministers. See Apostolate 863.

Ministry of reconciliation 1442

The ministry of reconciliation refers to the Church's act of reconciling others to God by exercising the power of *absolution*, or *forgiveness* of *sin*.

Minor Basilica

Minor basilica is a title given to certain important *churches* in Rome and other parts of the world. See Basilica.

Minor doxology

The minor doxology refers to the prayer, 'Glory be to the *Father*, and to the *Son*, and to the *Holy Spirit*. As it was in the beginning is now, and ever shall be, world without end. *Amen*.' It is one of the most commonly used prayers, and is frequently added at the end of other prayers. See Rosary. Also see Appendix of prayers.

Minor hours

The minor hours are those shorter hours of the *Divine Office* said throughout the day: *Terce, Sext*, and *None*. *Daytime Prayer* is usually recited only once daily as one of these three in the *Ordinary Form*. *Compline*, which is said at the end of the day, is also included among the minor hours. See Liturgy of the Hours 1174, 1178.

Minor logic

Minor logic is another name for *dialectics* or *formal logic*. It is concerned not with the *truth* of the content of thought, but with the process itself. See Logic. Also see Major Logic.

Minor orders

Traditionally, there are seven separate *degrees* of *Holy Orders* in the Western Church. They are divided into major and minor orders. *Minor orders* are *porter*, from the Latin word 'porta,' meaning gate; *lector*, from the Latin 'legere,' meaning to read; *exorcist* from the Greek 'exorkizein,' meaning to banish an *evil spirit*; and *acolyte* from the Greek 'akolouthos,' meaning follower. After *Vatican II* the minor orders and the major order of subdeacon were abolished in the *Ordinary Form* of the *Roman Rite*.

Miracles 548

A miracle is a marvelous event or *mighty and wondrous deed* that occurs within human *experience* and that cannot have been brought about by human power or explained by the *operation* of any known natural agency. It is not a breach of the *laws* of *nature* nor a suspension of them but an effect wrought independently of natural powers and laws such that only God can be considered to be the immediate and direct *cause*. For this reason, miracles must be ascribed to the special intervention of God. *Catholics* are bound to accept the existence of miracles, but the *miraculous* character of any occurrence must be settled by the evidence.

In miracles, God produces *sensible* effects that *transcend* the operation of natural causes, such as instant healing or control over the *laws* of *nature*. In working miracles, God does not contradict himself because nowhere has he bound himself to operate only according to the laws of nature. The Lord of nature is not limited or restricted by nature.

In the *New Testament*, the words, signs, and wonders are used in referring to miracles.

When the Greek word 'semeion,' meaning sign, is used for miracle in the New Testament, it does not mean a miracle so much as a manifestation of divine intervention. It is used when the sign or miracle is being used as evidence of *Christ's divinity*.

When the Greek word 'dynameis,' meaning power, is used for wonders worked by *Jesus* and his disciples, it is being used to describe a special manifestation of the power of God by some *supernatural* activity.

Understanding miracles as a function of power is essential to the *understanding* of Christ and the Church. The healing miracles of Christ reveal him as the Savior who removes the consequences of *sin*. They represent the power of his example, his word, and his Church by which he wills to save mankind.

Miraculous/Miraculously

Miraculous means having the nature of a *miracle*, wonderful, marvelous, or *supernatural*. See Miracles.

Missa 1332

'Missa' is the Latin word for *Mass*. It received this name because the *liturgy* in which the *mystery of salvation* is accomplished concludes with the sending forth of the *faithful* to fulfill *God's will* in their lives with the words, 'Ite missa est,' usually translated as 'Go, the Mass is ended.' The word 'missa' is commonly translated as Mass. More literally translated, it is 'go,' it is the dismissal.' See Mass.

Missa Cantata

In the *Latin Rite*, a sung *Mass* is also known by its Latin equivalent, *Missa Cantata*. See Mass 1332.

Missa plana

Missa plana is another name for *Low Mass*. See Low Mass.

Missa privata

Missa privata is another name for *Low Mass*. Since *Vatican II* with its renewed emphasis on the communal and *ecclesial* nature of the liturgy, the use of this term is discouraged. See Low Mass.

Missa Sicca

See Dry Mass.

Missal

A missal is a book containing all the *prayers* recited by the *priest* at the *altar* during *Mass*.

In the *Extraordinary Form*, the missal contains all the

texts of the Mass, but in the *Ordinary Form*, the missal usually only contains those texts said by the *priest*, while the readings and antiphons are found in the *lectionary* and the Graduale, respectively.

A hand missal is a smaller book with all the texts of the liturgy. It is useful since it allows one to prepare better for Mass and to follow along while assisting at Mass. This is especially true if the Mass is not being celebrated in one's own language.

Missio/Mission

'Missio' is a Latin word meaning sending forth or mission. This word occurs at the end of *Mass*, 'Ite missa est,' or 'Go, the Mass is ended,' and is the probable source of the word Mass.

Mission of the Holy Spirit 485

The word *mission* is used to describe both the visible and the invisible extensions of the *processions of the Divine Persons* in the *Trinity*. The *Incarnation* is the mission of the *Second Person*; the indwelling of the *Holy Spirit* is the mission of the *Third Person*. The Father is not sent, because he does not proceed but is the Person from whom the other *Divine Persons* proceed. Hence, he does not have a mission in this sense.

Missions do not involve movement or change in God; rather, they involve a *grace* that produces a new way of being related to him in those to whom they are sent.

Missionary

A missionary is one sent by the Church to preach the *Gospel* or to teach the *faith* in a given place. See Missionary mandate.

Missionary mandate 849

The missionary mandate is the command of *Christ* to the *Apostles* to 'go forth and make *disciples* of all nations' in Mt 28:19–20. The whole purpose of the Church is to spread the *Gospel* with the help of the *Holy Spirit*, who guides and sustains her after Christ's *Ascension*.

Miter

A miter is the liturgical headdress worn by the *Pope, cardinals, bishops,* and *abbots* in the *Latin Rite*. It is made of two pieces of stiffened and ornamented silk or linen rising to a point with two fringe lappets that hang from the back. Miters are always removed when the *celebrant* prays. There are three kinds of miters: the golden, the simple, and the white. They may be interchanged according to the solemnity of the occasion and *liturgical season*.

The miter, *crosier, pectoral cross,* and *episcopal* or *pontifical ring* used by bishops are signs of their episcopal office and *authority*.

Mitigated

Mitigate comes from the Latin word 'mitigare,' meaning to make mild, soft, or tender. In English, it means much the same: to make milder, less painful, moderate, or less rigorous. See Carmelite.

Mixed marriage 1633, 1635

A mixed marriage, or *marriage* of mixed *religion*, is a marriage between a *Catholic* and a *baptized* non-Catholic who is a member of an *ecclesial* community not in full *communion* with the *Catholic Church*. A mixed marriage is prohibited except by express permission of the competent *ecclesiastical* authority (Canon 1124). The *local ordinary* can grant permission for a "just and reasonable cause" (Canon 1125).

To receive this permission, the Catholic party must be prepared to remove the danger of falling away from the *faith* and promise to do all that is possible to have all children baptized and raised in the Catholic faith. The other party must be informed of the promises the Catholic party has to make in order to enter such a marriage and be aware and accept the *obligations* required of the Catholic party. Both parties must be instructed on the essential ends and purposes of marriage, which may not be excluded by either party.

Though dispensations may be obtained for such unions, the Church never favors them because they can become sources of serious difficulty.

In the 1983 *Code of Canon Law*, when the non-Catholic party is not baptized, a *diriment impediment* called *disparity of worship or cult* is incurred. Without a *dispensation* from this impediment, such a marriage is both *illicit* and *invalid*.

The parties in such a marriage must not go through a form of marriage before a non-Catholic minister unless this is required by *civil law* to obtain civil effects.

Mixed religion

The expression 'mixed religion' refers to a marriage between a *baptized* non-Catholic and a *Catholic*. Such a marriage, without dispensation from the bishop, is *illicit* but *valid*. See Disparity of Cult 1633, 1635.

Modality/Mode

A mode is a manner or way of *acting* or *being*. It is the way in which something has being, and is distinct from the *substance* itself, such as being sick. See Trinity, Holy 232.

Mode of expression 43

A mode of expression is the way or manner in which some thought is communicated in spoken or written form.

Modesty 2521

Modesty is a *moral virtue* that

guards *chastity* and enables *man* to observe restraint over external actions, dress, and conversation. It "protects the intimate center of the *person...* refusing to unveil what should remain *hidden...* It guides how one looks at others and behaves toward them in conformity with the dignity of persons" (CCC 2521).

"Modesty protects the mystery of persons and their love. It encourages *patience* and moderation in loving relationships... It inspires one's choice of clothing. It keeps silence or reserve where there is evident risk of unhealthy curiosity. It is discreet" (CCC 2522).

It objects to the "voyeuristic explorations of the human body in certain advertisements," and to media that goes "too far in the exhibition of intimate things" (CCC 2523).

Monastery

Monastery comes from the Greek word 'monasterion,' meaning to be or stand alone. Originally, it was used to indicate a *cell* inhabited by a *hermit.*

Because such cells began to cluster together as others came to live under the guidance of a holy *hermit,* a single building composed of multiple *cells* was formed. The term monastery came to be applied to the building. It became the dwelling place of a community of *persons* who lived a life of contemplation and seclusion, and where the members met together to recite the *Divine Office* in common. Now it refers to the residence of a group of people who live together under the *rule* of a *superior.*

Monasticism refers to the *mode* of life followed by those who retire from the world to devote themselves to prayer. St. Benedict (c. 480–550 A.D.) introduced monasticism to the West. The influence of monasticism on Western culture is impossible to overestimate because the monasteries preserved *classical learning* during the *dark ages* of the Barbarian invasions.

Because such persons *consecrate* their lives to *prayer* and contemplation, they are referred to as consecrated persons. See Enclosed. Also see Enclosure; Consecrated Persons 1672.

Monastic

Monastic comes from the Greek word 'monozein,' meaning to be alone. It refers to the manner of life lived by some *religious* who live apart from the world in what are called *cloistered monasteries.* See Eremitic Life 920. Also see Monastery.

Monasticism

Monasticism refers to a form of *religious* life followed by those who retire from the world to devote themselves to *prayer.* It is characterized by life in a community of *monks* or *nuns* bound together until death under a *common rule* of life by their *religious profession*. See Benedictines. Also see Dark ages; Monastery.

Monk

The name monk was originally applied to *hermits* or anchorites, but, even in the early Church, the name was applied to men living a community life in a *monastery*. See Abbey. Also see Cenobites.

Monophysite heresy / Monophysitism / Monophysites 467

The Monophysite *heresy*, from the Greek 'monos,' meaning one and 'physis,' meaning *nature*, professed that there was only one nature in *Christ* because his humanity was entirely *absorbed* into his *divinity*. It held that his Body was not of one *substance*, like other men, and, thus, was not really *human*. It was the opposite of *Nestorianism* and logically implied the denial of Christ's humanity. For Monophysites, Christ had only one nature, and it was *divine*. The Church teaches that Christ has two natures, one human and one divine, but that he is only one *Person*.

Monotheism

Monotheism is the *belief* in only one God. See Theism.

Monothelitism

Monothelitism is a word from the Greek 'monos,' meaning one, and 'thelema,' meaning will. It affirms the existence of one single *will* and one *operation* in the *Person* of Jesus *Christ*. The *Council of Constantinople III* (680–681 A.D.) defined the *Catholic doctrine* that Christ has two wills, and two natural operations, one *divine* and one *human*, without division, change, partition, or confusion. They are not contrary to one another but the human will freely follows and is subject to the *divine will*. See Council of Constantinople III 475.

Monsignor/monsignori

In a great part of the English speaking world, 'monsignor' is the title of an *honorary prelate* who has no special *jurisdiction* or power. There are three types of monsignori: *protonotaries apostolic, prelates of honor of His Holiness*, and *chaplains of His Holiness*. Honorary prelates wear a garb similar to that of *bishops*. Outside the English speaking world, 'monsignor,' meaning 'My Lord' in Italian or its equivalent in other European languages is a title, given to all prelates except *cardinals*, who are addressed as Eminence. See Particular church 833. Also see Prelature.

Monstrance

A monstrance is a vessel used to exhibit the *Blessed Sacrament* during *holy hours*, pro-

cessions, or the *Benediction of the Blessed Sacrament*. It is often made as a sunburst with metal 'rays' radiating from the exposed Eucharistic *host*. The host itself is held in a *'lunette,'* which is inserted into the monstrance. See Tabernacle 1379.

Montanism

Montanism was a second century *heresy* started in Phrygia (in Asia Minor) about 156 A.D. by Montanus, who, together with Maximillia and Prisca, claimed to have been inspired by the *Holy Spirit*. Montanus preached that the *second coming* of *Christ* was *imminent*. He held that post-baptismal *sins* could not be forgiven by the *sacrament* of *Confession*.

Its most significant convert was Tertullian who converted to these *beliefs* in 207 A.D. Pope Innocent I excommunicated their leaders, and the *sect* declined quickly. However, small groups of adherents did persist until the sixth and even the ninth century. See Heresy.

Moral/morals

Moral relates to the use of *free will*. It is a *judgment* of whether behavior is right or wrong according to whether or not it conforms to the *divine plan* or will. See Canonical age. Also see Moral act.

Moral act

Any action proceeding from a deliberate and free *act of the will* is a moral act. It is morally *good* or bad to the degree that it is chosen with *knowledge* of its conformity or non-conformity with the norm of true goodness. *Morality*, as applied to *volitional acts*, is a quality given an act elicited with knowledge of its conformity or non-conformity to the good. This goodness or badness of an act is referred to as its *morality*. See Human act 154.

Moral circumstances 1754

Moral circumstances are those external conditions that affect the quality of an act. Striking a parent would add an offense against *piety* to the act of *aggression*. The place where the offense takes place can affect its *gravity*, such as a murder in a *church*. Time can be a circumstance affecting the *morality of an act*. Over-eating on a fast day can make a harmless act sinful on such a day.

Some circumstances aggravate an offense, such as stealing a large amount of money as opposed to stealing a lesser amount. Other circumstances may lessen the *guilt* of a *sin*, such as insufficient *knowledge* or lack of clear *intention*.

Moral conscience 1777

Moral *conscience* refers to the dictate of reason "present at the heart of the *person*, enjoins him at the appropriate moment to do good and to avoid *evil*." It is also a *judgment* of "particular choices, approving those that are *good* and denouncing those that are *evil*" (CCC 1777).

Moral conscience "bears witness to the *authority of truth* in reference to the supreme Good to which the *human* person is drawn, and it welcomes the commandments. When he listens to his conscience, the *prudent* man can hear God speaking" (CCC 1777).

Moral evil 311, 312

Moral evil, also called *sin*, is *man's* misuse of the gift of *free will* by *deviating* from the dictates of *conscience* and the *divine law*. Moral evil is the only real *evil* because it is a perversion of the *will of God* expressed in the *moral law*, and therefore involves *guilt* and *punishment*. It is evil because it renders man unable to attain his *ultimate end*.

Moral evil only comes into being by the exercise of man's free will, which is a *contingent cause*. The will produces moral evil by choosing to reject the *divine plan*.

Moral evil can only exist if man chooses it. By accepting to cooperate with God's *grace*, man can avoid moral evil.

Moral holiness

Moral *holiness* is the union with God resulting from *mor-*

ally good acts performed through the *grace* of God. A *person* is morally holy who lives in union with God in the state of *sanctifying grace*. Living in this manner unites him to God by allowing him to share in the *divine life*. All men are called to moral holiness. See Holiness 2013.

Moral imperatives 2415

Moral imperatives are the *divine laws* that govern the use of things and that impose a *duty* or *obligation* that demands *obedience*, such as *justice* in dealing with others. See Integrity of Creation.

Moral intention

Moral intention is the direction of the *will* toward an act having a specific *end* or purpose. An intention may be either in agreement with or contrary to the *will* or *law* of God. See Intention 1750, 1752.

Moral law 1950, 1952

In a specific sense, the moral law refers to the *Decalogue*, or *Ten Commandments*, which represent the *divine will* regarding *human* behavior.

In a broader sense, it refers to an *ordinance* whose contents correspond to the *Decalogue* and that is recognizable and *valid* for all men, and *justified* independently of the Christian *faith* as it relates to the *moral order*.

The moral law is also referred

to as the *natural law*. As natural law, it is distinct from *revealed law* and refers to the way a *rational* creature participates in the *eternal law*. Natural law is derived entirely from the *rational order*. It governs the proper direction of human actions toward its eternal destiny or *ultimate end*. Every rational *being* is subject to the natural law from birth because it contains only those duties that can be derived from *human nature* itself and grasped by the unaided light of *human reason*.

The observance of the moral law gives rise to the *moral order* or *social harmony* that reason prescribes between *man* and himself, man and *society*, and man and his creator.

The observance of the moral law gives rise to the *moral order*, the *harmony* intended by God to exist between God and man, nature and society.

Moral order

The moral order is the application of the *understanding* of what is right to *human* behavior. The moral order is based upon *knowledge* that relates to the *nature* and application of the distinction between right and wrong in *human* acts.

The moral order is that knowledge concerned with *virtue*, *vice*, and the *rules* of right conduct. As a subject of study, it is the body of requirements to which actions must

conform in order to be judged as right or virtuous. See Moral Law 1950.

Moral perfection 1770

Moral perfection refers to the relatively perfect conformity of the *will* of *man* with the *will of God*. Such conformity of the will constitutes the union of man with God on earth and is perfected in *heaven*.

The perfection of Christian life consists *essentially* in *charity*, which is *love* of God and neighbor. Love of God and neighbor consists in keeping the commandments: 'If you love me, keep my commandments' (Jn 14:15).

Moral permissiveness 2526

Moral permissiveness refers to the lax attitude toward offensive behavioral practices and types of entertainment regarding matters of *morality*. Such laxity rests on an erroneous conception of *human freedom*. True freedom is only achieved by allowing oneself to be educated in the *moral law* and by cultivating respect for the *truth*, *purity of heart*, and in the moral and *spiritual dignity* of *man*.

Moral sense

The Church teaches that primary *moral principles* are self-evident and arise from *man's* power of *reason*. Moral sense is the inborn notion of right and wrong found in all men. It is called *synderesis*, which consists in the natural tendency to love the good and hate *evil*. Moral sense is developed by instruction and conduct. See Conscience 1706.

Moral sense (of Scripture) 117

The moral sense of *Scripture* is the interpretation of Scripture as a guide to *ethical* behavior or just action.

Moral virtues 1804

Moral *virtue* refers to the *habits* and dispositions leading to the performance of *morally good acts*. Moral virtues are perfected by *deliberate* choices made in conformity to the *divine law* as it is known by right *reason*. The moral virtues, that are acquired through *human* effort, may be *infused* in the *soul* by God along with the *theological virtues*.

The four moral virtues, also called the *cardinal virtues*, are *prudence*, *justice*, *fortitude*, and *temperance*.

The development of the moral virtues, which enable the *person* to choose the good with ease, is the goal of *natural* moral life. They are directly concerned with behavior and are distinguished from *intellectual virtue*, which is primarily concerned with the development of the power to know *truth*. *Knowledge* of the truth is necessary in order to live a more virtuous life.

The acquired virtues are prerequisites for the *theological* *virtues*, which are freely given *supernatural* gifts of God enabling man to attain his final *destiny*. The theological virtues are conferred at *Baptism* together with the infused moral virtues.

The theological virtues are *faith*, *hope*, and *charity*. They have God as their object and unite man to him through *sanctifying grace*, which enables man to choose the good with greater ease. When moral virtues are strengthened by the infused theological virtues of faith, hope, and charity they become supernatural virtues, that is, habits and dispositions entirely beyond the reach of man's *nature*, which enable him to attain his supernatural end more easily. See Prudence 1806; Also see Justice 2407; Fortitude 1808, 1831; Temperance 1809, 2341, 2407, 2517.

Morality

Morality is that quality of a *human act* by which it is judged to be in keeping with or contrary to the *law of God* according to the dictates of *conscience*. Morality refers to the character of goodness or uprightness of those human acts that are in accord with right conduct and consistent with *ethical* principles.

The *morality of an act* depends on the *nature* of the *object chosen*, the purpose or *end* desired in choosing it, and the circumstances under which the choice is made. See Sources of morality 1750.

Morality of an act

The morality of an act refers to the degree to which it is in conformity with the *moral law*. When the *intellect*, by *reasoning*, determines the morality of an act and judges its morality, it is called *conscience*. The constitutive elements of the morality of acts are object, *intention*, and motive.

First, the morality of an act depends on the *nature* of the *object chosen*, which is the *good* towards which the *will deliberately* directs itself. This good must be in keeping with the *rational order* of good and *evil* attested to by conscience.

Second, the morality of an act depends on the *end* or the goal of the act, that is, the good anticipated by the action.

Third, the morality of an act depends on the circumstances that accompany that act, including its *consequences*, that influence its moral goodness, for example, the size of a *theft* or acting out of fear. Circumstances do not change the moral quality of an act. They cannot make an act that is evil in itself either good or right. See Sources of morality 1750.

Morally good act 1755

A morally good act is an act that has as its goal an object that is *good*, that is chosen for an upright reason and that is performed under circum-

stances that would not make the act evil.

Morally invincible ignorance

Ignorance is morally *invincible* when the needed *knowledge* cannot be obtained by the amount of care and diligence that an ordinarily *prudent* man would exercise under similar circumstances. *Unintentional ignorance* can diminish or remove the *imputability* of a *grave* offense. See Conscience 1706, 1778.

Morning Prayer

Morning Prayer is the hour of the *Divine Office* said in the morning. Its Latin name is *Lauds*. It is one of the *major hours*, and the *Benedictus* (Lk 1:68-79) is sung or recited during it. See Liturgy of the hours 1174, 1178.

Mortal sin 1855

Mortal sin "destroys *charity* in the *heart* of man by a grave violation of God's *law*; it turns man away from God, who is his *ultimate end* and his *beatitude*, by preferring an inferior *good* to him" (CCC 1855).

It is called mortal or deadly because, in separating the soul from God and destroying *charity* in the heart, it deprives the soul of *supernatural* life.

Because mortal sin destroys *sanctifying grace* in the *soul*, it "necessitates a new initiative of God's *mercy* and a *conversion* of *heart* which is normally accomplished within the set-

ting of the *sacrament of reconciliation*" (CCC 1856).

In order to receive the sacrament of Reconciliation, one
must confess all mortal sins
according to number and kind.
This confession must also be
accompanied by the firm *intention* of *reformation of life*. For
absolution, *true contrition* or
attrition is also required, and
the *penance* assigned must be
performed. Confessing sorrow
for mortal sin privately or at
the *penitential act* at *Mass* is
not sufficient, and one must
receive absolution before going
to *Holy Communion*.

In order for a sin to be mortal,
there are three conditions that
must be met: the object of the
sin must be *grave matter*, the
sin must be committed with
full knowledge, and the sin
must be given *full consent*.

Mortification

Mortification is the performance of acts of *self-discipline*.
As a practice of *asceticism* it
may be *spiritual* by curbing
self-love or it may be physical
by means of self-inflicted *aus-
terity*. Mortification is practiced for the *expiation* of past
sins for oneself or for souls in
purgatory. See Penance 1459.

Mosaic law

Mosaic law refers to the *law*
that Moses received from God
and transmitted to the people
of Israel in the desert. It presents the body of *civil*, *moral*,
and *religious* legislation found
in the last four books of the
Pentateuch, traditionally
ascribed to the *prophet* Moses.

The foundation of the Mosaic
law is the *Decalogue* in *Exodus* 20. The *Covenant* is found
mainly in Exodus 20–30. Civil
legislation is found mostly in
Exodus 18–23 and *Deuter-
onomy* 20–23. Moral laws are
found in Exodus 20–23 and
Leviticus 11–20. Religious and
ceremonial precepts are found
in Exodus 25–30 and *Leviticus* 1–27. See Law of Moses.
Also see Genesis.

Mother of all Prophecy

The brief, mysterious message of victory of the seed of
Woman over the brood of the
serpent found in Gen 3:15 is
referred to as the *protoevangelium*. It is considered to
be the first announcement of
God's plan for man's *redemption*. The *Fathers* and *Doctors
of the Church* have seen the
woman announced in the protoevangelium as *Mary*, who,
as the Mother of *Christ* the
Redeemer, would be the *New
Eve*. The first Eve brought
death and *sin* into the world;
the New Eve brought life and
redemption. For this reason,
she is sometimes also called
the Mother of all Prophecy,
since all *prophecy* centers on
the *mystery* of redemption
and, in a sense, is contained
in this first prophecy-promise.
See Coredemptrix. Also see
New Eve 411.

Mother of God 971

Because she gave birth to *Jesus Christ*, a *Divine Person* who is both God and man, *Mary* is truly the Mother of God. The witness of countless *Fathers of the Church* attests that this was the *belief* of the early Church who called her *Theotokos* from earliest times.

Theotokos, literally 'God-bearer,' means Mother of God. It is still the principal title of the *Virgin Mary* in the *liturgy* of the *Oriental Church*. This title was already in use by the third century.

In about 427 A.D., this title became the center of a dispute between *orthodox Christians* and the followers of Nestorius (d. 451 A.D.), who denied Mary's divine maternity. Nestorius was first censured at the *Council of Ephesus* in 431 A.D., which declared, 'if anyone does not acknowledge that Emmanuel is truly God and that, therefore, the holy Virgin is Mother of God since she gave birth according to the flesh to the Word *begotten* of God the Father, let him be *anathema*.'

This does not mean that Mary generated the Godhead, just as no mother generates the soul of her child. It means that Mary is the mother of a Person who is God. This fundamental *dignity* is the *justification* for the great honor the Church pays to her.

In the *Latin Church*, the equivalent term for Theoto-kos is *Deipara*, meaning God-bearer. See Council of Ephesus 466.

Mother of the Living 726

Adam called the woman that God fashioned for him Eve. The creation of Eve from Adam's rib signifies the equality and communality of man and woman. The name he gave her, Eve (Hawwah), means life in *Hebrew*. He called her Eve 'because she became the mother of all the living' (Gen 3:20).

Because of their *sin* of disobedience in the *Garden of Eden*, Adam and Eve lost the *preternatural gift* of *immortality* and separated themselves from the *grace* of God. In order to restore man to *grace*, God promised a *redeemer*, saying to the Serpent, 'I will put enmity between you and the woman, and between your offspring and hers; she will strike at your head, while you strike at her heel' (Gen 3:15).

The woman's promised offspring was to be *Christ*, the *new Adam*, who would bring new life by restoring man to God. *Mary*, the Mother of the *Incarnate Son*, would be the *New Eve*, the Mother of those restored to life by Christ.

The notion of the New Adam and New Eve, reflected in the writings of St. Paul (e.g., Rom 5:12–21 and 1 Cor 15:45–50), is expressly mentioned by St. Irenaeus (130–200 A.D.) in the second half of the second century. In the writings of St. Augustine (354–430 A.D.) and other *Church Fathers*, Christ is portrayed as the *new Adam*, falling asleep on the Cross and, from his side, the Church, as the new Eve, is born.

The title Mother of the Living came to be applied to Mary in *recognition* of her *spiritual motherhood* of all humanity redeemed by her Son. As the new Eve, Mary is the spiritual Mother of all the living in the time of grace and redemption. See Hyperdulia.

Motherhouse

A motherhouse is an *autonomous monastery* that retains *jurisdiction* over another monastery, called a daughter house, which is derived from it. It also refers to the administrative headquarters of an institute for *religious* women. The administrative headquarters of some religious institutes is called the *generalate*. See Priory.

Motives of credibility 156

The motives of *credibility* are those considerations, apart from *revelation* itself, that moves one to believe a revelation that claims to be of *divine* origin and absolutely true. By the motives of credibility one is not moved to believe because what is revealed appears to be true in the light of *natural reason*, but because of the *authority* of God who reveals it.

Revealed truth, therefore, is distinct from the motives of credibility. However, so that the submission or *obedience of faith* might also be in accord with reason and freely given, God willed that the external proofs of his revelation, such as *miracles* and the fulfillment of *prophecies*, be accessible to reason and should accompany the internal *grace* of the *Holy Spirit* necessary to make the act of *faith*.

Closely related to, but not identical with, the motives of credibility are the motives of *credentity*, that is, the credibility of something is so persuasive that it *morally* obliges one to believe. See Credentity, Motives of.

Motu proprio

A motu proprio is a *document* drawn up and issued by the *Pope* on his own initiative and not in response to any petition or request. It is always personally signed by the Pope. See Constitution.

Movable altar

When the altar table is not a single consecrated stone, but rather is a frame surrounding an *altar stone*, it is called a movable, or portable, altar. The altar or altar stone has five crosses cut into it to represent the five wounds of *Christ*. Many altars in the U.S. are not fixed and have an altar stone set in them. This stone is in fact the *altar of sacrifice*. See Altar 1182.

Mozarabic Rite

The name Mozarabic Rite is a *corruption* of the arabic word 'mustarib,' meaning an arabic Christian living in the Moorish parts of Spain. It is more appropriately called the *Rite* of Toledo or the Visigothic Rite. It is a *Latin liturgy* of the *Gallican Rite* family, formerly used throughout the Iberian peninsula (Spain) but only preserved today in a chapel of the Cathedral of Toledo in Spain. A number of families belong to the rite *canonically* and by inheritance.

With local variations, this liturgy was once used in all of Gaul. The *marriage* rite, in which the *spouses* are tied together with a *yoke* of colored ribbons, is still used in Spanish South America. See Latin Rite.

Municipal

Municipal means having to do with a city or town or its local government. See Ordinance.

Munificence

Munificence is the willingness to expend one's wealth, talents, or *virtues* lavishly according to the dictates of good *judgment* and right *reason*. See Fortitude 1808, 1831. Also see Moral Virtues 1804.

Myron 1183, 1289

The *Eastern Churches* use the name 'myron' for *sacred chrism*. The word 'myron' is the Greek name for scented oil.

Myrrh

Myrrh is a fragrant smelling but bitter tasting gum resin extracted from several Arabian and African plants used in making perfume and *incense*. See Frankincense.

Mystagogia

See Mystagogy.

Mystagogy 1075

Literally, mystagogy means the teaching of a *mystery*. It refers to the *liturgical catechesis* used to initiate people into the mystery of *Christ*. It especially refers to the post-baptismal *catechumenate*, or the period of instruction for adults immediately following the reception of *Baptism*.

Teaching the mystery of Christ proceeds "from the visible to the invisible, from the *sign* to the thing signified, from the *'sacraments'* to the 'mysteries.'" (CCC 1075). It presents what is fundamental and common to the whole *Church* in *celebrating* the mystery in its *liturgy* and the sacramental order.

It is proper to continue the study of the *faith* throughout one's life in order to ensure continual maturation in the faith. This naturally occurs in participation in the liturgy and sacramental life of the Church. See Post-Baptismal Catechumenate 1231.

Mysteries of redemption

In *theology*, mystery refers to the *revelation* to *man* of the *divine plan* in which the *love* of God redeems man in the life and revelation of the *Incarnate Word*. *Salvation* is a process of being constantly drawn into the *mystery* revealed in *Christ*.

The mysteries of *redemption* are those particular elements of the divine plan, encountered by *faith*, love, *knowledge*, and experience, that, by *grace*, lead to salvation. These mysteries become clear to the eyes of faith through the reception of the *sacraments*, *meditation*, *prayer*, *virtuous* living, and growth in the *spiritual life*. They will be fully revealed in the *beatific vision*. See Mysterion 774; Mystery/ mysteries/mysterious 359; Liturgical year.

Mysteries of the Incarnation
512

The mysteries of the *Incarnation* refer to the major events in the life of *Christ*: his conception, birth, *Passion*, *Crucifixion*, death, burial, descent into *hell*, *Resurrection*, and *Ascension* into *heaven*.

Mysterion 774

Mysterion is a Greek word translated into Latin by *mysterium* and *sacramentum*. Sacrament, or 'sacramentum,' is a Latin word originally indicating something offered to guarantee fidelity to a commitment. It is the *mystery* revealed, and emphasizes the visible *sign* of the hidden reality of *salvation*. It is called the *mystery of salvation*. This visible sacramental sign is God's guarantee of the *truths* concerning salvation. Mysterium, or mystery, is the hidden reality of salvation, which is *Christ*. The saving work of his *sanctifying* humanity is revealed and active in the Church's sacraments, which the *Eastern Church* calls 'the holy mysteries.'

Mysterium 774

Mysterium refers to the *mystery of salvation*, the hidden reality of *Christ* in the visible sign of the *sacrament* or 'sacramentum.' It is 'mysterion' in Greek.

Mystery / Mysteries / Mysterious
359

The term mystery comes from the Greek word 'mysterion,' meaning something closed or secret. When it is applied to anything that is hidden or not completely known or understood it is a *natural mystery*.

In *theological* usage, mystery refers to a *truth* that is totally inaccessible to unaided reason but which can be comprehended in some way once God reveals it.

Mysteries whose *natures* can be comprehended once they are known, such as *creation* by a personal God, are called *preternatural* mysteries.

Other mysteries are not contrary to *reason* but so far *tran-*

scend it that, even after *revelation*, they remain directly impenetrable to *created intelligence*. Such a mystery can only be known through *faith* because its true nature is never known completely or in itself but is understood only by *analogy* to things *man* can know. Such mysteries are called *supernatural mysteries*. The revelation of the *Trinity* is such a strictly supernatural mystery, whose essence in itself cannot be understood directly but only by analogy to created things. In *heaven*, man will understand directly by a special gift called the *lumen gloriae*, the *beatific vision*.

Mystery of faith

The phrase 'mystery of faith' refers to the *Paschal mystery*: the *Passion*, death, *Resurrection*, and *Ascension of Christ*. The *liturgy commemorates* the mystery of *faith* with one of three responses: 1) 'We proclaim your Death, O Lord, and profess your *Resurrection* until you come again;' 2) 'When we eat this bread and drink this Cup, we proclaim your Death, O Lord, until you come again;' and 3) 'Save us, Savior of the world, for by your Cross and Resurrection you have set us free.' See Paschal mystery 571, 1085.

Mystery of iniquity 675

The mystery of iniquity refers to the whole plan by which God saves *man* in *Christ*. It includes the plan of *salvation* for fallen man and the role that *sin* plays in the world.

It also refers to the *diabolical* deception by which *Satan*, the father of lies, offers man apparent solutions to his problems at the price of *apostasy* from the *truth* and *perdition*.

Mystery of man 359

Man is a *mystery* to himself. To know himself, man must know his *origin*, purpose, and *eternal destiny*. These are things about himself that he cannot know except through *revelation*. By becoming man through the *Incarnation*, *Christ* revealed the answers to those questions. In this way, Christ reveals man to himself. The mystery of man only becomes clear in the mystery of the *Word made flesh* because humanity has its origin from Adam and is fulfilled by Christ as the *new Adam*. The first Adam became a living *soul* from the earth below, the new Adam, a life-giving spirit from above (cf. 1 Cor 15:45). Christ not only reveals to man his true destiny but also gives him the *grace* to be united with his maker in the life of the *Spirit*.

Mystery of salvation

The mystery of salvation refers to the hidden reality of *Christ* in the action by which the *soul* is freed from *sin* and its *consequences* and is enabled to attain the *beatific vision* in *heaven*. *Salvation* is not only a reward but also the attainment of man's *ultimate end*.

Salvation depends entirely on the love and *mercy* of God, but it is only achieved by *free choice* in cooperation with *divine grace*. See Mysterion 774.

Mystical

See Mystical interpretation.

Mystical Body

The *faithful* are bound to one another and to *Christ* in a *spiritual*, but real, body by virtue of their *Baptism*. That body is Christ's Body, but the baptized united in it as its members do not lose their own personhood. They are bound to Christ neither by a physical union nor by a merely moral union, like the citizens of a state or members of a corporation, but by a unique mysterious bond characteristic of *grace*. Membership in it is necessary for *salvation* because, through it, the *merits* of *redemption* are applied to man. The *Mystical Body* includes the *Church Triumphant* and the *Church Suffering* as well as the *Church Militant*.

As the source of her life, the soul of the Mystical Body is the *Holy Spirit*, but the phrase *soul of the Church* is used in a *metaphorical* sense to refer to all those in the Church who are actually in the *state of*

grace and being *sanctified* by the action of the Holy Spirit. See Communion of Saints 1475 Also see Spiritual Worship 2031.

Mystical interpretation

Mystical is used to describe something spiritually significant, symbolic, or *allegorical*. For example the phrase 'Mystical Rose' is used to refer to the *Virgin Mary*, the Church is referred to as the *Mystical Body* of *Christ*, and contemplation is referred to as mystical prayer. A mystical interpretation is one that refers to or describes something in terms of its *spiritual* significance. See Immolation; Liturgical seasons.

Mystical prayer

Mystical prayer is another name for *contemplative prayer*, which St. Teresa of *Jesus* described as 'nothing else than a close sharing between friends; it means taking time frequently to be alone with him who knows and loves us.' See Contemplative prayer 2709.

Mystical sense

The mystical sense of *Scripture* is the meaning of a passage in reference to the *truth* or event of which it is a *type*, *symbol*, or *foreshadowing*. For example, the term *Paschal Lamb* appears in the *Old Testament* as a *type*, or figure, of *Christ* the *Paschal sacrifice*.

The mystical sense is also called the *typical* or *allegorical* sense. See Senses of scripture 115.

Mystical union 2014

Mystical union is the goal of *spiritual* progress, that tends to an ever more intimate *union with Christ*. It is called mystical "because it participates in the mystery of Christ through the *sacraments*—'the holy mysteries'—and, in him, in the *mystery* of the *Holy Trinity*" (CCC 2014).

Mystical union is the soul's union with Christ in *contemplation*. Mystical union also refers to the union that occurs during *contemplation* and higher forms of *mental prayer*. Its primary characteristic is the presence of God, felt as a *spiritual* touch without images, and as a direct experience that is obscure and partly incomprehensible. Its effect is an increase of *charity*, *humility*, and *self-sacrificing devotion*.

There are three stages of mystical union.

1) The *prayer of quiet* is a union in which the *soul* is more *conscious* and certain of God's presence within it.

2) *Ecstatic union*, or ecstasy, is a vivid act of contemplation accompanied by the loss of awareness of one's surroundings and in which the soul is rapt in God and receives spiritual illumination.

3) *Spiritual marriage*, also called *transforming union*, is the highest degree of closeness and intimacy of the soul's union with God. The *consciousness* of the presence of God in the soul becomes clear and abiding in a practically indissoluble union.

N

National Council

A National Council was, in times before *Vatican II,* a meeting of the dioceses of a whole nation and often subject to a *primate* and presided over by him. Its *decrees* bound only those participating in the council. See Council.

Natural/Naturally

'Natural' comes from the Latin word 'naturalis,' meaning by birth or according to *nature.* Natural means in accord with what is found or expected in nature. It is something that is not artificial or manufactured, but found in the state provided by nature. Natural refers to something *innate* and not acquired, normal, usual, or customary. See Infused knowledge. Also see Innate.

Natural acts

Natural acts are those that can be performed using *human faculties* without *sanctifying grace.*

As a *human being,* man is a *rational animal* that acts, grows, feels, has the power of locomotion, *procreates,* thinks, and wills. Because these *operations* flow from his nature as a rational animal they are called natural acts. See Born from above.

Natural Family Planning (NFP)

Natural family planning is a method of regulating *procreation* (birth) through using *knowledge* about a couple's *fertility.* It involves learning to identify their mutual fertility and applying that knowledge either to trying to conceive a child or to postpone *conception* by engaging in or refraining from the *conjugal act* at the appropriate times.

It differs from *artificial birth control* because, rather than using the conjugal act as a means for selfish satisfaction, it serves to strengthen *conjugal love* and respect for the *marriage covenant* by enabling the *spouses* to exercise *continence* and self-mastery. It develops *authentic* mutual *love* and cultivates a generous commitment to a fruitful married life in loving sacrifice for their children. It allows the *graces* of the *sacrament* of *Matrimony* to make each *spouse* a means of *grace* and *holiness* for the other.

Natural family planning helps spouses come to know one another's role as mother and father and appreciate the mystery and privilege of parenthood. This holy reverential love for each other provides an example of *sacrificial love* for their children. See Regulation of procreation 2368.

Natural law 1952, 2036

Natural law is the original *moral* sense written in the *heart* of every *man* that enables him to discern by *reason* alone what is *good* and *evil*, true and false.

"The natural law states the first and essential *precepts* which govern the moral life. It hinges upon the desire for God and submission to him, who is the source and judge of all that is good, as well as upon the sense that the other is one's equal" (CCC 1955).

Natural law is distinct from *revealed law*. It is called natural law because everyone is subject to it from birth. It contains only those *duties* that can be derived from *human nature* itself and its essentials can be grasped by the unaided light of *human reason*.

St. Thomas taught that natural law is the participation of a rational creature in the *eternal law*. Natural law is also called the *natural moral law*.

Natural moral law 1952, 1954, 1955, 1958, 1959, 2036

The natural moral law is the original *innate moral* sense that enables man to discern, by *reason* alone, the *good* and the *evil*, the *truth* and the lie.

It is written in the *soul* of every man because it is *human reason* ordaining him to do good and avoid evil.

The "command of human reason would not have the force of *law* if it were not the voice and interpreter of a higher reason to which our *spirit* and our *freedom* must be submitted" (CCC 1954).

It is called natural because reason, which decrees it, belongs to *human nature*. Its principal *precepts* are expressed in the *Decalogue*.

Natural mystery

The term mystery comes from the Greek word 'mysterion,' meaning something closed or secret. When it is applied to anything that is hidden or not completely understood, but could be known by the use of *natural reason*, it is a natural mystery. See Mystery 359.

Natural order

Natural order refers to the way things are directed to the purposes for which they were made, or the way they are properly related to other things. See Grace 35.

Natural reason

Natural reason refers to man's *rationality* or capacity to reason unaided by the gift of *faith* or *supernatural revelation*. See Will of God 309. Also see Ethical; Revealed truth; Motive of credibility 156.

Natural virtue

Natural virtues are *virtues* that can be acquired through practice and become *habits* of doing good.

The *moral virtues* of *fortitude, prudence, justice,* and *temperance* are natural virtues that can be acquired through practice. They are called *cardinal virtues* because they are the virtues to which all other virtues are related.

In a broad sense, the cardinal virtues function according to an *ordinance* whose contents correspond to the *Decalogue*. They are recognizable and *valid* for all men and can be justified independently of the *revealed* law of the *Christian faith*.

Because the *theological virtues* of faith, *hope,* and *charity* are *supernatural virtues*, they cannot be acquired by *human* effort and must be *infused* by God through the reception of the *sacraments* or by special *grace*. See Virtue 1768, 1803.

Nature

Philosophically, the term 'nature' refers to that *essential* quality of a thing that makes it to be what it is and constitutes its fundamental or remote *principle* of acting. See Human nature 404. Also see Human person 2222.

Nave

The nave is the section of a *church* that accommodates the people. In Western Churches, it is customary to have pews and kneelers in the nave. See Church 752.

Necessary being

A necessary being is a *being* whose non-existence is impossible. See Theologia 236.

Necessary cause

Causes are called necessary when their effects come about as the direct result of the *nature* of an *operating* cause. Necessary causes may also be called *secondary causes* because they effect changes by virtue of their *created nature*.

God wills that *secondary causes* act according to their natures either by necessity (necessary causes) or contingency (*contingent causes*). An example of a necessary cause would be the falling of objects that directly results from the action of gravity. Gravity is the necessary operating cause of the effects it brings about. An example of a contingent cause would be a seed that will grow into a plant only under suitable conditions. The seed can act as a cause of a plant only in the presence of certain conditions, such as proper sunlight, water, and soil. See Primary cause. Also see Contingent cause; Secondary cause.

Negligence 1736

Negligence is a form of *involuntary action* resulting from lack of attention to what ought to be done, either because of carelessness or lack of ordinary awareness while doing something.

In the case of harm or injury, negligence does not remove the requirements for *restitution* required by *justice*, but it may reduce *culpability*.

Neopagan

Neopagan refers to adherents of *paganism* under new guises. See Neopaganism.

Neopaganism

Non-*Christians* are generally referred to as pagans. *Pagan* more properly refers to those who *worship* false gods, such as the powers of nature, statues, or *anthropomorphic* (human-like) deities. Certain animals were even considered gods by some *sects*. Neopaganism refers to new varieties of false gods, such as crystals, exaggerated concern and preoccupation with the body, physical or sexual prowess, and media-created celebrities.

The *cult* of the body is a popular *neopagan* notion that *sacrifices* anything for the sake of fame or *sensuality*. Other examples include placing excessive *value* on physical beauty or success in sports, idolizing media personalities, conspicuous consumption, and *material* wealth. By its selective preference for the strong over the weak, such values lead to the *perversion* of *human* relationships and the *corruption* of Christian values. See Cult of the body 2289.

Neophytes

Neophyte comes from the Greek words 'neos,' meaning new, and 'phutos,' meaning gown. It refers to those who have entered on a new and better way of life. See RCIA 1232.

Nestorian heresy/Nestorianism/Nestorians

The Nestorian heresy is the erroneous teaching of Nestorius, *Bishop* of Constantinople (c. 428–431 A.D.). His followers are called Nestorians.

Nestorius taught that there were two *persons* in the incarnate *Christ*, a *Divine Person* and a *human* person named *Jesus*. The human person of Jesus was the dwelling-place of the *Word*, the Divine Person, and it was Jesus alone who was born of *Mary* and died on the Cross.

The teaching of Nestorius was condemned by Pope St. Celestine I and again by the third *ecumenical council* at Ephesus, 431 A.D. The Church teaches that Christ is one Divine Person who *assumed* a *human nature*. Christ thus has two natures, one divine and one human. Mary, therefore, is really the *Mother of God* because she gave birth to a single person, Jesus Christ, who is God incarnate. See Council of Ephesus 466.

New Adam

Christ is seen as the New Adam of the *new creation* in 1 Cor 15:22, 45 and in Rom 5:12. The notion of a New Adam and *New Eve* is mentioned by St. Irenaeus (130–200 A.D.) in the second half of the second century. In the writings of St. Augustine (354–430 A.D.) and other *Church Fathers*, Christ is portrayed as the new Adam falling asleep on the Cross and from whose side is born the Church as the New Eve. See Bride of Christ 796. Also see Mother of the living 726.

New Code of Canon Law

The revision of the *Code of Canon Law promulgated* by Pope John Paul II on January 25, 1983, is sometimes called the 'New Code of Canon Law.' See Code of Canon Law.

New Covenant

The New Covenant is the *New Testament*. The New Covenant is also referred to as the *New Dispensation*. The *Old Testament* recorded the history of *salvation* from the *creation* of the world and the establishment of the *Old Covenant* with *Israel*.

The *Divine plan* under the Old Covenant was oriented to a *prophetic* preparation for the coming of *Christ*, the *Redeemer* of all men under the New Testament. The covenant of Christ presented in the New Testament infinitely surpasses and supersedes the Old Covenant by fulfilling it.

The Church teaches that the Old Testament remains an indispensable part of *Sacred Scripture* and is *divinely* inspired. The Covenant it established has never been revoked. The *mystery of* salvation presented in a hidden way in the Old Covenant is fully revealed and fulfilled in the New Covenant. See Old Covenant 1093. Also see Old Testament 121; New law 1965.

New creation

In Gen 3:15, after the fall of *man*, a mysterious message of victory of the seed of Woman over the brood of the serpent was promised. Referred to as the *protoevangelium*, this promise is considered the first announcement of God's plan for man's *redemption* through the birth of *Christ* and the advent of the *New Covenant*. This redemption would bring about a *new creation* restored in Christ and fully realized in what the Book of Revelation (Rev 21:2) refers to as a *new heaven* and a *new earth*.

The new creation is brought about by a *New Eve*, the *Blessed Virgin*, and a *New Adam*, Christ. Through *Baptism* man is born again, given *sanctifying grace*, adopted as a son of God, and given a share in the *divine life*. See Born of Virgin 502.

New Dispensation

New Dispensation is another name for the *New Covenant*.

New earth/new heaven 1043

The creation of a new *heaven* and new earth is mentioned in Rev 21:1. This describes the change that will occur on the last day when heaven is occupied by the risen *glorified bodies* of the *saints*.

At the end of time, the *Kingdom of God* will come in its fullness. After the *last judgment*, the Church "will receive her perfection... in the *glory* of heaven" (CCC 1042). This mysterious renewal, which will transform both humanity and the world, is referred to as the new heaven and new earth.

New Eve 411

The brief, mysterious message of victory of the seed of Woman over the brood of the serpent found in Gen 3:15 is referred to as the *protoevangelium*. It is considered the first announcement of God's plan for *man's redemption*. The *Church Fathers* and *Doctors of the Church* have seen the woman announced in the protoevangelium as *Mary*, who, as the Mother of *Christ* the *Redeemer*, would be the New Eve. The first Eve brought death and sin into the world; the New Eve brought life and *redemption*. For this reason she is also called the *Mother of All Prophecy*, since all *prophecy* centers on the *mystery* of

redemption and, in a sense, is contained in this first prophecy-promise. See Coredemptrix.

New fire

The *blessing* of the new fire is the first *ceremony* of the *Easter Vigil*. The *Easter candle* and the candles of the congregation are lighted from the newly *blessed* flame. The lighted Easter candle is taken into the *church* in procession during which three stops are made and the words 'Lumen Christi' (light of *Christ*) are sung. The congregation responds 'Deo Gratias' (Thanks be to God).

New Law 1965

"The New Law is the *grace* of the *Holy Spirit* given to the *faithful* through *faith* in *Christ*. It works through *charity*; it uses the *Sermon on the Mount* to teach us what must be done and makes use of the *sacraments* to give us the grace to do it" (CCC 1966).

The *Beatitudes* do not replace the original *Decalogue* of the *Old Testament*, but infuse the Decalogue with a new *understanding* of *love* of God and neighbor. This love releases the hidden potential of the *Ten Commandments* and *begets* new demands of them constituting the *essence* of the *moral* behavior they prescribe.

The Beatitudes do not add new external *precepts*, but aim to reform the heart, the root of *human acts*. They bring the law to its fulfillment through imitation of the perfection of the heavenly Father; particularly through forgiveness of enemies in *emulation* of divine *generosity*.

The Beatitudes, called the *Commandments of the New Testament*, are the work of the *Holy Spirit* and through him they become the interior law of *charity*.

The *New Law* fulfills and surpasses the *Old Law* and leads it to its perfection. The Beatitudes fulfill the *divine* promises by elevating and orienting them toward the *kingdom of heaven*. The New Law is also called the Law of Love or *New Covenant*.

New moon

New moon is that phase of the moon in which its disk is unlit and invisible, which happens when the moon is in conjunction with the sun. The times and dates of successive new moons are the point of reference for calculating the *synodic month* and devising the *lunar calendar*.

New Roman Breviary

The *Liturgy of the Hours* is sometimes called the New Roman Breviary.

New Testament

The Bible is divided into two parts, the Old Testament and New Testament. The *Old Testament* or *Old Covenant* contains forty-six books (although some systems of counting make it forty-five), and the New Testament or *New Covenant* consists of twenty-seven books.

The New Testament is the fulfillment of the Old Testament and includes what *Christ* said and did while he was on earth. It is the *New Law*, operative since the coming of Christ, that will remain until the *end of time*. See Sacred Scripture 102. Also see Bible.

Nicene Creed

Nicene Creed is another name for the *Nicene-Constantipolitan Creed*. See Nicene-Constantinopolitan Creed 195.

Nicene-Constantinopolitan Creed or Niceno-Constantinopolitan Creed 195

The Nicene-Constantinopolitan Creed is also called the *Nicene Creed*. It draws its great *authority* from the fact that it stems from the first two *ecumenical councils* held in 325 A.D. and 381 A.D. It is professed in common by all the great Churches of both East and West to this day. See Creed 13.

Night Office

The 'night office' refers to that part of the *Divine Office* that is prayed in the middle of the night or in the early morning. In the *Extraordinary Form*, this is called *Matins*, and was changed to the *Office of Readings* in the *Ordinary Form*.

The Office of Readings, while being suitable for any time of the day, can still be said as a night office. See Liturgy of the Hours 1174, 1178.

Night Prayer

Night Prayer is one of the *minor hours* of the *Divine Office*, and is said after *Vespers* and before retiring for the night. In Latin, Night Prayer is called *Compline.* See Liturgy of the Hours 1174, 1178.

Nihil Obstat

The Latin phrase 'nihil obstat' means 'nothing stands in the way.' It is a formal *judgment* by an examiner appointed by the *Bishop* of the *diocese* that, in terms of essential *orthodoxy*, a book contains nothing contrary or injurious to the teaching of the Church. The book may then be granted the 'imprimi potest' (it can be printed) or *'imprimatur'* (let it be printed), which is the formal permission of the appropriate *ecclesiastical authority* for the book to be printed. This authority is usually the local Bishop of the *diocese.*

The nihil obstat appears at the front of the book together with an imprimatur, to assure the reader that the material is printed with the consent of the Bishop or *religious superior* and contains *orthodox Catholic* teaching. See Diocese 833.

Nocturn

The hour of *Matins* in the *Divine Office* according to the *Extraordinary Form* is divided up into nocturns. Most days have one nocturn of nine *psalms* and three readings, but first and second class *feasts* have three nocturns, each with three psalms and three readings.

This structure is not present in the *Office of Readings*, but an echo of it may be seen in the option to extend the Office with additional *canticles* and a *Gospel* reading when the Office is said as a *vigil* service on the evening before a major feast.

Nonconformist

Nonconformist is a term now applied to the principles and practices of *Protestants* in England and Wales who are members of *religious* bodies other than the Anglican. The principal nonconformist *denominations* are the Baptists, Congregationalists, and Methodists. See Sectarians.

Non-consummated marriage

Until the *marriage consent* is confirmed by *sexual intercourse*, a marriage is nonconsummated. Before consummation, a marriage is only *ratified* and can be dissolved under certain conditions. See Indissolubility 1644.

None

None, Latin for the ninth hour of the day (3pm), is a *minor hour* of the *Divine Office*, and is called *Mid-afternoon Prayer* in English. It is part of *Daytime Prayer*. See Liturgy of the Hours. 1174, 1178.

Non-sacramental marriage

A non-sacramental marriage is a *marriage* where either one or both of the *spouses* are not *baptized*. If a baptized *person* and an unbaptized person want to marry, they must be *dispensed* from the *diriment impediment* of *disparity of cult* in order to *validly* contract marriage. A non-sacramental marriage is a true marriage according to the *natural law* and is thus *indissoluble* by any *human authority*. See Sacramental Marriage 1631.

Non-volitional

'Non-volitional' refers to an act that is not *deliberate*, intentional, or willed. It is an *act of man* but is not a *human act* and therefore does not involve a question of *morality*. See Act of Man. Also see Passions 1763.

Notaries/Notary

'Notary' comes from the Latin 'notarius,' meaning secretary or one who composes or *authenticates* documents. A notary is an official appointed to compose documents for various *Roman Congregations* and offices. See Protonotary Apostolic.

Novena

The word novena comes from the Latin word 'novena,' meaning ninefold or consisting of nine. The term is used to refer to the recitation of prescribed *prayers* and devotions for nine consecutive hours, days, weeks, or months. There are numerous novenas listed in the *Enchiridion of Indulgences* (formerly called the Raccolta) to which *indulgences* have been attached.

The number nine is used in memory of the number of days spent in prayer in the *Cenacle* between the *Ascension* and *Pentecost*. See Tradition 78, 174.

Novice

The term 'novice' refers to a *person* undergoing a period of probation called the *novitiate*. It lasts for a period of not less than one year. It is required in order to determine fitness for *religious profession* in a *religious institute*.

Prior to entering the novitiate, candidates for religious life are known as *postulants*. Upon entering the novitiate, they are clothed with the *habit* of the religious institute. A person cannot become a novice before completing his seventeenth year of age. A novice may freely leave or be dismissed from the community without *reason* at any time. See Religious Life 925. Also see Novitiate.

Novitiate

Novitiate refers to the period of time a *novice* spends before being accepted into a *religious institute* by *religious profession.* It is a period of probation of not less than one year required to determine fitness for life in the *religious* institute. During this time, novices are clothed with the *habit* and learn the *rule,* history, and special *charisms* of the institute.

Before becoming novices, candidates to the religious life are called *postulants.* A *person* cannot start the novitiate until they have completed their seventeenth year of age. A novice may freely leave or be dismissed without *reason* at any time. See Religious Life 925.

Novus Ordo

In 1976, long after the 1969 decision on the revision of the liturgy was made, Pope Paul VI casually referred to the revision in a speech as the 'Novus Ordo Missae' or the New Order of Mass. It became customary to use 'Novus Ordo Missae,' or simply 'Novus Ordo,' as a term referring to the entirety of the revised rite of Mass.

Some who disagreed with the revisions adopted the term Novus Ordo in a pejorative manner, using it as a general condemnatory term for the present-day Church, 'the Novus Ordo Church.' The expression 'Novus Ordo' itself appears in no official Church document in reference to the revised form of the *Roman Rite Mass.* See Ordinary Form.

Nucleus

The nucleus is the central mass of *protoplasm* present in most animal and plant cells containing most of the *hereditary factors* necessary for such functions as growth and *reproduction.* See Genetic inheritance 2275.

Null and void

The word 'null' comes from the Latin word 'nullus,' meaning none or not any. When a *marriage* is declared null, it is declared never to have existed and so is without *legal* force. Void means empty, ineffective, and not binding.

An attempt to marry is rendered null and void when it conflicts with a *natural, divine,* or *ecclesiastical law* that makes it impossible. See Nullity of a marriage 1629.

Nullity

Nullity is a formal judgment or decree of an *ecclesiastical* court that a reputed *marriage* is *invalid* and has no binding legal force. The marriage never existed. See Nullity of a Marriage.

Nullity of a marriage 1629

When a *marriage* is declared null, it is without *legal* force. An attempt to marry is rendered *null and void* when it conflicts with a *natural, divine,* or *ecclesiastical law* that makes it impossible.

Such an obstacle is called a *diriment impediment.* It may

arise from a condition in the *person*, something he has done, or some circumstance that arises from the relationship of the *persons* attempting marriage. This would be the case in the absence of *matrimonial consent* or the omission of the proper *canonical form* of *celebration* required for *validity*.

In such a case, the union entered into, even in good faith, is, in fact, not a true marriage. When a diriment impediment is discovered, such a union must either be declared null by *judicial* process or *regularized* by *simple convalidation*. In such cases, the Church, after examination by an *ecclesiastical tribunal*, can declare a nullity of the marriage, that is, that the marriage never existed. In this case, the persons are still free to marry if natural *obligations* of their attempted union are discharged. See Convalidation of a marriage.

Numbers

Numbers is the name of the fourth book of the *Bible*. It received its name because it begins with the census numbering the people of *Israel*. See Law of Moses.

Nun

In general, nun refers to a member of a *religious institute* for women living in a community under the *vows* of *poverty*, *chastity*, and *obedience*.

More accurately, nun refers to religious women under *solemn vows* living a *cloistered*, *contemplative life*, as distinguished from a religious sister. The latter term is usually employed to designate one whose vocation involves active ministry outside the confines of a cloister. See Consecrated person 1672.

Nunc dimittis

The 'Nunc Dimittis' are the first two Latin words of the song of Simeon found in Lk 2:29–32 at the presentation of the Child *Jesus* in the *temple* where Simeon says, 'Now let your servant be dismissed.'

It is recited daily in the *Liturgy of the Hours* at *Compline* and is sung during the distribution of candles on the *feast* of the *Purification* (also known as the Presentation of Our *Lord* or Candlemas). See Antiphon.

O

O Antiphons

Antiphon comes from the word 'antiphona' in Latin meaning alternating. An antiphon is a short verse from a *psalm* or other passage from *Scripture* recited before and after a psalm or between verses of a psalm.

The seven antiphons sung after the *Magnificat* from December 17 to December 23 are referred to as the major or great antiphons. They are called the O Antiphons because each begins with 'O.' They are chanted to particularly beautiful *Gregorian melodies* invoking the name of *Christ* using titles derived from the *Old Testament prophecies*. The O Antiphons form the basis for the most widely used *Advent hymn*, 'O Come, O Come, Emmanuel.' See Advent 524.

Oath 2149

An oath is a calling on the *divine* name as witness to the truth of a statement.

It is an act of the *virtue of religion.*

Obedience 531, 2216

Obedience is the *moral virtue* by which one recognizes the *authority* of a *legitimate* *superior* and complies with his commands.

In children, *obedience* is a manifestation of *filial respect.* As long as a child lives at the home of his parent, he should obey them in all they ask of him when it is for his good or that of the family. Children should also obey the reasonable demands of the teachers to whom their parents have entrusted them.

By virtue of the *vow* of obedience taken by *religious*, their *superiors* may oblige them to obey in personal matters as well as matters pertaining to the *rules* of their *order* and legitimate directives of Church *authorities.*

For the *clergy* and *laity*, obedience means accepting and following the will of Church authority as closely as possible, especially in matters touching the fulfillment of pastoral duties for the *clergy* and of the fulfillment of duties pertaining to one's *vocation* in life for the *laity.*

The obedience of *Christ* in the routine of his *hidden life* inaugurated his work of restoring what the disobedience of Adam had destroyed. See Evangelical counsels.

Obedience of faith 144, 2087

The obedience of faith is the personal response of man to the God's self-revelation in *Christ*.

The word obedience comes from the Latin 'ob audire,' meaning 'to hear from.' In this sense, 'hear' refers to the accepting response of an individual and community to the disclosure of the *Divine plan* in *revelation*.

Man's response to God's will revealed by Christ in the Church is made possible through the graced capacity to hear and respond to God's revelation completely and without reservation.

Through the obedience of faith, man freely entrusts his whole life to God, offering the full submission of his *will* and *intellect* to what God has revealed. See Charism of infallibility.

Object chosen 1750

The object chosen is one of three sources of *morality*. It refers to the goal or *end* toward which the will freely directs itself. It is another way of indicating the *object of choice*. See Sources of morality 1750.

Object of choice 1755

The object of choice is the goal or *end* toward which the will freely directs itself. The object of choice can *vitiate* or make an act sinful in its entirety. Some acts, such as *fornication*, are always wrong because choosing them always entails a *disordered will*, that is, *moral* evil.

Objective

A thing is objective when it is perceived or known to be an extra-mental *reality*, not a mere fiction or product of the *mind*.

Objective can also mean unbiased, without prejudice, detached, or impersonal. Objective is the opposite of *subjective*. See Objective norm of morality 1751.

Objective certitude

One has objective certitude when the *truth* of a choice which he believes to be true is in fact true, that is, when one's *perception* of *reality* actually corresponds to the reality being perceived. See Right Conscience 1706, 1776.

Objective faith

Faith can be considered from an *objective* or *subjective* point of view. In the objective sense, it refers to all the saving *truths* contained in *Scripture*, the *Creeds*, *council definitions*, teachings of the *Magisterium*, and writing of the *Doctors* and *saints* of the Church. In the subjective sense, it refers to the personal *act* whereby one actually believes those saving truths. See Faith as a theological virtue 1814.

Objective norm of morality

1751

The objective norm of *morality* is the norm of morality as expressed by the *rational order* of *good* and *evil* attested to by the *voice of conscience.*

This objective norm of morality that determines whether an act is good or evil, is outside *man* himself, that is, it is *objective*, not *subjective*. The norm is none other than God himself who alone is good.

Objective redemption

Objective redemption refers to the *redemption* in itself as a *reality*. In this sense *Christ* is the primary, universal, and efficient *cause* of redemption. Through his *Passion* and death Christ restored *man* to the friendship of God and procured his *salvation*. See Coredemptrix.

Objectively

Objectively is the state of being objective, that is, perceiving an object distinct from the *mind* as real and actual without bias or prejudice.

Oblation

An oblation is an offering; especially the act wherein a *victim* of *sacrifice* is offered to God. See Anaphora 1352.

Obligation/Obligatory

An obligation is a *duty* or responsibility. See Moral imperatives 2415. See Canonization.

Occult

Occult comes from the Latin word 'occultus,' meaning hidden or concealed. It is applied to *knowledge* known only to members of certain *societies.*

It is also applied to *human acts* which are not publicly known but are known privately. See Sorcery 2117.

Octave

An octave is a period of eight days extending from the day of a *liturgical feast* to the seventh day after the feast. A *commemoration* is offered at *Mass* and in the *Divine Office* each day of the octave. The numerous octaves in the *Roman Rite* except for two were abolished after *Vatican II*. Today the only octaves observed in the universal Church in the *Ordinary Form* are those for *Easter* and *Christmas*. Observance of the other octaves is retained only in the *Extraordinary Form*.

Offertory 1350

The term offertory refers to that point when the *priest* offers up the bread and wine during the *Mass*. This takes place after the *Gospel* or the *Credo* when it is recited.

The priest first offers the bread with a prayer, 'Receive O Father, etc.' (in the *Extraordinary Form*) or 'Blessed are you, etc.' (in the *Ordinary Form*) before the priest offers the wine he adds a few drops of water into the *chalice* signifying the *human* and *divine* *natures* in *Christ* and his union with his people. Then he offers up the chalice with the *prayer*, 'We offer to thee O Lord, etc.' (in the Extraordinary Form) or 'Blessed are you, etc.' (in the Ordinary Form).

Offertory collection or collection 1351

From the earliest times, *Christians* brought along with them the bread and wine for the *Eucharist* as well as gifts to share with those in need. This gave rise to the custom of the *offertory* collection.

The term collection refers to the universal custom of gathering contributions of money during the offertory for the support of the Church and the poor.

The offertory collection is a survival of the earlier practice of making offerings of bread, wine, candles, *incense* etc. at the offertory of the Mass. The *medieval mass-penny* formed the link between these two customs.

The personal *Mass stipend* today represents these older offerings.

Office

An office is the *duty* of service associated with one's station or position, in the Church or a task to be performed as an *obligation*. The three offices of the Church are to *teach*, to *sanctify* and to *govern*.

It can also refer to one of the canonical hours of the *Divine Office*. See Officium 1255. See Liturgy of the Hours 1174, 1178.

Office of Readings

The Office of Readings is an hour of the *Divine Office* consisting of *psalms* and readings from *Sacred Scripture* and the *Fathers of the Church*. Its equivalent in the *Extraordinary Form* was recited during the night and called *Matins*. In the *Liturgy of the Hours*, it retains its character as a *night office*, but may be recited at any time of the day. See Liturgy of the Hours 1174, 1178.

Officium 1255

'Officium' is a Latin word meaning *office*. An officium refers to any *ecclesiastical* function or *duty*.

Oikonomia 236

'Oikonomia' is a Greek word meaning 'house administration or stewardship,' from which is derived the modern word *economy* or economics in reference to commercial affairs.

In Church usage, oikonomia refers to the *economy of salvation*, which is God's plan for the *glory* of his Son and our *salvation*. It is revealed in the *Person* and work of *Jesus*, and is the administration of God's House, which is the Church and home of the Holy Family.

It is by way of the oikonomia

that *theologia* is revealed to us. See Economy 1066.

Oil of chrism

The oil of chrism, also known as *sacred chrism*, called 'oleum sanctorum' in Latin, is olive oil mixed with a small amount of *balsam* and blessed by the *Bishop* at the Chrism *Mass* on *Holy Thursday*. It is one of three holy oils and is necessary for the administration of the *sacrament* of *Confirmation*. It is also used in the sacraments of *Baptism* and *Holy Orders* and in the consecration of *churches*.

Anointing with chrism signifies the full diffusion of *grace*. See Anointing. Also see Holy oils.

Oil of Catechumens

The oil of *catechumens*, called 'oleum catechumenorum' in Latin, is olive oil that is blessed by the *Bishop* on *Holy Thursday* at the Chrism Mass.

In the rite of *Baptism*, it is used to anoint the chest and between the shoulders of the *person* to be baptized. It is also used to anoint the palms of the hands of *priests* during the rite of *ordination*.

The oil symbolizes the priestly and royal power of *Christ* in which the *faithful* participate by virtue of Baptism, which confers on them a royal *priesthood*. See Holy oils. Also see Sacred chrism 1183.

Oil of the sick

The oil of the sick, in Latin, is called 'oleum infirmorum.' It is olive oil that is *blessed* by the *Bishop* on *Holy Thursday* at the Chrism *Mass*. The oil of the sick is used in the administration of the sacrament of the *Anointing of the Sick*. See Holy oils 1183.

Old Covenant 1093

The Old *Covenant* refers to the *solemn ritual* agreement that served the function of a written contract in early *Old Testament Hebrew* history. The Old Covenant was written on tablets of stone by the finger of God himself. This contrasted with the *New Testament* or *New Covenant* between God and *man* made by *Christ* and written in the heart through love.

Old Law 1952, 1962

The Old Law refers to the *Ten Commandments* revealed by God to Moses on Mt. Sinai.

The Old Law is the first stage of *revealed law*. Its *moral precepts* are summed up in the Ten Commandments or *Decalogue* which lay the foundations for the *vocation* of *man*, which is union with God.

The Decalogue is a light offered to the *conscience* which makes the call and ways of God known to man and protects him from *evil*. It is *holy*, *spiritual*, and good but still imperfect, because it shows what must be done, but does not itself give the strength and *grace* of the *Holy Spirit* to fulfill it.

Because it cannot remove *sin*, the Old Law remains a *law of bondage*. It prepares and disposes the chosen people, and each *Christian*, for *conversion* and *faith* in the Savior. St. Augustine observed that the law was given so that man would seek *grace*, and grace was given so that man could observe the law.

Old Testament 121

The Old Testament is the forty-six books of the *Bible* which record the *history of salvation* from the creation of the world. It included the establishment of the *Old Covenant* with *Israel* in preparation for the appearance of *Christ*, who initiated the *New Covenant*. The *Church* teaches that the Old Testament is an indispensable part of *Sacred Scripture* and is *divinely* inspired.

The *covenant* it established has never been revoked. It is present in a hidden way in the *mystery of salvation*. The *economy* of the Old Testament was oriented to a *prophetic* preparation for the coming of Christ, the *Redeemer* of all men.

Ombrellino

Ombrellino comes from the Italian for 'little umbrella.' It is a canopy that is held over the *Blessed Sacrament* like an umbrella when the Blessed Sacrament is carried from place to place in processions.

It can also refer to the gold and red umbrella given by the *Pope* to a *basilica*.

Omen

An omen is a thing or event that is supposed to foretell a good or evil future event. To *augur* is to foretell or prophesy using omens. See Superstition 2111. Also see Augur.

Omnipotent/Omnipotence 270

Omnipotent means all powerful. Omnipotence is the quality of *infinite* unlimited power or almightiness. Strictly speaking, omnipotence is an *attribute* of only God himself, whose power alone is subject to no limit.

Omniscient/Omniscience

Omniscience means all knowing. It refers to God's *knowledge* of all that is or can be, even our most secret thoughts.

The primary object of *divine* knowledge is God himself without any medium by which he *apprehends* (understands) his *nature*. The secondary object of *divine* knowledge is everything else, the purely possible, the real, and the conditional future.

By his *omniscience*, God knows the whole sphere of the possible with a knowledge which encompasses all real things past, present, and future. However, the *temporal* difference between them does not exist for the divine knowledge since all is simultaneously present to God.

God also foresees the future free acts of *rational* creatures with *infallible* certainty. The future free *acts* foreseen follow *infallibly* not because God substitutes his *will* for the *free will* of his creatures, but because he does not interfere with the freedom he foresees they will exercise. See Kenosis. Also see Truly human knowledge of Christ 473.

Ontological/Ontology

The word 'ontology' comes from the Greek 'ontos,' *being*, and 'logos,' discourse. It is the science of being in its most general aspects, its primary *attributes*, determinations, and *categories*, and referred to as general metaphysics. In ontology, 'being' means the opposite of 'nothing' and includes everything that really exists or can have existence. The highest *principles*, which are immediately derived from the concept of being, are: 1) the principle of identity, which means that everything is what it is and whatever is, is necessarily so and cannot be otherwise; 2) the principle of non-contradiction, which means that it is impossible to be and not be at the same time; and 3) the principle of the excluded middle, which means that between being and not being there is no middle ground.

The primary determinants of being are 'act' and 'potency.' *Act* is anything that perfects and determines a thing in its order of being. *Potency* is the capacity or aptitude for something. The relation between act and potency is the relation of the completing to the complete, or the perfecting to the perfectible.

The capacity to act is determined by the *nature* of a being. Nature is *essence* viewed as the source of *operations*. The nature of *man* limits his operations to the capacities of his powers and faculties as a *human being*.

Baptism effects an ontological change or change in the very nature of those who receive it. Through the grace of Baptism, a person is born again into the *supernatural* order and begins to live supernaturally, that is, he becomes capable of acting in a way that is beyond his *created* nature as a man. See Born from above 526. Also see Systematic philosophy.

Openness to fertility 1652

Openness to *fertility* means that *spouses* must do nothing in their *conjugal act* that prevents *conception*.

By its *nature*, married love is ordered to the *procreation* and education of children, which is only possible when the spouses give themselves to one another without reservation in true love. True married love, and the *family* life that flows from it, is directed to disposing the spouses to cooperate valiantly with the love of the *Creator* and Savior who, through them, daily increases and enriches his family.

Operation/Operating

An operation is any act, movement, or process by which choices are made and executed.

Christ is one *Person* with two *natures* each having a *will* by which the function of choice is carried out. His two wills function as two distinct *natural* operations: one *divine* and one *human* without division, change, partition, or confusion between them. They function in perfect *harmony* because the *human will* is freely subject to the *divine will*. See Monothelitism.

Opus Dei

'Opus Dei' is a Latin phrase meaning the 'Work of God.' St. Benedict (480–550 A.D.) used this phrase as the name for the *Divine Office*. His *monks* were instructed to prefer nothing to it because it was the most important element of the *Monastic* life.

Opus Dei is also the name of an institution of the Church, founded in 1928 by St. Josemaria Escriva and approved as a *prelature* by the *Holy See* in 1982. Its official name is the Prelature of the Holy Cross and Opus Dei.

There are two independent branches of Opus Dei, one for men and another for women. The woman's branch was established in 1930. *Priests* belong to Opus Dei as well as married *persons* who wish to dedicate themselves to *Christian perfection*.

Opus Dei is a *personal prelature* and is headed by a *prelate* appointed by the *Roman Pontiff*. Opus Dei was the first personal prelature established by the *Holy See*.

In many ways a personal prelature is like an *institute* of *consecrated life*, but its members do not take *vows*. The *laity* is dedicated to the work of the prelature by way of special agreement made with it. See Personal prelature. Also see Liturgy of the Hours 1174, 1178.

Oracle

The word 'oracle' comes from the Latin word 'oraculum,' meaning a *divine* pronouncement. The Greeks applied the term to the place where people came to consult *deities*, to the answer they received, and to the medium or seer who communicated the answer. See Prophetic text 715.

Oral

Oral refers to the method of passing on the teachings and *traditions* of the Church by word of mouth. All the preaching of *Christ* and the *Apostles* was oral. The content of the *New Testament* itself had its origin in *Oral Tradition*. It is through Oral Tradition that the New Testament is accepted as the *Word of God*, called *revelation*. See Tradition 78, 174. Also see Catechizing.

Oral Tradition

The *Word of God* is found in both *Scripture* and Oral Tradition. The word was spoken before it was written. This spoken word handed down from the time of the *Apostles* is Oral Tradition.

Christ died in 33 A.D., but the oldest manuscripts of the *Gospels* date from 40 or 50 A.D. Luke and Mark weren't Apostles, so what they knew of Christ came from information provided them by those who were first-hand witnesses. There was no list of the books of the *New Testament* in Scripture itself. They could only have been determined by Oral Tradition.

The Church distinguishes between *human tradition* and *Sacred Tradition*. *Human* tradition consists in manmade *laws* that can change, such as the rule of not eating meat on Friday. Sacred Tradition is considered part of the unwritten Word of God believed through the centuries. Because it came from the Apostles, it is called the *Apostolic Tradition*. See Tradition 78, 174. Also see Oral.

Orans 2679

Orans refers to *Mary* as the prayer figure of the Church.

It also refers to a posture of praying with outstretched arms depicted on tombs found in the *catacombs*. The figures are said to represent the *souls* of the deceased.

Oratio Dominica 2765

'Oratio Dominica' is the *liturgical* Latin name for The *Lord's Prayer*.

Oratory/oratories

An oratory is a place designated by permission of the *ordinary* for *divine worship* for the benefit of some community or assembly of the *faithful* who gather there. An oratory is distinguished from a private chapel, which is established for the exclusive use of one or more *persons*. The permission of the *local ordinary* is required for the establishment of a private chapel and for sacred celebrations to take place therein. It is appropriate for oratories and private chapels to be blessed.

The *Blessed Sacrament* is reserved in the *church* or principal oratory attached to the house of a *religious institute* or other house of piety. It may be reserved in other oratories and *chapels* with the permission of the *local ordinary*.

Sometimes, oratory simply refers to a small, private place for *prayer* without any *canonical* status. See Prayer corner 2691.

Ordained minister

An ordained minister is one who has received the *sacrament* of *Holy Orders*. See Holy Orders 1536.

Order 1537

In Roman antiquity, the term order designated an established *civil* body, especially a governing body.

Christ established the governing body of the Church and assured its continuity by means of the *sacrament* of *Holy Orders*, by which *spiritual* power is handed on and *grace* conferred for the *confection* of sacraments, especially the *Eucharist*.

Orders are also groups designated as bodies with specific characters and functions organized in a *hierarchical order*; *deacons, priests, bishops*. See Ordinatio 1538.

Order of Funerals 1686

The Order of Funerals is the *liturgical celebration* during which the Church expresses her *efficacious* communion with the deceased and with the community gathered for the funeral services. It proclaims *eternal life* to the community.

In Latin the 'Order of Christian funerals,' is called the '*Ordo Exsequiarum.*' 'Ordo' means *order* or *rite*, and 'exsequia' means funeral rites. There are three distinct rites associated with the Order of Funerals: 1) the Vigil for the Deceased; 2) the Funeral Lit-

urgy, normally celebrated as a *Mass* (Funeral Mass); and 3) the Rite of Committal.

The Funeral Mass is held in a *church*. A Funeral Liturgy held outside Mass may take place in a church or a funeral home. The Rite of Committal takes place at the place and time of committal of the deceased.

The order of the Funeral Mass comprises four principal elements:

1) "A greeting of *faith* begins the *celebration*. Relatives and friends of the deceased are welcomed with a word of 'consolation' (in the *New Testament* sense of the Holy *Spirit's* power in *hope*)" (CCC 1687).

2) "The *liturgy of the Word* [including the *homily*] during funerals demands very careful preparation because the assembly present for the funeral may include some *faithful* who rarely attend the liturgy, and friends of the deceased who are not *Christians*" (CCC 1688).

3) "The *Eucharistic Sacrifice*," which "is the heart of the *Paschal* reality of Christian death" (CCC 1689).

4) "A farewell to the deceased is his final 'commendation to God' by the Church" (CCC 1690).

Orders

'Orders' is another term for the *sacrament of Holy Orders*. See Holy Orders 1536.

Ordinance

An ordinance is an *authoritative* command similar to a *municipal statute* or regulation. See Law 1951.

Ordinary

'Ordinary' is a *canonical* term referring to a *person* with authority over a *particular church* or its equivalent. Ordinary power refers to the power attached to a specific *office*.

In *Canon Law* there are two types of ordinaries. A *local ordinary* is one having authority over or in a particular church. *Residential bishops* are local ordinaries as are those comparable to bishops in *law*, such as *vicars general* and *episcopal vicars*. All local ordinaries must have received the *sacrament* of *Holy Orders*. Residential ordinaries must be a *bishop*. *Superiors* of clerical *religious institutes* or clerical *societies of apostolic life* are called ordinaries, but are not local ordinaries. See Local ordinary. Also see Episcopal vicar; Vicar General.

Ordinary and universal Magisterium 2034

The ordinary and universal Magisterium is the ecclesial instrument founded by and on *divine authority* to teach the *revealed truths* of *Christ* with the *charism of infallibility*.

There are two forms of the Magisterium: solemn and ordinary. The *solemn Magisterium* is exercised only rarely by formal and *authentic* definitions of *councils* or *Popes* teaching *ex cathedra*. The *ordinary Magisterium* is exercised continually by the *bishops* in communion with and under the guidance of the *Pope* in their universal teaching concerning *faith* and *morals*. As condition for exercising this authority, those enjoying it must intend to teach in the name of Christ in obligatory fashion. Both forms are *infallible*.

The ordinary Magisterium is exercised continually in dealing with the practices associated with faith and morals and is referred to as the *universal Magisterium*. Teachings concerning faith and morals contained in pontifical documents are part of the ordinary Magisterium, and, as such, require the *religious assent* of the *faithful*.

Ordinary Form of the Roman Rite

The Ordinary Form of the Roman Rite is the *liturgical* form of that Rite based on the directives of *Vatican II* for the reform of *liturgy* and promulgated in 1969 by Pope Paul VI. The name ordinary was given this form only later by Pope Benedict XVI in his motu proprio *Summorum Pontificum* when he approved the *celebration* of the *liturgy* according to the never-suppressed liturgical books authorized in 1962 by Pope St. John XXIII.

Both forms are expressions

of the same *lex orandi* of the *Roman Church* and in no way lead to a division in the *lex credendi* or rule of *faith*. They are two usages of the one *Roman Rite*. See Rite 1203. Also see Extraordinary Form of the Roman Rite; Roman Rite.

Ordinary jurisdiction

Ordinary jurisdiction is the right to exercise the *authority* attached to an *ecclesiastical office*. The *Pope* exercises ordinary *jurisdiction* over the entire Church, *bishops* exercise it over their *diocese. Pastors* exercise this right in the internal *forum* (in *Confession*) over members of their *parish*. See Coadjutor Bishop.

Ordinary Magisterium

See ordinary and universal Magisterium 2034.

Ordinary of the Mass

The ordinary of the *Mass* is the general name for all the *prayers* and *ceremonies* that do not change with various *feasts*; it is also called the *common of the Mass*. See Anaphora 1352. Also see Canon of the Mass.

Ordinary Time

Ordinary Time is part of the post-*Vatican II* revision of the *liturgical* calendar. Before 1970, the *Sundays* of Ordinary Time were referred to as *Sundays after the Epiphany* and *Sundays after Pentecost* respectively.

Ordinary Time is a single *Liturgical Season* divided into two parts that occur outside of the liturgical seasons of *Advent, Christmas, Lent,* and *Easter,* and which celebrate specific aspects of the *mystery* of Christ. According to *The General Norms for the Liturgical Year and the Calendar,* the days of Ordinary Time, particularly the *Sundays,* 'are devoted to the mystery of *Christ* in all its aspects.'

The first period of Ordinary Time begins on the Monday after the Baptism of the Lord, and lasts until *Ash Wednesday*. The second division of Ordinary Time is much longer and begins on the Monday after *Pentecost Sunday*. It continues until *Evening Prayer* I of the First Sunday of Advent, which marks the beginning of a new liturgical year.

When Ordinary Time resumes after *Pentecost* Sunday, the selection of readings depends on the length of the season for the year. If it has thirty-four weeks, the number of the week to be used is that following the last week used before Lent. When there are thirty-three weeks, the week that would follow consecutively after Pentecost is omitted to ensure that the last two weeks of Ordinary Time proclaim the coming of the *Kingdom of God*.

The season of Ordinary Time has several other interesting features. First, the word ordinary in 'Ordinary Time' does not mean 'customary, normal, usual, or average.' Here it means 'not seasonal' in the sense that it is not part of the seasons of Lent, Easter, Advent or Christmas. The Liturgical readings chosen for thirty-four Sundays of Ordinary Time and their week days are ordered to instruction on how to live the *Christian faith* in daily life. It celebrates the complete mystery of Christ rather than a specific aspect of the mystery of Christ as do the other Seasons.

Another characteristic of Ordinary Time is that not all weeks have a corresponding Sunday. See Liturgical colors; Liturgical Year 1168, 1171.

Ordinatio 1538

The Latin word 'ordinatio' literally means incorporation into a *rank*, an *ordo*, or *order*.

The Church has established various bodies which *tradition* calls *taxeis* or *ordines*. The singular of ordines is ordo, for example, *ordo episcoporum* (order of *bishops*), *ordo presbyterorum* (order of *priests* or presbyters) and *ordo diaconorum* (order of *deacons*). Other groups referred to as orders include *catechumens, virgins*, and widows. See Ordination 1538.

Ordination 1538

Ordination is the *liturgical rite* by which the *sacrament* of *Holy Orders* is conferred on men by their *Bishop*.

Ordines 1537

Ordines, is the Latin word for *orders* and refers to designated bodies with specific characters and functions. See Order. Also see Ordo.

Ordo 1537

An ordo is an organized body or rank, also called an *order*. One is incorporated into an ordo or rank by *ordination*. The Church *hierarchy* consists of three ordos: the *ordo episcoporum*, the *ordo presbyterorum*, and the *ordo diaconorum*.

Ordo diaconorum

'Ordo diaconorum' is the Latin for 'order of deacons.' The duties of the *deacon* are to minister at the *altar* and to *preach*. He can administer *Baptism*, preside at funerals and be the minister at *marriages*. Deacons are the third *hierarchical order*. See Order. Also see Ordo 1537.

Ordo episcoporum

'Ordo episcoporum' is the Latin for 'order of bishops.' The *bishops* are the first *hierarchical order*, possessing the fullness of the *priesthood*. See Order. Also see Ordo 1537.

Ordo exsequiarum

The Ordo exsequiarum is the Latin for *Order of Funerals*. See Order of Funerals 1686.

Ordo presbyterorum

'Ordo presbyterorum' is the

Latin for 'Order of *Priests.*' Their chief duties are to offer the *Sacrifice of the Mass*, administer the *sacraments* of *Baptism*, *Eucharist*, *Reconciliation*, *Anointing of the Sick*, assist at *Matrimony* and preach the *Gospel*. Priests are the second *hierarchical order*. See Ordo 1537.

Organic presentation 18

An organic presentation is an exposition of the systematic connection or coordination of parts forming a unified organized and systematic whole. Organic presentation is important because the *truths* taught by the Church are always understood in light of one another.

Organic synthesis 11

An organic synthesis is a quality of information which renders it organized and *coherent*. It brings together into an integrated and unified whole everything required to gain a comprehensive *understanding* of a subject.

Oriental

Oriental comes from the Latin word 'orientalis,' meaning eastern. See Oriental Church. Also see Magus.

Oriental Church

In Catholic terminology, 'Oriental Church' refers to Catholics who belong to the *Eastern Catholic Churches.*

Oriental Orthdox

The Oriental Orthodox are a body of independent *churches* in *communion* with each other and that accept only the first three *ecumenical councils*. The Oriental Orthodox are not in communion with the *Eastern Orthodox*, who accept the first seven ecumenical councils and who separated from the *Catholic Church* much later. The individual churches that compose the Oriental Orthodox are the *Armenian*, *Coptic*, Eritrean, Ethiopian, Malankara, and *Syriac* Orthodox.

The Oriental Orthodox saw the *Council of Chalcedon* as a capitulation to *Nestorianism*, and refused to accept the language of "one *person*, two *natures*." While they have been accused of being "*Monophysites*," the Oriental Orthodox themselves reject Monophysitism and profess "miaphysitism," which, unlike Monophysitism, does not deny that *Christ* shares in our humanity. Recent ecumenical *dialogue* has cleared away misunderstandings and established that there is a common Christology expressed with different terms.

Original cell of social life 2207

The first and most elementary *social* unit or community of *persons* is the *family*. In the family, husband, and wife are called to give themselves permanently to one another in love and the gift of life. The *authority*, stability, and life relationships created by the family form the foundations of freedom, security, and fraternity within all human relationships as well as the initiation of new life into the larger *society*.

Original Holiness

'Original holiness' refers to the state of *grace* enjoyed by *man* in the *Garden of Paradise* before the *fall*. It is also called the state of *original innocence* or *original justice*.

In the state of original holiness, man enjoyed the perfect ordering of his whole *person* to God, resulting in a perfect inner *harmony* with God, with his wife, and with all creation. His *intellect* was clear and in harmony with his *will*. Being completely governed by reason he was entirely open to *divine* guidance.

Because he freely chose to live in accord with the divine plan he was *holy*. This *holiness* constituted his likeness to God, the all holy one. In holiness, his *soul* was committed to *justice* with a firm and constant will to give God and others their due. It was the basis of his state of *harmony*, peace, and *love*. For this reason, the state of original holiness or *justice* is also referred to as the state of *original innocence*.

Original innocence

Original innocence refers to

the condition of man in the *Garden of Eden* before the loss of *sanctifying grace* and the *preternatural gifts* through *original sin*. Original innocence is also called *original holiness*.

Innocence is not proven holiness and can be lost, as indeed it was when Adam and Eve freely chose not to live in accord with the *divine plan* by sinning. *Christ* and *Mary* chose just the opposite and made it possible for man to reacquire his lost innocence through *Baptism*. See Fallen State 404. Also see Preternatural gift.

Original justice 376

Original justice is the state of *holiness* in which God *created man* with a perfect ordering of his whole *person* to God, resulting in a perfect inner *harmony* between himself and God, between man and woman and between man and all *creation*. Man enjoyed the *preternatural* qualities and gifts of *infused knowledge, integrity, impassibility* and *immortality*, which were conferred on him as representative of the entire *human* race.

Original sin 389

Original sin is the *sin* incurred when our first parents disobeyed the commandment of God not to eat of the fruit of the *tree of the knowledge* of *good and evil*. By their sin they lost the grace of *original holiness* or *justice.*

Original sin also refers to the sinful state into which all the children of Adam, except *Mary*, are born. The essential *consequence* of original sin was the loss of *sanctifying grace* in the *soul.* This condition is inherited from our first parents by virtue of the *solidarity* of the *human* race under the headship of the first Adam. Because of it, *man* is radically wounded and turned from his true purpose, union with God.

Neither Mary nor *Christ* inherited original sin because they are not under the moral headship of the first Adam: Christ, because he is the *New Adam,* and Mary, because, in virtue of her *Immaculate Conception,* she is only under the moral headship of Christ.

The effects of original sin are the loss of *sanctifying grace, concupiscence* of the flesh (the general tendency to uncontrolled self-love), mortality (being subject to death), and loss of *impassibility* (freedom from suffering). Through sin, man's *intellect* was darkened and his *will* weakened. He no longer clearly saw his purpose and could not easily choose it because his will was weakened.

Baptism, by restoring to the believer the innocence lost by Adam's fall, removes original sin but does not remove its consequences in *human nature.*

Orthodox/Orthodoxy

Orthodox comes from the Greek word 'orthodoxa,' meaning right opinion. Orthodox is an adjective applied to those who profess true *doctrine* in all its *integrity.* It is used in this sense in reference to the *true faith* of the Church.

Orthodoxy is also used to describe right *belief* or teaching as opposed to *heterodoxy* or *heresy.* To be orthodox, a teaching must be part of the body of *revealed truth* called the *deposit of faith* entrusted to the *Apostles* by *Christ.* The deposit of faith is preserved by the Apostles and their successors with the guarantee of *infallibility* for the guidance of the Church. See Deposit of faith 1202. Also see Eastern Orthodox, Oriental Orthodox.

Ouija board

An ouija board is a board bearing letters, numbers and other symbols, with a movable indicator which points to them. It is used during the *seances* of *spiritualism* to convey messages from spirits. See Divination 2116.

Our Father 2759

At their request, *Jesus* himself taught his *disciples* to *pray* (Lk 11:1) and entrusted to them and to his Church the fundamental *Christian prayer,* which we call the Our Father. The prayer, as found in Lk 11:2-4, contains five petitions; in a more developed form in Mt 6:9–13, it contains seven petitions.

The name of the prayer comes from the first words: Our Father. The Our Father is also called *The Lord's Prayer*, the *Pater Noster,* and the *Oratio Dominica.* See Appendix of prayers.

Our Lady

Our Lady is the most popular title for the *Blessed Virgin* in *Catholic piety* and *devotion.* The first recorded use dates from c. 750 A.D.

Over-zealous treatment 2278

Over-zealous treatment refers to medical procedures or treatments that are burdensome, dangerous, extraordinary, or disproportionate to the outcome expected.

Such treatment may *mor-*

ally be discontinued when the *intention* is not to cause death. The inability to impede death is merely accepted. If possible, the patient should make this decision, otherwise it should be made by those *legally* entitled to act for the patient and who will always respect his reasonable *will* and *legitimate* interest.

Even if death is considered imminent, the ordinary care owed to the sick, such as food and water, cannot legitimately be interrupted. Painkillers to relieve their suffering, even at the risk of shortening their life, can be in *moral* conformity with *human dignity* provided death is not willed either as an end or means, but is only foreseen and tolerated as inevitable.

P

Pagan /Paganism

A pagan is one who practices *idolatry*. Today, 'pagan' refers to a *person* who has abandoned all *religious belief* and become totally irreligious. *Atheists* are not really pagans because they simply reject God and refuse to serve him.

Paganism refers to the beliefs of pagans. See Neopaganism.

Palliative 2279

A palliative is anything used for relieving pain, suffering, or distressing symptoms of disease without curing the underlying condition, such as the use of painkillers.

Pallium

A pallium is a *liturgical* vestment symbolic of the fullness of *episcopal authority*. Only the *Pope* and *archbishops* wear the Pallium. It may be granted to a *bishop*, but in this case it is purely ornamental.

The pallium is made from the wool of two lambs blessed in the Church of St. Agnes in Rome. It consists of an inch-wide circular band ornamented with six crosses with a pendant strip attached to the front and back. It is worn around the neck and shoulders on top of liturgical *vestments*. See Archbishop.

Palm Sunday

Palm Sunday or *Passion Sunday* is the *Sunday* before Easter. It *commemorates* Jesus' triumphant entry into Jerusalem by the *blessing* of palms and a procession before *Mass*. During the *Liturgy of the Word*, the Passion according to the *Gospel* of St. Matthew is read or sung. Palm Sunday is the beginning of *Holy Week*. See Holy Week.

Palmistry

Palmistry is a type of *divination* which attempts to tell a *person's* character or fortune by interpreting the lines on the palms of the hands. See Divination 2116.

Panagia 493

The *Fathers* of the *Eastern Rite* call the *Mother of God* by this title. It means the all-holy. A medallion with a small icon of the Panagia is worn along with the *pectoral cross* by *bishops* of the *Byzantine Rite*.

Pange lingua

The Pange lingua is the beautiful *hymn* sung at *Vespers* on the *Solemnity* of *Corpus*

Christi. In English it is referred to as "Sing my the tongue the Savior's glory." It was composed by St. Thomas Aquinas and is used as a *processional* hymn on *Holy Thursday, Corpus Christi*, and at other occasions in honor of the *Blessed Sacrament*. The last two stanzas are sung at *Benediction of the Blessed Sacrament*. See Altar of repose.

Pantheism 285

Pantheism is the *religious belief* or *philosophical theory* that God and the universe are identical, implying a denial of the personality and *transcendence* of God. The *doctrine* holds that God is everything and everything is God. This teaching is contrary to the *faith* of the Church, which believes that there is a personal God who is at once *transcendent* and *immanent*.

Pantocrator 2749

'Pantocrator' comes from the Greek meaning 'all-mighty,' and refers to the Lord as *Creator* of all things.

Papal

Papal is an adjective used in referring to things associated with the *Pope*. See Chamberlain.

Papal bull

A *papal* bull is the most weighty and *solemn* form of papal letter. The name comes from the name of the disk-like leaden seal attached to such a document which is called a 'bulla' in Latin. See Brief.

Papal enclosure

Papal enclosure is the strictest form of *cloistered* life. See Cloistered.

Papal household

The Papal Household is a *prefecture* of the *Roman Curia* which manages the *papal* living quarters. The *prefect* in charge is a *titular bishop* with a staff and a secretary. He is responsible for arranging audiences with the *Pope*, and supervises non-*liturgical* papal *ceremonies*. See Prelature. Also see Prefecture.

Papyrus

Papyrus is a tall water plant abundant around the Nile River from which writing material was prepared by ancient Egyptians, Greeks, and Romans. Papyrus paper was made by soaking and pressing slices of the soft spongy center of the stalk, and laying them cross-wise to form sheets, which were then dried in the sun. See Scroll.

Parables 546

The word 'parable' comes from the Greek word 'parabole,' meaning comparison or placing besides for the purpose of comparison. A parable is a *fictitious* narrative or *allegory* used to illustrate a *moral* or *spiritual* truth. Over thirty-two parables of *Christ* are reported in the *Gospels*.

Parables expose an affinity that exists between the *natural* and *spiritual* orders, and are used to reveal a *religious* and moral *truth* hidden in the design of God.

Paraclesis 2678

A paraclesis is a *litany* to the *Blessed Virgin* used in the *Byzantine Church*.

Paraclete 692

A 'paraclete' is one who is called to take one's side to aid. It is often translated as *counselor* because he acts as an *advocate*.

The term is sometimes applied to *Christ* but is generally used to refer to the *Holy Spirit*. Christ speaks of the Holy Spirit as another Paraclete whose function it is to teach, to bear witness, to take Christ's place among the *Apostles*, and to convince the world of *sin*.

Paradise

Paradise is another name for *heaven*, the state of bliss in which the blessed enjoy the *beatific vision*. The *Garden of Eden* is also referred to as paradise, the place where *man* enjoyed the friendship of God in the state of *original innocence*. See Cherubim. Also see Garden of Eden.

Parchment

Parchment was often used as a substitute for *papyrus* as a writing surface because it was more readily available. Parchment is the skin of an animal, usually a goat or sheep, prepared as a surface on which to write or paint. University degrees were written on parchment, and even today they are referred to as a 'sheep-skin' for this reason. Because parchment is associated with beautiful and important documents, there are specialty papers that are treated to resemble parchment and used for stationary. See Scroll.

Parish 2179

A parish is a community of the *faithful* established by a *bishop* within his *diocese* and entrusted to a *pastor*. Parish and diocese were identical during the first four centuries; hence every pastor was a *bishop*. But with the rapid increase of the *faith* among the people, it became necessary to set up communities smaller than a diocese placed under the *authority* of *priests* called pastors.

Parishes are generally territorial units with boundaries, embracing all the *Christian faithful* within the territory. Pastors have *jurisdiction* only over those who reside within the boundaries of their parish, and the pastor is installed by the Bishop. These are called *territorial parishes*.

Besides territorial parishes there are *personal parishes*,

which are established based upon *rite*, nationality, language, or some other determining factor.

Parousia 830, 1001

Parousia is a Greek word meaning the coming of a royal personage. It is applied to *Christ* and his *second coming* at the end of time. See Marana tha 671, 1130, 1403, 2817.

Parrhesia 2778

Parrhesia is from the Greek 'para,' meaning beyond, and 'rhesis,' meaning speaking. It means praying with "straightforward simplicity, *filial* trust, joyous assurance, humble boldness, [and] the certainty of being loved" (CCC 2778). It expresses the filial quality which should characterize Christian *prayer*.

Parricide 2268

Parricide is the killing of a parent by their child.

Partakers of the divine nature 460

Through *redemption*, *Christ* gives his followers all the *graces* they need to lead a *supernatural* life of *holiness* and achieve *sanctification*. By entering into communion with the Word through *Baptism*, men receive the gift of *adoption* as sons of God. The divine Son, to make us sharers in his *divinity*, assumed our *nature* so that he, made man, might make men godlike by being *partakers of the divine nature* through adoption as sons. By this, it is not meant that men cease to be creatures by *nature*, but that by the *grace* of adoption, or *sanctifying grace*, they now can lead a *spiritual life*, or know and *love* according to the *divine* manner of knowing and loving. See Theosis.

Partial indulgence 1471

A partial indulgence remits part of the *temporal punishment* due to *sin*. See Indulgence.

Participation 1913

Participation refers to the "*voluntary* and generous engagement of a *person* in *social* interchange. It is necessary that all participate, each according to his position and role, in promoting the *common good*" (CCC 1913).

Participation is primarily achieved by fulfilling one's personal responsibilities, such as "the care taken for the education of his *family*, by conscientious work, and so forth." In this way, "*man* participates in the good of others and of *society*" (CCC 1914).

Particular church 833

'Particular church' is a phrase used by *Vatican II* to describe distinct bodies within the universal Church, such as *dioceses*, *vicariates*, *territorial abbeys*, and *prelatures*.

The *Catholic* or universal

Church enjoys a priority of existence over the particular churches which comprise it; however, it exists in each particular church. This means that the universal Church is not the sum of all the particular churches, but that the existence of a particular church presupposes that of the *Catholic Church* and, in one way or another, depends on it. Each particular church is under the care of a *bishop* or his legal equivalent. It is the Bishop who grants permission for priests to hear *confessions*, serve as pastors, and hold diocesan offices. *'Faculties'* generally refers to the permission to hear confessions, preach, and *celebrate Mass*.

Neither the *diocese* nor the Bishop is an *appendage* of the *Holy See*; rather, the One, Holy, Catholic, and Apostolic Church exists and functions in each particular church.

Particular examination of conscience

A particular examination of *conscience* is one that focuses on a particular fault, *virtue*, *duty*, or Commandment. By focusing one's effort on acquiring a particular virtue or rooting out a particular *vice* or *sin*, one can more easily achieve a *reformation* of life. See Examination of conscience 1454. Also see Ten Commandments.

Particular judgment 1022

"The *New Testament* speaks of judgment primarily in its aspect of the final encounter with *Christ* in his second coming, but also repeatedly affirms that each will be rewarded immediately after death in accordance with his works and *faith*" (CCC 1021). Man will receive his *"eternal* retribution in his *immortal soul* at the very moment of his death, in a *particular judgment* that refers his life to *Christ*" (CCC 1122). At this time, the *soul* will immediately enter into the *beatitude* of *heaven* (or, if necessary, following the *purification* of *purgatory*), or the *eternal punishment* of *damnation*. Because death ends all possibility of rejecting or accepting the *grace* of *conversion* of heart, one's eternal *destiny* depends on the state of the *will* at the time of death.

Particular ministries 1143

Not all members of the *common priesthood* have the same function. Some, those *consecrated* by the *sacrament* of *Holy Orders*, act in the *person* of *Christ* and preside at the *celebration* of *Mass* and the administration of the *sacraments*.

Those not *ordained* by Holy Orders can assist at the *liturgical* celebration in other roles, such as servers, readers, commentators, and *choir* members. They also serve the *People of God* in a variety of *apostolic* efforts, which bring the *sanctifying* presence of the Church to the world.

Such service of the *laity* to the community is called a particular ministry or *apostolate* because they are not acting in the name of the Church as such, but for the community.

Part-principle

The *hylomorphic* *theory* explains bodily existence in terms of two *principles*; *prime matter* and *substantial form*. Prime matter is the common *substratum* of all bodies. In itself, prime matter is wholly undetermined because, in order to exist, it has to be some kind of body. A second principle is required to make it a particular kind of body. This principle is called 'substantial form,' and it cannot exist except when it makes prime matter to be something in particular. Thus, since neither component can exist without the other, they are considered part-principles. See Form 365.

Pasch/Paschal

Pasch comes from the *Hebrew* word for *Passover*, the *feast* which *commemorates* the passing over of the homes of the children of Israel when God struck down the first-born of the Egyptians in Ex 12:27. Now, the word has become synonymous with *Easter*. See Easter.

Paschal candle

Paschal candle is another name for *Easter candle*. It is a large candle into which five grains of incense have been encased as a symbol of *Christ's* five wounds.

It is *blessed* on *Holy Saturday* at the beginning of the *Easter Vigil* and is a symbol of the risen Savior who is the light of the world. The candle is used to bless the *baptismal water* during the Easter Vigil. It remains in the sanctuary during *Paschal time*, being lighted during all *liturgical* services. After Paschal time ends, it is removed from the sanctuary and is lit only for *Baptisms* and funerals. See New fire.

Paschal Lamb

The *paschal* lamb was the animal which the *Hebrews* were ordered to slaughter and consume at the beginning of their *exodus* from the bondage of Egypt. See Paschal sacrifice 613.

Paschal mystery 571, 1085

The Paschal mystery is also called the *Easter mystery*. It refers to the *Passion*, death, *Resurrection*, and *Ascension* of *Christ* as *supernatural* events.

Paschal comes from Pasch, the *Jewish* feast of the *Passover*, which *commemorates* the *Hebrews'* deliverance from Egypt. The Pasch is a figure of the deliverance of *man* from *sin* achieved by the life of Christ, especially through his *Crucifixion* and death. The Paschal mystery is the central mystery of the *Christian faith* and is *celebrated* during the *Easter Triduum*.

Baptism and the *Eucharist* recall the fullness of the *paschal* mystery and dispense its benefits to us.

Paschal sacrifice 613

The Paschal *sacrifice* refers to *Christ's Passion* and death on the Cross at the time of the *Jewish feast* of *Passover*, when the *paschal lamb* was slain. The Church sees Christ as the new Paschal sacrifice in referring to his death on the Cross.

Paschal time

Paschal time refers to the *liturgical* period from *Easter Sunday* through *Pentecost*, a period lasting fifty days. This period is also called the *Easter Season*. See Easter Season 2042. Also see Easter mystery.

Passion

Passion, in reference to our *Lord*, refers to the human sufferings *Jesus* endured which culminated in his cruel death on the Cross. See Paschal mystery 571.

Passions 1763, 1767

Passions are movements of the *irrational sensitive appetites* accompanied by notable bodily alterations. Examples of passions are strong *emotions*, drives, or excitements such as *anger*, fear, *lust*, *hate*, etc.

Passions, in themselves, are

neither *good* nor *evil*. They become *morally* significant only to the extent that they effectively engage *reason* and the *will*, or when the will does not place obstacles in their way. Passions should always be governed by *reason*.

The disorder in the passions resulting from original sin is often referred to as *concupiscence*. When it arises spontaneously, passion is said to be *non-volitional* and, because it makes calm reflection difficult at times, it lessens the *volitional* character of acts performed under its influence.

When passion is *deliberately* stimulated, it renders *acts* performed under their influence at least indirectly voluntary and therefore morally *imputable*. Passions are good when they contribute to good actions and evil when they contribute to evil acts. Emotions and feelings, which are part of the passions, can be elevated by supporting acts of *virtue* or be perverted by supporting acts of *vice*.

Passiontide

The period of two weeks from the Fifth *Sunday* of *Lent* through *Holy Saturday* is known as Passiontide. During this latter portion of the Season of Lent, the *veiling of images* has been traditionally observed, a custom which may continue to be observed in the present day. See Liturgical seasons. Also see Veiling of images.

Passover

The Passover is the *Jewish feast* of deliverance from bondage in Egypt. It *commemorates* the night when the *angel* of death passed over the houses of the *Jews* but killed the firstborn of the Egyptians. The Jews were spared because they had marked their doorposts with the blood of the lamb.

This was a figure of the Blood of *Christ* which would save men from *eternal* death. Just as the Passover was the greatest feast of the Jews, *Easter* is the greatest feast of Christians. See Pascal mystery 571.

Pastor 1560, 2179

The word 'pastor' comes from the Latin word for shepherd. It is the title given to a *priest* entrusted by his *Bishop* with the care of souls in a *parish*.

The Bishop is the true pastor of all in his *diocese* and has the responsibility and *duty* to care for, teach, *sanctify*, and rule his flock in the name of *Christ* and the Church. He shares this pastoral responsibility with priests who serve as pastors under him.

Pastors enjoy certain *canonical* rights and *obligations* in respect to those entrusted to their care and certain *authority* over the activities and properties, which belong to the parish entity.

All pastors must be appointed by the Bishop and serve at his discretion. Pastors must obey their Bishop, and members of a parish owe obedience to their pastor.

Pastoral

Pastoral refers to the office of caring for souls entrusted to *bishops* and *priests* in the Church. This consists in the administration of the *sacraments* and nurturing the life of the *Gospel* in the *faithful* through instruction and preaching the Gospel to the whole world. See Elements of catechesis 6.

Pastoral Epistles

The Pastoral Epistles are the *Epistles* of Titus and Timothy in the *New Testament*. They are called Pastoral Epistles because they treat of the duties of the *episcopal* office. See Epistle.

Paten

A paten is the shallow, thin, concave dish used to hold the large *host* to be *consecrated* and consumed by the *priest celebrating* the *Mass*. The paten is made of precious metal, or at least plated with gold. Any priest may bless a paten.

When the *Eucharist* is received on the tongue, the *server* holds a paten (Communion plate) with a handle beneath the chin of the communicant to catch any fragments of the *consecrated Host* that may fall off. See Chalice.

Pater Noster

The first two words of the *Our Father* in Latin are 'Pater Noster.' It is also called the Lord's Prayer because he taught it to his *disciples* (Lk 11:1). *The Catechism of the Catholic Church* considers this prayer the perfect prayer (cf. 2776). See Our Father.

Patience

Patience is the ability to bear suffering, provocation, or delay with calm self-control. See Wrath 1866.

Patriarch 61

A patriarch is the father and ruler of a *family* or tribe. The title refers to one of the twelve sons of Jacob, from whom the tribes of *Israel* were descended, or the fathers of the race, Abraham, Isaac, and Jacob, and their forefathers.

In Christianity, a patriarch is a *bishop* who holds the highest rank, after the *Pope*, in the *hierarchy* of *jurisdiction*. The Pope is the Patriarch of the West, and the *Eastern Catholic Churches* have their own patriarchs as well. A patriarch is a major or minor patriarch depending on whether or not he holds the see or title to one of the five great patriarchates. There are only five genuinely patriarchal sees: Rome, Constantinople, Alexandria, Antioch, and Jerusalem. In those *Eastern Churches* not in union with Rome, the Patriarch is the head of the national Church.

The founders of old *religious institutes* are, at times, referred to as patriarchs. St. Benedict is the patriarch of Western *monks*; St. Basil is patriarch of Eastern monks. St. Dominic is also referred to as a patriarch as is St. Francis (patriarch of the poor).

Patriarchal basilica/church

The patriarchal basilicas are the major Roman *basilicas* of the *Catholic Church*. The Basilica of St. John Lateran is called an Archbasilica for the *Pope* as *Patriarch* of the West; St. Peter's is the basilica for the Patriarch of Constantinople; St. Paul's Outside the Walls is the basilica for the Patriarch of Alexandria; St. Mary Major's is the basilica for the Patriarch of Antioch; St. Lawrence's Outside the Walls is the patriarchal church for the Patriarch of Jerusalem, but it is not always considered major. See Basilica.

Patriarchal ,

Patriarchal, *national, plenary* and *primatial councils* are meetings of a whole *patriarchate*, nation, or several *provinces* subject to a *primate* and presided over by him. See Council 465.

Patriarchate

A Patriarchate is the territory governed by or under the *jurisdiction* of a *patriarch*. See Patriarch 61. Also see Nicaea II 476.

Patrinus
The Latin term 'patrinus' and the term *'sponsor'* have much the same meaning. A sponsor is a person who promises to give special help and guidance to one who receives the *sacrament* of *Baptism* or the sacrament of *Confirmation*. See Sponsor 1311.

Patristic
Patristic is the adjectival form of *Patristics*. See Father of the Church. Also see Apostolic Fathers; Patristics.

Patristics
Patristics is the study of the writings of *Christian* writers of antiquity who are referred to as the *Fathers of the Church*. It is also called *Patrology*. See Father of the Church. Also see Apostolic Fathers.

Patrology
Patrology is the study of the writings and sermons of early Christian writers whose *holy* lives and witness dramatically influenced the defense, definition, and *propagation* of the teaching of the Church. It is also known as *Patristics*. See Fathers of the Church.

Pauline Epistles
The Pauline Epistles are the thirteen Epistles (fourteen if *Hebrews* is counted among them) of St. Paul found in the New Testament that were named for the *person* or community to whom they were written. See Epistle.

Pauline privilege
The Pauline privilege is a provision in *Canon Law* whereby the *marriage* of two non-*baptized persons* united in a *consummated* marriage is dissolved if one is converted to the *faith* and the other either refuses to live in peace with the *Christian* or allow them to perform their religious duties. The former marriage is dissolved only when the new marriage is contracted by the baptized spouse. This privilege is based on the teaching of St. Paul in 1 Cor 7:12–15. Hence, it is called the Pauline privilege. Also see Polygamy 1610.

Peace 1909
Peace is the stability and security resulting from a *just* order. True peace can only exist where there is *justice*.

Public *authority* has the *duty* to ensure the stability and security of society and society has the right to *legitimate* personal and collective defense to preserve its stability and order.

Pectoral cross
The word 'pectoral' comes from the Latin word 'pectus,' meaning breast. A pectoral cross is usually a golden cross,

often ornamented with precious stones, suspended by a gold chain or silk cord over the chest. It has been worn by *bishops* as a sign of their *office* since the seventeenth century. It may contain *relics* of a *saint* or *martyr*. See Panagia.

Pelagius / Pelagianism / Pelagians 406

Pelagius (c. 400) was the author of a *heretical doctrine* called Pelagianism. The principal tenets of Pelagianism were the rejection of *original sin*; that death is not the result of the *fall*, but a *law* of *human nature*; that *Baptism* is not necessary to remove original sin, but merely a title of admission to the *kingdom of heaven*; and that *grace* is not necessary for *salvation*.

The Church condemned all these *beliefs* at the *Council of Ephesus* in 431. See Council of Ephesus.

Penance 1459, 1460

Penance is a *virtue* that moves a sinner to acknowledge his *sin*, fills him with sorrow, and gives him to a firm resolve to *amend* his life. The determination to amend his life is manifested by the performance of some act of self-*mortification* or undergoing the *penalty* imposed by *ecclesiastical* authority. The motive for penance must be *supernatural* and based on a consideration of the goodness of God and his *love*, not mere natural remorse or fear of punishment. Penance is required for forgiveness of sin even in *Confession*.

As a sacrament of the *New Law*, the *sacrament of Penance*, also called Confession, is the *rite* in which, by the *absolution* of the *priest*, sins committed after *Baptism* are forgiven when they are confessed with sorrow and a firm *purpose of amendment*.

There are several types of Penance.

1) *Private penance* is done by an individual at his own discretion for the sake of making *reparation* for sin. It may take the form of *mortification*, prayer, or any good work performed in the spirit of *repentance* or *compunction* for sin.

2) *Public penance* refers to a *discipline* of the Church required for notorious crimes in the past. Those doing public penance were referred to as *penitents* and, formerly, were organized into four degrees, through which they had to pass, a) *weepers*, who were excluded from divine service; b) hearers, who attended only the *liturgy* of the *catechumens*; c) kneelers, who knelt apart from the congregation, and d) standers, who were excluded from the *offertory* and *Holy Communion*.

Such penance sometimes lasted for a period of days or years or even for life. The concept of years and days associated with *indulgences* granted by the Church refers to such periods of penance. This *penitential discipline* was relaxed in the eleventh century but existed in modified and unofficial forms until the eighteenth century in Ireland and England. Public penance may not be imposed for secret offenses.

3) *Canonical penance* refers to prayers and good works, such as *fasting*, *almsgiving*, *pilgrimage*, and *retreat*, imposed by *ecclesiastical authority* on those guilty of offenses against *Canon Law* in order to obtain release from *canonical penalties*. Public canonical penance may not be imposed for secret offenses.

4) *Sacramental penance* is the *prayer* or other good work imposed by the priest in the *sacrament of Reconciliation* before granting absolution. Performing this penance is evidence of true sorrow and a purpose to amend one's life.

Penitent

A penitent is a *person* who is sorry for having done wrong and is willing to make *atonement*. It also refers to a person who is receiving the *sacrament* of *Penance*. See Sacrament of forgiveness 1424.

Penitential

Penitential means expressive of penance or performing acts of *penance*. See Double consequence of sin. Also see Penance.

Penitential abstinence

Penitential abstinence refers to *abstinence* undertaken for the benefit of the *soul*, such as the practice of refraining from the eating of meat on Friday in honor of the *Passion of Christ*.

Penitential abstinence is not intended to deny the goodness of *created* things or punish the body. Its purpose is to unite the *person*, through the practice of self-*sacrifice*, to the sacrificial love of Christ and free him from self-indulgence, which hinders devotion in *prayer* and ardent *charity*. See Fast Days. Also see Days of abstinence 2043.

Penitential act

The penitential act follows the greeting that begins *Mass*. It is an invitation to the *faithful* to recall their *sins* in preparation for participation in the *Eucharistic Sacrifice*. After a brief silence, the congregation makes a *general confession* by reciting the *Confiteor* or some other petition for forgiveness. It concludes with an *absolution* by the priest. This is not a substitute for *sacramental Confession*, and someone in the state of *mortal sin* may not receive *Holy Communion* on the basis of this penitential act.

During the *Easter season*, the penitential act may be replaced with a sprinkling of water in memory of the *forgiveness of sin* in *Baptism*. See Introit.

Pentateuch

'Pentateuch' refers to the name given to the first five books of the *Bible*. It takes its name from the Greek word 'pentateuchos,' which means 'book of five volumes.' The *Jews* refer to the Pentateuch as the *Torah* or the *Law*.

The five books of the Pentateuch are *Genesis*, *Exodus*, *Leviticus*, *Numbers*, and *Deuteronomy*.

Some scholars make the use of *Eloi* or *Jahweh* for the name of God in the *Pentateuch* as grounds for ascribing authorship to different parts of the Pentateuch. Following this interpretation, they use the terms *Elohist* and *Jahwist* to identify different sources for the material it contains. See Law of Moses.

Pentecost 696, 731, 1287, 2623

'Pentecost' means 'fiftieth' in Greek. It is the *solemnity celebrated* forty-nine days after *Easter* and is ranked with it as the major solemnity of the Church.

The solemnity *commemorates* the descent of the *Holy Spirit* on the *Apostles* in the *cenacle* and the foundation of the Church.

In England, Pentecost is called *Whitsun* or *Whitsunday* because of the white *baptismal* robes worn by those baptized on *Holy Saturday*. See Sunday 2175. Also see Cenacle.

Pentecostalism

Pentecostalism is a movement that developed in the early twentieth century. Its central tenet was a second *blessing, Baptism of the Holy Spirit*, in which one is exalted by the Holy Spirit himself who acts not only on the *emotions* but also through the outpouring of gifts resembling those of the first *Pentecost*, such as the speaking in *tongues* and the gifts of *prophecy* and of healing. These gifts were manifested in revival meetings.

After *Vatican II*, the movement arose among Roman *Catholics* to restore the *charismata* or spiritual *gifts of the Holy Spirit*, especially speaking in tongues, healing, and prophecy, to a central place in the life and *worship* of the Church. It is known as the *Charismatic Renewal*. See Charismatics.

Pentecostals

Pentecostals is the name given to members of pentecostal *sects*. See Pentecostalism. Also see Charismatic Renewal.

People of God 782, 831

In the face of the chaos caused by *sin*, God has been calling people back to himself. The people who have responded are called the People of God.

As a group, their origin is Abraham and his response of *faith* to the call of God. Later came the nation of *Israel* and the *Old Covenant*. This Covenant was fulfilled by *Christ*, and now the People of God are those united to Christ by *Baptism*.

The People of God are not limited to one nation or time; rather, its scope is universal and its call is to every *person*.

This is a "gift from the Lord himself whereby the *Catholic Church* ceaselessly and efficaciously seeks for the return of all humanity and all its goods, under Christ the Head in the unity of his *Spirit*" (CCC 831).

People of the poor 716

The people of the poor are "those who, humble and meek, rely solely on their God's *mysterious* plans, who await the *justice*, not of men but of the *Messiah*" (CCC 716).

They are "the great achievement of the *Holy Spirit*'s hidden *mission*" (CCC 716) to prepare mankind for *Christ's second coming*.

Per se 2366

'Per se' is a Latin expression meaning of itself or in itself. For example, *abortion* is, per se, evil.

Perception

Perception is the *act* by which the *mind* grasps an understanding of objects, or qualities by means of the senses. See Cognition.

Perdition

Perdition refers to the loss of the soul by *damnation*. See Golden rule 1970.

Perennial

Perennial comes from the Latin word 'perennis,' meaning lasting through the year. In English it has much of the same meaning, that is, lasting or continuing for a long time. See Communion of Saints 1475.

Perennial philosophy

Because of its comprehensiveness, completeness, *coherence*, and consistency *Scholastic philosophy* became known as the *perennial* (that is, enduring) *philosophy* of the schoolmen. It survives today as the most continuously existent, comprehensive, and consistent system of philosophic thought known to man.

Perfect

Perfect means whole or compete; having all the qualities proper to its *nature*. See Habits of the will.

Perfect contrition 1452

The word contrition comes from the Latin word 'contero,' meaning to rub away or pulverize.

The Church uses the word to refer to the condition of being bruised in *heart* or filled with sorrow or affliction of *mind* for some fault or injury done. *Contrition* is "the sorrow of the *soul* and the detestation for the *sin* committed, together with the *resolution* not to sin again" (CCC 1451).

Perfect contrition "arises from a *love* by which God is loved above all else" (CCC 1452). It is contrition moved primarily by the love of God.

Sin is forgiven by perfect contrition even before it is confessed, but the *obligation* to confess *mortal sin* still remains. *Deliberate* failure to confess such a mortal sin is a mortal sin itself.

Perfection

Perfection consists in *holiness*; therefore, for man it always has a *moral* sense. Only God is perfectly holy, but men can become *perfect* because in Mt 5:48 we read: 'So be perfect, just as your *heavenly* Father is perfect.' St. Thomas teaches that this commandment is binding on all in the sense that they must love God above all things and *abstain* from *mortal sin*.

It implies that they should try to remove all things that hinder the full commitment to God, as is seen from the words of *Christ* to the rich young man who observed the *law* from his youth. When he asked what further he must do, Christ told him, 'If you wish to be perfect, go, sell what you have and give it to the poor, and you will have treasure in heaven. Then come, follow me' (Mt 19:21). This is interpreted as a *counsel*, not a command.

The *evangelical counsels* are

ways of excluding common hindrances to the full commitment of the *heart* to God. All are obliged to exercise them according to their *state of life*.

On earth perfection is accomplished by the observance of the *law*, the practice of *virtue*, the use of the *sacraments*, and *prayer*. In this life perfection is judged by how well one exercises the *theological virtues* of *faith*, *hope*, and *charity* or love of God and neighbor. See Grace of original holiness 399.

Perichoresis

Perichoresis is the Greek term for the Latin word *circuminsession* (literally, sitting in each other), which comes from 'circum,' around or in, and 'sedere,' to sit or remain. It refers to the mutual *immanence*, indwelling, communion, or fellowship of the *Persons* of the *Holy Trinity*. Each Person is equally God, really distinct, yet fully within the others without ceasing to be distinct.

Circuminsession was also used to describe the relationship between the two distinct *natures* in the Person of Jesus *Christ*, but the term is now usually reserved to the Holy Trinity. See Trinity, Holy 232.

Periodic continence 2370

Periodic continence, at times referred to simply as *sexual abstinence*, refers to the method of birth regulation based on self-observation and limiting *sexual intercourse* to *infertile* periods.

This form of continence is in conformity with the *objective* criteria of *morality* because it respects the bodies of the *spouses*, encourages tenderness between them, and favors the education of an *authentic* freedom. See Sexual abstinence.

Perishable

Perishable refers to things that may perish or are liable to spoilage or deterioration. Things that are perishable are not lasting. See Resurrected body.

Perjury 2152, 2476

Perjury is making a promise under *oath* with no intention of keeping it or not keeping it once it is made. Most commonly, it is a false statement given in court under an oath to tell the *truth*.

Perjury is a *grave* offense because such an act contributes to the condemnation of the innocent or *exoneration* of the guilty or the increased punishment of the accused. It gravely compromises the exercise of *justice* and the fairness of *judicial* decisions. Perjury is asking God to witness a lie and is gravely contrary to the *virtues* of *religion* and *justice*.

Permanent character

A permanent character refers to a *seal* or irremovable mark of identification. The sacraments of *Baptism, Confirmation* and *Holy Orders* confer, in addition to grace, a *sacramental character* or *seal* by which the *Christian* shares in *Christ's priesthood* and is made a member of the Church.

This *configuration* to Christ, is brought about by the *Holy Spirit*. It is indelible and remains forever in the Christian *soul* as a positive disposition for *grace*, a promise of *divine* protection, a *vocation* to divine *worship* and service to the Church. Should a Christian be condemned to *hell*, the seal remains as a cause for shame and mockery. Because Baptism, Confirmation and Holy Orders confer a permanent character they cannot be repeated. See Baptism 1213.

Permanent deaconate/deacon / diaconate 1571

Vatican II restored the permanent deaconate as a proper and permanent rank in the *hierarchy*. The "permanent diaconate, which can be conferred on married men, constitutes an important enrichment for the Church's *mission*" (CCC 1571). Permanent deacons may not marry without a special *dispensation*. Deacons who are married may not contract another *marriage* after the death of their *spouse*.

Permanent deacons perform a variety of *pastoral* services, and some function as directors of parishes without a permanent *pastor*. They assist the *Bishop* and *priests* in the celebration of the *Eucharist*. They administer *Baptism*, distribute *Holy Communion*, bless marriages, proclaim the *Gospel*, preach, preside over funerals, and various other ministries of *charity*. Deacons may not administer the *sacrament* of the *Anointing of the Sick*.

Permanent deacons are not called to the priesthood. Deacons who go on to become priests are called *transitional deacons*.

Permanent or fixed altar

A permanent or *fixed altar* is one that cannot be moved. It has three parts: a top of stone, supports for the top, and a *sepulcher* or place in which bones of a *saint* or a *martyr* have been sealed. The stone top is the altar, properly speaking, and is what is consecrated. If a small *altar stone* is only inserted into a larger structure, it is called a *moveable altar*. See Altar 1383.

Permanent state

Permanent means long lasting or intended to endure indefinitely without change. See Consecrated life 916.

Permission 1635

Permission refers to the action by which one is allowed or given leave, liberty, or license to do something.

Perpetual

A thing is perpetual when it is permanent or endures for a long time without interruption. See Marriage 1603. Also see Matrimonial consent 1625.

Perpetual virginity

Mary was the Mother of *Christ*, who was *begotten* by the *Holy Spirit*, so her child had no earthly father. *Ever Virgin, Aeiparthenos*, is a title of the *Blessed Mother*. It comes from the Greek 'aion,' meaning ever and 'parthenos,' meaning virgin or maiden. The perpetual *virginity* of Our Lady means that the Blessed Virgin was a virgin before, during, and after giving birth to Christ. See Mary's virginity 496.

Perpetual Vows/Perpetual Profession

Perpetual vows, or perpetual profession, refer to the definitive profession of the *vows* of *poverty*, *chastity*, and *obedience* that a *person* takes in an *Institute of Christian Perfection*. Perpetual vows are preceded by *temporary vows*, which bind for a certain period of time. See Religious profession.

Persecution

Persecute means to afflict, harass, constantly injure, cause distress, or oppress cruelly. See Fortitude 1808, 1831.

Person 251, 252, 363, 2222

A person is an 'individual *substance* of a *rational nature*' according to Boethius. In Thomistic *philosophy*, person is defined as an individual, complete, *subsistent*, rational *substance*. In order that this definition might correctly fit the *Divine Persons*, St. Thomas qualified individual substance as subsisting in three really distinct ways or persons; otherwise, since the divine substance is but one and individual, there could have been but one person in God, when in fact there are three.

'Subsistent' refers to the mode of existence in which a thing is self-contained or *autonomous* in its operation. Something subsistent is able to exist and function independently of another *created* thing, for example, a tree. In God the divine substance or nature subsists in a threefold way in three really distinct Persons.

'Substance' refers to something that exists in and for itself and not in another. It is opposed to an *accident*, which must inhere as a quality in something else to exist, like color.

Man is a subsistent substance with the power of *reason*. Man is subsistent because he is self-contained and autonomous in his *operation*. He is a substance because he is complete and exists independently of other created things and

does not inhere in something else.

By nature, the *human person* is neither body nor *soul* but a subsistent rational being arising from a *substantial union* of the two. *Angels* are complete and subsistent rational beings without bodies.

Human beings, angels, and God are persons because they alone have *intellect* and *will* and can exist independently of others and do not need to inhere in something else in order to be.

Personhood is the source of *human dignity* and constitutes the *image of God* in man. Because God made man as a person, having intellect and *free will*, God can communicate with him and call him to himself in *love*, and man can freely respond to his loving call.

The Church uses person or *hypostasis* in referring to the Persons of the *Trinity*, the Father, the Son, and the *Holy Spirit*, who are really distinct yet not separate and so at the same time exist in full communion with each other in the unity of the Trinity. In this communion or *fellowship* of Persons, each is equally God, really distinct from yet fully within each other without ceasing to be distinct. This is called their *circumincession* (literally, tending to be in each other) or *circuminsession* (literally, sitting in each other). There is in God only one nature but three Persons. When the *Second Person* of the Trinity, became flesh at the *Incarnation*, he remained one *Divine Person*, and he assumed a *human nature* without losing his *divine nature* and became the God-man.

Another definition of person is that of Richard of St. Victor: the 'incommunicable existence of an *intellectual* nature.' This definition is preferred by St. Bonaventure (1221–1274 A.D.) and Bl. John Duns Scotus (1266/70–1308 A.D.). Incommunicable existence means that every intellectual nature, one capable of thought and love, has a unique character really distinct from and irreducible to that of any other similar nature, a mode of existence called personal. In this way the difficulty posed by the word 'individual' in the definition of Boethius is avoided, whether this difficulty arises from the individuality of the *divine nature*: individual, but not one person, or that of the *human nature* of *Christ*: individual, but not a human person.

Personal parish

A personal parish is one that is established based upon *rite*, nationality, language, or some other determining factor. It is distinguished from a *territorial parish*, which embraces all the *Christian faithful* within a certain geographical territory. See Parish 2179.

Personal or private prayer 2664

Personal or private prayer is the *prayer* of an individual acting alone.

Personal prelature

A personal prelature is a special type of *prelature* established by the *Holy See* under the *jurisdiction* of a *prelate* appointed by the *Roman Pontiff*. Its purpose, as defined by its statutes, is to carry out a special *pastoral* or *missionary* work in different territories for specific *social* groups.

It resembles an *institute* of *Christian perfection*, but its members do not take *religious vows*. The first personal prelature to be established was the *Opus Dei*. See Particular church 833. Also see Prelature; Opus Dei.

Personal responsibility 1914

A personal responsibility is anything for which one makes himself accountable as an individual. For example, the care and education of the family or conscientious work. It is by assuming personal responsibility that one participates in promoting the good of others and *society*.

Personal sin 404

Personal *sin* is a *deliberate act* of the *will* by which a *person* acts in opposition to the *divine will* as interpreted by *conscience*. It arises from the sinner's own free will as opposed to *original sin*, which is a state of *concupiscence* into which each *human being*, except *Mary*, is born as a result of the *fall* of Adam and Eve in the *Garden of Eden*.

Perverse

See Complaisance.

Pervert/Perversion

To pervert means cause to turn away from what is right, especially respecting *morality*. It is also used to describe *persons* who practice *sexual immorality* with the same sex or children. See Pornography 2354. Also see Neopaganism.

Petition, Prayer of 2629, 2734

In the *prayer* of petition, we express an awareness of our relationship to God as one of complete dependence. In it we ask God for his *blessings* and help.

The first movement of the prayer of petition is to ask for *forgiveness*. It is centered on the desire and search for the *Kingdom of God* in keeping with the teaching of *Christ*.

Petrine Privilege

The Petrine Privilege is also called the *privilege of the faith*. It generally involves the circumstance of a *marriage*, though not exclusively, between two *persons* one of whom is *baptized* and one who is non-baptized at the time of their marriage. Even when *consummated*, such a marriage is not *sacramental* and,

under certain conditions may be dissolved by the *Pope*, in virtue of the privilege of the faith, in favor of the *Catholic* party. Occasionally, however, the exercise of the Petrine privilege may also involve a sacramental marriage, *valid* (ratum) but never consummated. The power of the Pope to dissolve such marriages is *vicarious*, viz., not properly his power, but properly that of *Jesus*. Hence, it may only be exercised in accord with the conditions stipulated by Jesus.

A petition for the Petrine Privilege is initiated at the *diocesan* level and sent to the *Holy See* for the conclusion of the process and a final decision.

Before 1989, this process was handled by the *Congregation for the Doctrine of the Faith*, but now it is in the care of the *Congregation for Divine Worship and Discipline of the Sacraments*.

The Petrine Privilege differs from the *Pauline Privilege*. See Pauline Privilege. Also see Polygamy 1610.

Petty/pettiness

Petty means worthless, trivial, insignificant, or relatively unimportant. See Magnanimous.

Pharisaic/pharisaical

A *person* is pharisaic when he pretends or gives the impression of being highly *moral* or *virtuous* when this is not true.

It is being *hypocritical.* See Scandal 2282.

Pharisaical scandal

Pharisaical scandal consists in being disedified or scandalized by the *good* actions or behavior of another. It arises when a *person's* own *moral* weakness finds an occasion of *sin* in the good *acts* of another because of their own *evil* dispositions. *Pharisaical* scandal should not be considered *scandal.*

Pharisees 575

Pharisees refers to a party among the *Jews* who had no intercourse with the *Gentiles.* As a *sect,* they were distinguished by the strictly *literal* interpretation of the *law* and their *scrupulous* observance of *tradition* and *ceremony.*

Because they had become exclusive, formal, proud, and *self-righteous,* they provoked the *indignation* of *Jesus* as recorded in Mt 23:1–7, and especially in verses 13–36, where he says: 'Woe to you,' referring to the Pharisees, in seven contexts.

The name comes from a *Hebrew* word meaning 'to separate.' They believed in the *angels* and the *resurrection of the dead.*

Phenomenon

Phenomenon comes from the Greek word 'phainomenon,' meaning to appear. In English it means any fact, circumstance, or experience that is apparent to the *senses.* It also refers to the appearance or observed features of anything experienced as opposed to the reality or the thing in itself. Another meaning is an extraordinary occurrence. See Spiritism or spiritualism 2117.

Philia

Philia refers to the love of friends chosen because of mutual compatibility and similar *values.* See Love 218.

Philosophy/philosophical/philosophically

Philosophy comes from the Greek words 'Philos,' meaning to love, and 'sophia,' meaning *wisdom.* It is the study of *being* in its ultimate reasons, causes, and principles acquired by *reason* alone. Philosophical is the adjectival form of philosophy. See Scholastic philosophy. Also see Scholastic theology.

Phlegmatic

Phlegmatic is a type of *temperament.* Temperament identifies a *person's* customary frame of *mind* or natural disposition. *Persons* with a phlegmatic temperament are dull, sluggish, and *apathetic.* See Temperament.

Phos Hilaron

'Phos Hilaron' in Greek means gladdening light. It is the name given to the most ancient and famous *hymn* of *thanksgiving* in the *Byzantine liturgy*. See Psalmi idiotici.

Physical evil 311

Physical *evil* is the privation of a *natural good* or the absence of something that satisfies some desire. In practice it is often identified with things that cause some degree of pain.

Physical evil is different from *moral* evil, which is the privation of some good necessary to attain *eternal happiness*. The pain arising from moral evil involves both *eternal* and *temporal* suffering.

Evil can be distinguished as evil of fault or evil of punishment. Evil of fault is the *culpability* or blame that results from a disordered choice of the *will*. It entails liability to either *temporal* or *eternal* punishment or both, depending on the *gravity* of the disorder of the choice.

Though evil is always opposed to good and perfection, it is not a pure negation of *being* but a negation of some good proper to the *integrity* of a being. Because it is only a privation, it is not in itself real except in the sense that it presupposes the good that it deprives. For example, blindness is the absence of sight in a being whose *nature* it is to have sight. It is a lack of something, not an additional thing.

Physical evil is an involuntary deprivation of good in the *material* order resulting from a *necessary cause*. It is evil only from the perspective of the physical integrity and well-being of a *person*. Physical evil is the absence of something required for the *material* perfection or well-being of the body. The physical needs of the body are always *subordinate* to *spiritual* needs of the *soul*, that is, those things the soul needs to attain its *ultimate end*.

Everything that God allows to happen to man in the physical order is for his *spiritual* or *eternal* good. Even *suffering* should be seen and accepted as a gift from God and as a means for spiritual *perfection*. When it is accepted as the *will of God*, suffering can unite man to *Christ* and make it possible for him to share in Christ's *redemptive Passion*. All suffering is part of God's providential plan for man's *spiritual* perfection.

God permits physical evil and suffering to occur in the world for our spiritual good. As *Catholics*, we believe that we will receive the grace to accept suffering we cannot avoid, such as sickness, because it is the *will of God* and a gift given for our spiritual welfare.

Physically invincible ignorance 1793

Ignorance is said to be physically invincible ignorance when the needed *knowledge* cannot be obtained by any amount of care and diligence.

See Ignorance. Also see Unintentional ignorance 1860.

Piety 1675, 1831

Piety is an attitude of *reverence* and *obedience* toward God, *religious* practices, and articles. More generally, it refers to fervor in the fulfillment of religious *duties*.

Articles of piety refers to such things as *rosaries*, statues, *crucifixes*, medals, and the like that are intended for personal rather than public or *liturgical* use.

Piety as a *gift of the Holy Spirit* makes us affectionate and grateful to parents, relatives, and country. It also makes us just because it fills our heart with a dutiful respect and *reverence* for God, which then extends to all men because they are children of God.

The *spiritual and corporal works of mercy* arise from the gift of piety, which forms a bond of union between members of the *Church Suffering*, *Church Triumphant*, and *Church Militant*.

Through devotion to the service of mankind for the love of God, piety spreads through the whole earth soothing misery, assuaging pain, instructing the ignorant, counseling the doubtful, and sheltering the homeless in *Christ's* name.

The gift of piety completes the infused *virtue* of *justice*, which is the inclination of the *soul* to render to everyone what is his

due and to God the *adoration* we owe him as our creator.

Pilgrim

A pilgrim is a *person* who undertakes a journey to a *sacred* place as an act of *religious devotion*. The journey itself is called a *pilgrimage*. See Pilgrimage.

Pilgrim church

The *Church Militant* is also called the Pilgrim Church. See Church Militant.

Pilgrimage

A pilgrimage is a journey to a *holy* place made as an *act* of *devotion* and *piety*. Such a journey is undertaken to *venerate* a *saint*, to seek a spiritual favor, pray for a cure, perform an act of *penance*, or fulfill a promise. In the eighth century a pilgrimage was imposed on public sinners in place of *public penance*. See Penance 1459, 1460. Also see Canonical Penance.

Pious

Pious is the adjectival form of *piety*. See Piety 1675.

Plan of the mystery 1066

The plan of the *mystery* refers to the plan of the good pleasure of God for all *creation*, especially its *redemption*. It is confessed in the *Creed*, which reveals how the Father accomplishes the mystery of his *will* by giving his beloved *Son* and his *Holy Spirit* for the *salva-*

tion of the world and the *glory* of his name.

Plenary council

The word plenary comes from the Latin word 'plenus,' meaning full. A plenary council is a formal convocation or *council* of all the *archbishops*, and *bishops* of the same *episcopal conference*. Plenary councils are convoked by the episcopal conference with the approval of the *Apostolic See*.

A plenary council is distinguished from a *provincial council*, the latter of which pertains to an *ecclesiastical province*.

Both plenary and provincial councils enjoy the "power of governance, especially legislative power. [They] can, therefore, determine whatever seems opportune for an increase of *faith*, for the ordering of common *pastoral* action, for the direction of *morality* and for the preservation, introduction and defense of a common ecclesiastical *discipline*" (Canon 445). *Acts* of such councils must be reviewed by the Apostolic See (Canon 446).

The decisions of some plenary councils have later been extended to the universal Church. When the entire Church is summoned to a universal council it is called an *ecumenical council*. See Council 465.

Plenary indulgence 1471

A plenary indulgence is one, which remits all the *temporal punishment* due to *sin*. See Indulgence.

Polemical/Polemic 575

The term polemical is the adjectival form of the word polemic. Polemic itself is derived from the Greek 'polemos,' meaning war. The stem of the word is '-pellet,' meaning to shake or cause to tremble, and came to refer to a controversial argument or discussion, especially argumentation against some opinion or *doctrine*. As a method of conducting *theological* controversy, it is opposed to *irenics*.

Political community 1910

The political community is the association of men formed into a governmental group called a state for the purpose of defending and promoting the *common good* of a society, its citizens, and institutions.

Polyandry

Polyandry is the practice of one woman having several husbands. Neither polyandry nor *polygamy*, one man having several wives, is in accord with the *moral law*. Both are also contrary to the *natural law* since they are incompatible with the good estate of *marriage*.

The nature of *conjugal community*, which must be exclusive and undivided in its nature, is radically contradicted by polyandry because it directly negates the plan of God revealed from the beginning and because it is contrary to the equal personal *dignity* of man and woman, who in *matrimony* give themselves with a *love* that is total and, thus, unique and exclusive.

A polyandrist who desires to convert to Christianity is obliged to repudiate all but the first of the husbands with whom she has shared *conjugal life*. A woman who simultaneously has several non-baptized husbands may keep one of them, if it is difficult for her to remain with the first (Canon 1148). This marriage of a polyandrist can be *valid*, but it is possible that it is *invalid* if *indissolubility* had been expressly excluded when the marriage was contracted. If converted, she may profit from the *Pauline Privilege*.

She who has lived in polyandry has a *grave duty* in *justice* to honor the *obligations* contracted in regard to her former husbands and children. See Polygamy 2387.

Polygamous

Polygamous means engaging in or characterized by *polygamy*. See Concubinage.

Polygamy 1610, 1644, 2387

Polygamy is the practice of one man being married simultaneously to more than one woman. Because of the hardness of men's hearts, the *Mosaic Law* tolerated polygamy, but polygamy is contrary to *divine law*.

Polygamy is an offense against the dignity of women and is contrary to *conjugal love*, which must be undivided and exclusive and, by its nature, requires the *inviolable fidelity* of the *spouses*.

Conjugal community is radically contradicted by both polygamy and polyandry because they directly negate the plan of God revealed from the beginning and because it is contrary to the equal personal *dignity* of man and woman, who in *matrimony* give themselves with a *love* that is total and, thus, unique and exclusive.

A polygamist who desires to convert to Christianity is obliged to repudiate all but the first of the wives with whom he has shared *conjugal life*. A man who simultaneously has several non-baptized wives may keep one of them, if it is difficult for him to remain with the first (Canon 1148). This *marriage* of a polygamist can be *valid*, but it is possible that it is *invalid* if *indissolubility* had been expressly excluded when the marriage was contracted. If converted, he may profit from the *Pauline Privilege*.

He who has lived in polygamy has a *grave duty* in justice to honor the *obligations* contracted in regard to his former wives and children. Also see Polyandry.

Polytheism 2112

Polytheism is the *belief* in and *worship* of more than one god. *Catholics* believe in only one God who is three *Persons*, yet only one in *essence*.

Pontiff/Roman Pontiff 882

Pontiff comes from the Latin 'pontifex,' meaning bridge builder. It refers to a *high priest* who makes a bridge between God and *man*. Since the *Bishop* is the *High Priest* in his *diocese*, he is technically a *pontiff*; however, in English speaking lands, the title is only used in referring to the *Pope* as the *Supreme Pontiff*.

Pontifical family

Pontifical family refers to all those *persons* in the immediate service of the *Pope* who fulfill duties in his household. In an extended sense, it includes all domestic *prelates*, *chamberlains*, *lay* and *clerical* workers, and various guards. See Prelature.

Pontifical Institute

A pontifical institute or institution is one which offers specialized studies in such areas as *philosophy*, *theology*, *Canon Law*, *Scripture*, *sacred* music, or *Christian* archeology. They offer undergraduate as well as graduate degrees.

Pontifical Mass

A Pontifical Mass is a *Mass celebrated* by a *bishop* with those *ceremonies* proper to a bishop. The Papal Mass is a special form of the Pontifical Mass.

Pontificale Romanum

The Pontificale Romanum is the book containing the *prayers* and *ceremonies* for certain *rites* ordinarily reserved to *bishops*, such as *Confirmation*, *Holy Orders*, coronation of a *sovereign*, and *consecration* of a *church*. See Consecration of a virgin 923.

Poor Clares

Poor Clares is a *monastic* community of *nuns* founded by St. Clare (1194–1253 A.D.) under the inspiration of St. Francis of Assisi. They were the most *austere* among the *religious institutes* of the time. They emphasize *mortification, Eucharistic Adoration,* and chanting the *Divine Office*. See Contemplative.

Poor in spirit 2546

The poor in spirit are those who live in simplicity and detachment from worldly possessions. Living in a spirit of abandonment to the *providence* of the Father in *heaven* frees them from anxiety about tomorrow. Trust in God is a preparation for the *blessedness* of the poor who the *beatitude* says will see God.

Pope 882

The word pope comes from the Greek word 'pappas,' meaning father. Pope is the title of the visible head of the *Catholic Church*, the *Bishop of Rome* and successor of St. Peter. By reason of his office he is the *Vicar of Christ* with full, supreme, and universal power over the entire Church. The Pope is elected by the College of Cardinals.

He is called Pope because he exercises his *authority* in a paternal way after the example of Christ as the servant of the servants of Christ.

Popular devotions 1674

Popular devotion is the *religious* sense of the *faithful* which finds expression in various forms of *piety* surrounding the Church's *sacramental* life, such as *devotion* to the *Blessed Sacrament*, the *Blessed Virgin*, *veneration* of *relics*, visits to *sanctuaries*, *pilgrimages*, *retreats*, *processions*, *Stations of the Cross*, the *Rosary*, *religious medals*, *novenas*, etc. Such devotions may be public or private.

Pornography 2354

Pornography is any form of communication, whether written, graphic, or electronic, that is intended to excite *lascivious* or *erotic* feelings.

The word comes from the Greek meaning 'writing about *prostitutes*.' The *evil* of pornography consists in removing sexual acts from the intimacy of the partners in order to display them to third parties.

It offends against *chastity*

because it *perverts* the *conjugal act*, which is essentially the intimate giving of *spouses* to one another alone. It *gravely* injures the *dignity* of the participants, the actors, vendors, and the public, because each becomes an object of base pleasure and *illicit* profit for others.

Viewing pornography leads to *impurity* of thoughts and *lustful* behavior. *Impurity* tends to hardening of the heart and perverts one's *perception* of others, seeing them only as objects of selfish pleasure. Pornography is deeply *addictive* and destroys one's capacity for true intimacy.

The chief means of overcoming *addiction* to pornography are *prayer*, *fasting*, reception of the *sacraments*, and the guidance of a good *spiritual advisor*. See Lust/lustful 1866, 2351.

Porter

Porter is the lowest of the four *minor orders*. He serves as the doorkeeper.

Post-apostolic

Post-apostolic refers to the period after all the *Apostles* died. This period of time started with the death of the last surviving apostle, St. John, in 96 A.D.

Post-baptismal catechumenate 1231

The post-baptismal catechumenate is the further instruction in the *faith* required for the flowering of *baptismal grace* into *spiritual* growth after *Baptism* for *adults*. The Catechism of the Catholic Church has its proper place here. This instruction is more properly called *mystagogia* and should continue, in some form, throughout life. See Mystagogy 1075.

Post-mortem

The term 'post-mortem' is a Latin term adopted into English usage that means 'after death.' A post-mortem is the medical examination of a corpse to determine the cause of death. It is also called an *autopsy*. See Autopsy 2301.

Postulancy

Postulancy is the period of time a *person* spends in preparation to be clothed with the *religious habit* as a *novice*. During this time, the individual wears civilian clothes and follows the *community* life. It can last from several months to several years depending on the community's customs, the maturity of the postulant, and other particular circumstances. It ends when the person is clothed with the religious habit and becomes a *novice*.

Postulant

A postulant is a *person* preparing to be clothed in the *religious habit* as a *novice*. See Religious life 925.

Postulate/Postulated

Postulate comes from the Latin word 'postulare,' meaning to demand. It is used in reference to a principle or fact that is assumed to be true and can serve as the reasonable basis for action or argumentation. See Synderesis or synteresis 1780.

Potency

Potency is the capacity or aptitude for something. The relation between *act* and potency is the relation of the completing to the completable or perfecting to the perfectible. See Ontological.

Potential

Potential is an adjectival form of potency. See Ontological. Also see Will of God.

Poverty

As a *virtue*, poverty refers to detachment from material goods and greater concern for spiritual realities.
Religious take a vow of poverty, which is the renunciation of the ownership of *material* goods. For the *laity*, it takes the form of moderation and self-denial in the use of material goods. See Evangelical counsels 915. Also see Evangelical Poverty; Poverty of heart 2544.

Poverty of heart 2544

Poverty of heart is the *spirit of detachment* from riches that is *obligatory* for entrance into the *Kingdom of God*.

Christ bids his *disciples* to direct their affections rightly lest they be hindered in the pursuit of *charity* by the use of worldly things and adherence to riches, which is contrary to the spirit of *evangelical poverty*.

Power of the keys 553, 981

The power of the keys is an expression used in Mt 16:19 by which complete *ecclesiastical authority* of *orders*, *jurisdiction*, and *doctrine* was conferred by *Christ* on St. Peter and his successors.

It is often used to refer only to the power to *forgive sins* exercised in the *sacrament of Penance*, but this is not completely accurate since the power extends beyond this single sacrament to all matters of *faith* and *morals*.

Practical contradiction

A practical contradiction involves a choice between two contradictory propositions to be made here and now.

Applied to *morality*, it means that we are faced with giving *assent* to one of two propositions, one of which is *immoral* the other *moral*. See Certain conscience.

Practical faith

Practical faith is *faith* that affects behavior and moves the *will*. It is distinguished from *speculative faith*, which merely recognizes *revealed truth* in *theory*, but apart from behavior. See Faith 26, 146.

Practical knowledge

Knowledge can be considered as practical or speculative. Practical knowledge is knowledge that is put to specific, practical use to solve problems or produce results. *Speculative knowledge* simply enriches the *mind* with *truth* apart from any application to specific purposes.

Practical materialism

Practical *materialism* is a form of *atheism*. It denies the existence of God by restricting *man's* needs and aspirations only to space and time. In this way it rejects *divine providence*, *grace*, man's *obligations* to and dependence upon God, and *eternal life*. See Atheism 2124.

Practical reason

Reason is the ability to think *coherently* and to *logically* draw *valid conclusions* from facts or *premises*.

Practical reason is the application of the powers of reason in actual situations by making *judgments*, weighing alternatives, or applying the process of reasoning in solving real world problems. See Prudence. Also see Wisdom; Reason.

Praise

Praise is the recognition of another's good qualities or

deeds. It is the approving recognition of excellence in another.

Praise is associated with *glory*, which is the response of an individual to *knowledge* of outstanding goodness that elicits admiration.

St. Thomas distinguished between formal and objective glory. Objective glory refers to the fundamental goodness that gives rise to the need to praise another's excellence.

The knowledge of the goodness itself that is the basis of *glory* is called formal glory. Thus, because God knows himself perfectly, he must glorify himself perfectly. Man can give glory according to the degree he knows the goodness of God. The rest of creation gives glory only by reflecting the goodness of the *creator* because it cannot know God's goodness. See Glory 293. See Prayer of praise.

Praxis

Praxis is derived from the Greek word 'prattein,' meaning 'do.' It refers to practice as distinguished from *theory*, and, hence, to the actual practices or customs through which the *faith* of the Church is manifested as opposed to the merely intellectual teaching of the faith. See Doxology 2641. Also see Didache 2760.

Prayer 2098, 2559, 2567, 2623, 2664, 2738, 2744

"Prayer is the raising of one's *mind* and *heart* to God" (CCC 2559). Prayer is communion with God through *Christ* in the Church, it is "the living relationship of the children of God with their *Father* who is good beyond measure, with his Son *Jesus Christ* and with the *Holy Spirit*" (CCC 2565), and it is the work of the Church in the *liturgy*.

Prayer is the highest exercise of the *virtue of religion* and includes *worship*, thanksgiving, *repentance*, *reparation*, and *petition*. Prayer is the source of all our good.

It is an article of *faith* that prayer is necessary for *salvation* and should be made frequently. Good works are regarded as *virtual prayer* because of the mental attitude that accompanies them.

We pray primarily to God, but we ought to pray also to the *saints*, to our *guardian angel*, and, especially, to our *Blessed Mother* in order that, through their *intercession* and *merits*, God may deign to hear us.

Prayer can be *mental* or *vocal*. It is mental when it takes place in the heart or mind and is called *prayer of the heart*. It is vocal when it is uttered aloud alone or with others. Mental prayer is also called *personal* or *private prayer*.

Prayer may be *meditative* or *contemplative*. Meditative prayer consists in reflection on *divine truths* or *mysteries*. Contemplative prayer is the focusing of the mind and heart on the goodness of God in loving *adoration*, with ardent faith and *love*. Meditative prayer grows into contemplative prayer and is the fruit of God's favor.

Prayer may be *individual* or *public*, that is, the personal prayer of a single *person* praying alone and in private, or public, that is, prayer with others as in the *liturgy*.

Prayer has also been classified as *private* or *liturgical*. Private prayers are recited alone or with others in the form of special *devotions*. Liturgical prayer is the official prayer of the whole Church as in the *Mass*, *sacraments* and *Divine Office*.

When one of his disciples asked 'Lord, teach us to pray,' *Jesus* himself taught them to pray and entrusted to them and his Church the fundamental *Christian* prayer, which we call the *Lord's Prayer*.

Prayer as communion 2565

Prayer considered as communion is the "living relationship of the children of God with their *Father* who is good beyond measure, with his Son *Jesus Christ* and with the *Holy Spirit*" (CCC 2565). Prayer, in this aspect, is the way we enter into union with the whole *Trinity*.

"The life of prayer is the habit of being in the presence of the thrice-holy God and in communion with him. This communion of life is always possible because, through Baptism, we have already been united with Christ" (CCC 2565). We have been filled with his *sanctifying grace* and further united with him through the *Eucharist* and the other *sacraments*. "Prayer is Christian insofar as it is communion with Christ and extends throughout the Church, which is his Body" (CCC 2565).

Prayer as covenant 2562

Prayer is a *covenantal relationship* between God and man in *Christ*. It is an action of God and man springing forth from both the *Holy Spirit* and ourselves, wholly directed to the Father in union with the *human will* of the *Son of God* made *man*. In prayer, man enters into the *covenant* relation, in which he makes God his God and God makes man his *adopted son* in Christ. This familial bond is a *covenant* and formed by prayer.

Prayer corner 2691

A prayer corner is a place set aside for *private prayer*, which may contain a copy of the *Scriptures*, statues, *icons*, and even candles. The prayer corner is a kind of small *oratory*. When it is set up in the home, it fosters prayer in common in the *family*. A prayer corner is called a *home shrine* at times.

Prayer group 2689

A prayer group is the gathering together of a number of

persons to pray together and support one another through discussion of the *spiritual life, Scripture, catechism*, or spiritual books. The group usually meets on a regular schedule and has the same persons in attendance. See Schools of prayer.

Prayer of adoration

The prayer of adoration is man's response to God's gifts, returning *blessing* to him who is the source of every blessing. It is man blessing God who has *blessed* him. In adoration, man recognizes that he is a creature before his *creator* and exalts the greatness of the *Lord* who made him. See Forms of prayer 2625.

Prayer of intercession 2634

The prayer of intercession is praying on behalf of others for their needs and desires.

In the prayer of intercession, we pray as *Jesus* did; "He is the one intercessor with the Father on behalf of all men, especially sinners" (CCC 2634). *Interceding* on behalf of others "is characteristic of a heart attuned to God's *mercy*" (CCC 2635). *Christian intercession*, a participation in the intercession of Christ, is an expression of the *communion with the saints*.

Prayer of petition 2629, 2734

The prayer of petition is asking the Father for what we need or want.

It expresses our awareness of our relationship with God and our complete dependence on him. In the prayer of petition, we ask God for his *blessings*. "The first movement on the prayer of petition is asking *forgiveness*" (CCC 2631). Every petition "is centered on the desire and search for the kingdom to come, in keeping with the teaching of *Christ*" (CCC 2632). The *Lord's Prayer* is our model for prayer of petition. See Holy day/Holy day of obligation.

Prayer of praise 2639

The prayer of praise is the most immediate *recognition* that God is God. It gives him *glory* not for what he does, but for who and what he is. The prayer of praise embraces all other forms of *prayer*, and carries them toward him who is their source and goal.

The *Eucharist* contains and expresses all forms of prayer. It is the pure offering of the whole *Body of Christ* to the glory of God's name. It is the perfect *sacrifice* of praise.

Prayer of quiet

Prayer of quiet is a form of *prayer* that takes place in a state of union with God in which the *soul* becomes more *conscious* and certain of God's presence. The soul rests in the peace of the *divine presence*, bound closely to the object of its love. See Mystical Union.

Prayer of thanksgiving 2637

The prayer of thanksgiving expresses gratitude to God for his many *blessings*. It characterizes the *prayer* of the Church in the *celebration* of the *Eucharist*, which gives thanks for the work of *salvation*.

Prayer of the heart

The prayer of the heart is also called *interior prayer*. It consists in prayer carried out in the *mind* and *heart* of an individual. See Prayer 2664.

Preaching Friars

Dominican Friars or Preaching Friars are members of the Dominican order. They are also called Preaching Brothers. See Dominicans.

Pre-catechumenate

Initiation into the *Catholic Church* begins with an extended period of preparation generally referred to as the *catechumenate*. It begins with the pre-catechumenate or inquiry stage, and generally consists in a series of meetings in which the *person* asks questions, gathers information or corrects misunderstandings about the Church, and decides whether or not to continue preparation for reception into the Church. See RCIA 1232.

Precept

A precept is a command given to a particular *person* by his *ecclesiastical superior*. It binds the *person* wherever he may be, but it cannot be enforced outside the *jurisdiction* of the *superior*.

Precept also refers to the rules of life and conduct that must be followed to attain *salvation*, such as the *Ten Commandments*. Members of the *Catholic faithful* are also bound by the *precepts of the Church*.

Besides precepts, the *New Law* also includes the *evangelical counsels* of *poverty*, *chastity*, and *obedience*. The *virtuous* life of the *Gospel* always calls for a *generosity* that goes beyond exact observance of precepts. This ideal of whole-hearted and free service takes the form of *counsels*. The counsels are *rules* of life offered to those who, not satisfied with the minimum observances, aim at greater *moral* perfection by removing even obstacles to *spiritual* growth.

The distinction between the precepts and the counsels is drawn in relation to *charity*, the *perfection* of *Christian* life. The precepts are intended to remove what is incompatible with charity and the counsels aim at removing whatever is not contrary to charity but might hinder its development. See Evangelical counsels 915.

Precepts of the Church 2041

The precepts or *commandments of the Church* are *obligations* relating to the *moral life*, which is "bound to and nourished by *liturgical life*. The *obligatory* character of these positive laws decreed by *pastoral authorities* is meant to guarantee to the *faithful* the very necessary minimum in the spirit of *prayer* and *moral* effort, in the growth in *love* of God and neighbor" (CCC 2041).

The precepts of the Church are:

1) Assist at "Mass on *Sundays* and *holy days of obligation* and rest from servile labor" (CCC 2042). Holy days of obligation vary from country to country.

According to the *Code of Canon Law*, the Sunday rest is from: "those works and affairs which hinder the worship to be rendered to God, the joy proper to the Lord's day, or the suitable relaxation of *mind* and body" (Canon 1247).

2) *Confess* one's sins at least once a year.

3) Receive *Holy Communion* at least once a year during *Easter Time* (this is called the *Easter duty*).

4) *Fast* and *abstain* on the days appointed by the Church.

5) Provide for the needs of the Church.

Though these precepts bind under pain of *sin*, certain circumstances can *dispense* a person from keeping them.

Precursor 718

The word 'precursor' comes from the Latin meaning fore-runner. It refers to St. John the Baptist who prepared the way for the Lord.

Predestination 600

Predestination is defined by St. Augustine as 'the *foreknowledge* and preparation of the *blessings* of God by which whomsoever are saved are saved.'

St. Thomas tells us that predestination is 'the plan of transmission of the *rational* creature to his last end, a plan preexisting or foreseen in the divine mind.' For both these great Doctors predestination involves both an *intellectual* and volitional aspect in the mind of God: foreknowledge and preparation. In the words of St. John 'this is love, not that we loved God first, but that he loved us and sent us his Son to be an *expiation* for our sins' (1 Jn 5:10). The election of anyone to *glory* is not contingent on foreseen *merit*, but simply on God's *love*. In a word, our first *grace* and, therefore, everything following upon this first grace is radically gratuitous, a gift of *mercy* given prior to any consideration of future merit. In a word, if we arrive in heaven, it is precisely because of grace. At the same time, that prior love on God's part makes possible our merit as well.

It is *heresy*, however, to conclude from the revealed fact of predestination that God does not have a serious intention to save all men and that

Christ died only for some, not for all. God willed to save all and makes possible the *salvation* of all. But he endowed *man* with *free will* and foresaw that some would not accept his *grace*, and so he did not include these in the number of the *elect*.

God does not condemn anyone to hell regardless of his merits or demerits, but only because when man chooses to *sin*, he freely rejects salvation. Predestination precedes merit and makes merit possible, somewhat like how our creation precedes any work of *value* on our part and makes that work possible.

Reprobation, however, only follows upon our sins. Thus, if anyone attains the glory of *heaven*, it is first of all because of God's love and grace, but not without merit. He has, first of all, God to thank for this. Hence, there is a very significant difference between predestination and the reprobation of a sinner who definitively refuses God's love. Predestination is always prior to any consideration of merit, a pure unconditional gift. Reprobation in Catholic *belief* is always contingent on the demerit of man.

If anyone is in *hell*, it is simply because he refused God's love and union with him. He has no one to blame but himself. He is there by his own choice. Why one would make such a choice is an unfath-omable *mystery*, but it is not a reason to deny the truth of predestination.

Because this mystery is a mystery of God's intellect and *will*, in great part beyond our *apprehension* in this time of *pilgrimage*, it is impossible for us to make *valid* inferences from what has been revealed, e.g., that because the saved are predestined prior to any consideration of their merit, therefore the reprobate are condemned prior to any consideration of their demerit. This is a heresy more than once condemned by the Church. But neither can we conclude that because the condemnation of the damned is on the basis of their demerit, therefore, as the *Pelagians* have always argued, the glory of the elect is first granted them on the basis of their merit. In revealing, then, the true nature of predestination and of reprobation, God has wisely *abstained* from telling us who may be in heaven or hell. He has told only enough to enable us to appreciate two things. First, at the speculative level of *theology* any explanation that adopts aspects of one or another of the two extremes just mentioned, predestinationism or Pelagianism, is false. And at the practical level, the wisdom of an old practical *axiom* governing the correct conduct of our lives during a time of pilgrimage cannot be overstressed in view of peace of mind: work as though everything depends on you and pray as though everything depends on God. Anyone living thus 'in fear and trembling' will reach heaven without knowing beforehand if he is predestined or not predestined among the elect.

Predicate/Predicated

To predicate is to affirm or deny that something is a quality, *attribute*, or property of a subject.

In *logic*, the term proposition refers to a *judgment* expressed as a sentence. It consists of a subject and a predicate. In the *proposition*, the predicate affirms or denies something about a subject.

The subject of a *proposition* is that part of the proposition about which something is said or predicated. In the proposition 'John is happy,' the subject of the proposition is John.

The predicate of a *proposition* is the assertion or statement made or denied about the subject of the proposition. In 'John is happy,' 'happy' asserts something about John. Thus, happy is being predicated about John. See Proposition.

Preface

The preface is the *prayer* of *thanksgiving* that forms the *solemn* introduction to the *Canon* or *anaphora* of the *Mass*.

In the *Latin Rite*, the pref-ace is recited or sung by the *celebrant;* in other *rites* it is recited silently with an *ekphonesis* (raising of the voice) before the *Sanctus*.

It is strictly forbidden to accompany the singing of the preface by playing the organ or some other instrument. See Anaphora. Also see Canon of the Mass.

Prefect

A prefect is the *person* officially responsible for insuring that the specific duties of a *prefecture* are carried out. See Prefecture.

Prefecture

The word prefecture is derived from the Latin word 'praefectus,' meaning overseer, head, or supervisor. A prefecture is a department with specific duties under the direction of a *prefect* who is officially responsible for insuring that the specific duties of a department are carried out. See Papal household.

Preferential love 2448

Preferential love is a love that shows prior favor, choice, special liking for, or estimation of someone before or above others.

Those "oppressed by poverty are the object of a preferential love on the part of the Church which, since her origin and in spite of the failings of many of her members, has not ceased to work for their relief, defense, and liberation through numerous works of charity" (CCC 2448).

Prefiguring 720

To prefigure means to represent something beforehand by a figure or type.

Prelapsarian man

Prelapsarian man means man before the *fall*. The word comes from 'pre,' before, and 'lapsus,' fall in Latin. Prelapsarian man refers to the state of man in *Eden* before the fall from *grace* with God through the *original sin*. See Integrity. Also see Original sin 389; Preternatural gift.

Prelate

A prelate is a *cleric* who has some form of *ecclesiastical jurisdiction*. See Prelature.

Prelate nullius

A prelate nullius refers to someone who has independent *jurisdiction* over a district which is not under the jurisdiction of a *diocesan bishop*. He is usually a *titular* bishop, but even if he is not, he has the same *ordinary jurisdictional* powers and *obligations* as a bishop (Canon 370). He may administer *Confirmation*, *consecrate churches*, and vote in an *ecumenical council* if summoned. See Prelature.

Prelates of Honor of His Holiness

Prelates of Honor are hon-

orary *prelates* who have no special *jurisdiction* or power. Outside the English-speaking world, all prelates enjoy the title of *Monsignor*, or its equivalent, meaning in English: My Lord. In the English-speaking world only prelates of honor are called *Monsignori*. One grade of prelate of honor enjoying the title Monsignor is that of Prelate of Honor of His Holiness. See Monsignor, Also see Prelature.

Prelature

Prelature refers to the office of an *ecclesiastical* dignitary of higher rank and *authority*. A *prelate* ordinarily has some form of ordinary ecclesiastical *jurisdiction*, such as a *bishop*, *archbishop*, *metropolitan*, *patriarch*, the *abbot* or *prior* of a *religious* house, or the *superior* of a religious *order*. A prelate who has independent jurisdiction over a district not under the *jurisdiction* of a *diocesan bishop*, such as an abbot, is called a *prelate nullius* to distinguish him from a bishop.

There are also honorary prelates, in the English-speaking world addressed with the Italian title of *Monsignor*, who have no special jurisdiction or power. There are three types of prelates of honor: *Protonotaries Apostolic*, *Prelates of Honor of His Holiness*, and *Chaplains of His Holiness*. Honorary prelates wear a garb similar to that of bishops.

Domestic prelate is an honorary distinction conferred by the *Pope* on priests in recognition of special *merit*. They are considered members of the *Papal Household*.

The Papal Household is the *prefecture* of the *Roman Curia* that manages the living quarters. The *prefect* in charge is a *titular bishop*.

Pontifical family refers to all those persons in the immediate service of the Pope who fulfill duties in his household.

A *personal prelature* is a special type of prelature established by the *Holy See* under the *jurisdiction* of a prelate appointed by the *Roman Pontiff*. See Particular church 833.

Premise

A premise is a statement or assertion that serves as the basis for an argument in *logic*. It is sometimes called a *proposition*. See Reason. Also see Deductive.

Prenatal diagnosis 2274

Prenatal diagnosis refers to a medical diagnosis made to assess the physical condition of a *fetus*. Such a diagnosis is permitted "if it respects the life and *integrity* of the *embryo* and the *human* fetus and is directed toward its safe guarding or healing as an individual... It is gravely opposed to the *moral law* when this is done with the thought of possibly inducing an *abortion*, depending upon the results: a diagnosis must not be the equivalent of a death sentence" (CCC 2274).

"One must hold as licit procedures carried out on the human embryo which respect the life and integrity of the embryo and do not involve disproportionate risks for it, but are directed toward its healing the improvement of its condition of health, or its individual survival."

"It is *immoral* to produce human embryos intended for exploitation as disposable biological material" (CCC 2275).

Presbyter

Presbyter is another name for *priest*. See Presbyterate 1536.

Presbyterate 1536

The presbyterate refers to the office of the *priest*. The term *presbyter* is used to distinguish between priests and *bishops*. The word comes from Greek and means *elder*; is used in referring to someone appointed to oversee the life of a community.

A bishop has the fullness of *Holy Orders*, and the priests who assist him receive and exercise their *ecclesial* role and function under his *jurisdiction*. The body of priests who serve under the Bishop is also called the presbyterate.

Presbyterium 1567

'Presbyterium' refers to *priests* who serve as the

prudent cooperators, supports, and instruments of the *Bishop*. They constitute, with their Bishop, a college called the *presbyterium* in Latin or *presbyterate* in English.

"Priests can exercise their *ministry* only in dependence on the bishop and in communion with him... The bishop considers them his co-workers, his sons, his brothers and his friends, and that they in return owe him love and obedience" (CCC 1567). See Presbyterate.

Presbytery

The presbytery is a term that can be used to refer to the whole *choir* of a large *church*, but usually refers to the space between the *choir-stalls* and the *altar* steps. See Church 752.

Presentation

In the third stage of *Christian initiation*, after three *scrutinies*, candidates are presented with the Creed, and on the Fifth *Sunday* of *Lent* they are presented with the *Lord's Prayer* and *anointing*. These presentations indicate a more intimate relationship to the *faith* that they are going to accept at their *final initiation* on Holy Saturday. See RCIA 1232

Presentation in the temple 529

The presentation in the temple refers to a *Jewish* ceremony in which the first-born

male was formally offered or presented to God in the *temple*. It was a *religious* act of thanksgiving for the *salvation* of the first-born of the *Israelites* from the avenging *angel* during the final plague in Egypt before the *Exodus*.

As a *Christian feast*, it refers to the *ceremonial Jewish* presentation of *Christ* in the Temple recorded in Lk 2:22–39.

Presumption 2092

Presumption is a *vice* opposed to the *virtue* of *hope*.

"There are two kinds of presumption. Either *man* presumes upon his own capacities (hoping to be able to save himself without help from on high), or he presumes upon God's almighty power or his *mercy* (hoping to obtain his *forgiveness* without *conversion* and *glory* without *merit*)" (CCC 2092).

Of itself, presumption is a *mortal sin*, but only acting or appearing presumptuous is *venial*. One can overcome the sin of presumption by *prayer*, receiving the *sacraments*, and cultivating the gift of *fear of the Lord*.

Preternatural

The term preternatural is composed of the Latin prefix 'preter': beyond, and the word 'naturalis,' meaning natural. A thing is called preternatural when it surpasses the *attributes*, powers, and *exigencies* normal for a particular kind of *created nature,* but not those of every created nature. Thus, *angels* possess qualities and powers, such as acute *intelligence,* that is natural for them, but preternatural for men.

The term *'supernatural'* refers to gifts that surpass the *exigencies,* powers, and attributes of all creatures, for example, *sanctifying grace.* See Spiritism 2117. Also see Preternatural gift.

Preternatural attributes

Natural *attributes* are those powers, characteristics, or qualities of a thing needed for it to be a particular kind of *being.* Contrasted with these are preternatural attributes, which are powers and characteristics above and beyond the powers and characteristics required to be a particular kind of *being.* They perfect the being, but they do not change the *nature* of the being receiving them.

Before the fall, our first parents enjoyed the preternatural attributes of *infused knowledge, integrity, immortality,* and *impassibility.* These gifts were consistent with their human nature and perfected it, but they did not change *human nature.* See Preternatural gift. Also see Original sin 389; Original justice 376.

Preternatural gift

A preternatural gift is a favor granted by God beyond the powers or capacities of the *per-son* enjoying it or of the *nature* on which it is bestowed, but not necessarily beyond those of every person or beyond the normal conditions of every creature.

Preternatural gifts perfect a particular nature but do not raise it beyond the limits of its *created* order. The gifts of *infused knowledge, integrity, immortality,* and *impassibility* in *man's* first parents in the *Garden of Eden* were preternatural gifts.

The gift of infused knowledge was both *secular* and *spiritual.* Because Adam and Eve were created as adults and were the first teachers of their children, the gift of knowledge was *miraculously* conferred on them. The gift of integrity refers to a total absence of *concupiscence* by virtue of which man's whole sensitive and imaginative life were completely under the control of and ruled by reason. Through the gift of *immortality,* man was free from death, he would not die. By the gift of *impassibility,* man was free from suffering. This did not mean that man could not feel pain, but that he was free from pain caused by fallen nature.

Preternatural gifts are distinguished from the *supernatural* gifts that make possible actions beyond our nature and belong only to God, such as *habitual* or *sanctifying grace.* See Original justice 376.

Preternatural mysteries

Preternatural *mysteries* are mysteries that can be comprehended or understood once they are known by *revelation*, such as creation by a personal God. See Mystery 359.

Prevenient grace

Prevenient comes from the Latin word 'praevenire,' meaning to come before or precede. Prevenient grace is a form of *actual grace* given as an *inspiration* or *illumination* of the *Holy Spirit* preceding an *act of the will*.

Prevenient grace is the beginning of all *salvific* actions by *man* because it serves to enlighten the *mind* and stir up the will to the work of *salvation*.

In the arousal of the will by *actual grace*, there are two stages. The first is prevenient grace, which moves the will spontaneously and makes it incline to God. The second stage is *cooperating grace*, which continues to arouse the will and supports it while it acts.

Prevenient grace may be freely accepted or rejected. If it is accepted, it is because of a further grace, or the same grace under a different aspect called *consequent* or *cooperating grace*.

Thus, it comes about that God first moves us to act in a salutary way through prevenient grace and then gives us further grace to freely accept a movement already begun, making it fruitful by our cooperation. See Grace 35.

Pride 1866

Pride is a high or exaggerated opinion of one's own qualities, attainments, or estate that gives rise to a feeling and attitude of superiority over and contempt for others. The *capital sin* or *vice* of pride is opposed to the *virtue* of *humility*.

Pride is manifested in three ways: contempt for *lawful authority*, contempt for equals and inferiors, and the desire to surpass others. *Ambition, presumption*, and *vainglory* are forms of pride.

Because pride is part of every sin, it is perhaps the most difficult sin to overcome. Efforts to practice *humility*, a life of *prayer*, frequent *examination of conscience*, reception of the *sacraments*, and the effort to avoid even *venial sin* are all necessary to combat pride. The practice of voluntary *penance* and *fasting* can strengthen our resolve to overcome pride with the *grace* of God.

Priest/Priesthood/Priestly

Priest is another name for *presbyter*, that is, a member of one of the three orders of *ordained ministers*. The term priest comes from a Greek word meaning *elder*, but in English priest designates a *person* whose primary ministry is *sacerdotal*, from the

Latin word 'sacerdos': one who sacrifices.

For many *Protestant* groups a presbyter is simply an elder who governs, but does not offer *sacrifice*. The chief *duty* of a *Catholic* priest is to offer the *Sacrifice of the Mass*. The office of the priest is called the *presbyterate*.

Priesthood is the state of being a priest. See Holy Orders 1536.

Priest of the first order

'Priests of the first order' are *bishops* because they have the fullness of the *priesthood*. They can *ordain* other *priests* and bishops and are the successor of the *Apostles* for their *dioceses*. See Major orders.

Priest of the second order

'Priests of the second order' are priests who assist the *Bishop* in caring for the *faithful* with preaching, offering the sacrifice of the *Mass* and administering the *sacraments*. See Major orders.

Priesthood of Christ

By his *Incarnation, Christ* offered to the Father all the acts of his life in his death on the Cross. In this supreme *sacrifice* he was both *victim* and *priest*. The priesthood of Christ is the only priesthood of the Church. It is manifested in the ministerial priesthood conferred by *Holy Orders* in which certain men are set aside to *perpetuate* the Sac-

rifice of *Calvary* through the *Mass*, to administer the *sacraments*, and preach the *Gospel*. See Sacerdos 1554.

Priesthood of the faithful

By virtue of their *Baptism*, all *Christians* have a *sacerdotal* function and *dignity*. By becoming man, the Son of God became united with all mankind and through *Baptism* he makes men participators in the *priesthood of Christ*. With Christ as their head, the baptized offer worship, *sacrifice*, and *glory* to God, especially in their *celebration* of the *Eucharist*. The baptized are a *priestly people*.

The priesthood of the faithful is distinct from the ministerial priesthood that is conferred by *Holy Orders*. See Priestly people 784, 901.

Priestly Code

The Priestly Code is part of the *Torah*. It is not found in the Torah in one place, but is scattered throughout the *Pentateuch*. It is referred to as the Priestly Code because the strictly *cultic* and *ritual* content could have no one in mind except those responsible for public *worship*. See Genesis.

Priestly office 897

The priestly office or *duty* of those in *Holy Orders*, by virtue of *ordination*, is to offer the *Mass, praise*, and thanksgiving to the *divine* majesty in the name of the Church. See Priestly people.

Priestly office of the laity or faithful

By virtue of their *Baptism*, all *Christians* have a *sacerdotal* function and *dignity*. Dedicated to *Christ* and *anointed* by the *Holy Spirit*, they are called and prepared so that all their works, *prayers*, *apostolic* activities, *family* life, daily work, relaxation, and even their hardships can become *spiritual sacrifices* acceptable to God through Christ. By the *holiness* of their lives, the *laity* *consecrate* the world to God and offer him their *worship* by uniting themselves to the *Sacrifice of the Mass*.

By becoming *man*, the *Son of God* became united with all mankind and, through Baptism, men were made participators in the *priesthood of Christ*. The baptized are a *priestly people*. See Priestly Office 901.

Priestly people 901

The phrase 'priestly people' is a way of referring to the *priesthood of the faithful*. By virtue of their *Baptism*, all receive a *sacerdotal* function and *dignity*. See Priestly Office of the laity or faithful.

Primacy

Primacy means first in rank. It is applied to the *Pope* who, as *Bishop* of Rome, holds the primacy of *jurisdiction* and possesses full and supreme *teaching*, *legislative*, and *sacerdotal* powers in the *Catholic Church*.

This primacy was promised by *Christ* when he told Peter that Peter was to be the rock upon which he would build his Church. This primacy is a *dogma* of the Church.

Failure to acknowledge this primacy of the Pope is basic to the *schisms* that separates other *Christian* communities from the Church of Rome.

Primary cause

The primary cause is the first uncaused *cause*. Everything that exists, has its *being* either of necessity or by participation. The being of whatever exists by participation is caused and has an imparted or shared being ultimately from a being which is itself necessary and uncaused. This shared existence or being comes about by a direct creative act of God, the first uncaused cause.

Created beings are called creatures because they came to be out of nothing by the act of *creation*. God cannot share his own being, which is *infinite* and indivisible, because God's being is himself.

There is no cause outside of what God wills to create. His act of creation is absolutely free because he has no need of *creatures*. Not even God's goodness moves him necessarily to create.

God is changeless or *immu-*

table. He can *decree* changeable things without himself being changed. In creating, he remains the primary cause of all that is not him, but because the things he creates are not necessary beings, they can change. They came from nothingness into being by the act of *divine creation.*

Creatures can be true causes, but only secondarily, because whatever they produce already exists *potentially* in some way. Things can come into existence from *secondary causes* either as products of natural forces or as products of *man's* activity.

God wills that *secondary causes act* according to their *natures* either by necessity or *contingency.* Causes are *necessary causes* when their effects come about as a result of their nature acting as an operating cause. The weathering of stone results from the necessary action of weather.

Other causes act by contingency. They require other conditions outside of themselves in order to produce their effects. Seeds can only grow when temperature, moisture, and light are present in certain measure; without these the seed will not produce a plant. The seed is a contingent cause because it depends on something outside of itself in order to function as a cause. Thus God wills things to be changeable because created beings are in some way interdependent by their *natures.*

God does not impose necessity on *free will* or on contingent causes. On the other hand, nothing that occurs in this world is outside the order of *divine providence* and the intelligent design of the *Creator* of the universe.

Man is created with a free will. Free will is a contingent cause because the effects of *free choice* depend on the choices that man makes. See Divine providence 302. Also see Divine plan; First cause 308.

Primary sense of Scripture 115, 116

The primary or etymological sense of *Sacred Scripture* refers to the meaning derived from the origin and history of the words used to express Scripture, or from the study of their elements and history. It is also called the *literal* sense. See Literal sense of Scripture. Also see Senses of Scripture 115, 116.

Primate/Primatial

A primate is a *bishop* who is not a *patriarch* but has *jurisdiction* over all the *metropolitans* of a district or country. The position is no longer recognized by the 1983 *Code of Canon Law,* but numerous *archbishops* still retain the title. See Council 465.

Prime

Prime is the hour of the *Divine Office* that comes after *Lauds*. Lauds is the praise offered to God at dawn, and Prime entrusts the day and its labors to God. It is not found in the *Ordinary Form*, but is still prayed in the *Extraordinary Form*.

Prime matter

Prime matter is that aspect of a material *being* that makes it a *material* body. Prime matter is a *part-principle* and requires *substantial form*, which gives it a specific *character*, in order to be or exist. This understanding of the *nature* of being is referred to as the *hylomorphic theory*. See Form 365.

Principle

A principle is that from which something proceeds or flows in any way or on which it depends as its origin or source of *being* or *action*. Principle is distinct from *cause* because, although every cause is a principle, not every principle is a cause. For example, in Christianity the truths of *faith* are principles of *moral* conduct but are not the causes of virtuous conduct. See Dualism 285.

Principle of solidarity 1939, 1940, 2407

Solidarity is a bond of brotherhood and *charity*, a kind of *fraternal* union imposed on us by our common origin and the equality of all men by which we are all one and united in a common bond.

The principle of solidarity is the quality on the part of communities that unites them in some respects, like interests, sympathies, or aspirations. International solidarity is required for the *moral order*. World peace depends upon it.

Solidarity may also refer to the shared *moral* responsibility of two or more *persons* in carrying out a single *action*, usually very complex, for example, a bank robbery or the commission of an *abortion*.

Prior

Prior is the title of the *superior* of a *Priory*. See Superior. Religious. Also see Priory.

Priory

Smaller houses, or offshoots of an *abbey*, are called *priories*. Priories remain either financially or *jurisdictionally* dependent on their founding abbey or *motherhouse*. See Particular church 833. Also see Abbey.

Private chapel

A private chapel is established for the exclusive use of one or more persons. The permission of the *local ordinary* is required for the establishment of a private chapel and for *sacred celebrations* to take place therein. A *bishop* may establish for himself a private chapel, which enjoys the same rights as an *oratory*. It is appropriate for oratories and private chapels to be blessed. See Oratory.

Private confession

Private confession refers to the secret auricular *confession* of *sins* to a *priest* in order to receive *absolution*. See General confession.

Private consistory

A private consistory is one in which only *cardinals* participate. See Consistory.

Private Mass

'Private Mass' can refer to an unscheduled/unannounced *Mass* or a Mass *celebrated* in private. In previous times, it was also used to describe a *Low Mass*.

The term has been discouraged and replaced with "Missa sine populo," or "Mass without a congregation," to underline that the "Mass is not something private, even if a *priest* celebrates it privately; instead, it is an act of *Christ* and of the Church" (Bl. Pope Paul VI, *encyclical Mysterium Fidei*, 1965)

Private or personal prayer 2664

Private or personal *prayer* is the prayer of an individual acting alone. See Prayer.

Private penance

Private penance is *penance* done by an individual at his own discretion for the sake of making *reparation* for *sin*. It may take the form of *mortification*, *prayer*, or any good work performed in the spirit of *repentance* for sin. See Penance 1460.

Private revelation 66

A private revelation is a *manifestation* from God to private individuals for their own personal *spiritual* welfare and that of others. It is different from *pubic revelation*, which is found in *Sacred Scripture* and *Tradition* and given to the entire *human* race as necessary for its *sanctification* and *salvation*.

At times, *private revelations* may be approved and recognized by the *authority* of the Church, but they are never objects of *divine faith* binding one in *conscience* to believe on God's *authority* or according to the mind of the Church.

Private revelations take the form of *supernatural* visions, words, locutions, divine touches, or, often, a combination of these.

Privileged community 2206

According to *The Catechism of the Catholic Church*, the "relationships within the *family* bring an affinity of feelings, affections and interests, arising above all from the members' respect for one another. The family is a privileged community called to achieve a 'sharing of thought and common *deliberation* by the *spouses* as well as their eager cooperation as parents in the children's upbringing'" (CCC 2206).

Pro-choice

Pro-choice refers to a politically inspired *legal fiction* promoted by *libertarians* to justify an individualistic interpretation of *sexual morality*, particularly regarding *artificial birth control* and *abortion*. It is fictional because it is based on a false mechanistic interpretation of the human faculty of *procreation*, centering exclusively on sexual pleasure and totally excluding God and the *Divine Plan* from sexuality. See Reproductive rights. Also see Regulation of procreation 2368; End of marriage 2366.

Problem of evil

See Question of evil 309.

Procession of Divine Persons

The expression 'procession of Divine Persons' refers to the manner in which the *Divine Persons* are related to one another within the *Trinity* itself. The Son is said to proceed from the Father by *generation*. It is through procession by generation that the Son is *begotten* of the Father.

The *Holy Spirit* proceeds from the Father and the Son as from a single *principle* by *spiration*, an act of mutual *love* of the Father and the Son. Spiration is distinguished from generation, which is

applied only to the Son. The Father is not said to proceed because he is the origin without origin of the processions, and his relation to the other Persons is implied in their relationship to him. For this reason, he is called the First Person. By reason of their one, uncreated being, all three Persons are first in relation to creatures and all creatures are dependent for their being on the Divine Persons.

Because these processions are *eternal* aspects of the Trinity they cannot be understood as meaning that they follow one another as *cause* and effect or in sequence as do creatures. They occur within the Trinity itself as part of its *nature*.

Because of the *Incarnation* of the Son, the notion of his generation from the Father is more easily grasped though it remains mysterious. The origin of the Holy Spirit through spiration is harder to grasp because, though it is an inter-Trinitarian act, it differs somehow from generation.

To express the Church's teaching on this matter and defend the *divinity* of the Holy Spirit against the *Macedonians*, the first *Ecumenical Council* of Constantinople in 381 declared that the Holy Spirit proceeds from the Father. To ensure that this statement was not misunderstood to mean that the Holy Spirit proceeded from the

Father alone, the term *'filioque'* was later added to the *Nicene Creed*. See Mission of the Holy Spirit 485.

Processions

Processions are *sacred* functions in which the *clergy* and people parade from one place to another. They may take place within the *church* or outside. They are public *acts* of homage to God to honor him or his *saints*. They ask for *divine* favor, give thanks for *blessings* received, or beg pardon for *sins*. See Solemn.

Proclamation of the Gospel

The proclamation of the *Gospel* is the announcing of *Christ* to the world to make him known and loved by all. It takes place by speaking, writing, all forms of communication, and especially by reflecting the *virtue* of Christ in one's own life and behavior.

This proclamation is the *duty* of every *Christian* by virtue of his *Baptism*.

Additionally, during the *Liturgy of the Word*, the Gospel is not just read, but is 'proclaimed.' See Ambo 1184.

Proclivity to sin 1865

The proclivity to sin refers to the *perverse* inclination, tendency, propensity, or predisposition to *evil* that by clouding the *intellect* can corrupt the concrete *judgment* of *good* and evil. Though *sin* tends to reinforce and reproduce itself,

it cannot completely destroy the *moral sense* in the *heart* of *man*. God's *grace* is always sufficient to overcome the attraction of sin. By God's *grace*, man can overcome this inclination to evil. Practicing *virtue* makes it easier to choose the good.

Procreate/Procreative/Procreation

Procreate comes from the Latin word 'procreare,' meaning to create on behalf of, that is, with God. The word in English means to *beget* young.

The Church does not use the word *reproduction* in reference to begetting children. Reproduction suggests that begetting a child is an act entirely under *human* control and a process by which a purely biological product is produced. Used in this mechanistic or impersonal sense, reproduction provides the *philosophical rationale* for the notion of 'reproductive rights' used to justify *artificial birth control* and *abortion*. Because they are *persons*, humans must be 'procreated' because they have *immortal souls*. Animals are produced by purely biological processes because they have mortal animal souls, not spiritual and immortal souls.

The Church teaches that children are always a gift of God and he is the essential *agent* in their *creation*. She uses the word *procreation*, not reproduction, in order to indicate that man shares in God's creative act of procreating children. The close association of the *conjugal act* with the *divine* act of creation gives this *act* its *dignity* and makes it *holy*. For this reason the conjugal act must always be open to the gift of God's creation to be *morally* good. See Regulation of procreation 2368, Also see End of marriage 2366; Domestic church 1655, 1656.

Prodigal son

The Prodigal Son is a *parable* of *Christ* found in Lk 15:11–32. The parable reveals the boundless *mercy* of God. It narrates the *exile* and homecoming of a son who demanded his inheritance before his father's death, squandered it, and returned *repentant* to his father's house. His father forgives him and restores him to the family bestowing on him a robe and ring, symbols of *authority*. See Purity of vision.

Profanation/Profaning

Profanation means being violated, defiled, or *desecrated*. *Profaning* or unworthily treating the *sacraments* and other *liturgical* actions, as well as *persons*, things, or places consecrated to God, is called a *sacrilege*. It is a *grave sin* especially when committed against the *Eucharist*. See Sacrilege 2120.

Profane writing

Profane writing is writing that is *secular* in nature, not *sacred*. It does not imply an unfavorable *judgment*. See Canon of Scripture 120.

Profession, religious

See Religious profession. Also see Religious life 925; Consecrated life 916.

Profession of faith 187

The profession of faith is also called the *Creed* or *Symbol of Faith*. It is a brief summary of the *essential* elements that a *person* must profess in order to be a member of the Church. The profession of faith was intended especially for candidates for *Baptism*. It is called a creed because it begins with the word *credo*, meaning 'I believe.'

Professional secret 2491

Professional secrets consist of *knowledge* possessed by those in public office, soldiers, physicians, lawyers or others to whom confidential information is given under the seal of secrecy.

Such secrets must not be shared with others except in unusual circumstances where keeping the secret would cause very great harm to the one who confided it, to the one who received it, or to a third party, and the harm can only be avoided by divulging the *truth*.

The secret of the *sacrament* of *Penance* refers to the *inviolable* secrecy, which must be observed by the *confessor* and all others, such as translators, someone who overhears a confession, or someone who may otherwise have knowledge of matter confessed in the sacrament of Penance.

It is a crime for a *confessor* in any way to betray a penitent by word or in any other manner or for any reason. A *priest* who reveals such matter incurs a *latae sententiae excommunication* that can be *absolved* only by the *Pope*. See Secret of the Sacrament of Reconciliation 2490.

Progress, earthly 1049

Progress in an earthly sense refers to *material* and *intellectual* development, moving to higher stages by way of continuous improvement. Such earthly progress is implied in the command to man to increase and subdue the earth given in *Genesis*.

In regard to the Church, progress is not limited merely to quantitative or materialistic increase in membership in the Kingdom of *Christ*. The Church must bear fruit in the *Holy Spirit*. This *spiritual progress* focuses on the *morality* of *man's* behavior and his conformity to the *divine plan* or *will of God*. Spiritual progress contributes to the *salvation* of *souls* and forming of *human society* into the *Kingdom of God*. It is through the spiritual progress of individuals in society that man is con-

formed to Christ and grows in *holiness*.

Prohibiting impediment

Prohibiting impediments, also called hindering impediments, are obstacles that make *marriage illicit* or illegal but not *invalid*. Hindering impediments were dropped in the 1983 *Code of Canon Law*; however, the impediment of *mixed religion* still requires the permission of the *Bishop*. See Impediment. Also see Diriment impediments; Nullity of a marriage 1629.

Prokimenon

A prokimenon is a short prayer, often a *psalm* verse, recited before beginning *meditation* or *spiritual reading* as a means of preparation or recollecting one's thoughts.

In the *Byzantine Rite* the prokimenon is the psalm verse chanted before the Epistle. See Psalter 2585.

Promises 2147

A promise is an assurance given to another *person* stating that one will do, or refrain from doing, some specified act in the future. Because such a promise involves *fidelity* and *truthfulness*, it binds a person in *justice*. See Promises to God 2101.

Promises to God 2101

Promises to God are assurances given to God that one will do, or refrain from, doing some specified *act* in the future. *Christians* make *sacramental promises* to God in *Baptism*, *Confirmation* and *Holy Orders*. What are often referred to as promises made at *Matrimony* are really *vows*.

Out of personal *devotion*, Christians may also make a promise to God to perform certain acts such as *prayers*, *almsgiving*, or making a *pilgrimage*. *Fidelity* to such promises is a sign of respect and love for a faithful God.

A promise is different from a vow, which is a *deliberate*, *obligatory*, and free promise made to God concerning a possible and better good that must be fulfilled by reason of the *virtue of religion*. Once made, the person making a vow cannot *dispense* himself from it; rather, if it is dispensable, he must seek dispensation from the proper Church *authorities*. The possibility of being dispensed and how high of an authority would be necessary to dispense it depends on the matter and manner of the vow.

Promoter of justice

The Promoter of Justice is the official appointed by the *Bishop* to act as judge in a *diocesan* court. The *Vicar General* often discharges this office. See Diocese 833.

Promotor of the Faith

At the stage of a *person's* cause for sainthood leading to *beatification*, a person called the Promoter of the Faith, also called the *'Advocatus Diaboli'* or *Devil's Advocate*, is appointed. He exercises the full *authority* to examine the candidate's life, *virtues*, writings, reputation for holiness, and any *miracles attributed* to the person's *intercession*.

The Promoter of the Faith may not always be appointed, because today the role of the Promoter of the Faith has changed. The *Relator*, not the Promoter of the Faith, is now responsible for supervising this process. It is his *duty* to raise all possible *legitimate* objections to approval. This function may be filled either by the Relator himself or by a person distinct from the Relator.

After beatification, another proven miracle must take place through the intercession of the *beatus* before he is formally declared a *saint*.

In the case of a *martyr*, the requirement of two *miracles* is not necessary for *canonization*, but for others this second extensive scrutiny of the candidate's *holiness* is undertaken. See Canonizing 828. Also see Canonization.

Promulgate/Promulgation

To promulgate means to make known officially. See Synod 887.

Proof for the existence of God

31

The proof for the existence of God is not proof in the sense of the *natural sciences,* but a cumulative conviction resulting from converging and convincing arguments. Because God cannot be subjected to controlled experiment; he cannot be proven *empirically.* Self-evident *truths* cannot be proven empirically either, but this does not make them less certain. See Divine providence 302.

Propagation

Propagation means spreading ideas or customs. Propagation of the *faith* refers to the act of spreading the *Gospel* through the whole world in *obedience* to the command of *Christ.* See Fathers of the Church 11.

Proper/Proper of the Mass

The proper of the *Mass* refers to those parts that change according to the *feast* or *liturgical season.*

Proper of Saints

The Proper of Saints refers to the *liturgical* passages appointed to be recited for the *feasts* of *saints* throughout the year. See Liturgical seasons.

Proper of Seasons

The Proper of Seasons refers to the *liturgical* passages appointed to be recited for the days of the *liturgical sea-* sons. It parallels the *Proper of Saints.* See Liturgical seasons.

Prophecy

The term prophecy is often associated, almost exclusively, with the notion of predicting the future, but this is not what it primarily represented to the *Israelites,* for whom prophecy was a form of *divine* guidance to the meaning of divine *revelation* for the future.

The futuristic aspects of prophecy were present, either because the *prophet* offered an analysis of the present and announced the *consequences* of current behavior if the words from God he spoke were not accepted, or because, especially in the *Old Testament,* he indicated the conditions and time of the fulfillment of the divine promise of a Savior toward which all *divine revelation* and guidance is directed.

The origins of prophecy are vague. Moses is called a *prophet* and other Israelites in his time exercised this *charism.* Before the *Jewish* monarchy was established there appeared groups called 'sons of the prophet.' They were organized for *worship* in the form of *cultic* song and dance, but they do not seem to have been directly associated with the temple *cult.* As associates of Elijah and Elisha, they lived in a community outside of a town acting as aids and messengers for their leaders. The sons of the prophet identified themselves with the cause represented by the prophet.

The *biblical* meaning of prophecy is not necessarily the *foretelling* of what is to come, rather it refers to one who speaks, acts, or writes under the extraordinary influence of God to make God's *counsels* and will known to man. In time, the predictive aspect became more prominent because the consequences of disobedience were often proclaimed along with the message and because the divine message ultimately had reference to the future coming of the promised *Messiah*-Savior, the *Word Incarnate.*

The Church teaches that prophecy involves the certain prediction of a future event that cannot be known by *natural* means, in particular the *Incarnation* and the last things of this world. This distinguishes it from *revelation,* scientific forecasts, predictions, or conjectures about the future. Prophecy belongs to the *supernatural* order because, directly or indirectly, it makes known supernatural *knowledge* related to man's *ultimate end.*

Private revelations may include references to the future, but Our *Lord* tells us the day and hour of his final coming will not be included in genuine prophecies. See Charism. Also see Prophet; Prophetic formula.

Prophet

The English word 'prophet' is derived from the Greek word 'prophetes,' meaning one who speaks before others or on behalf of some other. In doing so, he communicates *divine revelation.* Today, prophet usually denotes the actual *person* who communicates divine revelation.

The prophet in ancient Israel was the authorized spokesman of the *divinity,* called to speak the truth fearlessly to the religious and political leaders of the people. The marks of a prophet were a *consciousness* of having been chosen and called by God, an awareness of having a message from God, and, with this awareness, the irresistible *mission* to make that message known in God's name.

Prophets are distinguished from the *oracles* or *seers* known in other ancient *religions* because of the *ethical* and *religious* content of their message. The prophet in *Israel* has no parallel in other *cultures* and *cults.* The resemblance between seers or diviners and *Israelite* prophets is merely in form.

The prophets do not appear to have been attached to any *temple* or *liturgical* cult. The 'sons of the prophet' seem to have been independent groups of worshipers, that is, they were not regular cult personnel, but were merely organized as disciples under a leader called a prophet who himself was not just an *ecstatic* worshiper, but another type of *religious* leader. The sons of the prophet identified themselves with the cause represented by the prophet they followed.

Moses was a supreme example of one who receives the *Word of God* and speaks it to Israel, and in that sense a unique type of *Christ* who is the one teacher of all, including the prophets of old. Christ as 'The Prophet' transcends Moses, as the *Son of God* in God's house, namely, Christ, transcends the mere servant there, e.g., Moses (Heb 3:1–6). See Prophetic Text 715. Also see Mosaic law.

Prophetic formula

Prophetic formula refers to the form of a prophetic statement indicating that what the *prophet* says comes from God. It is recognized by the words, 'Thus saith the Lord' or 'The word of the Lord.'

The term 'word,' in Semitic *culture*, was considered a *dynamic entity*. Words uttered with solemnity as in *marriage*, contracts, promises, *blessings*, and *curses* were rooted in the personality of the one uttering them.

The use of the expression: '*Word of God*,' in the *Old Testament* most often refers to the word of a prophet. The word of *Yahweh* came to the prophet as a dynamic and distinct reality, as it were, an extension

of the *person* of Yahweh. The words of prophecy are fulfilled when the reality of the word-thing reaches its fullness.

The *divine* utterance is the first recorded event in the Old Testament. There the word of Yahweh is a creative *agent* and creation becomes a word-thing.

In the *New Testament* the word signifies the *Gospel* proclaimed by *Jesus*, the Word of God. The *Second Person* of the *Trinity* uttered by the Father is called the Word, expressing the notion that he, as the ultimate reality or 'word-reality' on being uttered, will not be fulfilled until he unites all things to himself. Because with the *Incarnation* the 'word-reality' or ultimate reality exists in time, prophetic utterance now has reference, both to the past which it fulfills and to the future still to come which it in someway anticipates. See Prophetic Text 715.

Prophetic mission 905

The prophetic mission of *ordained ministers* and *laity* alike is to bear witness to the *Gospel* in word and example. The prophetic mission of the *baptized* and the ordained ministry alike is expressed in the words of *Christ* to 'Go therefore and teach all nations' (Mt 28:19).

Prophetic office 785, 904

The prophetic office refers to the *duty* of the *ordained min-*

isters of the Church and of the *laity* to bear witness to the *Gospel* in word and example. 'Go therefore and teach all nations' (Mt 28:19).

Prophetic people

A *prophet* is one called by God to speak in his name. By *Baptism*, Christians are called to live the *Word of God* and bear witness to all nations in his name. They are, therefore, a prophetic people.

Prophetic texts 715

Prophetic texts are oral or written utterances of a *prophet* as a declaration of the *divine will*. Prophecy is the *revelation* itself given under *divine inspiration* revealing the *will* or message of God.

The form of a prophetic statement indicates that what the prophet says comes from God. It is recognized by the words, 'Thus saith the Lord' or 'The word of the Lord.' Such words are called the *prophetic formula*.

Prophetic tradition 2697

'Prophetic tradition' refers to the instruction and guidance offered in the *Pentateuch*. It is dominated by certain *theological* ideas such as the election of *Israel* by *Yahweh* to be his people, the importance of observing the law, especially the repudiation of foreign gods, a broad humanitarian concern for fellow *Israelites* as well as foreigners, and confi-

dence in the power of Yahweh. It is also referred to as the *deuteronomic tradition*.

Propitiate/Propitiation

Propitiate means to regain favor, appease, or conciliate. A 'propitiation' is a *sacrifice* made to God to restore his favor. See Expiate 1459.

Propitiatory

On top of the *Ark of the Covenant* there was a gold plate called the 'kapporet' in *Hebrew*. It is translated as *'mercy seat,'* or *'propitiatory'* in English, the place where *Yahweh* receives *atonement*. Two *cherubim* facing each other were atop the Ark, so constructed that their wings overshadowed the 'kapporet,' where Yahweh meets Israel and reveals his commandments as from his throne. The overshadowing of the wings symbolized covering the eyes of God who in his *mercy* would not see the *sins* of the *Israelites*. See Kapporet. Also see Mercy seat.

Propitious

Propitious means favorably inclined or disposed. See Spiritism 2117.

Proportion (property of beauty)

See Beauty 341.

Proposition

In logic the term proposition refers to a judgment expressed as a sentence. It consists of a *judgment* about the relationship between a subject and a *predicate*. In the proposition, the predicate affirms or denies something about a subject. See Horns of a dilemma 589. Also see Predicate.

Proscribe 2110

In general, proscribe refers to the act of rejecting, condemning, or denouncing something as useless or dangerous and prohibited.

It is used in reference to teaching or practices contrary to Church teaching or practice.

Proscription 2262

A proscription identifies that which is prohibited, condemned, rejected, denounced, or declared useless, dangerous, or sinful.

Prosopon 467

Prosopon is the conception or external representation of one of the *Persons* of the *Trinity*. It is also used in Greek *theology* as an alternative to *hypostasis* to explain the plurality of Persons in the Godhead. The root meaning of prosopon means face, not person, and refers to the mask used by actors in the theater to represent different parts.

In incarnational *theology*, prosopon often refers to the appearance of the *human* and *divine natures* of the *Word Incarnate* as a single person and *hypostasis*. This can also

mean 'mere' appearance, but not really one person.

Because of this ambiguity, it was often used by *Nestorians* to mask or veil their denial of the *substantial union* of divine and human natures in the unity of a single *Person* in *Jesus*. It was used as a *justification* of their insistence on a merely *moral* union of two really distinct persons, the Divine Word and the human Jesus, who remained distinct after their union. This is why the Church frowns on the use of prosopon in incarnational theology. See Hypostasis.

Prostitution 2355

Prostitution is the act of soliciting and accepting payment for *sexual intercourse*. Prostitution does injury to the *dignity* of those who engage in it because it reduces a *person* to a mere instrument of sexual pleasure and is in itself a *grave sin*.

The one who pays for prostitution sins gravely against God and injures himself by violating the *chastity* to which his *Baptism* has pledged him, defiling his body, the *temple of the Holy Spirit*.

Prostitution is a *social* scourge and is often accompanied by other criminal behavior and slavery.

Protagonist 852

A protagonist is the chief personage in a drama or the principal character in the plot of a story. A protagonist may also be the leading personage in a contest, a prominent supporter of a cause, or even the most important individual in a situation or course of events.

Protestant

Protestants are *persons* who adhere to a religious group or *sect* that separated from the *Catholic Church* at the time of the *Protestant Reformation*. The name protestant was first used by Fredrick of Saxony who protested against an action of the *Diet of Speyer* in 1529 that *allowed* Catholic *worship*. Protestant comes from a Latin word meaning to witness against, namely, to protest.

Protestant sects hold a variety of *beliefs*, but generally they believe that *Jesus Christ* is *Lord* and *Redeemer* (although since the Reformation, and especially today, a great many claiming to be Protestant deny this central point of *Christian faith*); the *Bible* is the sole spiritual authority; there is a fellowship between God and each believer; God forgives *sin* in response to faith; the Church is the community of the followers of Christ; there is a *priesthood* of all believers so each Christian is responsible for his personal faith; Christians have a *duty* to learn and do the *will of God* in daily life; each Christian has the *obligation* to further the *Kingdom of God* on earth; and there is

an *eternal life* with God after death.

Points of greatest divergence between Catholic and Protestant belief are the Protestant rejection of the *Pope's infallibility* and *primacy of jurisdiction* in the Church; the *hierarchical* and *sacramental* role of *mediation* in the conferral of *grace;* the *invocation* and *intercession* of the *Virgin Mary*; and the authority of the *Magisterium* of the Church as final criterion of revealed *truth*.

Today, the term Protestant is interpreted as 'one who bears witness,' rather than one who protests against. See Pentecostalism.

Protestant Reformation

The Protestant Reformation refers to the major revolt against the *Catholic Church* that occurred in the sixteenth century. It was the result of a complex series of factors arising out of *humanism*, international politics, and economics, all of which came to focus on *theological* and *religious* issues. Prominent Reformation leaders include Luther, Calvin, and Zwingli. They believed that the Catholic Church had become deformed by human failures, misinterpretations, and errors and sought a return to what they considered to be the primitive *Christian* Church.

The Catholic *theologians* viewed this as an attack on

and rejection of the Church's *authority*, *doctrines*, and teaching. Numerous bitter confrontations followed during which the original intention of the reformers to restore Christianity was distorted and the *schism* hardened.

The *Council of Trent* was called to undertake a defense of the Church, but with the Protestants' refusal to participate, prospects for reconciliation became hopeless. Western Christianity became a house divided.

Having lost any final authority to which they could appeal, the Reformers soon began to disagree among themselves and the Protestant Reformation resulted in a number of isolated competing *sects* each with its own interpretation of the *Gospel*.

It was not until *Vatican II* that a framework for meaningful *dialogue* was created in a *decree* called 'Unitatis Redintegratio.' In it the Church offered a new basis for developing communication between the separated Christian denominations through *ecumenical* dialogue or *ecumenism*. Today, Christian leaders agree that the effectiveness of Christianity in preaching the word of *Christ* to the world is gravely hampered by the lack of unity among them. See Pentecostalism. Also see Ecumenism.

Protoevangelium 410

Protoevangelium is a Greek word meaning 'first *Gospel*.' It refers to the brief, mysterious message in Gen 3:15 of victory of the Woman (the *New Eve, Mary*) and her seed (the *New Adam, Jesus*) over the brood of the serpent. This is considered the first expression of God's plan for man's *redemption*, and for this reason Mary is referred to as the *Mother of all prophecy*. All *prophecy* originates and is contained in this first prophetic promise.

Protoevangelium also refers to the protoevangelium of James, a gospel of the infancy of *Christ*. It is the oldest *apocryphal* (not accepted as *canonical*) gospel. It dates from the early centuries of the Church.

Protonotary/Protonotaries Apostolic

Protonotary Apostolic refers to a member of the first college of *prelates* of the *Roman Curia*. It is said to have originated in the first century with the seven *notaries* appointed by *Pope* St. Clement to collect the acts of the *martyrs*.

There are four classes of Protonotaries.

1) De Numero participantium, of which there are seven. They have duties relating to the *canonization* and *beatification* of *saints*.

2) *Supernumerary*, an honorary distinction reserved to canons of *patriarchal basilicas* and eight Italian *cathedrals*.

3) Ad instar participantium,

an honorary title reserved to certain chapters of *canons* and individuals.

4) *Titular*, an honorary distinction conferred on *ecclesiastics* throughout the world who are not *domestic prelates* and do not belong to the *pontifical family*. See Prelature.

Protoplasm

Protoplasm is a semifluid, translucent colloid *essential* to the living matter of animal and plant cells. It consists largely of water, proteins, lipoids, carbohydrates, and inorganic salts. See Nucleus. Also see Genetic inheritance 2275.

Prototype

Prototype comes from the Greek word 'prototypon,' meaning original. A prototype is the first thing of its kind, the original, the model, or pattern that serves as a design for other things made like it. See Spiritual motherhood.

Providence, Divine 302

See Divine providence 302.

Providential/Providence

Providential means decreed by the *will of God*. See Divine providence 302. Also see Theism.

Province

A province is a territory under the jurisdiction of an *archbishop*. It includes his own *diocese* and at least one *suffragan* diocese. See Council 465.

Provincial council 887

A provincial council is a council of an *ecclesiastical province*, convoked by the *Metropolitan* of the *province*, with the consent of the majority of *suffragan bishops*.

The provincial council enjoys *legislative* power for the *ecclesiastical province* to which it pertains. It can "determine whatever seems opportune for an increase of *faith*, for the ordering of common *pastoral* action, for the direction of *morality* and for the preservation, introduction and defense of a common ecclesiastical *discipline*" (Canon 445). *Acts* of such councils must be reviewed by the *Apostolic See* (Canon 446).

Prudence/Prudent/Prudently 1806

"Prudence is the *virtue* that disposes *practical reason* to discern our true *good* in every circumstance and to choose the right *means* of achieving it" (CCC 1806).

As an *intellectual virtue*, *prudence* resides in a *faculty* of *understanding* called the practical *intellect*. It is gained both through the repetition of personal *acts* and through the *infusion* of *grace*. Prudence points out the golden mean between excess and defect in the other *cardinal virtues*.

As a *moral virtue*, prudence helps guide the *will* by assisting it in making choices in a reasonable way.

As the first cardinal virtue, it enables the *intellect* to recognize what is virtuous and what is not, how to do good and avoid *evil*.

Prudence is a *habit* of intellectual *discernment* that indicates to the will how the other moral virtues should be applied.

Prudence must not be confused with *timidity*, fear, or cowardice, nor with *duplicity* or pretense.

Prudent judgment 1780

Prudent judgment is the ability of *conscience* to recognize the *truth* about *moral* good, as defined by the *law* of *reason*, in a practical and *concrete* case and commanding the *will* to act.

With regard to advice from others, prudent *judgment* moves a *person* to act on counsel regarding a *moral* choice only after taking care to recognize and reject *evil* advice. Also see Conscience 1706.

Prudentially certain conscience

A prudentially certain conscience is one in which the reason for believing an *act* to be a *morally good* act is solid enough to justify action by an ordinarily *prudent* man. To act morally, a prudentially *certain conscience* is sufficient. See Conscience 1706.

Psalm

A psalm is one of the 150 poetic songs contained in the Book of Psalms in the *Old Testament*. See Psalter 2585.

Psalmi idiotici

The Latin word 'idiotici' is derived from the Greek word 'idiotikos,' meaning private, peculiar, or uneducated in the sense of not having formal training or an academic degree, not necessarily ignorant or stupid.

Psalmi iodiotici refers to poetic songs composed in the early centuries of the Church that were not accepted as part of *Scripture*. They came to be referred to as the private *person's psalms*.

The only examples of such psalms that have survived are the *Te Deum*, the *Gloria in excelsis Deo*, and the Byzantine *Phos Hilaron*. See Psalter 2585.

Psalmody

Psalmody refers to the singing of *psalms* in the *liturgy*. Psalmody was carried over from *Jewish religious* services, and was part of *Christian* liturgy from the beginning. See Criteria for singing and music in the liturgy 1157.

Psalter 2585, 2587, 2588, 2589

The *Old Testament* Book of *Psalms* consists of 150 poetic songs called the songs of praise or 'Tehillim' in *Hebrew*. The portion of the *breviary* or *Divine Office* containing the psalms is called the psalter. In the book of psalms, the *Word of God* becomes man's prayer in the *liturgical prayer* of the Church.

The other books of the Old Testament proclaim God's works and bring to light the *mystery* they contain. The words of the psalmist are sung for God. They express and acclaim the *Lord's* saving works. In the Psalms, the same spirit inspires both God's works and *man's* response. For *Christians, Christ* unites the two and in him the psalms continue to teach us to pray. The singing of psalms in *divine worship* was carried over into the liturgy from the *Jewish Temple worship.*

Psalm verses are frequently used as *antiphons* recited before and after psalms during the Divine Office. They are read before other readings or prayers to focus thought or attention.

In the *Byzantine Rite,* the verse from the psalter *chanted* by the reader before reading the *Epistle* or *Gospel* are called *prokimenon.*

Pseudo-reformation

The prefix pseudo- comes from the Greek 'pseudes,' meaning false. In English it means counterfeit, sham, or *fictitious.* A pseudo-reformation is a false *reformation.* See Reformation of life.

Psychic

The word psychic comes from the Greek word 'psychikos,' meaning *soul.* Psychic energy is energy from the *soul* or forces beyond the physical world. See Prophetic formula.

Psychological pain

The psychological pain of *hell* is the suffering of the damned resulting from an awareness of the consequences of its failure to seek *knowledge* and choose the *good.* It takes the form of *despair,* grief, and *depression* which makes any satisfaction, happiness, or rest of soul impossible. By this suffering, the *soul* shares the physical suffering of the body in the dark, loveless void of *perdition.* See Hell 633, 1033.

Psychology/Psychological

The word psychology comes from the Greek word 'psyche,' meaning *soul* or life principle, and 'logia,' meaning *knowledge.*

Psychological describes things related to psychology, the study of the *mind* and mental phenomena.

Rational psychology is the philosophy of the *human* mind and its *conscious acts,* or of the human *soul* on all levels of operation.

Experimental psychology investigates all kinds of conscious human behavior using scientific methods. It is an aid to rational psychology. See Imputable 2269.

Puberty

Puberty refers to the stage of physical development when sexual fertility becomes possible. Common *law* fixes it as fourteen for boys and twelve for girls. See Age of discretion 1457.

Public consistory

A public *consistory* is one in which *cardinals*, *prelates*, and *laity* participate. See Consistory.

Public life 1915

Public life refers to the engagement by an individual in the affairs, concerns, or service of the community or nation as a whole. It includes those activities of a *person* by which he comes into contact with the community, as opposed to his private or personal activities.

Public life of Christ

Of Christ's thirty-three years on earth only three are revealed in detail in *Sacred Scripture*. These are called his *public life*. The preceding thirty years are called his *hidden life* about which little is recorded in Scripture. See Hidden life/years of Christ 533.

Public penance

Public penance was a *discipline* of the Church required in the past for notorious crimes. Those doing public *penance* were referred to as *public penitents* and, formerly, were organized into four *degrees* through which they had to pass, 1) *weepers*, who were excluded from *divine* service; 2) hearers, who attended only the *liturgy of the catechumens*; 3) kneelers, who knelt apart from the *congregation*, and 4) standers, who were excluded from the *offertory* and *Holy Communion*.

Such penances lasted for days, years, or even for life. The 'years' and 'days' associated with *indulgences* granted by the Church refers to such periods of penance. This penitential discipline was relaxed in the eleventh century but existed in modified and unofficial forms until the eighteenth century in Ireland and England. See Penance.

Public penitents

The phrase 'public penitents' was used before the eleventh century to refer to *persons* who were under penitential *discipline*. Public penitents were organized into four degrees through which a person had to pass to regain *full communion with the Church* and receive her *sacraments*. *Public penance* was required to make public *reparation* for certain *grave* crimes, such as *idolatry*, murder, or *adultery*. See Public penance.

Public revelation 66

Public revelation is the *revelation* contained in *Sacred Scripture* and *Tradition*, and has been entrusted to the Church so that she may guide humanity to its *heavenly* purpose. Public revelation is the *supernatural manifestation* of God's *wisdom*, of his *will*, and is his self-manifestation.

Public worship

Public worship is a religious function intended for the community as opposed to private *persons*.

The *liturgy* is the public worship *Christ* gives to the Father and that the *faithful* give to Christ and, through him, to the Father. It is the *worship* of the *Mystical Body*. See Service 1551. Also see Ceremony; Rite 1203.

Pulpit

A pulpit is the raised platform from which the *priest* or *deacon* preaches and from which the words of *Scripture* are read to the people. See Ambo 1184.

Punitive

When an *ecclesiastical penalty* is intended as punishment for an offense, it is called a punitive or *vindictive penalty*. See Ecclesiastical penalty.

Pure in heart 2518, 2519

In *Scripture*, the thoughts, plans, *memory*, and affections of *man* are *metaphorically* seated in his *heart*, his innermost being. *Purity* of heart refers to the total freedom from any blemished purpose or desire in man's innermost search for God. In the *Beatitudes*, the reward for purity of heart is the direct vision of God.

" 'Pure in heart' refers to those who have attuned their *intellects* and *wills* to the demands of God's holiness, chiefly in three areas: *charity*; *chastity* or sexual rectitude; love of *truth* and *orthodoxy* of *faith*" (CCC 2518).

Purity of heart describes the condition of interior innocence that is preserved by *abstinence* from *sin*. A heart with such a *moral* purity is open to the *operation* of divine *grace*, which transforms it into the likeness of God. Because there is a relationship between purity of heart, of body, and of faith, the pure of heart are *blessed* with the vision of God.

Purgatory 1031, 1472

Purgatory refers to the state after death in which *souls* are *purified*, suffer the *temporal punishment* due to *sin*, and achieve the *perfection* in *holiness* required to enter *heaven*.

Sin has a double *consequence*. *Grave sin* "deprives us of communion with God" (CCC 1472). However all sin, even *venial sin*, also entails an unhealthy attachment to creatures, things, or *habits* that must be purified before the soul can attain the perfect *love* of God necessary to enter the bliss of *heaven*. Even when the guilt of sin is removed and communion with God is restored, we still must be purified from the second consequence.

All who die in God's friendship, but who are still imperfectly purified, are assured of *eternal salvation*. Since nothing imperfect can enter into the presence of God, the soul must first be purified of all earthly attachment to sin by the pain of intense longing for God in purgatory.

The Church teaches that the souls in purgatory can be helped by the *prayers* and *sacrifices* of the *saints* in heaven and the *faithful* on earth (cf. 2 Macc 12:39–46), and especially by the *Sacrifice of the Mass*. Since souls in purgatory can *intercede* for us with God, we can ask for their prayers.

The whole Church exists in three states that are bound to one another in a communion of *charity*. The souls in purgatory, being purified before entering the bliss of heaven, are called the *Church Suffering*. In charity they intercede for the *Church Militant* and *venerate* God in his saints in the Church Triumphant. See Communion of Saints 1475. Also see Three States of the Church 954.

Purification

The Purification is the *Feast* on February 2 commemorating the purifying of the *Blessed Virgin* done in accordance with the *Mosaic Law* forty days after the birth of *Christ*. It is also called the *Presentation of the Lord*. Here purification has the sense not of freeing the *Blessed Mother* from *sin* (for she was sinless), but of that offering of herself and of her Son as an example of perfect obedience to the *Law of Moses* and for the purification of the Church and her members.

Candles are blessed on this feast in *memory* of Simeon's *prophecy* referring to *Christ* as 'a light to enlighten the gentiles' (Lk 2:32). Another name for this feast is *Candlemas*.

Purification can also refer to the act of freeing someone or something from anything that impairs or changes the true *nature* of its *being* or its activity. Purifying *conscience*, for example, refers to the exclusion of self-will in the desire to perform the *will of God*. See Joyful mysteries of the Rosary. Also see Rosary 2678, 2708.

Purification of the social climate 2525

Purification of the social climate refers to the need for the communications *media* to show certain respect and restraint by cleansing itself of the widespread use of *eroticism* and *immorality* in advertising, language, television programing, movies, entertainment, newspapers, and magazines.

Modesty and *Christian purity* require such purification for the protection and preservation of purity in society. Christians must be alert and sensitive to offensive images and content in the media as occasions of *sin* and protect themselves from it by reducing their exposure to it as much as possible.

On the positive side, the *faithful* have a duty to become acquainted with and use sources of information that are not offensive and that support *morality* and Christian *values*. For this reason, *Catholics* have a duty to support Catholic television, radio, internet, and publications and to use them to further their own *spiritual* development.

Purified/Purifies

Purified means rendered free of impurities or pollution. It also means freed from or purged of guilt, *sin*, or *uncleanness*. See Reincarnation. See Justification 1266.

Puritanical

Puritanical means extremely strict in matters of *morals* and *religion*. See Righteous 1224, 1991.

Puritanism/Puritanical

Puritanism refers to a particularly rigid religious outlook or prudery especially regarding sexual *morality*. See Righteousness 1224, 1991.

Purity

Purity refers to the innocence consisting in *abstinence* from any kind of *sin*. It also refers to the simplicity of vision in which the *baptized* seek and find the *will of God* in everything.

Purity also refers to a state in which one refrains from unlawful satisfaction of the *sexual appetite*. In *Scripture*, it also means freedom from *moral corruption* or from *ceremonial* or sexual *uncleanness*.

Purity is distinguished from *chastity*, which is the control of the *sexual appetite* according to the dictates of right *reason*. See Chastity 915. Also see Grace of original holiness 399.

Purity of heart

Purity of heart describes the condition of interior innocence that is preserved by *abstinence* from *sin*. A *heart* with such a *moral* purity is the seat of *human* sentiment and is open to the operation of *divine grace*, which transforms it into the likeness of God. Because there is a relationship between purity of heart, of body, and of *faith*, the pure of heart are *blessed* with the vision of God. See Pure of heart.

Purity of intention 2520

The Catechism of the Catholic Church defines purity of intention as that "which consists in seeking the true end of *man*: with simplicity of vision, the *baptized person* seeks to find and to fulfill God's will in everything" (CCC 2520). It enables man to want what God wants and to *will* what God wills. See Purity of Heart.

Purity of vision 2520

The Catechism of the Catholic Church teaches that purity of vision is the fixing of the *heart* and *mind* on the *will of God*. *Man* achieves purity of vision by seeking his true end internally by *intention* and externally by his *acts*. This is done by disciplining his *imagination* and *emotions*, and refusing all complicity in worldly thoughts that may incline him to turn aside from the path of God's commandments.

Purpose of amendment

By purpose of amendment, we refer to the interior *resolution* to reject *sin* and avoid the occasions of sin that is required to obtain *forgiveness*.

In the *sacrament of Reconciliation* the purpose of amendment is manifested by the performance of the *penance* imposed by the *confessor* and other *voluntary acts* of *self-denial*, or undergoing the penalty imposed by *ecclesiastical authority*. See Penance 1459. Also see Confession.

Pusillanimity

Pusillanimity or *faintheartedness* is the fear of doing great or difficult things or being easily discouraged. It is a lack of *courage*, or *cowardliness*. The opposite of pusillanimity is *fortitude*. See Fortitude 1808.

Pyx

A pyx is a small metal vessel in which the *Blessed Sacrament* is kept or carried. It is the small round metal case used to carry *Holy Communion* to the sick. It should be enclosed in a silk bag and hung around the neck by a cord. See Sacred vessels.

Q

Quasi-privately 1140

The Latin word 'quasi' means seemingly or as if, but not really the same. Private, strictly speaking, means pertaining to one *person*; quasi-private means an action which is performed by many persons, but not as a strictly public act, hence similar to a private action of one person.

Liturgical services are not private functions but public *celebrations* of the Church, the *holy* people of God, united, and organized under the *authority* of their *bishops*.

Since liturgical services always pertain to the whole *Body of Christ* and have effects on it, they should be celebrated in common and as publicly as possible, rather than individually or quasi-privately.

Queen of heaven

The 'Queen of heaven' or '*Regina coeli*' is an Easter *anthem* dating from the twelfth century. During the *Easter season*, it replaces the *Angelus* and is also recited after *Compline*. See Appendix of prayers, Marian prayers: Queen of Heaven / Regina Coeli.

Question (or problem) of evil, The 309

The existence of *moral evil* and *injustice* is the most frequent argument advanced against the existence of God. *Atheists* argue that if the *creator* of the world were *good*, there would be no evil. But evil exists; therefore, either God is not good, is not credible, or does not even exist.

Responding to this argument requires making a distinction between physical evil and moral evil. In itself, *physical evil* is not a *being*, it is a non-being. It consists in the loss or privation of a good or perfection that should be present. It is the absence of something that is needed for a thing to act as it was intended to act. Blindness is an evil of this sort. It does not completely corrupt the *nature* of a thing, but deprives it of a capacity which it was *created* to possess.

As a privation, physical evil cannot preclude the existence of God because it is an absence or privation in something else that exists. Everything that exists is good, because existence is a *perfection*. Every perfection is desirable and what is truly desirable is good.

Existence is desirable because it is a perfection; therefore, everything that exists is good. Since physical evil is a privation, it does not have existence and is not created. Something that does not exist can be neither good nor evil.

Moral evil, however, is a rejection of a good that exists. Moral evil, or *sin*, is the deliberate rejection of a moral perfection that is the proper and intended object of *free choice*. *Sin* is evil because it disrupts the conformity that should exist between man's free choice and the norm of *morality* dictated by *conscience*. It is a freely chosen deviation from the *divine plan* in favor of the plan of a creature. When this rejection is known and formally approved of by the free choice of the *will*, it becomes moral evil.

Why then does God permit sin? God cannot be the author of evil. He can only be the *accidental* cause of physical evil because he does not will it for its own sake but for the conservation of the universal order. God cannot be the direct cause of moral evil because it can only be caused by the *free will* of man acting as a *contingent cause*.

God does not impose necessity on contingent causes, such as free will. He even allows man to cause moral evil by abusing the gift of free will. God made the use of free will of man necessary to achieve

man's *ultimate end*, and mysteriously draws good from the exercise of free choice acting as a contingent cause. This *mystery* is at the heart of *biblical* revelation, for instance, in the book of Job and in Psalms 36, 48, and 72.

Within the mystery of the *Passion*, death, and *Resurrection* of *Jesus*, we also see that physical suffering need not be merely punishment. It can become a *vicarious* sharing of the suffering of the innocent *Christ* for the *redemption* of sinners. The contrite acceptance of suffering can be the means for sinners, like the *prodigal son*, to *repent* and *convert*.

For the sinner, physical suffering is a means of doing *penance*. For the *saint*, it is a means for sharing in the vicarious suffering of the *crucified* Christ and making *reparation* for sin, as *Our Lady* asked at Fatima.

In the end, however, the will of the *Lord* will be triumphant. In the infinite goodness of God, *love*, *mercy*, and *justice* complement each other in resolving the question of evil.

Quicumque 192

Quicumque is a name given the *Athanasian Creed*. It received its name from the first word of that Creed, 'Quicumque,' in Latin meaning 'whoever.' This early statement of the Creed deals principally with the *Trinity* and

Incarnation and the *penalties* incurred by those refusing to accept these articles.

Quietism

Quietism is a *heresy* that taught that the way to God required man to abandon the use of all his *human faculties*. According to quietism, all *human acts*, even the reception of the *sacraments* are unnecessary to attain *holiness*.

This *doctrine* was condemned because God did not give man *reason, will, imagination*, and *memory* only to then make them useless. The use of *man's* faculties is necessary in order to overcome *temptation*, to *love* God, and to exercise *charity* toward others.

What *Catholic* doctrine refers to as the silencing of human *faculties* during *infused contemplation* is not their abandonment, but their use in a *divine* rather than human or creaturely mode. See Heresy 817. Also see Jansenism.

Quinquagesima

Quinquagesima is the third *Sunday* of the pre-*Lenten* season, called *Septuagesima*, in the *Extraordinary Form*, and means 'fiftieth,' indicating that it is about fifty days until *Easter*. It is the Sunday before *Ash Wednesday*.

R

Rabbi

Rabbi is a *Jewish* title applied to teachers and others of an exalted and revered position. In *New Testament* times, it was applied to one learned in the *Law of Moses* without reference to any office. See Canon of Scripture 120.

Rabbinical tradition

The oral and written *wisdom* of a people's history and customs is their *tradition*. The tradition preserved and transmitted by the *Rabbis* is referred to as Rabbinical tradition. See Ark of the Covenant.

Raccolta

The Raccolta was an official *Catholic prayer* book containing the prayers and *devotions* which the Church has enriched with *indulgences*. The conditions for gaining the indulgence, the amount of indulgence, and the date of the grant are listed with each prayer or devotion.

It was published by the *Sacred Penitentiary Apostolic* in the *Congregation of the Holy Office* (now called *Congregation for the Doctrine of the Faith*) by authorization of the *Holy See* in 1944 under the title of 'Preces et Pia Opera' (Prayers and Pius Works).

Translations of the Raccolta are published locally for the use of the *faithful*. Though it is now obsolete, it is still very useful.

Pope Paul VI's *Apostolic Constitution* on the Revision of Indulgences, 'Indulgentiarum Doctrina,' dated 1 January 1967, significantly changed the Church's approach to indulgences and called for an updated collection of indulgenced prayers and actions conforming to the new norms.

This updated book is the 'Enchiridion Indulgentiarum,' or *Enchiridion of Indulgences*. *Enchiridion* means 'at hand' in Greek, and is used to refer to a handbook or reference manual. See Indulgence 1471.

Rage

Rage is a furious and uncontrolled form of *anger*. See Wrath 1866.

Rancor

Rancor refers to a continuing bitter hatred and ill-will. See Wrath 1866.

Rape 2356

Rape is the crime of forcing another to submit to *sexual*

intercourse. It is the forcible violation of the sexual intimacy of another *person* and offends both *charity* and *justice*. Rape deeply wounds the respect, *freedom*, and physical and *moral integrity* to which every person has an *inalienable* right. It causes *grave* damage that can mark the *victim* for life, and is always an *intrinsically evil act*.

Rapture

Rapture is a sudden and violent form of *ecstasy* that cannot be resisted. It is possible to resist simple ecstasy at the outset only. See Ecstasy.

Rash judgment 2477

Rash *judgment* is the assumption, even tacitly, of the *moral* fault of another without sufficient grounds. To avoid rash judgment, everyone should be careful insofar as possible to judge the thoughts, words, and actions of others in a favorable way.

Ratify/Ratifying

Ratify means to sanction, approve, or confirm. See Sanction.

Ratiocination

Ratiocination is a mental process in which, from *truths* already known, one infers another truth contained in them and that necessarily follows from them.

Much of true *knowledge* is acquired directly by means of immediate *sense perception* and by analysis of fundamental *abstract concepts*. *Reality* can be so complex that there are truths that cannot be discovered by sense perception or by comparing concepts in a *judgment*.

In such cases a mediating *intellectual* process is required to discover *truth*. This process is called ratiocination or *reasoning*. See Understanding. Also see Reasoning.

Rational

Rational means based on or derived from the use of *reason*. It often implies the absence of *emotion* and a practical decision or choice. See Christian humanism 1676.

Rational animal

'Rational animal' is a *philosophical* definition of *man* that expresses the *essential* components of his *nature*. Man as a being consists of body and *soul*. The body has the *faculties* and properties of animals, but is radically adapted to the needs of a *spiritual*, rational soul. Thus, he is *material* or *corporal* in a distinctive way. In brief, the *vital functions* or operations of animals are nutrition, growth, vital generation, *sensation*, *appetency*, and locomotion. The body dies because it is composed of parts that disintegrate if the necessary conditions are not present to preserve them.

The soul has the *faculties*

and properties of a *spirit* and is simple and *incorporeal*, not subject to *corruption*. The soul has two faculties: the *intellect* and the *will*. The intellect is the capacity to know, the will is the *appetitive* power or power to choose. The will chooses on the basis of the knowledge presented to it by the *intellect*. The faculties of intellect and will constitute man a *person* made in the image and likeness of God.

The soul has an *extrinsic* dependence on the body, not an *intrinsic* dependence. It is not intrinsically dependent on the body because it is a spiritual *substance*. It can exist apart from it. It is extrinsically dependent on the body because, as a *substantial part* of a complete *human nature*, it depends on the senses of the body for its contact with the outer world. Being *spirit*, the soul has no parts and cannot disintegrate; therefore, it cannot die.

Man is a single *body-soul* composite and must not be understood as a body inhabited by a soul. See Soul 363. Also see Human nature.

Rational order

Rational means capable of *reasoning*. Order refers to a distinctive class. 'Rational order' refers to the class of things which pertain to *reason*. See Natural virtue.

Rationale

Rationale is the fundamental reason or rational basis for a statement or explanation. See Reproductive rights.

Rationalism/Rationalistic

Rationalism is the error of rejecting all *revelation* as a source of knowledge and giving *assent* only to what can be attained by the *natural* power of *reason* alone.

Rationalism denies revelation as a *valid* source of *knowledge* and argues that *human* reason is entirely self-sufficient and capable of knowing all that can be *known*. See Revelation 26, 50.

Rationality

Rationality is the quality or condition of being rational. See Natural reason.

RCIA 1232

The letters 'RCIA' stand for the *Rite of Christian Initiation of Adults*, which is the process of instruction in the *faith* given to adult candidates before their reception into the Church in the *sacraments of initiation*. The *person* receiving the instruction is called a *catechumen* if they are not baptized, but a candidate if they are baptized.

The corresponding instruction for children is called the *Rite of Christian Initiation of Children* or *RCIC*.

RCIC

The letters 'RCIC' stand for the *Rite* of Christian Initiation of Children. It is the instruction in the *faith* given to children before being received into the Church in the *sacraments of initiation*. The *person* receiving the instruction is called a *catechumen* if they are not baptized, but a candidate if they are baptized.

The corresponding instruction for adults is called the *Rite of Christian Initiation of Adults* or *RCIA*.

Real/reality

Real means something existing, actual, true, objectively so, not pretended or imagined.

Reality is the quality or fact of being real or *actual*. See Concept.

Real Presence

'Real Presence' refers to presence of *Christ* in the *Holy Eucharist*. In 1551, the *Council of Trent* declared that 'in the *sacrament* of the most Holy Eucharist is contained truly, really, and *substantially* the Body and Blood, together with the *soul* and *divinity*, of Our Lord *Jesus* Christ, and consequently the whole Christ.' Christ is actually, not *symbolically*, present. He is *objectively* present in the Eucharist, not only *subjectively* in the *mind* of the believer. He is *substantially* present with his *human* and *divine nature* as a *Person*, not a *spiritual* presence

merely imparting *blessings*. See Eucharist 1328.

Reanimation

Reanimation means to restore to life. See Resurrection of the dead 992.

Reason/Reasoning

The process by which the *intellect* determines *truths* that are not self-evident by using *logical* steps is called reason or *ratiocination*. Reason is the ability to think coherently and logically and draw *valid conclusions* from facts or *premises*.

Reason can be classified as *practical reason* when it is directed toward actions. It is called *speculative reason* when it is simply an act of pondering various aspects of a topic as speculation, imagination, or guesswork without taking action. See Soul 363. Also see Human reason.

Reborn 1270

The term reborn derives from Jn 3:3 where *Jesus* tells Nicodemus, 'Unless one is born anew, he cannot see the *Kingdom of God*.' Jesus teaches him that it is necessary to be born again of water and the *Holy Spirit* in order to be saved.

To the objection by Nicodemus that one cannot reenter his mother's womb to be born again, Jesus replies that biological birth is not the only form of birth, nor is it the more perfect form. *Spiritual* birth, though without a biological process, is a real birth, and a more perfect birth, because it involves the transmission of life from a *person* who *begets* to one who receives life, or is *begotten*.

The condition of man after *Baptism* and being reborn of the Holy Spirit is changed, and he becomes a *child of God*. In this *generation*, the Church, as a kind of extension of the *Virgin Mother of God*, is the Mother who begets men as adopted children of the Father and *spiritual* brothers and sisters of Jesus.

Whether one considers the 'second birth' of Jesus in becoming man (his first birth as *Son of God* was from eternity), or the second birth of men becoming children of God, both are uniquely effected by the power of the *Holy Spirit*.

Recapitulate 430

To recapitulate means to go over or repeat again, to summarize, or to restate briefly in a more concise manner.

Recapitulated in Christ 1138

Recapitulated in Christ refers to the gathering, uniting, bringing together, or summing up in *Christ* of all the promises, *prophecies*, and *graces* of God to man.

Recapitulation 518

Recapitulation is a *theory* that was especially elaborated by

St. Irenaeus (130–200 A.D.). It interprets *Christ* as effecting the restoration of fallen humanity to communion with God by his full and perfect headship over the entire *human family* and all *creation* and his perfect *obedience* to the Father. This restoration was first typified in the formation of Adam and Eve, and then progressively foretold in all the subsequent *revelations* of God before the *Incarnation* and the formation of the Church as his *Mystical Body*. Because *Christ experienced* all the stages of life, he brought all men into communion with God.

Reciprocity 1829

Reciprocity is the quality of a relationship marked by mutual action, influence, giving and taking, and concession of advantages or privileges.

Recognition

See Cognition.

Recollection

Recollection means to absorb oneself in *spiritual meditation* or *meditative* or *contemplative prayer*.

It can also mean to be aware of one's interior *spiritual* life. See Memorial 1363.

Reconciliation

Reconciliation is a sacrament of the *New Law*, also called *Penance* or *Confession*. It is the *rite* in which, by the *absolution* of the *priest*, sins committed after *Baptism* are forgiven when they are *confessed* with sorrow and *purpose of amendment*.

Reconciliation, in general, means to resolve differences, restoring *harmony* or friendly relations. See Penance 1459. Also see Confession.

Rectitude 415

Rectitude is the state of *justice* or friendship with God by which man lives in free submission to him by doing his *will*.

Redeem/Redeeming

Redeem comes from the Latin word 'redimere,' meaning to buy back. When *Christ* redeemed the world, he delivered it from *sin* and all its penalties through his sacrifice on the Cross. Through the *mystery* of his *Passion*, death, and *Resurrection*, Christ has restored *man* to the favor of God by *justifying* him. See Redemption. Also see Born under the law 422.

Redemption/Redemptive

Because of the loss of the state of *original justice*, *man* also lost the friendship of God. By his death and *Resurrection*, *Christ* blotted out man's *sin* and restored him to the friendship of God; delivering him from the slavery of sin by the payment of a ransom, not of gold or silver, but of the Pre-

cious Blood of *Jesus* himself. This restoration is referred to as redemption. See Image of God 705.

Redound

Redound means to have effect or results on others for good or ill. See Communion in charity 953.

Redress

Redress means to set right or remedy. It may also mean to make *amends* or satisfaction for a wrong done. See Armed resistance.

Reform/Reformation of life

'Reformation of life' refers to the change in behavior that results from true *repentance* and a *conversion* of *heart*.

Reformation may also refer to the efforts to correct defects in the administration of the Church. Attempts, however, to change *doctrine* or *discipline* immediately willed by *Christ*, or by the *Apostles* on direct orders of Christ, such as the reservation of *Holy Orders* exclusively to men, are forms of false or *pseudo-reformation*. See Conversion of heart 1430, 1888, 2608.

Reformation

See Protestant Reformation.

Refusing obedience to civil authority 2242

Citizens are obliged in *conscience* not to follow directives of *civil authorities* when they are contrary to the demands of the *moral order*, to the *fundamental* rights of *persons*, or the teachings of the *Gospel*. Refusal of *obedience* in such cases is justified by the distinction that must be made between serving God and serving the political community. One must always obey God rather than man in such cases because *civil law* is itself bound by the *divine law*.

Regeneration

Regeneration means being renewed, *reformed*, or reconstituted. It also means being spiritually *reborn*. See Common priesthood 1141.

Regina coeli

The 'Regina coeli' or *'Queen of heaven'* is an Easter anthem dating from the twelfth century. It is part of the *Liturgy of the Hours* recited during the *Easter season* at *Compline*. It is also recited in place of the *Angelus* during the Easter season. See Appendix of prayers, Marian prayers: Queen of Heaven/ Regina Coeli.

Regularize

Regularize means to restore to the correct form through the elimination of a condition or circumstance that rendered an *act invalid* or *illicit*. See Nullity of Marriage 1629.

Regulation of procreation 2368

The Catechism of the Catholic Church teaches that "for just reasons, *spouses* may wish to space the births of their children. It is their duty to make certain that their desire is not motivated by selfishness but is in conformity with the *generosity* appropriate to responsible parenthood" (CCC 2368).

In "harmonizing married *love* with the responsible transmission of life, the *morality* of the behavior does not depend on sincere *intention* and evaluation of *motives* alone; but it must be determined by *objective* criteria, criteria drawn from the *nature* of the *person* and his *acts*, criteria that respect the total meaning of mutual self-giving and human *procreation* in the context of true love; this is possible only if the *virtue* of married *chastity* is practiced with sincerity of heart" (CCC 2368).

"By safeguarding both these essential aspects, the *unitive* and the *procreative*, the *conjugal act* preserves in its fullness the sense of true mutual love and its orientation toward man's exalted vocation to parenthood" (CCC 2369).

Artificial birth control violates these two aspects of the conjugal act and has serious *moral* consequences. *Birth control* refers to the practice of engaging in *sexual intercourse* in a way that deliberately prevents *conception*. Some examples of artificial birth control are devices that prevent semen from reaching the egg or drugs that prevent ovulation. Such practices are referred to as artificial birth control or, more often, *contraception*. Drugs or devices that render the womb inhospitable to new life are not contraceptives but abortifacients. All of these are gravely contrary to *natural law*.

Intercourse should be the physical expression and consummation of love and should bond and increase affection by the pleasure of complete self-giving. This is impossible when the ultimate purpose of the act is deliberately avoided. Contraceptive intercourse becomes mutual *masturbation*; a degrading use of another for selfish pleasure.

However, not all methods of controlling *procreation* are *immoral*. For good reasons, a couple may find it *prudent* to avoid a pregnancy by simply agreeing mutually to *abstain* from intercourse during a woman's fertile times. This approach is characterized by true love, respect, and concern for the other. The self-restraint required becomes a sign of love. This practice of *periodic continence* is called *Natural Family Planning*.

Reincarnation 1013

Reincarnation is a *theory* that at death the *soul* moves from one body to another. According to the theory of reincarnation, when the soul is purified of worldliness it is freed by death for the state of bliss. A soul that is not purified enters another body that suits its character. This *transmigration* or movement of the soul continues until purification is attained. It is not clear what constitutes purification.

This *belief* is incompatible with the doctrine of *Christian redemption*, because while it appreciates the *immortality* of the soul, it does not appreciate the *person* as an individual. Christianity holds that perfect purification is freedom from sin.

Overcoming sin concludes, not in being free of the body in death, but in the *resurrection*, by God's *grace*, of man's own glorified body. Reincarnation is also called *metempsychosis*.

Relation 251

Relation refers to the position that one *person* holds with respect to another because of some *social* or other link between them. It is the particular *mode* or manner in which persons are mutually connected by circumstances.

In reference to the persons of the *Blessed Trinity*, the term relation is used to designate the fact that the distinction between the Persons of the Blessed Trinity lies in the relationship each has to the other two Persons. Also see Circumincession; Perichoresis.

Relative Chastity

See Chastity. Also see Absolute chastity.

Relator

The relator is the *person* in charge of coordinating a cause in *canonization* including the work of the *Promotor of the Faith*. He is not identical with the Promoter of the Faith, but by way of exception, may also hold the office of Promotor of the Faith.

Relic

A relic is an object associated with a *saint* such as part of the body, clothing, or something used or touched by them. There are three classes of relics. *First class relics* are parts of the saint's body. *Second class relics* are things the saint used during life. *Third class relics* are objects, such as cloth, that have been touched to a first class relic. Relics may not be sold or bought.

A fragment taken from the body of a saint, a first class relic, is placed in an *altar* or *altar stone*. A relic is usually bone, but it may also be other parts of the body that do not disintegrate easily, such as hair or fingernails. Relics that are not placed in the *sepulcher* of the altar are kept with *reverence* in what is called a *reliquary*.

It is customary to *bless* people with relics by making the *sign of the Cross* with the relic as a sign of *devotion* and as a prayer for the saint's *intercession* before the throne of God.

The custom of keeping relics arose from the deep devotion to the saints cultivated by the *faithful*, often in gratitude for *miracles attributed* to them. Devotion to the saints is an expression of the *communion of saints*. See Altar 1383. Also see Popular devotion 1674; Catacombs; Canonization.

Religion

The term religion is frequently used to identify *denominational* affiliation, such as Catholic, Lutheran, Baptist, etc.

It also refers to the *virtue of religion*, which is the virtue of *justice* as rendered to God. See Virtue of religion 2096, 2125. Also see Devotion.

Religious

A religious is any *person, clerical* or *lay*, who is a member of a *religious institute*. Religious can also mean devout, *pious*, godly, or conscientiously exact and careful about spiritual matters. See Religious institutes.

Religious assent 892

Assent is the acceptance by the *will* of the *judgment* of the *intellect*. In religious assent, the acceptance by the will is influenced by religious motives. It is an obedient acceptance of the Church's teaching imbued with and exhibiting the *spiritual* and practical effects of *religion*; with *piety, fear of the Lord*, and *devotion*.

Religious clergy

Religious clergy are *clergy* who are also members of a *religious institute*, bound by religious *vows* and living a community life. They are distinguished from *secular* or *diocesan clergy* who do not take religious vows and are not part of a religious institute. See Clergy. Also see Clerical orders; Cleric 934.

Religious Community

A religious community is a group of *religious* who publicly profess *vows* of *poverty*, *chastity*, and *obedience* and live a *common life* according to a common *rule* under the guidance of a *superior*. See Religious Institutes. Also see Religious Life.

Religious congregation

A religious congregation is a general term referring to a group of men or women who live in a *religious community*, lead a *common life*, and take *vows*.

In the 1983 *Code of Canon Law*, similar groups that do not profess vows, are referred to as *societies of apostolic life*. See Religious Life 925.

Religious foundation

A religious foundation is an endowment established to support some *ecclesiastical ministry* or institution. See Right to private property 2403. Also see Benefice; Canons.

Religious Institute

A religious institute is a *society* of men or women approved by *ecclesiastical superiors* in which members, in keeping with the *laws* of their association, make *temporary or perpetual vows* of *poverty*, *chastity*, and *obedience* and live a *common life* in a *religious community*. Institutes are either *clerical*, those in which a notable proportion receive *Holy Orders*, or *lay*, those in which only a few receive Holy Orders. Members of religious institutes are called *religious*.

For *canonical* approval by the Church, institutes must receive positive and formal approval from the *Holy See* or the *Bishop*. For such approval, they must have a *rule* or *constitutions* that determine their mode of governance and the *rights* of its members. See Religious Life 925.

Religious life 925

Religious life refers to the life lived within *religious institutes* that have been *canonically* erected by the Church and whose members give witness to the union of *Christ* with the Church. It is distinguished from other forms of *consecrated life* by its *liturgical* character, public profession of the *evangelical counsels*, and a *common life* lived in a *religious community*.

Entrance into the religious life begins with a period of trial called the *novitiate*, which is usually preceded by a preparatory period known as the *postulancy*. During the novitiate, the candidate is called a *novice*. During the novitiate, both the candidate and the community discern whether the *person* is really called to religious life in that community and should be allowed to make a *religious profession*. See Religious Profession. Also see Novice.

Religious medals

A religious medal is a flat wooden, plastic, or metallic disc having the image of a *saint* on one side and a *prayer* or *religious* symbol on the other. They are usually worn on a chain, but may also be worn attached to clothing by a clasp or pin.

Medals are *sacramentals* and are usually *blessed*. They may be considered as portable, miniature images of saints, *Christ*, or the *Blessed Virgin*. Some medals are commemorative pieces commemorating special religious events, such as *papal* and *jubilee* medals. See Popular Devotions 1674.

Religious profession

Religious profession refers to the taking of *temporary* or *perpetual vows* of *poverty, chastity*, and *obedience* in a religious institute.

Religious profession is preceded by a period called the *novitiate* during which *novices* live in the community life in

order to discern their *vocation*. See Religious Life 925.

Religious rule

A religious rule is a program of life and *discipline* approved by the *Holy See*. It is the plan according to which those who live in a *religious institute* do the work proper to their *apostolate* and grow in *Christian perfection*. See Consecrated virgin 922, 923.

Reliquary

A reliquary is a receptacle for the display and preservation of a *relic*. See Relic.

Remission

See remit.

Remit/remitted/remittance

Remit means to forgive or pardon. See Temporal punishment 1471.

Remnant 711

Remnant is a term used to refer to those who are left as survivors after great trials and to whom God will restore his favor. In *Scripture*, remnant often refers to those who survive the *wrath* of God by *exile*, etc., and become the object of the promises of restoration made to *Israel*. In this context, the remnant becomes a token of God's *fidelity* and saving power.

Reparation

Reparation means to make *amends* for some wrong done

to another. See Restitution 2412. Also see Justice 2407.

Reparation for injustice

Reparation for an *injustice* committed against another requires the *restitution* of stolen goods to the owner or the rectification of harm done to his *reputation*. This duty extends to all who, directly or indirectly, have taken possession of the goods of another and requires them to restore those goods, or their equivalent in kind or money. Restitution extends as well to the profit or advantages their owner would have *legitimately* obtained from them.

All who partake in *theft* or who have knowingly benefited from it are also required to make restitution in proportion to their responsibility and the share they took in what was stolen. See Commutative Justice 2411.

Repent

Repent comes from the Latin words 're,' again, and 'poenitere,' meaning to be sorry. It means to feel sorry, regretful, self-reproachful, *conscience*-stricken, or *contrite* for having done or having failed to do something. True *repentance* includes a firm *resolution* not to repeat the mistake in the future. See Contrition 1451. Also see Repentance.

Repentance

Repentance is another word

for *Contrition*. It is a deep sorrow for *sin* and a firm *resolution* to avoid sin in the future. See Contrition 1451.

Reprobation / Reprobate 603

Reprobation is the state of the damned who having rejected God condemn themselves *eternally*. The Church believes that, though God foreknows the *damnation* of those who die in *sin* and *preordains* their punishment, he does not unconditionally and positively *decree* that anyone will sin. Individuals condemn themselves to hell using their own *free will*. Only the gift of *freedom of the will* is preordained; its use is not. God wills the *salvation* of all, but *man* can refuse to accept his *mercy* and love and so *merit* a just sentence of condemnation. Those incurring damnation are said to be reprobate. See Predestination

Reproduction/reproduce

To reproduce means to produce again; that is to make, form, or bring into existence in some way. It is used in reference to the generation or propagation of a *species* by *sexual* or *asexual* processes.

The term *reproduction* is not correctly applied to *human* generation because it suggests that *begetting* a child is a biological act entirely under *human* control. The Church teaches that children are always a gift of God and he is an *essential agent* in their *creation*. She uses the word *procreation*, not reproduction, in order to indicate that man shares in God's creative act in begetting a child. Such close cooperation with God's creative act is what gives the *conjugal act* its *dignity* and makes it *holy*.

Reproduction is properly identified with the breeding of animals which do not possess an *immortal soul*. See Genetic inheritance 2275. Also see End of Marriage 2366; Regulation of procuration 2368.

Reproductive rights

The phrase 'reproductive rights' refers to a *legal fiction* established by *libertarians* to justify an individualistic interpretation of *morals* pertaining to sexuality, particularly regarding *artificial birth control* and *abortion*. It is fictional because it is based on a mechanistic interpretation of the human *faculty* of *procreation* and centers exclusively on sexual pleasure, totally excluding God and the *divine plan* from sexuality. Used in this mechanistic sense, it provides the *philosophical rationale* for the notions of 'reproductive rights' and '*pro-choice*,' which are used to justify artificial birth control and abortion.

The Church does not use the word *reproduction* in reference to *begetting* children. Reproduction suggests that begetting a child, a temple of God, is an act entirely under *human* control and one essentially no different from that of *brutes*. The Church teaches that children are always a gift from God and that he is the essential *agent* in their creation. She uses the word '*procreation*,' rather than reproduction, in order to indicate that man shares in God's creative act in producing children. See Regulation of procreation 2368. Also see End of marriage 2366.

Requiem Mass

Requiem Mass is another name for the *Mass of the Dead*. See Mass 1332.

Rescind/rescinded

Rescind means to revoke, repeal, or cancel. See Habitual intention.

Resentment

Resentment is a feeling of bitter hurt from a sense of being injured or offended. See Wrath 1866.

Reserved

To reserve the *Blessed Sacrament* means to keep some aside in a safe place, usually the *tabernacle*, for taking *Holy Communion* to the sick. See Church.

Resolution of amendment

Resolution of amendment refers to the firm and sincere decision of a *penitent* to avoid future occasions of the *sins* that were confessed in the *sacrament of Penance*.

The *purpose of amendment* includes the determination to avoid all *mortal* sin, the occasions of sin, and to use the means necessary to do this. It also includes the readiness to make *reparation* for the injury or harm done to others.

In *spiritual theology*, such a resolution implies a *conversion* of one's *moral* life made after due reflection and *prayer*. See Perfect Contrition.

Respect for the person 1907

One of the elements of the *common good* is respect for *persons* or the deferential attention, esteem, regard, honor, and *reverence* due to every *man* because of his *human dignity* and *inalienable rights*.

Society has the *duty* to permit each person to freely exercise his right to fulfill his *vocation* on earth and respond to his *eternal vocation* of bliss with God.

As a person, man is made in the *image of God* who endowed him with *intellect* and *will*. With the gift of intellect, man can *know* the true and the good. With the gift of *free will*, man can choose or reject the *truth* presented by the intellect.

God, who is *truth* and goodness itself, communes with man, calling him to *eternal* bliss. By his free response to God's call, man achieves his eternal *destiny*, which is to know and *love* God. The call to *union* with God is the source of man's *inalienable* rights and *society's obligations* to him.

Response of faith 1102

The response of *faith* is the *consent* and commitment given by those who accept *Christ* to the *covenant* between God and his people.

Responsible / Responsibility 1734, 1781

Responsible means that a *person* is accountable for his actions to the extent that they are *voluntary*. Responsibility makes a person answerable to others, or God directly, and liable in *justice* for the *consequences* of his *acts*.

Restitution 2412

Restitution is the action of restoring or giving back something to its proper owner or of making *reparation* for loss or injury caused by one's actions. It consists in giving *compensation* for damage inflicted on another.

It is *obligatory* if the action was deliberate, was the true cause of the damage, and the *evil* effects were foreseen. Restitution is an *obligation* of *justice* and *civil judgments* in these matters are binding in *conscience*.

Other non-material injury resulting from harmful *acts*, such as deceit or *calumny*, must also be repaired as far as possible. See Reparation for Injustice. Also see Commutative Justice 2411.

Resurrected body

At the *resurrection* of the dead, the body will be rejoined to the *soul*. It will be a true body having the same identity as the earthly body, but in a *glorified* state, *immortal* and *incorruptible*. The bodily resurrection of the dead is an essential element of the *Christian faith*.

Although all men, just and unjust, will rise, only the just will share in the glory of the *Resurrection* by being physically transformed with *glorified bodies*. *Man* does not know how the physical body will be glorified; how *perishable nature* will put on the imperishable; or how mortal nature puts on *immortality*.

The Church teaches that *resurrected bodies* of the just possess four qualities.

1) *Impassibility*: Freedom from all pain, suffering, or physical defects.

2) *Clarity*: The brightness of *glory* and splendor that overflows from the *beatific vision* and transforms the body.

3) *Subtlety*: The spiritual *docility* or *subjection* of the body, which takes on a *spiritual* character without ceasing to be a true body. Because it is a *perfection*, not a deprivation, of bodily nature, it is referred to as a *'spiritual body'* in 1 Cor 15:44.

4) *Agility*: The ability to move from place to place with great speed and serve as a perfect instrument of the soul, enabling the glorified body to exist in perfect *harmony* with all *creation* and know its wonders.

The bodies of the *reprobate* will also rise immortal and incorruptible, but not impassible and glorious. Just as the body partakes in the *moral* character of the *human person*, so it shall share in its *eternal* reward or punishment. It is the whole person who is punished or rewarded at the time of *judgment*. See Resurrection from the dead 992. Also see Glory 293.

Resurrection

Resurrection refers to the *reanimation* of a body to *eternal* life after death. Often it is used to refer to the *Easter mystery* when *Christ* rose from the dead after three days. See Resurrection from the dead 992.

Resurrection from the dead 992

The resurrection of the body refers to the *reanimation* of the bodies of the dead, whether saved or lost after the *last judgment*. The body, which will be rejoined to the *soul*, will be a true body having the same identity as the earthly body, but in a *glorified* state, *immortal* and *incorruptible*.

At the resurrection, *human nature* will reach a state of

ultimate *perfection*. God will grant incorruptible and eternal life to men's bodies when they are reunited with their *souls* through the power of *Jesus'* Resurrection. The risen bodies of the just will be *transfigured*, *glorified*, and *immortal*. The body together with the soul will share in *glorification* or *perdition*.

Resurrection of the body

Resurrection of the body is another way to refer to the resurrection of the *flesh*. See Resurrection of the flesh 990.

Resurrection of the flesh 990

The resurrection of the flesh is a formulation in the *Apostles' Creed* meaning that, not only will the *immortal soul* live on after death, but that even man's mortal body will come to life again at the *resurrection*. God will grant *incorruptible* life to man's body, reuniting his body and soul through the power of Jesus' Resurrection.

Retreat

A retreat is a period of time during which a *person* withdraws from ordinary life in order to *pray*, *meditate*, and receive instruction in the *spiritual life*. It is a form of popular *piety*. See Popular Devotions 1674.

Retribution

Retribution is the reward or punishment merited in *eter-*

nity for deeds done on earth. See Particular judgment 1022.

Retroactive/retroactively

Retroactive means applying an effect to something prior to its enactment or going into effect as of a specified date in the past. See Sanatio in radice.

Revealed law 1952

Revealed law is the guide to *human* behavior contained in the *Old* and *New Testaments*. It is also known as the *law* of the *Gospel*.

Revealed truth

Revealed truth is *knowledge* of God disclosed to *man* about himself and his *will*. Depending on how his *truth* is communicated, *revelation* can be *natural* or *supernatural*.

When it is communicated by the world of space and time, such as *creation*, or derived from the use of *natural reason*, it is said to be natural. Natural revelation thus is two-fold, once *objectively* from the *experience* of nature itself and again *subjectively* from the *reason* reflecting on this experience. In reference to this type of revelation, the *Old Testament* says that there are men who are naturally stupid 'who have not known God from things that are seen,' and those 'who have not been able to discover him who is by studying his works' (Wis 13:1). Supernatural revelation begins where natural revelation leaves off, and communicates God's revelation in a way that far exceeds that of nature. In his *providence*, God has willed to communicate his will personally by speaking to mankind 'through the *prophets*,' and 'through his Son who is the radiant light of God's glory and the perfect copy of his *nature*' (cf. Heb 1:1–2). There is a difference between these two kinds of supernatural communication. Before *Christ*, God spoke indirectly through his prophets, but in the *Person* of Christ, he spoke no longer through *human seers* but as man to fellow men. See Apostolic Tradition. Also see Motives of credibility 156; Deposit of faith 1202; Practical faith.

Revelation 26, 50

Revelation is the disclosure or communication of *supernatural knowledge* to *man* by God. The Church teaches that there are two sources of knowledge for man: *reason* and *revelation*.

Rationalism rejects all revelation as a source of knowledge and gives *assent* to nothing but what can be attained by the *natural* power of reason alone.

Revenge

Revenge means to inflict punishment or damage in return for some injury. See Anger 2302.

Reverence

Reverence is a feeling of deep respect, *love*, or awe for something held as *sacred* and worthy of *veneration*. See Piety 1675, 1831.

Right / rights 1930

In *law*, 'right' refers to an object to which one has claim or a moral *obligation* that is due from others.

As a *moral* quality, it refers to that by which a *person* is entitled to claim that something belongs to him, is due him, and is the basis for requiring others to perform or *abstain* from some act. Refusing a person his moral right is an offense against *justice*. A right is not dependent on one's ability to enforce it.

Because rights *inhere* in the *human person*, they are ordinarily *inalienable*. The duties imposed by the *Creator* on his creatures imply the rights to fulfill them.

The inherent rights of persons are called *human rights*. There are three types:

1) The rights of a *human person* include the right to: life, *freedom* under God, just laws, follow the dictates of *conscience*, marry, have *family* independence, have reasonable private property, and be treated as a person rather than as a thing.

2) The rights of a civic person include the right to: equal suffrage, political participation, political self-determination,

free investigation and discussion, equal rights before the law, and equal opportunity for equal ability.

3) The rights of a working and *social* person include the right to: choose work, organize in groups, earn a just wage, share in management and ownership, and have some social security.

Right Conscience

When *conscience* is certain that something it believes is true is in fact *objectively* true, the conscience is called a right conscience. One must follow a right conscience. See Conscience 1706.

Right of economic initiative 2429

The right of economic initiative is the right to undertake a business enterprise that makes *legitimate* use of one's talents in order to contribute to "the abundance that will benefit all" (CCC 2429) and to receive the just fruits of one's labor.

Right of succession

The right of succession refers to the right of a *Coadjutor Bishop* to become *Bishop* of the *diocese* when the present bishop dies. *Auxiliary Bishops* do not have this right. See Bishop 861.

Right reason

Right reason refers to thought or thinking that conforms to the laws of *logic* governing *valid* thinking processes and good *judgment*. It also means to support or justify something *coherently* and logically with *conclusions* based on *truth*. See Moral virtues 1804.

Right to a trial marriage 2391

"Some today claim a 'right to a trial *marriage*' where there is an intention of getting married later. However firm the purpose of those who engage in premature sexual relations may be, 'the fact is that such *liaisons* can scarcely ensure mutual sincerity and *fidelity* in a relationship between a man and a woman, nor, especially, can they protect it from *inconstancy* of desires or whim'" (CCC 2391).

Sexual intercourse is morally good only within the context of the definitive commitment of the life of marriage. Married love demands a definitive and mutual gift of self to one another until death.

Right to private property 2403

The goods of the earth are destined for the whole *human* race because these goods are intended to assure the security of human lives. The appropriation of property by private *persons* is *legitimate* for guaranteeing the freedom and *dignity* of the *person* and providing for the needs of those in his charge.

Private property refers to those goods a person justly

acquires as fruits of his labor and to which, in *justice*, he has a claim and may use for his own personal needs or the needs of those in his charge.

The *common good* requires respect for the *universal destination of goods* as well as respect for the right to private property. The legitimate use of things requires man to regard the goods he owns not merely as exclusive to himself but in common with others. His good can and should benefit others as well as himself.

Ownership makes the holder a steward of *providence* with the task of making his property fruitful and communicating its benefits to others.

Some have questioned the right of the Church to own and administer worldly property. The Church has upheld the appropriateness of owning worldly property as a *temporal* necessity to the fulfillment of her *divine mission*. With her goods, she provides for the needs of *divine worship*, a decent support for her ministers, the works of the *apostolate*, and a variety of works of *charity*, especially towards the poor and needy.

Righteous

Being righteous means to act in a just, upright, and *virtuous* manner, doing what is right. See Righteousness. Also see Justification 1266, 1987.

Righteous anger

Righteous anger is that *anger* that is roused against *sin* or *injustice*, whether caused by oneself or others. Such anger is not sinful. *Christ* showed such anger when driving the money changers from the *Temple*. See Anger 2302.

Righteous seed

'Righteous seed' refers to the descendants of David who would remain faithful to the *Covenant* and walk in the ways of the Lord. God also calls them *legitimate seed*, innocent of any charge or accusation. See Righteousness 1224, 1991.

Righteousness 1224, 1991

The *Hebrew* word 'sedek' has no single English word that adequately expresses its meaning. 'Sedek' is right conduct in the sense of good *moral* conduct and is usually translated as righteousness, *just*, or *justice*.

In English, 'sedek' is understood as righteous in the sense of being innocent of a charge. In general *Christian* usage, it refers to moral goodness and deliverance from *sin* through the saving work of *Christ*.

The interpretation of righteousness or justification is a central issue in Luther's teaching and was fundamental to his interpretation of *salvation*. His position was controverted by the *Council of Trent*, which held that moral righteousness was more than moral rectitude achieved by observance of the *Law*, it also extended to deliverance from sin by living a *spiritual* life of *faith* with the aid of *sanctifying grace.*

For the *Jews*, to seek righteousness is to seek *Yahweh*, because it is through good conduct that he is found. The righteous man serves God and lives by *fidelity* to his law. Such righteousness also implies a right or claim, because good conduct establishes a claim on Yahweh to deliver one from *evil*. In this sense it is translated as salvation, *deliverance*, or *vindication.*

Righteousness also refers to "the acceptance of God's righteousness through *faith* in *Jesus* Christ. Righteousness (or 'justice') here means the *rectitude* of divine love. With *justification*, faith, *hope*, and *charity* are poured into our hearts, and *obedience* to the *divine will* is granted us" (CCC 1991).

The word 'righteousness,' together with its *derivatives*, declined in general use among *Catholics* because the translators of the *Douay-Rheims Bible* preferred the words 'justice' or 'just.' *Puritanical* abuse of the term in a completely *moralistic* sense also contributed to its abandonment by *Catholics*. However, some recent *Scripture* translations have restored the word 'righteousness' for justice.

Rigorous

Rigorous means strict. See Legitimate defense by military force 2309.

Rising 997

By death, the *soul* is separated from the body. The body decays and the soul returns to meet God until it is reunited with its body at the end of the world. Only the bodies of the just rise *glorified*. Rising refers to the *belief* that God will grant *incorruptible* life to *man's* body by reuniting it with his soul through the power of *Jesus' Resurrection*. See Resurrection of the Dead.

Rite 1203

Rite comes from the Latin meaning in due form or with proper *ceremony*. It can refer to a particular *liturgical ceremony*; for example, the Rite of Christian Burial, or to the whole system of ceremonies, *prayers*, and actions prescribed for liturgical or *sacramental* acts by a particular *Christian church*. In this sense, 'rite' is used to identify a particular *tradition* with its own liturgical, *spiritual*, juridical, and cultural identity.

The *Catholic Church* embraces many rites, including the *Roman*, *Byzantine*, *Armenian*, *Chaldean*, *Coptic*, *Ethiopian*, *Syro-Malabar*, *Maronite*, and *Syrian* Rites.

A Catholic belongs to a rite they were *baptized* in. Usually this is the rite of their parents or, if their parents belong to different rites, of their father. Transferring from one rite to another ordinarily requires permission from the *Holy See*. In inter-*ritual marriages* (marriage between *persons* of different Rites), the wife may transfer to the husband's rite. See Latin Rite. Also see Eastern Church.

Rite of Christian Initiation of Adults 1232

The 'Rite of Christian Initiation of Adults' is the instruction in the *faith* given adult *catechumens* before being received into the Church in the *sacraments of initiation*. It is often referred to simply as *RCIA*.

Rite of Christian Initiation of Children 1232

The 'Rite of Christian Initiation of Children' refers to the instruction in the *faith* given young catechumens before being received into the Church in the *sacraments of initiation*. It is often referred to simply as *RCIC*.

Rite of Election

The Rite of Election is a *liturgical* landmark that takes place in the third stage of Christian initiation in preparing a candidate for the reception of the *sacraments of initiation* at *Easter*. The Rite of Election begins the First *Sunday* of Lent. It includes three scrutinies, presentations, and anointing. See RCIA 1232.

Rite of Exorcism

Exorcism refers to the driving out or expulsion of *evil spirits* from *persons* or things in cases of *demonic* possession by means of *adjuration* or a command in the name of God.

The Rite of Exorcism is the *ceremonies*, *prayers*, and actions prescribed for expelling evil spirits from *persons* in cases of demonic possession. See Exorcism 550, 1237, 1673.

Rite of the Holy Sepulcher

The Rite of the Holy Sepulcher refers to a rite used by the *Latin Church* in Palestine during the twelfth and thirteenth centuries.

The *Carmelite Rite* was based on the Rite of the Holy Sepulcher.

Ritual

The term ritual comes from the Latin word 'ritualis' or 'ritus,' meaning form. Ritual refers to the prescribed words and *ceremonies* for a *religious* service. It can also refer to the book which contains these prescriptions. See Old Covenant. Also see Rituale Romanum.

Ritual purity

Ritual purity consists in being free of some flaw or *uncleanness* which would bar one from contact with *holy* objects or places, especially the holy presence of God in *worship*. When that which was unclean or impure came into contact with what was holy, the results could even be death.

Because blood was associated with the *mysterious* power of life, any loss of blood necessitated *purification*. *Impurity* also arose from touching a corpse. Participation in war caused impurity because it brought a *person* into contact with foreign gods. See High Priest. Also see Unclean.

Rituale Romanum 168

The Rituale Romanum or Roman Ritual is a book containing the *prayers* and regulations for the *ceremonies* used to *celebrate* the *sacraments* and give *blessings* according to the *Roman Rite* of the *Latin Church*.

Rod of Aaron

A rod is a stick, sometimes called a staff, used as a walking stick. Rods were also used for defense, punishment, and measurement. They were also symbols of *prophetic*, *priestly*, and *royal office*. After Aaron was constituted priest, his rod was placed in the *Ark of the Covenant*.

Roman Breviary

The Roman Breviary is a book containing everything needed to recite the *Divine Office*. It is usually printed in several volumes, often with one for each season. Following *Vatican II*, a revised edition was approved by Pope Paul VI in 1970 under the title *Liturgy of the Hours*.

Roman Church

Strictly speaking, the Roman Church refers to the *diocese* of Rome, since the name of the *cathedral* city is used to identify the local church, e.g., the Church of Chicago is the Diocese of Chicago.

However, by extension, the term Church of Rome is synonymous with both the Western Church, because the *Pope* (the *Bishop of Rome*) is the *Patriarch* of the West, and the whole *Catholic Church*, since it is in union with the Pope. See Apostles' Creed 194.

Roman Congregations

A Roman Congregation is a body of *cardinals* responsible for the administration of Church affairs. The present list of congregations is organized as per the *Apostolic Constitution* 'Bonus Pastor' issued by Pope John Paul II on June 28, 1988. The Roman Congregations are listed in the Annuario Pontifico, the official annual directory of the Roman *Catholic Church*. The Roman Congregations are:

a) *Congregation for the Doctrine of the Faith*. Its purpose is to safeguard the teachings of the *faith*, examine *doctrinal* questions and writings, promote *theological* study, and oversee matters related to the

Petrine Privilege in *marriages*. The *Theological Commission* and *Biblical Commission* are attached to it.

b) *Congregation for the Oriental Churches*. Its purpose is to oversee all matters pertaining to the *Eastern Catholic Churches*.

c) *Congregation for Bishops*. Its purpose is to oversee all issues related to *bishops*. It supervises the Commission for Latin America.

d) *Congregation for Divine Worship and the Discipline of the Sacraments*. It has *authority* over the regulation and promotion of the *sacraments* and the *liturgy*.

e) *Congregation for the Causes of Saints*. It oversees all matters related to *beatifications* and *canonizations*.

f) *Congregation for the Clergy*. It has authority over the *clergy*, including *discipline*, preaching, and care for the Church's *temporal goods*.

g) *Congregation for Institutes of Consecrated Life and Societies of Apostolic Life*. It oversees all aspects of *religious institutes*, *third orders*, *secular institutes*, and *societies of apostolic life*.

h) *Congregation for Catholic Education* (for *Seminaries* and *Institutes* of Study). It has authority over all institutions of Catholic education.

i) *Congregation for the Evangelization of Peoples*. It supervises all *missionary* activity across the globe and has

control over various *societies*, *unions*, and *councils* to assist in the missionary undertaking. See Roman Curia.

Roman Curia

The *Roman Curia* consists of those bodies that assist the *Pope* in administering the universal Church. These include the *Congregations*, Pontifical Commissions, Pontifical Councils, *Tribunals*, and Curial Offices.

There is also a diocesan curia proper to the *Diocese* of Rome, but 'Roman Curia' does not usually refer to this. See Diocese 833. Also see Protonotary Apostolic.

Roman Missal

The Roman Missal is the *liturgical* book which contains all the *prayers* used in the *celebration* of *Mass*. It also includes the *sacramentary* or *ritual* part of the Mass used by the *celebrant* and the *lectionary* containing the readings from *Scripture* used by the *celebrant* and assisting ministers. See Lectionary. Also see Sacramentary.

Roman Pontiff

The Roman Pontiff is the *Pope* of the Roman *Catholic Church*, the successor of St. Peter, and the *Bishop* of Rome. See Excommunication 1463. Also see Pontiff 882.

Roman Rite

Roman Rite is another name

for the *Latin Rite* in the *Catholic Church*. It is the largest *Rite* in the Western Church. There are two forms of *liturgy* in the Latin Rite, the *Ordinary Form*, which employs the *Roman Missal* approved by Pope Paul VI in 1969, and the *Extraordinary Form*, which employs the Roman Missal of 1962 approved by Pope John XXIII.

The Ordinary Form can be celebrated either in Latin or in the *vernacular*, but the Extraordinary Form can only be celebrated in Latin. Because of this, the term 'Latin Mass' usually refers to the Extraordinary Form even though the Ordinary Form can also be celebrated in Latin. See Rite 1203.

Rosary 971, 2678, 2708

The Rosary is a *prayer* with sets of 10 *Hail Mary's* being recited while meditating with *Mary* on one or another mystery of *Jesus*. The beads are arranged into five groupings of ten beads called decades, and with a single bead in between them. Suspended from a religious *medal* joining the first and last decades is a *crucifix* and a group of three beads preceded and followed by a single bead.

The prayer begins at the crucifix with the recitation of the *Apostles' Creed* followed by an *Our Father* (the *Lord's Prayer*) on the single bead and a Hail Mary on each of the three following beads, and then the *Glory Be*. The Our Father on the remaining bead starts the first decade. The Hail Mary is recited on each of the beads in a decade. At the bead that separates the decades, the *Glory Be* ends the decade, and the Our Father begins the next.

Meditation on a *mystery* of the *faith* drawn from the *Gospels* accompanies the recitation of each decade of the Rosary. These meditations are called the *Joyful, Sorrowful*, and *Glorious* mysteries. Pope St. John Paul II gave the Church a fourth group called the *Luminous mysteries*. Different mysteries are used on different days of the week to encourage meditation on the life of *Christ*. The recitation of five decades of the Rosary ends with the prayer *Hail Holy Queen*. Meditation on the mysteries during the Rosary seems to have begun with Alanus de Rupe in about 1428 A.D.

The Rosary is a powerful prayer and the *faithful* have been asked to pray it by the *Blessed Virgin* herself in the numerous *apparitions* of modern times.

The use of beads as an aid to *memory* while reciting a set number of prayers is not *Christian* in origin, but it has been in use by the Church since earliest times. In the eleventh century, there arose the custom of reciting 150 '*Aves*' each day. This earliest version of the Ave, or Hail

Mary, consisted only in the words 'Hail Mary, full of grace, the Lord is with thee, blessed art thou amongst women and blessed is the fruit of thy womb.' The number 150 represents the number of *psalms*, and the recitation of the 150 Aves made it possible for the *laity* to identify with the liturgy recited in the *monasteries*.

Tradition holds that St. Dominic (1170–1221 A.D.) learned the use of the Rosary from the Blessed Virgin in a revelation. According to Pope Benedict XIV, this *belief* rests on a tradition of the *Dominican order* whose members used the Rosary as early as 1270. Pope Benedict XIV also mentioned that a *Confraternity* of the Rosary at Piacenza was granted *indulgences* by Pope Alexander IV (r. 1254–1261) in 1254.

A related devotion, introduced by St. Faustina, is the *Divine Mercy Chaplet*. See Vocal Prayer 2664. Also see Prayer. Also see Mysteries of the Rosary in the Appendix.

Royal office 786

All *Christians* are said to hold a royal office because by *Baptism* they share in the kingship of *Christ* who made himself servant of all. For the *Christian*, to reign is to serve Christ by serving others, especially the poor and suffering. With the help of *divine grace*, the Christian gains *dominion* over his *will* and the power to rule over his *evil* inclinations.

Rule

A rule is an organized set of regulations and methods of living the *evangelical counsels* in a community, e.g., the *Rule of St. Benedict* or the Rule of St. Augustine. Rules of *religious* communities govern their customs, daily life of *prayer* and work, and provide a support system for more effective *moral* living or service to others. See Benedictines. Also see Rule of St. Benedict.

Rule of law 1904

Rule of *law* refers to the sovereignty of the law over individual conduct in a *society* and the application of the law to all members of that society equally. It is opposed to rule by the whims of the powerful.

Rule of St. Benedict

The Rule of St. Benedict refers to the *monastic* regulations established by Benedict of Nursia in the mid-sixth century as a guide for his *monastery* at Monte Cassino. Derived from earlier rules of like nature by John Cassian (360–435 A.D.), Basil (329–379 A.D.), Augustine (345–430 A.D.), Caesarius of Arles (d. 542 A.D.), and the *Fathers of the Desert*, it was intended to serve as a guide for living the *religious life* in a community under the rule of the *abbot*.

The rule, noted for its *enlight-*

ened flexibility, was adopted by much of Western *monasticism*. St. Benedict is considered to be the Father of Western Monasticism and his *monks* are known as *Benedictines*. See Benedictines.

S

Sabbath 2175

The Sabbath is the seventh day of the *Jewish* week. It is derived from the *Hebrew* verb 'to rest' or 'to cease.' It was observed by resting from all work and joining in *divine worship* in *obedience* to the third *commandment*. This observance applied to slaves and animals as well as the ordinary *Israelite*.

Over time, *rules* for the proper observance of the day of rest became very detailed, so much so that it became a source of contention between *Jesus* and the *Scribes* and *Pharisees* and prompted the statement by *Christ* that 'The Sabbath was made for man, and not man for the Sabbath' (Mk 2:27).

Sacerdos 1554

Sacerdos is a Latin word that refers to the *ecclesial ministry* of *bishops* and *priests* but not deacons because the Church recognizes two *degrees* of participation in the *priesthood of Christ*; the *episcopacy* and the *presbyterate*. The *deaconate* is intended to help and serve the priesthood.

The English word *'priest'* comes from the Greek word for *elder*, but in English *Catholic* usage priest does not mean elder; it means what 'sacerdos' in Latin, or *sacerdotal* in English does: one whose office is to *sacrifice* or make *holy*.

Sacerdotal

Sacerdotal comes from the Latin 'sacer,' meaning holy or sacred. It is a quality applied to one who offers *sacrifice* or to those things pertaining to priests or *priesthood*. The *sacerdotal office* or *priesthood* has two degrees: the *episcopate* and *presbyterate*. See Sacerdos 1554.

Sacrament 1114

A sacrament is an outward sign instituted by *Christ* to confer *grace*, or the visible form of invisible grace. Both definitions originate with St. Augustine (354–430 A.D.). See Sacraments of Christ 1116.

Sacrament of Confession 1424

The *sacrament of Penance* is also called the sacrament of Confession, because in order to obtain *forgiveness* of *sin* through the sacrament, the disclosure or confession of *sins* to a *priest* is *essential*. This sacrament is also called the *sacrament of Reconciliation*.

Sacrament of conversion 1423

The sacrament of *Confession*, *Penance*, or *Reconciliation* is referred to as the sacrament of *conversion* because it makes "sacramentally present *Jesus'* call to conversion, the first step in returning to the Father from whom one has strayed by *sin*" (CCC 1423).

The *sacrament* of Confession was instituted by *Christ* in Mt 16:19. *'Amen* I say to you, whatever you shall bind on earth, shall be bound also in *heaven*; whatsoever you shall loose on earth, shall be loosed also in heaven.'

Sacrament of forgiveness 1424

The *sacrament of Penance* is also called the sacrament of forgiveness, because by the priest's *absolution* God grants the *penitent* pardon, *peace*, and *reconciliation* with God and the community of the Church.

Sacrament of Penance 1423, 1424

The sacrament of Penance is the *sacrament* by which sinners obtain pardon and *forgiveness* for *sins* committed after *Baptism*. In order to receive this sacrament worthily the sinner must confess his *sins* to a *priest* with a *contrite* heart and a firm *resolution* to *amend* his life.

Sacrament of Reconciliation 1424

The *sacrament of Penance* is called the sacrament of Reconciliation, because it imparts to sinners the merciful love and *reconciliation* with God and the Church.

Sacrament of regeneration

Baptism is called the *sacrament* of *regeneration*, because it gives *man* a new life in *Christ*. See Baptizein 1214.

Sacrament of the sick

The *sacrament* of the sick is another name for *Anointing of the Sick* or *Extreme Unction*. See Extreme Unction 1512.

Sacrament of unity 1140

The sacrament of unity refers to the Church herself as a sensible sign instituted by *Christ* to both *signify* and confer *grace*.

When the whole community *celebrates* the *liturgy* together, it is united with Christ its head. Together with him, each member becomes an outward sign of the Church uniting its members as the *Mystical Body* of Christ.

Sacramental absolution

Sacramental absolution is the *forgiveness of sins* imparted by a *priest* to an individual who has *confessed* his sins with sorrow and a firm *resolution of amendment*. See General absolution 1483.

Sacramental character

The *sacraments* of *Baptism*, *Confirmation* and *Holy Orders* confer an *indelible spiritual character* or seal of the *Holy Spirit* on the *soul* called the sacramental character. It is an everlasting sign of *divine* ownership, of the *person's faith* and of the expectation of both the *blessed* vision of God and hope of *resurrection*.

The sign is indelible because it remains even in one who loses the state of *grace*. It signifies that one who has received these sacraments has a special relation to *Christ*. It is called a character because it confers a permanent quality distinctly identifying the individual with unique abilities which enable him to perform certain works in the Church.

This *seal* or permanent mark is Christ's pledge of *eternal life*. It is also called the *seal of the Lord* or *Dominicus character*. See Seal of the Lord 1274. Also see Baptism 1213.

Sacramental dispensation 1076

The sacramental *dispensation* is the orderly management and administration by means of which the Church administers the channels of *divine grace* entrusted to her by *Christ*.

Sacramental economy 1076

The sacramental *economy* refers to the communication or *sacramental dispensation* of the fruits of *Christ's Paschal mystery* in the *celebration* of the Church's sacramental *liturgy*.

Sacramental epiclesis 699

The sacramental *epiclesis* is the *intercessory prayer* in which the *priest* begs the Father to send forth the *Holy Spirit* to grant the special *grace* of the *sacrament* being administered.

Sacramental grace 1129, 2003

Sacramental *grace* is the special "grace of the *Holy Spirit*, given by *Christ* and proper to each *sacrament*" (CCC 1129).

The fruit of sacramental life is *divine* sonship, the *Spirit of adoption* that makes the *faithful* partakers in the *divine* nature *(theosis)* by uniting them in a living union with the only Son, the Savior.

Sacramental grace is considered to be *habitual grace* when it refers both to the object of the sacrament and a title to the *actual graces*, necessary for the more perfect fulfillment of the purpose of the sacrament.

Sacramental marriage 1631

A sacramental *marriage* is one in which a *priest* or *deacon* assists at the *celebration*, receives the consent of the partners in the name of the Church and imparts the *blessing* of the Church on them. The presence of the priest or deacon and witnesses expresses the fact that marriage is an *ecclesial* reality.

The Church requires that sacramental marriage be contracted according to *canoni-*

cal form for several reasons: 1) sacramental marriage is a liturgical act; 2) marriage introduces the spouses into an ecclesial order conferring rights and duties in the Church, between themselves, and towards their children; 3) since marriage is a state of life, certainty about it is necessary and requires witnesses; and 4) the public nature of the consent of marriage helps the spouses remain faithful to it.

Sacramental orders

Sacramental orders refers to the sacrament of Holy Orders, which is a sacrament conferred by the imposition of the hands of a bishop which confers on a man the grace and spiritual power to sanctify others. There are three degrees of the sacrament: the deaconate, the priesthood, and the episcopacy. The three degrees constitute only one sacrament administered separately with three consecutively higher sacramental effects. See Holy Orders 1536.

Sacramental penance

Sacramental penance is the prayer or other good work imposed on the penitent by the priest before granting absolution in the sacrament of Confession.

The penance or prayers imposed in confession should be articulated with the lips though not necessarily aloud. This external evidence of the performance of sacramental penance is a vestigial form of public penance and is fitting as reparation for the offense of sin to the community. See Penance 1459.

Sacramental seal of confession 1467

Because of the delicacy and greatness of the ministry of forgiveness and the respect due persons, the Church declares that "every priest who hears confessions is bound under very severe penalties to keep absolute secrecy regarding the sins that his penitents have confessed to him. He can make no use of knowledge that confession gives him about penitents' lives" (CCC 1467).

This bond of secrecy is called the sacramental seal, and it forever binds the priest. It has no exceptions; not even the state has any authority here.

This should make the sinner less anxious about revealing his innermost failings in confession.

Sacramental sign 1152

A sacramental sign is the outward evidence of the sacrament. They are those things we can perceive with our senses and which symbolize the hidden mystery of grace. The Catechism of the Catholic Church teaches that it is "through the sacramental signs of his Church that the Holy Spirit carries on the work of sanctification." The sacraments "purify and integrate all the richness of signs and symbols of the *cosmos* and *social* life." They "make actively present the *salvation* wrought by *Christ*, and *prefigure* and anticipate the *glory* of *heaven*" (CCC 1152).

Sacramental theology

The word *theology* comes from the Greek word *'theologia,'* meaning the study of God. Theology is the formal study of the *nature* of God and his relations with the universe. Concentration on particular areas of theology gives rise to specialties such as *moral* theology, *Marian* theology, *dogmatic* theology etc. Sacramental theology is one such specialty that deals with the subject of the *sacraments*. See Council of Trent 406.

Sacramentals 1667

Sacramentals are *sacred* signs that "bear a resemblance to the *sacraments*. They signify effects, particularly of a *spiritual* nature, which are obtained through the *intercession* of the Church. By them men are disposed to receive the chief effect of the sacraments, and various occasions in life are rendered *holy*" (CCC 1667).

Sacramentals must not be confused with sacraments. *Christ* instituted sacraments; the Church institutes sacramentals. Sacraments impart *grace* by virtue of the confer-

ring *rite* itself, *ex opere operato*, but sacramentals impart grace according to the dispositions of the recipient and the *intercession* of the Church.

The sacraments cannot be changed or modified by either the minister or the community, but sacramentals may be changed, introduced, or fall out of use, according to the times. The number of sacramentals can vary.

Used in accordance with the mind of the Church, sacramentals are a means of receiving *actual grace* and are an extension of the sacramental principle of using *material* objects to signify *spiritual truths* and grace.

Some sacramentals are objects, such as *holy water*, *scapulars*, *rosaries*, medals, statues, and *icons*. Other sacramentals are actions. In general, these actions fall into six classes: 1) *prayers*, such as the *Our Father*; 2) dipping or sprinkling with holy water when conferring a *blessing*; 3) eating, such as *blessed* bread (which is different than the *Eucharist*); 4) confessing, such as in the *Confiteor;* 5) blessings of candles, houses, bells, palms, food before meals, etc.; and 6) giving *alms* in the name of Church, not as a private deed.

The Catechism of the Catholic Church teaches that sacramentals were instituted for the *sanctification* of certain *ministries* and certain *states of life.* They are associated with a variety of circumstances in *Christian* life and things useful to *man.* They always include *prayer* and a *sensible* sign.

Sacramentary

The sacramentary is the part of the *Roman Missal* containing the *prayers* and directives for the *Mass* and sacramental formulas but not the *readings* for the Mass. See Consecrated virgin 922.

Sacraments of Christ 1116

The sacraments of Christ refer to the seven *sacraments* of the Church: *Baptism, Confirmation* or *Chrismation, Eucharist, Penance, Anointing of the Sick, Holy Orders,* and *Matrimony.* The sacraments of the Church were instituted by *Christ* and may properly be called sacraments of Christ. Sacraments are actions of the *Holy Spirit* at work in the Church *sanctifying* the *faithful.*

Sacraments of eternal life 1130

The sacraments of the Church are also called sacraments of *eternal life* because in them the Church *celebrates* the *mystery* of her Lord until he comes again and becomes everything to everyone for all *eternity.*

In her *liturgy* the Church is drawn toward this goal by the *Holy Spirit*'s groaning, '*Marana tha.*' In her sacra-

ments, the Church already receives the guarantee of her inheritance and even now shares in *everlasting life* while waiting in *blessed hope* for the appearance of *Jesus Christ.*

The sacraments are signs that both *commemorate* what precedes them (the *mystery of salvation*) and demonstrate what Christ has accomplished, which is eternal glory. In the sacraments, man can enjoy a foretaste of eternal life already in this world.

Sacraments of faith 1123

The Catechism of the Catholic Church teaches that the "purpose of the *sacraments* is to *sanctify* men, to build up the *Body of Christ* and, finally, to give *worship* to God. Because they are signs they also instruct. They not only presuppose *faith,* but by words and objects they also nourish, strengthen, and express it. That is why they are called 'sacraments of faith'" (CCC 1123).

Sacraments of healing 1211, 1421

Because the new life as a child of God given at *Baptism* can be weakened and even lost through *sin, Christ* the Physician of *souls* has willed that his Church continue his work of healing *salvation.* For this purpose he has given the Church the two *sacraments* of healing: The *sacrament of*

Penance and the sacrament of *Anointing of the Sick.*

Sacraments of initiation 1211

The sacraments of initiation are the three *sacraments* that lay the foundation of every *Christian* life: *Baptism, Confirmation,* and the *Eucharist.*

Sacraments of salvation 1127

The Church teaches that "for believers the *sacraments* of the *New Covenant* are necessary for *salvation*" (CCC 1129).

The sacraments "are *efficacious* because in them *Christ* himself is at work: it is he who baptizes, he who acts in his sacraments in order to communicate the *grace* that each sacrament signifies" (CCC 1127). *Celebrated* worthily in *faith,* by virtue of the power of the *Spirit,* the sacraments work *ex opere operato,* that is, by the fact that the actions are performed.

Sacraments of service 1211

Holy Orders and *Matrimony* are "the *sacraments* at the service of communion and the *mission* of the *faithful*" (CCC 1211), because they are directed primarily towards the *salvation* of others. They contribute to personal salvation through service to others.

Sacraments of the Church 1117, 1118

The Church "has discerned over the centuries that among *liturgical celebrations* there are seven that are, in the strict sense of the term, *sacraments* instituted by the *Lord*" (CCC 1117). These are *Baptism, Confirmation* or *Chrismation, Eucharist, Penance, Anointing of the Sick, Holy Orders,* and *Matrimony.*

"The sacraments are 'of the Church' in the double sense that they are 'by her' and 'for her.' They are 'by the Church,' for she is the sacrament of *Christ's* action at work in her through the mission of the Holy Spirit. They are 'for the Church' in the sense that 'the sacraments make the Church,' since they manifest and communicate to men, above all in the Eucharist, the mystery of communion with the God who is love" (CCC 1118).

Sacramentum 774

Sacramentum refers to the "visible sign of the hidden reality of *salvation*" (CCC 774). The saving work of *Christ's sanctifying* humanity is revealed in the signs of the *sacraments.*

The Latin word 'sacramentum' originally denoted a valuable object that was deposited in a temple as expression and guarantee of one's *fidelity* to a given commitment. Applied to the sacraments, it firstly refers to the *fidelity* of Christ in conferring *grace* through the sacraments he instituted. Secondly, it refers to the fidelity that those receiving a sacrament pledge to Christ. The same sacramental sign expresses the fidelity of Christ and of the *Christian*. This is why unworthy or *sacrilegious* reception of a sacrament is so serious a *sin*: it is a form of lying to God.

Sacramentum exeuntium 1523

When administered to the dying, the *sacrament* of the *Anointing of the Sick* is properly called 'sacramentum exeuntium,' which means the 'sacrament of the departing' in Latin. This *anointing* "completes the holy anointings that mark the whole *Christian* life: that of *Baptism* which sealed the new life in us, and that of *Confirmation* which strengthened us for the combat of this life. This last anointing fortifies the end of our earthly life like a solid rampart for the final struggles before entering the Father's house" (CCC 1523).

Because of this connection with the passage out of this life, this sacrament came to be seen as one only given to the dying and became known as *Extreme Unction*.

Today, this sacrament is administered to those suffering from frailty or sickness as well as to the dying, and is referred to as the *sacrament of the sick*. A deacon may not administer this sacrament.

Sacred

Sacred comes from the Latin word 'sacer,' meaning *holy*. Something is sacred when it is *consecrated*, set aside for or belongs to God exclusively. Sacred things are set apart and dedicated to some *religious* purpose. See Sacramentals 1667.

Sacred anointing 1499

Sacred *anointing* is another name for the *sacrament* of *Extreme Unction*, now called *Anointing of the Sick*, since it is no longer reserved to those at the point of death.

Sacred art 2502

From earliest times, the Church has used art as an expression of the invisible glory of God whether in painting, sculpture, mosaics, architecture, *vestments*, or *sacred vessels*.

In sacred art, the true and beautiful are used to invoke and glorify the *transcendent mystery* of God in *faith* and *adoration*. For this reason, *bishops* are encouraged to promote sacred art in its various forms and remove from *churches* everything which is not in conformity with the *truth* of the faith and the *authentic* beauty of sacred art.

Sacred chrism 1183

Sacred chrism is one of three oils *blessed* by the *Bishop* during the Chrism Mass on *Holy Thursday*. It is olive oil mixed with *balsam*. It is used in the *sacraments* of *Baptism*, *Confirmation*, and *Holy Orders* as well as in the consecration of *churches.* It is also referred to as *myron* or *oil of chrism.* See Holy oils.

Sacred Liturgy

'Sacred Liturgy' is another name for the *Mass.*

Sacred office

An office is the *duty* of service associated with one's station or position, or a task to be performed as an *obligation.* When such duties pertain to *ecclesiastical* matters they are called sacred offices. The three offices of the Church are to teach, to *sanctify,* and to govern. See Officium 1255. Also see Interdict.

Sacred orders

Sacred orders is another name for *Holy Orders.* See Clergy. Also see Holy Orders 1536.

Sacred Scripture 102, 109

Sacred Scripture refers to the sacred writings of the *Old* and *New Testaments* that contain the *truth* of God's *revelation* to *man.* The Church teaches that they are the *Word of God* composed by human authors inspired by the *Holy Spirit.*

In the words of Sacred Scripture God reveals himself to man in the words of *human* authors writing under the *inspiration* of the Holy Spirit and have God as their primary author.

The Church holds that "all that the inspired authors or sacred writers affirm should be regarded as affirmed by the Holy Spirit... the books of Sacred Scripture firmly, faithfully, and without error teach that truth which God, for the sake of our *salvation,* wished to see confided to the Sacred Scriptures" (CCC 107).

Sacred Scripture is also referred to as the *Bible.* The Bible is divided into two parts, the Old Testament, containing forty-six (or, according to some, forty-five) books, and the New Testament, consisting of twenty-seven books. See Old Testament. Also see New Testament.

Sacred seasons

In her loving solicitude for the eternal welfare of her children, Mother Church, guided by the *Holy Spirit,* carefully strives to foster, and enrich the *spiritual life* of her children. The spiritual life of the Church revolves around a *liturgical year* which is divided into four cycles called sacred seasons and a *sanctoral cycle* of feasts. The four sacred *liturgical* seasons celebrate the life of *Christ* from before his birth to his *Passion,* death, *Resurrection,* and glorious *Ascension* into *heaven* and close with an account of the life of the early Church. The sanctoral cycle, which parallels the *cycles of the liturgical year* commemorates the life of the *saints* and *martyrs* whose lives proclaim the *Paschal mystery* exemplified by those who have suffered and have been glorified with Christ and the feasts of Our *Lord* and *Our Lady*. See Liturgical seasons.

Sacred species

Sacred species refers to the appearances of bread and wine that remain after the *consecration* changes their substance into the Body, Blood, *soul*, and *divinity* of *Christ* by *transubstantiation*.

The term species was used by the *Council of Trent* (*Denzinger* 1652) to refer to the *accidents*, such as size, weight, color, taste, and odor of the bread and wine which remain exactly the same after *transubstantiation*. These are not mere appearances as though the properties or accidents are unreal. But, they are only appearances because after *consecration* these accidents lack the natural *substance* that underlies them or in which they inhere and are sustained miraculously. See Consecration 1376.

Sacred Tradition 80, 95

Tradition comes from the Latin 'traditio,' meaning giving over, or handing down. *Christ* who summed up the entire *revelation* of the most high God commanded the *Apostles* to preach the *Gospel* which he fulfilled in his own *person* and *promulgated* with his own lips. This Gospel was the source of all saving *truth* and *moral* discipline.

This Gospel was handed on in two ways: 1) orally by the spoken words of the *Apostles* in their preaching and example and by the institutions they established; 2) in writing by the Apostles and others associated with them who, under the *inspiration* of the *Holy Spirit* committed the message of *salvation* to writing. This living transmission, accomplished by the Holy Spirit, is called Tradition. It is distinct from *Sacred Scripture*, but closely connected to it.

Through this Tradition the Church perpetuates her *doctrine*, life, and *worship* and all she is and believes to all generations. Because it is of God it is called *sacred*. See Oral Tradition.

Sacred vessels

The vessels required for the celebration of *Mass*, the *chalice* and *paten*, hold the place of honor among *sacred* vessels. Other sacred vessels include the following: 1) the *ciborium*, which resembles a covered chalice and holds the *Eucharist*; 2) the *pyx*, which is a container for the large Host used in exposition or a small capsule used to carry the Eucharist to the sick; 3) the *monstrance*, which is a large vessel used to expose the Host for *adoration* or during Benediction; 4) the *lunette* or lunula, which is a crescent shaped device used to hold the Host securely upright in the monstrance. It is sometime called a *capsula*.

Present regulations state that these vessels should be made of *materials* that are solid, noble (gold or silver) and that will not break easily. Vessels made of metal should be gilded if the metal will rust. Other materials prized in the region where they are used may be employed but *chalices* should always be made of non-absorbent material. Following *liturgical* custom the sacred vessels are *consecrated* using a prescribed *rite*. This may now be done by any *priest*. See Chrism. Also see Tabernacle 1183, 1379.

Sacrifice/sacrificial

Sacrifice is the highest form of *adoration*. In it a duly authorized *priest* offers a *victim* in the name of the people acknowledging God's supreme *dominion* over *man* and his complete dependence on God.

In sacrifice the victim is at least partially removed from *human* use and to the degree that it is destroyed it is an *act* of submission to the *divine* majesty. See Curse. Also see Sacrifice of the Cross.

Sacrifice of Calvary

The Sacrifice of Calvary is the same as the *Sacrifice of the Cross*. See Sacrifice of the Cross.

Sacrifice of the Cross

The Sacrifice of the Cross refers to the death of *Christ* by *Crucifixion* on *Calvary*.

With the institution of the *Eucharist* by *Jesus*, offering the same Sacrifice of the Cross in many places without in any way compromising the unity of the *sacrifice* becomes possible and permits all peoples to participate in that *sacrifice* throughout time. The *heavenly liturgy* under the *New Dispensation* may be found everywhere the *Catholic Church* is. See Three offices of Christ 783. Also see Synagogue; Temple.

Sacrifice of the Mass

See Mass 1332.

Sacrifice of the New Covenant

613

The *sacrifice* of the *New Covenant* is the *Paschal sacrifice*, that is, *Christ's Passion* and death on the Cross.

Sacrificial love

Sacrifice is any act of *eternal worship* which honors God as the principal end of *man* by the *oblation* of a visible creature. The term is also used *metaphorically* to apply to internal acts by which man, in the spirit of *self-sacrifice*, devotes himself to the service of God, a *reformation* of life and to the service of others in *obedience* to the command to *love* others as one loves himself for the love of *Christ*.

Sacrificial *love* then, refers to the internal *act* by which a *person* devotes himself to the *duties* of his *state of life* and service to others in a spirit of faithful and devoted *obedience* out of love for God.

The mutual dedication of *spouses* to the *spiritual* and *temporal* good of one another in the sacramental *covenant* of their *marriage* is a form of sacrificial love and the *means* by which spouses sanctify one another. See Love 218.

Sacrilege 2120

"Sacrilege consists in *profaning* or treating unworthily the *sacraments* and other *liturgical* actions, as well as *persons*, things, or places *consecrated* to God. Sacrilege is a *grave sin* especially when committed against the *Eucharist*" (CCC 2120).

Sacrilegious

Sacrilegious is the adjectival form of *sacrilege*. See Excommunication 1463.

Saint(s)

'Saints' was the name given to *Christians* in general in Col 1:2, but it soon came to be used to name those exhibiting extraordinary *virtue* and example. In the proper sense today saints are those who have exhibited heroic *virtue* in their lives and are honored by the Church through universal teaching *authority* or by a solemn *proclamation* called *canonization*. Official *recognition* of *sanctity* implies that the *person* is now in *heaven*, may

be publicly invoked and their virtues or death by *martyrdom* serves as a worthy witness and example to the *faithful*. See Object of faith.

Saint Savior

Saint Savior is a title given to some *churches* dedicated to God the Son as *Redeemer*. The *titular feast* is *celebrated* on August 6. The *feast* is also known as the Feast of the Holy Redeemer, but it is found only in the special calendar of some *dioceses* and *religious orders*, and is celebrated with proper *Mass* and *Divine Office* either on the third *Sunday* of July or on October 23. See Transfiguration.

Salvation

Salvation is the action by which the *soul* is freed from *sin* and its *consequences* and enabled to attain the *beatific vision* in *heaven*. It is not only a reward but the achievement of man's *ultimate end*. Salvation depends entirely on the love and *mercy* of God, but is only achieved by *free choice* in cooperation with *divine grace*. See Mysterion 774.

Salve Regina

Salve Regina means *Hail, Holy Queen*. It is one of the oldest *Marian antiphons* in the *Latin Church* and used from early times in the *Divine Office*. The author is probably Hermannus Contractus (d. 1054). After *Compline* in

Dominican usage it is accompanied by a procession. In the *Carmelite rite* it is recited at the altar steps before the last Gospel and before the blessing in the *Mozarabic rite*. See Dominican Rite. Also see Paraclete. 692.

Salvific

Salvific means causing *salvation*. See Fullness of time 484, 702. Also see Prevenient grace; Coredemptrix.

Sanatio in radice

'Sanatio in radice' is a Latin phrase meaning 'healing at the root.' It refers to the *judicial* procedure called *convalidation* by which an *invalid marriage* is given *legal* recognition by the Church. The *impediment* to *validity* of the marriage is *dispensed retroactively*. Renewal of consent is not required, and *canonical* effects are *attributed* to a *marriage* as if it were *valid* from the start. See Nullity of Marriage 1629.

Sancta sanctis 948

'Sancta sanctis' is a Latin phrase meaning, 'holy things for the holy.' It "is proclaimed by the celebrant in most Eastern *liturgies* during the elevation of the *holy Gifts* before the distribution of *communion*. The *faithful* (sancti) are fed by *Christ's* holy (sancta) Body and Blood to grow in the communion of the *Holy Spirit* (koi-

nonia) and to communicate it to the world" (CCC 948).

Sanctification

Sanctification involves being made *holy*. All men are called to the *vocation* of holiness. A *person* is said to be holy when he lives in union with God in the state of *sanctifying grace*, which unites him to God and allows him to share in the *divine life*. This is called *moral holiness*. See Sanctify.

Sanctify

Sanctify means to make *holy*. See Sacraments of Faith 1123.

Sanctifying grace 1999, 2000

Sanctifying *grace* is a free gift that God makes to us of his own life. It is *infused* by the *Holy Spirit* into the *soul* to heal and *sanctify* it. Sanctifying grace is an *habitual* gift, or a stable and *supernatural* disposition that perfects the soul itself to enable it to live with God and to act by his love in keeping with God's call. It is a vital principle of the *supernatural* life just as the *rational* soul is the vital principle of man's *natural* life.

Sanctifying grace is not a *substance* but a real quality that becomes a permanent part of the substance of the soul and which renews it by the fact of its presence. Sanctifying grace effects an *ontological* change in the soul by enabling it to become a *partaker of the divine nature*, an object of God's special *love, heir* to *heaven*, coheir with *Christ*, and a son of God. The state of sanctifying grace is *union with Christ*.

Although sanctifying grace is commonly associated with possession of the *virtue* of *charity*, it is distinct from it. Charity belongs to the *will* and sanctifying grace belongs to the whole soul, *mind*, will, and affections.

Sanctifying grace must not be identified with the indwelling of the Holy Spirit in the souls of the just or the *imputation* of the merits of Christ on the soul as a sort of garment. *Scripture* speaks of it as a garment only to indicate that it has an external origin in the *merits* of Christ. Sanctifying grace makes those who possess it *holy* by giving them a participation in the *divine life*. It is the life that Christ taught he has with the Father.

Sanctifying grace can only be lost in the soul by the commission a deliberate *mortal sin* and only *repentance*, at the instigation of God by actual grace, can restore it. For *Catholics* this implies reception of the *sacrament of Reconciliation*.

Sanctifying grace is also known as *habitual grace*. It remains *permanently* in the soul so long as no *mortal sin* is committed. It is distinguished from *actual grace*, which is a passing influence of the Holy Spirit on a *person* in moments of action, both interior and exterior. Such actions may be those which first move one to *conversion* or to those involved in persevering in the process of *sanctification*.

Sanctifying office 893

An office is a service or *duty*, responsibility, or function of the Church. The *Bishop* exercises the office of sanctifying as the steward of the *grace* of the *priesthood* and especially the *Eucharist*, which is the center of the life of the *particular church* and *sanctifies* the people.

The Bishop and *priests* also exercise the office of sanctifying the Church by their *prayers*, the ministry of the word and the *sacraments*, and by their example.

Sanction

Sanction is the act of a recognized *authority* confirming or *ratifying* an action. It is authorization, approval, or permission. See Canonizing 828.

Sanctity

In the absolute sense sanctity refers to the total *transcendence* of God referred to in the *Gloria* of the *Mass*, 'You alone are the Holy One, you alone are the *Lord*, you alone are the Most High.'

All other sanctity is by *participation*. The sanctity of a *person* is in proportion to the degree that he shares in the Divinity. Such sanctity consists in the possession of *sanc-*

tifying grace. Generally speaking, sanctity is used to describe persons who practice extraordinary *virtue,* especially love of God and neighbor. See Apostolic Fathers. Also see Saint; Grace of original holiness 399.

Sanctoral cycle

The *sanctoral cycle* is also called the *Proper of Saints.* It parallels the *cycles of the liturgical year* and commemorates the life of the *saints* and *martyrs.* Their lives proclaim the *Paschal mystery* exemplified by those who have suffered and been glorified with *Christ* and the feasts of Our *Lord* and *Our Lady.* The *Proper of Seasons* determines the liturgical passages appointed to be recited in the *Mass* and office to commemorate the individual *feast* or *mystery* of *faith* in the seasons of *Advent, Christmas, Lent, Easter* and *Ordinary Time.* See Liturgical seasons; Cycles A, B, C.

Sanctoral year 1172

The sanctoral year, or saints' year, refers to the commemoration of the *martyrs* and *saints,* which the Church does in an annual *liturgical* cycle. In this cycle she proclaims the *Paschal mystery* exemplified by those who have suffered and have been *glorified* with *Christ.*

Sanctuary

The sanctuary is that part of the Church in which the *altar* is located. It also contains seats for the *celebrant* and ministers, a *credence table* where vessels and other items needed for the *celebration* of the *Mass* are placed until needed, and the *aumbry* where the *holy oils* are stored. In the case of *cathedrals* it is the location of the *episcopal* throne and *choir-stalls* where the *Divine Office* is sung by *canons.* The sanctuary is called *sacred* space because of the activities that take place there and because frequently the *Blessed Sacrament* is reserved there. When this is the case there is a lighted red *sanctuary lamp* indicating the presence of the *Holy Eucharist.*

A sanctuary may also refer to a place of *devotion.* To such a place the *faithful* travel on *pilgrimage* to pray for a special *grace* or favor. See Church 752.

Sanctuary lamp/candle

A sanctuary lamp is a lamp containing a candle usually of wax in a red glass globe which continuously burns wherever the *Blessed Sacrament* is reserved. It represents *Christ's* abiding love and reminds the *faithful* to respond with loving *adoration* and respect in his presence. See Tabernacle 1183, 1379.

Sanctus

Sanctus is a Latin word meaning *holy.* It is found in

the *preface* as the *prayer* of thanksgiving forming the solemn introduction to the *Canon* or *anaphora* of the *Mass*. It is sung by the *celebrant* in the *Latin Rite* and ends with the Sanctus or *Tersanctus* (thrice holy) *hymn* of victory: 'Holy, holy, holy Lord God of hosts. *Heaven* and earth are full of your *glory*. *Hosanna* in the highest. *Blessed* is he who comes in the name of the Lord. Hosanna in the highest.' See Preface 1352. Also see Appendix of prayers: Prayers recited at Mass; Sanctus.

Sanguine

Temperament identifies a *person's* customary frame of *mind* or natural disposition. Persons with a sanguine temperament are warm, passionate, and cheerful. See Temperament.

Sanhedrin 591, 597

Sanhedrin was the name for the highest court of *justice* and supreme council in Jerusalem, during the life of *Christ*. It regulated *religious* and *civil* observances, enforced the *Law of Moses*, controlled *doctrinal* teaching and in a wider sense also the lower courts of justice. It had seventy-two members.

Satan

Satan is a *Hebrew* word meaning adversary. It is frequently used in the *New Testament* to refer to the *devil* or Lucifer. See Devil.

Scandal 2282, 2284

Scandal refers to any action or omission provoking or causing *immoral* actions in others by words or deeds.

Scandal is direct when one *deliberately* or willfully seeks to draw another into *sin* as in *seduction*. It is indirect when the sinful act of another is foreseen to be at least likely to lead another into *sin*.

Pharisaical scandal consists in being disedified or scandalized by the *good* actions or behavior of another. It arises when a *person's* own *moral* weakness finds an occasion of sin in the good acts of another because of their own *evil* dispositions. *Pharisaical* scandal should not be considered scandal.

Scapular

The word scapular comes from the Latin word 'scapula,' meaning shoulder. It is an outer garment worn by some *religious institutes*. Originally it was a work apron worn by *Benedictines* to protect their clothing. It consists of two strips of cloth joined at the shoulder so that one strip fell in front and one in back. It is worn over a tunic fastened by a belt. At times it may have a hood attached. It is a symbol of the *yoke* of *Christ*.

Tertiaries wear an abbreviated form of the scapular under their *secular* clothes. Scapulars vary in size and color to correspond to their religious *family*. They consist of two pieces of cloth about two by three inches joined by strings worn on the back and front under their regular clothes.

There are seventeen such scapulars recognized by the Church each being the badge of a *confraternity*. The five best known are the brown scapular of *Our Lady* of Mount Carmel, the red scapular of the *Passion*, the black scapular of the *Seven Dolors*, the blue scapular of the *Immaculate Conception*, and the white scapular of the *Blessed Trinity*.

Scapulars are worn with confidence in the *mercy* of God whose *blessings* are invoked by the wearing of the scapular. See Third order.

Schism 817, 1206, 2089

Schism is the obstinate refusal to submit to the *authority* of the *Pope* or willful and formal separation from the unity of the Church and *ecclesiastical* communion with members of the Church. The external act of schism *ipso facto* incurs *excommunication*. The *sacraments* may not be administered to schismatics.

The difference between *heresy* and schism is that in schism the grounds for separation are non-*doctrinal* while in heresy they are doctrinal.

Scholastic philosophy

Philosophy is the science that studies the ultimate *reasons*, *causes*, and *principles* of being using *reason* alone.

There was no *systematic philosophy* in the Church before the twelfth and thirteenth centuries. At that time a philosophy, largely an adaptation of Greek thought, drawn from Socrates (450–380 B.C.), Plato (427–347 B.C.) and especially Aristotle (384–322 B.C.), arose which is referred to as Scholastic philosophy. It was enriched by the thought of St. Augustine (354–430 A.D.). It was developed further by Alcuin (735–804 A.D.), St. Anselm (1033–1109 A.D.), Abelard (1079–1142 A.D.), William of Auvergne (1180–1249 A.D.), Alexander of Hales (1170/80–1245 A.D.), St. Bonaventure (1221–1274 A.D.), St. Albert the Great (1193–1280 A.D.), St. Thomas Aquinas (1225–1274 A.D.), and Bl. John Duns Scotus (1266/70–1308 A.D.). It reached its full perfection in the thirteenth century.

Scholastic philosophy reasons only from the light of *nature* and has no direct connection with *revelation*. It proves the existence of God from his works alone and does not investigate the revealed nature of God as *trinitarian* which is beyond reason. In this aspect it differs from many modern systems which claim to be a substitute for *revelation*.

The Schoolmen, or Scholastic philosophers taught that philosophy is the *handmaid of theology and faith* in three ways:

(1) It prepares the way for *faith* by establishing the spiritual nature of the *soul* and the existence of God.

(2) Though it cannot prove *revealed truth*, it can show that it is not contrary to reason.

(3) Wherever the provinces of philosophy and theology touch, the philosopher must correct his *conclusions* in light of the higher *certitude* of faith and divinely revealed truth.

Because of its completeness, *coherence*, and consistency it became known as the *perennial* philosophy of the Schoolmen, hence its name Scholastic philosophy. It survives today as the most continuously existent, comprehensive, and consistent system of philosophic thought known to *man*. See Scholastic theology.

Scholastic theology

Theology is the science which treats of God and things pertaining to him, such as *virtues*, Christian *doctrine*, *moral* behavior, the *spiritual life*, care of *souls*, and the derivation of *truths* of *revelation* and *dogmas*. Theology which is based on the system of *Scholastic philosophy* is called Scholastic theology.

It is an *axiom* of Scholastic philosophy that nothing can be true in *philosophy* which is false in theology. The Church does not teach philosophy,

she only declares those philosophical tenets which reject primary *truths* about *faith* and *morals* to be false. The correction of false reasoning she leaves to philosophers.

Divinely revealed truth finds in Scholastic philosophy a noble instrument for the exposition and scientific elaboration of *understanding* as it applies to the realm of theology. See Theologian 2038. Also see Scholastic philosophy.

School of prayer 2689

School of prayer is another name for *prayer groups*, the gathering together of a number of *persons* to pray together and support one another through discussion of the *spiritual life*, *Scripture, catechism*, or spiritual books. Participants usually meet on a regular schedule and have the same *persons* in attendance.

Science

Science comes from the Latin word 'scientia,' meaning to know, discern, or distinguish. Science is a body of systemized *knowledge* derived from observation, study, or experimentation. See Empirically. Also see Proof for the existence of God 31.

Scourge/Scourging

A scourge is a whip or other instrument, such as a strap of leather, used to beat condemned *persons*, often in

preparation for *crucifixion.*
See Crucified.

Scribes

Scribes were a class of well
educated *Jews* trained as
copyists and *notaries.* They
were referred to as lawyers
and *rabbis* but they were not
priests. Some were members
of the *Sanhedrin* and inter-
preters of the *law.* Because
they were devoted to preserving and defending the *law,*
they saw *Jesus* as a threat and
challenged him on many occasions. They ultimately took
part in plotting his death. See
Sabbath 2175.

Scripture/Scriptural

Scripture is another way of
referring to the book of *Sacred
Scripture* or the *Bible.*

Scripture refers to the words
by which God reveals himself
to man in the *human* words
of authors writing under
the *inspiration* of the *Holy
Spirit* with God as their primary author. The Church
holds that "Since therefore all
that the inspired authors or
sacred writers affirm should
be regarded as affirmed by the
Holy Spirit, we must acknowledge that the books of Scripture firmly, faithfully, and
without error teach that *truth*
which God, for the sake of our
salvation, wished to see confided to the Sacred Scriptures"
(CCC 107). See Inspiration
105. Also see Senses of Scripture 115.

Scroll

A scroll is a an ancient book
written on pieces of *papyrus,*
animal skin or *parchment*
each about six inches wide
and ten inches long. They
were sewn together and rolled
up around a stick. The reader
would unroll the scroll from
the stick and wrap it around
another stick as it was read.
The title of the book was written along the outside edge of
the scroll. Scrolls were costly
and highly prized. They were
carefully stored in leather
cases or clay containers. Large
scrolls were kept in a specially
built cabinet. See Synagogue.

Scrupulous

Scrupulous comes from the
Latin words 'scrupulosus,'
which literally means full of
sharp stones, or rough or rug-
ged. It came to be used to mean
the smallest quantity, very
exact, precise, or accurate.
We use it to refer to behavior
characterized by attention to
minute points of behavior or
duty. A scrupulous *person* is
excessively careful with attention to what is proper or right.

Applied to promptings of *conscience,* it describes persons
who for insufficient motives
imagine *sin* to be where it does
not exist or to view *venial sins*
as *mortal.*

Scrupulosity is dangerous to
the health of both body and
soul when it relies entirely on
personal *judgment.* Scrupulous persons should humbly

submit to the advice of their *confessor*. See Pharisees 575.

Scrutiny / scrutinies

The rite of *election* is a *liturgical* landmark which takes place in the third stage of *Christian* initiation. It includes the scrutinies which are careful examinations designed to prepare a candidate for the reception of the *sacraments of initiation* at *Easter*. It begins the first *Sunday* of *Lent* and includes three *scrutinies*, *presentations*, and anointing. See RCIA 1232.

Seal of the Lord 1274

Before reading and writing skills were common, seals served as signatures. Seals were carved into a hard surface, which could be pressed on sealing wax or other *material* to leave a distinctive mark. The Greek word for seal is '*sphragis*.' It refers to the image created by a seal, especially in sealing wax, to ensure the *authenticity* of a document. A *person's* seal was often hung by a cord around the neck or arm. The mark of the seal served as evidence of authenticity or ownership of things marked by the seal. The seal also served as a personal pledge of the one whose seal it was.

At *Baptism*, the Christian is marked with a *sacramental character* or the seal of the *Holy Spirit* with a sign of ownership and the person's *faith* and expectation of both the *blessed* vision of God and hope of the *resurrection*.

The *seal or invisible mark on the soul* is a permanent mark of the Lord placed on the soul of the baptized and is his pledge of *eternal life* and it is called the seal of the Lord or *Dominicus character*. See Seal or invisible mark.

Seal or invisible mark on the soul

By the sacraments of *Baptism*, *Confirmation* and Holy *Orders* the *soul* is marked with a seal of the *Holy Spirit* as a sign of divine ownership, of the *person's faith* and of expectation of both the *blessed* vision of God and hope of *resurrection*.

This *seal* or invisible permanent mark of the Lord placed in the soul of the *baptized* is *Christ's* permanent pledge of *eternal life* and a permanent sacramental *character* enabling the recipient to do certain works in the Church. It is also called the *seal of the Lord* or *Dominicus character*. See Seal of the Lord 1274.

Seance

A seance is a gathering in which a *person*, called a *medium*, tries to communicate with the dead. See Spiritism 2117.

Seasons of penance 1438

Seasons of *penance* refers to the periods during the *liturgical* year especially set aside for more intense *penitential* practice, such as *Advent, Lent* and all Fridays.

Secede(d)

Secede comes from the Latin word 'secedere,' meaning to withdraw or depart. Today it means to withdraw from membership or association with a group or organization. See Marcionism 123.

Second Adam

The Second Adam refers to *Christ*, who restored fallen man through the new birth of *Baptism*. See New Adam.

Second class relics

There are three classes of *relics. First class relics* are parts of the *saint's* body. *Second class relics* are things the saint used during life. *Third class relics* are objects, such as cloth, which have been touched to a first class relic. Relics may not be sold or bought. See Altar 1383. Also see Relic.

Second coming

On the night before he died *Jesus* promised the *Apostles* that he would 'return to take you with me' (Jn 14:3). At the *Ascension angels* appeared saying, 'This same Jesus will come back in the same way as you have seen him go there' (Acts 1:11). This return is referred to as the second coming. When this return will take place no one knows. Some early *Christians* thought it would take place soon, perhaps in their own lifetime.

The promise is intended as the basis of Christian *hope*. We must 'live *good* and *religious* lives here in the present world while waiting in joyful hope for the *blessings* which will come with the appearance of the *glory* of our great God and Savior, Jesus *Christ*' (Titus 2:13). See Advent 524. Also see Parousia 830.

Second conversion 1428

The Catechism of the Catholic Church uses the term second conversion in reference to *Christ's* continuing call to *conversion* throughout Christian life. *Baptism*, which grants a new life in the Christian, does not abolish *human* frailty or the inclination to *sin*. Hence, *conversion* must be a continual and uninterrupted task for the whole Church, which is *holy*, yet always in need of *purification* by constant *penance* and renewal.

St. Ambrose speaks of two conversions, the *conversion of water* in Baptism and the *conversion of tears* of *repentance*. The second conversion of tears has a *communitarian* dimension because the Lord continually calls the whole Church to *repentance*.

The conversion of tears is not a merely *human* work, because the *contrite* heart is drawn and moved by *grace* of the *Holy Spirit* to respond to the merciful *love* of God who loved us first.

Second Person of the Holy Trinity

The Church teaches that God is one in *essence* and three in *Persons*: the Father, the Son, and the *Holy Spirit*; each of whom is *consubstantial*, that is identical with the *divine substance*. *God the Son* is referred to as the Second Person of the Holy Trinity. See Trinity, Holy 232, 234, 237, 253. Also see Son, God the 240, 241, 242.

Second plank 1446

The second plank is a phrase used by Tertullian (c. 160–222 A.D.), as well as by the *Council of Trent*, to refer to the *sacrament of Penance* because it is a second rescue from the loss of *grace* in the shipwreck of *sin* after *Baptism*.

Second Vatican Council

The Second Vatican Council was the twenty-first *ecumenical council*. It is called simply *Vatican II* in references. It was opened by *Pope* John XXIII in St. Peter's *Basilica* in Rome on October 11, 1962.

In attendance were 2,300 *bishops* and *prelates*. Thirteen *commissions* prepared materials for deliberation by the Council. There were four sessions. The first opened on October 11, 1962 and closed on December 8, 1962. The second session opened on September 29, 1963 and closed on December 4, 1963. The third session opened on September 14, 1964 and admitted women to the working sessions for the first time in history. It closed on November 21, 1964. The fourth and final session opened on September 14, 1965 and closed with solemnities on December 8, 1965.

Pope John died on June 3, 1963 and Cardinal Giovanni Montini was elected Pope, taking the name Paul VI. The Council was continued under the new Pope.

The Council was distinctive in being *'pastoral'* rather than one of *dogmatic proclamations*. Two movements already present in the Church before the Council were reinforced by the Council and began to affect the entire Church. The first was the renewal of *biblical* study which profoundly deepened the Church's devotional *understanding* and *piety*. The second was the *liturgical* movement which adapted forms of *worship* in the lives of *Catholics*.

The Council produced and *promulgated* sixteen documents consisting of four *Constitutions*, nine *Decrees* and three *Declarations*. The *faithful* are encouraged to study and meditate on these documents because *Vatican II* provided a program which will continue for years to come. Some of these pronouncements have been seriously misinterpreted leading to much confusion.

Secondary causes 308

Secondary causes are *causes* whose *causality* depends on some other cause or being. Because creatures are dependent on God, the *first cause*, for their *essence* and *existence*, their causality is also dependent on the *first cause* which is the original uncaused cause or *Creator* of the Universe.

Secret of the Mass

In the *Roman Rite*, the *Canon of the Mass* was once recited by the *priest celebrant* in a low voice, as is still the case in the *Extraordinary Form*. These prayers, which could not be heard by the people, were sometimes referred to as the secret of the Mass.

Strictly speaking, the secret referred specifically to the prayer recited in a low voice by the *priest celebrant* at the end of the *offertory* and before the *preface*. See Anaphora 2770.

Secret of the Sacrament of Reconciliation 2490

The secret of the *sacrament of Reconciliation* refers to the *inviolable* secrecy, which must be observed by the *confessor* and all others, such as translators, or someone who overhears a *confession*, or who may otherwise have knowledge of matter confessed in the sacrament of Penance.

It is a crime for a confessor in any way to betray a penitent by word or in any other manner or for any reason. A *priest* who reveals such matter incurs *excommunication ipso facto* and can be *absolved* only by the *Pope*.

Sect

Where state *churches* are established, a sect is an organized body of dissenters from the established form of the *faith*. In countries where many faiths are recognized, a sect generally is a *religious* group lacking organization and less likely to endure. See Montanism.

Sectarian

Sectarian is a term applied to adherents of numerous *nonconformist* groups who have separated from the principal *Protestant denominations*. They adhere to a particular teacher or isolated *doctrine* which sets them apart from other denominations. Sectarianism manifests itself by a stress on non-essential matters rather than agreement about *religious truths* and a tendency to minimize *virtue* outside their own group. See Chiliasm.

Secular

Secular comes from the Latin word 'saecularis,' meaning worldly or *profane*. Secular relates to *temporal* and worldly things as distinct from things pertaining to the Church or *religion.* See Secular institutes 928. Also see Secular messianism 676.

Secular clergy

Secular clergy refer to members of the *clergy* who are not members of a *religious institute.* They are not bound by a *vow* of *poverty* or community life but they are bound by *celibacy* in the Western Church and promise *obedience* to their *Bishop.* See Clergy.

Secular institutes 928

A secular institute is a form of *consecrated* life in which *Christian faithful,* by living in the world strive for the *perfection* of personal *charity.* Their presence acts as a *leaven* working for the *sanctification* of the world as well.

Secular institutes are principally composed of *laypersons,* but may also include *clerics.* Their members profess the *evangelical counsels* of *poverty, chastity,* and *obedience,* but not by means of *public vows,* nor do they live a *community life.*

Members retain their *marital* or single state and occupation. They must pass through a period of probation before the taking of sacred bonds in the *institute.*

After taking perpetual bonds, they must have an *indult* from the *Holy See* to leave it, if the institute is of pontifical rite, otherwise from the diocesan *Bishop.* The Holy See recognized secular institutes in 1974, although they have been in the Church since the sixteenth century.

Secular institutes differ from formal *religious* institutes because the vows the members take are not technically public *vows of religion* and the members do not live a common life. They are states of Christian perfection with an *apostolate* in the world where they work for the extension of *Christ's* kingdom.

Secular messianism 676

Secular messianism is the *belief* that the *Messiah* will come as a political and earthly ruler who will destroy the enemies of Israel.

Seduction

Seduction comes from the Latin word 'seducere,' meaning to lead away or mislead. Seduction is the act of persuading or tempting someone to do something *evil* or wrong, especially to engage in unlawful *sexual intercourse.* See Scandal 2282.

See

The word see comes from the Latin word 'sedes,' meaning seat. In the Church it refers to the Church's *papal* or *episcopal authority* vested in the *Pope* and *bishops.* An *episcopal* see has definite territorial boundaries determined by the *Holy See* and is called a *diocese.* See Patriarch 61.

See of Peter

The See of Peter is also referred to as the *Apostolic See* or *Holy See*. It is the *Diocese* of the *Bishop* of Rome. Strictly speaking, Apostolic See could refer to any see founded by one of the *Apostles*, but when it is used with the definite article it refers specifically to the See of the Bishop of Rome, who is the *Pope*. Because he is the direct successor of Saint Peter he exercises supreme *authority* over the entire Church. Out of respect for his holy office he is referred to as His Holiness and his See is called the Holy See. See Apostolic See. Also see Holy See.

Seer

Seer is another word for *oracle*, or *visionary*. See Oracle.

Self-abnegation

Self-abnegation means lack of consideration for one's own interests or *self-denial*. See Humility 2546.

Self-control 1832

Self-control refers to mastery of oneself, that is, controlling, or directing one's *emotions*, desires, or actions.

After his *fall* from *grace*, *man* lost the *preternatural* gifts of *infused knowledge, integrity, immortality*, and *impassibility*. With the loss of the gift of integrity, man lost his power of total *self-mastery* causing him to struggle with *concu-*

piscence or the rebellion of the *flesh* throughout his life.

The rupture of man's friendship with God through *sin* destroyed his ability to achieve his *ultimate end* because he lost God's *grace*. In his *mercy*, God restored man to friendship and gave him the necessary grace to attain his end through *redemption*. God did not restore the preternatural gift of self-control or integrity but made it a means of achieving *salvation* with the help of grace.

Baptism removes *original sin* but not its consequences in *human nature*. Man must now achieve control over his body and its tendencies gradually through a life-long, difficult process requiring prolonged effort. With the help of *grace*, however, regaining *self-control* is possible. With grace, even with a weakened *will* and darkened *intellect*, fallen man still remains free to resist *temptation* and refuse consent to sin.

The practice of self-control restores the *harmony* in man's *nature* intended by God. We are meant to control our bodies and its *evil* inclinations according to *reason* and God's *law*. He will give us sufficient grace to regain self-control if we ask for it.

To prevent *concupiscence* from dominating us we must struggle against it with the help of God's grace and crucify the unruly desires of the flesh through self-discipline, *self-denial*, custody of the senses, *fasting*, *prayer*, and frequent reception of the *sacraments*. Also see Fruits of the Spirit 1832.

Self-denial

Self-denial is the act of giving up some *legitimate good* for the sake of a higher good or motive. See Self control 1832.

Self-discipline

Self-discipline refers to control of oneself, one's desires, actions, or habits. See Ascesis.

Self-indulgence

Self-indulgence means readily yielding to or satisfying one's desires. It also refers to the tendency to gratify one's wishes or not making demands on one's self. See Penitential abstinence. Also see Abstain/ Abstinence 2043.

Self-mastery

Because of the fall from *original justice* through *original sin*, *man* lost control over his body and its tendencies and must gradually regain it through a difficult life-long process requiring prolonged effort. With the help of *grace*, however, man can regain the *self-control* or self-mastery he lost through *sin*. With *grace*, even with a weakened *will* and darkened *intellect*, fallen man is still free to resist *temptation*, and refuse to consent to *sin*. Through the practice of *virtue*,

man restores the *harmony* in his *nature* intended by God. See Self-control.

Self-respect

Self-respect is the proper acknowledgement of one's own self-worth as a *person*. See Gluttony 1866.

Self-righteous

Self-righteous means filled with the conviction of being morally superior than others or being smugly *virtuous*. It also suggests *hypocrisy*. See Pharisees.

Self-sacrifice

Self-sacrifice is the offering of oneself or one's own interest for the benefit of another. See Love.

Seminary/seminaries

A seminary is a school dedicated to academic and *spiritual* training of candidates for the *priesthood*. The *Council of Trent* ordered the establishment of a seminary in every *diocese*. The seminary may be diocesan, regional, inter-regional, provincial, or pontifical. See Congregation for Catholic Education.

Semites

The Semites were a tribe of people who inhabited Asia and Africa. They are said to be descendants of Noah's son Shem. In historic times Western Asia, except for Asia minor, was Semitic and included the Babylonians, Assyrians, Canaanites and Arabians. See Garden of Eden. Also see Tree of knowledge of good and evil 396.

Sensation

Sensation comes from the Latin word 'sensatio,' meaning *knowledge* gained through the senses. Sensation is the power or process of receiving *conscious* sense impressions through direct stimulation of one of the senses, such as hearing, touching, tasting, smelling, or seeing.

Sensation differs from thought in two ways. Sensation is limited to *material* things, while thought is also about *spiritual* things. Sensation is always a *material* way of knowing, whereas thought may be about a material *reality* but is always a spiritual kind of *knowledge*. See Conscious.

Sense/Senses

The senses are specialized mechanisms or functions by which the nerves and brain are able to receive and react to a particular class of external stimuli. The reactions to stimuli results in a special kind of knowledge called *sense knowledge*.

Man has five senses: sight, hearing, taste, smell, and touch. The sense of touch is really composed of a number of distinct senses, such as, warmth, cold, pressure, pain,

and three other senses that react to the internal condition of the body called the kinesthetic sense, the visceral sense and the static sense.

The kinesthetic sense provides knowledge or awareness of position and movement of parts of the body. The visceral sense provides information about the nutritional system, the digestive tract, the circulatory system and respiration. The static sense affords information about positional equilibrium and orientation. See Material.

Sense knowledge

The stimulation of the organs of the *senses* results in sense knowledge. There are as many types of sense knowledge as there are senses.

They are generally classified as taste, smell, touch, hearing, and sight; however, there are others referred to as the internal senses, such as the synthetic sense that combines the data of various external senses into a composite *perception*.

Even when the objects that stimulate the senses are absent they can be made present to the *mind* with their different qualities through imagination.

Past events can be recalled, recognized, and placed in their location in time. Such recognition is called sensory memory.

Finally, man *experiences* certain innate unlearned tendencies or drive toward or away from specific objects and that are called *instincts*. See Sense perception.

Sense perception

The *senses* are specialized organs by which the nerves and brain are able to receive and react to a particular external *stimulus*. The reaction to a stimulus results in what is called *sense knowledge*.

Man has five senses: sight, hearing, taste, smell, and touch. The sense of touch is really composed of a number of distinct senses, such as, warmth, cold, pressure, and pain, and three other senses that react to the internal condition of the body called the kinesthetic sense, the visceral sense and the static sense.

The *experience* of sensing is called *sensation* which is a *conscious* awareness caused by the stimulation of a sense organ. It is through sensation that various *attributes* of stimuli are recognized.

By the *act* of *perception* the *mind* grasps an *understanding* of objects and recognizes the object which cause them. Because the stimuli come from objects, they convey information to the mind regarding the object. The act of perception always includes past sensations of the same kind and combines them with a current sensation to make it possible to identify or distin-guish between different kinds of mental experiences.

Sensation is seldom simply *experienced* without passing immediately to the experience causing the sensation. We don't just sense an ache, but feel a headache. We are not just conscious of a color but of a colored flower. *Consciousness* is filled with perceptions which are elaborations of underlying sensations, rather than simple sensations. See Senses. Also see Ratiocination. Also see Ecstasy.

Senses of Scripture 115

Senses of Scripture refers to ways in which *Scripture* may be understood. According to ancient *tradition*, one can distinguish between two senses of Scripture: the *literal* and the *spiritual*.

The spiritual sense is subdivided into the *allegorical*, *moral*, and *anagogical senses*. The profound concordance of these different senses makes it possible to apply all its richness to the reformation of the lives of those reading it. See Allegorical sense 117. Also see Anagogical sense; Moral sense.

Sensible

Sensible refers to that which can cause physical *sensation* or be perceived by the senses. See Miracles 548.

Sensitive appetite

Sensitive appetite is an inclination toward an object in the sensitive *order*. It corresponds to desire. Because *passion* resides in the sensitive appetite it is also called the *concupiscible appetite*. See Appetite, irascible.

Sensuality

Sensuality is the state or quality of being sensual. It is a fondness for or indulgence in pleasure derived from, based on, or appealing to the *senses*. It suggests the strong appeal of that which is pleasing to the senses and implies the gratification of the grosser bodily senses or *appetites*. See Neopaganism.

Sensus fidei 92

'Sensus fidei' is a Latin phrase meaning sense of the *faith*. It refers to the *supernatural* appreciation of faith by the whole *People of God*. It provides sensitivity to the relationship between an idea and the *truth* of the faith and helps us sense and identify erroneous teachings.

Separation 1649

Separation refers to a *canonical* judgment which requires *spouses* to live apart because of a situation in which living together becomes practically impossible, for example, where a partner constitutes a serious physical danger or gives *scandal* to the children.

In such cases, the Church permits physical separation

of the couple and their living apart. While separated, neither spouse is free to contract a new union because they remain married. Separation does not include *dissolution* of a *valid marriage*.

Septuagesima

In the *Extraordinary Form* of the Roman Rite, the three *Sundays* before *Lent*, called Septuagesima, constitute a period of preparation for the *Lenten season*. While violet vestments are worn, it is not a penitential season. These Sundays were referred to as Septuagesima, *Sexagesima*, and *Quinquagesima* Sunday. The words themselves mean seventieth, sixtieth, and fiftieth, and refer to the amount of time until *Easter* (the Latin name for Lent is 'Quadragesima,' which means 'fortieth'). This period of preparation does not appear in the *Ordinary Form*.

Septuagint 213

See Greek Septuagint 213.

Sepulcher

Sepulcher comes from the Latin word 'sepulchrum,' which is closely related to 'sepelire,' meaning to bury. 'Sepel-' at the beginning of the word 'sepelire' means to *venerate* or honor.

Sepulcher refers to a tomb or burial vault intended to honor and revere the dead. The cavity in an *altar* or *altar stone* which contains a *relic* or fragment of a saint's body is placed there to honor the saint's *memory*. *Churches* are often named for the saint whose relic is entombed in the altar. See Altar 1383.

Seraph

See Bronze serpent 2130.

Sermon on the Mount

The Sermon on the Mount was preached by *Christ* early in his *public life* on a hill near Capernaum. It is a comprehensive discourse that appears in Mt 5–7. It is included in shorter form in Lk 6:20–49. In it Christ presents the *New Law* and outlines the kind of life a follower of Christ must live in order to attain the *kingdom of heaven*. The sermon contains the *Beatitudes* and includes the *Lord's Prayer* and the *Golden Rule*. See New Law 1965.

Servant of God

Servant of God is the title given in the first step toward *canonization* of a *person* who is thought to have lived an exemplary life of *virtue*.

The process of canonization begins when a group approaches their *Bishop* and proposes an individual of outstanding virtue as worthy of canonization. This initial step in the formal process of inquiry leading to canonization is called the ordinary process. The Bishop of the diocese in which the person lived makes an inquiry into the *holiness* of the candidate and his life of virtue. This inquiry is conducted by a *tribunal* consisting of three judges, a *notary* and a *Promoter of the Faith* called the devil's advocate.

If the investigation seems promising, the Bishop submits his findings to the *Congregation for the Causes of Saints* for further study and examination.

If the Congregation approves, the candidate is referred to as 'Servant of God.'

At this time, permission is given for veneration of the candidate in a particular region or country but it does not grant permission to display his image in *church* or mention his name in the *Divine Office* or the *Mass*, which normally is required for public *veneration* in the proper sense.

The *Congregation for the Causes of Saints* further examines the candidate's virtues to establish that the individual did indeed practice heroic virtue or died a martyr's death. If so, the Congregation prepares a report. When the *Pope* accepts this report the person is called '*Venerable*.' See Canonization.

Servant songs 713

Servant songs are *Scriptural* passages, which proclaim the meaning of *Christ's Passion* and show how he will pour out the *Holy Spirit* to give life to the many by embracing the form of a slave.

Servant songs specifically refers to four portions of the Book of Isaiah: 42:1–7; 49:1–7; 50:4–11; and 52:13–53:12. In them, the outline of the Servant's personality is developed.

In the first poem, God calls him 'my chosen' and the Spirit-*anointed* bearer of divine *justice* to the nations. His mission is to open the eyes of the blind and bring freedom and light to captives. In the second song, the Servant himself speaks of being called to raise up and restore the preserved of *Israel*. In the third song the servant willingly submits to those who abuse him, being confident of God's support. In the fourth song, he accomplishes his mission by suffering on behalf of others.

Since early times *Christians* recognized *Christ* as the fulfillment of the servant songs. In various places in the *New Testament*, the servant songs provide a model for understanding the *Passion* and death of *Jesus*. In Lk 22:37 Jesus announces that he fulfills Is 53:12. Mt 8:17 cites the relation between Jesus and the words in Is 53:4 'he took our infirmities and bore our diseases.'

Server

A server is a non-ordained *person* who assists the *priest* in the *sanctuary* especially at *Mass*. Post-conciliar directives (Ordo Missae 1970 III, 81) provide that those who minister at the *altar* be *vested* in an alb or *surplice*. See Low Mass.

Service 1551

Service refers to the performance of the *duties* or attendance of a servant. It is the work done in *obedience* to and for the benefit of a master.

In the *ministerial priesthood*, service especially refers to the *celebration* of *public worship* and to providing for the *spiritual* needs of the *faithful*.

Servile fear

Servile fear is the fear of punishment like a slave has of a cruel master.

The gift of *fear of the Lord* is not prompted by the dread of punishment from God. Rather it inspires a *filial fear* which arises from the *experience* and *knowledge* of the utter *holiness* of God. This in turn inspires a detestation of *sin* because of the awareness of how it offends God's perfect love, *providence*, *justice*, and care for us. See Fear of the Lord 1831.

Servile work/labor 2042

Servile work is work, which formerly was considered the work of slaves as opposed to liberal work which was the work of the free *man*. The servile work forbidden by the third commandment of the *Decalogue* refers to labor, which is principally bodily, mechanical, or manual.

The exact meaning of work depends on traditional usage and common opinion. Work that is principally liberal, artistic, or intellectual is not considered servile even if it involves physical labor, such as stone carving, even when it is done for payment.

While the *Sunday* rest was formerly from, specifically, servile work, the Church currently directs the *faithful* to "refrain from engaging in work or activities that hinder the *worship* owed to God, the joy proper to the Lord's Day, the performance of the *works of mercy*, and the appropriate relaxation of *mind* and body" (CCC 2185). This perspective takes account that what is work for one *person* might be relaxing for another. For example, gardening may be a form of relaxation for an accountant, but not for a professional landscaper.

Also, direct service of religion, requirements of charity, or grave inconvenience can legitimately excuse one from the *Sunday* rest, but care should be taken that legitimate exceptions do not become the rule and that the Sunday rest is respected by *society*.

Seven Dolors of the Blessed Virgin

The seven dolors of the Blessed Virgin refers to the seven sorrows *Mary experi-*

enced in her association with *Christ*: The prophecy of Simeon in Lk 2:34–35; the flight into Egypt in Mt 2:13–21; the loss of Jesus in the *Temple* in Lk 2:41–50; meeting Jesus on the way to Calvary; the *Crucifixion*; the removal of Jesus from the Cross; and his burial in the tomb. The *feast* commemorating the seven dolors is held on September 15 and is called our Lady of Sorrows. See Scapular.

Sexagesima

Sexagesima is the second *Sunday* of the pre-*Lenten season*, called *Septuagesima*, in the *Extraordinary Form*, and means 'sixtieth,' indicating that it is about sixty days until *Easter*. It precedes *Ash Wednesday* by a week and a half.

Sext

Sext, a Latin reference to the sixth hour of the day (noon), is a *minor hour* of the *Divine Office*, and is sometimes called *Midday Prayer* in English. It is part of the *Daytime Prayer*. See Liturgy of the Hours. 1174, 1178.

Sexual abstinence

Sexual abstinence refers to refraining from *lawful sexual intercourse* at certain times for specific reasons. This abstinence is called *periodic continence* when it is practiced by married couples as a free and mutual decision for regulating *conception* according to *natural* methods approved by the Church. See Regulation.

Sexual appetite

Sexual appetite is an inclination toward sexual things which is frequently driven more by *passion* rather than *reason*. Hence, sexual appetite provides a fertile ground for *spiritual* combat. See Chastity 915.

Sexual identity 2333

Sexual identity refers to the personal appreciation, understanding, and acceptance, of being *created* man or woman in the plan of God. This implies acceptance of the *Christian* mode of living as male or female in a world where by *immoral* pressure the *natural* role of sexual activity is often rejected or *perverted*.

Sexual intercourse

Sexual intercourse refers to the sexual union of two *persons*. It is also called *copulation* or *coitus*. See Chastity 915. Also see Marital intercourse.

Sexual love

Marital or sexual love, refers to feelings centered on the *natural appetite* to seek *good* in *procreation*. It includes an *intellectual* element as well as a *sensitive* attraction toward another. Married love must be governed by *right reason*, that is, it must always seek the *spiritual* good and welfare of the beloved. *Spouses* become, by virtue of the *sacrament* of *Matrimony*, special channels of *grace* and expressions of the *will of God* guiding the spouses to mutual *sanctification*. See Love 218.

Sexually continent/Sexual continence

Sexual continence refers to *self-control* in the matter of sexual *appetite*. It may refer to refraining voluntarily from *intercourse* in *marriage* for sufficient *reason* with the consent of both parties. See Shewbread 2581. Also see Continence 1650.

Share in the Divine life

Through *Baptism* a *person* is born again into a *supernatural order* and lives in a way beyond his *created nature*. This rebirth enables *man* to share in the *divine life* through *grace*. His *natural* acts acquire a *supernatural character* by sharing in the life of *Christ* in the *Eucharist* while they are still on earth. Living the grace-filled life of *virtue*, man is united to God by *love* and grows in *holiness*.

By Baptism and incorporation into *Christ* man is cleansed of *original* and *actual sin* and infused with the *theological virtues* of *faith, hope,* and *charity*. We become a *temple of the Holy Spirit* and filled with *sanctifying grace*. We become members of the *Mystical Body* of Christ, *heirs to heaven* and partakers in the *divine nature* by an *adoption* as sons.

Man participates in the life of God by the *indwelling of the Holy Spirit* who raises his natural *human acts* to the supernatural level. This grace enables him to live a life of virtue opening his heart to union with him by living a life of virtue. By grace we can say with Paul, 'And I live now, not I; but Christ lives in me' (Gal 2:1). See Born from above 526.

Sheol 164, 633

The meaning of Sheol developed over time. According to Eastern thought, the world was structured into three parts: *heaven*, earth, and the underworld. This underworld consisted of the subterranean ocean beneath which Sheol was located. It was the abode of the dead.

The *etymology* of Sheol is uncertain. Originally, Sheol meant simply death or the grave. No one could be delivered from the power of Sheol, and one who entered could not return. It was a pit of darkness, worms, and dust, and seems to have represented the tomb. Those in Sheol were in a state of utter inactivity, a denial of all that is meant by *life*.

In early *Judaism*, those in Sheol could not remember, praise, or thank God. In Sheol, there is no work, thought, *knowledge*, or *wisdom*. The *Jews* personified Sheol as a monster that opens its mouth to devour and is never satisfied. At this time, the concept of punishment of the wicked after death had not yet developed, but those who chastise their sons could avoid Sheol.

In the later thought of Judaism, Sheol became a place only for the wicked, while the *righteous* were taken to paradise. This place of punishment was called *Gehenna*, which was developed from Sheol but distinct from it. God does not remember the dead in this deep dark region.

Sheol/Gehenna was represented in Greek culture by 'hades,' which was simply the abode of the dead.

In the New Testament, *Hades* became Hell. This was a place of torment, much like Gehenna. The power of the risen *Christ* was shown by his possession of the keys of death and Hades or Hell. At the end of time, Sheol or Hades will give up the dead for a final judgement.

Abaddon, meaning perdition in *Hebrew*, is named together with death and Sheol. In rabbinical literature it seems to be part of Gehenna. It is mentioned in Rev 9:11 as the name of an *angel* of the abyss.

Shewbread 2581

Shewbread designates what the *Hebrew* call the bread of the presence, or the bread of the face. The directions given in Lev 24:5–9 state that twelve loaves, each made from two-tenths of a measure of fine flour, are to be baked. They are to be set in two rows of six loaves each and sprinkled with pure *frankincense*. The bread was placed in the *holy* place on a table made of acacia wood constructed for that purpose. It was to be set before *Yahweh* each *Sabbath*. The loaves were offered to God not as food or as *sacrifice* but as a sign of gratitude for the benefits he granted his people.

When the fresh bread was laid out, the *priests* were to eat the loaves of the preceding week. *Laymen* could eat the loaves provided they were *sexually continent* for an undetermined length of time.

Incense and the bread, also called the Presence, were signs of the *holiness* and *glory* of God at once Most High and Most Near.

Shrine

In general a shrine is a *holy* place. It may refer to a box-shaped repository in which *relics* of a *saint* are preserved or an alcove in which a statue or sacred image is kept. In homes it is a space set aside for *devotional* purposes. Such home shrines are called *prayer corners*.

In Canon 1230, "By the term shrine is understood a *church* or other sacred place to which numerous members of the *faithful* make *pilgrimage* for a special reason of *piety*, with the approval of the *local ordinary*." Though a shrine might not necessarily be an *apparition* site or the tomb of a saint, public shrines frequently are the burial places of saints or places where *heavenly apparitions* occurred or where *miraculous* phenomena approved by the Church have taken place. See Prayer corner.

Shrove Tuesday

Because of the custom of going to *confession* just before Lent, the Tuesday before *Ash Wednesday* was called *Shrove Tuesday*. See Lenten season; Shrovetide.

Shrovetide

The three days before *Ash Wednesday* are called *Shrovetide*. The name is derived from the Old English 'scrifan,' meaning 'to shrive,' that is, *confession* of sins and performance of a *penance*. See Liturgical seasons.

Sibling

A sibling is one of two or more individuals who have the same parent or parents. See Fratricide 2268.

Sign

A sign is a motion or gesture that conveys information, such as agreement, or permission. The *sign of the Cross* is a sign of *belief* in the *Trinity*. See Sign of the Cross 1235.

Sign of the Cross 1235

The sign of the Cross is a *ritual* gesture, which makes a *profession of faith* by invoking the *Trinity* while tracing a cross by touching the forehead, breast, and the two shoulders. On entering a *church* the sign of the Cross is made with *holy water* as a cleansing of the *mind* in preparation for *prayer*.

Tertullian gives testimony to the use of the sign of the Cross that dates from the earliest times. 'In all our travels and movements, in all our coming in and going out, in putting on our shoes, at the bath, at the table in lighting our candles, in lying down, in sitting down, whatever employment occupieth us we mark our forehead with the sign of the Cross' (Tertullian, 160–225 A.D.).

The sign of the Cross is made frequently during *liturgical ceremonies* and before beginning any *spiritual* or *temporal* activity to *sanctify* actions and dedicate them to the *glory* of God.

The *Byzantine Church* makes the sign of the Cross holding the thumb and first two fingers together to represent the *Holy Trinity*. The other two fingers, represent the two *natures* of *Christ*. In the *Eastern Church* the sign of the Cross is made touching the shoulders right to left. In the Western Church it is made touching the shoulders left to right. See Appendix of prayers.

Signify

To signify means to be a sign or indication of something or to make it known. See Sacrament of unity 1140.

Signs of the covenant 1150

The chosen people received from God distinctive signs and symbols marking their *covenant* with God in their *liturgical* life. Among these liturgical signs were *circumcision*, *anointing*, and *consecration* of kings and *priests*, laying on of hands, *sacrifices*, and especially the *Passover*.

The Church sees in these signs a *prefiguring* of the *sacraments* of the *New Covenant*.

Signs of the human world 1146

Being body and spirit, man perceives *spiritual realities* through *physical* signs and *symbols*. Signs have an important place in *human* life because, as a *social* being, *man* uses signs and symbols of the human world to communicate with others through language, gestures, and actions. The same holds true for signs used in man's relation to God.

Signs taken up by Christ 1151

In communicating his message to man, *Jesus* made use of signs of *creation* to make known the *mysteries* of the *Kingdom of God*. He performs healings and illustrates his *preaching* with physical signs and symbolic gestures giving new meaning to the deeds and signs of the *Old Covenant*. He is himself the meaning of all these signs.

Silent consent

Silent consent is voluntary compliance with something presented as a *good*. It is manifested by some outward sign in cases whose nature admits of such consent, as in accepting a gift.

Silent consent is acceptance without verbal expression but manifested by some behavior or the refusal to *act*. See Consent 1627.

Simile

Simile is a figure of speech in which one thing is likened to something different by using the word 'like,' as for example in, 'Life is like a bowl of cherries.' See Analogy.

Similitude 43

Similitude is the quality or state of being like, resembling, or being similar to something else.

Simony 2121

Simony is the buying or selling of *spiritual* things. The term is traced to Simon, a Samaritan magician converted by the *Apostles* who attempted to purchase *spiritual* gifts from them (Acts 8:18–32).

Buying or selling something spiritual like a *sacrament* is strictly forbidden. Because they have their source in God it is impossible to appropriate

to oneself spiritual goods and behave towards them as their owner and master. Thus, one can receive them only from God without payment.

Simple convalidation

Simple convalidation is a form of *convalidation of a marriage* in which a *diriment impediment* rendering a marriage *invalid* has ceased. It consists in a simple renewal of *consent* on the part of one or both *spouses*. But if the impediment is public, then a new celebration of *marriage* must take place in which the spouses exchange consent according to *canonical form* (Canon 1158). See Convalidation of marriage.

Sin 386, 1849

Sin is an offense against God. It is, any thought, word, or deed contrary to the *law* of God, and therefore to his *holiness* and *justice*. Sin is also an offense against *reason, truth,* and *right conscience*. It is a failure in genuine *love* for God and neighbor caused by a perverse attachment to certain goods. It wounds the *nature* of *man* and injures *human solidarity*.

Sin is contrary to the *eternal law*. Sin sets itself against God's love for us and turns our hearts away from it. Sin may be either *venial* or *mortal*.

There are sins of *commission* and sins of *omission*. Sins of commission consist in performing *evil acts*, such as *theft*. Sins of omission consist in neglecting to perform an act which is required of us, such as missing *Mass* on *Sunday* without good reason.

Sinful inequalities 1938

Sinful inequalities refers to the excessive *economic* or *social* disparity which exists between people and is a source of *scandal* which militates against *social justice, human dignity* and even social and international *peace*. Because all men have equal dignity, we should always strive for fairer and more humane conditions for all.

Sins of commission

Sins of commission consist in performing evil acts, such as *theft*. See Sin.

Sins of irreligion 2118

Sins of irreligion are acts which are contrary to the first commandment of the *Decalogue* and *virtue of religion*. Such sins *tempt God* in words or deeds, such as *sacrilege*, and *simony*.

Sins of omission

Sins of omission consist in neglecting to perform an *act* which is required of us, such as missing *Mass* on *Sunday*, without good reason. See Sin.

Sins that cry to heaven 1867

The Catechism of the Catholic Church refers to four sins as 'sins crying to *heaven*' for *vengeance*. These are:

1) the blood of Abel, willful murder (Gen 4:10),

2) the sin of Sodom, *sodomy* (Gen 18:20),

3) The cry of the oppressed in Egypt (Ex 3:7–10), the oppression of the poor and the cry of the foreigner, the widow, and the orphan (Ex 20:20–22), and

4) defrauding laborers of their wages, injustice to the wage earner (Deut 24:14–15).

These are particularly wicked, because they are *grave* offenses against *human dignity* and *justice*.

Sister

Sister is a title for women religious. See Nun.

Skullcap

A skullcap is a small cap worn by *prelates*. It is white for the *Pope*, red for *cardinals*, purple for *bishops* and black for *abbots*. It is also called a *zucchetto*. See Abbey nullius.

Slander/Slanderer

Slander is also called *calumny*. It consists in verbal *defamation* of character whether spoken or written. It causes suffering and *social* harm to the victim. See Calumny 2477.

Sloth or Acedia 1866, 2094, 2733

Sloth is also called acedia or accedie from the Greek word meaning not to care or loss of interest in any good. It is a *torpor* of the *mind*, weakness of the *will*, lack of enthusiasm for *spiritual* growth and development, or lack of self-exertion on behalf of *virtue*. Sloth is one of the *capital* or *deadly sins*.

Sloth is opposed to *love* of God and fosters an undue love of pleasure, *lukewarmness* in *religion*, and discouragement or even *despair* in the pursuit of virtue. It increases the danger of omitting *grave obligations*, distraction of mind, torpor of spirit, and dislike of *prayer*.

"Spiritual writers understand by this [sloth] a form of depression due to lax *ascetical* practice, decreasing vigilance, carelessness of *heart*" (CCC 2733).

Sloth is a *sin* against *charity* in which one may "go so far as to refuse the joy that comes from God and to be repelled by *divine* goodness" (CCC 2094). Sloth begets a kind of regret for the gift of *faith* because of the troublesome *obligations* it may involve or entail.

Prayer, acts of *mortification*, frequent *confession*, and *Communion* help a *person* overcome sloth. Spiritual reading can also help restore a *zeal* for *holiness* by providing knowledge of *revealed truth*, encouragement in *reform*, and good examples to imitate.

Social

Social refers to anything having to do with *human beings* living together dealing with one another in matters affecting the common welfare. See Signs of the human world 1146.

Social class

A social class is a group of people considered as a unit based on economic, occupational, or *social* status, such as working class, middle class or upper class. See Class war.

Social justice 1929

Social justice is the respect *society* must show and guarantee for the *human person* and the *inalienable rights* which flow from human *dignity*. Society must provide the conditions that allow people to obtain what is their due according to their *nature* and *vocation*.

Social sin 1869

Social sin refers to *evil social* situations and *structures of sin*. These lead their *victims* to do evil. Such *sins* appear to be also a part of *society* or in some way to infect it, giving rise to what is known as a social sin. It is *sin* that all *society* approves and legalizes such that the situations and structures of the society contribute to these sins. A *Catholic*, or any good *person*, cannot be opposed to these sins, and still approve of or vote for the *legalization* of actions which give rise to them.

Making *immoral laws* like

the so-called right of choice regarding the lives of innocent children and popularizing immoral life styles in the media are examples of social sin.

Social well-being 1908

Social well-being is that element of the *common good*, which centers on *social duties*. The public *authority* must decide between various needs of particular citizens; however, "it should make accessible to each what is needed to lead a truly *human* life: food, clothing, health, work, education and culture, suitable information, the right to establish a *family*, and so on" (CCC 1908)

Socialism / Socialistic 2425

Socialism is a general term referring to a variety of *social theories* critical of contemporary society. Though socialism may mean different things, it most often stands for the ownership of all income-bearing wealth by the state so that it has complete control over production and distribution.

Those socialists who *advocate* taking over such control by means of force are called revolutionary socialists or communists.

Distributism is another alternative to the excesses of *capitalism* which stresses, not state ownership of income-bearing wealth, but fair distribution of wealth so as to support the *dignity* of all families.

This is a program closely associated with the English Catholic writer, G. K. Chesterton. He claimed that the differences between modern capitalism and socialism were merely incidental, both concentrating control of the means of production in the hands of a few powerful *persons*: the first in the hands of a few private persons, and the other in the hands of a few powerful politicians. The views of Chesterton greatly influenced Dorothy Day, foundress of the *Catholic Worker Movement*, and seems to have had a certain influence on the thought of *Pope* Benedict XVI.

Socialistic theories have arisen because of the excesses of *capitalism*, which can tend to exploit some to the advantage of others and concentrate power in the hands of few without regard to the *universal destination of goods*.

Socialistic theory

See Socialism.

Socialization 1882

Societies are necessary to *man* because he is a *social* being. Socialization is the process by which people adapt to life in society in order to live in *peace* and *justice* with others.

"To promote the participation of the greatest number in the life of a society, the creation of *voluntary* associations and institutions must be encouraged" (CCC 1882).

Socialization "expresses the natural tendency for *human beings* to associate with one another for the sake of attaining objectives that exceed individual capacities. It develops the qualities of the *person*, especially the sense of initiative and *responsibility*, and helps guarantee his *rights*" (CCC 1882).

Socialization can present dangers. Excessive state intervention threatens personal *freedom* and initiative, and the principle of subsidiarity counters this danger. According to the principle of subsidiarity "a community of a higher order should not interfere in the internal life of a community of a lower order, depriving the latter of its functions, but rather should support it in case of need and help to coordinate its activity with the activities of the rest of society, always with a view to the common good" (CCC 1883). Subsidiarity is opposed to all forms of *collectivism* and fosters true international order.

Societies of apostolic life 930

Societies of apostolic life are associations of *persons* whose members, without *religious vows*, pursue the particular *apostolic* purpose of their *society*. They lead lives in common according to a particular manner of life and strive for perfection of *charity* through observance of their *constitutions*.

Society/Societies 1880

"A society is a group of *persons* bound together organically by a principle of unity that goes beyond each one of them. As an assembly that is at once visible and spiritual, a society endures through time: it gathers up the past and prepares for the future" (CCC 1880).

In a society, each person is to use what he has received from the society to develop his own identity and, in turn, enrich society. *Man* "rightly owes loyalty to the communities of which he is part and respect to those in *authority* who have charge of the *common good*" (CCC 1880).

Sodomy

Sodomy refers to any form of unnatural *sexual intercourse*, such as intercourse with animals called *bestiality* and intercourse between two members of the same sex. See Sins that cry to heaven 1867.

Solar Calendar

The solar calendar is a system that measures the beginning, length, and divisions of a year revolution of the earth around the sun. One revolution around the sun is a solar year. It is divided into twelve solar months.

In the Solar calendar, time is divided into days, weeks, and months. A day is measured from midnight to midnight, 24 hours. Seven days make a week. Four weeks plus two or three days make a month. Twelve months make a year. See Lunar calendar.

Soldier of Christ

Soldier of Christ refers to the dedication to combat *concupiscence* and overcome *sin*. In the Western Church, *Confirmation* is the *sacrament of initiation* in which a *baptized person* receives the *Holy Spirit*, is strengthened in *grace*, and signed and *sealed* as a *spiritual soldier of Christ*. See Confirmation 1289.

Solemn

The word solemn is associated or connected with any *religious rite* or observance performed with extra *ceremony* and *reverence*.

It is applied to various *ecclesiastical ceremonies* or services that acquire a special character by virtue of additional use of singing, *incensing*, *processions*, and the assistance of additional *ministers*. See Solemn Blessing 1245.

Solemn blessing 1245

A solemn blessing is one performed with and accompanied by due formality and *ceremony* or one having a formal character.

Solemn Communion, First 1244

Solemn Communion refers to the first reception of the *Eucharist*. In the *Latin Church*, this takes place some years after

Baptism and is preceded by a period of *catechesis*.

It is referred to as Solemn Communion because the occasion is accompanied by a special *recognition* during the *liturgy* to *commemorate* the event formally. After *Mass*, there is usually a special celebration with friends and family and the Christian community accompanied by the giving of gifts to commemorate the event. See First Holy Communion 1244.

Solemn Magisterium

The solemn Magisterium is that use of the *authority* given by *Christ* to teach *infallibly*. It is exercised by formal and *authentic definitions* of *ecumenical councils* or *Popes* teaching *ex cathedra*. See Magisterium 83, 889, 890.

Solemn Mass

Solemn Mass, or 'Missa solemnis,' is the *Mass* in the *Extraordinary Form* celebrated with full *ceremony* by a *priest*, a *deacon*, and a *subdeacon*. The deacon and subdeacon parts may be done by either deacons or priests, and, with certain modifications and not without need, the subdeacon part may be taken by a *layman*. The Solemn Mass also incorporates *incense*, the singing of the Mass parts, and requires at least four *servers*.

In the *Ordinary Form*, the term 'Solemn Mass' can be

used to describe a Mass with more than usual solemnity.

Solemnity/Solemnities

Solemnity comes from the Latin word 'solemnis,' meaning 'stated, established, and appointed.' The highest *liturgical* rank of *feasts* in the liturgical calendar are called solemnities. Solemnities are celebrated with as much liturgical decorum as possible. See Corpus Christi.

Solemnity of the Mother of God

The *feast* of the *Circumcision* which was formerly *celebrated* on January 1, is today called The Solemnity of the *Mother of God*. It is a *holy day of obligation* in the United States. See Circumcision, Feast of 527. Also see Holy day/Holy day of obligation.

Solidarity 1939, 1940

Solidarity refers to the agreement, support, and unity existing between individuals of a group. It is expressed by friendship and *social charity*. It grows out of the *human* brotherhood and *Christian* charity imposed on all who have a common origin and equality and are ordered by the *Creator* to his *glory*.

As a principle, solidarity is the quality of communities, which unites them in some respect like interests, sympathies, or aspirations. International solidarity is required

for the *moral order* and world *peace* depends upon it.

"Solidarity is manifested in the first place by the distribution of goods and remuneration for work. It also presupposes the effort for a more *just social* order where tensions are better able to be reduced and conflicts more readily settled by negotiation" (CCC 1940).

The *virtue* of solidarity extends beyond *material* goods to include *spiritual* goods of the *faith* which are necessary for *man* to achieve his *ultimate end*.

Solidarity among creatures 344

'*Solidarity* among creatures' refers to the unity between all *created* beings as being created by *God* for his *glory*. See Solidarity.

Son Incarnate

The *Incarnation* refers to the act by which the *Second Person* of the *Trinity, Jesus, assumed a human nature* while retaining his *divine nature*. Through the Incarnation, the human and divine natures of the Second Person of the Trinity are united in a single *Person*. Because of his Incarnation, *Christ* is called the Son Incarnate. Also see Incarnate Word; Born of a virgin 502.

Son, God the 240, 241, 242

The *Holy Trinity* is the central and most sublime mystery of the *faith*. It teaches that God is absolutely one in *nature* and *essence* and relatively three in *Persons—Father, Son* and *Holy Spirit*—each of whom is *consubstantial*, that is, identical with the *divine substance.* The Church confesses one God in a consubstantial Trinity of three Persons, not three gods.

The Second Person is the true consubstantial Son of God, the *Word of God, begotten* of the Father from all eternity. The Word proceeds from the Father by way of the *intellect.* The intelligible activity of the Father is a vital action.

The Word became Incarnate and dwelt among us for our *salvation.* The *Incarnate Word*, Jesus Christ, the Son of God, has two natures, one *divine* and the other *human*, united to the one Person of the Word. He was born to a human mother, the *Virgin Mary.* He had no human father, but was born by the power of the Holy Spirit who came upon her. See Trinity, Holy 232, 234, 237, 253. Also see Father, God the; Holy Spirit.

Son of God 441

"In the *Old Testament*, son of God is a title given to the *angels*, the *Chosen People*, the children of *Israel*, and their kings. It signifies an adoptive sonship that establishes a relation of intimacy between God and his creature" (CCC 441).

In the *New Testament*, the term is used to refer to *Christians* in the *state of grace.*

When the *Messiah* was called 'son of God,' it did not necessarily "imply that he was more than *human* according to the literal meaning of these texts. Those who called *Jesus* 'son of God,' as the *Messiah* of Israel, perhaps meant nothing more than this" (CCC 441).

"Such is not the case for Simon Peter, when he confesses Jesus as 'the *Christ*, the Son of the living God' (Mt 16:18)" (CCC 442); he meant that Jesus was actually God's only Son. Jesus responded that this was a *revelation* from the Father. Later Jesus said, 'my Father and I are one' (Jn 10:30), to confirm that he is indeed God. See Son, God the.

Son of the Father
See Heirs to heaven.

Sons of the prophet
The sons of the prophet were groups organized for *worship* in *cultic* song and dance. They were not attached to any temple or *liturgical cult.* The sons of the *prophet* identified themselves with the prophet's cause. The distinction between the prophet and 'sons of the prophet' is not always clear.

The sons of the prophet associated with him and lived in communities outside of towns serving him as messengers and aids. Elisha called on them for music to stimulate him to deliver an *oracle* requested of him. See Prophetic texts.

Sorcery 2117

Sorcery is the use or practice of *magic* arts, enchantment, or *witchcraft*. Practitioners of witchcraft claim to have special *occult* powers over others received from *devils*. Even the attempt to resort to such practices is *gravely* contrary to the *virtue of religion*.

Sorrowful mysteries of the Rosary

Meditation on a *mystery* of the *faith* drawn from the *Gospels* accompanies the recitation of each decade of *Hail Mary's* of the *Rosary*. These *meditations* are known as the mysteries of the Rosary.

The mysteries of the Rosary are collected into groups of related *scriptural* events referred to as the *Joyful, Sorrowful, Glorious* and *Luminous* mysteries. The recitation of five decades and meditation on a set of mysteries ends with the prayer Hail Holy Queen.

The Sorrowful mysteries, prayed on Tuesdays and Fridays, are: The Agony in the Garden (Mt 26:36–46; Mk 17:26–42), The Scourging at the Pillar (Mt 27:15–26; Mk 15:1–15), The Crowning with Thorns (Mt 16:24–28; Lk 23:6–11), Carrying the Cross (Mk 8:31–38; Jn 19:17–22), The *Crucifixion* (Mk 15:33–39; Lk 23:33–46). See Rosary 2678, 2708.

Soul 363

The term soul refers to the innermost aspect of *man*, that by which he is made most especially in God's image. It is the *spiritual principle* in man, the principle of his life, *vital functions*, thought, and action.

The soul has two faculties: the *intellect* and the *will*. The intellect is man's *cognitive* or knowing faculty and is referred to as the *mind*. The will is his power to choose and tend toward attaining what he deems desirable. It is called his *intellectual appetitive* power or *intellectual appetite*. The ability of the intellect to recognize *truths* that are self-evident is called *intelligence*. When the intellect determines truths which are not self-evident by *logical* steps it is called *reason* or thinking. When the intellect is aware of itself and the world, it is called *intellectual consciousness*. When the intellect by reasoning determines the *morality of an act* and judges its morality, it is called *conscience*. When the intellect retains its *knowledge*, it is called *intellectual memory*.

The intellect and will are *supra-organic faculties* and do not depend *intrinsically* on any bodily member or organ. They are spiritual and inhere in the soul *innately*. It is difficult to determine which faculty: intellect or will, is superior. Because to know something is more *perfect* than to tend toward something, this would suggest that the intellect is superior, an opinion preferred by St. Thomas Aquinas. However, to achieve is more perfect than to simply know, suggesting that the will is superior in the opinion of Bl. John Duns Scotus (1266/70–1308 A.D.).

When man achieves the *beatific vision*, he will only use his intellect illumined by the special *grace* of the *lumen gloriae* or light of grace. Yet even in this state, the will perfectly and *eternally* seeks God in loving union. Since both of these faculties must work together in a single being, the issue of superiority is irrelevant for practical purposes. Either opinion, however, may be held by a *Catholic* without harm to *faith*.

The soul of man is commonly regarded as an entity distinct from the body, that is, the spiritual part of man in contrast to the body, which is the purely physical part. Man, however, is not a body inhabited by a soul but a single *body-soul* composite. Man is a *rational animal*, and must be both *material* and *rational* to be a *person*. Both the body and soul are united in eternity and share eternal bliss as a person chosen by God called by grace to union with him.

According to the *hylomorphic theory*, for a thing 'to be' requires a *substantial form* and *prime matter*. These are *part-principles*, which in every

case but man cannot exist independently of one another. The human soul, however, can exist separately from the body it informs. On this point there have been two errors condemned by the *Popes*. The first claims that the soul pre-exists the body. It only informs it as a consequence of some sin. The second claims the soul is not in principle *immortal* and so like an animal life principle ceases to exist at death.

Prime matter makes man *material* and substantial form makes him to be rational. Man, defined as a *rational animal*, is the union of these two *part-principles*.

Soul of the Church

The *Holy Spirit* is called the *soul* of the Church because he is the source of the life of her *Mystical Body*.

The phrase 'soul of the Church' is also used in a *metaphorical* sense to refer to all those in the Church who are actually in the *state of grace* and being sanctified by the action of the Holy Spirit. See Communion of Saints 1475. Also see Spiritual Worship 2031.

Souls in purgatory

The souls in purgatory, also called the *Holy Souls*, refers to the souls of the *just* in *purgatory* being purged of the *temporal punishment* due to *sin*. It is of *faith* that the souls in purgatory can be helped by the *prayers* and *sacrifices* of the *faithful* on earth. It is an *immemorial* custom in the Church to pray to these souls asking them to *intercede* for us with God. This practice is a beautiful expression of the *communion of saints*. See Communion of saints 1475. Also see Communion with the dead 958.

Sources of morality 1750

The sources, or constitutive elements, of morality are three: the *object chosen*, the *intention* or *end* that moves the choice and the *circumstances* under which the choice is made.

The object chosen is the *good* toward which the *will deliberately* directs itself. This object must always be in keeping with the *rational order* of good and *evil* attested to by *conscience*.

The end is the goal of the act, that is, the *good* anticipated by the action. A good end may never justify the use of an *immoral* means. If the end is *moral* but the means used to attain it are immoral the entire act is sinful. This is the meaning of the adage, 'The end does not justify the means.'

The *circumstances*, including the *consequences* that may accompany an act, contribute to the increase or diminution of its moral goodness, such as the amount of a *theft* or acting out of fear. Circumstances do not change the moral quality of an act. They cannot make

an act which is evil in itself either good or right.

Sovereign

Sovereign means superior to all others, having supreme *authority*. See Latria.

Special graces 2003

Special graces are gifts granted by God primarily for the good of others rather than for the good of *persons* who receive them. They are also called *charisms*.

Species

In general a species is a class of *persons* or objects possessing common *attributes*.

Since the *divine essence* or *being* is absolutely unique, it transcends all categories and *species* into which *created beings* naturally fall. See Divine nature. Also see Genetic inheritance 2275.

Species, Eucharistic

See Eucharistic species 1373.

Speculative faith

Speculative faith refers to a merely *intellectual assent* to *religious truth*, which does not affect behavior, but remains only in the *speculative order*. It is distinguished from *practical faith*, which always affects behavior. 'So also faith of itself, if it does not have works, is dead' (Jas 2:17). See Faith 146.

Speculative knowledge

Knowledge can be considered as practical or speculative. *Practical knowledge* is that knowledge which is put to specific practical use to solve problems or produce results. Speculative knowledge simply enriches the *mind* with *truth* and without application to specific purposes. See Knowledge 1831.

Speculative order

The speculative order refers to *knowledge* that is based upon, or characterized by *reasoning, induction, deduction,* or pure *theory,* in contrast to knowledge that is practical or positive, that is, based on *experience* and put to practical use. See Knowledge 1831.

Speculative reason

Speculative reason refers to the application of the powers of *reason* in purely *theoretical* thought processes in the nature of *meditation* or conjecture, which is unrelated to real or *concrete* problems or situations as such. It is contrasted with *practical reason,* which is immediately concerned with a real concrete situation. See Reason. Also see Speculative Faith.

Sphragis 698

Sphragis refers to the image created by a *seal,* especially in sealing wax, to ensure the *authenticity* of a document. See Seal of the Lord.

Spiration

Spiration comes from the Latin word 'spirare,' meaning to breathe (cf. Jn 3:5–8). Spiration refers to the mode by which the *Holy Spirit proceeds* or relates to the other two *Persons* of the *Trinity* as from a single *principle.* Spiration indicates an act of mutual *love* and denies procession by *generation* which is proper to the Son.

The Father is neither spirated nor generated. He is the origin of the processions of Son and Spirit, but himself without origin. Hence, the Father is called First Person, because first, absolutely speaking, is without origin. His relation to the other Persons is implied in their relation to him. See Holy Spirit 702.

Spirit/Spiritually

A spirit is something entirely immaterial and not dependent on matter for its existence or activity. When considered as the principle of life in man it is called the *soul.*

Spirit can also refer to the possession of a special quality, such as the *spirit of adoption.* It may be used to refer to a real intention, such as to follow the spirit of the *law.*

Spirit is also used as a synonym for *supernatural* to indicate how *spiritual being* always transcends in some way and in varying degrees what is merely *material.* But this often leads to confusion if not properly qualified. Only *divine* being or spirit absolutely transcends all other beings. When used of *angels* in relation to *man* or men in relation to material, spirit is used only relatively: to some, not all other beings. Finally it can mean not *corporal* or material. *Holy Spirit* refers to the *Third Person* of the *Blessed Trinity*. See Real Presence. Also see Holy Spirit 702.

Spirit of Adoption

In the *Old Testament Israel's* relationship with God was that of an *adopted* child. God referred to Israel as his first-born. 'Thus says the Lord: Israel is my son, my first-born' (Ex 4:22). 'For you are a people *sacred* to the Lord, our God, he has chosen you from all the nations on the face of the earth to be a people peculiarly his own' (Deut 14:2), and, 'When Israel was a child I loved him, out of Egypt I called my son' (Hos 11:1).

The New Testament refers to believers as children of God (Lk 20:36, Rom 9:26, Gal 3:26), and affirms their special and intimate relationship with God. However, it also distinguishes *Jesus'* unique relation to God as the only *begotten* (Jn 1:18 and 3:16) making the filial relationship of believers derivative and secondary in nature.

Paul uses the word *adoption* to describe the relation *persons* receive by virtue of

their *redemption* in Gal 4:3–7. For him adoption symbolizes God's love and acceptance of believers as his children.

The *adopted sonship* of the *faithful* takes place through *sanctifying grace* bestowed by the *Holy Spirit* in *Baptism* granting the power to overcome *temptation* and become *holy* by living life in the *Spirit*. By the life of the Spirit the redeemed cry trustingly 'Abba,' Father in prayer. Their prayer in the Spirit is filled with filial trust, joyous assurance, and the certainty of being loved. It is called *parrhesia*. It is this quality in *Christian* prayer that enables us to pray the *Lord's Prayer* in the *liturgy*. See Sacramental grace 1129, 2003.

Spirit of detachment

The spirit of detachment is the enlightened sense of the relationship which exists between *material* goods or pleasures and God and *spiritual* realities. It is exercised in respect to attachment to material goods, success, and prosperity regarding them to be of secondary importance compared to the ultimate purpose of life.

Detachment requires complete abandonment to the *will of God*. Detachment of the *will* is the hardest, most necessary and most *meritorious* form of detachment. It enables a *person* to abandon himself entirely in the will of God. Those who live in spiritual detachment live the words of the *Blessed Virgin*, 'Be it done unto me according to thy word.' See Poverty of heart 2544.

Spirit of the World

The phrase, 'spirit of the world' in general, refers to those pervasive attitudes and tendencies of *society* which serve as the primary motives or *values* which incline *persons* to focus too much on the materialistic and hedonistic inclinations of fallen *nature*. Such persons are called worldly. Worldly persons lack the self-discipline required for the bodily mortification needed to control their *appetites* to make them conform to right *reason* and the *divine law*.

In *Scripture* and spiritual writing, 'world' refers to everything *created*, the cosmos. Everything created is *good* in itself because it conforms to the creative *will of God*. Genesis describes the *man* God created as very good, because he is created in the image and likeness of God.

In a broad sense 'world' refers to whatever is *temporal*, changing, and imperfect. In this sense it can become a distraction from divine realities and absolute good and constitute a source of *temptation* for fallen man.

The expression 'spirit of the world' as used in the New Testament also refers to the forces of evil which oppose the work of man's *redemption* from *sin*. The fall of man from *grace* caused disorder in his relation with God, with himself, with his neighbor and between him and all *creation*.

All creation, including man, will only reach its goal and *perfection* when it is renewed and transformed into 'the new heaven and new earth' in the fullness of the *Kingdom of God* on the last day.

Until that time man journeying to heaven must overcome the three major obstacles to spiritual perfection referred to as the world, the flesh and the *devil*. Spiritual writers also refer to the spirit of the world as an attachment to earthly things, worldliness, or the pride of life.

To overcome the spirit of the world, some degree of self-discipline is required as a condition of *salvation* because *Christ* tells us, 'Unless you will be perfect go sell what thou hast and give to the poor' (Mt 19:21), and elsewhere he adds, 'If any man will come after me, let him deny himself, and take up his cross and follow me' (Mt 16:24). See Ascesis 1734, 2015, 2340.

Spirit of truth

The Spirit of Truth (Jn 14:16; 16:13) is the *Holy Spirit* sent by the Lord to guide the Church. He is also described as the Counselor (Jn 16:7). The word counselor is translated as *Paraclete* in some *Bibles*. See Holy Spirit 702.

Spiritism or spiritualism 2117

Spiritism, also called spiritualism, refers to the practice of attempting to make contact or communicate with the souls of the dead or *demons*.

The *person* who makes the supposed contact is called a *medium*. The sessions at which such communication is attempted are called *séances*.

During séances, apparently *preternatural phenomena* may be observed. Such phenomena are ordinarily fraudulent and result from abnormal but entirely natural *psychic* qualities possessed by the medium or those attending. But it is possible for such activities to create conditions *propitious* for *diabolical* intervention, which is *preternatural*.

Communication with the dead depends on God's *will*, not on the use of mediums. Spiritism is pure *superstition* and even attendance at such séances is entirely forbidden by the Church. Spiritism sins against the first commandment.

Spiritual

Spiritual is that which pertains to the *soul* or *mind* as distinguished from the body. Spirit is opposed to *material*, is positively immaterial, has no dependence on matter for its existence or activity, and may be *supernatural*.

The distinction between spirit and matter in *man* is unique. Man is a body-spirit composite. His spiritual soul is immortal and does not just inhabit the body, but is integral to his *nature*. His body and soul are *part-principles*, and their union constitutes a single *human nature*.

The spiritual faculties of *intellect* and *will* possessed by the soul make man a *person* in the *image of God*. True communication is only possible between *persons*. God made man a person because God wished to communicate man's *ultimate end* and purpose to him.

Man's soul is *eternal* because it is spiritual. It cannot die because it has no parts into which it can be reduced. This has implications for human *generation* and birth. Being spiritual, the soul of man must be *created* by God at the moment of *conception*. It cannot be supplied or produced by the parents. This is why the term *'procreation'* must be used for human generation. It expresses that parents produce children only with the help of God. The spiritual soul does not perish when separated from the body at death, and will be reunited with the body at the final *resurrection* to share in eternal glory or *perdition*.

In irrational creatures the soul is material, not immortal. It exists only so long as the creature is informed by it and ceases to exist at the death of the creature. Thus, animals are said to reproduce, not procreate. See Aeviternity/Eviternal.

Spiritual advisor

A spiritual advisor is a *person* who offers guidance to individuals to help them lead a life more completely under the *dominion* of the *Holy Spirit*. See Spiritual direction 2690.

Spiritual betrothal

Spiritual *betrothal* is a vision in which *Christ* promises to unite a *soul* to himself in *spiritual marriage*. See Mystical union 2014. Also see Spiritual marriage.

Spiritual body

The *Scholastic Theologians* teach that *glorified bodies* possess four qualities: 1) Freedom from all pain, suffering, or physical defects, called *impassibility*. 2) The brightness of *glory* and splendor that overflows from the *beatific vision* and transforms the body, called *clarity*. 3) The *spiritual docility* or subjection of the body, which takes on a spiritual character without ceasing to be a true body, which is called *subtlety*.

Because it is a *perfection*, not a deprivation of bodily nature, it is referred to as a 'spiritual body' in 1 Cor 15:44. 4) The ability of the spiritual body to move from place to place with great speed and serve as a perfect instrument of the soul enabling it to exist in perfect harmony with all creation and know its wonders is called *agility*. See Eviternity.

Spiritual direction 2690

Spiritual direction refers to the guidance or *counsel* given to individuals to help them lead a life more completely under the *dominion* of the *Holy Spirit*. Spiritual direction is the art of guiding *souls* in making *spiritual progress*.

A spiritual director leads a soul by helping it become ever more *docile* and sensitive to the promptings of the Holy Spirit who is the true *spiritual advisor*.

In spiritual direction, counseling is used to identify impediments to a more intimate union with the Spirit as well as to give encouragement and instruction in ways of living a life of greater *virtue* especially through a life of *prayer*.

Spiritual freedom 1828

Spiritual freedom refers to the ease with which *man* knows and understands what is true and good and becomes more ardent in choosing it. Because *truth* and goodness are necessary for the *perfection* of man, he is only really free when he becomes what his Creator intends by freely choosing it.

Endowed with *free will*, man is *created* with the power of *free choice*, but this does not mean that he cannot be bound to *obedience* without his *consent.* This is because he is naturally born in a state of dependence on others. He has *duties* and *subjugations* from which he cannot be freed.

Man is free only to reject *evil* and choose *good* with the *grace* of God. St. Augustine taught that man's *will* by itself is sufficient to choose *evil*, but it is not adequate to choose saving good without grace.

Man is truly free only when he chooses good, but fallen man, deceived by false goods, may choose evil under the guise of good. In his loving *mercy*, God has revealed what is good in the *Ten Commandments* and the *Beatitudes* to guide man to his *final end*. Through *faith*, God gives man the grace to recognize *truth* and what is good.

Baptism infuses in man the *theological virtues* (faith, *hope*, and *charity*), the *moral virtues* (*prudence*, *temperance*, *fortitude*, and *justice*), *sanctifying grace*, and the *gifts of the Holy Spirit*, to guide and strengthen him in his journey to *spiritual perfection* by enabling him to know and choose what is good and true.

In imperfect human *nature*, the impulses of the flesh and impulses of the spirit are at war. With the exercise of virtue, made possible through grace, the spiritual man gains ascendancy over the *flesh* and it becomes easier for him to *discern* and choose his true good.

Spiritual gifts

Spiritual gifts refer to the *graces* God grants to man to attain his *salvation*. The *gifts of the Holy Spirit* are infused in the soul with the *sacrament* of *Baptism* and strengthened within the soul at *Confirmation*. See Gifts of the Holy Spirit 1831. Also see Theological virtues 1812; Charismatic gifts 768.

Spiritual life 89

Spiritual life refers to the responses one makes to the call of God which through practice become integrated into his behavior during life.

A *spiritual person* is one who strives to make his response to God's call the dynamic center of his life, activities, and choices. Thus, the spiritual life is the work of a lifetime in becoming *conformed or configured to Christ* through *virtuous* living.

Spiritual marriage

Spiritual marriage or *transforming union* is the ultimate form of *mystical union* with God. The term occurs in St. Teresa's *The Interior Castle* and is used to describe the highest degree of closeness and intimacy of the *soul*'s union with God in which consciousness of the presence of God in the soul becomes clear and abiding.

Spiritual marriage effects a

complete surrender into the hands of God, with a thirst to suffer for him, and an ardent *zeal* for souls. It is preceded by a *spiritual betrothal* in which *Christ* promises to unite the *soul* to himself in a vision. It is not the absorption of the soul into God or dissolving two *persons* into one because God and creature always remain irrevocably distinct. See Mystical Union 2014.

Spiritual motherhood

The spiritual motherhood of the *Blessed Virgin* is understood from her relationship to the Church. *Vatican II* affirmed three aspects of this relationship: 1. As *prototype* of the Church; 2. As the preeminent member of the *Mystical Body*; 3. As *Mother of the Church*, a title proclaimed by Pope Paul VI on Nov. 21, 1964.

Mary represents and signifies the Church. As Mother of the *Redeemer* and as *Coredemptrix*, she is Mother of those reborn as *sons of God*. As the *New Eve*, her perfect *obedience* untied the knot of Eve's disobedience, and she became the Mother of the saved. She expresses in herself the *holiness* of the Church in which *Christ* is loved and his Mystical Body is *sanctified*.

What is said of the Church, is first true of Mary. Both are mothers and *virgins*. Both gave God the Father a *posterity*. Mary furnished the body for Christ the head of the Church. Christ *redeemed* the world through the perfect obedience of Mary, making her the Mother of Christ and Mother of the Church.

Mary is the preeminent member of the Church because she is not only the Mother of God, but also becomes the Mother of the Church, the Mystical Body of Christ and enjoys the title: Mother of the Church. See Mother of the Living 726.

Spiritual progress

Spiritual progress is improvement focused on the *morality* of *man's* behavior and his acceptance of the *divine plan* or *will of God*.

Such spiritual progress is vital to man because it is a reflection of growth in personal *holiness*, to the ordering of human society to the *Kingdom of God* and the *salvation* of *souls*.

It is through making spiritual progress that man is conformed to *Christ*, grows in holiness and, with the *grace* of God, achieves his *eternal* reward. Spiritual growth is manifested by increased ease in the practice of *virtue*. See Spiritual Direction 2690.

Spiritual reading

Spiritual reading (in Latin, 'lectio divina') refers to any serious reading intended to bring the *soul* nearer to God through *exhortation*, *exposition*, *meditation*, or example, which extends one's *knowl-*

edge of the *faith* or *holy* things. See Lectio divina 1177, 2708.

Spiritual relationship

A spiritual relationship is the *affinity* arising from active participation in the *sacraments* of *Baptism* or *Confirmation*. *Sponsors* in these sacraments become spiritually related to the one baptized or confirmed. The relationship which arises no longer constitutes an *impediment* to *marriage* with the *person* sponsored. See Godchild.

Spiritual sacrifice

Spiritual sacrifice refers to the *Sacrifice of the Mass* which is the unbloody *Sacrifice of the Cross*. Those who participate in the *liturgy* are united in the sacrifice spiritually by offering themselves with it and consuming the *Eucharist*. See Common priesthood 1141.

Spiritual sense 117

Spiritual sense refers to a way of interpreting *Scripture*. It is also called the *mystical or typical* sense. The spiritual sense expresses the *truth* God intended by means of a *figure* or *type*. The spiritual sense may take one of three forms: *allegorical, moral,* or *anagogical*.

The spiritual or mystical sense of *Scripture* refers to that meaning which a passage has in reference to some *truth* or event of which it is a type, symbol, or *foreshadowing*. The

Old Testament's reference to the *Paschal Lamb* is a type or figure of *Christ* our *Paschal sacrifice*. The mystical sense is also called the *typical* or *allegorical sense*. See Senses of Scripture.

Spiritual sloth 1866, 2094, 2733

Spiritual sloth, or acedia, is "a form of depression due to lax *ascetical* practice, decreasing vigilance, carelessness of heart" (CCC 2733). Spiritual sloth is sloth particularly in relation to one's *spiritual life* and duties. See Sloth.

Spiritual works of Mercy

A work of mercy is a work of *charity* done from concern and *compassion* for those in distress. The seven spiritual works of mercy are directed to the needs of the *soul*. They are: convert sinners, instruct the ignorant, counsel the wayward, comfort the sorrowing, bear adversities patiently, forgive offenses, pray for the living and dead. See Piety 1675. See Corporal works of mercy.

Spiritual worship 2031

Spiritual worship refers to the *moral life* by which we present the *offering* of our bodies as a living *sacrifice* to God in union with the *Mystical Body* of *Christ* in the offering of his *Eucharist*.

Sponsor 1311

A sponsor is a *person* who promises to give special help

and guidance to one who receives the *sacrament* of *Baptism* or the sacrament of *Confirmation*. The term sponsor is usually reserved for the member of the community who presents the adult candidate for admission to the *catechumenate* though not always involved in the final preparation for sacramental initiation.

Those who serve as sponsors must themselves be firm believers, must have received the *sacraments of initiation*, be able and ready to help those newly baptized or confirmed on the road of the *Christian* life.

The task of a sponsor is a truly *ecclesiastical* function or *officium*. In the 1983 Code, two Canons (892–893) deal with sponsors for Confirmation, and depend upon the chapter on baptismal sponsor (Canons 872–874). When celebrated together the same sponsors serve throughout the *rite*. Though the Latin term, *patrinus*, is used for both sacraments, the term sponsor usually refers to the member of the community who presents an adult candidate for admission to the *catechumenate*.

Canon 872 states the responsibility of sponsors: insofar as possible, the one to be baptized is to be given a sponsor to assist an adult in *Christian initiation*, or, with the parents, to present the infant at Baptism and to help the bap-

tized to lead a Christian life and to fulfill the obligations connected with it. The *liturgical* books define in fuller terms the function of sponsors.

Canon 873 sets the number and sex of sponsors to be employed for the candidate as only one male or one female sponsor or one of each sex.

Canon 874 deals with the qualifications of sponsors. Stated in brief, in order to be admitted to the role of sponsor, a person must fit the following qualifications.

1) A sponsor be designated by the one to be baptized, by the parents or one who takes their place, or, when necessary, by the *pastor* or minister. The person named must have the qualifications and intention of performing the role.

2) He must have completed his sixteenth year.

3) He must be a *Catholic*, be confirmed, received the *Holy Eucharist*, and live a life in harmony with the *faith*.

4) A sponsor must not be bound by any *canonical penalty*.

5) He may not be either the father or mother of the person to be baptized. The purpose of this is to indicate the difference between *natural* and *spiritual* parenthood. Baptized non-Catholics may only serve as witnesses, not sponsors, together with a Catholic sponsor.

Canon 892 takes up the responsibility of the Confirmation sponsor, requiring 1) that, as far as possible, a sponsor for the one being confirmed should be present at the Confirmation; 2) that the confirmed person acts as a true witness to *Christ* and faithfully fulfills the obligations connected with the sacrament. The general statements of responsibility of sponsors in this canon parallel those of Canon 872.

Canon 893 requires the Confirmation sponsor to perform the role and conditions for a baptismal sponsor listed in Canon 874. It is also desirable for the one who undertook the role of baptismal sponsor to be sponsor for Confirmation.

Spouse

A spouse is a *marriage* partner: a husband or wife. See Marriage bond 1640. Also see Adultery 2380; Spouse of the Holy Spirit.

Spouse of the Holy Spirit

Because *Mary* begot *Christ* by the overshadowing of the *Holy Spirit*, she is called the *Spouse of the Holy Spirit*. Her espousal to the Holy Spirit does not mean that she became the wife of the Holy Spirit and that the Holy Spirit was the father of *Jesus' human nature*. Rather, it means that she was united to the Holy Spirit in a perfect form of that true spousal love which unites husband and wife. By the power of the Holy Spirit the *divine nature* of

the *Second Person* of the Trinity *assumed a human nature* provided by the Blessed Virgin. St. Joseph, the virginal husband of Mary, was the foster father of the Christ child.

Her child is indeed the Son of God because his human and divine nature constitutes a single Person. See Full of Grace 722.

State of grace 1861

The state of *grace* refers to the condition of a *soul* that is free of *original sin* and *mortal sin*. The *virtues* and *gifts of the Holy Spirit* are present and active in the soul in this state which constitutes friendship with God, whereby there is personal *indwelling* of the *Holy Trinity*.

The state of grace transforms the soul enabling it to function at an entirely new interpersonal level with God. The state of grace can be lost through *grave sin* and regained with the grace of *repentance* and the *sacrament of Reconciliation*.

State of holiness and justice 375

The state of holiness *and* justice was the condition of *man* in *paradise*. It is also called the state of *original holiness*. Holiness refers to the *spiritual perfection, purity, sanctity,* and conformity to the likeness of God in which man was *created. Justice* refers to the conformity of all his actions to what is *morally* right, reasonable, and true.

State of life

State of life refers to a set of circumstances or *attributes* which characterize a group of *persons*. In the Church, state of life refer to groups of persons serving the Church in specific roles, such as *clerics*, *religious*, and *laity*. See Age of discretion.

Stations of the Cross

Stations of the Cross are also called the *Way of the Cross*. This *devotion* to the *Passion* of *Christ* consists of making fourteen *meditations* before a series of crosses called *stations*. Each station recalls the events which took place on the way to the *Crucifixion*, as well as at the scene of the Crucixion, concluding with the burial of Christ in the tomb. Those making the way of the Cross may either move from one station to another themselves or make responses to an officiating minister who makes the journey accompanied by a cross and two candles.

The stations themselves must consist of fourteen crosses *blessed* by one with *faculties* to erect stations. The pictures or sculptured figures which often accompany the stations alone do not suffice to obtain the *indulgences* associated with this devotion. The crosses are required, not the pictures or

statues. See Popular devotions 1674.

Statute

A statute is the same thing as a *law* or ordinance. See Ordinance.

Stele

The word stele comes from the Greek word 'stele,' meaning a post or slab. It refers to a pillar or stone slab engraved with an inscription or design to serve as a monument. Tombstones are common examples. See Table of the Law.

Sterile/Sterilization

Sterilization refers to a surgical procedure which renders a *person* sterile, that is, incapable of producing offspring.

The Church condemns direct sterilization: 'Equally to be excluded,' i.e., condemned with the same force as the use of artificial contraception is condemned, 'is direct sterilization, whether perpetual or temporary, whether of the man or of the woman' (Paul VI, *encyclical Humanae Vitae*, 1968).

In a 1975 statement, the *Congregation of the Doctrine for the Faith* clarified that 'any sterilization which of itself, that is, of its own nature and condition, has the sole immediate effect of rendering the generative faculty incapable of procreation, is to be considered direct sterilization, as the term is understood in the declarations of the pontifical *Magisterium*, especially of Pius XII. Therefore, notwithstanding any subjectively right intention of those whose actions are prompted by the care or prevention of physical or mental illness which is foreseen or feared as a result of pregnancy, such sterilization remains absolutely forbidden by the *doctrine* of the Church.'

The specific conditions permitting sterilization were outlined by Pope Pius XII: '1) that the preservation or functioning of a particular organ provokes serious harm or constitutes a threat to the complete organism; 2) that this harm cannot be avoided, or at least notably diminished, except by the amputation in question and that its efficacy is well assured; and 3) that it can be reasonably foreseen that the negative effect, namely, the mutilation and its consequences, will be compensated by the positive effect: exclusion of danger to the whole organism, mitigation of the pain, etc.' All these conditions must be fulfilled simultaneously.

Eugenics employs sterilization as a means of improving the *human* race by controlling *genetic inheritance*. Compulsory sterilization is *immoral* and sterilization of *persons* considered unfit is an unjust violation of their bodily *integrity*. See Eugenics 2268. Also see Artificial birth control.

Stewardship 2417

Stewardship refers to the administration, management, control, and responsible use of resources.

Stimulus

A stimulus is any *agent* which causes change in an organism or excites a sense organ to transmit a nerve impulse culminating in *sense knowledge*. See Sense perception.

Stipend

Stipends are *offerings* made to the *clergy* on the occasion of the administration of certain *liturgical rites*, namely, the *celebration* of *Holy Mass*, *baptisms*, *marriages*, and funerals. The amount of the *offering* is set by *bishops* of an *ecclesiatical province*, and they are not exacted from the poor.

Stipends are not to be considered payment for spiritual ministrations, but as part of the layperson's general *duty* to support the *pastor*.

Stole

A stole is a *liturgical vestment* consisting of a band of material several inches wide worn around the neck of a *priest* or *bishop*. The color of a stole varies with the liturgical season or the *feast* being *celebrated*. It must be worn by *clerics* when *celebrating Mass* and during the administration of *sacraments* or exercising their *order*. The *Pope* wears a stole always and everywhere as a mark of his universal *jurisdiction*.

A stole is also the sash worn over the left shoulder by *deacons* during the *celebration* of Mass or the administration of *sacraments*. The stole is the distinctive garment of a deacon and it is conferred on him at his *ordination*.

A *Carthusian nun* wears a stole when singing the Gospel during the hour of *Matins* in the *Divine Office*. See Consecration of a virgin.

Stole Fee

See Stipend.

Storge

Storge is family love. In a broad sense, it can refer to the bond formed between an individual and other *persons*, between animals and persons and between persons and things around him. See Love 218.

Structures of sin 1869

Structures of *sin* refers to those *social* situations and conditions that are contrary to *divine* goodness. They are the social expression and effect of personal sins and lead their *victims* to do evil in their turn. See Social sin.

Subdeacon/Subdiaconate

The subdiaconate was formerly one of the four *major orders* in the *Roman Rite*. It was received before being ordained *deacon*. See Major

Orders. Also see Cleric 934; Age of discretion 1457.

Subjective certitude

Subjective certitude is the state of a *conscience*, which believes something to be good which is *objectively* wrong or *evil*. This is called an *erroneous conscience*.

Conscience may be an erroneous conscience either because of *vincible* or *invincible ignorance*. Vincible ignorance is ignorance in the absence of *knowledge*, which a *person* can attain. Invincible ignorance is absence of knowledge under circumstances in which *knowledge* cannot be obtained without extraordinary effort.

An erroneous conscience must be obeyed, but the person has the *duty* to learn what the Church teaches on *moral* issues in order to form a *correct conscience*. See Conscience 1706.

Subjective faith

Faith can be taken in an *objective* or subjective sense. In the subjective sense, it refers to the *acts* and dispositions by which *doctrines* are believed and practiced. It is in this sense that faith is considered one of the three *infused theological virtues*.

Though subjective faith is primarily a disposition of the *intellect*, it also involves an *act of the will*. It is more than the *adoption* of a *conclusion* based on sufficient evidence or argument, it is the *grace* of God moving the will to believe. Faith is required for *salvation* and is infused into the *soul* at *Baptism*. See Faith as a theological virtue 1814. Also see Objective faith.

Subjective redemption

Subjective *redemption* refers to the application of the *merits* of *Christ* to the *redeemed*. These *graces* are conferred through the maternal mediation of *Mary*. See Mediatrix 969.

Subjectively certain

A *person* has subjective *certitude* when he believes something to be true which is not true in *reality*. See Conscience. Also see Subjective certitude.

Subjugation

Subjugation is the noun form of the verb subjugate. It comes from the Latin word 'subjugare,' the combination of 'sub,' meaning under and 'jugum,' meaning a *yoke*. Animals were controlled and made to perform work by being placed under a yoke. Subjugate means to bring under control, subdue, or make subservient to. See Spiritual freedom 1828.

Subordinate

Something is said to be subordinate when it is of a lower rank, power, or importance. Things are important in proportion as they pertain to

man's eternal *destiny*. Earthly things are judged good in so far as they lead *man* to union with God. See Physical Evil 311.

Subordinationism

Subordinationism is a *heresy*, which denied that the *Second Person* of the *Blessed Trinity* existed from all eternity and was *coeternal* with the Father and *Holy Spirit*. It taught that the Second Person came forth from the Father and was *divine* but only at the time of the *Incarnation*. See Heresy 817.

Subsequent grace

Subsequent grace is another name for *grace of cooperation*. It is the form of *actual grace* which assists us in an operation, which is already begun and accompanies every *supernatural* act. It may also be called assisting or *concomitant grace* because it is associated with the use of *human freedom* in carrying out the *will of God*. See Grace of cooperation. Also see Grace 153.

Subsidiarity, principle of 1883

Societies depend on *socialization* to achieve their cohesion, but socialization can present dangers. Excessive intervention by the state in socialization can threaten personal *freedom* and initiative.

As a protection against this, the Church has elaborated the principle of subsidiarity according to which "a community of a higher order should not interfere in the internal life of a community of a lower order, depriving the latter of its functions, but rather should support it in case of need and help to coordinate its activity with the activities of the rest of society, always with a view to the *common good*" (CCC 1883). Nothing should be done at a higher level that can be done at a lower level. Levels of communities move upward from the *family*, to the city, county, state, and nation.

Subsistent/Subsistence

A thing that is subsistent is capable of existing *substantially*, that is, as a *substance* and existing by itself or in itself, independently, and not in another substance. It has completeness in itself and its own way of *acting* or *being*.

Subsistent *created* beings exist in themselves and by themselves, but not of themselves. Only God is capable of existing of himself, that is, without the dependence, which results from being created. When a subsistent material being is an *intellectual* or *rational* being, it is said to be a *person*.

Subsistence is the status or condition of being subsistent. See Human person 251, 252, 2222.

Subsists 1958

Subsists means to exist in or continues to exist. See Subsists in.

Subsists in 816, 1958

To subsist in means to reside or inhere in. In this context, the only true Church of *Christ* subsists in, that is, has its *being* or existence in the *Catholic Church* in a certain complete manner, form, state, or condition. Subsists in also refers to that which is wholly preserved, sustained, or supported by the Catholic Church.

Substance 251

Scientifically, a substance is an element or chemical compound. *Philosophically*, a substance is a *being* whose *nature* it is to exist in itself, by itself and for itself, needing no other subject in which to *inhere* in order to exist.

God exists not only in, but by, for himself and of himself. Because he is being itself he exists in himself. Because God is uncaused, God exists by himself. Because he is *infinite*, he exists for himself. Because he exists without beginning, he exists of himself.

The Church uses the term substance to designate the *divine* being in its unity. See Human person 251, 252, 2222. Also see Hypostatic union; Hypostasis; Substantial union.

Substantial

Substantial means belonging to *substance* rather than

to *accidents*. *Eucharistic consecration* produces a substantial change called *transubstantiation*. It is a total change in substance from bread and wine to the Body and Blood of *Christ*, while the accidents of bread and wine remain. See Substance. Also see Substantial union; Accident.

Substantial form

Substantial *form* is that which makes a thing to be what it is. It is that which gives *prime matter* a specific *character* and determines or makes a thing to be the particular thing that it is. Prime matter is that which makes a thing bodily. Substantial form determines the kind of body it is.

Prime matter makes a thing *material*, substantial form makes it a particular kind of material thing. Prime matter is potentially anything that a substantial form makes it, such as a dog, tree, *man*, or stone.

Substantial form and prime matter are *part-principles*. They cannot exist apart from one another because for a thing to be, it has to be something, and that requires both matter and form.

Man is composed of body and *soul*. The soul is the substantial form of the body, but it is incomplete without prime matter, which makes it bodily. When the substantial form of man, his soul, is united to prime matter, he becomes a bodily *person*.

In the case of *human nature*, however, and only human nature, the substantial form, or soul, unlike the vital principle of irrational animals, is capable of *subsisting* separated from the body after death. Man's soul is *created* and comes to exist in a body only at the moment of *conception*.

The human soul is the substantial form of man. It is *endowed* with the powers of *intellect* and *will*, which enable him to know and to choose. Man's soul is by nature *immortal* because man is created for *eternal* happiness. *Knowledge* makes it possible for him to know God and the purpose for which he was created: to know, *love*, and serve God and be to happy with him forever. To achieve this purpose, man must freely choose to accept the *divine plan*.

This explanation of the *nature* of material being is known as the *hylomorphic theory*. The theory itself is called *hylomorphism*.

By this *theory*, we understand that man is not a body inhabited by a soul but a single *body-soul* composite. For this reason, both his *glorified* body and his soul together must share in man's *eternity*. See Hylomorphic Theory. Also see Form 365; Soul 363.

Substantial part

A substantial part is one of great or considerable worth, possessing very important qualities or *essential* elements. See Rational animal.

Substantial union

Substantial union is a term employed in Christology to describe the precise nature of the union between the *divine* and *human natures* in *Jesus*, the God-man. Substantial union is of two kinds: in the *person* and in the nature, because both person and nature are realities pertaining to the order of *substance* as distinguished from *accident*.

A substantial union of two distinct substances in the unity of a single person is known as the *hypostatic union*, of which we have but one example: the *Incarnation*. A substantial union of two distinct substances, e.g., *soul*, and body in man, to form a single nature, is known as a unity of nature.

In the hypostatic union, two natures, one human and one divine, are *substantially* united but remain distinct, complete natures substantially united in a single person. *Man* is a single nature consisting of body and soul constituting a single human nature, which is neither the soul alone nor the body alone.

An *accidental* union is one based not on unity of person or of nature, but only in some accidental perfection or qual-

ity of the person or nature, such as friendship, mutual love, cooperating in the production of the same effect, etc. In this case two persons or two natures remain substantially distinct, even if united accidentally.

Nestorius conceived the *Incarnation* as an accidental union of two distinct persons, one human, one divine. The *Monophysite heresy* conceived the Incarnation as a substantial union, but in nature, not in the person. See Hypostatic union.

Substratum

A substratum is any part, *substance*, or element which lies beneath and supports another, such as a foundation. In *metaphysics* substratum refers to the events or *causes* which act on a substance and change it, such as *attributes* which inhere in it or changes which occur in it. See Part-principle.

Subtlety

Subtlety is a quality *attributed* to the *resurrected* body by *Scholastic Theologians*. Subtlety refers to the complete subjugation of the body to the *soul* and the assumption of a *spiritual character* without ceasing to be a body. Subtlety may also refer to the sharp-mindedness needed to grasp and distinguish metaphysical and spiritual concepts. See

Resurrection from the dead 992.

Succession

Succession means to follow another in office. See Bishop.

Suffragan Bishops

In the Western Church the title *Metropolitan* is added to that of an *archbishop* who presides over a *province* encompassing neighboring dioceses with their bishops, called *suffragan bishops*. Among Anglicans a suffragan bishop is the equivalent of an *auxiliary bishop* among *Catholics*. See Metropolitan.

Suicide 2281

God is the *sovereign* Master of life. "We are *obliged* to accept life gratefully and preserve it for his honor and the *salvation* of our *souls*. We are stewards, not owners, of the life God has entrusted to us" (CCC 2280).

"Suicide contradicts the natural inclination of the human being to preserve and perpetuate his life. It is *gravely* contrary to the just *love* of self" (CCC 2281). It offends the love of neighbor by unjustly breaking *solidarity* with family, nation, and others to which man has *obligations*. It is gravely contrary to love of God.

Responsibility for suicide can be diminished by *psychological* disturbances, anguish, or fear of *suffering* or torture.

We need not despair of the eternal salvation of one who commits suicide because God's *mercy* can always provide the opportunity for *repentance*. "The Church prays for *persons* who have taken their own lives" (CCC 2283).

Sunday 2175

Sunday, the day *consecrated* to the Lord, is observed on the first day of the week. At times it is referred to as the *Sabbath*, but it is not the same day as the *Jewish Sabbath* named in the third commandment of the *Decalogue*.

The *New Law* of *Christ* abrogated the observance of the Sabbath on Saturday, the last day of the week and transferred it to Sunday, the new *eighth day* of *salvation*. The eighth day which is the day of the *Resurrection* has a sunrise, but no sunset, hence *symbolically* has no day following it. In this sense Sunday, the day of Christ's Resurrection from the tomb, becomes the celebration of the risen Savior, who died once and dies no more, and our anticipated, *sacramental* sharing in the *eternal, blessed* life of *Jesus*. Sunday became the weekly *commemoration* of the Resurrection and the coming of the *Holy Spirit* at *Pentecost* both of which took place on Sunday.

Sunday also commemorates the eighth day of creation, the day of *eternity*, and is added to the seven-day week as a sign of *perfection*.

The Sunday observance fulfills the *obligation* of the third commandment of the *Decalogue*. The *law* of the Church prescribes the obligations of assisting at *Mass* and resting from "work or activities that hinder the worship owed to God, the joy proper to the Lord's Day, the performance of the *works of mercy*, and the appropriate relaxation of *mind* and body" (CCC 2185).

Other ways of keeping the day *holy* include attending other church activities, participating in *Scripture* and *Catechism* discussion groups, *spiritual* reading, the recitation of additional *prayers* and acts of *charity*.

The proper *celebration* of Sunday as a *holy day* includes proper relaxation of mind and body by means of recreational pursuits as long as they do not interfere with observing the rest and *spiritual* renewal Sunday should afford.

Sunday Obligation 2180

When the Christian mystery supplanted the *Old Law* of the *Sabbath*, with the day called Dominica, meaning day of the *Lord*, or *Sunday*, *Catholics* were obliged by Church *law* to attend the sacrifice of the *Mass*. This is called the Sunday obligation. In 1970, the *Congregation for the Clergy* decreed that the *faithful* may satisfy the Sunday *precept* by attending Mass on the evening of the preceding Saturday. The grant also applies to the obligation to assist at Mass on *holy days of obligation* as well.

Sundays after Pentecost

Ordinary Time is divided into two parts. The second part begins on the Monday after *Pentecost Sunday* and continues until the first Sunday of *Advent*. The Sundays in the first part were formerly called *Sundays after the Epiphany*. See Liturgical seasons. Also see Ordinary Time.

Sundays after the Epiphany

Ordinary Time is divided into two parts. The first falls between the Baptism of the Lord and *Ash Wednesday*. The *Sundays* in this period were formerly called Sundays after the Epiphany, and included the Sundays of *Septuagesima*, *Sexagesima* and *Quinquagesima*. This first period is interrupted on the Tuesday before Ash Wednesday. See Liturgical seasons, Ordinary Time.

Sung Mass

The term Sung Mass, or 'Missa Cantata' in Latin, refers to *Mass* celebrated in the *Extraordinary Form* of the *Roman Rite*, in which the *priest* is not assisted by a *deacon* or *subdeacon* and sings the parts of the Mass as in a *Solemn Mass*. It is an intermediate between the Solemn Mass and the *Low Mass*, and lacks exact rubrics of its own. Its *ceremonial* is usually some combination of the Solemn

Mass and Low Mass, admitting considerable variations such as the use of *incense*; when and where to sit, stand, and kneel; and the number and roles of the *servers*.

The term may also be used to describe a Mass in the *Ordinary Form* when the *liturgical* texts are sung by the *celebrant* and the congregation.

Super-essential

Super-*essential* refers to the literal translation of the Greek words 'artos epiousios' used in the *Lord's Prayer*. 'Artos' is 'bread' or 'loaf' in Greek and 'epiousios' means 'super-essential.' Together, they are translated as 'daily bread.'

The word 'epiousios' is used in no other place in the *New Testament*. See Bread of Life. Also see Body of Christ 787, 789, 790, 1381.

Superfluous

Something is said to be superfluous when it is not useful, needed, or wanted. See Benefice.

Superior, religious

A religious superior is anyone having *authority* over others by virtue of *ecclesiastical* rank in the Church or some entity within it, such as *religious institutes*.

Titles of such superiors in religious communities vary, but some of the more common are *father superior*, *mother superior*, *prioress*, *abbess*,

guardian, *warden*, *prior*, *superior general*, *minister general*, and *abbot*. See Convent.

Superior general

Superior general is the title of the *superior* of certain *religious institutes*. See Superior, religious.

Supernatural 1998

Supernatural refers a power which surpasses the *nature* of a *created being*, but is added to it out of God's gracious initiative, such as the call to *eternal life* and *sanctifying grace*.

Whatever is supernatural neither constitutes a thing's *essence* nor is a necessary consequence of it. The supernatural is not something that an *essence postulates* as if its being and activity would be impossible without it. Rather, it is a special gift of the *divine* goodness itself given above and beyond the *natural* possibilities and requirements of a created being.

Supernatural gifts

A supernatural gift is not something that a *created* being requires for its existence and activities. It is a special gift of divine goodness added to a *nature* above and beyond its *natural* capacities and requirements.

Supernatural mystery

Supernatural mysteries are those which are not contrary to *reason*, but which exceed it so that even after being known by *faith* they remain indemonstrable to *created intelligence*. Such mysteries can only be known through faith because their true *nature* is only known by *analogy*. The *Trinity* is a supernatural mystery. See Mystery 359.

Supernatural virtue

Supernatural virtue refers to the *infused moral* and *theological virtues*. These are said to be *supernatural* because they are beyond the reach of man's *natural* powers and enable him to attain his supernatural end. They are infused because they are free gifts of God and form a disposition of the *soul*. See Virtue 1768.

Supernumerary

Supernumerary is the title of a class of *prelates* of the *Roman Curia*. It is an honorary distinction reserved to *canons* of *patriarchal basilicas* and eight Italian *cathedrals*.

The term supernumerary is also used to identify members of *Opus Dei* who may be married and live with their *families*. They follow the same spiritual life as the members who handle the administration and *spiritual direction* of members of the *prelature* who are called numeraries. Supernumeraries contribute some of their income to support the work of Opus Dei. See Prelature.

Superstition 2111

Superstition refers to the *attribution* of *magical* power to certain practices or objects, such as *charms*, etc.

Suppress

To suppress is to abolish by *authority*. See Liturgical seasons.

Supra-organic

Supra-organic comes from the Latin words 'super,' meaning over or above and 'organum,' meaning tool or implement. Supra-organic means beyond, above, or outside of an organ or body. When used in reference to the *intellect* and *will* in *man*, it means that they exist in the *soul* rather than the body as the instrument of the soul. See Soul 363.

Supreme cause

The supreme cause is the *first cause* from which all effects arise. It is the only uncaused cause. See Wisdom 295 1831.

Supreme pontiff

The title Supreme Pontiff comes from the Latin 'pontem facere,' meaning to make or build a bridge. It originally referred to the Roman emperor as head of the college of priests in pagan Rome because he was seen as the bridge builder between men and the gods.

The emperor Gratian gave the title to the *Pope* in 375 A.D. because he was the *Vicar of Christ* on earth and supreme *pastor* of the Church. The letters 'P.M.,' or 'Pont. Max.' written after the Pope's name mean Pontifex Maximus, in English, Supreme Pontiff. See Authentic Teachers 2034.

Surplice

A surplice is a loose fitting outer garment worn by *clerics* over a *cassock* in *choir*, *processions*, or when administering *sacraments*. *Laymen* when serving at *liturgical* functions often use it, but it is generally the distinctive dress for the lesser *clergy* and *priests* except when *celebrating Mass*. The name surplice comes from a Latin word 'superpelliceum,' meaning over fur because it was worn over the fur coats in cold climates. See Clerics 934.

Surrogate womb

Surrogate comes from the Latin word 'surrogare,' meaning to elect in the place of another or a substitute. A surrogate womb is one substituted for the *natural womb* of a mother by artificially implanting a *fertilized* egg into the womb of another woman to carry a child to term.

This procedure is *immoral* because it dissociates the sexual *act* from the *procreative* act and brings a child into existence by an act other than that by which two *persons* freely give themselves to one another in the state of *marriage*. See Heterologous artifi-

cial insemination and fertilization 2376.

Suscipiat

The suscipiat is the *prayer* recited by the *faithful* when the *celebrant* says 'Pray brethren,' etc. after washing his hands at the end of the offertory before beginning the *Canon of the Mass*. See Appendix of prayers; Prayers recited at Mass; Suspicion.

Suspension

Suspension is a form of *ecclesiastical censure* by which a *cleric* is forbidden to exercise his *office*, *jurisdiction*, or the enjoyment of his *benefice*.

A suspension from office forbids one to exercise any or all the powers received by *ordination* and any act of *jurisdiction*. Suspension from benefice deprives the *cleric* of the fruit of a benefice. A benefice is the right to revenues attached to some *sacred* office. The revenues may arise from property owned by the benefice, from some obligatory contributions made by some *person*, from the *voluntary* offerings made by the *faithful*, and from *stole fees* paid according to *diocesan statute* or custom. See Censure.

Symbol of Faith

The Symbol of Faith refers to the *Creed*, also called the *Profession of Faith*. See Profession of Faith 187.

Symbolic/symbolically

Something is symbolic when it stands for or represents something else. A fish was used by early *Christians* to represent *Christ*. See Truly, really, and substantially contained 1374.

Symbolon 188

The Greek word symbolon refers to one half of a broken object, which is presented as a token of *recognition*. When one of the two half parts was presented to another *person* possessing the other half and found to match, it could serve to verify both bearers' identity.

In the Church, it refers to a collection of statements, called a *creed*, which constitute a summary of the principal *truths* of the *faith* which must be believed and which is recited to identify one as a *Christian* to other Christians. See Symbol of Faith.

Synagogue

Synagogue is a Greek word meaning assembly. It refers to the building where the *Jews* gathered for public *worship*.

The synagogue is different from the *Temple* which is the place where *sacrifice* was offered. There was only one Temple, but after the *Babylonian exile*, synagogues were built wherever Jews lived. The *scrolls* containing the books of the *Law*, the *Pentateuch*, from which the Jews read the

Torah, were kept in the synagogue.

The *Jewish religious* service consists of *blessing* of God, *prayers*, readings from scrolls containing the *law* and *prophets* and exposition of the *Scriptures*.

In the *New Testament* with the institution of the *Eucharist* and of the priesthood by *Jesus*, the possibility of offering the same *Sacrifice of the Cross* is possible in many places without in any way compromising the unity of the Sacrifice of *Calvary*. It also became possible to multiply *churches* and permit all peoples to participate in that sacrifice. The *heavenly* Jerusalem under the *New Dispensation* may be found everywhere as the *Catholic Church*. See Aramaic terms in the liturgy. Also see Exile.

Synaxis 1329

Originally, this Greek word meaning assembly, referred to any gathering for *divine worship* whether for the *Eucharist*, *prayer*, or *sacred* reading.

Today synaxis refers to any assembly gathered together for *liturgical* purposes, such as *Liturgy of the Hours*, the administration of *sacraments* and especially the Eucharist.

The *Divine Office* developed from the practice of gathering to pray or read together. It was also in this way that the *Mass* and Divine Office came to focus on the same *sacred mys-*

tery or *feast* being *celebrated* on the day in the *liturgical calendar*.

In the *Byzantine Church*, synaxis refers to a *rite* in which the people of God gather to honor *saints* connected with the mystery celebrated on the previous day.

Synderesis or synteresis 1780

Synderesis comes from the Greek word 'synteresis,' meaning spark of *conscience*. Synderesis is the instinctive, *infallible, habitual knowledge postulated* as the first principle of *moral* action; do *good* and avoid *evil*. Synderesis is an instinctive disposition and is distinct from *conscience*, which is a practical application of known *principles* judging the *morality* of a particular *act*. Conscience can be *objectively erroneous*, unless guided by the teaching of *Christ* and the Church.

Synderesis provides a sure point of reference for orientating *conscience*, and at the same time *postulates* the *judgments* of a right conscience. The presence of synderesis also explains why acting against conscience and God's *law* always results in *guilt*, and why the *human heart* cannot rest until it rests in God. See Conscience.

Synod 887

A synod is an assembly that may be held at the level of the universal Church or for a *diocese*.

In the case of the universal Church, the assembly is known as the Synod of Bishops. It is "a group of *Bishops* selected from different parts of the world, who meet together at specified times to promote the close relationship between the *Roman Pontiff* and the Bishops. These Bishops, by their counsel, assist the Roman Pontiff in the defense and development of *faith* and *morals* and in the preservation and strengthening of *ecclesiastical discipline*" (Canon 342). The Synod of Bishops may convene in a general assembly to address concerns of the universal Church or in a special assembly to address concerns of a particular region (Canon 345).

In the case of a *diocese*, the assembly is known as a *diocesan synod*. It is "an assembly of selected *priests* and other members of *Christ's faithful* of a particular *church* which, for the good of the whole diocesan community, assists the diocesan Bishop" (Canon 460). Any *decrees* emanating from a diocesan synod are approved and promulgated on the sole authority of the diocesan Bishop, who then forwards the text of the decrees to the *Metropolitan* and to the *episcopal conference*.

Decrees of a diocesan synod bind only in the diocese of

the Bishop who called it. See Council 465.

Synodal judge

A synodal judge is a member of a group of *clerics*, who are competent canonists, approved in a *diocesan synod* and appointed by the *Bishop* to serve as judges in *ecclesiastical* cases. See Diocese.

Synodic month

A synodic month is the average period of time between successive *new moons*: twenty nine days, twelve hours, forty-four minutes and 2.7 seconds. See Lunar calendar.

Synonymous

A word having the same or nearly the same meaning as another word. See Rite 1203.

Synoptic Gospels

The *Gospels* of Matthew, Mark and Luke are called the synoptic Gospels because they follow the same general plan and offer the same comprehensive view of the life and teachings of *Jesus*.

The Gospel of John, which is not classed as a synoptic Gospel, was written to record special proofs of the *divinity* of *Christ*. See Gospel.

Synthesize

Synthesize means to bring together into an organized whole. See Coredemptrix.

Syrian Rite

The Syrian Rite is used by the Syriac *Catholic Church*, the Syriac Orthodox Church (part of the *Oriental Orthodox* communion), and by the *Maronite Church* to some extent. This is also called the West Syrian Rite to distinguish it from the East Syrian, or *Chaldean*, Rite.

It is substantially the *liturgy* of fourth century Antioch. The language used is Syriac or Aramaic, but some Arabic is used as well. *Holy Communion* is received under both *species*. *Baptism* by immersion is followed by *Confirmation* and Communion under the species of wine. The Jacobite Syrians make their *confession* before the *priest* at the door of the *church*. The *altar* is usually in full view. There are pictures but no statues in the church. *Byzantine* type *vestments* are worn and *bishops* always wear a small hood. Sometimes a Western *miter* is worn. The Syrian Rite has its own *Canon Law* and is governed by the *Patriarch* of Antioch in Beirut. *Celibacy* is obligatory since 1888 but the obligation can be *dispensed* and some priests are married. St. Ephrem was of this rite and he was declared a *doctor of the church*. His *feast* was extended to the whole *Latin Church* in 1920. See Rite 1203.

Syro-Malabar Church/Rite

Syro-Malabar *Christians* live

in southwest India, and often call themselves Saint Thomas Christians because they trace their religious ancestry to St. Thomas the Apostle. Today they form three groups:

1) The first group are those in union with the *Pope*. These are about half a million in number, and use the Syro-Malabar Rite. They include those who were converted from *Nestorianism* in 1599 A.D. by the Portuguese missionaries and Malankarese, the latter being reunited with Rome in 1930 A.D.

2) The Nestorian party called the Mellusians originated in the *schism* from native *Catholics* led by *Bishop* Mellos in 1874 A.D.

3) The party of Jacobites or *Monophysites*, who rejected the *Council of Chalcedon* (451 A.D.), got their name when they went into schism in 1653 A.D. because they were prevented from approaching the Nestorians and could only get help from the Jacobite *Patriarch* of Antioch. It may be doubtful whether they actually profess the Monophysite *heresy*, but they do deny the *primacy* of the Pope. Their *sacraments* and *Holy Orders* are *valid*. They have suffered from frequent quarrels since 1816 A.D. Those who have been much influenced by Anglican missionaries became Reformed Jacobites. Each group of Indian Christians has its own *liturgy*. See Rites. Also

see Oriental Church; Eastern Church.

Systematic and organic

Systematic refers to the organization or arrangement of things so related that they form a unit or organic whole. In *catechesis*, it refers to a set of facts, principles, or rules classified and arranged into an orderly way to reveal the *logical* plan linking various parts into a unified whole.

Organic refers to a part of the body composed of specialized tissue adapted to the performance of a specific function. In catechetical instruction it refers to the organization of facts and *principles* so that they reveal a *logical* plan which unites them into an organized whole in which each part contributes to a comprehensive *understanding* of the *truths* taught. See Catechetical instruction.

Systematic philosophy

Systematic means carefully organized and arranged into a complete, coherent, and consistent method or plan. *Scholastic philosophy* is called a systematic *philosophy* because it considers all the major philosophical questions in a developmental sequence. Philosophy is sometimes divided into physics and *metaphysics*. Typically metaphysics is divided into: 1) *logic*, the science of correct thinking; 2) *epistemology*, the *validity* or *truth-*

value of human *knowledge*, from *experience* and the use of the *intellect*; 3) *ontology*, also referred to as general *metaphysics*, which is the study of *being*, its primary *attributes*, determinations, and *categories*; 4) *cosmology*, the study of the corporeal universe and its ultimate constitution; 5) rational *psychology*, the study of the whole *man* as a sentient, vegetative, *rational* organism, his *soul*, *intellect*, *free will* and *destiny*; and 6) *ethics*, the study of the *laws* which determine right and wrong using *human reason* alone. See Scholastic philosophy.

Systematic theology

Systematic theology is another name for *dogmatic theology*. See Dogmatic theology 88.

T

Tabernacle 1183, 1379

A tabernacle is a box-like receptacle wherein the *Blessed Sacrament* is reserved or kept in *churches*. It may be made of wood, stone, or metal, but should be immovable and locked to prevent danger of *profanation*.

A *tabernacle veil* usually covers the tabernacle. The interior is usually lined with silk and a linen cloth, and a *corporal* covers its floor. Its contents are usually the *sacred vessels*; *ciborium* containing the *consecrated Hosts* for *Holy Communion* and a *capsula* or *lunette*, which contains the larger Host inserted into the *monstrance* for *Benediction* or *Exposition* of the Blessed Sacrament.

In the past, the Tabernacle was universally the central focus of the parish Church and located in the center of the main *altar*. Today, it may be located in other areas deemed more suitable to private *prayer*, although still prominent, easily recognized, and still serving to focus attention on the *recognition* of the *doctrinal* centrality and significance of the *Real Presence* in the life of the Church community.

A *sanctuary lamp* is kept burning in the *sanctuary* before the tabernacle as a sign that the Blessed Sacrament is being reserved. The Blessed Sacrament may not be reserved in more than one place in a *church*.

In the *Byzantine Church*, the tabernacle, called the *artophorion*, is always located on the main altar.

Tabernacle veil

A tabernacle veil is a decorated cloth completely covering the top and sides of the *tabernacle* divided in the front so that the door may be opened. It is normally *unlawful* to leave the door of the tabernacle uncovered, no matter how beautiful it may be, when it contains the *Blessed Sacrament*. The veil may always be golden, silver, or white, or it may follow the liturgical color of the day, but it must never be black. Often a second curtain is hung inside the door. See Tabernacle 1183, 1379.

Tables of the Law

Tables of the Law refers to the stone tablets on which were written the *Ten Commandments* (Ex 24:12 and Deut 9:9). The tablets themselves were small *steles* like those other nations used to publicize their *laws*.

The purpose of the *Ark of the Covenant* was to serve as a container for the stone tablets on which the *Ten Commandments* were written. It was the association of the Law as the *Word of God* that gave rise to the concept that the Ark was the throne of God or his footstool. Thus the Ark came to represent the presence of God in the midst of the people.

The Ark of the Covenant is a type of *Our Lady* as *Mother of God*, because in her God *Incarnate* is found present for the first time. *Mary* is so invoked in the *Litany of Loreto*. See Ark of the Covenant.

Tarot cards

Tarot cards are a set of cards bearing pictures of certain traditional *allegorical* figures used in *fortune telling*. See Divination 2116.

Taxeis 1537

Taxeis is a Greek word which refers to the Latin word *'ordines'* translated as orders in English. *Orders* are *ecclesiastical* groups designated as bodies having specific characters and functions.

Te Deum 168

Te Deum are the first two words of a beautiful *hymn* of *thanksgiving*. It is also known as the *Ambrosian hymn*, but St. Ambrose (340–397 A.D.), though he probably used it,

did not compose it himself. See Psalmi idiotici.

Teaching office

The teaching office is a service, *duty*, responsibility, or function in the Church. The teaching office refers to the *responsibility* of the Church to teach the *faith*.

In the Church, the *hierarchy* actually has three *offices*: to *teach*, to *sanctify* and to *govern*. The teaching office is also known as the *Magisterium*, the office of sanctifying as the *priestly* office and that of governing as the royal office. These offices reflect and are extensions of the *prophetic*, priestly, and royal *dignity* of *Christ*. See Office.

Temperament

According to medieval physiology, a temperament is one of four conditions of the body or *mind*. Temperament identifies a *person's* customary frame of mind or natural disposition. They are called *sanguine, phlegmatic, choleric*, or *melancholic*, each of which is *attributed* to a corresponding humor. *Persons* with a sanguine temperament are warm, passionate, and cheerful. Persons with a phlegmatic temperament are dull, sluggish, and *apathetic*. Persons with a choleric temperament are quick tempered, *irascible* and easily irritated. Persons with a melancholic temperament are sad, gloomy, depressed, and pensive.

Temperance 1809, 2341, 2407, 2517

Temperance is the *cardinal moral virtue* that moderates the attraction of pleasure and provides a balance in the use of *created* goods. It ensures the mastery of the *will* over instinct, and keeps *natural* desires within proper and honorable limits.

The *virtues* of *modesty*, *chastity*, and *abstinence* are parts of the virtue of temperance; hence it is opposed to *gluttony*, *lust*, and drunkenness. This virtue not only moderates the drive for pleasure but also our drive for *violence*.

Because our *society* is focused on pleasure without temperance, it is filled with love of violence. In order to restrain our love of violence, we must restrain our love of pleasure. Temperance does much to bring peace into our lives.

Temple

According to the *Law* of the *Old Testament* the temple was the only place where *sacrifice* could be offered. For this reason it constituted the center of *Jewish worship*. Because the Temple was located in Jerusalem, the city itself was also considered a *holy* place.

Since the Jews gathered in large numbers to *celebrate* the *feasts* of their *faith*, the *pilgrimages*, festivals, *sacrifices*, and evening offering were held in Jerusalem and it became the natural center of Jewish *secular* life and education.

With the institution of the *Eucharist* by *Christ* as the continuation of his *Sacrifice of the Cross* in every place and time, it became possible in a real sense for the Holy City to be everywhere the Church *celebrates* and reserves the *Eucharist*. See Filial prayer 2599. Also see Mercy seat 433.

Temple of the Holy Spirit 1695

By the *grace* of God, the *faithful* become temples of the *Holy Spirit* through *Baptism*. They are justified in the name of *Christ* and the Spirit, and called to *sanctification* by the work of the Spirit in them. 'Do you not know that you are God's temple, and that the Spirit of God dwells in you?' (1 Cor 3:16).

The *temple* is God's dwelling place. It is used for the exercise of the priestly *rites* of *prayer* and sacrifice. Through *Baptism*, the faithful are united to Christ who is the true temple of God and the place where his *glory* dwells.

The *sacrament of Baptism* not only *purifies* from *sins* but makes the baptized a new creature, an *adopted son* of God, partaker of the *divine nature*, member of Christ, co-heir with him, and a temple of the Holy Spirit.

The *indwelling of the Holy Spirit* makes the Church the

temple of the living God and prompts the faithful to act and bear fruit in *charity*. By the healing of *sin*, the Spirit renews the faithful through a *spiritual* transformation, and enlightens, and strengthens them to live as children of light.

Through the life of the Spirit in them, the faithful believe in God, hope in him, and love him. Through it they have the power to live and act under the promptings of the Spirit. Through the Spirit, the faithful grow in *holiness* by the practice of *moral virtues* and so are *sanctified*.

Temporal

Temporal describes anything that lasts only for a time and whose existence or activity will cease. What is temporal is the opposite of *eternal* and is applied to what is of this world as opposed to what is *heavenly*. It may also refer to what is *material* in contrast with what is *spiritual*. See Millenarianism.

Temporal consequences of sin

The *temporal* consequences of *sin* are such things as suffering, illness, death, and the frailties *inherent* in life. It also includes the weaknesses of *character* and inclination or attraction to sin, which remain after *sin* is forgiven by *Baptism* or the *sacrament of Reconciliation*. The temporal *consequences* of *original sin*

are referred to as *concupiscence*.

The attachment to sin caused by concupiscence remains after *forgiveness* and is a hinderance to complete attachment to the *will of God*. Since nothing imperfect can enter *heaven* this attachment must be *purified* either on earth or in *purgatory*. See Concupiscence 405. Also see Temporal punishment 1471.

Temporal goods

Temporal good refers to those *created material* things and possessions, required to maintain life, health, and the exercise of one's talents.

Temporal goods of the Church refers to those material things required to carry out her *mission*; for example, those things required to conduct *divine worship*, to provide support of the *clergy*, to exercise various works of charity and carry out her *apostolate* to the poor. See Congregation for the clergy.

Temporal punishment 1471, 1472

Temporal punishment is the punishment due to *sin* after the guilt of sin has been forgiven. Temporal punishment is punishment in the present life or in *purgatory* as opposed to the *eternal punishment* of *hell*. It may be considered as the *temporal consequences* of sinful acts, especially in the form of any earthly attachments, which might remain even after sin has been forgiven.

Temporal punishment can be removed in this world through *purification*, which results from performing good works or it can be *remitted* by *indulgences*. If one is not sufficiently purified at the end of life in this world, purification must be completed in *purgatory* because *Scripture* teaches that nothing imperfect can enter the *kingdom of heaven*.

Only the *just* enter purgatory. Those in purgatory are assured of *eternal life* after their purgation and *perfection*. Purgatory is not a second chance for *heaven*.

Temporary Vows

Religious take *vows of poverty*, *chastity*, and *obedience* when they enter a *religious institute* in a *ceremony* called *profession*. In order to allow *persons* time to carefully discern if they are called to *religious life*, they are initially only permitted to make temporary vows.

After a period of temporary profession, religious may take *perpetual vows* that bind definitively. See Religious Profession. Also see Religious Life 925.

Tempt or tempting God 2119

The Catechism of the Catholic Church defines tempting God as "putting his goodness and almighty power to the test by word or deed" (CCC 2119).

Tempting God wounds the respect we owe our *Creator* and *Lord* because it always harbors some doubt about his *love, providence,* and power.

Temptation

Temptation refers to an invitation to *sin* by persuasion or offering some form of pleasure. Temptation arises from the world, the flesh or the *devil*.

The world tempts with the attractiveness of bad example and pressure to conform to the ways of the world and its *values*. Temptation comes from the *flesh* in the form of urges to *carnal* or *spiritual concupiscence* by the tendency toward the *capital sins*. *Demonic* temptation arises at the instigation of the *devil* who ever encourages all forms of *avarice, selfishness, pride,* and other sins. See Holy Water. Also see Jansenism.

Ten Commandments

The Ten Commandments are referred to as *Ten Words* and as the *Decalogue*. The commandments were given to Moses by God on stone tablets on Mount Sinai. They appear in two somewhat different formulae in Ex 20:1–17 and Deut 5:6-21. See Ten words 2058.

Ten words 2058

Ten words is another term for the *Decalogue* or *Ten Commandments* written by the hand of God on two tablets given to Moses on Mount Sinai

(Deut 5:22). See Ten Commandments.

Terce

Terce, a Latin reference to the third hour of the day (9am), is a *minor hour* of the *Divine Office*, and is called *Midmorning Prayer*. It is part of the *Daytime Prayer*. See Liturgy of the Hours. 1174, 1178.

Terminate

Terminate means to end in or conclude in some way. See Voluntary act 1734.

Territorial abbey

See Abbey nullius.

Territorial parish

Parishes are generally territorial units with boundaries, embracing all the *Christian faithful* within the territory. *Pastors* have *jurisdiction* only over those who reside within the boundaries of the parish of which they are installed as pastor by the *Bishop*. These are called territorial parishes.

Territorial parishes are distinguished from *personal parishes*, which are established based upon *rite*, nationality, language, or some other determining factor. See Parish 2179.

Tersanctus

The Tersanctus (thrice holy) is a hymn of victory beginning with the words, 'Holy, holy, holy Lord God of hosts. *Heaven and earth are full of thy glory.*

Blessed is he who comes in the name of the Lord.' See Preface 1352. See Sanctus.

Tertiary/Tertiaries

Tertiary is a member of a *third order*. See Third Order.

Tetragrammaton

JHWH are the four consonants of the name of God as revealed to Moses. His name was considered too *sacred* to be uttered aloud and was written only using the consonants of the word. These four letters are referred to as the tetragrammaton. IHVH, and *YHWH*, are other forms of the tetragrammaton. See YHWH 206.

Thanksgiving after meals

Thanksgiving after meals is a prayer of thanks offered to God for his gifts. See Appendix of prayers Thanksgiving after meals.

Theft 2408

As taught by *The Catechism of the Catholic Church*, theft is "usurping another's property against the reasonable *will* of the owner. There is no theft if consent can be presumed or if refusal is contrary to *reason* and the *universal destination of goods*" (CCC 2408). The prime example is "when the only way to provide for immediate, essential needs (food, shelter, clothing...) is to put at one's disposal and use the property of others" (CCC 2408).

Any form of unjust taking and keeping the property of another is against the seventh commandment even if it does not contradict *civil law*. Business fraud, unjust wages, price gouging, taking advantage of *ignorance* or hardship of others, are all forms of theft. *Justice* toward others, not legality, determines the sinfulness of theft. Robbery is theft accompanied by *violence*.

Theism/theistic

Theism is the general *belief* in the existence of a personal *providential* god and admits the possibility of *revelation*. It may take on different forms such as *monotheism* (belief in one God) or *polytheism* (belief in several gods) or *henotheism* (belief in one god who is chief among several).

Theism differs from *deism*, which is belief in the existence of God on purely *rational* grounds without reliance on *revelation* or religious *authority*. It takes the position that God *created* the world and *natural law* then takes no further part in its functioning. See Christian humanism. Also see Deism 285.

Theologia 236

'Theologia' is a Latin word meaning *theology*, the study of God as known from *revelation*. Theology is especially the study of the *mystery* of the *internal* life of the *Trinity*.

Theologia is revealed to us through *oikonomia*, the works of God, and theologia in turn illuminates oikonomia. In the Western Church study of the oikonomia is also known as theology, although subordinated to the study of the *Trinity*.

In the *Eastern Church* study of the oikonomia is called just that. This mode of dividing theology into two great parts is reflected in the terminology of *Blessed* John Duns Scotus (1266/70–1308 A.D.): theology of *necessary being*, that is a *being* which cannot not be, or the study of God, *Triune* and one; and theology of *contingent being*, whose nonexistence is possible. He organized oikonomia around the absolute *primacy* of *Christ*. See Oikonomia 236.

Theologian 2038

A theologian is a *person* trained in the science of *theology*. See Scholastic theology.

Theological

The word theological comes from the Greek word 'theologia,' meaning the study of God. As an adjective it refers to things having to do with or based on *theology*. Theology is the formal study of the *nature* of God and his relations with the universe. Different forms of theology are expounded by various religious *denomina-*

tions. See Apathy. Also see Protestant Reformation.

Theological Commission

The International Theological Commission is an international group of *theologians* created by Pope Paul VI to assist the *Congregation for the Doctrine of the Faith* in examining certain *doctrinal* questions. It is attached to the Congregation for the Doctrine of the Faith. See Congregation. Also see Congregation for the Doctrine of the Faith.

Theological graces

Theological graces refer to the *infused moral* and *theological virtues.* They are called *supernatural* because they are beyond the reach of man's *natural* powers and enable him to reach his *supernatural end.* They are called *graces* because they are free gifts of God and form a disposition of the *soul.*

These graces animate *moral* life and give it a special *character* by adapting *man's faculties* for participation in the *divine nature.* These gifts enrich and enhance the *moral virtues.* The moral virtues are prerequisites for the theological virtues, which are the gifts of grace enabling man to attain his final destiny. See Theological virtues 1812.

Theological tradition

Theological tradition refers to the *understanding* and interpretation of Church teaching

and *doctrine* preserved, developed, and handed down by *theologians* who are judged as *orthodox* by the *Magisterium.* See Apostolic Fathers. Also see Fathers of the Church.

Theological virtues 1812

The theological virtues are *faith, hope,* and *charity.* They are the foundation of Christian *moral* activity. They *animate* moral life and give it its special *character* by adapting man's *faculties* for participation in the *divine nature.*

They are called *theological* because they have God as their primary object. Theological virtues unite *man* to God through *sanctifying grace* enabling man to choose the good with greater ease.

The theological virtues enrich and enhance the *moral virtues.* The moral virtues are prerequisites for the theological virtues, which are gifts of *grace* enabling man to attain his final *destiny.* See Virtue.

Theological virtues in prayer
2656, 2657, 2658

"*Prayer* is the raising of one's *mind* and *heart* to God or the requesting of good things from God" (CCC 2559). It is through prayer that we experience communion with God through *Christ* and the Church. Through prayer, we are opened to the movement of the *Holy Spirit* to the redeeming *mercy* of God. In prayer everything is drawn to God, the source of prayer. "One enters into prayer as one enters into *liturgy*: by the narrow gate of *faith*" (CCC 2656).

Acts of faith, *hope*, and *charity* are necessary for *salvation* and are required for growth in *holiness*. Faith is a divinely *infused virtue* that enables us to give *assent* to the *truths* of salvation. Through acts of faith in prayer, we foster the growth of faith in our lives. Hope is the infused virtue that enables us to rely on God's *grace* and salvation, and look forward to achieving our salvation and fulfillment in him by prayer. Charity is that infused virtue that enables us to *love* God for his own sake, as he does, and oneself and others for his sake, in loving all as he does. Growth in the *theological virtues* is the ultimate aim of *Christian* life.

Theology

The word theology comes from the Greek word 'theologia,' meaning the study of God. It is the formal study of the *nature* of God and his relations with the universe. Different forms of theology are expounded by various religious *denominations*. See Apathy. Also see Protestant Reformation. Also see Scholastic theology.

Theophany 204, 697, 707, 2059

Theophany comes from the Greek meaning a *manifestation* of God. A theophany is any manifestation of God to man as in the case of Moses on Mt. Sinai.

The *Epiphany* is sometimes called a theophany because of the manifestation of the *Christ* Child to the *Magi* from the East. God also manifested himself in theophanies and to Peter, James and John, in the *Transfiguration* of *Christ*, when he manifested his *glory* before his death and *Resurrection*.

Theory/Theoretical

Something is called theoretical when it is primarily concerned with *abstract* understanding, not the practical application of *knowledge* to something. The theoretical is only concerned with *principles* and methods, not practice or application. It is the opposite of applied *knowledge*. See Assent. Also see Praxis.

Theosis

Theosis is a Greek term meaning *divinization* or *deification*. In Catholic *theology*, it refers to the participation in the *divine nature* by the *grace* of *adoption* as sons brought about by *Baptism* and through the fruits of the *sacramental life*. It does not mean that the creature ceases to be a creature and becomes divine in his *being*. See Sacramental grace 1129.

Theotokia 2678

Theotokia is a Greek word meaning *Mother of God*.

Theotokion

A theotokion is a short *hymn* in honor of *Our Lady* sung in the *Byzantine Church*. See Troparia 1177.

Theotokos 495

Theotokos means '*Mother of God.*' It is the principal title of the *Virgin Mary* in the *Oriental Church*. The title was used already in the third century and was first sanctioned at the *Council of Ephesus* in 431 A.D. The equivalent Latin term is *Deipara*, meaning God-bearer.

Third class relics

There are three classes of relics. *First class relics* are parts of a *saint's* body. *Second class relics* are things the saint used during life. Third class relics are objects, such as cloth, that have been touched to a first class relic. Relics may not be sold or bought. See Altar 1383. Also see Relic.

Third order

A third order is an association "whose members live in the world but share in the spirit of some *religious institute*, under the overall direction of the same institute, and who lead an apostolic life and strive for *Christian perfection*" (Canon 303). Members of third orders are called *tertiaries*.

The purpose of third orders is to bring the spirit of the *religious life* into the *secular* world and *sanctify* its members. See Congregation for Institutes of Consecrated Life and Societies of Apostolic life. Also see Dominicans, Secular institutes.

Third Person

The Third Person of the Holy Trinity is the *Holy Spirit* or Holy Ghost. See Trinity, Holy 232, 233, 234, 237. Also see Divine missions 258; Divine Persons.

Three offices of Christ 783

The office or work of *Jesus* is threefold. First, *Christ* came to *redeem man* from *sin*. This is asserted in *Scripture*, in the writings of the *Fathers*, and in the *Creed*. *Redemption* constitutes Christ's *priestly office*. The *Word Incarnate* is the *mediator* between God and man in the *Sacrifice of the Cross*.

In the *Person* of Christ, both the *divine* and *human natures* are united. In his human nature, he was able to suffer and die in satisfaction for sin. Because in his *divine nature* he is God, this satisfaction had *infinite value* and could compensate for the *infinite* dishonor to God's majesty caused by sin.

The second office of Christ was *prophetic*. Christ came to bear witness to the *truth* that man might have life and have it more abundantly. He revealed the *Trinitarian nature* of the Godhead. He explained the *mysteries* of the kingdom and established a Church to continue his teaching and *prophetic office* for all time so that men might live *righteously* and *justly* before God and follow him into the *kingdom of heaven*.

The third office of Christ is his *kingly office*. The *Prophets* of the *Old Testament* foretold him as king and the *anointed one* of God, the *Messiah*. When he was lifted up on the Cross all power was given him in *heaven* and on earth. He exercises his kingship by drawing all things to himself through his death and *Resurrection*.

Three states of the Church 954

The three states of the Church refers to the fact that among the members of the Church some are *pilgrims* on earth: they are called the *Church Militant*. Others have died and are being *purified*: they are called the *Church Suffering*. Still others are already in *glory* contemplating God himself: they are called the *Church Triumphant*.

All share in different ways the same *communion in charity* towards God and neighbors. In the *Spirit* they form one Church, and cleave together in *Christ*.

The three states are bound to one another in a communion of charity. The souls in *purgatory*, being purified before entering the bliss of *heaven*, are called the Church Suffering. In charity they *intercede* for the Church Militant and venerate God in his *saints* in the Church Triumphant.

The saints in heaven enjoying the *beatific vision* are called the Church Triumphant. They intercede for the Church Suffering and the Church Militant before the throne of God.

The Church Militant intercedes for the Church Suffering and venerates the Church Triumphant before the throne of God asking for its *intercession* for the earthly *pilgrims*.

Timidity

Timidity refers to fearfulness, lack of confidence, or cowardliness in making decisions and taking action. See Prudence 1806.

Tisri

Tisri is the Babylonian name for the first month of the *Jewish civil year*. It corresponds to the month of the *ecclesiastical* year which includes parts of September and October in our calendar. This name replaced Ethanim after the *Babylonian exile* or captivity. See Day of Atonement 578.

Titular

Titular means title. It is an honorary distinction conferred on *ecclesiastics* throughout the world who are not *domestic prelates* and do not belong to the *Pontifical Family*. See Prelature. Also see Protonotary.

Titular Archbishop

A titular archbishop is a *prelate* who holds the rank and title of *Archbishop* without episcopal jurisdiction or specific archiepiscopal duties. Examples of titular archbishops would include an archbishop who has retired or is serving as coadjutor to a governing archbishop and entrusted with special duties. It also includes archbishops who are not *metropolitans*, that is, without *suffragan* diocesan bishops subject to them. See Archbishop.

Titular feast

When a *church* is *blessed* or *consecrated* it is given a name of a *Divine Person*, *mystery*, *sacred* object, or a *saint*. The name of the *saint* whose *relics* are entombed in the *altar stone* is usually the name of the church. This name is *celebrated* in the *liturgical* calendar and that *feast* is called the titular feast. See Altar 1182, 1383.

Tongues, Gift of

The gift of tongues is one of the *preternatural gifts* given to the *Apostles* on *Pentecost*. It is also called *glossolalia*. It is the ability to speak and be understood by all who hear. It is accompanied by the gift of *interpretation of tongues* which is the ability of hearers to understand someone speaking in a foreign language. See Charism. Also see Glossolalia.

Tonsure

Tonsure is a *ceremony* in which a man's head is shaven in five places to form a cross, so signifying his being set aside to serve the crucified Savior, and he is vested with a *surplice*. Tonsure makes a *person* a *cleric* and prepares him for the reception of *minor* and *major orders*, but it is not itself considered an order. Since *Vatican II* it has been replaced by a ceremony known as initiation into the *clerical state*. See Cleric 934. Also see Clerical orders.

Torah/Tora

Torah/tora in *Hebrew* means instruction of God. This instruction consists of the *revelation* of God to Israel together with the body of *Jewish theology* contained in the *Pentateuch*, the first five books of the *Old Testament*. See Genesis. Also see Pentateuch.

Torpor

Torpor refers to sluggishness, stupor, or *apathy*. It is characteristic of *Sloth* or *Acedia*. See Sloth 1866.

Total continence

Total continence is also called *total sexual abstinence*. It refers to the total abstinence from sex, which is required by the sixth commandment of the *Decalogue* of all unmarried *persons*.

Total continence is also part of the total gift of self of those who embrace the *evangelical counsel* of *chastity* and those in *Holy Orders*. See Continence 1650.

Total sexual abstinence

Total sexual abstinence is required by the sixth commandment of all single *persons*. Total abstinence is also part of the total gift of self of those who embrace the *evangelical counsel* of *chastity* and those in *Holy Orders*. See Total continence.

Traditio 2769

Traditio is the Latin word for *tradition*. It means handing on.

Tradition 78, 174, 688

In Church usage, Tradition, written with a capital letter, refers to the living transmission of the message of the *Gospel* in the Church. It refers to the oral preaching of the *Apostles*, and the message of *salvation* written under the *inspiration* of the *Holy Spirit* (*Sacred Scripture*) which are conserved and handed on by the Church through the *apostolic succession* as the *deposit of faith*.

In Church usage, when tradition is written with a small letter, it refers to what has been handed down by a series of *authentic* Church teachings through time. This includes various *pious* customs and practices, such as *novenas*, which may change with the passing of time, because they are not specifically part of the *revelation* of God to the Church.

Transcendent / Transcendence 285, 440

The word transcendent is used to describe that which utterly rises above, surpasses, exceeds, or goes beyond in some respect, quality, or *attribute*. God is transcendent because he surpasses everything, in every way he is incomparable, and incapable of *categorization*. Transcendent is the opposite of *immanent*. Transcendence is the state of being transcendent.

Transcendent event 647

A transcendent event is an occurrence or happening, which transcends, surpasses, or excels all others.

Transcendental attributes of being

There are three general aspects or elements of *being*: *unity*, *truth*, and goodness. These are called *transcendental attributes* of all being.

The attribute of unity implies the idea of indivision or undividedness in a being's inner reality which separates it from all other things. The attribute of *truth* consists of the conformity of a being with its *nature*. A thing is what it is by virtue of its nature and *essence*. The attribute of goodness means that every positive reality is *good* and in some way perfect because *actuality* itself is a kind of *perfection*. The notion of perfection of being gives rise to the attribute of *beauty*, but beauty is not interchangeable with being like the other three are, and therefore not a transcendental, properly speaking. Also see Beauty.

Transcends 42

That which transcends rises above, surpasses, exceeds, or goes beyond in some respect, quality, or *attribute*.

Transfiguration 554

The Transfiguration refers to the unveiling of the *divine glory* of *Christ* witnessed by Sts. Peter, James and John as related in Mt 17:1–13; Mk 9:3–12; and Lk 9:28–36, just before Christ went to Jerusalem to undergo his *Passion* and death.

The feast of the Transfiguration is observed on August 6. Its institution is commonly *attributed* to *Pope* Calixtus III (1455–58), who promoted the feast to obtain God's help against the Turks. It is the *titular feast* of *churches* dedicated to *Saint Savior*. It is also customary in the *Byzantine Church* to bless fruit on this occasion.

At the Transfiguration, Christ permitted the divine light momentarily to pass from his Godhead and *soul* to become visible as an interior light shining from his body. The

glory of Christ's soul did not shine forth from the moment of his *conception* in order that he might work out the *mystery* of our *redemption* in a body capable of suffering. Nevertheless, he was not deprived of the power to transmit the glory of his *soul* to his body as he did at the Transfiguration.

Various reasons have been offered for the Transfiguration. 1) Christ wanted to bolster the *faith* of the *Apostles* before his *Passion* and death so they could understand that just as his glory was hidden in his *human* form, his victory over death would be concealed in the *Crucifixion*. 2) Christ wanted them to know he was truly *divine* by the witness of Moses and Elijah and the voice of God speaking in the cloud (Lk 9:28–36; Mt 17:1–8; Mk 9:2–8). 3). He wanted all *Christians* to hope for their own glory at their resurrection as they are transformed by Christ's *graces*.

Transforming union

Transforming union is another term for *spiritual marriage*. See Spiritual marriage.

Transmission of the Faith 74

Because "God desires all men to be saved and to come to the *knowledge* of the *truth*" (CCC 74), he provided a means by which whatever he revealed to his Church through *Christ* should be transmitted down the ages. He gave this mission to the *Catholic Church* who has, through the laying on of hands, faithfully and infallibly proclaimed the message through all ages.

Transgression(s)

Transgression comes from the Latin word 'transgressus,' meaning to step or pass over. In English it means to overstep or break a *law* or commandment. See Born under the Law 422.

Transitional deacon

A transitional deacon is a *deacon* who will ultimately be ordained a *priest*. Transitional deacons commit themselves to a *celibate* life and the daily recitation of the *Divine Office*. They may administer *Baptism*, distribute *Holy Communion*, preach during the *liturgy* and witness *marriages*. Deacons who will not become *priests* are called *permanent deacons*. See Permanent Diaconate 1571.

Transmigration

Transmigration from the Latin 'trans' across or over and 'migrare' to move from one place to another or migrate. It is also known as *metempsychosis* which is derived from the Greek 'meta,' change, and 'empsychosis,' meaning after living. The *theory* of transmigration holds that the *soul* migrates from one body to another after death until it

is *purified* of worldliness and freed by death for the state of complete bliss. It is not clear exactly what constitutes purification. Transmigration is incompatible with the *doctrine* of *redemption* and misrepresents its *character*. See Metempsychosis.

Transubstantiation 1376

Transubstantiation refers to the total and substantial change of bread and wine into the Body and Blood of *Christ*, which takes place at the moment of *consecration* in the *Mass*. The Greek *Fathers* referred to this change as 'meta-ousiosis,' which means change of *being*.

The term was used to describe the *Eucharistic mystery* by the *Fourth Lateran Council* in 1215. Later, the *Council of Trent* formally called the conversion of the whole *substance* of the bread and wine into the substance of the Body and Blood of Christ transubstantiation. In transubstantiation the total substance: matter as well as form, that is, the total, not partial substance of bread and wine, becomes the total reality of Christ's Body and Blood. Only the appearance or properties of bread and wine remain.

Because this is revealed to us by Christ himself, we are absolutely certain of its *truth*. It is more reasonable to doubt the existence of bread and wine revealed by our senses than to doubt that they are the Body and Blood of Christ after consecration. This is called the *mystery of faith*.

Treatise

A treatise is a formal systematic article or book on a particular topic or subject. It contains a discussion of facts evidence, principles, and *conclusions* based on this information. See Didache.

Tree of Life

The expression '*tree of life*' was a common ancient symbol for *immortality*. The footnotes in the *Douay-Rheims Bible*, referring to Gen 2:9, explain that the tree of life was so called because by eating of its fruit *man* would be preserved in a constant state of health, vigor, and strength, and would not have died at all.

The tree of life is said to typify the Cross, whose fruit is the *Eucharist*, the *Bread of Life*, or the *Body of Christ* given for us and the Blood he shed for us. See Garden of Eden.

Tree of the knowledge of good and evil 396

The tree of the *knowledge* of *good* and *evil* is a *symbol* of the *insurmountable* limits that *man*, as creature, must freely recognize and respect with trust in God.

For the *Semites*, to know means to *experience* in any way. Because good and evil are terms of polarity, or extremes, they signify a totality, that is, a total experience of both good and evil. To experience evil is to know or experience *sin* by rejecting the *will of God*.

To know sin is to refuse to accept our condition as creature because it is a rejection of his plan for our *ultimate end*. This requires rejecting God's plan for *creation* by attempting to substitute our own *will* for his trying to make ourselves his equal.

Catholic *exegesis* is against regarding the tree of the knowledge of good and evil as a mere *allegory*. Though not all details need be taken literally, the expression as a whole must be regarded as real history. Adam fell by choosing his will over God's will, that is to say, he rejected *divine authority* as such. This is what makes the malice of *original sin* so terrible, and why its *consequences* for the family of Adam are so terrible. But realization of this helps immensely to appreciate the greatness of divine *mercy* and love involved in our *redemption* and the beauty of divine *grace* revealed in the Immaculate Heart of *Mary*.

Tribunal

A tribunal is an *ecclesiastical* court. See Diocese 833. Also see Ecclesiastical tribunal.

Trinitarian

Trinitarian means having to do with the *Holy Trinity*. It is at times used to refer to one who believes in the *doctrine* of the Holy Trinity, or to a member of a *religious* community known as Trinitarians. See Trinity, Holy 232.

Trinitarian nature

Trinitarian nature refers to the *mystery* of the *Trinity*, one nature and three *Persons*. See Trinity, Holy 232, 233, 234, 237, 253. Also see Beatific vision 1028.

Trinity, Holy 232, 233, 234, 237, 253

The Catechism of the Catholic Church teaches that "the *faith* of all *Christians* rests on the Trinity" (CCC 232). "The mystery of the Most Holy Trinity is the central *mystery* of Christian faith and life. It is the mystery of God in himself. It is therefore the source of all the other mysteries of faith, the light that enlightens them. It is the most fundamental and *essential* teaching in the 'hierarchy of the *truths* of faith'" (CCC 234).

The Church teaches that the Holy Trinity is inaccessible to *reason* alone but God has "left traces of his *Trinitarian* being in his work of *creation* and in his *Revelation* throughout the *Old Testament*" (CCC 237). The mystery remained inaccessible to Israel before the *Incarnation* and the sending of the *Holy Spirit*.

Following *Apostolic Tradition*, the Church confessed at the *Council of Nicaea* (325

A.D.) that the Son is *consubstantial* with the Father, that is, one only God with the Father.

The *Council of Constantinople* (381 A.D.) retained this expression in its formulation of the *Nicene Creed* and confessed that the only *begotten Son of God* was eternally begotten, not made and is *consubstantial* with the Father. In addition this Council also defined that the Holy Spirit is consubstantial with the Father and Son.

In her teaching of the *dogma* of the Trinity, the Church confesses one God in a consubstantial Trinity of three Persons, not three gods. The First Person is the *Father*, the *Second Person* is the *Son* and the *Third Person* is the *Holy Spirit*. The Persons do not share one *divinity* between them, but each Person is God whole and entire. Each Person 'is' what the other two 'is.' By *nature* there is but one God. The *Fourth Lateran Council* teaches that each Person is that supreme reality, namely, the divine *substance*, *essence*, and nature.

The *Divine Persons* are truly distinct from one another. "God is one but not solitary. 'Father', 'Son', 'Holy Spirit' are not simply names designating *modalities* of the *divine being*, for they are really distinct from one another" (CCC 254). They are distinct from one another in their relations of origin, the

Father generates, the Son is *begotten* and the Holy Spirit proceeds. "The divine Unity is *triune*" (CCC 254).

The *procession* of the Word from the Father is called *generation* and the procession of the Holy Spirit from the Father and the Son is called *spiration*. These processions are *eternal* and *immanent*.

Because the real distinction of Persons from one another does not divide the divine unity, the real distinction between them resides solely in the relationships, which relate them to one another. The three Divine Persons are co-equal, co-eternal and *consubstantial* and deserve equal glory and *adoration*.

They are called Persons in view of their relations, but they are one in nature and substance. Because of this substantial unity, each Person is wholly in the other two Persons. This in-existence of really distinct Persons in the Trinity is known as *circumincession* in Latin and *perichoresis* in Greek.

The whole *divinely* established *economy* of *creation* and *salvation* is the common work of the three Divine Persons because, since they have one and the same nature, they must have one and the same *operation*.

They are not three *principles*, but one principle of everything that exists outside of the Trinity. Each Person performs the common work according to his unique personal property. The Church confesses one God and Father from whom all things are, one Lord *Jesus Christ*, through whom all things are and one Holy Spirit in whom all things are (cf. Rom 11:36).

The *divine missions* of the Son's *Incarnation* and the gift of the Holy Spirit show forth the properties of the Divine Persons. We do not speak of the Father, from whom all things come, as having a mission in this sense, because he is the First Person from whom the others originate, but is himself unoriginated because the first One cannot be absolutely first and also from another.

Trinity Sunday

Trinity Sunday is the *Solemnity* of the Most *Holy Trinity*. It is *celebrated* on the first *Sunday* after *Pentecost*. See Easter duty.

Triune

Triune means being three in one. See Trinity, Holy 232, 233, 234, 237.

Troparia 1177

Troparia are the short responses offered after reading the *Word of God* during the recitation of the *Divine Office* or *Liturgy of the Hours*.

The singular form of the word is troparion and is a *generic* name for short *hymns* in the *Byzantine Church*.

There are various classes of

troparia used in the Byzantine Church: the *theotokion* is in honor of *Our Lady*, the *kontakion* refers to the *feast* of the day, and the *apolytikion* precedes the dismissal.

True contrition

When *contrition* is heartfelt, it is called true contrition and refers to the sincerity of the sorrow and firmness of the *resolution* to reform one's life. See Contrition 1451.

True faith

True faith is *orthodox faith* which means that it is consistent with the body of *revealed truths* contained in the *deposit of faith* entrusted to the *Apostles* by Christ. The deposit of faith is preserved by the Apostles and their successors with the guarantee of *infallibility* for the guidance of the Church. See Deposit of faith 1202.

True human knowledge of Christ 473

The operative word in this phrase is 'true.' It means that *Christ's human knowledge* is genuinely human; and that his human knowledge is the most perfect form of knowledge possible to *man*. In *biblical* terms this is a particular application of the saying: Christ is like us in all things but *sin* (cf. Jn 8:46).

Over the centuries the Church has insisted that the human knowledge of Christ includes knowledge that is *beatific, infused,* and *experiential*. Since he is a *Divine Person* with two *natures*, one divine and one human, he is a man without sin. Because of the unique condition of being one Person with two natures, he cannot both know and not know simultaneously, nor be able to know a *truth* without error and with error at the same time.

Further, it is not possible for Christ to have been ignorant or subject to error during his time on earth because to admit this possibility would be to allow that he might be in error concerning his personal identity and mission. To admit the possibility of such error would allow him be in error concerning the formation of *conscience* and discernment of *temptation*. If he were ignorant or subject to error he would be incapable of providing his *disciples* with infallible guidance in following him. Christ definitely implies such guidance in his claim to be the one Teacher of all (cf. Mt 23:10).

To object that such *infallibility* is incompatible with genuine experimental knowledge as is ordinarily found in men during their life time, fails to make an important distinction. Ordinary modes of human knowing, both before and after Adam's fall, are not normative of the most perfect mode of knowing possible to man, namely, that of the God-man without *sin*. This is not to ascribe *omniscience* or unlimited human knowledge to Christ, nor is it to deny that he grew in knowledge during his life (cf. Lk 2:52). It does affirm that this growth in knowledge and grace took place in a manner we have not experienced. Whereas we grow in knowledge by learning what we did not know and in a manner subject to error, Christ learned experimentally and without danger of error what he already knew in another way. See Kenosis.

Truly, really, and substantially contained 1374

'Truly, really, and substantially contained' is a phrase from the *Council of Trent*, session 13, canon 1, where the Council affirms the correct understanding of *Christ's Eucharistic presence* against specific errors of two groups of *Protestant* reformers.

The first group, known as sacramentarians, held that Christ was present in the Eucharist only as a truth is present in the sign pointing to it, or only as a *person* is present in a figure or statue representing him.

The second group, mainly Calvinists held that Christ was present in the Eucharist only to the degree that a worker is present where the effect of his work is felt.

Christ, however, is not present merely as a sign, but as the truth being signified. He is not present merely as in a figure or representation or a merely *symbolical* way, but as the reality represented.

Finally, he is not present merely to the extent that he is working in the *hearts* of those who consume the Eucharist as a sign of him, but in his very *substance subsisting* therein. Thus the Church believes that, in the Eucharist, Christ is truly, really, and substantially present or contained.

Truth 215

Truth refers to the degree of *veridicality* (correspondence), conformity, or agreement that exists between an *intellectual* representation and the reality it represents.

Moral truth is the agreement or conformity between acts and *intention* and the *moral law* as presented by *conscience*.

Revealed truth is that truth communicated to *man* by God in *revelation* and which the Church has proposed for our acceptance. Some revealed truth is formal and *explicit* such as the articles of the *Creed*. Other revealed truth that is formal and explicit is found in *dogmatic* pronouncements *infallibly* made by the *authority* of the *Vicar of Christ*, such as the *Immaculate Conception* of *Mary*, the *Mother of God*.

Other truths are considered to be virtually revealed because they are implied in some formally revealed truth, such as the inability of *Christ* to *sin*.

Truth of being

The *attribute* of *truth* is the conformity of a *being* with its *nature*. A thing is what it is by virtue of its *nature* and *essence*. See Transcendental attributes of being.

Truthfulness 2468

Truthfulness is uprightness in *human* action and speech. It is also called sincerity or candor. *Truth* is determined by the agreement that exists between the *mind's* understanding of something and the expression of that understanding in word or action.

Truthfulness as a *virtue* consists in showing oneself true in deeds and truthful in words, by guarding against *duplicity*, *dissimulation*, and *hypocrisy*.

The virtue of truthfulness is related to *justice* because it gives to another what is his due. We owe it to others to be honest in word and deed.

Truthfulness must keep a just balance between what ought to be expressed and what ought to be kept secret; it entails both honesty and discretion.

Type 117

A type is anything that represents, *foreshadows*, or symbolizes something else. The fulfillment of a type is called an *antitype*.

Typical sense

The typical sense of *Scripture* is the meaning which a passage has in reference to some *truth* or event of which it is a *type*, symbol, or *foreshadowing*. It is also called the *mystical sense*. See Allegorical sense 117.

Typological 1094

Typological refers to a method of *biblical catechesis* in which the newness of *Christ* is revealed by means of the *figures* or *types*, which announce him in the deeds, words, and symbols of the *Old Testament*.

Typology 130

Typology is the study of *types*. In *Scripture*, a type is a *person*, thing, action, or event in the *Old Testament* that the *Holy Spirit* presents as a *foreshadowing* of some future event often in the *New Testament*. See Allegorical Sense 117.

Typos tou Patros 1549

'Typos tou Patros' is a Greek phrase meaning 'living image of God the Father.' It was used by St. Ignatius of Antioch (35–107 A.D.) of the *ordained* ministry, especially *bishops*, indicating how the presence of *Christ* as head of the Church is made visible to the *faithful*.

Tyrocinium

Tyrocinium (in the military) or *novitiate* (in religious life) is similar to apprenticeship in the crafts. An apprentice is called a tyro or a *novice* in other fields. It is a period of trial during which he learns a craft and is bound to serve a master for a certain number of years in order to master its details and duties.

The practice of *chastity* can be considered a sort of apprenticeship. See Apprenticeship in self-mastery 2339.

U

Ultimate end

An *end* is the purpose, goal, or outcome of an act or *intention*. The ultimate end is the last in a series of ends for which a *person* strives. In the case of *man* his ultimate end is union with God in the *beatitude* of *heaven*. See Beatitude 1719; Beatific vision 1028; Physical evil.

Unadulterated

Unadulterated means pure and genuine. See Born of a Virgin 502.

Uncertain conscience

An uncertain or *doubtful conscience* is one, which is unable to decide whether an *act* conforms to the *moral law*, or not. One is never allowed to act morally with an uncertain or doubtful conscience.

For right action a *prudentially certain conscience* is sufficient, that is, there is solid enough reason to justify an action by an ordinarily *prudent* man. See Conscience 1706.

Unclean/Uncleanness

Unclean is the state of being tainted and in need of *purification* because of the presence of impure elements. One could be *ceremonially* or *ritually* unclean without reference to *moral purity*.

Among the *Jews, marriage*, childbirth, contact with the dead, or being in the presence of lepers produced an unclean state. *Christ abrogated* this aspect of the *Mosaic law*. See Ritual Purity.

Understanding 1095, 1101, 1831

As a *gift of the Holy Spirit*, understanding enables one to get a better grasp of the *mysteries* of *revelation* and *religion* and have a greater attachment to them in times of difficulty. The *habit* of easy and prompt use of understanding is an *intellectual virtue*.

Understanding is also used in reference to the *intellect* engaged in the act of making a *judgment*. It is distinguished from *reason*, which designates the intellectual activity involved in *ratiocination*, or *reasoning*.

By understanding, *man* forms ideas, makes judgments and comparisons, grasps the meaning of things and estimates their *value*. Understanding distinguishes man from *brute* animals.

Unequivocally

Unequivocally means absolutely clear and plain, not admitting of mistakes. See Capitalism 2425.

Uniate

The *Eastern Churches* which have returned to *Catholic* unity are sometimes referred to as 'Uniate.' See Eastern Church.

Unintentional ignorance 1860

Unintentional ignorance is *ignorance*, which is not the result of personal choice either through neglect or *conscious* rejection of related *knowledge*.

Because it is not the result of an *act of the will*, it can diminish or even remove the *imputability* of a *grave* offense.

Unintentional ignorance may be *ignorance of fact* or *ignorance of the law*. No one, however, is deemed ignorant of the *principles* of the *moral law* written in the *conscience* of every *man*.

Unintentional killing 2269

Unintentional killing is the taking of *human* life in an act in which the death was not foreseen, intended, or sought, as a definite *end* by the *will*.

Union with Christ

Union with Christ is *holiness*. Progress or growth toward holiness begins with keeping the *commandments*, accepting the *will of God* in all things, and doing good works by practicing *virtue*.

Supernatural holiness

depends on living the *theological virtues* of *faith*, *hope*, and *charity* infused in the *soul* at *Baptism* with *sanctifying grace*. Sanctifying grace is a habitual *supernatural* disposition that perfects the soul and enables it to live with God and to *act*, by his *love*, in response to his call to *holiness*. It renews the soul by its presence by enabling it to partake in the *divine nature* through *adoption* as a *son of God*, an object of his special love, and *coheir* to *heaven* with *Christ*.

Sanctifying grace is required for union with God, because through such grace *man* shares in the *divine life* which *sanctifies* him. Through grace, man is infused with the virtues and *gifts of the Holy Spirit*, which strengthen and increase the holiness of life in the soul. See Sanctifying grace 1999. Also see Mystical union 2014.

Unitive

Unitive refers to that which promotes or is conducive to union. See Unitive and procreative aspects of marriage. Also see Lust 1866.

Unitive and procreative aspects of marriage

The *unitive* aspect of *marriage* refers to the union which results from the mutual and exclusive self-giving for life in the context of true *love* in marriage. The unity is of such a nature that it cannot be broken by the *spouses* once the marriage is *validly* established.

The unitive aspect of marriage is inseparably associated with *procreation* which in its fullest sense expresses a mutual unifying *love* and orients it to the exalted *vocation* of parenthood. See Regulation of Procreation 2368.

Unity of being

The *attribute* of *unity* in *being* refers to the idea of indivision or undividedness in a being's inner reality which separates it from all other things. See Transcendental attributes of being.

Universal destination of goods
2403

The universal destination of goods refers to the *belief* that, since the entire earth was entrusted to all mankind, all have the *right* to share in its bounty. The *dignity* of *man* demands that he have access to those *material* things, which he needs.

The *common good* requires both respect for the universal destination of goods and respect for the *right to private property*.

Universal Magisterium

The ordinary *Magisterium* is exercised continually in the universal practices associated with *faith* and *morals* and is referred to as the universal Magisterium. *Encyclicals* are part of the ordinary Magisterium and as such require the *religious assent* of the *faithful*. See Ordinary and universal Magisterium 2034. Also see Magisterium 83, 889, 890.

Unleavened (bread)

Unleavened bread is bread made without yeast. See Host. Also see Leavened.

USCCB

USCCB is the acronym for the United States Conference of Catholic Bishops. This is the proper *episcopal conference* for the *Catholic hierarchy* in the United States. It is a *canonical* entity governing the Church in the United States, and a public policy arm. See Holy day/ Holy day of obligation.

Usurious 2269

Usurious means taking or charging excessive interest on loaned money or being exacting in respect to the payment of interest.

V

Vainglory

Vainglory is the *vice* of inordinate love of or desire for *praise* and honor. It is particularly dangerous when praise and honor is undeserved or sought from unworthy men and when it obscures the sense of grateful dependence on God.

To desire and attempt to preserve a good reputation is not vainglory or sinful. See Pride 1866.

Valid/validly

Valid means binding under *law*. See Indissolubility 1644. Also see Validity 1635.

Validity 1635

Validity is the quality of being true and actual, well founded in fact, or properly established, and really being what it claims to be.

In *marriage*, validity establishes a bond between *spouses*, which by its very nature is *perpetual* and exclusive.

For validity in *Christian* marriage, partners must be *baptized*, freely express consent before an approved *ecclesiastical authority*, and be free to marry, that is, not impeded by any *ecclesiastical* or *natural law*.

The natural law requires that the spouses must have the physical capacity to complete the *procreative conjugal act* because marriage is ordered to the procreation and education of children. For this reason the sexual act must always remain open to procreation.

An act may be *valid* and still be *illicit*. That is, it may be properly established but not lawful.

Value/Values

In its most general sense a value is that quality in a thing which effectively satisfies a *human* need. Usefulness implies a relationship between a *person* with a need and an *object* which satisfies that need. This relationship gives an object use value.

Some things have value because they can be exchanged for something else; such things have exchange value. This is because the use value of one thing is deemed equal to the use value of the other things for which they are exchanged.

Some things have use value which is widely recognized. Such things have *intrinsic* value, such as gold or diamonds. Other things have a use value which is totally *extrinsic* and useful only to particular individuals, such as an heirloom or lock of hair from a beloved.

Things have value in proportion to their ability to satisfy human needs. Because *man* is a *rational animal*, he has both *physical* and *spiritual* needs. Since in man, his physical animal *nature* is necessary for his rational nature, use value must be considered in terms of both animal and rational needs.

The higher *faculties of the soul*, the *intellect* and *will*, are exercised through the *mediation* of man's animal faculties, his bodily *senses*. Man's will enables him freely to choose to conform or not conform to the *divine plan* as known by the intellect. The divine plan for man, his *ultimate end*, is union with God. Man attains this end by ordering his choices to conform with that end. The rational faculties of the soul determine the criteria for all human values whether physical or *spiritual*. Things have use value for man in proportion as they are ordered to his ultimate end.

Any need which conforms with man's ultimate end is called a true good. True good is the supreme value. In proportion as man chooses the truly good he is *holy* and *righteous* before God.

Sin consists in choosing something which is not in conformity with the *divine* plan for man's ultimate end. The faculty of choice is always directed to *good*, so when through sin *evil* is chosen, it is done under the guise of good but based on deception. Such good is called *apparent good*. See Hierarchy of values 1886.

Vatican II

Vatican II is the common way to refer to the *Second Vatican Council*. See Particular church 833.

Veiling of images

On the Fifth *Sunday* of Lent *crucifixes*, statues, and pictures (*icons*) were traditionally covered with purple cloth during the last two weeks before *Easter*. The veiling of images recalled the words in the *Gospel* of the day, which is still proclaimed in the *Extraordinary Form* of the *Roman Rite*: 'They took up stones to throw at him: but *Jesus* hid himself, and went out of the temple' (Jn 8:59).

This custom of veiling images may continue to be observed. The unveiling of the Cross prior to *veneration* on *Good Friday* also remains an option. See Liturgical seasons.

Venerable

Venerable is a title given to a *person*, not yet proclaimed a *saint* or even *blessed* by the Church, but is judged to have lived the cardinal and *theological virtues* to a heroic degree. Private *devotion* is permitted for a venerable. See Canonization.

Venerate/veneration

Venerate means to treat with deep respect or reverence. It is not *adoration*. See Nicaea II 476. Also see Adoration.

Venereal

Venereal refers to *sexual love* or serving to arouse sexual desire. It can also refer to diseases transmitted chiefly through *sexual intercourse*. See Lust/lustful.

Vengeance

Vengeance is the desire to return injury for injury as punishment or *retribution* for a wrong, injury, or damage one has suffered. See Wrath 1866.

Venial sin 1458, 1855, 1862

Venial sin is an offense against God that does not separate the sinner from God as his last end and so does not destroy *charity* in the *soul* or deprive the soul of *sanctifying grace*, though it offends and wounds or weakens the soul. Venial sin can be forgiven by the reception of *Holy Communion*, an *act of contrition* or *sacramental Confession*.

A venial sin may be committed in two ways. First, it may be committed when the matter itself is not *grave* and otherwise is not aggravated by the sinner's *intention* or by various circumstances. Such is ordinarily the case with 'white lies.' Second, a venial sin may be committed when the matter is *grave*, but the commission of the sin is not fully deliberate. But *commission* of a venial sin always manifests a disordered affection for *created* goods, which impedes the soul's progress in the exercise of *virtue*, and it incurs *temporal punishment*.

Venial sin of itself does not deprive the sinner of *sanctifying grace*, friendship with God, or *charity*. Though it does not incur the loss of *eternal* happiness, the attachment to *sin* must be purified in *purgatory*. Deliberate and unrepented venial sin disposes us, little by little, to commit *mortal sin*.

Veridicality

Veridicality refers to the degree of correspondence between what is held as true and external *reality*. See Truth 215.

Vernacular

Vernacular refers to the native language of a country or place. It is ordinary language commonly spoken as opposed to literary language which is found in books. See Low Mass.

Vernal equinox

The word 'vernal' comes from the Latin word for spring, 'vernalis.' The word equinox comes from the Latin word 'aequinoxium,' meaning equal night. The vernal equinox occurs when the sun crosses the plane of the earth's equator at the beginning of spring. In the northern hemisphere, this happens about March 21, but slight variations in the exact date and time occur each year. For the purposes of calculating the date of *Easter*, the Church assigns March 21 as the date of the vernal equinox, even though it may not correspond to the exact date of its occurrence in a given year. See Liturgical seasons.

Vespers

Vespers is the hour of the *Divine Office* said in the late afternoon or evening. The term comes from 'vesper' in Latin, and is also called *'Evening Prayer'*. It is one of the *major hours*, and the *Magnificat* (Lk 1:46–55) is recited or sung during it. The liturgical observance of *Sundays* and *solemnities* begins the previous evening with First Vespers, also called Evening Prayer I. See Liturgy of the Hours 1174, 1178.

Vestigial

Vestigial describes something which is only a trace, mark, or sign of something that no longer exists, like a footprint left by a *person* on a beach. See Public penance.

Vestments

Vestments are the *ceremonial* attire worn by *ministers* when *celebrating* the *Mass* and administering *sacraments*. See Stole.

Viaticum 1331, 1517

Viaticum is the Latin word meaning 'traveling provisions.' It is used to refer to the food for the voyage through death to *eternal life*.

Viaticum is the name given the *Holy Eucharist* when it is given to one who is dying or one in danger of death as *spiritual* food for the journey into *eternity*. It is usually given at the same time as *Extreme Unction* or *Anointing of the Sick*.

Vicar

A vicar is one who acts in the place of another. See Vicar General.

Vicar General

The Vicar General is a *deputy* appointed by a *Bishop* to assist him in governing his *diocese*. On behalf of the Bishop, he exercises *episcopal jurisdiction* in *spiritual* and *temporal* matters to the extent the Bishop wishes.

He forms one *tribunal* with the Bishop so there can be no appeal from a sentence of one to the other. He takes precedence over all other diocesan *clergy* and has the *privileges* and dress of a *titular protonotary apostolic* while in *office*. See Diocese.

Vicar of Christ

Vicar of Christ is another

name for *Pope*. The Pope as the visible head of the Church, the *Mystical Body* of *Christ*, represents Christ on earth and acts as his representative with full *authority* in matters relating to it. See Truth 215.

Vicariate

Vicariate refers to the office or authority of a *vicar* or to the office or work done by an apostolic vicar.

Vicariate may also refer to the district administered by a vicar. An apostolic vicariate is an *ecclesiastical* district in a *missionary* territory that is not yet developed enough to be a *diocese*. See Particular church 833.

Vicarious

Vicarious comes from the Latin word 'vicarious,' meaning substituted. It means to take the place of another *person* or thing.

Vicarious suffering is pain endured or performed by one person in place of another. *Christ* suffered and died for mankind to *merit salvation*. See Question or problem of evil.

Vice 1768

A vice is a lasting disposition of the *soul* inclining it toward *evil* and thus *moral* depravity. A vice is a sinful *habit*.

Victim

A victim is a living being offered to God in *sacrifice*. As a

sacrifice the victim is actually or equivalently given up in an act of *adoration* or *expiation*. It is the acknowledgement of God's supreme *dominion* and man's complete dependence. The destruction of the victim, called *immolation*, is a *voluntary* surrender of the victim as an offering or *oblation*. The immolation and oblation constitute the sacrifice. See Oblation.

Vigil

The word vigil comes from the Latin word 'vigil,' which means watch. By *immemorial tradition* the Church has kept the day preceding a *feast* as a day of preparation, and this day is known as a vigil. Services may be held on the night of the vigil as a *spiritual* preparation for the feast. See Holy Week.

Vincible ignorance

Vincible ignorance is the absence of *knowledge* under circumstances in which knowledge can be obtained with ordinary effort. See Conscience 1706.

Vindicate/vindicated

Vindicate means to clear from all criticism, guilt, or blame. It also means to defend against all opposition and to justify. See Last judgment 1038.

Vindictive penalty

When an *ecclesiastical penalty* is intended as punishment for an offense it is called a *punitive* or vindictive penalty. See Ecclesiastical penalty 1463.

Violence

Violence refers to the use of excessive physical force to cause injury or destruction. It may also refer to the merciless use of power in violation of another's *rights* or sensibilities. See Wrath 1866.

Virgin

See Virginity. Also see Aeiparthenos 499.

Virgin Birth

The Virgin Birth refers to the preservation of the *virginity* of the *Blessed Mother* during the birth of *Christ*. Mary remained a virgin before, during, and after giving birth to Christ. She is venerated as the *Ever Virgin*.

The Virgin Birth must not be confused with the *Immaculate Conception*, the *doctrine* that the *Blessed Virgin Mary* was in the first instant of her *conception*, by a singular *grace* and privilege of God in view of the *merits* of Christ, preserved from all stain of *original sin*. See Immaculate conception 491.

Virgin Mary

The Mother of Jesus was named *Mary*. Because she remained a *virgin* before, during, and after the birth of *Christ*, she is honored with the title Virgin Mary. See Virgin Birth. Also see Mary's Virginity 496.

Virginal conception

The *dogma* that the Mother of *Jesus* conceived *Christ* without carnal *intercourse* and gave him birth without injury to her *virginity* and that she remained a *virgin* all her life is expressed in all the *Creeds* of the Church. *Mary's* virginal conception was foretold in the *Old Testament* by Isaiah, 'Behold a virgin shall conceive and bear a son and his name shall be called Emmanuel' (Is 7:14).

The virginal conception must not be confused with the *Immaculate Conception*, the *doctrine* that the *Blessed Virgin Mary* was in the first instant of her conception, by a singular *grace* and privilege of God in view of the *merits* of Christ, preserved from all stain of *original sin*. See Born of a Virgin 502. Also see Virgin birth. Also see Immaculate Conception 491.

Virginity 1619

Virginity refers to both a physical and *moral* state. Physically, virginity consists in bodily *integrity* and *morally*, it consists in the practice of complete *sexual abstinence*. Physical virginity may be lost by violation against one's *will* without losing moral virginity.

There is no special *virtue* of virginity and in a given case, it is preferable to *marriage* only if it is chosen directly for God's sake in order to belong to him and serve him in a special way.

Christ, according to St. Matthew (Mt 19:12), and the *Council of Trent* both taught that virginity in itself is preferable to marriage because the root of *Christian* virginity is to seek a more radical love of God alone and a more perfect union with him.

Virtual intention

An *intention* is *virtual* when it is no longer accompanied by the attention which preceded its *elicitation*, yet still influences a *person's* activity. See Intentional homicide 2268. Also see Intention 1752.

Virtual prayer

Virtual prayer refers to actions which though not formally called *prayer* are considered prayer for practical purposes because the attitude of *mind* which accompanies them involves an awareness of the presence of God and the intention to do his *will*. Because such acts are a form of communion with God they constitute a form of prayer. See Prayer 2098.

Virtue/Virtuous 1768, 1803

Virtue is an *"habitual* and firm disposition to do the good... The virtuous *person* tends toward the *good* with all his *sensory* and *spiritual* powers; he pursues the good and chooses it in *concrete* actions"

(CCC 1803). Because virtue is habitual, it enables man freely to practice the good and makes choosing good easier.

Growth in virtue is the ultimate aim of *Christian* life because it opens the heart to the movements of the saving *grace* of God. The goal of the virtuous life is to become good by conforming behavior to the *will of God*. This means that virtue firmly fixes the *will* on good. There are different types of virtue:

Moral virtue refers to those firm attitudes, stable dispositions, and habitual perfections of *intellect* and will which govern our actions, order our *passions*, and guide our conduct according to *reason* and *faith*. It makes *self-mastery* and the joy of leading a morally good life possible and easier.

Moral virtue is perfected by the repetition of *deliberate* virtuous *acts*. It is directly concerned with the *human* ability to choose *moral* good or avoid moral *evil*. The fundamental moral virtues are *prudence, justice, fortitude*, and *temperance*. They are also known as the *cardinal virtues* because all other virtues are governed by them. They are enriched and enhanced by the *supernatural virtues*. The moral virtues are prerequisites for the *theological virtues* which are gifts of grace enabling man to attain his *final end*.

Natural virtue refers to habits, which dispose one to *act* in accordance with right reason. It is not so much connected with special grace as right reason and is acquired by the repetition of virtuous acts.

Intellectual virtue refers to the habit and disposition for good, which is primarily concerned with the development of the power to know *truth*.

Theological virtue refers to the virtues of faith, *hope, and charity*. These have God as their source and object and by uniting us to him through *sanctifying grace*; they enable us to choose the good with greater ease. The theological virtues are supernatural virtues which enrich and enhance the natural moral virtues.

Supernatural virtue refers to the *infused* moral and theological virtues. These are referred to as supernatural because they are beyond the reach of *man's* natural powers and enable him to reach his supernatural end. They are infused because they are free gifts of God and form a disposition of the *soul*.

Virtue of religion 2096, 2125

The virtue of religion is the *virtue* of *justice* as it relates to God. Men give to God due *worship* and *reverence* by the virtue of religion. It consists in the constant and firm *will* to give God his due.

Virtues related to this virtue are *piety, devotion*, and reverence. In some ways it is a forgotten virtue in modern life where devotion and piety are seldom actively cultivated.

This virtue is directly sinned against by *idolatry, superstition, false worship, sacrilege* and *blasphemy*. Practices of *magic, sorcery*, and *divination*, by which one attempts to tame *occult* powers and gain *supernatural* power over others, as well as the wearing of *charms* to avoid *evil*, are also contrary to the virtue of religion.

Indirectly the virtue of religion is commonly offended against by failing to adopt and develop *devotional* practices, neglecting the life of *prayer* and lack of reverential behavior in the presence of the *Blessed Sacrament*.

Visible bonds of communion in the Church 815

The multiplicity of peoples and *cultures* gathered together in the unity of the Church is always threatened by *sin*. St. Paul (Eph 4:3), therefore, exhorts *Christians* to maintain the unity of the *Holy Spirit* in the bond of peace. This bond of unity rests above all in *charity* which binds all in perfect *harmony*. The visible bonds of communion in the Church are: 1) The profession of one *apostolic faith*; 2) the *celebration* of *liturgy* and *sacraments*; 3) *apostolic succession* through the *sacrament* of *Holy Orders*.

Visionary

A visionary is a *person* who sees visions; a *prophet* or *seer*. The term is also applied to persons whose ideas or plans seem impractical or too idealistic.

Vital function/operation

Vital means concerned with or manifesting life. A vital function or operation is something *essential* for life. See Rational animal.

Vitiate 1755

To vitiate is to make or render something *morally* corrupt, or to make something depraved, bad, impure, or defective.

Vocal prayer 2664, 2700

Vocal prayer is the use of spoken words by which the *heart* is turned to God. Vocal prayer is an *essential* element in the *Christian* life. *Christ* teaches us vocal prayer in the *Our Father*. Vocal prayer is the form of *prayer* most readily accessible to groups, but even *interior prayer* cannot neglect vocal prayer. Because prayer is internalized to the degree we become aware of him to whom we speak, vocal prayer becomes an early form of *contemplative prayer*.

Vocation

A vocation is the call of God to a distinctive *state of life* in which a *person* can reach *holiness*. The first vocation of the *Christian* is the universal call to holiness in the Church. See Sanctification. Also see Holiness 2013.

Voice of Conscience

Conscience is a *judgment* of practical *reason* whereby a *person* recognizes the *moral* quality of a *concrete act* that he is going to perform, is in the process of performing, or has already completed or omitted. This judgment is called a voice because it is presented to *consciousness* as a command. The *intellect* is called conscience when by *reasoning* it determines the *morality of an act* by judging its conformity to *natural* or *revealed law*. The process of reasoning is like speaking to oneself because it is conducted entirely by the *conscious* intellect. See Objective norm of morality 1751.

Volitional act

A volitional act is defined as an *act of the will* that *terminates* in an objective, which is willed as an *end* in itself or as a *means* to an end. Such an act is also called a *directly voluntary act*. See Voluntary Act 1734. Also see Imputable 2269.

Voluntary act 1734

A voluntary act is an *act of the will* that *terminates* in an objective, which is willed as an *end* in itself or as a *means* to an end. Such an act is also called a *directly voluntary act*.

Voluntary doubt 2088

Voluntary doubt is the disregard or refusal to hold as true what God has revealed and the Church proposes for *belief.* It may result in the rejection of a teaching of the Church because one judges it unreasonable.

Vow 2102

A vow is a deliberate and free promise made to God concerning a possible and better *good* that must be fulfilled by reason of the *virtue of religion.* A vow is an *act* of *devotion* in which the Christian dedicates himself to God or promises some good work and from which he cannot *dispense* himself.

Vows of religion

Vows of religion are those whereby *religious* bind themselves to practice the *evangelical counsels* of *poverty, chastity,* and *obedience.* See Evangelical Counsels.

Vulgate Bible

The Vulgate is a Latin translation of the *Bible.* The Latin Vulgate is chiefly the work of St. Jerome (342–420 A.D.) commissioned by Pope Damasus I (r. 366–384 A.D.) in 382. After the *Council of Trent* declared that the Latin Vulgate is to be held *authentic* in public readings, disputations, sermons, and exposition, it became the official biblical text of the Church.

The authentic or *authoritative character* of the Vulgate does not imply any preference for this version above the original text or of versions in other languages, but is a direction to regard it as authoritative among Latin translations. It involves the *belief* that the Vulgate substantially represents original text and is free from *doctrinal* error. The present official edition is called the Clementine because it was issued under the auspices of Pope Clement VIII (r. 1592–1605 A.D.).

The Latin Vulgate was translated into English at Rheims and Douay, France, and this English translation became known as the *Douay-Rheims Bible.* See Righteousness 1224. Also see Douay-Rheims; Sacred Scripture 102.

W

Warden

Warden is the title of the *superior* of certain *religious* communities. See Superior, religious.

Way of the Cross

See Stations of the Cross.

Weepers

Weepers is the name for a *degree* of *public penance* once practiced in the Church.

Those doing public penance were referred to as *penitents* and, formerly, were organized into four degrees through which they had to pass, a) weepers, who were excluded from divine service; b) hearers, who attended only the *liturgy of the catechumens*; c) kneelers, who knelt apart from the congregation, and d) standers, who were excluded from the *offertory* and *Holy Communion*. See Public penance. Also see Penance 1459, 1460.

Whitsunday/Whitsun

In England *Pentecost* is called Whitsun or Whitsunday because of the white garments that were traditionally worn on this day. See Pentecost 696, 731, 1287, 2623.

Will

The *soul* has two *faculties*:
the *intellect* and the *will*. The intellect is man's *cognitive* or *knowing* faculty and is referred to as *the mind*. The *will* is his power to choose and tend toward attaining what he deems desirable. It is called his *appetitive* power.

The intellect and will are *supra-organic* faculties and do not depend *intrinsically* on any bodily member or organ. See Soul 363.

Will of God

The will of God refers to the *eternal plan of God* as it relates to all *creation* and to each individual *person's* whole life. Everything God *created* is perfect in itself as he willed it. Even deformities or disabilities are to be accepted as the expressions of God's perfect love and *man's* greatest *good* regardless of personal likes or dislikes. The will of God is revealed as the *divine plan* expressed in his *divine providence*.

To some extent, the will of God can be known by the light of *natural reason*, but the *mystery* of divine love and the *grace* of *salvation* which are part of the divine plan are only grasped through the gift of divine *revelation* and revealed clearly in the teaching of his

Church. The Church guides man to his *final end* by her teaching, the graces of the *sacraments*, a life of *prayer*, and her guidance in *moral* behavior. In this way the will of God becomes known to those who sincerely wish to accept his will by doing it.

God's will, like his knowledge, is absolutely independent of all that is extra-divine. God is *infinite*. In his will there is no movement from *potency* (possibility) to *act* (*being*), no sequence of individual acts leading to a result. The *divine will* is a single successionless act of willing and identical with his *divine essence*.

God's will is changeless or *immutable*. God is the *primary cause*. Without himself changing, he wills things outside himself which are subject to change, and capable of acting as *secondary causes*. Unlike God, secondary causes change because when they act they fulfill their *potential* and become more perfect.

God cannot will *evil*, because being perfect, his infinite power residing in his will is really identical with his *wisdom* and *truth*. Willing evil is not the exercise of a positive power, but merely manifests the limitations of a created will not yet *impeccable* seeking to fulfill desires incompatible with the *truth* and *wisdom* of God.

Evil itself is not a thing, but the absence of something that should be present. Evil only exists as the privation of some good. Since God is all perfect good, no privation can exist in him.

God never wills evil directly, but as an accident, that is, as a property of something which is good. When he allows physical pain or disasters, he wills a good which can only be attained by enduring the absent good in the spirit of resignation to his *omniscient* will. God never wills *moral evil* in any way because it is against the *nature* of God who is *absolute good*.

God's will is manifested to man through reason and revelation in the form of *precepts*, prohibitions, and *counsels*. The manifestation of the divine will in the *natural* and *revealed law* is not inconsistent with the *omnipotence* and *immutability* of the *Creator*. We must not think of the divine will as a reflection of our *experiences*. Rather we should recognize that the omnipotence of God and his power to work *miracles* is at the service of his loving kindness. We should see in his immutability the guarantee of his *fidelity* and reliability, nowhere so manifest as in the *Incarnation* and the *sacrifice* of his only-*begotten* Son for our *salvation* and in the stupendous miracle of the *Eucharist*. See Divine providence 302. Also see Question or problem of evil 309; Physical evil 311; Moral perfection 1770.

Wisdom 295, 1831

As a gift of the *Holy Spirit*, wisdom is the perfection of the *knowledge* by which God *created* and relates to the world according to his plan. The gift of wisdom enables *man* to know the *divine* purpose and plan of God's wisdom and enables the *just* man to judge all things from the divine perspective according to divine standards. Wisdom does not imply extraordinary mental ability but rather the *contemplation* of all things in God.

As an *infused theological virtue*, wisdom cultivates in the soul a readiness to respond to divine guidance and see things more easily from the divine perspective. As an *intellectual* virtue, wisdom is a *habit*, which perfects the *intellect* enabling it to pursue inquiry into the nature of *truth* and search for the *supreme cause* of things, their *essence* and *final end*.

Wisdom differs from knowledge, which perfects the judgment of *practical reason*. Wisdom perfects the judgment of *speculative reason*.

In *Scripture*, wisdom refers to the personification of God's wise dealing with man and plan for redemption.

In general, wisdom may refer to either the perfection of knowledge or the accumulation of information in a particular field through study or human *experience*. From this arises the tendency to associate wisdom with age.

Witchcraft

Witchcraft refers to the practices of a witch or witches. It is the exercise of powers supposed to be possessed by *persons* in league with the *devil* or *evil spirits*. Witchcraft is gravely opposed to the *virtue of religion*. See Magic or Sorcery 2117.

Word made flesh

The Word made flesh refers to the *Incarnation*, the act by which the *Word of God*, the *Second Person* of the *Blessed Trinity assumed a human nature* while retaining his *divine nature*. Through the Incarnation, the human and divine natures of the Second Person of the Trinity are united in a single Person. See Incarnation 461. Also see Christ 436.

Word of God

The Word of God refers to the *Second Person* of the *Blessed Trinity*. 'In the beginning was the Word and the Word was with God, and the Word was God' (Jn 1:1). Saying that the Word was with God distinguishes the Word from the Father, but because he was God he shares the *divine nature*. The Word is also called the 'logos,' Greek for statement or utterance, the intelligible expression of the mind of God.

The Word of God also refers to *Sacred Scripture* which, with *Sacred Tradition*, having God as its author, contains, and is the Word of God, the *revelation* of God's *person* and will. See Domestic church 1655. Also see Incarnation.; Sacred Scripture.

Words of institution
The words of institution are the specific words used by *Christ* at the *Last Supper* when he instituted the *Eucharist* in Mt 26:26–29; Mk 14:22–25; and Lk 22:1–21. See Chaldean Church/Rite.

Work of God
St. Benedict (480–547 A.D.) referred to the *Divine Office* as the 'Work of God,' and required his *monks* to pray it. See Liturgy of the Hours 1174, 1178.

Works of mercy 2447
Works of mercy are charitable actions by which we come to the aid of our neighbor. There are two types of works of mercy depending on whether the acts relate to *spiritual* or bodily necessities.

The *spiritual works of mercy*, aid our neighbor spiritually. They are: instructing the ignorant, counseling the doubtful, admonishing sinners, bearing wrongs patiently, forgiving offences willingly, comforting the afflicted, and praying for the living and the dead.

Works that aid our neighbor bodily are called *corporal works of mercy*. They consist in feeding the hungry, giving drink to the thirsty, clothing the naked, sheltering the homeless, visiting the sick, ransoming the captive, and burying the dead. For their scriptural basis cf. Mt 25:31 ff.

Worship
Theologically, to worship is to show deep religious *reverence* or *devotion* toward, or to *venerate* as a deity. The unique reverence paid to God as the supreme being is called *latria*. The honor shown saints is called *dulia* and should be referred to as veneration rather than worship. The veneration shown to *Mary* the Mother of God, because of her singular *holiness* in being without *sin*, is called *hyperdulia*.

In general, worship is the acknowledgement of another's *dignity* or superior position. See Virtue of religion 2096, 2125. Also see Synaxis 1329; Spiritual worship 2031; Sabbath 2175.

Wrath 1866
Wrath is a strong feeling of *resentment* against another or an inflammation of the *mind* with an inordinate desire for *aggression* and *vengeance* against someone or something. Wrath is also called *rage, anger,* or *ire.* See Anger 2302.

XYZ

Yahweh

Yahweh is the mysterious *Hebrew* name God revealed to Moses in the burning bush. It is translated as 'I am Who Am.' Because the *Jews* never spoke the name of God, they used the term *Adonai*, meaning literally, 'my Lords,' in reference to God, as a substitute for the term Yahweh. See YHWH 206. See Tetragrammaton.

Yahwist

Yahwist is another word for Jahwist. See Jahwist.

YHWH or JHVH 206

YHWH are the four consonants of the name of God as revealed to Moses. His name was considered too sacred to be uttered aloud and was written only using the consonants of the word. These four letters are referred to as the *tetragrammaton*. IHVH and JHWH are other forms of the tetragrammaton.

God's name appears in the *Old Testament* as Yahweh (YHWH) or Jahveh (JHVH). The word *Jehovah* grew from a false reading of the name of God as found in the current *Hebrew* text. Yahweh is probably the correct pronunciation of the *sacred* name.

Yoke

A yoke is a wooden frame fixed with loops which is fitted on the necks of oxen to harness them for pulling a cart or plow. See Subjugation.

Zeal

Zeal is a strong *emotion* or intense enthusiasm moving a *person* to work for a cause with great dedication and *devotion*. It is an impelling desire to advance the Kingdom of *Christ*, sanctify *souls* and advance the *glory* of God by making him better known and *loved*. See Spiritual marriage.

Zen

Zen is the name of a school of meditation that arose about the sixth century A.D. in China as Mahayana Buddhism.

Meditation is widespread among all forms of Buddhism but the Zen School teaches a particular manner of meditation which is regarded as the high point of *Buddhist* meditation. It is characterized by its orientation toward the *experience* of enlightenment. Enlightenment is a super-clear experience of *reality* and the unity of all *being* that is attained suddenly through meditation by the exercise of a sort of psychic technique. The most important element of this technique is meditation while sitting in an upright position with legs crossed, called the lotus position. An Indian monk Bodhidharama (638–715 A.D.) is regarded as the founder of Zen but his biographical details are not historically certain.

There is little doctrinal difference between schools of Zen Buddhism but the practice of Zen itself differs according to each monastery. Buddhism has exercised a significant influence on Japanese culture since the thirteenth century.

The practice of *centering prayer* originated in the mid-seventies out of *dialogues* of a Trappist *monk* with *Buddhist, Hindu,* and Zen masters. The techniques it employs are neither *Christian* nor *prayer*. The Church cautions *Catholics* against engaging in centering prayer. See Centering prayer.

Zucchetto

A zucchetto is a small skullcap worn by prelates. It is white for the *Pope*, red for *cardinals*, purple for *bishops* and black for *abbots*. See Abbey nullius.

Ω

Index of dictionary entries
by Paragraph number.

611

616

PART FOUR
Christian Prayer

Bibliography for
A Catechetical Dictionary

Addis, Wm. E. & Arnold, Thomas, *A Catholic Dictionary*, 16th Edition Revised (St. Louis MO: B. Herder Book Co., 1957).

Aquinas, Thomas, *Summa Theologica* (Rome: Marietti, 1950).

Attwater, Donald, Ed., *A Catholic Dictionary*, Third Edition. (Rockford IL: Tan Books and Publishers, 1997).

Beal, John P., Coriden James A., Green, Thomas J., editors, *New Commentary on the Code of Canon Law* (Maywood, NJ: Paulist Press, 2000).

Bittle, Celestine N., O.F.M.Cap., *Cosmology, From Aether to Cosmos.* (Milwaukee, WI: The Bruce Publishing Company, 1941).

_____.*Epistemology , Reality and the Mind.* (Milwaukee, WI The Bruce Publishing Co., 1939).

_____.*Logic, The Science of Correct Thinking.* (Milwaukee, WI The Bruce Publishing Co., 1935).

_____.*Ontology, The Domain of Being.* (Milwaukee, WI: The Bruce Publishing Company, 1941).

_____.*Psychology, The Whole Man.* (Milwaukee, WI: The Bruce Publishing Company, 1945).

Bretzke, James T, S.J., *Consecrated Phrases. A Latin Theological Dictionary* (Collegeville, MN: Liturgical Press, 1998).

Broderick, Robert, ed., *The Catholic Encyclopedia* (New York: Thomas Nelson Inc. Publishers, 1976).

Bunson, Matthew, *Encyclopedia of Catholic History* (Huntington, Indiana: Our Sunday Visitor Publishing Division, 1995).

Butler, Trent C., ed., *Holman Bible Dictionary* (Nashville, TN: Dolman Bible Publishers, 1991).

Caparros, E., Sox, J., Lagges, P., Editors, *Exegetical Commentary on the Code of Canon Law* (Chicago, Ill.: Midwest Theological Forum, 2004).

Catechism of the Catholic Church, Second edition (Washington D.C.: U.S. Catholic Conference, 1997).

Christopher, Rev. Joseph P. And Spence, Rev. Charles E., *The Raccolta* (New York: Benziger Brothers, Inc. 1943).

Code of Canon Law, Latin-English Edition (Washington, D.C.: Canon Law Society of America, 1983).

Congregation for the Causes of Saints, New Laws for the Causes of Saints Promulgated in 1983 (vatican.va/roman_curia/congregations/csaints/documents/roc_con_doc_07021983_norme_en.html: donwloaded 2013).

Copleston, Fredrick, S.J., *A History of Philosophy*: Three Book Image edition (Garden City, NY: Image Books, 1985).

Cox, Ignatius W., S.J., *Liberty Its Use and Abuse*, Third Revised Edition (New York: The Declan McMullen Co., 1956).

Denziger, Henry, Trans. Roy F Deferrer, *The Sources of Catholic Dogma* (Fitzwilliam, N.H.: Loretto Publications, 2002).

Dictionary of Mary (New York: Catholic Book Publishing Co., 1985).

Diekamp, Franciscus, *Dogmaticae Theologiae Manuale Volumen 1.* (Tornaci: Typis Societatis S. Joannis Evangelistae,1944).

The Enchiridion of Indulgences, Norms and Grants, Authorized English Edition (Issued by the Sacred Apostolic Penitentiary, 1968) Formatted into electronic text June 2, 1998.

Fehlner, Peter Damian Ma., F.I., *St. Maximilian Ma. Kolbe, Martyr: Pneumatologist: His Theology of the Holy Spirit* (New Bedford, MA: Academy of the Immaculate, 2004).

Flannery, Austin O.P., *Vatican Council II: The Conciliar and Post Conciliar Documents*, New Revised Edition (Collegeville, Indiana: Liturgical Press, 1992).

Franciscus, E., & Hoffmann, Adolphus, O.P., *Theologiae Dogmaticae Manuale*, Volumne IV (Paris: Desclee & Sociorum, 1946).

Glenn, Paul J., *An Introduction to Philosophy* (London: B. Herder Book Co., 1945).

General Instruction of the Roman Missal (Rev Ed) (Liturgical Documents) (Washington D.C., United States Conference of Catholic Bishops, 2011).

Genicot, E, S.I., & Salsmans, Ios. S.I., Editors, *Institutiones Theologiae Moralis*, Volumen Primum, Editio Sextadecim Le Edition Universelle, S.S.(Brussels: Uitgeverij Universum, N.V., 1946).

Hardon, John A., S.J., *Modern Catholic Dictionary* (Bardstown, KY: Eternal Life, 1999).

Herve, J.M., *Manuale Theologiae Dogmaticae*, Volumen III, Editio Decima Octava (Westminister, MD: The Newman Bookshop, 1946).

The Holy Bible (Douay Rheims Version. Rockford, Il: Tan Books and Publishers, Inc., 1971).

Ignatius Catholic Study Bible: New Testament, Second Edition, RSV (San Francis: Ignatius, 2001).

Klein, Rev. Peter, *The Catholic Source Book* (Orlando, FL: Harcourt Religion Publisher, 2007).

Kocik, Fr. Thoma, *Loving and Living the Mass* (Bethesda: Bacchus Press, 2007).

Liturgy of the Hours According to the Roman Rite (New York: Catholic Book Publishing Co., 1975).

Mackenzie, John L, S.J., *Dictionary of the Bible* (New York: Macmillan Publishing Co. 1965).

Martins, Cardinal Jose Saraiva, C. M.F. *New Procedures in the Rite of Beatification* (Baltimore, MD: L'Osservatore Romano English Edition, October 19, 2005).

Murphy, Dennis J. MSC Ed., *The Church and the Bible* (Theological Publications in India, Indoor Printers, New Delhi 2007).

Stein, Jess, Ed., *The Random House Dictionary to the English Language* (New York: Random House, Inc., 1967).

McBride, Alfred O. Praem. *Images of Mary* (Cincinnati, Ohio: St. Anthony Messenger Press, 1999).

Miravalle Mark S.T.D., Editor, *Mariology: A Guide for Priests, Daecons, Seminarians and Consecrated Persons* (Goleta, CA: Seat of Wisdom Books, Queenship Publishing, 2007).

Mounce, William D., ed., *Mounce's Complete Expository Dictionary of Old and New Testament Words* (Grand Rapids MI: Zondervan, 2006).

Murphy, Dennis J., MSC Ed., *The Church and the Bible* (Theological Publications in India, Indoor Printers, New Delhi 2007).

New American Bible: St. Joseph Edition (New York: Catholic Book Publishing Co., 1986).

Noort, G. Van (Gerardrus) Msgr. Trans.& Rev. by Castelot, John J. S.S. and Murphy, William S.S. *The Sources of Revelation* Volume 3 - Divine Faith (Westminister, MD: The Newman Press 1961).

Phillips, R.P., *Modern Thomistic Philosophy*, Vol. II, Metaphysics (Westminster MD: The Newman Press, 1948).

Pope Benedict XVI, *Summroum Pontificium*, motu proprio 1962. English translation on the website of the Holy See (http://www.vatican.va/holy_father/benedict_xvi/motu_proprio/documents/hf_ben-xvi_motu-proprio_20070707_summorum-pontificum_en.html).

Pope Paul VI *Concistoro segreto per la nomina di venti Cardinali, 24 maggio 1976*. Vatican.va.

Professors of the Pontifical Biblical Institute, *The Psalms: A Prayer Book* (New York: Benziger Brothers, Inc., 1946).

Radin, Max Ed. Greene, Lawrence G., *Radin Law Dictionary* (Dobbs Ferry NY: Oceana Publications, Inc., 1955).

Rahner, Karl, ed., *Encyclopedia of Theology* (New York: The Seabury Press, 1975).

Ratzinger, Joseph Cardinal, Prefect, *Norms on the Preparation of the Process for the Dissolution of the Marriage Bond in Favour of the Faith*. (Rome: www.vatican.va/roman_curia/congregations/cfaith/documents/rc_con_cfaith_doc_20010430_favor-fidei_en.html. April 30, 2001).

Sabetti, Aloysio, S.J. & Barrett, Timotheo, S.J., *Compendium Theologiae Moralis*, Editio Trigesima Quarta (New York: Frederick Pustet Co. Inc., 1939).

Simpson D. P., *Cassell's New Latin Dictionary* (New York: Funk & Wagnalls Co., 1959).

Stein, Jess, Ed., *The Random House Dictionary to the English Language* (New York: Random House, Inc., 1967).

Stelten Leo F., *Dictionary of Ecclesiastical Latin* (Peabody MA: Hendrickson Publishers, Inc., 1995).

Stravinskas, Rev. Peter M. J., Ed., *Our Sunday Visitor's Catholic Encyclopedia* (Huntington IN: Our Sunday Visitor Publishing Division, 1991).

Tanquery, Ad., Bord, J.B., ed., *Synopsis Theologiae Dogmaticae Fundamentalis*, Editio Vigesima Quarta (Tourney: Desclee & Co, 1937).

Appendix of
Commonly used Prayers

Sign of the Cross
(Traditional)

In the name of the Father, and of the Son, and of the Holy Spirit. Amen. See Sign of the Cross 1235

The Our Father (Pater Noster)
(Roman Missal)

Our Father who art in heaven, hallowed be thy name. Thy kingdom come, thy will be done on earth as it is in heaven. Give us this day our daily bread, and forgive us our trespasses as we forgive those who trespass against us. And lead us not into temptation, but deliver us from evil. Amen. See Our Father 2759.

Hail Mary (Ave Maria)
(Traditional)

Hail Mary full of grace, the Lord is with thee. Blessed art thou amongst women, and blessed is the fruit of thy womb, Jesus. Holy Mary, Mother of God, pray for us sinners, now, and at the hour of our death. Amen. See Rosary. Also see Hail Mary.

Glory be to the Father (Minor doxology)
(Traditional)

Glory be to the Father, and to the Son, and to the Holy Spirit. As it was in the beginning, is now, and ever shall be, world without end. Amen. See Minor doxology.

Morning offering
(Traditional)

My God I offer you this day, all that I think or do or say, uniting all with what was done by Jesus Christ your only Son.

Guardian Angel prayer
(Raccolta)

Angel of God my guardian dear to whom God's love commits me here, ever this day be at my side to light and guard to rule and guide.

Grace before meals
(Traditional)

Bless us O Lord and these thy gifts which we are about to receive from thy bounty through Christ our Lord. Amen.

Thanksgiving after meals
(Traditional)

O my God we give thee thanks for these and all thy benefits which we have received from thy bounty through Christ our Lord. Amen.

Night prayer
(Traditional)

Now I lay me down to sleep and pray the Lord my soul to keep. If I should die before I wake, I pray the Lord my soul to take.

Prayer for a happy death
(Traditional)

I believe in thee, I hope in thee, I love thee, adore thee, O Blessed Trinity, one God. Have mercy on me now and at the hour of my death save me. Amen.

Fatima Prayer
(Our Lady of Fatima)

O my Jesus, forgive us our sins, save us from the fires of hell. Lead all souls to heaven, especially those most in need of thy mercy.

Prayer for the faithful departed
(Traditional)

May the divine assistance be always with us and may the souls of the faithful departed rest in peace.

Eternal rest grant unto them O Lord and perpetual light shine upon them.

Come Holy Spirit
(Traditional)

Come, Holy Spirit, fill the hearts of the faithful and kindle in them the fire of your love. Send forth your Spirit. And you will renew the face of the earth.

LET US PRAY. O God, who taught the hearts of the faithful by the light of the Holy Spirit, grant that, by the gift of the same the Spirit, we may be always truly wise and ever rejoice in his consolation. Through Christ our Lord. Amen.

Act of Faith, Hope and Charity
(Unknown)

Almighty and everlasting God, give me an increase of faith, hope, and charity; and that I may deserve to obtain that which thou didst promise, make me to love that which thou dost command. Through Christ our Lord. Amen.

MARIAN PRAYERS

Praying the Rosary

Make the sign of the Cross (above) Recite Apostles' Creed (below) Recite Lord's Prayer (above) on first bead. Recite three Hail Mary's (above) on next three beads. Recite the Glory be to the Father (above). Repeat last three steps reciting Hail Mary's on the next ten beads meditating on a mystery (below). Recite the Hail Holy Queen (below) after the last mystery.

Apostles' Creed (Credo)
(Traditional)

I believe in God, the Father almighty, creator of heaven and earth, and in Jesus Christ his only Son, our Lord, who was conceived by the Holy Spirit, born of the Virgin Mary, suffered under Pontius Pilate, was crucified, died, and was buried. He descended into hell; on the third day he rose again from the dead. He ascended into heaven, and sits at the right hand of God the Father almighty; from thence He shall come to judge the living and the dead. I believe in the Holy Sprit, the holy Catholic Church, the communion of saints, the forgiveness of sins, the resurrection of the body, and life everlasting. Amen.

Mysteries of the Rosary
(Traditional)

The mysteries of the Rosary are collected into groups of related scriptural events referred to as the Joyful, Sorrowful, Glorious and Luminous mysteries. Each mystery is divided into five related scriptural events which are used on different days of the week to encourage meditation on the life of Christ. The recitation of five decades and meditation on a set of mysteries ends with the prayer Hail Holy Queen (*found below*).

The Joyful mysteries, used Saturdays and Mondays, are: The Annunciation (Lk 1:26–38), The Visitation (Lk 1:39–56; Jn 1:19–23), The Nativity (Mt 2:1–12; Lk 2:1–20), The Presentation (Lk 1:22–35), The Finding of Jesus in the Temple (Lk 21:44–50).

The Sorrowful mysteries, used Tuesdays and Fridays, are: The Agony in the Garden (Mt 26:36–46; Mk 17:26–42), The Scourging at the Pillar (Mt 27:15–26; Mk 15:1–15), The Crowning with Thorns (Mt 16:24–28; Lk 23:6–11), Carrying the Cross (Mk 8:31–38; Jn 19:17–22), The Crucifixion (Mk 15:33–39; Lk 23:33–46).

The Glorious mysteries, used Sundays and Wednesdays, are: the Resurrection (Mt 28:1–10; Lk 24:1–12), The Ascension

(Mt 28:16–20; Lk 24:44–53), The descent of the Holy Spirit (Jn 14:15–21; Acts 2:1–11), The Assumption (Jn 11:17–27; Rev 21:1–6), The Coronation of Mary (Mt 5:1–12; Rev 12:1).

The Luminous mysteries, used Thursdays, are: The Baptism of Jesus in the Jordan (Mt 3:13–17; Mk 1:1–9; Lk 3:21–22; Jn 1:29–31), The Wedding at Cana (Jn 2:3–5, 7–10; Lk 6:27–28, 37), The Proclamation of the Kingdom (Mk 1:14–15; Lk 4:18–19), The Transfiguration (Mt 5:14, 16; Lk 9:30–33), The Institution of the Eucharist (Jn 13:1; Mt 26:18; Lk 22:15–16).

Hail Holy Queen
(Traditional)

Hail holy queen, Mother of Mercy, our life our sweetness and our hope. To thee do we cry, poor banished children of Eve. To thee do we send up our sighs; mourning and weeping in this valley of tears. Turn, then, most gracious advocate, your eyes of mercy towards us. And after this our exile, show unto us the blessed fruit of thy womb, Jesus! O clement, O loving, O sweet Virgin Mary!

R. Amen

V. Pray for us O holy Mother of God.

R. That we may be made worthy of the promises of Christ.

Memorare
(St. Bernard)

Remember, O most gracious Virgin Mary, that never was it known that anyone who fled to thy protection, implored thy help, or sought thy intercession was left unaided. Inspired with this confidence, I fly unto thee O virgin of virgins, my Mother. To thee I come, before thee I stand sinful and sorrowful. O Mother of the Word Incarnate, despise not my petitions but in thy mercy hear and answer me. Amen.

Angelus (Angelus Domini)
(Traditional)

(Recited three times a day: morning, noon, evening.)

V. The angel of the Lord declared unto Mary.

R. And she conceived by the Holy Spirit.

Hail Mary full of grace, etc.

V. Behold the handmaid of the Lord.

R. Be it done unto me according to thy word.

Hail Mary full of grace, etc.

V. The Word was made flesh.

R. And dwelt among us.

Hail Mary full of grace, etc.

V. Pray for us O holy Mother of God.

R. That we may be made worthy of the promises of God.

Let us pray. Pour forth, we beseech thee, O Lord thy grace into our hearts; that we to whom the Incarnation of Christ thy son was made known by the message of an angel, may by his Passion and Cross, be brought to the glory of His Resurrection; through Christ our Lord. Amen.

Queen of Heaven/ Regina Coeli
(Traditional)

(Used instead of the Angelus during easter season.)

V. Queen of heaven rejoice, alleluia.
R. For the Son you were privileged to bear, alleluia.

V. Has risen as he said, Alleluia.
R. Pray for us to God, Alleluia.

V. Rejoice and be glad, O Virgin Mary, Alleluia.
R. For the Lord has truly risen, Alleluia.

Let us pray:

O God, who by the resurrection of thy Son, our Lord Jesus Christ you have brought joy into the world. Grant that through the intercession of the Virgin Mary, his Mother, we may attain the joys of eternal life. We ask this through Christ our Lord. Amen.

Canticle of Mary (Magnificat)

(Raccolta)

My soul doth magnify the Lord: And my spirit hath rejoiced in God my Saviour.

For he hath regarded the lowliness of His handmaiden: for, behold, from henceforth all generations shall call me blessed. For He that is mighty hath done great things to me: and holy is His Name.

And His mercy is from generation to generations, to them that fear Him. He hath shown might with his arm: He hath scattered the proud in the conceit of their heart. He hath put down the mighty from their seat, and hath exalted the lowly.

He hath filled the hungry with good things: and the rich he hath sent empty away. He hath given help to His servant Israel, being mindful of His mercy. As he spoke to our fathers, to Abraham and his seed forever. Amen.

Prayers Recited at Mass
(Roman Missal)

Confiteor

I confess to almighty God, and to you my brothers and sisters, that I have greatly sinned in my thoughts and in my words in what I have done and in what I have failed to do, through my fault, through my fault, through my most grievous fault; therefore I ask Blessed Mary ever virgin, all the angels and saints, and you, my brothers and sisters, to pray for me to the Lord our God.

The Gloria

Glory to God in the highest, and on earth peace to people of good will. We praise you, we bless you, we adore you, we glorify you, we give you thanks for your great glory, Lord God heavenly king, O God almighty Father.

Lord Jesus Christ, Only Begotten Son, Lord God, Lamb of God, Son of the Father, you take away the sins of the world, have mercy on us; you take away the sins of the world receive our prayer; you are seated at the right hand of the Father, have mercy on us.

For you alone are the Holy One, you alone are the Lord, you alone are the Most High, Jesus Christ, with the Holy Spirit, in the glory of God the Father. Amen.

The Nicene Creed (The Credo)

I believe in one God, the Father almighty, maker of heaven and earth, and of all things visible and invisible.

I believe in one Lord, Jesus Christ, the only Begotten Son of God, born of the Father before all ages. God from God, Light from Light, true God from true God, begotten, not made, consubstantial with the Father; through him all things were made.

For us men and for our salvation he came down from heaven, and by the power of the Holy Spirit was incarnate of the Virgin Mary, and became man. For our sake he was crucified under Pontius Pilate, he suffered death and was buried, and arose again on the third day in accordance with the Scriptures. He ascended into heaven and is seated at the right hand of the Father. He will come again in glory to judge the living and the dead, and his kingdom will have no end.

I believe in the Holy Spirit, the Lord, the giver of life, who proceeds from the Father and the Son, who with the Father and the Son is adored and glorified. He has spoken through the prophets. I believe in one holy, catholic, and apostolic Church. I confess one Baptism for the forgiveness of sins and I look forward to the resurrection of the dead and the life of the world to come. Amen.

Suscipiat

May the Lord accept the sacrifice at your hands for the praise and glory of his name, for our good and the good of all his holy Church.

Sanctus

Holy holy holy Lord, God of hosts. Heaven and earth are full of thy glory. Hosanna in the highest. Blessed is he who comes in the name of the Lord. Hosanna in the highest.

Agnus Dei (Lamb of God)

Lamb of God, you take away the sins of the world: have mercy on us. Lamb of God, you take away the sins of the world: have mercy on us. Lamb of God, you take away the sins of the world: grant us peace.

Communion response

Lord, I am not worthy that you should enter under my roof, but only say the word and my soul shall be healed.

Prayer to Michael the Archangel
(Traditional)

St. Michael the Archangel, defend us in the battle, be our protection against the malice and snares of the devil. May God rebuke him we humbly pray; and do thou, O Prince of the Heavenly host, by the power of God, cast into hell Satan and the other evil spirits who roam about the world seeking the ruin of souls. Amen.

PRAYERS RECITED FOR CONFESSION

Beginning Confession

Bless me Father for I have sinned. My last confession was made --- weeks ago. Since then I have committed these sins.

Psalm 50

(Douay-Rheims Bible)

Have mercy on me, O God, according to thy mercy; according the multitude of thy tender mercies blot out my iniquity.

Wash me yet more from my iniquity, and cleanse me from my sin. For I know my iniquity, and my sin is always before me.

To thee only have I sinned, and I have done evil before thee that thou mayst be justified in thy words, and mayst overcome when thou art judged.

For behold, I was conceived in iniquities; and in sin did my mother conceive me.

Lo, thou hast loved truth: the uncertain and hidden things of thy wisdom thou hast made manifest to me.

Thou shalt sprinkle me with hyssop, and I shall be cleansed: thou shalt wash me, and I shall be made whiter than snow.

To my hearing thou shalt give joy and gladness: and the bones that have been humbled shall rejoice.

Cast me not away from thy face; and take not thy holy spirit from me.

Create a clean heart in me, O God: and renew a right spirit within my bowels. Cast me not away from thy face, and take not thy holy spirit from me.

Restore unto me the joy of thy salvation, and strengthen me with a perfect spirit. I will teach the unjust thy ways, and the wicked shall be converted to thee. Deliver me from blood, O God, thou God of my salvation and my tongue shall extoll thy justice.

O Lord thou wilt open my lips, and my mouth shall declare thy praise.

For if thou hadst desired sacrifice, I would indeed have given it: with wilt burnt offerings thou wilt not be delighted.

A sacrifice to God is an afflicted spirit: a contrite and humble heart, O God, thou wilt not despise.

Deal favorably, O Lord, in thy good will with Sion; that the walls of Jerusalem may be built up.

Then shalt thou accept the sacrifice of justice, oblations, and whole burnt offerings: then shall they lay calves upon thy altar. Then shalt thou accept the sacrifice of justice, oblations, and whole burnt offerings: then shall they lay calves upon thy altar.

Act of Contrition
(Traditional)

O my God, I am heartily sorry for having offended thee because thou art so good and deserving of all my love. I detest all my sins because I dread the loss of heaven and the pains of hell. I firmly resolve, with the help of thy grace, to confess my sins, to do penance and amend my life. Amen

OTHER PRAYERS

Prayer before communion
(Byzantine prayer)

O Lord I believe and profess that you are truly Christ, the Son of the living God who came into the world to save sinners, of whom I am the first.

Accept me as a partaker of your mystical supper, O Son of God; for I will not reveal your mysteries to your enemies, nor will I give you a kiss as did Judas, but like the thief I confess to you:

Remember me, O Lord when you shall come into your kingdom.

Remember me O Master when you shall come into your kingdom.

Remember me O Holy One, when you shall come into your kingdom.

May the partaking of your holy mysteries, O Lord be not for my judgment or condemnation, but for the healing of my soul and body.

Lord I also believe and profess that this, which I am about to receive, is truly your most precious body, and your life-giving blood, which, I pray make me worthy to receive for the remission of all my sins and for life everlasting. Amen

O God be merciful to me a sinner.

O God, cleanse me of my sins, and have mercy on me.

O Lord, forgive me for I have sinned without number.

Spiritual communion
(St. Francis)

I believe that you, O Jesus, are present in the most holy Sacrament. I love you and desire you. Come into my heart. I embrace you. Oh, never leave me. May the burning and most sweet power of your love, O Jesus Christ, I beseech you, absorb my mind that I may die through love of your love, who were graciously pleased to die through love of my love. Amen.

Soul of Christ
(Early fourteenth century prayer)

Soul of Christ be my sanctification; Body of Christ be my salvation; Blood of Christ fill all my veins; Water from Christ's side, wash out my stains; Passion of Christ my comfort be; O good Jesus listen to me; In Thy wounds hide me; Never to be parted from Thy side; Guard me should the foe assail me; Call me when my life shall fail me. Bid me come to Thee above, with all Thy saints to sing Thy love, World without end. Amen.

Morning Offering
(St. Francis de Sales)

O Jesus, through the Immaculate Heart of Mary, I offer you my prayers, works, joys, and sufferings of this day, in union with the Holy Sacrifice of the Mass throughout the world. I offer them for all the intentions of Your Sacred Heart: the salvation of souls, reparation for sin, the reunion of all Christians.

I offer them for the intention of our Bishops, and of all members of the Apostleship of Prayer, and in particular, for those recommended by our Holy Father this month.

Consecration
(St. Francis de Sales)

I vow and consecrate to God all that is in me: my memory and actions to God the Father; my understanding and words to God the son; my will and thoughts to God the Holy Spirit; my heart, body, tongue, senses, and all my sorrows to the sacred humanity of Jesus Christ; 'who was willing to be betrayed into the hands of wicked men and suffer the torment of the cross.

Oblation to the Sacred Heart
(St. Margaret Mary)

O Eternal Father, permit me to offer You the Heart of Jesus Christ, your well-beloved Son, as he offers himself in sacrifice. Graciously receive this offering on my behalf and receive all the desires, all the sentiments, all the affections, all the movements, and all the acts of this Sacred Heart. They are all mine, since He immolates Himself for me, and since I intend to have no other desires henceforth but His. Receive them in satisfaction for my sins, and in thanksgiving for all His benefits. Graciously receive then, all the merits of the Sacred Heart of Your Divine Son which I offer, and grant me in return all the graces which are necessary for me, especially the grace of final perseverance. Receive them as so many acts of love, adoration, and praise which I offer Your Divine Majesty, since it is by Your Divine Son alone that You are worthily honored and glorified. Amen.

Notes

Notes

Notes

Notes

Notes

Notes

MARIAN CATECHIST APOSTOLATE

The mission of the Marian Catechist Apostolate is to form catechists doctrinally and spiritually for the teaching of the Catholic Faith. Simply put, it is to help others to know, love and serve God in this world in order to be happy with him forever in Heaven. Marian Catechists have as their motto the words of the Blessed Virgin Mary to the servants at the wedding feast of Cana: *Do whatever He tells you* (John 2:5).

Marian Catechists must be heroic souls, trained catechists who are committed to the conversion of our secularized society through the New Evangelization advanced by Pope Saint John Paul II and his successors. One of the actions taken by Pope Saint John Paul II to reverse the dismal global trend of declining faith in God was to ask Saint Mother Teresa of Calcutta to prepare her Sisters, the Missionaries of Charity, not only to care for the immediate material needs of the poor, but also to evangelize them, to teach them about God's immeasurable love for them and about his desire to be united with them in Heaven for all eternity.

Saint Mother Teresa was directed to Servant of God Father John A. Hardon, S.J., for the help she needed to prepare her Sisters to evangelize the poorest of the poor. Father Hardon was an eminent theologian and master catechist, the author of over forty major works of theology, spirituality and catechesis, and one of the world's most respected authorities on the Catholic Faith. He began to teach the Missionaries of Charity and, at the same time, he began to prepare the texts that would eventually become a set of home study courses to be used by the lay faithful. Still today, the Missionaries of Charity, along with countless lay members of the Church, use Father Hardon's courses to prepare themselves to be effective witnesses of the Faith to all they meet.

Father Hardon was responding to Saint John Paul II's call for a New Evangelization when he founded the Marian Catechist Apostolate. He established the Marian Catechist Apostolate in order to form catechists, both spiritually and doctrinally for the teaching of the Faith. He was elated when His Eminence Raymond Leo Cardinal Burke, then-Bishop of La Crosse, Wisconsin, decided to use his home study courses to form catechists in the Diocese of La Crosse. On December 12, 1999, the Feast of Our Lady of Guadalupe, then-Bishop Burke established the Marian Catechist Apostolate as a Public Association of the Faithful. The Apostolate has been placed under the patronage of Our Lady of Guadalupe, Patroness of all America and Star of both the first and the new evangelizations.

Shortly before Father Hardon's death on December 30, 2000, he asked Cardinal Burke to assume leadership of the Marian Catechist Apostolate. Cardinal Burke accepted and remains today the Episcopal Moderator and International Director of Father Hardon's apostolate of catechesis.

Dr. Joseph Fisher is passionate about catechesis. For ten years, he directed Adult Religious Education at St. Bernadette's Church in Albuquerque, New Mexico, and taught the *Catechism of the Catholic Church* to adults, to the Carmelite Nuns of Santa Fe, and to high schoolers at Our Lady of Perpetual Help Byzantine Catholic Church. He reviewed and evaluated the *United States Catholic Catechism for Adults* for the Archdiocese of Santa Fe, in preparation for its publication by the USCCB. He has since worked with the RCIA program in Des Moines, Iowa, and presently teaches adult catechism at Sacred Heart Parish in Newton, Iowa, where he resides.

In addition to teaching catechism, Dr. Fisher has been a dedicated scholar and academic. Professor Emeritus of Drake University (Des Moines, Iowa), he studied theology at Holy Cross Abbey (Canon City, Colorado) and at St. John's School of Theology and Seminary (Collegeville, Minnesota). He also holds degrees in philosophy, English and Spanish from Benedictine College (Atchison, Kansas) and in statistics and educational psychology from the University of Iowa. Besides teaching at Drake, he also taught at Texas Christian University (Ft. Worth, Texas), and as guest professor at the University of Panama (Panama City, Panama).

Dr. Fisher has traveled extensively in Europe and South America for the International Reading Association, and in South America for the United Nations, in the area of literacy. He was a final evaluator for the American College Testing (ACT) Program. For fourteen years, he edited the *Journal of College and Adult Reading and Learning.* He has published for McGraw-Hill.

Dr. Fisher and his wife Kay have been married for 63 years, and are the parents of nine children, 13 grandchildren and three great-grandchildren.

THE ACADEMY OF THE IMMACULATE

The Academy of the Immaculate, founded in 1992, is inspired by and based on a project of St. Maximilian Kolbe (never realized by the Saint because of his death by martyrdom at the age of 47, August 14, 1941). Among its goals the Academy seeks to promote at every level the study of the Mystery of the Immaculate Conception and the universal maternal mediation of the Virgin Mother of God, and to sponsor publication and dissemination of the fruits of this research in every way possible.

The Academy of the Immaculate is a non-profit religious-charitable organization of the Roman Catholic Church, incorporated under the laws of the Commonwealth of Massachusetts, with its central office at Our Lady's Chapel, POB 3003, New Bedford, MA 02741-3003.

AcademyoftheImmaculate.com

Special rates are available with 25% to 60% discount depending on the number of books, plus postage. For ordering books and further information on rates to book stores, schools and parishes: *Academy of the Immaculate, P.O. Box 3003, New Bedford, MA 02741,* Phone *(888)90. MARIA [888.90.62742],* E-mail *academy@marymediatrix.com.* Quotations on bulk rates by the box, shipped directly from the printery, contact: *Franciscans of the Immaculate, P.O. Box 3003, New Bedford, MA 02741, (508)996-8274,* E-mail: *fi-academy@marymediatrix.com.* Website: *www.marymediatrix.com.*

80075984R00361

Made in the USA
Columbia, SC
03 November 2017